THE UNIVERSITY OF

Cambridge

an 800th Anniversary Portrait

THE UNIVERSITY OF

Cambridge

an 800th Anniversary Portrait

Editor Peter Pagnamenta

III THIRD MILLENNIUM
PUBLISHING, LONDON

UNIVERSITY OF CAMBRIDGE
800 YEARS
1209~2009

THIRD MILLENNIUM PUBLISHING

In one respect this book is the culmination of ten years of particularly rewarding publishing with individual Cambridge colleges – beginning with my own, Clare. Using both words and pictures we have sought to communicate how such communities, each with its own unique character and ethos, can draw strength from the values and traditions of the past, while at the same time being totally engaged with the present. What we have found to date to be true of Clare, Corpus Christi, Girton, Trinity Hall, St John's, Pembroke and Gonville & Caius is of course true of the University of Cambridge itself. It has been a great privilege for a youthful publishing company to provide this portrait of a venerable university in its eight hundredth year.

Julian Platt

Title page: King's Parade from Gonville & Caius. Photograph by Dan White, 2007.

Front endpapers: From Senate House Hill on Degree Day Morning, 1863, *by Robert Farren (see page 292).*

Rear endpapers: Degree Day 2007. Photograph by Hiroshi Shimura.

Above: Old Court, Peterhouse. Photograph by Hiroshi Shimura.

The University of Cambridge: An 800th Anniversary Portrait

Managing Editor: Catharine Walston
Editorial Assistant: Fred Bosanquet
Design: Matthew Wilson and Susan Pugsley
Production: Bonnie Murray
Project Manager: Christopher Fagg

Copyright © The University of Cambridge and
Third Millennium Publishing Limited

Individual authors retain copyright in their own contributions.

First published in 2008 by Third Millennium Publishing Limited,
a subsidiary of Third Millennium Information Limited

2–5 Benjamin Street, London
United Kingdom, EC1M 5QL
www.tmiltd.com

ISBN: 978 1 903942 65 9

British Library Cataloguing in Publication Data

A CIP catalogue record for this book is available from the British Library.

Printed by Cambridge University Press

Editor's Note

When we were embarking on this book, some people expressed doubt as to whether it would be possible at all. I was warned that this would be a difficult, even a dangerous task. How could a book, with a finite number of pages, possibly meet all the expectations that different readers would have for it, depending on their standpoint in the University today or their own particular experience of it in the past? So a few explanations, even disclaimers, are needed. This is not a linear history of the whole 800 years, or an encyclopaedic guide to every part of Cambridge activity. As the subtitle suggests, we have tried to produce a wide-angled picture of the University coming up to the 800th anniversary in 2009, showing at least the range of teaching and research, and giving an impression of extracurricular life, using many voices. There are inevitable omissions. Though some of the early history is here too, the main stress is on the last 60 years in which so much has changed so fast, and on the present day.

Among the several strands that make up the book, the first is the personal recollections of alumni, which are woven throughout. The soliciting of first hand testimony is a hit or miss process, and there are imbalances in the way different generations respond. Many are suspicious of these general exhortations. So we need to thank all who overcame their inhibitions, and followed so well the stern guidelines requesting a sharp focus. It has been possible to use only a portion of what was received, and contributions have been edited.

The second strand comes with the illustrations. As well as the many picture sources credited separately, we owe thanks to a talented list of photographers who are graduates or have strong Cambridge connections, and who allowed us to use their work. They include Antony Barrington Brown, Christopher Angeloglou, Phillip Brown, David Thomas, Hiroshi Shimura, Ihsan Aslam and Michael Derringer. We should also thank the *Varsity* cartoonists over the years, including the most recent, Anna Trench.

Commissioned articles provide the third strand. I am grateful to all who agreed to write about complex subjects in a very limited number of words, and submitted to deadlines that some academics regarded as brutal, so gracefully and effectively. I owe a special and personal debt to two contributors in particular. Apart from writing their own pieces, Professor Malcolm Longair and Professor Ron Laskey gave invaluable help with the assembly of the sections that deal with the physical sciences and technology, and with the biological and medical sciences. While doing this they found themselves drawn into the editorial grind more deeply than they might have wished. If this resulted in a temporary loss to science, it was our gain. I am also grateful to our Advisory Committee, who gave wise guidance, understood the constraints, and were supportive throughout.

We have adopted a rather loose running order, and the book is intended to work as an anthology, so that research is treated next to poetry and spiritual life comes before sport. To the reader who complains that this kaleidoscopic view is confusing, one response would have to be that the University itself has never been logically organized, and its many facets, layers, overlaps, and dazzling fragments form its essential character and identity. But to help those who would have liked a more rigorous plan, the design incorporates a gentle colour key, which may allow readers with specific interests to find their way around more easily. A full list of acknowledgements and thanks appears at the end of the book.

Peter Pagnamenta

Advisory Committee

Professor Alison Richard
Vice-Chancellor, University of Cambridge, Chair

Professor Tony Badger
Master, Clare College
Paul Mellon Professor of American History, Faculty of History

Professor John Barrow
Professor of Mathematical Sciences, Department of Applied Mathematics and
Theoretical Physics

Dame Gillian Beer DBE
Emerita King Edward VII Professor of English Literature, Faculty of English

Professor Paul Cartledge
A.G. Leventis Professor of Greek Culture, Faculty of Classics

Professor Andy Hopper
Professor of Computer Technology and Head of Department,
the Computer Laboratory

Professor Deborah Howard
Head of Department of History of Art and Professor of Architectural History,
Faculty of Architecture and History of Art

Professor David McKitterick
Librarian, Trinity College and Honorary Professor of Historical Bibliography

The Right Honourable Michael Portillo
Peterhouse, 1972
Former Cabinet minister, journalist and broadcaster

Professor Martin Rees OM, FRS (Lord Rees of Ludlow)
Master, Trinity College, Professor of Cosmology and Astrophysics,
Institute of Astronomy, President of the Royal Society and Astronomer Royal

Professor Colin Renfrew (Lord Renfrew of Kaimsthorn)
Emeritus Disney Professor of Archaeology, Department of Archaeology,
Faculty of Archaeology and Anthropology

Karl Sabbagh
King's College, 1961
Writer, television producer and director

Dr David Starkey CBE
Honorary Fellow, Fitzwilliam College
Historian, writer and broadcaster

Dr Liba Taub
Director and Curator, Whipple Museum of the History of Science,
Department of History and Philosophy of Science

Dame Jean Thomas DBE, FRS
Master, St Catharine's College
Professor of Macromolecular Biochemistry, Department of Biochemistry

Professor Mark Welland FRS, FREng
Professor of Nanotechnology, Department of Engineering: Chief Scientific Adviser
to HM Government, Ministry of Defence

HRH The Duke of Edinburgh, Chancellor of the University since 1976.

The real significance of the 800th anniversary of the founding of a university at Cambridge is that the institution has not just survived for that long, but that it grew into an institution with a level of scholarship and research to compare with the most respected universities anywhere in the world.

That achievement is certainly worth celebrating, but it is inevitable that people who identify with a particular teaching department, or a research group, or a college, or in dedicated pursuit of some extra-curricular activity, may not know much about what is going on just a short distance away. One of the advantages enjoyed by a Chancellor is the chance to see the University as a whole; to get a sense of the entire eco-system and its prevailing ethos. As I move around the Faculty buildings and laboratories, the courtyards of the Colleges, the new institutes and construction sites, and meet staff and under graduates, and post graduates, I am struck by the fact that so many people, whose day to day preoccupations are so different, can still share the same values and are able to appreciate the unique character of the wider institution.

This book, with its anthology format, tries to catch the essence and character of modern Cambridge. I believe that, in doing that, as well as recording the academic achievements and research successes, it reflects the hopes and tensions, the concerns and anxieties of a vital and energetic organism.

Cambridge is a complex place, and I believe that it is this complexity that should be cherished, because it is the sum of its diffused parts that has made the university what it is today; a challenging environment and an exceptionally rewarding place to work and study.

Contents

Cambridge through the seasons:
Spring p10, Summer p86, Autumn p222, and Winter p288.

Notes: The design incorporates a colour code giving a separate tint to different Cambridge themes and focuses:

History, inheritance and overview sections have a blue tab
University policy and administration are tabbed with grey
Academic and research chapters are marked with orange
Undergraduate life and extra-curricular sections are in green.

Dates shown after alumni contributions mark years of matriculation, or for graduates and researchers, the date of arrival in Cambridge.

Introduction

'The real quest is not for knowledge, but for understanding...'

GORDON JOHNSON

We mark the passing of 800 years, and that is indeed a remarkable span for any institution. But history is never an even-flowing stream, and the most remarkable thing about modern Cambridge has been its enormous growth over the past half-century. Since I came up as an undergraduate in 1961 the student population has more than doubled (from just under 9,000 to just over 18,000), graduate students now constitute about a third of the whole; just as notable, around half of all students are now women. More students have meant more teachers, and, even more significantly, more scholars devoted solely to research: every category has more than doubled in numbers. This huge increase has been partly absorbed by an expansion of the colleges: they all have more students and more Fellows than they did 50 years ago; and, since 1954, no fewer than 11 of the 31 colleges are either brand new foundations, such as New Hall, Churchill, Darwin, Wolfson, Clare Hall, Lucy Cavendish and Robinson, or have been conjured up as new creations from existing but quite different bodies, like Homerton, Hughes Hall, Fitzwilliam and St Edmund's.

From being a university primarily driven by undergraduate education, Cambridge's reputation is now overwhelmingly tied to its research achievements, which can be simply represented by the fact that more than three-quarters of its current annual income is devoted to research. This has brought not just new laboratories but new buildings to house whole faculties and departments: in the mid-20th century few faculties (and those mainly in the sciences) had a physical manifestation beyond, perhaps, a library and a couple of administrative offices. As late as the 1960s, the History Faculty existed as the Seeley Library (then in the Cockerell Building beside the Senate House, now the Caius College Library) and a tiny bolt-hole in Green Street presided over by the formidable Miss Box. Now it has a remarkable (if controversial) building on the Sidgwick Site, surrounded by buildings for Law, Music, Divinity, English, Philosophy, Criminology, Classics, Modern and Medieval Languages, and Asian and Middle Eastern Studies.

Left: The new Centre for Mathematical Studies on Wilberforce Road.

Right: Magdalene bridge at 9am.

Previous pages: Spring on the Backs. Photograph by Hiroshi Shimura.

Physically, the University has burst out of the old town centre: the University Library, Selwyn and Newnham no longer form outposts on the western frontier, since beyond and between them lie new colleges and scientific departments relocated to West Cambridge from old places in the city centre; Peterhouse, Engineering and Chemistry no longer stand sentinel to the south, since distant on the road to Colchester lies Addenbrooke's Hospital (itself moved from Trumpington Street) with the Clinical School and a vast array of bio-scientific research laboratories and institutes.

Growth on this scale, in so few decades, is unprecedented in the long history of the University. It has not been without its discomforts; we should not underestimate the ferocity of battles fought to get to where we are. It is simply not true, though it is often alleged, that University politics are vicious because little is at stake. It is a highly controversial thing to decide what (and who) to teach, and which frontier of knowledge to advance upon next and where to make the investments that might support these decisions; it is hard also to define our role in the affairs of the state and its many agencies, or our relation

to business and industry, to alumni and other well-meaning friends; and it is difficult to determine just where to strike the bargains that bring in the resources needed for the University's work. It is because the University is so relevant and important to our society's well-being that it is the focus of so much attention, and a place of real struggle for power and influence.

However, Cambridge has prospered and stands amongst the foremost universities of the world. Despite the change of scale, Cambridge has retained the quality of a great university: a place where enquiry is encouraged and tested and where critical thought is the order of the day. The University brings together a wide range of disciplines and, loosely, pursues them all. There has been no plan to catch them up in some great common, coherent and directed research project that would solve the problems of the age, though some of what is learnt here is directly relevant to work beyond the University, and some of what is discovered has immediate practical application. For all of its size, Cambridge is still a collection of colleges and departments, separate and overlapping disciplines. The parish government is often criticized for being a bit anarchic, and this at times frustrates some

within and annoys authorities without. But it remains fundamentally a place of individual scholarly creativity and clear educational purpose.

Cambridge attracts the best students and academics because they find the University and the colleges stimulating and enjoyable places in which to live and work. The students are thrown in with similarly able minds, learning as much from each other as from their teachers; the good senior academics know better than to be too hierarchical or to cut themselves off from intellectual criticism and debate. We so easily believe that what we spend our waking hours thinking about must somehow be an advance on what is known or understood already. Earlier generations have thought the same. They were sure that they were right as well. In the sciences there is often agreed progress, but even here there will be conflicting ideas and uncertainties. One generation dismisses another: not even Erasmus or Newton, Darwin or Keynes stand unscathed by the passage of time; nor can we be but humbled, especially in our day when so much information is so easily accessible, by the vast store of knowledge which we can approach but never really control. Our library and museum collections bring us into contact with many lives lived in the past. They serve as symbols of the

continuity of learning, or the diversity of views, of an obligation to wrestle with fact and argument, to come to our own conclusions, and in turn to be accountable for our findings. The real quest is not for knowledge, but for understanding.

It is remarkable that Cambridge should have had a University for so long. We take it for granted. We assume that Cambridge has always been an important centre of learning, and that what has been will be forever. But history tells us otherwise. The University and the colleges have a chequered past. More often than not, however, teachers and students here have been conscientious and followed their vocation. They have sought out and promoted knowledge, and been the guardians of much that is good in our culture. They have remained close to the interests and needs of our society at large, asking hard questions, challenging established ways of thinking, and incorporating new understanding in what is taught and learned. We celebrate a great history; but we can look forward to a future only by knowing what it is that makes the genius of the place.

Gordon Johnson *is President of Wolfson College and Provost of the Gates Cambridge Trust.*

Above: Panorama from the tower of the University Library, May 2008.

Impressions and perspectives

NJABULO NDEBELE, BELA BOLLOBAS, BILL JANEWAY, HENRY LOUIS GATES, ANITA DESAI, VAHNI CAPILDEO, GUOHUA CHEN

I remember the Swiss Air DC-10 flight from Johannesburg to Zurich on an October evening in 1973: my first intercontinental flight. I was on my way to Cambridge.

Going to Cambridge sealed my love for Lesotho. Its government granted me a passport to travel to the UK, offering tremendous opportunities for me not possible in my oppressed country: South Africa. I remember the thrill of landing at Heathrow from Zurich. The immigration official asked what I was coming to do in the UK. I was going to study at Cambridge, I said. He said 'how wonderful!'. I remember feeling good.

Although this was my first visit to the United Kingdom, I had nevertheless been there countless times before in my imagination, through British novels, drama, music, film and colonialism. At Cambridge, I fell in love immediately with the prolonged greyness of the Michaelmas term with its short days and long nights. I soon bought a bicycle, and loved cycling in crowds, weaving my way through traffic. I would take in all of Cambridge on my bike.

I remember the small world of the Wolfson flats for married students at Churchill College: Americans, Canadians, Nigerians, Tanzanians, Indians, South Americans, Australians, the Irish, the British, and of course, South Africans from Lesotho.

The British summers came with their long days that allowed our son and other 'third world' children at the Wolfson flats to play outside long after their British friends had been sent to bed. I remember cycling my son to nursery school, and how motorists on Huntingdon Road smiled strangely at me as they passed. Then I realised they were amused by my three-year-old son, who, in his seat behind me, imitated every signal I made with my arms.

What makes for a great university? It must be the community of scholars who attract others from all over the world to learn from them. There he was, George Steiner, coming out of his room one staircase below mine. He greeted me warmly. I was too awed to ask him many questions. I remember coming out of Raymond Williams's lecture at the Sidgwick Centre and then seeing him open the boot of his

car, put his coat and case in it, and then drive away with a woman who had been waiting for him. The ordinariness of greatness!

I remember that Joseph Needham, Master of Caius College invited us to a reception at his college. As the evening wore on I saw him sit on the floor in front of Mpho, my wife, for a chat. The ordinariness of legend!

I remember meeting Wole Soyinka at the Churchill College bar for a drink. He too was in residence there. Many years later I was to preside over a graduation ceremony where, on behalf of the University of Cape Town, I conferred an honorary doctorate on him.

I remember Frank Kermode's elegant lectures; Colin McCabe's demanding lectures on James Joyce; and Iain Wright's probing tutorials on the Russian novel. I remember that Henry Louis 'Skip' Gates and I attended the same lectures on film theory by Stephen Heath.

I loved being at Cambridge, and savoured the joy of tribal solidarity against Oxford. What if I had gone to Oxford? Could it have been the other way round? I remember meal time at Churchill College and how I wished there was more noise and laughter in the dining hall. I remember being a member of the Gods at Churchill College and that I

> *"Cambridge, wet, cold, abstract, formal as it is, is an excellent place to write, read and work."*
>
> **Sylvia Plath, writing to her mother, 1956, from *Letters Home*, 1975**

Left: Byron's pool, now a city nature reserve, where not only Byron but Rupert Brooke and Virginia Woolf would swim in the Cam.

Prospectus CANTABRIGIÆ Occidentalis

Castellum	5. Coll: Iesu.	9. Bibliot: Trinitatis	13. Eccl St Andreæ	17. Aula Claræ	The Prospect of CAMBRIDGE from the West.	1. Castele Prison	
Agger Castelli	6. Bibliot: divi Iohannis	10. Eccl: St Michaëlis	14. Eccl: Btæ Mariæ	18. Aula Katharinæ		2. Castle Hill	
Eccl: St Petri	7. Coll: divi Iohannis	11. Eccl: S:S: Trinitatis	15. Eccl: St Edvardi	19. Coll: Reginense		3. St Peters Church	
Coll: Magdalen	8. Coll: Trinitatis	12. Coll: Caij	16. Sacel: Coll: Regalis	20. Montes Hogmagog		4. Magdalen Colledge	

The Prospect of Cambridge from the West, *1688, by David Loggan. University Library, Cambridge.*

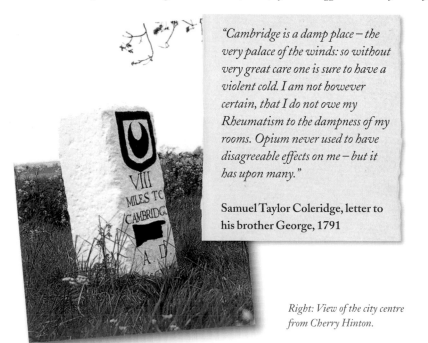

"Cambridge is a damp place – the very palace of the winds: so without very great care one is sure to have a violent cold. I am not however certain, that I do not owe my Rheumatism to the dampness of my rooms. Opium never used to have disagreeable effects on me – but it has upon many."

Samuel Taylor Coleridge, letter to his brother George, 1791

Right: View of the city centre from Cherry Hinton.

acted in Tim Cribbs's production of *The Splendour and Death of Joaquin Murieta* by Pablo Neruda.

And then I was in the second division soccer team of Churchill College. We won and we lost. I remember cycling to the Cambridge Railway station just to look at trains. I remember browsing at Heffers; walking at the university Botanic Garden; marvelling at the American Cemetery.

I loved being on Burrell's Walk alongside the UL, on my way to just about anywhere.

I remember seeing my name on the notice board on King's Parade. I had passed! But why was it another BA and not an MA? Later the BA became an MA. The ways of Cambridge!

I remember that at Cambridge I became an international citizen, and suddenly felt light-years away from the parochial oppressiveness of South Africa. When would my country be part of the world? It now is.

Njabulo Ndebele *is a novelist and was Vice-Chancellor and Principal of the University of Cape Town.*

...lledge	9. Trinity Libary	13. St. Andrews Church	17. Clare Hall
...brary	10. St. Michael's Church	14. St. Mary's Church	18. Catharine Hall
...Colledge	11. Trinity Church	15. St. Edwards Church	19. Queens Colledge
...olledge	12. Keys Colledge	16. Kings Coll. Chappel	20. Hogmagog hills

O n 1 October 1963 I arrived in Cambridge from communist Hungary. I was 20, and that autumn I should have started my third year of undergraduate studies in mathematics in Budapest. Up to then I had lived all my life in the claustrophobic atmosphere of a dictatorship, so being in Cambridge was an exhilarating experience beyond my imagination. I was overwhelmed by the magnificent and well kept buildings, the amazing lawns and gardens, the wealth of the country, the quaint customs, and the polite and disciplined people in the streets. I was also greatly relieved that – at least to my untutored eyes – England was alive and well: after all, in my communist homeland it was hammered into us that capitalism had run out of steam and was about to collapse.

I was even more surprised to see how well Cambridge undergraduates lived: many had money of their own, went to stay with friends in the country and took their girlfriends to restaurants; some owned cars and spent their holidays abroad; many were looking forward to well-paid jobs in the City. The world was their oyster. I was amazed that the porters treated the undergraduates with respect, as if they were 'adults': in Budapest an undergraduate was much closer to a child than to a grown-up.

That I ever managed to get to Cambridge was a miracle. I had known of Cambridge as an unattainable place, a place one can long for but cannot hope to reach. For me, Cambridge's reputation rested on Newton, Cayley, Maxwell, Russell, Whitehead and the legendary Hardy-Littlewood partnership; strangely, it never occurred to me that Littlewood might still be alive. Although I was considered to be the best student in Budapest, had already written a joint paper with the globetrotting legendary mathematician Paul Erdős, and was not asking for any financial assistance from the Hungarian authorities, the drawn-

out process of obtaining permission to leave the country for a year was a humiliating experience. That Trinity became my college in Cambridge was due to sheer luck: one of Erdös's best friends, Harold Davenport, was in Trinity, and he arranged my admission.

The style of doing mathematics in Cambridge was very different from what I had been used to in Budapest. There I had attended an endless stream of lectures, examples classes, special seminars and discussions from morning till evening, hardly having time to eat: in Cambridge it wasn't even possible to schedule more than 24 lectures a week. As I did not fit into the standard mould, I chose my courses myself, without much input from my Director of Studies: I chose a mixture of courses in IB, Part II and Part III. The supervision system amazed me: I was supervised on my own and my supervisors were outstanding; in fact, all four were Fellows of the Royal Society. At no place in the world are undergraduates looked after so well!

Mathematics was (and is) very highly regarded in Hungary – it is not by chance that mathematical competitions had existed in Hungary many decades before they were started in other countries – and several of my professors there were among the best in the world. However, with a few exceptions, the lecturers were much more easy-going in the sense that they did not feel obliged to cover a certain amount of material come what may, and did not consider it a disaster if most of their lecture had to be redone the next time. In Cambridge it was new to me that there was a syllabus for every course, known to all the students, not only to the lecturers. I admired the precision, speed and efficiency of the lecturers, who miraculously managed to fit the material into 24 lectures. By and large, the lectures were free of backtracking and corrections, although I was rather disappointed to see that several lecturers relied on their handwritten notes to help them out in difficulties, and some of them (God forbid!) even copied their notes onto the board. In Budapest this was not done.

In addition to its 'serious' side, Cambridge held many other attractions for me: the sports clubs, the plays, concerts and films in various colleges, the bridge parties and punting trips, the formal dinners, and all the exciting people I could meet. The small size of Cambridge enabled me to revel in the wealth of societies from the Union to sports clubs: using my bike I could be at my destination within five minutes.

Having always been a keen sportsman, I played soccer, tennis, squash, table-tennis and bridge, did modern pentathlon and gymnastics, fenced, ran cross-country and rowed (very badly, but enjoying it immensely, as I had never thought that I'd row in an eight). I did pentathlon against the Army, and in the Christmas break went to Paris with the Cambridge University Fencing Team to fence (and lose) against some of the best clubs there.

Yet another reason why I owe a great debt to Cambridge is that I got to know the great physicist, P.A.M. Dirac, and his wife, who was of Hungarian origin. Professor and Mrs Dirac more or less adopted me, and at the end of the year even came to visit me in Budapest. They showed me the country houses around Cambridge, and Paul Dirac

Cambridge from Castle Hill, 1894, by Henry William Brewer (d.1903). Fitzwilliam Museum.

Above: Old Court in Corpus Christi where Christopher Marlowe had rooms in 1581.

Right: Trinity Lane.

took me to swim in ice cold waters, which I felt compelled to enjoy, since he did. It gave me immense joy to stay in close touch with them until they both died.

At no year of my life from the age of ten did I do as little mathematics as in 1963–4: I was sure that I could do plenty of mathematics in Hungary and was convinced that I'd never again have a chance to take advantage of all the opportunities that Cambridge had to offer. I am very happy to say that I turned out to be wrong, although the route back to Cambridge was far from easy.

A year and a half after my return to Budapest I received a scholarship from Trinity to do a PhD, so I applied again for permission to leave Hungary. I was refused in no uncertain terms. My application for permission to go to Paris to do a doctorate was similarly unsuccessful. Next came Oxford, with the same result. At that point, in my mind I left Hungary for good: I promised myself that if I were ever allowed to go to the West, even for one minute, I would not return.

Evenutally, in early 1969, after a year in the Soviet Union and a painful delay of six months, I was finally allowed to leave Budapest for Oxford. As I had promised myself, I did not go back to Hungary, so I cut short my Oxford fellowship and reactivated my old scholarship to Trinity. When in October 1969 I returned to Cambridge, I knew that I had come home.

Bela Bollobas is a Fellow of Trinity College, an external member of the Hungarian Academy of Sciences and Jabie Hardin Professor at the University of Memphis.

I arrived in Cambridge in the early autumn of 1965, after four years in Princeton's Woodrow Wilson School for Public and International Affairs. There I had been a model student for lessons whose general import was: 'All problems of public policy are problems of management … and we have the intellectual tools to manage them, from the national economy and the international monetary system to the balance of terror with the Soviets and the occasional guerilla war in some far-off jungle.' Now, from a highly structured academic environment, with weekly classes and lectures and graded examinations in each course, I arrived as a candidate for acceptance as a research student with virtually no formal requirements whatsoever, save to convince my supervisor to recommend me to the Faculty of Economics as worthy of such status.

And so I had the extraordinary luxury to read. I had been drawn to Cambridge in the first place by reading Keynes at an impressionable age. Now my one academic task was to produce an essay for Michael Posner, Director of Studies in Economics at Pembroke, which would convince him that I 'understood' *The General Theory*. Even as mainstream economists, on both sides of the Atlantic if not yet on the banks of the Cam, were adopting mathematical formalism as their methodological programme, I immersed myself in Keynes's prose, most compelling and subversive when he spoke of the 'extreme precariousness' of our long-term expectations … on the basis of which we nonetheless are compelled to make commitments of irreversible economic and financial significance.

In parallel with Keynes I read Dickens. I picked up *Little Dorrit* under the guidance of a close friend at Newnham, who was working for Q.D.

Leavis. I found myself drawn ever more deeply into the moral education of, first, Arthur Clenham, and then that of the other heroes of Dickens's later novels, Pip, of course, most of all. The moral universe of the mature Dickens unfolded in parallel with the inescapable uncertainty of the economic and financial world that Keynes expounded. In each case, the individual actor was faced with the compelling need to decide and act with no sureness of outcome, on the basis of no simple or simplistic utilitarian calculus, and to live with the consequences. The message was all the more powerful as, from Vietnam through Detroit and Newark to

Cambridge, Senate House Passage, *1843, by Joseph Murray Ince.*
Fitzwilliam Museum.

Wall Street, the world proved recalcitrant to the pretensions of positivist social science. Cambridge was not an ivory tower, isolated from these events. Rather it was an environment in which my capacity for critical examination of them was radically deepened.

That first year with Keynes and Dickens that Cambridge gave me was decisive. Indeed, I had been rendered temperamentally unfit for my intended career as an academic economist in the United States, at a time when tenure-track jobs were still quite widely accessible, even for the mathematically challenged. Through the 40 years since, Dickens (see the episode of the Muffin Bubble in *Nicholas Nickleby*) and Keynes (see chapter 12 of *The General Theory*) were of inestimable value in surviving, even exploiting, the cycles of Fear and Greed that episodically dominate the world of entrepreneurial finance in which I have lived professionally since Cambridge. Of greatest value, Cambridge provided the cultural space in which to absorb the obligation to triangulate a morally defensible course through a world of contingency and chance.

Bill Janeway studied at Cambridge as a Marshall Scholar and is a senior advisor at Warburg Pincus and director of several US companies and non-profit organisations.

When I was growing up in the 1950s, when my cousins would say that they wanted to become professional baseball players such as Hank Aaron or Willie Mays, I would respond that I wanted to be a Rhodes Scholar, attending Oxford or Cambridge, after graduating from Harvard or Yale. At the beginning of my senior year at Yale, in the Fall of 1972, I applied for every fellowship that I could identify that would take me to Oxford or Cambridge. To say that I was reasonably confident that I would be selected for one of them would be an understatement. I was certain that, for all of the wrong reasons, they would find the candidacy of an Afro-American (as we identified ourselves then) who hailed from the hills of eastern West Virginia, a fairly attractive proposition. And no doubt that sense of entitlement, barely disguised, no doubt, is precisely what led to my serial rejection by the Rhodes, the Marshall, and the Fulbright selection committees! It came down to one last possibility, and that was something called a Mellon Fellowship, an exchange between Clare and Yale.

Upon the advice of a lapsed girl friend, I decided to stop pretending that I was some sort of faux Englishman, be myself, and just admit that I wanted to study at Cambridge not because of a specific academic programme, but to experience what it would be like to be black in a country that did not have the long and painful history of slavery and Jim Crow segregation that America had; a country in which, by most accounts, it had somehow become possible for class to trump one's race as a primary criterion of social classification. As a twenty-one-year-old black man born in America, I could scarcely imagine such a thing. Besides, I told the interviewers, I had learned far more about being black in America than I had learned about Africa and Africans (and I had learned quite a lot about both), while living for a year in Africa, and

Roofline of Gonville & Caius, 2007.

I would treasure the opportunity to get to know myself – the 'blackness' of my self, as it were – in a similar manner, but this time, through English eyes. Truth be told, I had no idea even of what subject I wished to study at Cambridge. Perhaps it was the simplicity of my appeal, perhaps it was just the temper of the times, but, to my astonishment, I was awarded one of the year's two fellowships.

With tears streaming down my face, I phoned my parents to share the news. Once my father had called my mother to the 'extension phone', as it was called then, I shouted at them that "You'll never believe it, you'll never believe it, I got a Mellon Fellowship to Cambridge!"

'You're the first Negro to win a Mellon Fellowship?' my daddy responded, deadpan.

'Humph, then they are going to rename it the Watermelon Fellowship from now on!'

So, armed with my Watermelon Fellowship, I set off, sailing on the QE II the day after Yale graduation.

So very much of what I have become, as a scholar of literature and African and African American Studies, as a person, as an African American, I can without romance or sentimentality trace back to my years at Clare and Cambridge. I realized, when I met in my first week or so my fellow Clare student, Anthony Appiah, and my supervisor in African literature, Wole Soyinka, that I didn't, actually, want to be a doctor or a lawyer; rather, all along, I had longed to become a scholar, a professor, a writer and a teacher. And that the avocation I had long enjoyed for sheer pleasure – reading literature, of any nationality – was actually the vocation I so longed to pursue. Unlike back at Yale, where the highest calling among my friends had been the law, or business, medicine, or journalism (soon, the lawyers would become investment bankers), at Cambridge, by contrast, at least among my two closest friends, the highest calling was the academy. Appiah had come up to Clare as a medical student, but migrated to Philosophy as soon as he could; and Wole Soyinka had come to Cambridge from Nigeria as an Extraordinary Fellow at Churchill in political exile, having survived 27 months of imprisonment during the Nigerian Civil War. For both, the life of the mind was nature's highest calling. Appiah would become the first African to take the PhD in Philosophy at Cambridge, and a double first, while Soyinka would become the first African to win the Nobel Prize in Literature. It was they who were my guides, the Virgils who ushered me back through the Middle Passage to embrace an Africa, with all of my senses and all of my intellect, that I had presumed long lost to the sons and daughters of its diaspora.

And it was with them, one rainy night the first week of October of 1973, at an Indian restaurant, that we made a drunken pledge that the three of us would fulfil W.E.B. Du Bois's dream of editing an *Encyclopedia Africana*, the black equivalent of the *Encyclopedia Britannica*. A pledge, a fantasy, really, that would forever enshrine the intellectual and personal friendship of a Nigerian, a Ghanaian, and a black West Virginian descended from slaves, who had been thrown together because of the accident of time and place, to meet and bond, of all places, at the University of Cambridge. Twenty-six years later, on Martin Luther King's birthday on January 19, 1999, dedicated in memory of Harvard's first black PhD, William Edward Burghardt Du Bois, and in honor of Nelson Mandela, the *Encyclopedia Africana* was born.

Henry Louis Gates *is Director of the W.E.B. Du Bois Institute for African and African American research at Harvard University and Alphonse Fletcher Professor.*

"I am one of the fortunate few to have been embraced by Britain's two oldest universities. Before I went to the other place by the Isis, I saw the river Cam when I came up to study for my Economics Tripos at St John's.

In the beginning was St John's. The colour light blue is one of my favourites and is often seen on my head. My memories of my days in Cambridge are deep. I was taught by teachers like Nicholas Kaldor, Joan Robinson, Maurice Dobb and Professor R.C.O. Mathews. I have vivid recollections of the economist Piero Srafa working at the Marshall Library.

It was here that I became a contemporary of Amartya Sen, Jagadish Bhagwati, Mahbubul Haq and Rehman Shobhan – all renowned economists from South Asia who became lifelong friends. My teachers and my peers in Cambridge taught me to be open to argument and to be fearless and lucid in the expression of one's opinions.

These virtues, and a relentless desire to pursue intellectual truth were inculcated in me at Cambridge. In many important ways, the University of Cambridge made me."

Manmohan Singh. Extract from his speech of acceptance when conferred with an Honorary Doctorate in Law in 2006. He studied Economics at St John's College between 1955 and 1957 before going on to take a doctorate at Oxford. Manmohan Singh became Prime Minister of India in 2004

Lent Term, 2008.

my life (nor did I again), sit at the high table (it actually was raised a few inches above the level of the dining hall floor, I noted with surprise; I had imagined this was a figure of speech) and dine with the other Fellows. I came to know the high tables and Fellows of other colleges in Cambridge: collegiality was a word, like Cambridge, that became a reality; to make acquaintances and friends who remain friends today, Cambridge friendships being of as enduring a nature as the University

In the years when I lived in India, Cambridge to me was the picture, the rich oil painting, by Virginia Woolf in *A Room of One's Own*. I did not think of it as other than a painting; not a reality, and certainly not one I could aspire to owning or even visiting. And when the life to which I did aspire, a writer's life, in India, seemed, in 1986, a steadily more grey and lonely and melancholy one, an exercise in decline, a letter arrived from Girton College offering me the Helen Cam Fellowship. It seemed to come from nowhere: I had not applied for it, I knew no one at Girton or, in fact, in Cambridge, but here was the invitation to step into that imagined, unreal world of Cambridge. Who was I to refuse it? I accepted.

The memories of arrival remain very bright and crisp-edged: the porters' lodge, being escorted through the orchard to an ivy-draped Victorian pile in which I was given rooms, the french windows looking out over a sheep meadow, the desk where I settled down to revise and complete the novel I had brought with me to work on, *Baumgartner's Bombay*. All these images remain for me lit by the happiness I felt at being allowed to live such a life, filling my days with the work I wished to do and that, so unexpectedly, those around me wished me to do as well. Opposition was entirely absent, support ever present.

The fellowship lasted a year; during it I would walk through the apple orchard, singing aloud although I had never done that before in

itself. I bought myself the most decrepit second-hand bicycle I could find to fit unobtrusively into the picture, and on it I explored the town and the meadows around it, stopping sometimes on my way to Madingley Hall or back to help myself to blackberries from the hedgerows, and look out onto the patchwork landscape so suitable for watercolours and so celebrated by English landscape painters. There was the University, its towers and turrets and spires, and there were the fens, sunk into their ancient legends and mythology, and the life of the colleges, till then only imagined and half believed in, now offering themselves like the landscape itself, sunlit or rainswept, with such openness, saying 'Here, take, have'.

Extraordinary as the scene and the experience of Cambridge were, what was perhaps most unexpected and overwhelming of all was that here of all places, one I had never considered a 'real' place on a map at all, my books were known, had been read, and I was considered, as I had been invited, a writer. This had never happened in India. Perhaps it is always so in the country of one's birth, where one can only be known as someone's daughter, or sister or mother; certainly not anyone to be taken 'seriously'. Carlos Fuentes, who held the Simon Bolivar Chair at the University the same year I was there, confirmed this by saying to me, 'Of course: at home one's friends see one as their spitting partner – the one they used to have spitting matches with' ('I'm not sure I have the verb right) 'and that is what one is when one returns. One has to leave to acquire another identity, the one of one's own making.'

One stage of that new identity was coming to know the students at Cambridge – in the most informal way, since I had not been assigned any 'duties' as such. To begin with, I had a small group come over to read to me what they were writing privately, outside the lecture rooms, and this was followed by invitations from student groups in other colleges, sometimes to talk about writing and sometimes to talk of the literature of India which at that time had not yet become a standard genre in the English-speaking world. These meetings had a certain tentative quality, they were beginnings, filled with promise rather than any certainties or agendas.

If I had not had that year which Cambridge provided, then I do not think I would have had the courage to go on to the United States and boldly embark on the profession of teaching creative writing courses at their generous colleges (an experience I had never had and did not know the first thing about). It was Cambridge that gave me a boat, a *sail*, and the wind that caused me to cross the Atlantic to earn my own living at last, stand on my own feet and have any trust in myself at all.

Anita Desai has published more than a dozen novels, including Fire on the Mountain, *and is now John E. Burchard Professor Emerita of Humanities at MIT.*

Above: Market Square and Great St Mary's, 2008.

Left: The Market Square, *1930, by Henry Rushbury.*

1939 poster.

There are streets in cities where, it seems, a person could walk blindfold, never having set foot before in that particular pattern. Such streets rush that stranger, insist on destination, fixed purpose. Not in Cambridge. The instant I quit the overheated coach, my clothes slapping cold upon me, I have to draw breath. The sky drains itself, silvering over fens, towards felt, imagined coastline. Turning the corners, I continue in wonder. Will a parking lot open a threat, or the line of sight rest on a juncture of well-inhabited stone?

The quality of physical space can (I believe) encourage the ability to think actively, not reactively; thoughts forming that are unexpected, perhaps important or necessary; that are allowed time, too, for perspectives to build themselves. Cambridge as a dedicated space – the river a line of time; the colleges' wall-lengths no exclusion zone, rather palazzi, temple complexes, villages, lightened to paper cut-outs by their contained human energies – pleased my residual Hindu idea that the brahmchari (every person in the first stage of life) is best given to study, contemplation and dialogue, the foundation for whatever else that life grows to be. *Not the real world?* That phrase confuses happenstance with reality… *but colour: you must miss that? Leaving Trinidad for Cambridge?*

People who otherwise did not speak like one another spoke alike on that point. These welcomers' anxiety was so silvery that it would have been unkind to reassure them with contradictory truths: my research fellowship on the literature of medieval Iceland, a republic in the year 1000, did not seem that distant to me from the fierce independence of my own gulf-stream republic in the year 2000; besides, in my experience much of Trinidad had been two colours. The blue and white convent girl, constrained for 'safety' to travel by car, stepped almost nowhere on her island's soil, watching above her garden or from approved friends' windows the holiday-white hippos and pegasuses in a solidly blue sky; then the effects of rain (nearly six months of it) seem to belong to a non-airconditioned Outside… England was where I really got to know weather; and, from that first, 45-minute walk (fallen leaves thickening deliciously over shoes' borders) to Girton College (I did not yet know that its ancient presiding spirit was Hermione Grammatike, the female mummy whose surname celebrated her learning), Cambridge struck itself into my muscle and bone with the pedestrian intimacy of a Fenland town.

And there is no avoiding the full-length mirror in the central market square. There the woman, part impresario, part abbess, holds a ballgown stall, an affair of curtains behind which random girls vanish, re-emerging in Hollywood she-dragon glitter and scales, or maidenly velvet languishments, at all seasons the celebrants of transformation glow, bare-armed. So even carnival finds a counterpart?

In Cambridge, I have walked my way home.

Vahni Capildeo was educated in Trinidad and at Oxford. She has published three books of poetry and was a Research Fellow at Girton College in 2003–4

"*Sometimes I think Cambridge wonderful, at others a ditch full of clear water where all the frogs have died. It is a bird without feathers, a purse without money; an old dry apple, or the gutters run pure claret. There is something in the air I think which makes people very awake.*"

Ted Hughes, letter to Olwyn Hughes, February 1952, from *Letters of Ted Hughes*, 2007

After I started school in China in 1960 I kept hearing and reading about the expression 'temple of knowledge'. For example, 'it was so and so, or such and such a book or radio programme that led me into the temple of knowledge'. In my mind, however, the expression remained just a vague concept until the spring of 1990, when I came from Beijing to Cambridge to see Dr Yan Huang, a friend of mine who was then a research Fellow at Churchill College. Dr Huang kindly took me to see some of the most famous colleges in the city. When we walked over the Wren Bridge and saw the façade of the New Court bathed in bright sunshine, the vague concept of the temple of knowledge suddenly became vivid in my mind. It was the classical architectural design of the New Court that had invoked in me the metaphorical image of the Temple of Knowledge and it was at that moment that I said to myself, 'If only I could come and study here!' Although Dr Huang explained to me that the New Court was mostly student dormitories plus a few offices, the image of the temple of knowledge that it represented took root in my mind and has remained there to this day.

Shortly afterwards, my dream came true. St John's College awarded me a Benefactors' Research Studentship to study for a PhD in Shakespeare's language. After I came to Cambridge, I found that 'temple of knowledge' meant much more than the superficial image of a beautiful, classical-style college building. In a deeper sense, the real temple of knowledge in Cambridge is the University Library. It not only has an enormous collection of books but also provides the best service a university library can provide. In Chinese the term for a library's collection of books is *cangshu*, which literally means 'hide book'. In other words, a library is a place where books are hidden. In many libraries readers are not allowed to access the books by themselves and it is very difficult to obtain permission to see the rare books 'hidden' in a library. Not so in the UL. Most of the books are on open shelves and students have easy access to the well-kept rare books and manuscripts departments.

Temples are places where gods and goddesses or saints and immortals are worshipped. Temples of knowledge also have their gods and goddesses and saints and immortals. In this sense, each college in Cambridge is a 'temple of knowledge', and its distinguished Fellows and students are the gods and goddesses, saints and immortals, whose statues, portraits or names can be seen in the college chapels or halls. Some, like Newton, Bacon, Milton and Wordsworth, are bigger gods; others are less well-known. As long as they have contributed in some

Left: New Court, St John's College.

The river at Grantchester.

way to the world of knowledge and to humanity in general, they are immortal. Unlike religious gods, they are there not to be worshipped, but to be emulated and surpassed. Living in the temples where great thinkers, scientists, scholars and literary figures once lived, one is bound to be influenced by them and aspire to join them. Wordsworth was a typical example. In his lengthy biographical poem *Prelude*, he described the initial stage of his student life in Cambridge:

We sauntered, played, or rioted; we talked
Unprofitable talk at morning hours;
Drifted about along the streets and walks,
Read lazily in trivial books, went forth
To gallop through the country in blind zeal
Of senseless horsemanship, or on the breast
Of Cam sailed boisterously, …

This might still be true of Cambridge students today. But Wordsworth went on to say:

In this new life. Imagination slept,
And yet not utterly. I could not print
Ground where the grass had yielded to the steps
Of generations of illustrious men,
Unmoved. I could not always lightly pass
Through the same gateways, sleep where they had slept,
Wake where they waked, range that enclosure old,
That garden of great intellects, undisturbed.

Undoubtedly, Wordsworth's feelings are shared by all academics and students at Cambridge University. Such is the power of a great academic institution with its 'generations of illustrious men'.

Although Oxford and Cambridge are equally well known in China, most Chinese, including state leaders, feel a closer affinity for the latter. This is because several of Cambridge's 'illustrious men' are forever remembered by Chinese people for what they themselves did for China. The earliest Cambridge sinologists Sir Thomas Francis

Wade (1818–95) and Herbert Allen Giles (1845–1935) developed the famous Wade-Giles system of romanising the Chinese language, William Empson (1906–84) taught the best and brightest young intellectuals in China during and after the Second World War, and Joseph Needham (1900–95) undertook the mammoth task of uncovering the lost history of science and civilisation in China. Shoulder-to-shoulder with the above-mentioned 'illustrious men' stands Xu Zhimo, a young Chinese poet who studied at King's College, 1920–2. The most famous poem written by this celebrated modern poet is 'Taking Leave of Cambridge Again'.

There is an old Chinese saying: 'It doesn't matter whether a mountain is high or not, as long as an immortal lives there, it becomes famous. It doesn't matter whether a pool is deep or not, as long as a dragon lives there, it becomes efficacious.' The University of Cambridge is a famous temple of knowledge, not because it has beautiful architecture or well-stocked libraries, but because it has engendered so many intellectual immortals and will continue to inspire countless more.

Guohua Chen *is a professor and Deputy Director at the Beijing Foreign Studies University.*

Taking Leave of Cambridge Again (6 November 1928)
by Xu Zhimo

Softly I am leaving,
    Just as softly as I came;
I softly wave goodbye
    To the clouds in the western sky.

The golden willows by the riverside
    Are young brides in the setting sun;
Their glittering reflections on the shimmering river
    Keep undulating in my heart.

The green tapegrass rooted in the soft mud
    Sways leisurely in the water;
I am willing to be such a waterweed
    In the gentle flow of the River Cam.

That pool in the shade of elm trees
    Holds not clear spring water, but a rainbow
Crumpled in the midst of duckweeds,
    Where rainbow-like dreams settle.

To seek a dream? Go punting with a long pole,
    Upstream to where green grass is greener,
With the punt laden with starlight,
    And sing out loud in its radiance.

Yet now I cannot sing out loud,
    Peace is my farewell music;
Even crickets are now silent for me,
    For Cambridge this evening is silent.

Quietly I am leaving,
    Just as quietly as I came;
Gently waving my sleeve,
    I am not taking away a single cloud.

New translation (2008) by Guohua Chen
with Wendy Fillipich

再別康橋

輕輕的我走了，
    正如我輕輕的來；
我輕輕的招手，
    作別西天的雲彩。

那河畔的金柳，
    是夕陽中的新娘；
波光裏的艷影，
    在我的心頭蕩漾。

軟泥上的菁荇，
    油油的在水底招搖；
在康河的柔波裏，
    我甘心做一條水草！

那榆蔭下的一潭，
    不是清泉，是天上虹；
揉碎在浮藻間，
    沈澱著彩虹似的夢。

尋夢？撐一支長篙，
    向青草更青處漫溯，
滿載一船星輝，
    在星輝斑斕裏放歌。

但我不能放歌，
    悄悄是別離的笙簫；
夏蟲也為我沈默，
    沈默是今晚的康橋！

悄悄的我走了，
    正如我悄悄的來；
我揮一揮衣袖，
    不帶走一片雲彩。

Above: '*Meng hu ji*', *literally* Fierce Tiger Collection, *the book of poems by Xu Zhimo (1920), published in Shanghai in 1931. The poet was killed in an aircrash later that year.*

What happened in 1209?

CHRISTOPHER BROOKE

The highly educated clerical elite of the 12th century travelled far in search of good masters. From all over Christendom – and especially from Britain and western Europe – they went to Bologna to study law and to Paris to study theology. As the 12th century turned into the 13th, they increased very rapidly in numbers and sought learning nearer home: some of the leading masters of the day – that is, academic teachers with university degrees – united to form provincial universities at Oxford and Cambridge.

For universities to grow and flourish – then as now – a variety of contradictory demands had to be met. The first universities north of the Alps were formed by groups of masters. They needed fees and patronage; they needed towns with ample lodgings for their students; they needed books; above all they needed the recognition and support of the authorities of the Church, and they needed peace and quiet and independence. Then, as now, the last was the most difficult to secure.

There had been schools in Oxford for much of the 12th century, and towards the end of the century they grew into a corporation of masters and apprentice students, a *universitas* or university. But in the early 13th century life was anything but peaceful. Pope Innocent III and King John were at loggerheads over the appointment of Cardinal Stephen Langton as Archbishop of Canterbury. In 1208 the pope laid an interdict on England and all the churches were closed; for six years they were silent, and in 1209 King John was excommunicated. Also in 1209 a serious riot broke out in Oxford; the schools were closed and masters and students dispersed. The St Albans monk Roger of Wendover (not the most reliable of chroniclers, but a contemporary with access to good information) says that some of the masters moved to Cambridge. A few years later, king and pope were reconciled (1214) and Stephen Langton played a leading role in bringing John and the barons together to agree to Magna Carta (1215). By the 1220s the tiny, young university of Cambridge had a chancellor; in the 1230s its privileges were confirmed by King Henry III and Pope Gregory IX.

Left: The Saxon tower of St Bene't's Church, which was built in 1025. The oldest extant building in Cambridge, St Bene't's served as the college chapel to Corpus Christi College from the 14th to the 16th centuries. The rough stonework of the tower is original, and would have been there in 1209 when the first masters arrived.

Thus it seems likely – one cannot say more – that the arrival of Oxford masters in Cambridge in 1209 marked the beginning of the University, and that they came from the environs of St Mary's Church in Oxford to St Mary the Great in Cambridge. But why did they come to Cambridge? Oxford was in the vast diocese of Lincoln, almost as remote from the authority of bishop and cathedral as it could be. Cambridge was in the tiny diocese of Ely, barely far enough from Ely not to be under the bishop's eye. But there was no cathedral chancellor in the monastic chapter at Ely to claim authority over the university chancellor in Cambridge; and in 1209 there was no bishop at Ely.

Below: Charter of Edward I, 1291/2, confirming the privileges of the University. The illuminated initial shows the king presenting the charter to a Doctor of Canon Law, a Doctor of Civil Law and two kneeling Doctors of Theology. Their degrees can be deduced from their academical dress. (University Archives, Luard 7*)

Eustace, Bishop of Ely, was in exile at the time; the pope had given him a dangerous role as one of the organizers of the interdict.

The real answer seems to be, however, that some of those founding masters, at least, were coming home: Master John Grim was of a Cambridge family and in the service of the Bishop of Ely; Master John Blund may also have linked Oxford, Cambridge and Ely. If they sought peace, independence and freedom, Cambridge was in some respects an ideal choice and 1209 an ideal moment. In the long run these first Cambridge masters knew Bishop Eustace well, and when he returned from exile were able to win his acceptance of what was now (however sketchily) a university in the making. They were men of considerable stature: Master John Grim had been master of the schools at Oxford, and Master John Blund may possibly be identified with an eminent figure at Paris and in Oxford, who was later close to Henry III and very likely one of those who inspired him to grant his charters for Oxford and Cambridge. It is certainly the case that Cambridge would not have survived if the masters had not been able to combine the tradition of independence – to run their own affairs, to organize their own syllabuses – with a measure of official approval. Above all, the support of the king was to be crucial: it is to Henry III and his advisers that Oxford and Cambridge owed the strange monopoly they held in England down to the 19th century.

Henry III's charter was issued in 1231. Meanwhile, in 1209, St Francis of Assisi began to form the Order of Friars Minor, shortly followed by St Dominic and the Dominicans. Hitherto the universities had been chiefly (though not exclusively) manned by secular clergy. The orders of friars were vowed to poverty; humble folk preaching to the humble and working among them. But very soon, and especially in northern Europe, they won many recruits among university students, and these recruits transformed both the orders of friars and the universities. Long before the colleges of secular clerks came into being (Peterhouse was founded in 1284), several houses of friars were established in Cambridge: the Franciscan in 1226 and the Dominican by 1238. They were to disappear in the 1530s when Henry VIII dissolved the monasteries; but the precinct of the Franciscan house survived to become Sidney Sussex College, and the precinct of the Dominican house is preserved in the ample campus of Emmanuel – the most visible reminder today of the University before the colleges.

Christopher Brooke *is Dixie Professor Emeritus of Ecclesiastical History and a Life Fellow of Gonville & Caius College.*

Above: Joseph John Howard, Clare College clerk, examines the remains of an early Master which were discovered in the college chapel, 1935.

Below: Aerial view of Emmanuel College, whose grounds contain the precinct of the house of friars of the Order of St Dominic, founded in 1238 as one of the earliest manifestations of the University.

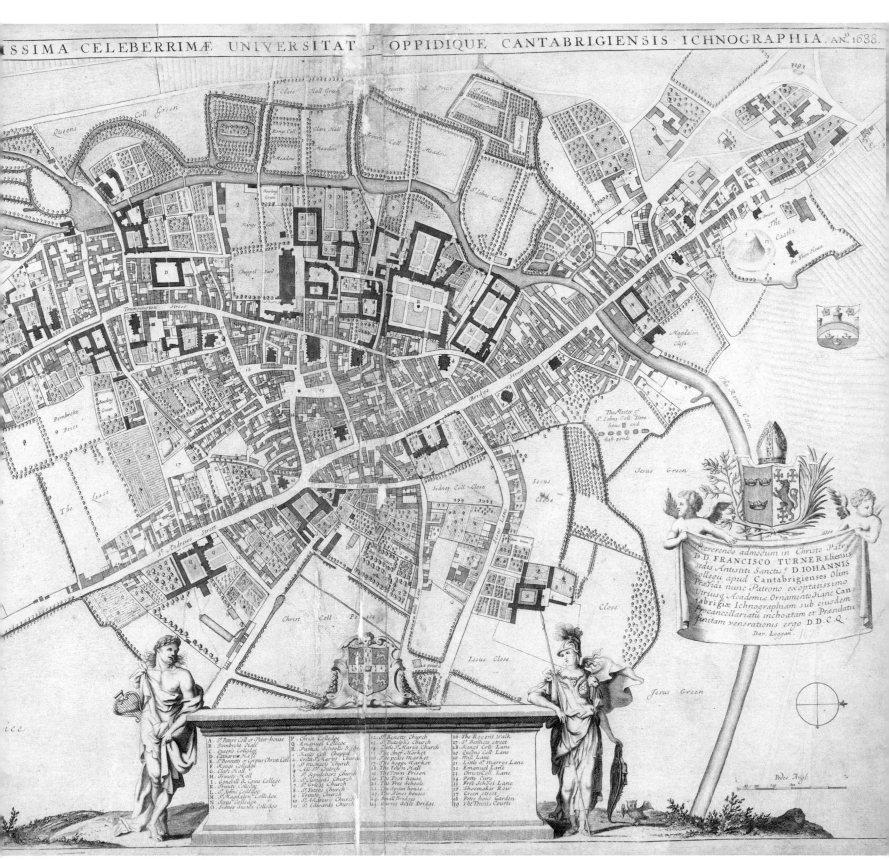

Map of Cambridge by the prolific engraver David Loggan, who had mapped and illustrated Oxford and its colleges (1675) before he began work on his Cantabrigia Illustrata, *which included this map, published 1690.*

Early Statutes

The earliest recorded copy of the statutes of the University, preserved, not in Cambridge, but in Rome, is the Angelica manuscript (right). These are among the earliest, if not the earliest statutes to survive of any university in Europe, depending on whether they can be described as a complete corpus of statutes or just a selection. The thirteen chapters are as follows:

1. Chancellor, elected by Masters, may appoint deputy, who must be approved by the Masters, if he is to be absent for more than a short time. Shall hear all suits of scholars, unless the atrocity of the offence requires the concurrence of the Masters. Must execute the Masters' sentences when brought to his attention. May not make new statutes without consent of the Masters.
2. Qualifications and duties of Masters, including regulations for disputations.
3. Dates for the beginnings and endings of terms.
4. All Masters obliged to attend admission of new Masters, and on days when university business is to be discussed, and to abstain from disputations on such days.
5. Academical dress.
6. Masters' court: to hear actions, with some cases, e.g. rents, excluded.
7. Office of rectors [proctors]: duties are, with burgesses, to assess rents, ensure fair prices for victuals, order times of lectures, disputations, obits, etc., maintain discipline.
8. Office of bedells: to order the schools, serve writs, announce times of lectures, etc., attend ceremonies.
9. Sureties to be given in jurisdictional cases, to attend the outcome.
10. More on judicial proceedings.
11. Rights of scholars and penalties for delinquency.
12. Hostels and rents.
13. Exequies.

Some of these statutes appear also in the earliest Proctors' Books, and indicate, for example, that the Chancellor is to be elected annually. The general tenor shows that the university was essentially governed by the Regent Masters, i.e. those who, having graduated MA, were obliged not only to teach but to concern themselves with the business of the University. (Biblioteca Angelica, Rome, MS 401, fol. 54r)

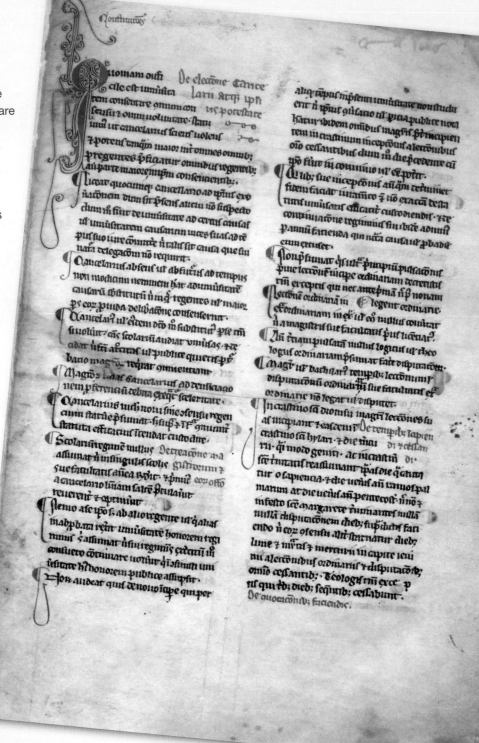

These Elizabethan statutes (below) remained in force until the middle of the 19th century. They mark a decline in the power of the Regent Masters, as exemplified in the Angelica MS (opposite) and an increase in the powers of the Heads of Houses (non-existent, of course, in 1250, as the first college, Peterhouse, was not founded until 1284).

Elizabeth has executed her best signature at the top of the page, and at the bottom William Cecil, Chancellor of the University, has inserted in his own hand the place and the date of signing: Reading, 26 September 1570. (Cambridge University Archives: Luard 187)

In earlier centuries statutes had mostly been enacted piecemeal. Although a new code had been promulgated in the reign of Edward VI, this was doomed to be soon superseded. Elizabeth's statutes turned the 'Caput Senatus', first instituted late in the 14th century and appointed on an *ad hoc* basis, into a body annually appointed. The Caput had originally comprised the Vice-Chancellor, a representative Doctor in each of the Faculties of Divinity, Law and Medicine, a Doctor from one of the religious houses and one representative each of the Regent and Non-Regent Houses. (Non-Regents were persons who had fulfilled their obligations as Regent Masters and were either senior MAs, or Bachelors or Doctors of higher faculties.) By Elizabeth's time, of course, the religious houses had been abolished; otherwise the composition of the Caput remained unchanged. All business to be put to the vote in the University had to pass through the Caput, and every member had a right of veto.

It was succeeded as an executive committee by the Council of the Senate in 1856. Until then the constitution of the University had remained stable, although, fortunately, the statutes regarding the syllabus had become a dead letter.

Elisabeth Leedham-Green is a Fellow and Archivist of Darwin College, Ancient Archivist of Corpus Christi and author of *A Concise History of the University of Cambridge* (1996).

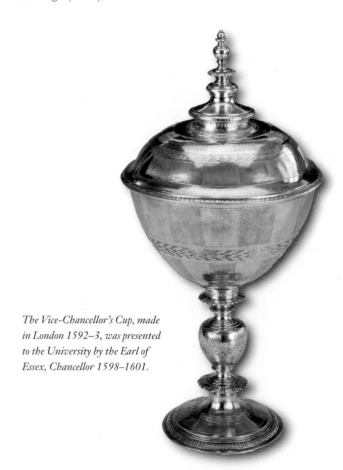

The Vice-Chancellor's Cup, made in London 1592–3, was presented to the University by the Earl of Essex, Chancellor 1598–1601.

Opening the Doors

Who comes to Cambridge?

RAY JOBLING

Visitors to Cambridge cannot but encounter the University and the colleges. It probably lives up to everyone's idea, maybe ideal, of a 'university city'. In term time certainly the students are everywhere, thousands of them, apparently constantly on the move. Outsiders come, of course, with preconceptions founded upon images and a narrative built up over decades, resting upon anecdotes, press coverage, and fiction going back decades and thereby firmly planted in the popular mind. The students are expected to be young, bright, ambitious, and full of obvious (even loud and obtrusive) social confidence born of family origin and fostered in a public school background... with attitudes and accents to match. Perhaps a brainy, studious, select few will reveal humbler origins. Whatever, they all play rugger, row, sometimes chat in cafés, and always cycle furiously. It adds up to a notional finishing school on the one hand, and an academic hothouse on the other. The city streets, and more so the college courts, seemingly offer a glimpse of the country's traditional elite.

The reality is more complex. Cambridge University now provides not just undergraduate education and first degrees to British school-leavers, but also advanced courses and research for the PhD for those who have already graduated – increasingly from other universities. Whereas the former remain largely British, though the numbers from other countries are growing, among the graduates those from abroad have now become a majority. Cambridge is in this educational sense, as in its research, a university with a clear and important international role and mission. The culture and feel of the student community has been changing accordingly... more mature perhaps, certainly more cosmopolitan, serious, and fully committed to scholarship. Cambridge stands at the pinnacle of the academic hierarchy, topping the league tables, and if the students are to be seen as an elite, that judgement must rest on their academic qualifications and intellectual strengths. They, both undergraduate and graduate alike, indisputably work longer and harder on average than their predecessors. Their working days can be long and spent increasingly in laboratories on sites well away from the historic centre, and the arts faculties have also to some extent moved out. College libraries now offer students 24-hour access, an opportunity appreciated and accepted.

Left: Open day tour for prospective new students, 2007.

Right: A demonstration outside what is now the Cambridge University Press bookshop in front of the Senate House against the admission of women to the title of degrees during the vote on 21 May 1897. It was another 50 years before the vote was carried in favour of women graduates.

"The University has swallowed at least two revolutionary proposals. These are the admission of post-graduate members of the new college without preliminary degrees, and the inclusion in its midst of a college which is mainly specialist in character. To add to these a proposal for a co-educational college would be like dropping a hydrogen bomb in the middle of the University!"

Jock Colville, Private Secretary to Sir Winston Churchill, advises that the new Churchill College to be built in Cambridge should not be opened to women, 1958.

On 4 July 1998 over 900 women between the ages of 68 and 96 responded to the invitation to come to Cambridge to accept the apology of the University for failing to recognise women for so long. It was 50 years from the admission of women as full members of the University. The fit processed on foot from Newnham to the Senate House and were cheered as they walked through the streets. The less fit and those from Girton were taken by bus with a motor cycle escort and drove down Trinity Street the wrong way to the astonishment of the crowd who looked at the signs on the buses. When they read them they clapped enthusiastically, many of the women with their hands high above their heads.

I had one year not being a member of the University but attending lectures with the men, taking the same exams, but no gown. In October 1948 we wore gowns for the first time but the women's gowns were made with sleeves open only below the elbow; these sometimes caught on the open handles of the cars of the day, bringing their wearers off their bikes. Within a short time a sewing woman was brought in to cut away the sleeves to the shoulder, removing the risk.

Enid Woolett
(1947)

In my day it was very relaxed. A letter from my housemaster, one from my tutor and, yes, one from my rowing coach! That was all that seemed to be necessary and, as for an interview! My parents wanted to re-visit Cambridge, since we used to live there during the war, so we all trooped in to see the Tutor for Admissions together. There followed 15 minutes or so of small talk. I seemed to be an extra, not being called upon to speak a word! Finally, everyone rose and we were ushered out of the door, nothing having been mentioned about my admission.

Worried stiff, I blurted out: 'When will I know if I have been accepted or not?'

T for A: 'Oh, dear chap. Don't worry about that. Once we've accepted a man, just let us know when you would like to come up to the University.'

I don't remember ever receiving any sort of formal acceptance, but I arrived and no one objected, so I stayed for four years in one of the most stimulating environments in the world.

Alan Shrimpton
(1957)

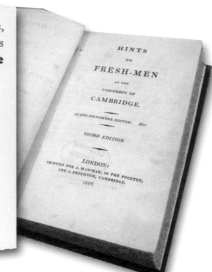

Advice from Hints to Fresh-men at the University of Cambridge, *1807.*

"Dear Sir,
I will be obliged to you to order me down 4 Dozen of Wine, Port, Sherry—
Claret, & Madeira, one Dozen of Each; I have got my Furniture in, &
begin to admire College Life. Yesterday my appearance in the Hall in my
State Robes was Superb, but uncomfortable to my diffidence."

George Gordon Lord Byron, letter to John Hanson (1805)

More generally, the student body reflects changes occurring in the wider society over recent times. In the 1950s, even into the 1960s, the colleges still relied for their admissions upon links with schools built up over a long period, particularly in the independent sector. Contacts were undeniably important in this process, and while without doubt the already privileged thus secured yet more advantage, there is ample evidence that the system was far from wholly exclusive. There were undergraduates who were very definitely by no means privileged in their backgrounds. This was the era of College Entrance and Scholarship Examinations, confirming a determination to assess academic potential in a more formal fashion than via the legendary interview alone. They gave the gifted grammar school 'scholarship boys' (still mainly boys) their opportunity – clever, articulate and ambitious. By the mid-1960s a great expansion in higher education was under way, reflecting not just the transformation of secondary education but also greater demands for professional and managerial talent, and also rising popular aspirations. The term 'first-generation student' came into use. Older universities expanded and new ones were founded. Cambridge in turn adapted accordingly. During the 1970s and 1980s of course the colleges changed their statutes to become co-educational establishments.

Matriculation at Girton, 1979, the year in which men were admitted as
undergraduates to what had been the first women's college.

Michaelmas, 2007.

A scholarship student from East Ham Grammar School, I was one small drop in the post-war, Labour-sponsored tidal wave that was changing Britain from a society of privilege to one of merit. Cambridge, with prescience and daring, absorbed about 6,000 of us in three years. This influx of raw talent must have delighted the faculty. Our parents were mostly labourers and trades people. We were often the first family member, ever, to enter a university. My grandmother washed floors to keep me in school. Of course there were challenges. Professional counselling did not exist at Cambridge, and some made bad academic choices or just drowned. I did not even understand the *title* of one of my first maths courses! However, I think we, in our different ways, have justified the faith that Cambridge and our families had in us.

Richard Mansfield
(1954)

In my entrance examination it seems that what interested my examiners most was my free topic essay on the good works of Adolf Hitler following his publication in 1925 of *Mein Kampf*. At my interview my views were intensively probed. 'Was I an active Fascist?' came one question. My opinions of the later Hitler seemed to put minds at rest and my schoolgirl image must have seemed unthreatening too.

It has always been amazing what Hitler got away with and how he got people of high position to help him. But perhaps I should not be surprised. In 1950 I arrived at Newnham porters' lodge with my substantial luggage for my first term. I was told which room I had been given in Peile. As I moved with some difficulty in that general direction a woman, in what I must say struck me as eccentric attire, asked if she could help me with my awkward load. Remembering my father's briefing that there would be staff to assist me, I accepted help and on arriving at my room I said a polite thank you, giving her a silver sixpenny piece for her prompt aid. It was accepted with a smile. She smiled very kindly at me again next day when I was formally introduced to her – the Vice-Principal.

I was reading Modern Languages and had several brilliant lecturers, who were academically strong but had appalling accents. One of them, recently deceased, invited me courteously not to attend his lectures when he'd planned to read out lengthy passages in the foreign tongue. The intense care and interest shown for my studies by my tutors were unsurpassable. However, afternoon lectures were not infrequently skipped in favour of tennis, and I played against Oxford in each of my three years. Dancing at the 'Dot' was regarded as important too, where it could be argued that tangos at least provided the colouring of another country and occasionally a new word – not in the books.

Elvira Kinsman Young
(1950)

A literary critic, particularly one of the Freudian persuasion, might make much of my first memory of dining in. There I was in hall, looking down at my soup. I took up a spoon and stirred. And stirred again. But without result: the substance just would not combine with the liquor. Then I realized that I had been trying to dissolve the college arms emblazoned in the bowl. Apart from possible symbolism, the incident was revealing. I was one of Tom Sharpe's grammar school tykes, from a home that did not run to armorial crockery, though certain of the Fellows would probably have been surprised to discover we had by then got beyond chipped enamel pannikins.

There were, I think, three interviews in college. The one that sticks, well, let's say in my memory, was with Mr Camps. I waited for what seemed hours by his black-painted door only to be greeted in his disconcertingly halting manner with the words: 'Ah yes, I… know your… brother, so I… don't… need to talk to you,' and be sent on my way.

Christopher Smith
(1957)

Until 1963, the colleges conducted their own independent admissions, although the Scholarship Examination was run by an inter-college Board of Examiners. With the boom in applications in the early 1960s, the group system was adopted, where candidates applied to a group of colleges and sat a central entrance examination. This was then abandoned in 1985 in favour of places offered based on interview and A level grades.

I had hoped it would be the best of times; in many ways it turned out to be the worst of times. A little lad from Lowestoft Grammar School, I had no idea for instance about 'eating in hall' – as far as I recall I had never eaten with anyone except my godparents, who had brought me up. I didn't possess a tie, and was too poor to own a suit. I had never even shared a room with anyone except my younger brother. The year I 'came up' (the social implications of that still thunder across the years), the intake to my college was about 100, of which no more than a handful were from other than a public school. Thus, the entire language and manners and rules which I was expected to understand and conform to were mysterious, even alien. I was made to feel isolated, unwanted and definitely unwashed. And when the student in the next room to me committed suicide towards the end of my first term, I was not surprised. The image of his coffin being taken down the staircase haunts me to this very day.

Tony Palmer
(1960)

I was an unlikely candidate – a 30-year-old lone parent working as an apprentice carpenter and joiner – when Clare College accepted me as a mature student.

Switching from a 40-hour week at the joinery shop to being an architecture student provided interesting contrasts. The joinery shop operated under a controlled factory regime that, nevertheless, tolerated much unfairness. As the only woman there, I was accustomed to harassment by my fellow apprentices, but that was mild compared to the bullying they meted out to each other.

There was nothing like that at Clare College, where I was treated as an individual and never felt patronised, but the Department of Architecture was a different matter. Although it prided itself on its liberal and radical culture, it also tended to marginalise outsiders. I remember protests by women students about being assigned to study kitchens while the men did structures, and it was not unknown for male students to add pictures of naked women to their projects to spice them up.

Yvonne Jerrold
(1974)

I was not born to Cambridge as many of my contemporaries seemed to be; my school knew virtually nothing about Oxbridge. When the time came for my interview, a couple of teachers set up a mock interview for me; good of them, but it was more of a mockery. I had no idea what to

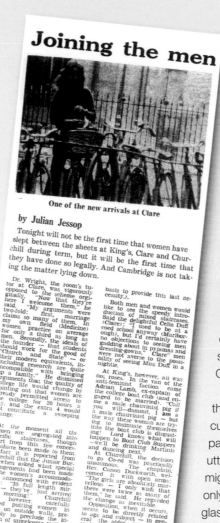

Joining the men

One of the new arrivals at Clare

by Julian Jessop

Tonight will not be the first time that women have slept between the sheets at King's, Clare and Churchill during term, but it will be the first time that they have done so legally. And Cambridge is not taking the matter lying down.

Varsity October, 1970

expect, and must have seemed pretty *aggrieved* to the interviewers. They asked what I saw myself doing in ten years' time and my answer was snappy in both senses: 'Not married with children, if that's what you are getting at' (they weren't). I can only assume they saw some potential behind my feistiness, and I thank them for that.

Alison Cawley
(1979)

I was raised in the Iron Age, a life ruled by Bangladeshi rural superstition and splashed with Islamic culture – though technically, I lived in 1980s London. No unmarried women beyond 18, no notions of a solar system and certainly no bicycles for girls. And then I was suddenly an undergraduate at Trinity College, Cambridge.

Rice and curry, burgers and chicken wings – that is to say, I come from a world without cutlery. Presented at my first formal dinner with a parade of multifarious metal apparatus, I was utterly disorientated by what possible end this might serve. The dazzle of silver was matched only by the radiance of an absurd array of glassware – it was the rituals of decanting, rather than any inclination to drink itself, which prompted me into the forbidden realm of intoxication, the sin of sharabi. Just three inquisitive sips of sherry, wine and port; more than enough for my virgin mind to soar to a delicious madness that compelled me to hitch up my sequin-embroidered saree around my waist and dance the Trinity Great Court Run.

A room of my own was a dream that I'd harboured in the most rebellious recesses of my mind, since I developed a love of reading, accomplished only illicitly with the secret light from a hidden torch or the snatched light from a streetlamp outside the window. And now, I had the right to close my own door and sit at my own desk – though I will confess to doing the second far less frequently than the first.

In my past life, knowledge was forbidden, education was corrupting and independence of mind was the most dangerous thing. And now, I walked in libraries that held all the knowledge of all the ages, libraries that chimed the death of the adolescent marriage and motherhood that should have been my fate, the same my sisters had submitted to without even a sullen frown. I sought out the secluded corners of the oldest libraries and sat in nests of illuminating dust, reading to my heart's content.

I discovered Newton and atheism, Huxley and drugs, Woolf and sex. I partied at clubs, bops and balls. But I was ever the outsider. I launched myself into happy society, though I was weighed down with the sorrow of loneliness. In our globalised world, outlandish creatures like me are becoming a more familiar presence at Cambridge, and I hope they will also become more accepted and nurtured than I was. But there is certainly a happy ending to my story: to the continuing horror of my family, I now ride my bicycle everywhere.

Jobeda Ali
(1993)

I am a wheelchair user, paralysed from the neck down. I was possibly the first female tetraplegic undergraduate at Cambridge (although I don't know that for certain). During the last 15 years Cambridge has made strong efforts to increase the number of disabled students and to cater for their needs. While I was at the University, I lived at Bridget's, a hostel for disabled students at both Cambridge University and Anglia Polytechnic University (as it was then called). A few years ago Bridget's closed down, enabling disabled students to live in colleges alongside their able-bodied peers.

I was very fortunate in having an enlightened Director of Studies, and a supportive tutor who helped me as much as they could. However, I did come across the occasional attitude problem from the other staff. One supervisor suddenly asked me in the middle of a session on Cicero: 'How do you get up in the morning, Victoria?' It was not the question I was expecting at that moment – I had great difficulty in keeping a straight face!

Victoria Brignell
(1994)

Travelling up before my interview, nightmare scenarios and nagging questions of self-doubt were marching through my mind just as quickly as the flat countryside rushed past the train windows. Coming straight from an average comprehensive sixth-form college, I remember feeling petrified, mainly because this was the first time I had ever had an interview upon which so much hinged, and because my mind was flooded with images of vast numbers of students at the best independent schools up and down the country undergoing finely honed preparations for interview success.

The actual interview went badly; a minor difference of opinion on an academic issue soon proved highly flammable. I was disconcerted and by the time I had climbed out of the hole I had dug myself, it was too late. Days later I received a call from the University informing me that I had been 'pooled'. I scrabbled around frantically to find out what it actually meant. But before I could worry about it further, Christ's College had asked me to attend a day of interviews and these went well.

Sam Higton
(1996)

King's Parade.

Applications and undergraduate numbers grew at this time, and simultaneously the college admissions system and selection processes came to be more closely scrutinised as the need to demonstrate academic and social fairness became an imperative. The intercollegiate entrance examinations receded and reliance on A-level performance, plus interview, became the norm. Colleges still jealously guarded their autonomy in the admissions field, but steadily came to see that alignment of policies and procedures would benefit everyone. It was to be decades however, well after 2000, before the University itself would become a formal partner in the admissions process, joining in strategic planning and policy deliberation. This was very much in response to the introduction of government requirements and 'targets' aimed at widening participation and access. In the interim, without question, the colleges did begin to trawl more widely for potential talent, gradually at first but then with gathering momentum, proactively recruiting rather than simply sifting through applications as they came in. Admissions offices were established and staffed with professionals. Tutors, initially alone and then in teams, began to tour the country visiting schools, seeking to stimulate interest among gifted sixth-formers who would not otherwise have contemplated studying in Cambridge.

Through the 1990s the admissions recruitment efforts began to have impact, bringing forward a larger, wider pool of applicants, often the ablest and most promising students in their schools. The outcome is that the undergraduates who now come to Cambridge have school-leaving academic results unsurpassed by any other British university. Sadly, however, in the nature of things the hopes of many were to be dashed in the face of rising demand but only limited space and places, generating wider disappointment and doubt in the process. A tide of

When I arrived from East London I quickly realized that, the 'Cambridge experience' would be exactly what I made it. I did try my hand at some of the activities that were typically associated with the University: I woke up at 6.30am to go rowing (I won't pretend this happened more than three times!), I churned out the ridiculous number of essays that my Social and Political Sciences (SPS) Tripos required, attended 'Bops' where everyone was stupidly drunk and moved 'interestingly' to some seriously cheesy music, and lasted until the 5.30am survivors' photo at May balls. And it didn't take long for me to admit that the style of singing in my college choir was just way too different from what I was used to and enjoyed while I was a member of the my sixth-form college's Gospel Choir.

At the top of my list of priceless memories I have to place the night of Cambridge's first Urban Talent Show; being pounced on at the Freshers' Fair by the founder of the University's African Caribbean Society; and the pleasant surprise I felt when people like Makosi (as opposed to less surprising guests like Richard Dawkins) from Big Brother (2005) were invited to speak at the Union.

In my second year, in the capacity of co-president of the Black and Asian Caucus, the most memorable event for me was the launch of a mentoring scheme which linked professionals and students from ethnic minority backgrounds. Unsurprisingly, my degree had to take priority over the scheme's continuation. However, one of its aims – to dispel stereotypes about Cambridge – continued to be fulfilled on the occasions when I and other students showed AS level students around the city and colleges. I shouldn't have been surprised when one of the prospective applicants found me on Facebook, the social networking site, used by the majority of students (and some lecturers!). Facebook was useful for organising events, viewing photos and staying in contact. It was also a huge distraction! Anyway, simpler things like how stunning St Catharine's College is at night, riding my bike past King's College in the summer, and paying £5.30 for a three-course meal in a beautiful hall, will always be the important sprinklings on the multi-layered cake of my Cambridge experience.

Amifa Tholley
(2005)

Material supplied to schools by Cambridge University Admissions Office, some of it produced by GEEMA (Group to Encourage Ethnic Minority Applications), which was set up in 1989 to promote greater diversity.

The entrance to the Downing site.

criticism rose with increasingly pointed accusations of class, race and gender bias, in outcomes if not by deliberate intent. Yet the Cambridge colleges had already begun to address the underlying issues, and they were not reluctant to expose their admissions procedures to public scrutiny. A few colleges took the initiative in steps to encourage and facilitate ethnic minority admissions, later to be universally embraced in a full-blown intercollegiate outreach scheme, with more two-way visits, summer schools, mentoring programmes, and the like. St John's were the first (in Lambeth), then quickly followed by others, in establishing substantial ongoing working partnerships with Local Education Authorities in disadvantaged areas to encourage academic ambition and support learning, in the process awakening interest in the prospect of Cambridge. Not widely enough known is that it has been integral to these efforts that the colleges added significant resources to schools to encourage achievement more generally, reaching down the schools to pupils as young as 12 years old.

The undergraduates now being admitted are better qualified than ever they were. The student body is larger and more diverse socially, and in its ethnic and racial mix, than it was 20 years ago, and dramatically more so than in the 1960s. The University draws in students from a vastly wider range of schools than in earlier eras. It is by no means as yet a statistical reflection of the encompassing British social structure, but this reflects no lack of college or University will or effort. It remains an issue that while the University and colleges are fully and genuinely committed to being open to all the talents, candidates still have to be encouraged and persuaded to come forward from a wide social and educational background. The contributory factors are deeply entrenched and persistent in the host society, its culture and its key institutions, notably secondary education. These have to be addressed if there is to be continuing progress.

Ray Jobling is a lecturer in sociology, and Fellow and former Senior Tutor at St John's College.

Enabling mission

ANIL SEAL

It is a truth universally acknowledged that every leading university which wishes to remain in the front rank must keep its doors open to talent, both from home and overseas. This, and its corollary that academic merit and purses deep enough to meet the costs of study, do not always, or even frequently, go together.

So, the decision of government, more than a quarter of a century ago, to triple the fees paid by overseas students, ostensibly to cover 'real costs', represented a grave threat to Cambridge's international standing. That increase provoked an outcry abroad and in the sadly diminishing circles of domestic enlightenment. It is to Cambridge's credit that it responded to the challenge, first by defying the fiat from on high by a somewhat quixotic revolt, and soon after by giving a committee the remit of helping overseas students and devising schemes of awards for the longer term.

In its turn, this in 1982 encouraged the Local Examinations Syndicate, as Cambridge Assessment was then called (which had done well by examining many students from the new Commonwealth), to give £10 million to establish the Cambridge Commonwealth Trust, our first step towards putting into place a 'needs blind' system of admission for talented students from abroad, an important milestone in Cambridge's history.

Lecture theatre.

Cambridge Commonwealth Trust: first meeting of trustees under the chairmanship of HRH The Prince of Wales, October 1982.

The gift from the syndicate, generous though it was, remained dwarfed by the resources of the Rhodes Trust in Oxford, which then supported about 180 scholars, whereas our new trust had funds to give awards to at most a quarter of that number. With an optimism unfettered by realism, our trustees settled on a target to be achieved, if not in the 20th century, then in the next millennium: of supporting twice as many scholars in Cambridge as Rhodes did in Oxford. Within five years, the Cambridge Commonwealth Trust had achieved that aim; and today, the two sister trusts (the Commonwealth Trust and the Overseas Trust for countries beyond the Commonwealth which was set up in 1988) help to support ten times as many scholars in Cambridge as Rhodes does in Oxford.

Between them, these two trusts have already helped more than 13,500 overseas students to take up their places in Cambridge, and their third sister trust, the Cambridge European Trust, has in the past decade helped 3,300 students from the EU.

Behind these statistics, the visible tip of an iceberg of almost titanic dimensions, there lies unremitting hard work and commitment by the trustees, by those who work for the trusts, by their many collaborators and

Arriving from warm and sunny Singapore to bleak, wet, wintry England for my interview, I wondered how anybody survived more than a few days there, much less a few years. Having the surname Wong meant that I was the last person in the line-up. One young man burst out of the interview room saying that he had never felt so stupid in his entire life. The rest of us made sympathetic noises.

At the interview, I was relieved to be asked for the definition of resistance (in physics). I replied with the simple equation. I was then asked if there were any resistors in the room. After pointing to all the obvious ones – the light bulb, the kettle, the heater – I looked at my interviewers and cautiously pronounced that everything in the room was a resistor, that electricity could run through anything as long as the voltage was high enough, for example when lightning strikes. I could sense that that was the answer they had hoped for and felt somewhat relieved.

Ting Hway Wong
(1992)

For the entire two months before I left for Cambridge, almost every conversation I had about my impending move included the phrase: 'You'll have to get a bicycle, of course.' Even the otherwise taciturn official at Gatwick who examined my visa reminded me of my impending cycle necessity. And so, as I mentally listed all the things I would need in my transition from the undergraduate to graduate world and in my new designation as an ex-pat, I placed 'bicycle' right at the top.

My third morning in Cambridge, one of my housemates and I headed out to register with a doctor. He suggested cycling, and I decided that, since my first bike ride in a decade was as likely to end with a trip to the doctor as not, we might as well kill two birds with one stone. I wobbled my way down the street, fighting the urge to ride on the right and cringing when a bus passed us with (in my harried estimation) mere centimetres to spare. My first steps at Cambridge were often like that first bike ride; I sometimes got lost along the way and ended up on the wrong side of the road.

One of the main adjustments involved the Oxbridge system itself. The American structure seemed more directed, requirements clearer. By comparison, the English system was riddled with unknowns. My supervisor at Penn, the wonderful Jonathan Steinberg, summed up the situation with an insightful brevity I didn't fully appreciate until a few weeks after my arrival. Responding to my statement that my plan was to simply do my best at whatever I was told to do, he replied, 'But, no one is going to tell you to do anything'. Such was the essence of the Cambridge experience, this realisation that no roadmap would be forthcoming, that it must rather be constructed, with all the uncertainty and anxiety that accompanies such an undertaking.

Such a system carried its own rewards, including the opportunity to study with experts, several of whom became excellent mentors; confidence and pride in not only exceeding expectations but in setting them as well. Like at Penn, the international mix of the programme was

Outside Trinity Gate, October 2007.

also a tremendous asset. Each student offered unique perspectives of current debates and historical issues, informed by their diverse backgrounds. Our different strengths and areas of expertise made seminar discussions and feedback on research both richer and more challenging. Supervisors and other professors provided valuable input on structuring research and honing dissertations, but other students were an equally vital part of the process.

There were also more intangible rewards. I left the first few meetings of one seminar, entitled 'Making History, Ending History' wondering if history would in fact be the end of me. I soon found I wasn't alone. Together my course-mates and I represented a variety of places, but we all sometimes viewed life on the Cam as a formidable challenge. As we adjusted, we met often, in the library, in college, cafés or pubs. We met to study, to commiserate, to eat and chat aimlessly. Our conversations careened wildly (often like my early bike riding) from movies to what exactly a supervisor's scrawled 'fine' in the margins might mean. Just as the variety of students enhanced the intellectual experience, it also offered close-knit groups created by the experience of life at the University. Thus international diversity became a key component of the Cambridge experience and one of its many strengths.

Melissa Clapper
(2006)

friends in Cambridge and far beyond, and, above all, the strategy of putting together packages of support from several different sources to enable as many of the best students as possible to take up their places at Cambridge.

Not surprisingly, this enterprise has helped to keep Cambridge at the top of the league of world-class universities and has immeasurably fortified its international role in the wider world. For example, the Malaysian Commonwealth Studies Centre, generously funded by Malaysian sources, has helped many students from the Commonwealth and from Malaysia, has planned an international and Commonwealth university in Malaysia, organised meetings of Commonwealth Finance and Cabinet Secretaries, and, for the past six years, been behind one of the most significant initiatives in the Commonwealth, an informal Commonwealth Club which promotes electoral democracy, in which Election Commissioners with responsibility for more than a billion-and-a-half voters meet annually (and to good purpose) in Cambridge. The unique library of the Commonwealth Society has been rescued and brought to Cambridge; and it is generally recognised that Trinity's laudable initiative in setting up the Newton Trust has owed much to the example of the Cambridge Trusts, with which it shared a founder director for the first 12 years of its existence. Most recently in this odyssey of achievement, mention must be made of the setting up of the Gates Cambridge Trust, with the largest single endowment that any university in this country has ever received, a munificent benefaction which may not have come Cambridge's way quite so smoothly if the Cambridge Trusts had not ensured Cambridge's place as a critical hub on the global map of today.

Yet mere statistics and these few words cannot convey the hard work on the one hand, and the excitement and gratification on the other, of helping to give young people from so many countries the

In part, I pursued a graduate degree at Cambridge to be among the English. I suspect that this motive – which falls at the intersection of admiration, curiosity, adulation and condescension – has been shared by many US students at the University over the last 200 years. At my college's 2004 annual dinner, giddy from drinking to the health of the Queen, I scanned the others who shared my table. To my right, at the end of the bench, an Italian. To my left, eight more nationalities were strung out without repetition: Canadian, then Australian, Serbian, Japanese, Greek, German, South African, Slovenian, and – finally – an Englishman (this list is accurate… I wrote it down). While my short-lived conception of Cambridge as some sort of English preserve had been destroyed months earlier, I was still impressed at the heterogeneity of the graduate community around me, in which my English friends played a proportionate role. I left the University a little confused, with my appreciation of international experiences intact and my nation-centric world view shattered.

Jordan Jacobs
(2003)

opportunity to study here. If Cambridge is to have as distinguished a future as it has a past, this great enterprise will need to continue to prosper, drawing on the support of our alumni and the many collaborators who have, in an exciting two-and-a-half decades, enabled the trusts to make a contribution to Cambridge which others have deemed to be quite unique in the annals of this university's history.

Anil Seal *is the former Director of the Cambridge Commonwealth and Overseas Trusts and a Fellow in History at Trinity College.*

Bill Gates, who has donated over £100 million for the Gates Trust and other University developments, visiting Cambridge in 1997.

Coming up in 1967

I first saw Cambridge during my school's half-term holiday in October 1962, the week of the Cuban Missile Crisis when Kennedy and Khruschev were threatening to make revising for Tripos an increasingly irrelevant activity. It was love at first sight.

I was visiting my brother who had just gone up to Caius to read Law. We were Jewish boys from Manchester; our parents had left school at 14, our grandparents were illiterate immigrants from Eastern Europe. The Cambridge I saw in 1962 seemed very traditional: students on bikes racing down Trinity Street between lectures, gowns to be worn after dark, the streets patrolled by bulldogs, fines of six shillings and eight pence levied for minor infractions of the arcane rules; but the appeal of the university town was instant and overwhelming.

Five years later I matriculated in my own right, having doggedly believed in that destiny despite the deep and understandable scepticism unwittingly demonstrated by most of my teachers. Staying overnight in Tree Court for my interview in September 1966, I was amused by the arrival in the morning of a jug of hot water, borne by a porter, who greeted me with that unique mixture of deference and contempt I came to know so well. I never had the slightest doubt that I would be offered a place. I belonged in Cambridge.

By October 1967 the place had moved on quite significantly since that first sight of it five years earlier. Gates were still shut in college at midnight, but I was allocated a room in the new building in Harvey Court in West Road, where there were no gates but there was running hot water.

There were plenty of traditions still intact but we were very aware of the student radicalism which had started at the University of California at Berkeley in the early years of the decade, and was spreading slowly over the campuses of Western Europe. Our generation believed it was in the vanguard of significant social and political change. This was demonstrated in my first term, when Harold Wilson arrived in the market place and was pelted with eggs. A few months later, great attempts were made to overturn Denis Healey's car with the Minister of Defence still inside it. What a politically articulate lot we were.

This radicalization altered the social balance of Cambridge life. All my friends tended to have arrived in Cambridge from grammar schools rather than public schools. We knew no sense of inferiority which might have been the case in the previous decade, when public schoolboys and their attitudes still predominated.

By far the worst aspect of Cambridge life was the unhealthy 10:1 ratio of men to women. In my second year I fell in love with a very attractive first year historian who unfortunately lived in Girton. There was a statuesque row of necking couples lined up outside the gates in the final minutes until the clock struck midnight. The parting of sweet

sorrow was followed by the inevitable Long March of the men back into town along the Huntingdon Road, all of us contemplating an overnight stay and risking the possibility of rustication. Sex was much discussed, but, I suspect, less widely practised until colleges went co-educational in the 1970s. I missed Swinging London and the sexual revolution. I only had four Manchester City trophies and three one-day Lancashire cricket cups to show for my years as an undergraduate.

Nevertheless, I revelled in what Cambridge had to offer – acting in one production for the Mummers or the ADC every term, writing on sport and films for *Varsity* and playing football, cricket and tennis for Caius. It wasn't all roses – I was quite unhappy there for much of the time – but Cambridge made me what I am and I shall always remain thankful I was there.

Colin Shindler is a TV writer and producer, and novelist. His autobiography, *Manchester United Ruined My Life*, was published in 1999.

Christopher Angeloglou

Hiroh Shimura

Coming up in 1994

Right back in sixth form, when I was thumbing through prospectuses for prospective universities, Cambridge seemed to offer something other places couldn't. I didn't even need to open the prospectus – you could just tell from the cover. It was brown, you see. And not in some retro 1960s-style rust-interior sense either, just a really boring brown. Yup – Cambridge was the place where I wouldn't have to worry about the fact that I wasn't particularly trendy or hip or whatever the cool word for cool was in those days. All the other university prospectuses looked like ads for dating agencies, crammed with pictures of beautiful and trendy people having a beautiful, trendy time being beautiful and trendy. And laughing, lots of laughing.

By contrast, the students photographed in Cambridge's prospectus looked like they were, well, studying for their degrees. So it was a no-brainer for me: I would apply to Cambridge, where I could exercise my grey matter rather than my genitals.

Being at a comprehensive school in Hounslow, I perhaps relied on that prospectus more than I otherwise would have. I also consulted an 'alternative' prospectus published by the Students' Union, which purported to show the unofficial, untamed underbelly of Cambridge life. But flicking through that thing merely strengthened my resolve, after it memorably described Christ's College as 'a mug of Horlicks'. And so it was to Christ's College that I applied.

I remember friends telling me I should buy a snappy suit for the interview. Instead I made do with the most tasteless hand-me-down bottle-green blazer that a podgy uncle had outgrown. I paired it with oversize navy trousers – the only non-denim pair I owned – and couldn't have looked more ridiculously untrendy if I tried. But I didn't care. I'd found my kingdom of geeks.

So, imagine my surprise during Freshers' Week to find the majority of fellow students were neither boring, geeky nor asexual.

I felt like I'd stepped from the grainy paper of the *Hounslow Chronicle* into a glossy collage of the *Tatler*'s society pages, and those über-trendy fashion shoots in *Dazed & Confused*. As if I didn't feel intimidated and inadequate enough, when Freshers' Week drew to an end, I discovered all these beautiful and trendy students were actually clever too.

When I sought comfort squandering my student maintenance grant on the latest CDs, by some uncanny coincidence I found they captured perfectly what I was feeling, particularly tracks like 'The Beautiful Ones' by Suede, 'Common People' by Pulp, 'Loser' by Beck and, my university anthem, 'Creep' by Radiohead.

That's not to say Cambridge didn't provide some sanctuary for us aspirant geeks. In fact, the division between us and them was so stark that we even gave them a collective acronym: BPs, which stood for either Beautiful People or Buttery People, because they all hung out and laughed and flicked their shampoo-ad hair in the college bar (which for some reason that I still don't know was called the Buttery). Don't get me wrong – they were nice people. They just weren't geeks.

I remember trying to articulate all this adolescent angst to a student in the year above me. He suggested that, evolutionarily speaking, we had all been geeks at school. After all, how else could we have attained the A-Level grades necessary for admission? The BPs were simply taking advantage of their relatively superior bone structures to just play at being hip. In other words, it was all an act and therefore the rest of us shouldn't feel intimidated.

But now, with the benefit of both hindsight and having spoken with pupils in various schools and colleges, I think his explanation of the BP syndrome was just plain bollocks. Instead, the answer is much less about pretence, and potentially much more useful. Whatever is said about the pros and cons of public schools versus state schools, one difference seems to matter more than any other: public schools create a culture where, put cheesily, it's cool to be clever; where there's no trade-off between being a studious geek and being socially and sexually successful.

This was by far the most powerful cultural shock Cambridge hit me with. If only every student could benefit from the same thing, regardless of what school or university they find themselves in.

Gautam Malkani read Social and Political Science at Christ's College before becoming a journalist. His first novel, *Londonstani*, was published in 2006.

Changes in teaching and curriculum

MELVEENA MCKENDRICK

I arrived in Cambridge as a new research student at Girton in the October of 1963 and before the end of my first year had started to supervise undergraduates. Four years later I married a history don at Caius and my Cambridge course was set. Now, as Pro-Vice-Chancellor for Education, I look back over 40 years as supervisor, tutor, senior tutor, director of studies, lecturer, professor and chair of my faculty, and reflect on the changes I have witnessed. From outside, little in Cambridge may appear to have changed. Gowns might have disappeared from lecture and examination rooms, but we still have our colleges, our supervision system and our Tripos, we still have our bright students, and we still take pride in our predominantly academic-led and bottom-up governance. These are all crucial aspects of our identity, our distinctiveness. The view from the inside, however, is very different. Not only have the pace and intensity of academic life in Cambridge greatly increased over 40 years, but to be a student here now is in some significant ways also a very different experience, not least because with the change in the age of majority in 1973 all undergraduates over the age of 18 officially became adults overnight.

The most visible change, instantly noticeable in lectures and college halls, is the dramatic rise in the female student population. Between 1968 and 2006, while undergraduate student numbers overall rose from 8,271 to 11,731, the proportion of women undergraduates rose from 11 per cent to 50 per cent. Even if one includes graduate students, the proportion of women is 48 per cent. So from being in the 1960s still a fair simulacrum of a boys' public school Cambridge has

> There is a SIREN, to whose strains you must be deaf, if you would be wise, if you would be honoured, if you would be happy. Her name is neither *Parthenope, Ligeia,* nor *Leucosia.* It is SLOTH*. *Vitanda est improba* SIREN, DESIDIA †.

become, at student level at least, a thoroughly mixed community. The effect this has on student culture and social life I leave to the reader's imagination. Interestingly, the arts/sciences balance has changed only minimally: in 1968, 52.4 per cent of undergraduates read arts subjects and 47.6 per cent read sciences; by 2006, the arts and sciences had swapped places, with 47.2 per cent reading arts and 52.8 per cent sciences. These figures are heartening in two respects: they show that in spite of the advance of the sciences Cambridge still provides a flourishing broad-based education across all major subject groups; and they suggest a healthy take-up of science overall by female students, even if women are still relatively thin on the ground in areas like mathematics and physics.

Broad-based as education in Cambridge still is, it has by no means stood still. The highest-profile development has been the arrival and proliferation of Masters degrees, predominantly the one-year MPhil. There are now 96 of them: some are taught degrees, a small number are research degrees; many of them serve either as a path into doctoral research or as the prelude to a different career altogether. They range from Anglo-Saxon, Norse and Celtic, through Modern Society and Global Transformation, to Micro- and Nanotechnology, and the students they attract have contributed to a marked extent to the

> *"We have mathematical lectures, once a day – Euclid and algebra alternately. I read mathematics three hours a day – by which means I am always considerably before the lectures, which are very good ones. Classical lectures we have had none yet – nor shall I be often bored with them. They are seldom given and, when given, very thinly attended."*
>
> **Samuel Taylor Coleridge, letter to his brother George, 1791**

Left: Examination under way in the Senate House, 2007.

Top right: More advice from Hints to Fresh-men at the University of Cambridge, *1807.*

Along with about 11 other undergraduates I embarked on a Part II in Zoology in October 1953; in those days it was only a small group who were allowed to study the subject due to laboratory space. One of our lecturers was the distinguished mathematician Sir Ronald A. Fisher who taught us statistical theory in a small teaching room in the laboratories. He was a small man resplendent with beard whose writing was even smaller and he wrote in minute letters in chalk on a blackboard. Every now and again one of us would shout out (in hindsight rather rudely) 'Write larger!' Whereupon he would turn around at us and glare, and turning back to the board would write 'LARGER' in splendid huge capital letters. The board by the end would be crammed with small writing and the word LARGER would appear about once a paragraph! He was greatly loved and admired but, if the truth be told, not a very good teacher.

Ian Beer
(1951)

Lectures in theology varied from the extremely entertaining (Henry Chadwick on the Early Church was always packed out) through the bewildering (we called Rowan Williams 'the Divine' because of his eminent incomprehensibility) to the extremely tedious (one lecturer marched in and read from his book for an hour, then swept out). Each subsequent week the class diminished until by week 4 he glanced at me, commented: 'So you've come to face the barrage alone, have you?' and proceeded to read the next chapter. I didn't go again.

Margaret Hobbs
(1979)

Left: The last wooden spoon to be presented before the descending-order system was abandoned. Wooden spoons had been given each year from the early 19th century to the student who passed the Mathematical Tripos with the worst degree. This one was made from an oar and awarded in 1909 to C.L. Holthouse, a student at St John's College and enthusiastic member of Lady Margaret Boat Club.

disciplines; critical theory and gender studies are embedded in many subjects; economics has absorbed econometrics; and the study of history is now more international, with a greater emphasis on a thematic rather than narrative approach, and on social, economic and cultural history.

In the sciences, Cambridge's research-led teaching has inevitably been a guarantee of growth and change as cutting-edge research is increasingly carried out across the boundaries of science's traditional divisions. Across the biological sciences, physical sciences and technology, the need for collaboration over cross-disciplinary course content has become a live issue: engineering has introduced bioengineering to its Tripos, while teaching in chemical engineering and biotechnology have been brought closer together.

Since I arrived in Cambridge all those years ago the nature of teaching and learning has also changed dramatically. Lectures, practicals and supervisions, of course, still survive, but classes and seminars are more widespread, not least at Master's level. The arrival of the electronic age has been transformative. Course information, bibliographies, hand-outs, feed-back questionnaires, access to library catalogues, and in some cases lecture notes, are available on the University's website for students to access at will, and virtually all communication with students takes place by email. There is extensive

expansion of postgraduate numbers generally in the University. There has been considerable movement, too, in undergraduate studies, with new or reconfigured Triposes in Computer Science, Education, History of Art, Linguistics, Management Studies, Manufacturing Engineering, Medical and Veterinary Sciences, and Social and Political Sciences. The content of existing Triposes has changed with the times as well: literary studies now extend to the present day and other continents and reach into other

Working area in the Cavendish Laboratory.

provision of learning materials on subject websites, including interactive materials; and computer-aided language learning is available to students across the University. Electronic support for learning and teaching and its administration is also strong. A major advance has been the development of a collection of online tools for University members to use in their teaching, learning and research (CamTools). There are online reporting systems for supervisors, and a significant step forward in transparency and communication has been the arrival of an electronic data base (CamData) that provides students and the outside world with information relating to courses, student statistics and quality assurance, as well as with links to other relevant University sites. All of these developments have been very positive and in terms of learning support have a particularly valuable role to play in easing the transition between school and university studies: many students who come to Cambridge these days do not have the knowledge basis we could traditionally count on, nor have they had the chance to develop the habit of independent study.

The other major development in educational culture in recent times was the introduction into higher education in the early 1990s of a government-driven regime of quality assessment and control that marched under the banners of accountability, transparency and cost-effectiveness. Quality Assessment became the bane of our lives. I was reliably told at the time that on the occasion of the University's first institutional (University-wide) audit, it took two large pantechnicons to transport the required paperwork to London. The cost in terms of time and energy spent in producing it was vast. When the Faculty of Modern Languages received a week-long teaching quality visit, 12 external assessors visited 91 teaching sessions (one of them, perhaps unsurprisingly, fell asleep in a seminar). The disruption it created that week and in the months of intensive preparation beforehand was, again, vast. The new quality culture, at first bitterly resented, in the course of time came to be accepted with resignation, an evolution helped along by the government's eventual recognition that the approach had been heavy-handed and excessively costly, and that a

> *"On coming up you will be allocated a Tutor and a Director of Studies. Your Tutor's main responsibility is your general welfare, and he is sometimes said to stand in loco parentis… It has been suggested that you should treat your Tutor as if he were your immediate superior officer in the Army; your Director of Studies as if he were your uncle by marriage, and your Supervisor as if he were a rather distant cousin.*
>
> *College teaching in Cambridge is in most cases very good, but in many faculties the lectures organised by the University are poor. Take your Supervisor's advice on lectures at first, but temper it with your experience. If you find that a particular lecturer is the world's worst, cut him and spend the time more profitably with a book."*

Varsity Handbook, **1950–1**

I was a NatSci studying zoology and other biological stuff at Pembroke in 1980–3. Computers were simply not part of our life. As part of our course we had one afternoon in the Computing Labs when we did something on the mainframe: all I can remember was shuffling a stack of punched cards and being utterly bored. It seemed arcane and had no relevance to our work or our lives.

A couple of years later I came back to Cambridge to visit a friend who was doing a PhD at Trinity and I was amazed that a corner of the JCR had been equipped with ten or so Apple Macs and laser printers for the students to use. I did not quite appreciate at the time the significance of the moment. I now realise that it was the very earliest inkling of the personal computing and internet communications revolution that, over the past 20 years, has utterly transformed our daily lives in all spheres of work, study, relationships and entertainment.

I and my contemporaries were the last generation of students to experience an entirely computer-free life at Cambridge. That moment can now be seen as a significant watershed in the 800-year history of life and work at the University.

John Stewart
(1980)

As a school leaver in 2003, I was well-versed in the modern art of passing examinations to order. GCSEs, AS levels, A levels; each qualification seeming meaningless in itself, and valuable only as a passport to the next level. I was cynical before my years, having learned to write in sentences that would echo the mark-scheme of my examiner, and ensure that he or she was utterly convinced I knew my subject (or at least that I had wit enough to memorise the targets).

My earliest supervisions at Cambridge out-footed me, and inspired me to think again. With two long years before my first set of English Tripos exams, there was no need to economise with a veneer of learning (despite the huge breadth of the reading lists!). There was time to mature, and space in which to be challenged – as I constantly was by my enquiring tutors. One of the rituals which tried me most at the time, and which I most value now, was their insistence on probing with further and yet further questions, until no thoughtless assertion of mine had been left untried. The then unwelcome scrutiny taught me to consider my words: to know when to defend my ideas and to recognise when to concede them to another's point of view.

In three all too brief years, Cambridge enabled me to discover what a joy it is to learn. I remember leaving the University Library in my final year, 2006, consumed in thoughts about all I had been reading that morning, and acknowledging for the first time the way that my understanding was extending like a network of caves in all directions as I, like a potholer, uncovered new and unexpected gems of knowledge each day.

Amy Morrish
(2003)

It's in the catalogue hall that you first discover them. Probably not until your second year when the University Library finally beckons and you climb those formidable steps into its stern embrace. As you walk through to the Reading Room you come upon the relics of a bygone age – and the elder statesmen of your department leafing slowly through them. They lift the substantial volumes from below, rest them on the shelf and search, presumably with method, until satisfied and then toddle off towards the book stacks.

Up until the moment I experienced this it seemed a truth self-evident both to me and my fellow arts student friends that studying and computers were inseparable bedfellows. Newton, the library catalogue, was almost the first thing mastered upon arriving fresh-faced – just type in the reference, and within seconds you are told the exact locations of the required tomes, which are there for the taking. And if, whisper it, you didn't actually want to read the book in question, Jstor, an online database containing back copies of hundreds of scholarly journals, tempted you with instant access to all the book reviews you could ever need. In half-an-hour the taut summaries of your reading list would sit before you, saved neatly on your hard drive ready to be pillaged and presented as if they were the fruits of your own toil.

You could, I'm told, go for three years without actually picking up a real book but (honestly) most of us didn't. For me, the biggest shift came halfway through my second Michaelmas Term when, after losing yet another set of notes to one-too-many late night kebabs, the pen and paper were abandoned for the safety of MS Office. When it came to my dissertation, I quickly realised that without my trusty laptop I would have drowned in paper in no time. How do you find a reference when no search function is at hand? Why make a trip across the Atlantic, or even to the British Library, when the artefacts you are to study can be viewed online, from the comfort of your own room?

Whatever the tactile pleasures of the written word, all those who have made the transition would assert that the few holding out in the safety of the UL are not saving a lost art for the next generation but missing out on a world of efficiency, immediacy and order. But maybe those are the watchwords only for this generation of students.

Tom Ebbutt

(2002)

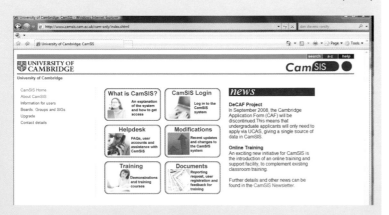

lighter touch should in future be applied. It was helped along too, however, by the grudging recognition that, overly intrusive as it had been, in many respects the process had proved fruitful. What it had achieved was, effectively, the professionalisation of teaching. We learned to reflect on our methods, procedures and standards, and on the nature and aims of our courses, and to articulate them. We realised we had to produce transparent criteria for our classing of candidates. The introduction of student feedback made us think harder about how we lectured and supervised. This in turn led not only to the end of the practice of talking to the top left-hand corner of the lecture room but to the production of more and better teaching support materials – when I first came to Cambridge there was scarcely a booklist or hand-out in sight in my department. All faculties and departments now have

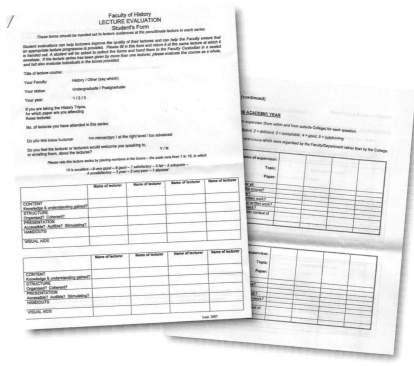

Above: Form for undergraduates reading history to comment on their lecturers. Feedback on courses and the quality of teaching is now collected in all departments.

Left: Garret Hostel bridge from Jerwood Library, Trinity Hall

committees or individuals with specific responsibility for educational issues. Largely as a result of this new concentration on effective teaching and learning support, the third class degree has virtually withered away and even the 2:2 (lower second) is in serious decline – the days when either was considered a respectable outcome for the undergraduate with other interests to pursue have long gone.

Collegiate Cambridge has an international reputation for its excellence in learning and teaching, a reputation borne out by approval by external bodies, by our leading position in national and international league tables and by the employability record of our graduates. There are undoubtedly tensions in the system: most palpably the underfunding of teaching and the uncertainty with regard to future fee levels, and the pressure to concentrate on research placed on academics by the Research Assessment Exercises which determine research funding. There are also certainly many challenges ahead. We must make sure that the Tripos continues to meet our needs in a changing and increasingly competitive world – which raises issues such as interdisciplinarity, modularisation, borrowing of papers, and flexibility and collaboration generally. We must make sure, too, that it is responsive enough to meet the challenges of access and widening participation. It will also be essential to continue to attract and retain high-flying academics dedicated to teaching as well as research, and to provide at both undergraduate and graduate levels the bursary support necessary to attract the best students whatever their background. In the face of tensions and challenges alike, the crucial thing is that we strive to preserve the Cambridge values enshrined in our Learning and Teaching Strategy. We have two overarching aims: excellence of student learning opportunities at both undergraduate and graduate level, and a stimulating environment for all those who teach and support student learning in the University. The symbiotic relationship between students and teachers is the defining characteristic of the Cambridge experience.

Melveena McKendrick is Professor of Spanish Golden-Age Literature, Culture and Society, and Pro-Vice-Chancellor for Education.

> *"As an undergraduate I was persuaded that the Dons were a wholly unnecessary part of the university. I derived no benefits from lectures, and I made a vow to myself that when in due course I became a lecturer I would not suppose that lecturing did any good. I have kept this vow."*
>
> Bertrand Russell, *The Autobiography of Bertrand Russell*, 1967

Physical Sciences and Technology

Probing new frontiers

MALCOLM LONGAIR

Cambridge has been at the forefront of the physical, mathematical and technological sciences throughout its history. It is a daunting task to maintain and enhance the legacies of such giants as Isaac Newton, Ernest Rutherford, J.J. Thomson, G.H. Hardy, Frank Whittle, Maurice Wilkes, to mention only a few of the most prominent personalities of our heritage. While excellence in mathematics has been part of Cambridge's scientific culture from the very beginning, most of the great developments in the experimental sciences and technology belong to the 20th century. From the college-based University of earlier centuries, the physical and technological science departments grew phenomenally during the last century in response to fundamental discoveries, the need for larger and more expensive facilities and the increasing importance of these disciplines for society at large.

The formal presentation of the science syllabuses and examinations remain the responsibility of the University departments, but teaching within the colleges through the supervision system remains at the core of learning and understanding in Cambridge. Particularly over the last 50 years, there have been major changes in the undergraduate teaching programmes in the physical, mathematical and technological sciences. Much of this has been driven by advances in the disciplines but the expectations of the students have also evolved. They are as brilliant and creative as ever, but they come with somewhat different preparation from the expectation of 50 years ago – their education is broader but in less depth. A particular challenge is the need to provide mathematical support and the difficulty students have in relating the mathematics to the physical phenomena they are describing. Nobody is pretending there is an easy way of doing this; if there were, we would have discovered it long ago. But this challenge is part of the process of replacing school understanding with university and professional thinking at the highest level.

The change from a three-year to a four-year course for essentially all the physical sciences has been a wonderful success and enabled Cambridge to produce superbly trained undergraduates who are eagerly sought worldwide as graduate students. Research project work is now part of the undergraduate syllabus for all physical science and technology

The European Southern Observatory VLT/VLTI site at Cerro Paranal in Chile, 2007, where Cambridge astrophysicists make observations on the most advanced telescopes available.

departments and is a joy to supervise. Each year a few undergraduates produce outstanding innovative research which is published in such prestigious journals as *Physical Review Letters*. A second feature is the expansion of the syllabus to cover a much broader range of topics which are important for students in their later lives and for society at large. There are now examinable courses in entrepreneurship, education, medical physics and environmental science which would have been unthinkable 50 years ago.

The last 50 years have seen fundamental changes in the way in which Cambridge departments in the physical and mathematical sciences carry out their research programmes. From a period when much scientific work could be carried out on a laboratory scale with modest resources, most physical science and technology departments are now dependent upon access to expensive and often large-scale facilities to maintain their research programmes at the cutting edge. At one end of the scale there is participation in huge projects, such as the Large Hadron Collider at CERN, the telescope facilities of the European Southern Observatory and the Diamond synchrotron radiation facilities. Even in areas which are traditionally thought of as being desk-based, such as applied mathematics and theoretical physics, many programmes are reliant upon access to massive and expensive computing facilities. Cambridge has been extraordinarily successful in winning the resources from the research councils and other bodies to participate in and carry out research in essentially all frontier areas.

The message of these examples is that Cambridge is a research-driven university, supported by a very large body of outstanding graduate students, research fellows and post-doctoral workers. These individuals are crucial to the maintenance of the vitality and regeneration of the research programme. While the staff members continue to be the leaders and inspiration of research, the pressures of teaching, management and accountability as well as the increased intensity of international competition and co-operation in research have meant that many of the best scientists cannot spend as much time at the coal-face as in the past. Despite these pressures, Cambridge physical sciences and mathematics continue to be amazingly productive and are undoubtedly in the very top rank internationally according to any metric.

Physics and astronomy

MALCOLM LONGAIR

Physics and astronomy are traditionally thought of as 'fundamental' physical sciences. Yet the subjects are not just 'intensive', but also 'extensive', giving rise to new disciplines. A classic example is James Watson and Francis Crick's discovery of the double-helix structure of the DNA molecule, which was made in the context of understanding the X-ray diffraction analyses of biological molecules in the Cavendish Laboratory. In turn, this led to the foundation of the Laboratory for Molecular Biology which developed a life of its own and resulted in the award of numerous Nobel Prizes in the biological and life sciences. In astronomy, the new discipline of astrobiology is rapidly becoming a reality as a result of the discovery of a large population of extra-solar planets. It is only partly in jest that the motto of the Cavendish Laboratory is: 'Physics is what physicists do'. In physics and astronomy, the very best researchers are appointed and are then supported to pursue their scientific instincts wherever their research takes them.

On the very large scale, particle physics, inaugurated by the discoveries of the electron and the nucleus by Thomson and Rutherford, continues to probe the very nature of matter itself. Cambridge particle physicists are deeply involved in the forthcoming experiments at CERN to discover the Higgs boson and new types of elementary particle. These experiments may provide insight into the nature of the dark matter which we know dominates the large-scale structures in the Universe we live in. A crucial spin-off of these massive endeavours was the need to handle and communicate huge bodies of data. The World Wide Web and the internet were invented at CERN and life without these would nowadays be unthinkable.

From the earliest days of the computer, pioneered in the Computer Laboratory with machines such as EDSAC, Cambridge physicists and astronomers have been at the cutting edge of exploiting their capabilities. I fondly remember my own first cosmological simulations of 1964 carried out on the EDSAC 2 computer. Large-

Above: E.T.S. Walton operating the Cockroft Walton machine, the simplest form of linear ion accelerator, in 1932.

Right: The Helium-3 Spin-Echo Spectrometer, in the new Cavendish Laboratory, 2007.

J.J. Thomson and Ernest Rutherford

1895 was a key year for the development of research in Cambridge. For the first time, the University allowed students to come to Cambridge from other universities to study for higher degrees. J.J. Thomson had been Cavendish Professor of Experimental Physics since 1884 and, among the first generation of foreign students, Ernest Rutherford came to the Cavendish Laboratory from New Zealand. 1895 was also the year in which X-rays were discovered by Roentgen and in the following year Becquerel announced the discovery of radioactivity. Thomson and Rutherford responded to these discoveries by changing the course of their researches, Thomson to study the origin of X-rays and cathode rays and Rutherford radioactivity.

By 1897, Thomson and his principal assistant Ebenezer Everett had carried out a remarkable series of experiments in which they determined the charge-to-mass

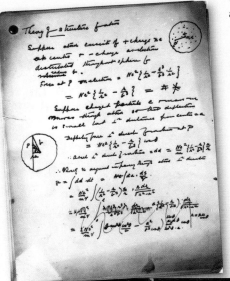

Left: Ernest Rutherford's notes on the structure of the atom.

Below: The 1897 Cavendish Laboratory research group photograph, which includes J.J. Thomson (seated, centre) and Ernest Rutherford (seated, far right). C.T.R. Wilson, the inventor of the cloud chamber, is standing second from the left.

ratio of the cathode rays. Thomson concluded that the cathode rays, which had been named electrons a few years earlier by Johnstone Stoney, were the first known sub-atomic particles. They went on to demonstrate that the β-particles ejected in radioactive decays and the particles ejected in the photoelectric effect were exactly the same subatomic particles, the electrons. Thomson continued his studies of the electron, providing the first estimate of its charge using the newly developed Wilson cloud chamber in 1899. His electron studies culminated in his demonstration with Barkla that the number of electrons in atoms was roughly half their atomic weight, showing that the number of electrons in the atom could not account for the total mass of atoms.

Rutherford was an experimentalist of genius who, almost single-handedly, established the physics of radioactivity. He elucidated the radioactive decay chains involving elements heavier than lead. In turn, this led to the first reliable estimates of the age of the Earth, supporting the view of the geologists that it was more than 700 million years old. After a period at McGill University in Canada, he accepted the Chair of Physics at Manchester University where he carried out a brilliant experiment in which he demonstrated that the α-particles released in radioactive decays are the nuclei of helium atoms. In 1911 he discovered the atomic nucleus in α-particle scattering experiments and made the first estimates of the size of the nucleus. On his return to Cambridge as Cavendish Professor in 1919, he discovered nuclear disintegration induced by fast α-particles.

Thomson and Rutherford were awarded Nobel Prizes for their pioneering experiments which were to usher in a new epoch in experimental and theoretical physics.

I remember cycling down King's Parade to get to my first lecture in the Cavendish labs (in those days situated in the heart of the city, in Free School Lane), my black undergraduate gown, christened with gravy by a careless waiter at formal hall the night before, flowing in the breeze behind me. I made my way into the lecture hall, a grand amphitheatre filled with gowned apprehensive freshers like myself, awaiting the entrance of the lecturer in the pit at the bottom.

It is hard to describe the shock as Professor Pippard made his entrance. What did I expect? I had expected someone who had reached the dizzy heights of professorship to be ancient, white-haired, with dust on the shoulders of his gown and the remains of the morning's toast and marmalade clinging precariously to his white beard, looking crabby and bored at the prospect of yet another lecture, yet another intake of undergraduates. I did not expect a 30-something-year-old man bouncing into the hall as if on his way to a basketball match. I did not expect this youngster with a full head of dark hair and a smile on his face. The lecture was amazing and enthralling, delivered with obvious enthusiasm. As he revealed each new idea he made it seem as if he were sharing some secret, revealing something he had just discovered that morning and not yet shared with anyone outside the lecture hall. I think that was the moment when I relaxed and began to enjoy myself.

Alan Williams-Key
(1966)

The ATLAS barrel toroid magnet being assembled at CERN, 2006. This went into operation in 2008 and the Cambridge HEP Group made a leading contribution to the large silicon detector which tracks particles as they emerge from the collision region.

scale computing now plays a role as an essential tool in all fields of physics and astrophysics. Michael Payne and his colleagues have developed procedures which enable *ab initio* quantum mechanical computations to be carried out for very large molecules. These are of the greatest interest to drug companies who can predict how complex pharmaceutical molecules interact. Another example is their demonstration of how the bulk properties of matter have their origin at the quantum level, for example in the propagation of cracks in pure materials.

Low temperature physics has long been a strength of the Cavendish Laboratory. In its modern incarnation, by pushing to extremely low temperatures and high pressures, Gil Lonzarich and his colleagues have discovered new states of matter in simple materials which promise to provide deep insights into the behaviour of more complex materials which are high temperature superconductors. At these very low temperatures, strange quantum processes dominate their behaviour. Advances in semiconductor technology led by Michael Pepper have enabled the direct manipulation of the wave-functions of semiconductor devices, one of the most remarkable discoveries being the anomalous quantisation of resistance at very low temperatures in the presence of a magnetic field. Some other aspect of strongly correlated electron physics must be involved.

A different approach to semiconducting devices has been pioneered by Richard Friend and his colleagues through the discovery of semiconducting polymers which involved a tight collaboration between polymer chemists and physicists. These materials can be created by bench-top chemistry rather than by the traditional complex processes of semiconductor manufacture, and find application in light-emitting

Stephen Hawking

Stephen Hawking's triumph over the debilitating effects of motor neurone disease is an inspiration to everyone. His immense creativity since he contracted the disease in the late 1960s is utterly astonishing. But what did he do to merit his iconic status as one of the greats of modern science?

Most scientists would single out two areas in which his work has been profoundly original. The first concerned the conditions under which there must be singularities in black holes and in the early stages of the Big Bang picture of modern cosmology. He and his colleague Roger Penrose adopted an entirely new geometric approach to these mathematically complex problems and came up with theorems about the existence of singularities which could be tested by observations of our Universe. They discovered a general set of conditions under which there would necessarily have to be a singular point in the early Universe and the conditions under which collapse of material to a black hole is inevitable.

The second area was Stephen's own discovery. According to classical general relativity, the black surface of a black hole is the point of no return for the matter and radiation which collapse towards it. In a brilliant analysis, Stephen showed that this is not strictly true if quantum processes are considered close to the black surface of the black hole. According to quantum mechanics, there is a finite probability of radiation or particles escaping from the hole. Stephen showed that a temperature could be associated with the black hole, which is proportional to its mass, and hence eventually a black hole could radiate away from its own mass. This was an analysis of the greatest complexity, carried out long after he was able to put pen to paper. In turn these insights have led to the study of the thermodynamics of black holes and how the law of entropy increase can be related to black hole physics.

These were but two of the subjects in which Stephen has made profound contributions to relativity and fundamental physics. In the volume published in celebration of his 60th birthday a few years ago, his many students and colleagues paid due tribute to the extraordinary influence his thinking has had upon so many different aspects of contemporary astrophysics and fundamental cosmology. In 2007 the Centre for Theoretical Cosmology was established in the Department of Applied Mathematics and Theoretical Physics, supported by the Stephen Hawking Trust Fund, with the aim of furthering the world-leading research in fundamental cosmology by Stephen and his colleagues.

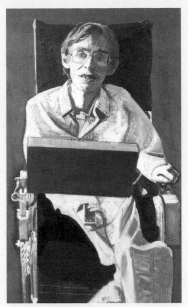

Stephen Hawking, Lucasian Professor of Mathematics and a Fellow of Gonville & Caius. Portrait by Paul Gopal-Chowdhury.

diodes, solar cells and as transistors. Already, these devices have been used in displays and the spin-off company Cambridge Display Technologies has proved to be an outstanding success with investors.

The physics of biology and of medicine are examples of the extensive nature of physics research. These initiatives developed from the recognition that there are many ways in which a physics-led approach has the potential to produce new insights into biological and medical processes. Examples include the understanding of the physics of hearing and the remarkable realisation that the glial cells in the retina act as optical fibres, channelling light through the scattering layers. These and many other programmes at the interface between physics, biology, biochemistry and medicine will be advanced through the construction of a new building dedicated to the physics of medicine and cognate disciplines, which will be opened in December 2008.

New groups and sectors are formed in response to developments in experimental and theoretical capabilities. The Atomic, Mesoscopic and Optical Physics group was formed recently to study quantum optics, cold atoms, mesoscopic systems and quantum electronics. The Detector Physics group runs a major facility for designing, manufacturing and testing new generations of superconducting detectors for astrophysics and the applied sciences. The Nanophotonics group constructs new materials in which atoms are arranged in sophisticated ways on the nanometre scale.

Astrophysics and cosmology are among the most active areas of the physical sciences in Cambridge. In the 20th century, strength in astrophysical and cosmological theory built on the legacy of Arthur Eddington and Fred Hoyle. Based in the Department of Applied Mathematics and Theoretical Physics, Stephen Hawking has made many contributions to general relativity and cosmology, which have culminated in the recently founded Institute for Theoretical Cosmology. At the Institute of Astronomy, Martin Rees's many contributions

Cavendish Laboratory notice board.

The physical setting for lectures was still the wooden benches and big traditional blackboards of the Arts School in the New Museums site and the Mill Lane lecture rooms. And the blackboards really were wide. Ray Lickorish promised that the triangle inequality has 'a one-line proof. As long as you start well to the left on the board'.

Enthusiastic and idiosyncratic teaching was much appreciated. Colin Sparrow in optimisation lectures made a point of stopping half-way for a brief interlude. Often this involved quoting from a US field survival guide ('Playing dead when approached by a bear') to great effect. As part of fluid dynamics, Keith Moffat performed the now-illegal act of lighting up and blowing big smoke rings from a cardboard box machine of his own invention. He also memorably invited students to try *sucking* out a match, to prove the non-linearity of fluid flow. A mustachioed friend, who tried this later, reported a singed upper lip and a still burning match.

Martin Hyland managed to make (linear) algebra I sexy as well as receiving celebrity-style rounds of applause on entering the room. Generating such enthusiasm for vectors is a hard trick to pull off. It was partly due to his appearance dressed as a mad scientist's younger brother (baggy sweater and round rimless glasses). But mostly it was due to his intelligent intensity in communicating the material, delivered with style and humour.

In Lent 1988, a Ib lecture series called 'A Short History of the Universe' was given by Stephen Hawking. Already chair-bound and speaking with his new synthesised voice, he delivered seven magnificent lectures. This was genuinely a masterclass, with one of the leading cosmologists explaining advanced research to second years in digestible but not patronising language. That it was also entertaining and non-examinable cemented its popularity.

The fact that such memories are still fresh after 20 years proves that the commitment of gifted researchers to teaching the next generation is one of the great advantages that distinguishes Cambridge mathematics. QED.

Martin Baxter
(1986)

to astrophysics have included his pioneering papers on relativistic aberration effects which account for a wide range of phenomena in high energy astrophysics, including the appearance of superluminal motions in quasars, the existence of extraordinarily powerful sources of gamma-rays from quasars and the physics of extragalactic gamma-ray bursts.

The Cavendish Astrophysics Group has concentrated upon experimental astrophysics, building on Martin Ryle's pioneering initiatives in radio astronomy. His great achievement was the practical implementation at Cambridge's Lord's Bridge Observatory of the principles of aperture synthesis which enable radio telescopes of very high angular resolution and sensitivity to be constructed by adding together coherently the signals from small separated antennae. The remarkable structures of all types of high energy astrophysical

A computer-generated projection of the ALMA array in Chile when the telescopes are in place in 2012.

explosions have been studied in detail and cosmological studies have been carried out, since the sources extended to cosmological distances. Antony Hewish studied the short time-scale fluctuations of the intensities of the radio sources with a large telescope array at the Lord's Bridge Observatory. The use of this telescope resulted in the discovery of pulsars, the first examples being neutron stars which are crucial for understanding high-energy astrophysical phenomena. These experimental initiatives led to an extension of aperture synthesis techniques to study fluctuations in the Cosmic Microwave Background Radiation and also to the infrared and optical wavebands, as well as the Atacama Large Millimetre Array (ALMA) which employs the same techniques at sub-millimetre wavelengths.

Between the extremes of pure theory and experimental astrophysics is the huge spectrum of observational and interpretative astrophysics. This includes major groups working at the Institute of Astronomy in the theory and observation of accretion discs, X-ray, gamma-ray and high-energy astrophysics, helio- and astero-seismology, astrophysical cosmology and large-scale simulations of the formation of galaxies and large-scale structures in the Universe. The observers have won observing time on all the most advanced telescopes available to astronomers: the Hubble Space Telescope, the Very Large Telescope in Chile, the Gemini Telescopes in Hawaii, the XMM-Newton X-ray Observatory, and so on. They are also deeply involved in the next generation of large international projects, including the James Webb Space Telescope, the ALMA sub-millimetre array, the European Extremely Large Optical-Infrared Telescope and the Square Kilometre Array.

Cosmology has been a traditional strength of the three Cambridge groups and these will be brought together in the Cambridge Kavli Institute for Cosmology under the directorship of George Efstathiou, ensuring that Cambridge remains a world force in all aspects of these studies.

Malcolm Longair is Jacksonian Professor of Natural Philosophy, Professorial Fellow and former Vice-President of Clare Hall. He was Head of the Cavendish Laboratory from 1997 to 2005.

Sir Isaac Newton, *1709–12, by James Thornhill, Trinity College.*

Isaac Newton

For William Wordsworth (St John's), Isaac Newton's statue in Trinity College portrayed a disembodied genius, a solitary scholar with a superhuman intellect:

The marble index of a Mind for ever
Voyaging thro' strange seas of Thought, alone.

Now Cambridge's most famous alumnus, Newton researched at Trinity for over 30 years, and is celebrated for three major contributions to modern science: establishing the laws of mechanics and gravity, analysing sunlight, and insisting on an experimental methodology. To the horror of many, in the 1940s Wordsworth's vision was attacked by another eminent Cantabrigian, John Maynard Keynes, who declared that Newton 'was not the first of the age of reason. He was the last of the magicians…' By examining Newton's manuscripts – including the many alchemical documents purchased by Keynes himself – historians are revising Newton's image as the world's greatest scientist.

Newton was not a scientist (a word invented only in 1833, by William Whewell, Master of Trinity), but a natural philosopher for whom theology and alchemy were as crucial as mathematics for learning about the world. His own beliefs differed significantly from the tenets of modern Newtonianism. A deeply religious man, Newton concealed his heretical faith in Arianism (which denies the divinity of Christ) and created a universe pervaded by an ever-present God. Unlike the scientists who later modified his theories, Newton believed that the behaviour of the cosmos is not entirely predictable, because God intervenes in its operation from time to time.

Extract from the annotated
first edition of Principia
Mathematica, *1686.*

Newton's ideas were not immediately accepted, and some of them have been abandoned. In his alleged flash of inspiration under an apple tree – an anecdote first narrated by Newton himself – Newton decided that the same mathematical laws can be used to describe how the moon circles around the Earth and how an apple is pulled down towards the ground. Critics attacked his concept of invisible forces stretching out through the cosmos, accusing him of reintroducing magic's occult powers. Inspired by alchemy, Newton conjectured instead that gravity is carried by invisible weightless particles comprising an aether filling the whole of apparently empty space, a model that remained influential into the 20th century.

Newton paved the way to the future, but for his own ideas he looked backwards. 'If I have seen further,' he wrote, 'it is by standing on the shoulders of giants.' When investigating rainbows, he decreed that they must have seven colours to conform with the principles of mathematical harmony developed by Pythagoras. Drawing from his prolific alchemical research, Newton conceived the Earth as a living organism surrounded by aethereal spirits and revived by comets carrying vital matter in their tails. Although he devised a form of calculus, Newton preferred geometry, the mathematical language of the Greeks: it was not until the early 19th century that the Cambridge Analytical Society campaigned to import the techniques of Newton's great rival, Gottfried Leibniz.

Keynes's manuscripts are now, along with many others, electronically available: future historians will continue to reinterpret Newton's life and legacy.

Patricia Fara is an affiliated lecturer in the Department of History and Philosophy of Science and Senior Tutor of Clare College.

Mathematics: the great tradition

Martin Hyland

Mathematics is the historic subject at Cambridge. In the century following Newton it was made central to intellectual life in the University. An oral examination in mathematics was introduced for all students, followed a little later by a major innovation: a series of written papers. This, the famous Mathematical Tripos, is the model for written university examinations in the modern world.

The Tripos became an intense training in mathematical technique and was spectacularly successful, nurturing a series of great mathematical scientists (Green, Stokes, Kelvin, Maxwell, Rayleigh, J.J. Thompson). But the 19th-century Tripos seems strange today. There was no University or college teaching (private coaching filled the gap), and little encouragement to study anything outside a narrow range of exam questions. The system lasted until 1907 when major (and highly contentious) reforms modernised and broadened the syllabus.

Through the 20th century mathematics developed in tandem with the University, becoming thoroughly international in outlook. Departments were founded: Applied Mathematics and Theoretical Physics (DAMTP) in 1959, and Pure Mathematics and Mathematical Statistics (DPMMS) in 1964. In 2002 the faculty came together in the new Centre for Mathematical Sciences, designed to encourage synergy between the departments. Over these years the Mathematical Tripos has changed relatively little. We teach a more modern syllabus, but as the 1907 reformers wished, we still attempt to educate in mathematical understanding rather than cram for examinations. We still set hard

The Centre for Mathematical Sciences. The move of the Department of Applied Mathematics and Theoretical Physics (DAMTP) and the Department of Pure Mathematics and Mathematical Statistics (DPMMS) to the new premises was completed in 2002.

Nobel Prize certificate awarded to Paul Dirac in 1933 for the discovery, with Erwin Schrödinger, of new productive forms of atomic theory.

problems, and the most common style of question, bookwork followed by a rider, would seem perfectly familiar to our predecessors.

Cambridge is the centre of a distinctive British style of applied mathematics, in which the mechanics of fluids and solids is prominent. Nowadays mathematical modelling of real fluid phenomena, deriving striking consequences from good simplifying assumptions, is supplemented by judicious use of computer simulation. Our interests include environmentally critical areas – the atmosphere, ocean and ice caps – and more exotic processes such as magnetoconvection in stars. The physics of the earth is a longstanding concern: exciting work on volcanoes and the earth's core is focused in the Institute of Theoretical Geophysics, a joint venture with Earth Sciences. A further strength is applied analysis encompassing numerical methods, order and chaos in non-linear systems, and the systematic derivation of approximate equations to describe real-world systems. We have exceptional expertise in practical questions: complex fluids in industrial processes, noise from jet engines, the flow of water round hulls and air over wings. Work in fluid mechanics is best linked to experiment, and the purpose-built G.K. Batchelor Fluid Dynamics Laboratory is in constant use.

Cambridge interest in general relativity and cosmology goes back to Eddington in the 1920s. The group led by Stephen Hawking is at the forefront of research. Hawking famously discovered that black holes were not black; properties of black holes and the early universe remain major concerns. Cambridge quantum mechanics stems from Paul Dirac, Nobel Prize winner for his foundational work. I vividly remember his 1969 Rouse Ball lecture in which he stressed that ideas such as his prediction of anti-matter were arrived at by considerations of mathematical elegance. Dirac's successors display the same spirit. A major challenge for theoretical physics is to reconcile general relativity and quantum mechanics. Cambridge is a world centre for work on major candidate theories, supergravity, string theory and its extensions to M-theory and D-branes. We also study applications of quantum physics, such as quantum computing and quantum fluids.

Pure mathematics, neglected in 19th-century Cambridge, has blossomed since the 1907 reforms. Initial momentum came from Hardy and Littlewood who introduced rigorous analysis, and themselves made many important contributions to analytic number theory. Hardy's collaboration with Ramanujan is legendary. The University has maintained its reputation in hard analysis. Spectacular results on arithmetic progressions in the prime numbers have recently been obtained by analytic means. Researchers in this area are closely linked to a distinctive school of combinatorics built up in the last 30 years. The algebraic side of number theory derives from Louis Mordell, who came

Quite different was the course of lectures on quantum mechanics that I attended in my second year. The lectures were given by the Lucasian Professor of Mathematics, Paul Dirac, who in his mid-twenties had produced his relativistic theory of quantum mechanics which accounted naturally for electron spin and predicted the positron, antimatter, and the mutual annihilation of colliding electrons and positrons. He shared the 1933 Nobel Prize for Physics with Erwin Schrödinger. Dirac was an inspiring person and a superb lecturer.

Norman Greenwood
(1948)

Memorable lectures included: Dr Babbage of Magdalene on geometry. He would fill an enormous blackboard in the Arts School from top to bottom with very neat script, ending puce in the face on his knees as he completed the final line. 'Facedesmic polyhedra' stick in the mind, though that sort of geometry has disappeared.

Dr Atiyah of Trinity, barely any older than us National Service veterans, with many years left to qualify for his Fields Medal. He did groups and abstract algebra, bubbling with enthusiasm the while.

Dr Abdus Salam of Trinity on electricity and magnetism. He was another obvious enthusiast, who went on to a Nobel Prize in Theoretical Physics. His blackboards were well planned, but he would then think of something, 'rope off' a space and fill it with his afterthoughts.

Jonathan L.G. Pinhey
(1954)

in 1906 as a self-taught schoolboy to England from the US to take the Entrance Scholarship Examination. Mordell was followed by a long line of exceptional Cambridge researchers, and algebraic number theory is now a major speciality in DPMMS. The most celebrated achievement stemming from the Cambridge school is the proof by Andrew Wiles of Fermat's Last Theorem.

Cambridge algebra and geometry originated with the work of Philip Hall and William Hodge in the 1930s. Hodge revolutionised geometry by studying the equations of mathematical physics, and links he uncovered between analysis, geometry and physics still continue as the focus of research. Hall had a major impact on modern group theory, and his successors were heavily involved in the classification of the finite simple groups. Abel Prizes awarded in 2004 to Michael Atiyah (once a student of Hodge) and in 2008 to John Thompson, testify to an enduring influence in the two subjects. Surprising new connections are now emerging with number theory, and remarkable progress has recently been made in the classical area of algebraic geometry.

*Mathematical Tripos
examination paper, 1884.*

In Cambridge many sciences (astronomy, physics, computer science) stemmed from mathematics, and other subjects (economics, philosophy) were influenced by mathematicians. But the traffic has not all been one way. Statistics began in the sciences, in particular with the study of observational error in astronomy. The first appointments were in agriculture; and the great statistician Fisher was Professor of Genetics from 1943. The Statistical Laboratory was founded as late as 1947, and was then incorporated into DPMMS. As statistics has become ever more important within the sciences, it has become imperative to give the subject greater focus, and a Statistics Initiative has been launched to do that. The Statistical Laboratory also encompasses all kinds of probability. The study of networks, fundamental for modern communication, is a particular strength, with links to computer science. A newer area, mathematical finance, shares interests with the Judge Institute of Management. Finally, modern biology has produced a range of mathematical challenges with serious statistical content. The Cambridge Computational Biology Institute has been set up in DAMTP to promote research. Mathematical biology offers research opportunities to both departments and is the most recent subject area to be introduced in the Mathematical Tripos.

With exhilarating progress being made in established areas, and the introduction of fresh applications, Cambridge mathematics is active on a broad front. This breadth is a strength, as major progress often involves connections between apparently unrelated phenomena, and finding such links counters the centrifugal tendencies inherent in so extensive a subject. Benefits are also felt by undergraduates. The Mathematical Tripos covers a greater intellectual range than any comparable mathematics course. Most of our students will find some area which particularly appeals to them and in which they can shine.

Breadth demands openness and a toleration of difference, and that is part of our inheritance. Our undergraduates still come largely from the UK, and what we care about at this level is sheer mathematical aptitude. In research, we welcome the very best wherever they come from: about half our research students are from abroad. In return we export our own. Cambridge mathematicians are found all over the world. What Cambridge gave and still gives is opportunity: the opportunity to learn and research in an environment which cherishes independent ideas; and the opportunity and the encouragement to excel.

Martin Hyland *is Head of the Department of Pure Mathematics and Mathematical Statistics, Professor in Mathematical Logic and a Fellow of King's College.*

Hardy and Littlewood

Following the acrimonious debate between Newton and Leibniz in the 17th century over the invention of calculus, British mathematicians closed their minds to the ideas coming from the Continent for almost two centuries, and so the great discoveries of the 19th century that revolutionized analysis passed them by. From Newton's death until the beginning of the 20th century, Britain failed to produce a pure analyst of the highest rank, as mathematics had become an ancillary to natural philosophy. This sorry state of affairs was remedied by G.H. Hardy (1877–1947) and J.E. Littlewood (1885–1977), who by the 1920s had created a school of mathematics second to none, and transformed Britain into one of the major powers in hard analysis and number theory.

For most of their lives, Hardy and Littlewood lived in Cambridge as Fellows of Trinity College. Littlewood had the same set of spacious rooms in the most beautiful court of Trinity for 67 years. They formed a legendary partnership, the most successful in the history of mathematics: they wrote 100 joint papers in an age when joint work was very rare, with their first paper published in 1912 and the last 36 years later, after Hardy's death.

Hardy and Littlewood made fundamental contributions to many branches of analysis and number theory: convergence and summability of series; inequalities; additive number theory, including Waring's problem and Goldbach's conjecture; Diophantine approximation; harmonic analysis, probabilistic analysis, and non-linear differential equations. Their work on the Riemann Hypothesis helped it to become the most famous conjecture not only in number theory but in all of mathematics: the Holy Grail for many mathematicians.

Even when they were near-neighbours in Trinity, they liked to communicate in writing rather than words, with porters scurrying back and forth across the college with their mathematical notes. Their collaboration was based on a number of negative 'axioms'. Thus, it was completely indifferent whether what they wrote to each other was right or wrong; neither was under any obligation to read what he had received from the other; nor did it matter if one of them had not contributed the least bit to a paper published under their common names.

In addition to collaborating with each other, Hardy wrote wonderful papers with the Indian genius Srinivasa Ramanujan, and Littlewood proved groundbreaking results with his brilliant former pupil, R.E.A.C. Paley, and with Hardy's former student, the formidable Mary Cartwright, who later became Mistress of Girton.

In his left-wing sympathies and anti-war stance Hardy was influenced by Bertrand Russell, his senior by five years. He was an ardent atheist, never went into a church, and refused to enter the college chapel even for formal business, like electing new Fellows. As a game, he considered God his personal enemy, who maliciously denied him happiness. When he was about to cross a stormy

Channel, he would try to outwit God who might be preparing to drown him by sending a postcard to his friends announcing that he had just solved the Riemann Hypothesis. Surely God would not let him perish if after his death his name would be covered in glory as the man who proved the Riemann Hypothesis.

Although Hardy was very shy, he loved to be the centre of academic life. Through his voluminous research, the best of which he did with Littlewood, many books and numerous students, he changed the mathematical landscape in Britain. He was a brilliant writer and lecturer; in Cambridge he led the move to abolish the Mathematical Tripos (although he did not succeed in this, the Tripos was reformed, very much for the better); he did much to improve the standing of the London Mathematical Society; and he co-ordinated the efforts to find jobs for mathematicians escaping from Hitler. Much earlier, after the First World War, as President of the Union of Scientific Workers, he had worked to allow German scientists to attend international conferences.

Hardy loved cricket, and was an accomplished batsman and real tennis player. He was fond of intellectual games like picking cricket teams of humbugs, bogus poets and bores. His Trinity team was inordinately strong (Byron, Thackeray, Maxwell and Tennyson could not be certain of their places), while Christ's, for example, started extremely strongly with Darwin and Milton, but faded rapidly. He judged mathematicians by comparing them to cricketers: for many years his highest praise was 'in the Hobbs class', but later changed to 'the Bradman class', with Archimedes, Newton, Euler, Gauss, Darwin, Einstein and a handful of others rated that highly, and also, sadly, Lenin.

In his personal dealings Littlewood was not shy at all and did not suffer fools gladly: in his prime he was considered the rudest man in Cambridge. However, unlike Hardy, he shunned public appearances and never went to conferences, giving rise to the joke that he did not exist and was only invented by Hardy to have someone on whom he could blame his mistakes.

Littlewood was an even more powerful mathematician than Hardy: he revelled in attacking hard concrete problems like the Riemann Hypothesis. Hardy considered him to be the finest mathematician he ever knew. 'He was the man most likely to storm and smash a really deep and formidable problem; there was no-one else who could command such a combination of insight, technique and power.' Littlewood was stocky, well built and agile. In his youth he was a keen sportsman: a good gymnast, a hard-hitting batsman, the stroke of a

G.H. Hardy and J.E. Littlewood in Trinity College, c.1930.

college Eight, an enthusiastic Alpine skier, and a passionate and excellent rock climber.

Most vacations he spent in Cornwall, where he guarded a secret. In an age when a public scandal would have meant resigning his fellowship, he had a daughter by a married woman. Calling her his 'niece', he had grave doubts about whether he was right to sacrifice family life for the life of a college Fellow dedicated to mathematics, and fell into a severe depression. For several decades he worked way below his capacity whilst still achieving much more than many top mathematicians.

When in 1969 I returned to Cambridge for good, I was amazed to find Littlewood alive as Hardy had been dead for 20 years. He was still very sharp, still loved mathematics in all shapes and forms, and his great knowledge of classical mathematics was very much in evidence, but he had become much warmer, was happy to sit for the portrait busts my wife made of him, and was grateful to her for the love she gave him. Sadly, his former students tended to shy away from him, believing that they would not be welcome.

A few years after we got to know Littlewood, he told my wife the truth about his 'niece'. My wife eventually prevailed upon him to acknowledge that she was his daughter, after much persuasion. His low-key 'announcement' greatly relieved him, and from then on he became much happier. By then his life revolved around the college: for many years he was the Senior Fellow but in attitude he remained young. He steadfastly refused to preside over dinner, and unfailingly voted for change, such as admitting women.

He was a great raconteur: after almost every dinner he was to be found in the Combination Room drinking claret in the company of Fellows and visiting academics, turning the evening into a special occasion. He was a demigod even for the giants of mathematics and physics. When in the mid-1970s I went to collect the great physicist Paul Dirac to take him to dine at High Table in Trinity, and told him that he would sit next to Littlewood, to the amazement of his wife, Dirac went upstairs and changed into a previously shunned new pair of trousers she had bought for him months earlier. The Combination Room in Trinity still hasn't recovered from losing Littlewood, its main link to a golden age.

Bela Bollobas is a Fellow of Trinity College, an external member of the Hungarian Academy of Sciences, and Jabie Hardin Professor at the University of Memphis.

Millennium Mathematics for the Millions

Mathematics is a Cinderella subject. It lies at the root of much of modern commerce, engineering and science, and yet its role is often uncredited, its actors unrecognised, and its script unknown. This has had many unfortunate consequences for the place of mathematics in our general culture, and for the esteem in which it is held amongst outsiders.

In 1998 mathematicians in Cambridge realised there was an urgent need to improve the public appreciation of mathematics and its teaching and learning in schools, and the Millennium Mathematics Project (MMP) was conceived. In the following year I moved to Cambridge to become its first Director. Our idea was to use new technologies to engage directly with school students of all ages, using the expertise that already existed in the Faculty of Education and the Mathematics Departments, and to inform the general public about the importance and beauty of mathematics. We aimed to raise the aspirations of young people who might otherwise be discouraged from pursuing mathematics beyond the minimum requirements of the school curriculum. By drawing upon the mathematics in the world around them, in sport, art, commerce, nature, technology and science, we wanted to show how mathematics can tell you things that you cannot learn in any other way – and that it is also fun. We had to awaken curiosity and sustain interest by showing them some of the fascinating parts of mathematics, and their unsuspected applications and interconnections.

Since then, the MMP has developed as a medley of programmes designed for different audiences and purposes. The largest is NRICH, our online website, which focuses on active problem solving. It posts ten issues a year, which contain carefully constructed mathematics problems, tagged both by their stage in the school curriculum and degree of difficulty. Youngsters from all over the world send in solutions. We publish only their solutions on the site – not ours. If problems are unsolved then that is how they stay: tough nuts for the future. The NRICH philosophy has led to a range of books and professional development programmes for teachers.

Our commitment to new technologies meant that from the outset we used video conferencing to link clusters of schools to mathematicians in Cambridge and elsewhere through our Motivate project. Pupils work on mathematics projects between these conferences and then present and discuss their team's work with the other video-linked groups in their cluster. The MMP engages in a host of other activities. These include an award-winning online e-magazine, PLUS, about the applications of mathematics and the diversity of career paths it offers, public talks, 'road shows' that visit schools around the UK, including one about the mathematics of codes that visits schools for a programme built around a real Second World War Enigma machine, a multilingual online mathematics Thesaurus, the Stimulus project which sends undergraduates into local schools to assist teachers, provision of further mathematics teaching in schools where it cannot be offered, and special pupil-and-teacher programmes in disadvantaged areas.

It has been satisfying to see this example of 'outreach' really starting to register. Last year we worked with more than 1,200 schools, received more than 190 million hits on the websites and 9 million site visits, up 60 per cent on the previous year. If you want to see what it looks like, make a start at www.mmp.maths.org.

John D. Barrow is Professor of Mathematical Sciences and Director of the Millennium Mathematics Project.

Jonathan Evans lecturing in the Wolfson Room on the foundations of quantum mechanics.

Engineering

Ann Dowling

Engineering at Cambridge began with the election of James Stewart to the newly established Professorship in Mechanisms and Applied Mechanics in 1875. It has grown steadily over the years and now involves about ten per cent of the University's students and staff. Stewart's pioneering lectures were attended in 1877 by Charles Parsons, who went on to build the first turbo-generator, which became the standard way of using steam to generate electrical power. It is striking how the same issues of energy generation and its efficient use drive many of our activities today.

The Mechanical Sciences Tripos was established in 1892 and the teaching of engineering blossomed under the leadership of Charles Inglis (Head of Department 1919–43); in 1939 about one-fifth of all engineering graduates in the UK were from Cambridge. The Tripos provided a broad foundation in engineering science and its practical application. Frank Whittle studied in the department 1934–7, obtaining first class honours in the Mechanical Sciences Tripos after only two years of study and developing his ideas for the jet engine in his third year.

The appointment of Lord Baker as Professor of Mechanical Sciences and Head of Department 1943–69 was transformational. He not only saw ambitious building plans through to completion, he also brought research into the forefront of the department's activities, establishing its leadership in the development of a wide range of new

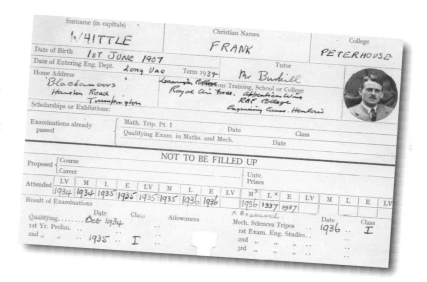

Undergraduate record card of Frank Whittle,
inventor of the jet engine, while studying in the Department of Engineering.

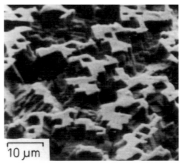

Above: An early micrograph obtained with SEM1.

Above: A prototype of the first production Scanning Electron Microscope, developed by Charles Oatley's research team, 1965. Charles Oatley was Professor of Electrical Engineering at Cambridge from 1960 to 1971.

technologies. Baker's own research was in the plastic design of steelwork, which saw early application in the 'Morrison' air-raid shelter. Over 1.25 million of these table-sized shelters were distributed to householders in the Second World War, saving many lives. Since then the Department's research has had huge impact. Charles Oatley's research led to the world's first production Scanning Electron Microscope, commercialised through the Cambridge Instrument Company, an early 'spin-out'. One of Oatley's research students, Alec Broers, now Lord Broers, used the SEM to conduct some of the earliest experiments in electron beam microfabrication and now seen as a precursor to nanotechnology. Research results on soil mechanics, robust control, gas turbines, material sciences, photonics and many more have gained international recognition and wide-scale industrial application.

In response to the growing importance of new fields of engineering, the department established an additional Tripos, the Electrical Sciences Tripos, in 1962. The Advanced Course in Production Methods and Management followed in 1966 and the

I discovered when I arrived at Cambridge that I was one of five girls amongst 250 men reading mechanical sciences, now titled engineering. Many years later we discovered there had only been nine girls ever before reading that subject.

I had never done technical drawing – it was not a subject in girls' grammar schools, and changing schools had meant that I had to give up physics. However, incredibly, I passed and they said I would be taking my degree in two years with a long vac term. That was a real sweat – two hours technical drawing every afternoon, my mind boggled at projection and cross-section. However, as a lovely East End woman said on the 50th anniversary of VJ day, 'you didn't make a fuss in those days or someone would say, "Didn't you know there's a War on"?'

Our Head of Department, Professor Inglis, insisted we could not specialise in our first year even in those circumstances, so we covered structures, applied mechanics, thermodynamics (including indicator diagrams for steam engines, morning after morning, not very useful in aeronautics), management, psychology, timber, surveying, electricity, hydraulics, carpentry. How lucky we were in that very broad course. Aeronautics did not come into it until the second year, with lectures by Dr Piercy of Queen Mary College. Professor Melville Jones had gone to war.

Beryl Platt
(1941)

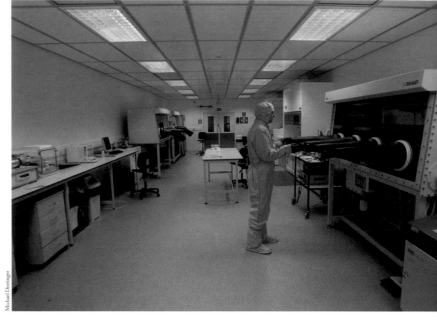

Michael Derringer

A clean room in the Nanoscience Centre, completed in 2003, on the West Cambridge Site.

A 3D silicon nanostructure fabricated using chemical vapour deposition.

Ghim Wei Ho

Production (now Manufacturing) Engineering Tripos in 1979. One of the aims of the change in the undergraduate course in 1988, when the three-year BA degree was expanded into a four-year MEng, was to provide scope for more project-based work – because we believe that engineering students learn best by doing and not just through lectures and examples papers. There are now projects in each year of the course, building on the ever-popular structural design-build-and-test exercise in the first year, through a robot competition in the second year and a variety of design-and-build and computer-based team activities in the third year, to a substantial final-year project which the students work on throughout the academic year for about half their time. These

projects not only help students develop creativity and the ability to integrate engineering ideas and concepts, they also dramatically illustrate the multidisciplinary skills needed to address any engineering challenge – and the reason for our integrated course, in which all undergraduates study a common course for most of their first two years irrespective of their final engineering area. The MEng course continues to evolve and a new specialisation in Engineering for the Life Sciences started in 2007.

Over the years the engineering course has become more outward-looking and foreign languages (French, German, Spanish, Japanese and Chinese) are now offered as an integral part. Another international dimension comes through student exchanges. There has been an exchange scheme with the Massachusetts Institute of Technology since 2000. Our students who have spent their third year at MIT return for their final MEng year with great enthusiasm and a wider perspective. The department is now starting a similar exchange with the Ecole Centrale in Paris.

The department research strategy is 'to address the world's most pressing challenges with science and technology'. This has required us to identify where we should target new resources, and engineering for the life sciences, cognitive systems, and sustainable development – particularly sustainable energy – have been selected as areas of particular importance. It has also led to changes in our ways of working, with more emphasis than ever on team work and on collaboration with other disciplines.

A real change that I have seen in the time that I have been working in the department has been an increase in the ambition and scope of research projects. Nearly all research projects now involve a number of members of the academic staff and several (in some cases large teams of) full-time researchers. This proves to be an excellent way for those involved to learn from one another as they come together to address complex themes that would be impossible working in isolation. It also really enhances the training of our PhD students as well as being great fun. We now have about 200 research associates and over 600 PhD students working in the department. The number of contract research staff has nearly doubled over the last six years and there are over 40 per cent more research students. In the past, the research going on in the Department was almost invisible to the undergraduates. But under the UROP (Undergraduate Research Opportunities Programme) scheme introduced in 2003, we now offer undergraduates the chance to work for payment with a research team. This is proving to be very popular.

Addressing major challenges has also made us develop new ways of working with industry and other stakeholders. Some involve significant, established partnerships with industry, such as the University Gas Turbine Partnership. This is a multifaceted and sustained collaboration involving over 20 academic staff and 90 research students and post-docs collaborating with Rolls-Royce plc on the development of environmentally friendly aircraft engines. There are other models and, for example, the Centre for Applied Photonics and Electronics (CAPE) was established with support from a small set of strategic, non-competing industrial partners to invent and develop electronic and photonic materials, processes, components and systems. Notable successes to date include the development of the next generation holographic displays and biomolecular solid state sensors. In addition, an Integrated Knowledge Centre in advanced manufacturing technologies for photonics and electronics links our Electrical Engineering and Manufacturing Divisions with the Cavendish Physics Laboratory and the Judge Business School and a wide range of companies and organisations.

The department has nearly £30 million of current research contracts related to energy, which include ultra efficient low-emission transport (air and ground-based), novel fuels, power generation by wind, sun and ground heat sources, and the integration of distributed power generation with the grid. Our research in energy includes a new initiative, Energy Efficient Cities, a collaboration between the Departments of Engineering, Architecture and Chemical Engineering, the Computer Laboratory, the Judge Business School and the BP Institute. The aim is to reduce the energy demand in cities by using novel technologies in an integrated approach to urban planning, the design of buildings, transport systems and district and micro-power generation.

All this has put pressure on space and many of the new activities are taking place in new buildings at West Cambridge. The Nanoscience Centre, completed in 2003, is an interdisciplinary centre addressing nanotechnologies. The new Electrical Engineering Division building has bought in over 3000m² of extra space at West Cambridge, and construction has just begun on a new building for the Institute for Manufacturing. Currently there are builders everywhere on the Trumpington Street site, constructing laboratories for new Engineering for Life Sciences activities and refurbishing space for the Centres of

My research was in the then-emerging field of nanotechnology with supervisor Mark Welland. I had recently completed building a combined electron microscope and tunnelling microscope, following in a long tradition of microscope development at Cambridge. This microscope was designed to locate, and image in 3D, structures with dimensions on the nanometre scale. I arranged to meet a friend at King's and we took our gowns so we could avoid the queues to attend the carol service. After the service I returned to the lab and commenced one final attempt to image the nanoscale wires I had been trying to image for weeks. Just as I was thinking about packing up for the year, the wires came into view. They had never been seen before in 3D and I continued experimenting with imaging these nanostructures into the early hours of Christmas Eve. After two years' development the new microscope had achieved its goal. I cycled into the cold December morning knowing I had something significant to show my supervisor over mince pies and Christmas cake later that day.

Grahame Rosolen
(1989)

I had considered myself a physicist at school, and had decided to read engineering with the romantic notion that I would build things: things like bridges and aeroplanes. But when I started at Cambridge in 1983, I knew almost nothing about the practice of engineering. Even when I left Cambridge, I had little idea of what would be required of an engineer beyond technical skills: communications skills, political skills, and – perhaps most importantly of all – a sense for the business that drives any engineering activity. Those skills can't be taught in a few short years at university, and are learned – if at all – over years of professional practice. Realization of what Cambridge did give to me and to my fellow engineers has been slow to come, formed over a quarter of a century as an engineer and an operator of the products of engineering. It gave us perhaps the most important quality an engineer can have at the start of his or her career: breadth. We studied civil, mechanical, electrical, and aeronautical engineering, and were required to take holiday courses in more practical areas like surveying or metrology. I still don't build things at work (that's what my garage is for!), but through engineering jobs at two Fortune 100 companies, a stint as a graduate researcher at MIT, and a decade at NASA designing and flying spacecraft, I've never had an assignment that wasn't made more interesting and successful through the application of this breadth.

Like most in engineering, my current job – I'm a NASA astronaut, and flew on a 2006 shuttle mission to the International Space Station – does not require mastery of any one field of engineering. Instead, it requires me to be conversant in many: from software testing to heat transfer to structural design. But near the end of my 13-day space flight, when I was able to look down 300km at Cambridge as it receded at nearly 30,000 km/hr, I thought of none of this. Instead, I pictured the Backs in summer, and I remembered my friends.

Nicholas Patrick
(1982)

Cambridge will always be many places for me: The market town which I knew as a boy growing up in the Fens, before the Science Park was built, when the cattle market was still thriving; the peculiar world of the Lab of Molecular Biology with its colourful models where my parents worked since soon after is was opened in 1962; and my primary school, with its retired missionary headmistress who kept discipline by parading the classrooms with snakes.

But that was life on the other side of the town/gown divide. I came back after a year in South America and four more at Imperial College with an invention, and a research grant from the California Energy Commission to enable me to take things further. I approached the University to see whether its reputation for embracing 'blue skies' research projects would extend as far as mine, and via a series of strokes of good fortune, I was admitted to develop my invention under the supervision of Prof. Nick Collings, later to be written up for a PhD.

Life on the inside revealed another set of parallel worlds, co-existing within a few hundred yards of one another. The long echoing corridors of the Engineering Department at night couldn't seem further away from a rowdy hall in college, just a few hundred yards away. I began discovering countless hidden enclaves of land which I never knew existed as a child, making the town feel like it was created by M.C. Escher.

My academic journey through Cambridge was an interesting and fruitful one. Its anarchic structure nurtures the exploration of the rich territory that lies on the boundaries between disciplines, in the no-man's land where no-one has yet thought to venture. However, at times, academic life in Cambridge can be lonely and frustrating. The sort of really innovative research that is associated with a multitude of small research groups often leaves research students to fend for themselves. It dawned on me at some point later that this is how it has always been: Clerk-Maxwell and Rutherford didn't fit neatly into laboratories awaiting their arrival. The building blocks of great things were all around them, but they would have to figure out how to put them together on their own.

Cambridge gave me something that few places can: resources, and the freedom to exploit them. Long may others be able to say the same.

Tom Smith
(2001)

Sustainable Development, Engineering Design and Computational Fluid Dynamics, bringing them together to facilitate their interactions. We have also begun to address the fact that, with substantial research interests in energy-efficient buildings, we do not set a very good example ourselves. There are plans to remedy this and to use the Trumpington Street site as an exemplar of the roles of good practice and novel technologies in reducing the carbon footprint of existing buildings, and buildings account for over 40 per cent of the energy usage in the UK. One aspiration is to use an appropriately instrumented building as

Above: The Electrical Engineering Division's new building at West Cambridge.

Right: Some of the Silent Aircraft Initiative Research team, including Ann Dowling (centre), Alex Quayle (far right) and the silent aircraft model.

Affinity is a prototype solar electric vehicle, designed and built by Engineering Department students to undertake the first solar-powered journey from Land's End to John O'Groats. It is a precursor to Cambridge University's first entry in the World Solar Challenge in 2009.

communication and teaching tool. We are finding that our students really 'want to make a difference', and final-year options related to energy, sustainability and reduced environmental impact are very popular. The students also recognise the considerable employment and market possibilities in these areas.

Our contributions to solving some of the world's most pressing challenges are not only through our research but also, and perhaps particularly, through the commitment, enthusiasm and innovation of our graduates.

***Ann Dowling** is Professor of Mechanical Engineering, Director of the University Gas Turbine Partnership with Rolls-Royce, and Head of the Division in which research in aeronautics and energy is carried out.*

I found the studying very tough, very much in at the deep end. It was quite a shock. Some of the problems we were set seemed just impossible. The encouragement and help we got from our supervisors were staggeringly varied. Some were brilliant research people, who often weren't very good at teaching. Some were good teachers but had more modest reputations. Dr Roberto Cipolla stands out for his ability to realise that he needed to stop teaching us about the subject of control systems; instead he taught us how to get through the exam. I believe he was well rewarded by a decent set of results.

It was interesting to see group dynamics at play in the seating arrangements of LT0, the biggest lecture theatre in the Engineering Department. The 300 students initially grouped themselves mostly by college, and that then morphed into like-minded people: boaties at the back rushing in after an early morning on the river; foreigners sitting right at the front, like teachers' pets.

David Reid
(1991)

I came to Cambridge to take up a PhD in Mechanical Engineering with Professor Dowling at the Engineering Department. At the beginning of the programme I joined the Silent Aircraft Initiative (SAI), a three-year collaborative project in partnership with MIT. The SAI was a unique opportunity, with a research team totalling more than 35 people over the course of the project. My own contribution has been on the subject of landing gear noise, which I was surprised to learn is one of the dominant noise sources, even on today's aircraft!

One of the main objectives of the SAI was to develop collaboration between industry and the universities around a substantial technical challenge. In this respect, the project was very successful and exciting. Around every six months we would receive feedback on our designs from Boeing and Rolls-Royce about the technical implementation of our design, but also from stakeholders such as test pilots, airlines and airport operators. These discussions provided vital technical input but also identified a need to clearly define and integrate individual research contributions on a regular basis.

The final design of the Silent Aircraft was a major achievement. As a team we proposed a new conceptual aircraft which would be almost imperceptible above typical traffic noise and is predicted to be 25 per cent more fuel-efficient than the best of today's aircraft. When it was launched, the project created a substantial amount of interest in the research being done at Cambridge and received global news coverage.

Participating in a focused research team at the same time as completing an individual PhD has been a challenging and rewarding process. Students participating in the project had to provide regular team updates and work towards important project deadlines. The success of the project has also created additional challenges, such as communicating complex research initiatives to the wider public and dealing with significant media interest.

Alexander Quayle
(2004)

Computing: building the future bit by bit

Peter Robinson

The idea that machinery could be made to perform repetitive computations is not new: Charles Babbage had his first ideas for a calculating machine before 1820, and pursued them until his death in 1871. His ideas were difficult to implement in a system that was totally mechanical, and progress had to wait until the Harvard Mark 1 machine was constructed in the early 1940s. That machine was basically mechanical but made use of relays and magnetic clutches. It was during the Second World War that ideas for fully electronic calculations emerged, to be exploited once the war had ended.

The Computer Laboratory, then called the Mathematical Laboratory, had been founded in 1937 to be a resource for the University on scientific computation. Its development was effectively stopped by the war, but it began to gain momentum in 1946 and set about building a stored-program computer under the guidance of Maurice Wilkes. By May 1949, the EDSAC (Electronic Delay Storage Automatic Calculator) worked as a complete system, including input and output peripherals, and was the first such machine anywhere to do so.

Within a year the EDSAC was offering a round-the-clock service with operators during the day and self-service at night (as long as the machine continued working). Wilkes was particularly keen that the machine should provide a service to the whole University rather than being kept as the preserve of its inventors. 'Automatic computing' was enthusiastically promoted through a summer school, a book and even a film. The computer was heavily used for theoretical chemistry, molecular biology, radio astronomy and many other disciplines, contributing to research in molecular biology and radio astronomy that led to Nobel Prizes. Wilkes was quick to see the need for people who were well trained in the use of computers, and what became the Diploma in Computer Science began in 1953, the world's first taught course in computing. Teaching has expanded steadily over the years and there is now a full three-year Tripos in which students learn topics totally unimagined when the diploma started.

Ever since the early days, the Computer Laboratory has retained its emphasis on the practical side of computer engineering – something that distinguishes it from many competing institutions which only came into being after you could buy computers and no longer had to make them. Research in the laboratory during the 1950s led by Wilkes and David

South façade of the William Gates Building, home of the Computer Laboratory, at night.

Wheeler built up the basic stock of knowledge that has subsequently sustained the subject: programming (including the invention of sub-routines, recursion and hash tables), computer architecture (notably micro-programming) and libraries for Fourier transforms and numerical analysis. EDSAC 2 was commissioned in 1957, providing much greater speed and capacity and improved programming tools.

The arrival of Titan in 1964 was followed in 1967 by a round-the-clock multiple-access system, provided to users generally in the University. This was sustained by research led by Roger Needham in time-sharing systems and high-level programming languages, and supported early work on computer-aided design and interactive graphics using a satellite computer. In 1970 a separate University Computing Service was established in the Laboratory under the direction of David Hartley. Building on its inheritance of innovation and quality gained in the early years, the Service maintained the Laboratory's traditions by first providing an innovative but professional service on a succession of IBM mainframes, and then building a comprehensive communications network. A highlight of the latter was the establishment in 1992 of the Granta Backbone Network: a 30km duct and fibre network interlinking all departments and all colleges throughout the City of Cambridge. Today the Service provides comprehensive facilities in support of distributed computing.

Logbook recording the daily performance of the EDSAC machine, 1949.

EDSAC

When I returned to Cambridge in September 1945 to restart the Maths Lab after the war, I had the extreme good fortune to possess exactly the right experience. Not only was I a thoroughly experienced electronic engineer, but I had done some computing with a desk machine as part of my PhD project on ionospheric radio wave propagation.

My later contacts with Lennard-Jones and his group had brought home to me how effective a desk machine could be if it was used with determination. In other groups, where pioneering computers were being built, there seemed to be an assumption that even the earliest machines would be powerful enough to enable an effective start to be made on major projects, such as numerical weather prediction. I knew better, but I did see what a godsend even the most primitive digital computer would be to research students in many disciplines, who at present were limited by what they could do with a desk machine. Accordingly, as soon as the EDSAC was working well enough, we made it available to students. This policy was entirely successful. Students showed their results to their research supervisors, who in turn passed on the good news to other senior people in the University. In this way, knowledge of what was possible was spread from the bottom upwards, as it should be.

Maurice Wilkes was Director of the Mathematical Laboratory (later the Computer Laboratory) from 1945 to 1980 and is Emeritus Professor of Computer Technology.

Above: Maurice Wilkes at the opening of the William Gates Building in 2002. The Green Door is from the Corn Exchange Street building, the original home of the laboratory, which was demolished in 1969. It was saved and now has a plaque bearing the names of retiring members of the laboratory, who are 'shown the door'.

Research in the laboratory broadened in the last quarter of the 20th century to embrace not just computer hardware (the CAP computer, local area networks and the Rainbow display) and software (distributed systems, security and multimedia), but also formal methods (modelling and verifying hardware and software, automatic theorem proving), communication between people and computers (speech and language processing, graphics and interaction, security and privacy), and applications (databases, image processing and bioinformatics).

The Computer Laboratory was focal to the development of computers during the second half of the 20th century, but what of the 21st century? The development of computing, and information and communications technology as a whole, depends on reinvention and transformation to drive innovation. There is certainly more of everything – more processors on a chip, more connections, more calculations, more data – but progress has also meant rethinking relations between different system elements, like hardware and software, or between different layers, like operating system and applications, or computer and network.

The laboratory's research is committed to rethinking what computers are like, what they do, and how they do it. This involves work on formal theory and practical implementation, on system operation and user advantage, and on human–computer relationships. Our research vision for the future is focused on the idea of sustainable development, both technically in computing itself and for the world: making computer

systems themselves sustainable because they are more flexible, more robust, and more adaptive; making computing applications more sustainable because they fit with the physical and social constraints imposed by their environments; and making societies and economies more sustainable by applying computers to the best use of natural, technical and human resources. Thus we are researching across the spectrum from hardware compilation to biological modelling.

The Computer Laboratory is equally committed to ensuring that its students are fully informed about the current state of the art, and are

Right: Interior atrium, known as 'The Street'.

Programmers queueing to use EDSAC 2 in the old Mathematical Laboratory on the New Museums Site, 1957.

My recollection of the building that formerly housed the Mathematical Laboratory is by no means sharp, but I can recall an entrance, square onto the street, roughly between today's goods entrance to the Department of Materials Science and Metallurgy and the rear stairs to the Titan Teaching Rooms. It was a three- or four-storey building, and the layout had been arranged and rearranged so that the entire building was configured, physically and spiritually, around EDSAC 2.

This great beast, notable at the time for the huge size of its main memory (4K), occupied the central core of two floors. The heart of the machine was on one floor, just about where the Babbage Lecture Theatre is today. It was a valve-machine, and the kit that cooled the valves which took more power than was needed to run the computer, was on the floor below. Around this throbbing core were laid out various lecture rooms, offices, and the room that housed the students enrolled on the Diploma in Numerical Analysis and Automatic Computing.

There were eight or ten of us. There was just one other undergraduate. By virtue of our junior status, we two were entitled to sit for the Diploma in Computer Science but could not expect to be awarded it. We all mucked along very well for the year (after Tony Pearson had drawn attention to my annoying habit of talking aloud to myself while programming). The atmosphere was entirely different from the undergraduate teaching I had experienced for the previous two years. Hitherto, it had been… inspiring, yes, but daunting as well, to sit at the feet of intellectual giants of the likes of Hoyle, Taunt, Batchelor, Polkinghorne, Atiyah, who swept in to deliver their 60 minutes' worth of distilled genius and then swept out again, leaving me to limp back to college and salvage what I could from my wretched notes. In the Mathematical Laboratory, by contrast, the mood was informal and relaxed. Maurice Wilkes was a benign directorial presence, though he seldom ventured out into the mêlée of the public thoroughfares.

The main attraction of the diploma course was the opportunity to learn programming on EDSAC 2. I have no idea how programmers exercise their craft nowadays – my most recent experience was 30 years ago, using FORTRAN and BASIC, which were a doddle because you simply assigned a name to a variable and wrote algebraic or logical statements using the names. On EDSAC 2, you had to imagine a lattice of 4,000 pigeon-holes and keep track of what you were putting in them. The machine-code instructions comprised three parts: {number} letter(s) {number}. So, for example, 39f100 meant 'Read in a value from tape and store it in pigeon-hole 100.' The most exotic instruction was 120f0. The input/output station had an oscilloscope attached to it, to which one could fix a camera: the instruction 120f0 meant 'Take a photograph of whatever is appearing on the oscilloscope.'

With the program drafted, the programmer's next step was to punch it out on paper tape, using a teleprinter with a conventional keyboard. The machines that did the tape-punching could produce any combination of five holes, thus providing scope for 30 characters. 'All blank' and 'All holes' had no effect. The machine code used 0–9 and a subset of the 26 alphabetic characters. Prudent programmers would leave an inch of blank tape between each block of characters making up a program-line because, if we made a programming error (and we frequently did), it would be necessary to excise the offending block and splice in a correction. Kids nowadays? – they don't know they've got it made.

And to what end was this programming effort directed? We each had a dissertation topic to tackle. A few were self-selected. Susan Nightingale chose to write a program that harmonized Church of England chants according to the accepted rules of classical harmony. Besides my own, that is the only topic I can remember, probably because it appealed to me greatly and I was envious and admiring of her imagination in lighting on it.

Adrian Williams
(1957)

thoroughly equipped to meet the challenges of the future. We will continue to ensure that they have a proper training in both principles and practice – for example in system theory, design and engineering – to contribute as computer science and technology professionals to all areas of employment where computing has or acquires a role. We will continue to educate our graduate students so that they will be the innovators of the future. We believe that by continuing at the forefront of computing and computer science research we will both advance the field itself and ensure that our teaching is forward-looking and of high quality, so that our graduates will meet the emerging technical, economic and social challenges that global-scale information and communications technologies bring.

Computer science and technology move fast, and nobody knows where the action will be in five years' time. This is both stimulating and challenging. It is not easy both to remain influential in research and to continue to produce well-informed, independent, 'can-do' young people; but this is what the Computer Laboratory intends to stay good at.

Peter Robinson is Professor of Computer Technology and Deputy Head of Department at the Computer Laboratory.

Chemistry: the central science

JEREMY SANDERS

Chemists like to claim that chemistry is the central science, with the other sciences arranged in a circle or sphere around its edges. While this view of the world is arguable, it is certainly true that chemistry crosses the boundaries between physical and biological sciences, particularly in Cambridge. Its areas of interest range in scale from individual atoms to the entire earth's atmosphere. Chemistry teaching in Cambridge dates back at least to 1702, when our first chair was established (the early history is covered in *The History of the 1702 Chair of Chemistry at Cambridge*, ed. M. D. Archer and C. D. Haley, Cambridge University Press, 2005), but modern molecular biology, atmospheric science and plastic electronics can all trace their origins to chemical advances in Free School Lane in the early 1950s and in Lensfield Road since 1958.

The father of the present department was Alexander Todd. In 1944 he accepted the 1702 Chair and moved from Manchester to Cambridge with his research group. Vitamins, pigments, co-enzymes, DNA and RNA had all been discovered in plants and animals in earlier decades but their chemical structures were largely unknown, while their biological functions were a complete mystery. Todd's research group became expert in determining the structures of these 'natural products'; the ultimate proof of their structures was to synthesise them in the laboratory from smaller molecules of proven structure. In 1951 Dan Brown and Todd elucidated the basic structures of DNA and RNA – this knowledge allowed Watson and Crick to discover the DNA double helix. Around the same time, Todd's group developed methods for making the nucleoside and nucleotide building blocks used by DNA and RNA. Todd was awarded the 1957 Nobel Prize for these discoveries, which led to the development of molecular biology and biotechnology as academic disciplines, clinical tools and worldwide businesses.

Today, it is relatively easy for chemists to determine the structures of natural molecules, so our attention in this area has turned to understanding and controlling their biological function. Two of Todd's current intellectual heirs in Cambridge are Chris Abell and Shankar

Above: The old chemistry laboratories in Pembroke St.

Left: Alexander Todd, Professor of Organic Chemistry 1944–71.

Antony Barrington Brown

Balasubramanian. Abell is investigating how vitamin mimics can inhibit enzymes in unwanted bacteria, and how to evolve new catalysts from existing enzymes, while Balasubramanian is trying to uncover the roles of recently discovered four-stranded DNA and RNA 'quadruplex' structures in biology. Each has also founded a flourishing spin-out company: Astex, co-founded by Abell with Sir Tom Blundell, is at the forefront of new drug discovery techniques, while Solexa (now part of a US company, Illumina), co-founded by Balasubramanian and David Klenerman, has developed a new, low-cost approach to DNA sequencing which may lead to each of us having access to our own complete gene sequences within a decade or two.

Ronald Norrish was elected to the Chair of Physical Chemistry in 1937. In the 1950s there was much interest in understanding the mechanisms of reactions that are initiated by light. Norrish and his

Above: Research on military poison gases produced by the Department of Chemistry during the Second World War.

Left: The largest scientific lecture theatre in Cambridge, in the Chemistry Department on Lensfield Road, with seating for 450.

Opposite: Peter Wothers demonstrating the principles of chemistry during National Science Week, 2007.

student George Porter developed flash photolysis as a technique for following chemical reactions during the first few microseconds after initiation by a flash of light. They studied reactions of simple molecules such as chlorine oxide (ClO) and ozone (O3). These might be thought obscure and boring, even in an academic context, but decades later these very reactions turned out to be crucial in leading to industrially induced ozone depletion in the upper atmosphere. The fundamental understanding and techniques developed in Cambridge in the 1950s led to Norrish and Porter being awarded a share of the Nobel Prize in 1967, and eventually to the 1987 Montreal Protocol that protects the ozone layer and all our lives. Professors John Pyle and Rod Jones are Norrish's current intellectual heirs in Lensfield Road, through the interdisciplinary Centre for Atmospheric Sciences. Pyle carries out massive computer simulations of all the chemistry and gas flows in the atmosphere, looking decades into the future to predict air quality across all the planet's continents, while Jones directs an aircraft project which determines the concentrations and fates of trace molecules at every level of the atmosphere, thereby increasing our knowledge and feeding information into Pyle's calculations. At the other extreme of length scale, S.F. Boys in the 1970s, and Nicholas Handy since then, pioneered the use of computers to calculate the properties of single

molecules from first principles, while the fundamental studies of surfaces and solids by Sir David King and Sir John Meurig Thomas have enabled us to understand and control fundamental aspects of industrially important catalysts.

Other strands of physical and theoretical chemistry have moved into the biological arena: David Klenerman uses electrochemical methods to look at cell surfaces and lasers to sequence DNA as mentioned above, while Carol Robinson has developed mass spectrometry to the point where she can look at giant intact biological machines such as ribosomes. Studies by Sir Alan Fersht, Chris Dobson, Jane Clarke, Michele Vendruscolo and Sophie Jackson of how proteins fold and unfold are transforming our understanding of how key proteins implicated in cancer might be controlled, and of the molecular basis of diseases such as Alzheimer's, Huntington's chorea and diabetes.

Chemistry is uniquely and literally creative: we design and synthesize new molecules that have never previously existed. Developing new ways of making molecules that might be used as drugs, plastics or in many other ways is at the heart of our teaching and research. Steve Ley, the current 1702 Professor, has invented many powerful new synthetic methods that are being adopted worldwide in organic chemistry, while Lord (Jack) Lewis and Brian Johnson opened up new areas of inorganic chemistry. In the 1980s, Andrew Holmes in chemistry was collaborating with Richard Friend in physics, trying to synthesise organic polymers which would be electrically conducting, rather like metals, when they accidentally discovered that one of their new materials glowed when an electrical potential was applied to it. Seizing on this chance observation, they created the entirely new field of light-emitting polymers and opto-electronics, and founded Cambridge Display Technology as a spin-out. If we can soon watch television on thin plastic sheets that can be rolled up and slipped into a pocket, it will be thanks to this seizing of the unexpected opportunity.

Alex Todd was the driving force in creating the great Lensfield Road building in the 1950s. Following major refurbishment and expansion in 1999–2003, this will be the heart of Cambridge chemistry for the foreseeable future. Over the years, thousands of under- and postgraduates have studied in the department and then contributed to society in a multitude of ways and professions outside chemistry, while our Open Days reach out to thousands of schoolchildren – and their parents and grandparents – every year. With around 60 academics and over 450 postgraduate and postdoctoral workers, we have a rich past and present to celebrate, and an exciting but utterly unforeseeable future to look forward to: the whole physical world consists of molecules, so what in the world isn't chemistry?

Jeremy Sanders is a Fellow of Selwyn and Professor of Chemistry. He was Head of the Department of Chemistry 2000–6, and is currently a Deputy Vice-Chancellor.

Dr 'Soapy' Saunders lectured on organic chemistry in my days – the late 1940s. One term's lectures were on hetero-cyclics. Drawing a formula on the board, he said: 'This is 3-methyl indole. I am now going to tell you something which you will remember all your life – perhaps the only fact that will remain of all you have learnt in this department. (Pause for effect; we waited agog). It is the malodorous element in human excrement… but it has a commercial use as the strawberry flavouring in ice-cream.'

How right he was!

Antony Barrington Brown
(1948)

It was one afternoon in 1968 at a seminar in the University Chemical Laboratories, Lensfield Road. One man dominated the proceedings. He sat in the audience and asked question after question in loud confident tones. At the end of the seminar I asked my course mate, Alan Horn, 'who was that Stentor who wouldn't give us peace at the seminar?'

'Huh! Don't you know him? That was F.H.C. Crick.'

The reference to Crick was sufficient. I had come to Cambridge in 1966 on the inspiration of Professor Lord Todd who gave a lecture on 'Phosphorylation' to the Department of Chemistry, University of Ghana in 1962. I had synthesized (±) desethyldihydrocleavamine by June 1967 and was struggling with the synthesis of other alkaloids. The vision of Crick fired my imagination and led me to synthesize (±) tubifoline, (±)-condyfoline, (±)-tubotawine and (±)-geissoschizoline under the supervision of John Harley-Mason of Corpus Christi.

B.A. Dadson
(1966)

Dr B.C. Saunders lectured in organic chemistry. He was a very good lecturer, a bit of a showman and a ladies' man, well dressed, fastidious and a perfect gentleman. His lecture experiments, always performed by a technician in a whiter than white lab coat, were something of a magical experience. During the Second World War, Dr Saunders worked on nerve gases and occasionally he would tell his students horrific stories of experiments he performed on himself, all of which were top secret at the time. The lady undergraduates worshipped him and he loved every minute.

Peter A. Barker
(1953)

Our Science Future

7

Keeping an edge

MARTIN REES

From Isaac Newton onwards, Cambridge has loomed large in the history of science. And its scientific excellence is being sustained. World-class scientists spend their lives here; the University's ambiance and traditions still attract good students; but we cannot be complacent. In today's global community, people are much more mobile. There is less inertia in institutional reputations. Cambridge needs to respond to the vibrant innovation in the US, and now in the Far East as well. Despite our high-scoring past, we are not immune to relegation from the premier league in the 21st century, if we let things slip. But I think we have every reason to look forward with optimism – to a century where Cambridge maintains its ascendancy in the sciences, and achieves even wider influence.

One should be cynical about the spurious precision of league tables. But there's no gainsaying Cambridge's research distinction, which is more than a match for any universities in mainland Europe or the Far East. Not least among our advantages is the collegiate structure. Colleges are crucial to the experience that Cambridge offers its students; but they are communities for the faculty as well, and foster cross-disciplinary contacts, to an extent that does not occur in universities in any other country (the US included).

The most talented students, the most original and creative researchers, cluster here in impressive constellations, and the interdisciplinary atmosphere brings the best out of them. It is this unique combination, coupled with the aesthetics of the surroundings, that enables Cambridge to retain the commitment of so many academics, despite the blandishments of careers elsewhere. These qualities, plus the uncovenanted benefit that English is a world language, should help to lure the best scientists and render Cambridge a magnet for mobile international talent.

We will need to change if we are to exploit new opportunities, both in teaching and in research. People everywhere in the world will be immersed in a cyberspace that is ever more information-rich and sophisticated. There will consequently be a broadening and democratisation of scholarship. Everyone will have access to the world's publications. Moreover, students or scholars in any university, anywhere in the world – and indeed skilled amateurs with their PCs – will be able to download from a 'virtual observatory', or from a library of genome data. They won't need to go to a central archive, any more than scholars in the humanities will actually need to visit a great library.

Cambridge can still keep its edge. It's hard to believe that virtual contact will replace – rather than just supplement – personal contact. Indeed, those who depend most on new technology, the innovators in Silicon Valley, and now in Silicon Fen too, benefit from being clustered together because they attach great value to actual propinquity. My own experience is that I can readily collaborate with long-time colleagues electronically, but it's hard to forge new collaborations unless they start with personal contact. Cambridge will always attract scientists to its laboratories; its distinctive lure cannot be eroded by technological advances. Our University's present-day scientists take pride in the great figures who worked here in past generations; indeed, we are inspired by them. But we will work in a different style, and on a different (and far wider) range of subjects. The map of learning is itself changing as knowledge expands. Two of our greatest 20th-century successes were in interdisciplinary subjects: radio astronomy and molecular biology. It will continue to be fruitful to focus on the interfaces between traditional subjects.

Enhanced computer power will transform the way we do our science. We can handle huge volumes of data. As an astronomer I can crash stars and galaxies together in a 'virtual universe' on a computer. Scientists in other fields can do 'numerical experiments' where they cannot do real experiments, and address questions such as: What do pollutants do to the world's climate? How do financial markets react to various externalities? And so forth.

Much front-line research – particle physics, or the human genome project, for instance – now demands quasi-industrial teamwork on scales too large for a single university. We will need to bring together consortia if we are to pursue big and time-consuming projects like these. But a lot of the best science, small innovative instruments as well as (of course) theory, will still come from individuals or modest-sized groups within a single university. There is still scope for scientists who like to be individualists.

The coastline of Peru, taken from the Discovery space shuttle in 2006 by Nicholas Patrick (1982), the first alumnus of the Department of Engineering to journey into space.

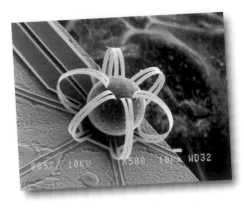

Left: Nanohand and its captured ball, only ~65μm, photographed by Jack Luo and Yong Qing Fu. This is used for capturing and holding cells without applying force to them.

There is a blurring of the boundaries between the University itself and other organisations affiliated to it. For instance, Cambridge is an intellectual power house in biomedical science, because the Medical Research Council, the Wellcome Trust, Cancer Research UK and other charities have endowed independent laboratories, as well as helping to fund the University's own research departments. This heavyweight research effort attracts bio-tech companies to the area. The links between academia and industry are equally benign in computer sciences and IT – this is all part of the 'Cambridge Phenomenon'. The University is now embedded in a 'greater Cambridge', a hotbed of scientific expertise encompassing the city and surrounding region.

Contacts between the academic world and business are forged not only at the level of start-up companies, but also through the daily interchange, in the lab cafeterias and college halls, between graduate students and their contemporaries who work for local companies.

Science offers immense prospects, but raises new ethical and security dilemmas. Novel technologies, bio- and nanotechnology, will be needed if the world's long-term energy requirements are to be met and conflicts over scarce resources to be avoided. The world's ever-growing population, empowered by advancing technology, poses threats to our climate and biosphere that could be irreversibly damaging.

Even the 'purest' of scientists hope that their work can be exploited for human benefit whenever possible. They may not develop such applications themselves, but should surely encourage them; conversely, they have an obligation to ensure that possible hazards are minimised. They should engage in dialogue with the wider public on these issues; academic scientists have a special obligation, since they have more independence than those in government or in commercial employment. The benefits of science are broader than 'wealth creation'; they encompass our entire quality of life. Scientists must strengthen their engagement with the unprecedented global challenges that will confront us all in the coming decades. The 21st century will confront us with unprecedented risks – events that may have a small probability, but whose consequences could be catastrophic, such as flu pandemics,

extreme weather, 'bioerror' and 'bioterror', global network breakdown. Policy makers are over-concerned about some of these, but in denial about others that may be even more threatening. There is urgent need for fuller scientific analysis, allied with a better understanding of public attitudes and of the appropriate economics.

Policy makers in government, in the private sector, and in international organisations have inadequate contact with the best science; moreover, in most academic institutions, science is too compartmentalised to allow optimal formulation of policies on issues that span many disciplines. Cambridge has an opportunity and an obligation to meet these needs.

The University has a concentration of expertise, spanning natural sciences, engineering, law, economics and other disciplines unmatched anywhere else in Europe. This expertise can crucially illuminate an ever-widening range of policy issues. We should take the lead in 'scanning the horizon' and identifying looming problems before it is too late.

Cambridge should not be an ivory tower. It should promote exchange of ideas between scientists and policy-makers in governments, the private sector and international organisations. That is why a Centre for Science and Policy is being set up in the University.

Right: Architect's projection of the new Sainsbury Laboratory for the Study of Plant Diversity and Development, being built in the Botanic Garden.

High on the agenda should be the challenge of clean energy and the replacement of fossil fuels. Many of the scientists who laid the foundations for nuclear energy were based in Cambridge, and our geophysicists have done work of immense value to the oil industry, but an even wider range of expertise is needed today. And the expertise needed is not purely scientific. The technical, strategic and economic aspects need to be tackled together. And we need internationally acceptable policies to mitigate (and adapt to) climate change, which has profound consequences for urban planning, water resources, land use and biodiversity.

Yet energy and climate change are not the only global issues to be addressed. Cambridge is a world centre for research in genomics, stem cells and related developments, all exciting in their potential for human health, but raising novel and perplexing ethical issues. Traditional categories are being transcended: we can't clearly say whether an assemblage of cells is an embryo, still less whether it is human.

And ever since the pioneering days of computing, Cambridge academics have been spearheading advances in information technology. The long-term potentials for society are astonishing, and may come upon us rapidly. Issues of security, surveillance, privacy, and the vulnerability of vast networks will surely loom large.

Future generations of students will live in a world still more deeply moulded by science than ours, with new opportunities and new threats. They won't flourish without flexible, interdisciplinary expertise. Science should remain part of our culture, and an inspiration, but it should be our responsibility to ensure that it is optimally applied, and that those who spearhead the advances are sensitised to the effects they may have on society, and to the ethical conundrums their work may raise.

We don't know what will be the 21st-century counterparts of the electron, quantum theory, the double helix and the computer, or where the great innovators of the future will get their formative training and inspiration. But it's not wishful thinking, given Cambridge's sustained record so far, to anticipate that the 21st century will be more influenced by the creative ideas that germinate in this small city than by the products of any other patch of ground in the world. It should be our goal to make this so.

Martin Rees *(Lord Rees of Ludlow) is Professor of Cosmology and Astrophysics, Astronomer Royal, President of the Royal Society and Master of Trinity since 1994.*

The Genius of Scale

8

Evolution of the colleges

MARILYN STRATHERN

The colleges weave their way through this book, as they do through students' lives. They are the context in which much learning and an impressive amount of teaching goes on. That every student is a member of a college at once introduces a complexity into Cambridge and simplifies everything.

Of course the University is as much added to the colleges as the other way round. Cambridge originally consisted of small societies of masters and scholars, not collectively known as a university until the early 14th century. But the modern University with its numerous separate departments and subjects has a much shorter history. The huge expansion of academic disciplines and constantly developing fields of study in the 19th century has added several layers of complexity. In the 20th, having to respond to financial constraints and managerial pressures, and not least making itself accountable to the public purse in terms of its research output (as through the national Research Assessment Exercise), gives it common cause with universities across the country, and across the world. It has also given the university half of Cambridge common cause with its colleges.

Colleges have similarly evolved, not least in terms of the professionalism of staff, communications networks, outreach programmes – and in their interactions with the University. At the start of the 21st century, there are more occasions for co-operation among themselves, and a greater degree of interdependence with the University, than anyone could have imagined a generation ago. Combined efforts to raise funds for student bursaries is a prime example. For this world-class research university is equally a world-class teaching university – and at a level that marks British universities generally, and Cambridge in particular, out from its international peers: undergraduate training. Here

Above: Lucy Cavendish College, 1970. Established to encourage mature women back to education, the group photograph was taken after the move from Silver Street to Lady Margaret Road, showing all students and staff. This was the last year before the college was allowed to admit undergraduates.

Left: Central Cambridge, including parts of Trinity Hall, Trinity, Gonville & Caius, Clare and the Senate House.

The neo-classical façade at Downing College, founded in 1800, and designed by architect William Wilkins, also responsible for buildings at King's and Corpus Christi.

Christopher Angeloglou

Above: Architect's original plan for Churchill showing courtyards.

Left: Winston Churchill with spade at the planting of an oak tree on the site of the new Churchill College, 17 October 1959.

colleges benefit the University beyond measure. The Cambridge college is a unique resource for small group teaching, and a unique formula for staff–student contact. At the heart is the fact those who admit the students are also going to be teaching them, but don't examine them (that is an external, University, matter). This is special to undergraduates. Colleges have always appreciated their masters and doctoral students, an ever-increasing proportion these days, but do not admit or teach them in the same way. They back up the research training the University offers with different possibilities for scholarly contact.

For undergraduates, the college is their first point of call, second- and third-year students often making a special point of welcoming freshers,

Tony Jedrej

and the home from which they will sally forth to lectures. The department or faculty may come to play an increasing part in their lives, especially in subjects where the laboratory looms large or where classes are organised by lecturers. But for many students, it is the college Director of Studies who sets up the supervisors for whom they complete reading assignments and write essays. College libraries, huge resources for personal study, invariably have lights burning late. Like their students, many teachers and researchers combine department and college lives too. A college is a company of people from all the subjects that the University encompasses, an exhilarating amalgam of interests and enthusiasms. Take any rowing eight or cricket side – or choir, drama society or dinner table – and any discipline could be there. What is so valuable about that form of collegiality is not just the lateral thinking it engenders but the knowledge it brings of others' work practices, pressures or preoccupations, and of what other parts of the University are like.

So colleges add their own administrative layers. They also simplify. *This is the genius of scale.* Each college is the University in microcosm, working democracies independently governed. And as residential institutions, colleges bring complexity down to the manageable proportions of daily life. Certainly none is quite like its neighbour in the way it organises its house staff, gardeners, cooks, electricians, not to speak of administrators, tutors, the bursar and the nurses. And alongside the quiet evolution of individual colleges whose identity

Left: The heads of all 31 Cambridge colleges, elected to their posts by their college Fellows, meet regularly in the Colleges Committee.

endures, new identities are created in response to new needs. The pioneering women's colleges led the way in the 19th century; in the 20th, specific Cambridge foundations have responded to the needs of graduate students, mature women students, and visiting scholars, and brought within the system educational professionals.

But the genius of scale has another side. Together the colleges have allowed the University to solve an organisational problem in a way that could never have been planned. Grow large, remain intimate. It can increase student numbers while also keeping students in relatively small communities. This could not be more significant for its continuing expansion. Cambridge has been able to grow while sustaining intimate working environments quite distinct from the laboratory or department.

The genius of scale is replicated throughout the system. Indeed it is the very replication of the colleges alongside one another that fosters the quality of education. Cambridge undergraduates experience an intimate attention to their work on a par with that offered to graduates. This makes a huge difference to standards and to the satisfaction they derive from their courses; no wonder the Cambridge drop-out rate is negligible. This is the scale-effect of the supervision system. It is well known that colleges also multiply access to resources such as libraries and other facilities; less well known perhaps is the replication of opportunities. Thus colleges pride themselves on the post-doctoral research fellowships they offer, from their own funds, across the disciplines, that start many scholars off on their careers.

Finally, colleges simplify what could otherwise be inordinately complicated. And they do that by a kind of unseen education. Life is never lived at one pace or in a single time frame, and that is a learning experience that the 31 colleges add to the University. One needs to develop the ability to move between places, to be both several kinds of person and still be one person. This is not just a question of diversity, but – and we return to this word – of complexity, of the ways in which situations fold in on one another. Students have to live that complexity: it is not something that anyone else can do for them. This kind of environment is also good for the brain. It nourishes the built-in ability to switch between modes of thinking. It fosters the capacity to move between contexts, in short, to manage something like the complexity students are going to find in the world beyond the University.

Marilyn Strathern *is William Wyse Professor of Social Anthropology and Mistress of Girton College.*

Above: Sidney Sussex College.

Right: Dining Hall at Girton. The college was founded in 1869 as the first residential college for women in the country, and moved to its present location in 1873.

Overleaf: Summer – Magdalene College. Photograph by Hiroshi Shimura.

Myth and reality

During the war, we all had to do some sort of military training. This was difficult for Nat Sci students as the timetable of lectures and practicals was very full. But the 7th Cambridgeshire Counter-Attack Battalion of the Home Guard fitted our needs as all the parades were in the evening or weekends. You might have thought from its name that this was some sort of elite corps, ready for anything. Actually, it would have disgraced Dad's Army. But we all had bicycles (which made us mobile) and 1917 rifles (though no bullets). It was supposed that we would ride out into the Fens to repel German paratroopers (hence counter-attack). Lucky indeed that we were never put to the test, or I would not be writing this more than 60 years later.

Graduating from schoolboy to manhood in the 1940s almost inevitably involved starting to smoke. Most freshers quickly equipped themselves with pipes, tobacco jars (bearing college crests), cigarettes and lighters. Smoking was then thought of as a harmless and rather sociable pastime: amazing to see what passion it has since aroused.

James McFarlane (1943)

THERE is a serious dearth of teaching staff in the University. For four days I have been asking different men if they have time to supervise my work and each has made the same reply: 'I have a lot of people on my hands already; perhaps you could try Mr Blank!'. The fourth Mr Blank – a cheerful pipe-smoking fellow of about 35 with a wife and two children – was willing to take me on. He had spent two joyless months looking for somewhere to live before he found his flat, and as he apologetically told me: 'Of course as far as French literature is concerned, I'm a bit rusty myself after five years in the navy.'

Supervisors are overworked and attendance at lectures has long passed saturation point. As the church clocks slowly chime out the morning hours, with traditional lack of synchronism, the streets are abnormally full of students walking or cycling between lectures. They move in surging groups through Petty Cury, fan out in the Market Square and force their way in fast currents down the passages and closes to lecture hall or lab. Outside the Arts School there is an unorganized crowd some one hundred strong, locked in a scrimmage of two mighty sides trying to gain entrance and exit. But in ten minutes the two sides have changed places and are going about their proper business: the outgoing students have found another door

Opposite: 6am, Trinity May Ball, June 2008.

Above: Emmanuel undergraduates carrying gas masks during the Second World War.

around the corner and the incoming crowd has been dispersed about the various lecture rooms. The first-comers have found seats and the late arrivals scrounge chairs or squat on the steps and platform beside the lecturer's rostrum.

These students are anything but homogeneous. There are the older men back from war service, many of them struggling to keep a family on their state grant; you see them soberly shopping on their free afternoons with wife on one arm and basket on the other. There are the freshmen who have spent some years in the forces, and for whom a student's life is novel and stimulating. Lastly there are the freshmen proper. Young and very fresh from the sixth form, they are slightly reverential of this older generation, which tends willy-nilly towards aloof segregation.

Extract from the diary kept by Kenneth Knight (1946) during his first term/on his return to Cambridge after army service

THERE was a tremendous feeling of freedom and relief in the air, a return to normal, back to sanity after the years of terror and, more frequently, boredom. A determination to enjoy life, a release from the stifling discipline of the services. It was the last year for the war

generation, those who had served and come up (for a two-year degree) thanks to a grateful and generous government. The University was full of ex-wing commanders, captains, oh! every sort and rank of soldiers, sailors and airmen, all discreetly and firmly civilian, but with experience beyond anything that, thank God, we know today. I myself had spent some three years on the lower deck, as I joined just after the war had finished, when the Admiralty was engaged in running the Fleet down and didn't really want any more of those damned amateurs. While it was tedious and rather uncomfortable, I now realize that I would not have missed it for worlds; it was a great experience.

Brian Russell (1948)

FOR a reason never disclosed the Senior Tutor believed that military service before going up would be educationally and personally beneficial, and also that spending one's first year out of college would be helpful in some equally mysterious way. As a result, 1949 saw me exchanging the spacious flat in northern Greece provided by the army for a small broom closet on the way to Histon provided by the College. The culture shock was massive. Moving after Christmas to King's Road (Newnham), and hoping to reduce the initial disappointment, I fell in with the widowed Mrs Hayward, a compassionate landlady of the finest traditional type, whose commands, however, were not to be ignored.

> *"It is a good idea to order a few hundredweight of logs to eke out your coal ration during the winter. Electric fires are forbidden to undergraduates in some colleges, but the small portable gas fires you can get are useful. A brick on a gas ring is a useful way of taking the chill off a room if you don't want to light a fire."*

Varsity Handbook, 1950

CHRIST'S COLLEGE
CAMBRIDGE

Date 16 June 1948.

Mr. Melinsky

DR. to the KITCHEN
(PLEASE MAKE CHEQUE PAYABLE TO THE STEWARD)

1948		£	s	d
14 June	1 bottle Sherry	1	0	0
	2 bottles Moulin Blanc	1	16	0
	2 " Port	1	16	0
	2 " Red Bordeaux	1	1	0
	Cup		15	10
	8 Tots			8
	8 White Wine Glasses			8
	16 Sherry Glasses		1	4
	1 Glass broken		3	6
	Cleaning, cooking and			
	carving 2 chickens		5	0
	Salad for 8		3	4
	New Potatoes for 8		4	0
	Sherry Trifle for 8		12	6
	Hire of Crockery etc.		7	8
	4 Cigars		10	8
		£8	17	6

'Write your essays on the table. The desk is full of rice.'

'Why?'

'For the next war, of course'.

'You moved his razor. Don't do it again.'

Everything in the house had to remain as on the day her husband left Cambridge to be killed in France.

'You can't go to the lavatory yet' (outside in the garden). 'The duck's in there. Wait until she's laid her egg.'

'Here's your breakfast. The cat got part of it out of the frying pan, but there's enough left. Eat up.'

In this freshman year, set texts were also a problem. Until then no-one had told me what to read; being widely read had been assumed. No matter. A genuine Cambridge education began at the beginning of my second year when I moved into excellent rooms in Walnut Tree Court and began to benefit from the pleasures and challenges of college life.

Michael Collie (1949)

IN my last year the chickens came home to roost; it looked as though I would fail my Finals. I gave up acting, and swimming gave me up. I had a wonderful Director of Studies called Roland Winfield. He had been an RAF doctor in the war, and flown eighty bombing missions to study air-crew stress and then become a parachutist. He was given a Fellowship, but did no research and not much teaching: this might be acceptable in Trinity, but not at St John's. As finals came closer, Roland gave me some blue pills and some pink pills. 'The pink ones are to give you three hours of sleep a night, which is all you can afford', he said, 'and the blue ones are to keep you awake while you do in a few months all the work you should have done in three years.'

James Cellan Jones (1949)

"*The ton or beau monde, pinnacle of arriviste ambition, divides its time between Trinity, Miller's, Newmarket, and London; the world of the cloth waistcoat and the flat cap, mainly composed of Legal and other Smoothies, is to be found in the E.S.U., the K.P., or the Pitt Club; the academic intelligentsia frequents the tea-room of the University Library; the politicians may be seen boring each other to extinction in the Union; the Cambridge writers and actors (few of whom either write or act) are often to be heard in the Copper Kettle and the Whim.*

The Bath is a rendezvous for many of Cambridge's tweedier citizens: the Pickerel for her jazzmen; the Baron for the Magdalene or Visual Arts contingent; and the Volunteer for what used to be known as the Hearties. Tulliver's is usually crowded with first and second-year lecture-goers; and one is given to understand that those who wear College scarves may be encountered in the Dug-out.

Each of these groups has its distinctive dress, speech, gestures, and mode of behaviour."

Varsity Handbook, 1950

Draghunting

In the late 1940s and early 1950s, runners had to be found to pull the drag around for the Cambridge University Drag Hunt. I was a member of the Cambridge University Hare and Hounds Cross Country Running Club and so was deemed suitable.

Bottles containing panther urine came by train from London Zoo and were collected from the Railway Station. The Drag was about the size of a brick and made of Hessian packed with cotton waste and attached to a rope about six feet long…the runners were briefed by the Master of the Drag Hunt, Marcus Kimball, and given a light lunch of cheese rolls and a glass of port. We were taken to the start of the course, usually to the west of Cambridge and told where there was any wire as this had to be avoided. The drag was then primed with the precious fluid and we set off over the heavy Cambridgeshire clays along the appointed route. Occasionally we were caught by the hounds and the drag hunt, but not often. The hounds were not fierce and seemed quite content to sniff the drag and then go off and do their own thing! The riders would jump off their horses with cries of 'hold my horse', which we did. The runners with whom I went were usually Roger Shaw (Caius) and John Denton (Trinity or Magdalene). Our reward was an invitation to the Drag Hunt dinner at the Pitt Club. The food and drink were stupendous – my memory is of Black Velvet, stout and champagne, as an aperitif with oysters.

Are there any of the other runners still running, or indeed still alive, I wonder?

**Archie Dunbar
(1948)**

Beagling

This picture of the Trinity Foot Beagles was taken in 1987 with the Master of Magdalene, Sir David Calcutt, at a time when all three masters of the pack were members of the College. Despite its name membership of the pack, which is now amalgamated with the South Herts, is open to all members of the University from whom it  continues to draw support. The pack traces its origins to 1862 and my son Dominic Armstrong, on the left of the photograph, was the fifth generation of the family to be involved.

When not out with the Beagles I was also a member of the 'Panther Club' referred to above by Archie Dunbar – alive but not necessarily running!

**Angus Armstrong
(1958)**

Ralph Lewin

BEER TRIPOS Pt. II

11.30 A.M. – 1.30 P.M.

JUNE 3RD

1952

"...in vino veritas..."

Left: Alexander Campbell and William Rice in their rooms in St John's, 1954.

I was an undergraduate during World War II between 1939 and 1941, and again between 1946 and 1947. When I returned to Downing a few years ago, I was delighted to note how much more comfortable and convenient college rooms and amenities are now, and wrote this:

Cold College Rooms

Our toasting forks we had to make
From straightened hanger wire
As we discussed philosophy
Before a glowing fire.
Bill shot down and Leo died
And Harry's old and grey –
So too am I as I recall
Our rooms of yesterday.
But now there is a telly set
Where once a scuttle sat.
Plug in the pop-up toaster and
Turn up the thermostat.

Ralph Lewin (1939)

For me, the point about Cambridge was and must be still, that wherever you are you're only 15 feet from a congenial person. And you know you'll not find that civilized delight ever again. Nor, unless you inhabit the South Bank, will you again encounter so much art and music and cinema and friendship and highest standards in so tiny an area. In the claustrophobia of sheer joy even time is constricting. Everything has to be crammed into eight weeks, but an hour…

Two vacations were for desperately catching up with the reading and the long vac was for menial jobs in hotels or Swedish forests. Travel was hitch-hiking, where you raced rival hitch-hikers across Europe. No money then, but more fun?

Yes, it *was* colder then. The Cam froze and suddenly everyone had skates. As you skimmed along under the bridges the ice sagged and then came up again, giving the sensation of skating on waves.

But there is a different Cambridge for each of us. Mine was the smell of last minute scenery and greasepaint in the ADC, and the brilliance of the Marlowe Society, who produced a mind-boggling *Troilus and Cressida*. My Cambridge gave me Fellini and Ingmar Bergman, the Rex Cinema, *Gamma Girton's Needle* and *Love's Labour's*

Ben Wray

Ben Wray

Above: The winter of 1962–3 was the coldest since 1740 with most of England under snow from late December to early March. The Cam was frozen to Grantchester.

Right: Guidance for new proctors on walking their rounds, 1946.

D.V. 109/2 x/j.
10

Notes on Walking

1. Never fine without an interview. Have notebook. Take men's initials. Note time and offence.

2. Go easy with the fines the first week of Michaelmas Term. Warn Freshmen. Zero hour in Mich. and Lent Terms = 7.30 p.m.

3. Don't let your constables dictate or take the lead.

4. Don't let them give chase in crowded streets unless the offence is serious.

5. Only let one constable go away from you at a time.

6. Don't argue in the streets; take name and "We can discuss that when you call".

7. Send men home if you suspect they may become noisy or commit street offences, or if you want to clear the streets. Don't allow argument; take note of time.

8. Make men without caps come for interview, but don't fine – at least for first offence.
When a man with a ragged gown or cap is ordered to get a new one, make him bring both the new and the old one when he calls; confiscate the latter.

9. Send out men found in riotous pubs. Take names and report to Tutor.

10. If the publican asks about the position, say that he is quite right to serve drinks, but that undergraduates must leave when requested.

11. Only raid low grade pubs if there are signs of obvious trouble.

12. Visit cinemas and stand about for a few minutes.

13. Look for unlocked doors of lodging houses. Report to Lodging Houses Syndicate.

14. Don't fine for smoking unless flagrant.

15. If you suspect a false name, take man to nearest College and borrow a white list; or send a constable home with the suspect.

16. Take names of men behaving improperly with girls, or if your men suspect the girl. Report to Tutor if undergraduate is in any doubt as to her name or where he met her.

17. Take car numbers if doubtful and report to Motor Proctor.

Lost, where the players strolled from the Downing College tennis courts fitting their rackets into presses as they declared the opening lines: 'tis but a three years' fast. The mind shall banquet, though the body pine.'

Peter Vincent (1953)

IMPATIENTLY and almost vengefully determined to do well academically after my two years' National Service in the Royal Navy, I worked hard on my English essays in that first term. But I also worked hard on seeking girlfriends: sated body would entail clear head for judicious writing. I visited jazz dances at the Rex Ballroom (Tuesday nights) and the Masonic Hall (Saturday nights). The joyfully improvised music seemed to mock the scripted pedantries of the Mill Lane lecture rooms. I would jive amateurishly with skilful partners in swirling skirts. I wore brown suede shoes, an old brown corduroy jacket, black shirt and black jeans which probably exuded wafts of sweat and stale tobacco, though after years of cigarette-smoking I believed myself odourless. At one of those Saturday-night dances, I invited a pleasant young woman to accompany me back to college. At that time, the rear wall of Pembroke (along Tennis Court Road, by the gate) was being reconstructed, so she and I were able to enter the college by squeezing through the builders' temporary fencing of wire and palings. We tiptoed along, hand-in-hand in the dark, past Orchard Building to the Victorian court and up the draughty staircase to my room. In the distance, the bells of the Catholic church chimed midnight.

Once inside that room, I experienced grim qualms. Suppose a porter burst in and found me there with a female? All porters had a master-key. It was strictly forbidden for any undergraduate to entertain a female in his college room after 9.30pm; indeed, an erring student could be sent down for such a gross offence. It would mean the end to my university career: goodbye, degree! Goodbye, job prospects! All those years of study, the essays, the tense exams, the memorizing of quotations and dates, the reading of thousands of works extending from *Beowulf* to Beckett, my annotation of the whole of Shakespeare's output, the struggles to improve my Latin and German, the nervous fear at those

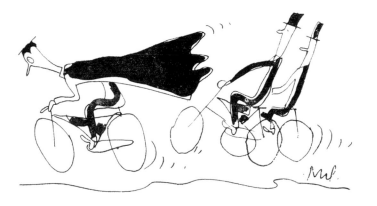

Rag Day

Rag Day in the 1950s showed considerable ingenuity. On one occasion, the gentlemen's lavatory under the market place was transformed into Tutankhamen's tomb and admission cost sixpence. There was also a group of rugby players dressed as members of an exotic harem, two on each side of Trinity Street, holding the shafts of a curtained litter, which completely blocked the road to traffic. A further burly figure would lean out and embrace any passing motorist or cyclist and only after payment was the litter raised to allow free passage. Individuality was welcomed, but anything considered unseemly was frowned upon, and the enterprising undergraduate dressed realistically as a sweep was nevertheless required to remove the notice fixed to his jacket reading 'Up your flue for one and two' (one shilling and two pence).

Peter Bryan
(1949)

Poppy Day in 1959.

interviews, and, most importantly, the patient encouragement and generosity of my parents as the years passed and I remained a student: all that would be wasted. Years of endeavour sacrificed for a few transgressive minutes!

So I decided to sleep in the armchair in order, should the worst come to the worst, to offer some mitigating circumstances. She undressed, slid into the bed, and soon appeared to be asleep. But as I sat there, the room gradually became colder and colder (for I had frugally turned off the gas fire), and the chair became less and less comfortable. I brooded miserably.

Eventually, I tiptoed across to the bed.

'Excuse me', I whispered, nudging her cautiously. 'I'm freezing. Would you mind moving over?'

Cedric Watts (1958)

THOUGH normally a fairly law-abiding individual, I transgressed University regulations shortly before graduating in summer 1960. I had ventured into the streets of the city without a jacket on and fell into the hands of a proctor doing his rounds. I boldly decided to cock a snook at hoary authority and, being aware that the appropriate fine was one-third of a pound (6s. 8d), I collected the requisite number of farthings (then still in circulation) to make up this amount. On turning up at the proctor's rooms at the appointed hour, I produced my collection of farthings (neatly packed in a small cloth bag) in payment of the expected fine. The proctor in question (Dr Redpath, a lecturer in English), had a rather sober mien, but took my impudent gesture in good part, as his addition to the wording of the receipt shows.

Graham Martin (1957)

MOSTLY we ate in hall, at least for the first meal of the evening. Three courses: soup, a roast of some kind and a substantial pudding. The Cuppers rugby team was treated to a special meal of steak on the eve of matches, in the unlikely belief that it would improve our performance the following afternoon.

Hall was early, 6.45pm in the first year, so after the activities of the evening we had to top up most likely with Bhuna Ghosht at the Indian restaurant in Regent Street near the Catholic church. If one did eat out it was either Indian or risotto, chips and mushrooms in the café upstairs in St Andrews Street. Once or twice a year we went to the Plough at Fen Ditton for a T-bone steak, then an almost mythological dish of such a size that allowed it to hang over both the left and right edges of the plate.

Will Wyatt (1961)

Varsity 1962

Cinema

During the late 1950s, the gentlemanly, rather severe Norman Higgins programmed the Arts Cinema with his finger firmly on the pulse of change in world film-making. Here one saw *Hiroshima Mon Amour*, *L'Avventura*, the great works of Ingmar Bergman, and revivals like Murnau's *The Last Laugh* or Pagnol's *La Femme du Boulanger*. Arguments about the New Wave, or the relative merits of Fellini and Visconti, helped pass the time while waiting in the queue that stretched down Market Passage.

As the 1960s advanced, many undergraduates cycled out to the Kinema in Gwydir Street for American rarities like Joseph Losey's *The Big Night*. John Cassavetes' *Shadows* also ran at the Kinema for some weeks.

Film was THE art form of the period, with two pages a week in *Varsity*, several more in the weekly *Broadsheet*, and even an entire issue of *Granta* in November 1960.

Peter Cowie
(1959)

Invitation to the mock funeral of a student sent down for failing his exams, October 1962.

IN my first weeks at the University in October 1962 a group of well bred undergraduates, who included Prince William of Gloucester, held a mock funeral through the streets of Cambridge, headed by a coffin in which lay the live body of one of their confrères, who had been sent down from Magdalene for failing his examinations. It featured in the national press, who were pleased with copy confirming general perceptions about the kind of people who were at the ancient universities. There certainly was a well-to-do group of patrician or would-be patrician undergraduates, who set themselves up with a swagger as the smart set and treated their more earnest studious contemporaries from less salubrious backgrounds with condescension. If these patricians had an ambition, it was to enjoy the place as much as their fathers and grandfathers had done in days when Cambridge was a better place, and when, as one remarked, the undergraduates were in tone with the college buildings rather than the Guildhall. Even if they were losing ground as admission became more competitive, they still cut quite a figure, and were indulged by dons who knew their families. 'As I was saying to William Gloucester' became a favourite opening gambit at parties. Many read history, but land economy was the course that had real class; but whatever the subject, they were generally happy to get by rather than to excel. Their most characteristic sporting activity was hunting or going out with the Trinity Foot Beagles, whose meets ended up with sumptuous teas in the plush country houses roundabout.

The Kinema, Mill Road, 1957.

The Arts Cinema, 1971.

Overleaf: May Week, 1961. The Cambridge University Madrigals Society sings on the Backs. Photograph by Christopher Angeloglou.

CLARE COLLEGE
MAY BALL
MONDAY 11th JUNE

Dancing to TOMMY KINSMAN
and THE JAZZ BAND

Full Supper Including a Bottle of Champagne
Running Buffet

Tickets obtainable at 4½ gns. at the Porters' Lodge

Cabaret by
CRANKS
The entire cast of the present
revue at the St. Martin's Theatre
By kind permission of John Cranko
"SAGITTARIUS" will play his Guitar in the "LAUTREC CELLAR"

I HAVE BY CHANCE
253
MAY BALL TICKETS
FOR SALE
AT THRICE THE PRICE.
APPLY IN PERSON (OR
IN OWN HANDWRITING)
TO
A. CAPONE X.13

"Cambridge today is
dominated by the professional
undergraduate"

Varsity 1960

Many drove sports cars that got them to London for debutante parties. A favourite haunt of theirs was the Tickell Arms at Whittlesford, run by old Malburian Kim Tickell, attired in knee breeches and silver buckled shoes. They were not to the fore in the main University sports or in the Union; they despised the political clubs, even CUCA (the Conservatives), which they complained was full of 'grey men'. They preferred exclusive dining clubs like the True Blue and the Beefsteak in Trinity. There was the University Pitt Club in Jesus Lane, with its panelled rooms and run like a London gentlemen's club, the 100 or so members of which were chosen by election. Journals like *The Field*, *Tatler*, *Sporting Life* and the *Daily Express* (for the William Hickey column) were in demand in the reading room, while earnest publications like *The Economist* and the *Financial Times* lay there unfingered. In-jokes appeared in a book provided for the purpose, while far-fetched bets decorated another volume. Waiters – all called George – joked familiarly with the members. It was all a final chapter in a way of university life depicted by Max Beerbohm's *Zuleika Dobson* or Evelyn Waugh's *Brideshead Revisited*, in another place at another time.

Charles Lysaght (1962)

Home of Rupert Brooke, the poet
The Orchard, Grantchester
MORNING COFFEE
TEAS · LUNCHES
OPEN EVERY DAY EXCEPT MONDAY
Easily accessible by footpath through Grantchester Meadows and by
road or river
Phone: TRUMPINGTON 2208
· During the winter months, kindly phone in advance

Breakfast at the Orchard, May Week, 1961.

月秋湖平 **HANGCHOW CHINESE RESTAURANT**
11-15 PETTY CURY (Entrance from Alexandra)
Open 12 Noon-11.30 p.m. Street, off Petty Cury) Tel. : Cambridge 51203
including Sundays
Finest English and Chinese Dishes by Expert Chefs. Parties catered for

We are open **ALL DAY**
from 8 a.m. to 11 p.m.
(except for Sundays, when
we open at 9·30 a.m.,
Mondays, when we are
closed from 5·30 p.m.)
For breakfasts, elevenses,
lunches, teas & dinners.
The Whim is licensed.
THE WHIM
10 Trinity Street, Cambridge,
telephone (0223) 52135.

Enjoy the good eastern food in
comfortable surroundings at the
NEW BENGAL RESTAURANT
Fully Licensed
43 REGENT STREET
SPECIAL THREE COURSE LUNCH FROM 33 p
ALSO CURRY TO TAKE AWAY IN HEAT RETAINING
CONTAINERS
SPECIAL PARTIES CATERED FOR
Open
Monday-Friday   12 noon-3 p.m.   6 p.m.-midnight
Saturday & Sunday   12 noon to midnight
For your table reservation 55845

NOW A FREE HOUSE
THE TICKELL ARMS
Whittlesford
Formerly The Waggon & Horses
(Née The Chequers)
CAMBRIDGE BUT SEVEN MILES VIA LITTLE SHELFORD
WINES ON DRAUGHT   HOT & COLD SNACKS ALWAYS
WORTHINGTON 'E'
SAWSTON 3128   YOUNGER'S SCOTCH ALE

Eating out in the 1960s.

"Women: Your Appearance
Strike the happy medium. Men loathe the girl who appears at an early morning lecture dressed and made up for Ascot. Equally unpopular is the girl who seems to have thrown a few shapeless garments over her pyjamas.

Be feminine, don't try to ape men in appearance and behaviour. No one gains more respect than the woman who does not set herself off as a feeble imitation of men, but who develops an individual approach to her work and her friends, and yet contrives to look neat and feminine."

Varsity Handbook, 1951

PERHAPS everyone recollects their time at Cambridge as the best of times. But we were constantly told that this was so. In 1965–8, we were neither too young nor too old for Swinging London, for dancing to the Sergeant Pepper album in the summer of love, for demonstrating in Grosvenor Square against the Vietnam war. Aged 18–22 we were, incontrovertibly, the right age at the right time.

But in 1965 Cambridge still seemed, compared with my gap year on a newspaper in then-booming Tyneside, staid. A spinsterly aura hung over Girton's Gothic corridors. But not having been to boarding-school – mine was a co-educational grammar, now gone comprehensive – I was amused by the feasts-in-the-dorm atmosphere and the annual singing of college songs. All Cambridge's rituals held a curious charm. I went to the Bumps, to a May Ball; I even went beagling.

Then, Dylan's 1965 mantra-song, 'The times they are a changin', began to ring true. The Union had its first woman president, the captivating Ann Mallalieu. *Varsity* had its first woman editor, Suzy Menkes. I was measuring out my life in *Varsity* articles. I interviewed Helen Brook, venerable founder of the Brook advisory centres which offered contraceptive advice to the unmarried: they opened in Cambridge in 1966, not a moment too soon for me. Lady Brook's enlightenment contrasted with the disapproval of Mrs Markwick, my moral tutor. Canon Montefiore, vicar of Great St Mary's, supported the clinic 'to avert tragedy'; however, sex outside marriage was, he said, 'almost always wrong'. But in our time the contraceptive pill made sex easier to negotiate, less shackled with guilt. And fashion, reflected in *Varsity*'s pages full of Biba, bell-bottoms, beads and flower-power, became sexier. We had discos, in unlikely venues like the Union cellars. Most of us were hardly touched by drugs; alcohol was quite dangerous enough. Yet for *Varsity* I wrote, in blissful ignorance, about LSD and psychedelic music.

Cambridge café society at the Guild, 1961.

The Cambridge Highland Band play in a Poppy Day parade , 1950.

Dancing

I was born to be a side drummer, so having served my apprenticeship at Loretto during the war, it was natural that I would look for opportunities in the Cambridge Highland Dance Club – never mind the Part 1 Economics – and within a year there were three. It cost a fortune to import a live band from the north, so Gordon advertised in *Cam* for volunteers; he got two accordionists – one could actually read music, the other was sent off to learn from Jimmy Shand records – Jim, a classical violinist, a flautist I think, and/or a double-bass player. With Gordon on piano and myself on drums, at least we got the tempo almost right, over a testing but successful two-year spell.

But this was not the only bonus for a successful amateur snare drummer. All sorts of 'flat race' dancers wanted a reel at midnight, two pipers with a drummer were just the job for the price of a bottle of whisky or a double ticket. The 'Pipe Major', a close friend, I recall, of Humphrey Lyttleton, was a lovely man, blown out of a tank during the recent disagreement with Germany, his aluminium leg an interesting challenge to kilt dress. The most widely remembered Highland events were the Poppy Day parades by the ad hoc pipe band through the streets with the dancers, raising cash for the British Legion in canvas sheet and tin bucket. None of this was the height of sophistication, but the 1949 undergraduate population had a wide range of maturity, from veteran to schoolboy. We therefore delighted in a post-war freedom to invent, to innovate.

Stephen Allan
(1949)

Behind our busy, upbeat frivolity we knew there were others of our number, sitting in mute despair in their solitary rooms where, every few weeks, one of them would be found dead. For *Varsity* I attended the inquest on a boy who had carefully sealed up the doors and turned on the gas. His mother, beautiful, proud, elegant, spoke in icy, disengaged tones. Had he written home about his depression? 'No', she replied. 'It wasn't his habit.' I often reflected on such irrecoverable family tragedies: a son at Cambridge, the zenith of aspiration; a son dead at nineteen, the nadir.

Throughout the early 1950s The Cambridge University American Square Dance Club attracted up to 14 Squares (112 dancers) every Friday evening during term time, at firstly the Milton Road School and latterly at Brunswick School (now closed). The high point of the club's existence was a 'Square Ball' held in a packed Guildhall in the Easter Term of 1955.

Derek J. Read
(1952)

Cambridge gave me a chance to participate in so much, both at college level, where I was a theatre and film club technician, an on/off cricketer and a chapel marshal, and also at the wider, university level. My happiest times outside academic life were with the Cambridge Dance Club, where I ended up as Vice-President, Events, in my final year, as well as dancing for the D Team and the B Team in the Varsity Match. I also had a long association with the Methodist Society and held several positions including being President for a term and organising the term's events. In my final year, I also joined the URNU, which gave me a chance to learn more about the navy and life at sea. The roles in the various societies gave me the skills necessary for organizing events, and for proper time-planning – something I bless in my current busy job, when I am trying to fit in research, administration and my teaching responsibilities.

Roz Halliwell
(1993)

When a group of friends decided that Cambridge needed a dancing club to support the increasing popularity of ballroom dancing in 1949, little did they know that they were laying the foundations of a club which would grow and flourish to become the largest annual membership society in Cambridge University and the largest dancing club of its kind in Europe. With over 2,000 active members each year and over 50 hours of classes a week, the Dance Club is not only a fantastic place to learn to dance but also a thriving social scene. Most come as beginners and, in some cases, stay with us for decades. I myself started going to ballroom, Latin and dancesport classes two years ago and have since been going to more classes than I have time for and have taken on an active role in the day-to-day running of the club.

For those who are keen there is the highly successful Cambridge University Dancesport Team, this year's winners of the Varsity Match against Oxford and IVDC Overall National Champions 2007. Our rock'n'roll and salsa teams also have an impressive competitive record.

Ana Kalabina
(2004)

Some of us cared enough about changing the world at large to march and sit-in: about apartheid in South Africa, the colonels' coup in Greece, the Arab-Israeli conflict, the Vietnam war, the Biafra war, and always, War on Want. WOW staircase lunches of bread and cheese were a daily option. Student activism became de rigueur. In 1967 Muriel

"I disliked my sitting-room from the first moment I saw it. It was chilly, bare and high; and the walls had been newly papered and painted, a bright, unfriendly brown. My few books huddled together, quite lost in the tall bookcase; and I had no photographs or menu-cards to break the long bleak black line of the mantelpiece. The grate didn't draw properly: the fire was difficult to keep alight and the chimney smoked. There were eight hard, leather, brown chairs, none of which I ever used. They had to be ranged along the wall or grouped round the table; making you feel, in either case, that you were surrounded by stiff invisible presences. Altogether, the place was like an old-fashioned dentist's waiting-room."

Christopher Isherwood, *Lions and Shadows: An Education in the Twenties*, 1938

Counselling

On 1 April 1969 the Vice-Chancellor opened the Cambridge University Medical Counselling Service with me as its first counsellor, or 'Mother Confessor' as the more excitable national newspapers called me. All the newspapers, both broadsheet and tabloid, were intrigued by the novelty of this institution, as Cambridge was only the second university in the country to have one. Busy tutors, whose role *in loco parentis* was coming to an end, were finding more of their time taken up by undergraduates with quite severe personal problems. GPs wanted a place where they could see their undergraduate patients away from their busy surgeries, and undergraduates wanted to be able to discuss their problems with a greater degree of anonymity and confidentiality. Accordingly, in true Cambridge fashion, a committee was set up with an Egyptologist as chairman, and after two years of deliberation, the Service came into being.

As a psychiatric social worker with psychotherapeutic training, I had worked in the Cambridge Psychiatric Department for 12 years and knew my way around. Nonetheless, there had been some opposition to the scheme from some tutors, and even a psychiatrist, and I approached the job with trepidation. A leaflet was distributed publicizing the service to both graduate and undergraduate students and all the colleges. During that first morning, April 1, nothing very much happened, but by the afternoon there were three people in the waiting room and three hundred were seen in the first year. Referrals came from the students themselves, from tutors, chaplains, GPs and sometimes friends. Interviews were by appointment and generally lasted an hour. Problems were sometimes work-related and, particularly in the arts subjects, often reflected an inability to cope with the flexible structure. Severe loneliness was common, as were psychosexual and general identity issues. I visited all the colleges and met all the tutors to allay their anxiety about confidentiality. The finance

Cambridge 54545
by Martin Adeney

THE Samaritan Service will open at 8.00 on Monday morning. From then on a round-the-clock watch will be maintained by volunteer counsellors at their headquarters at 35 Regent Terrace.

Handbills and posters advise: "If you are in despair and tempted to suicide and do not know where to turn for help, ring Cambridge 54545."

Above: Varsity, 1962.

Right: Sex advice booklet for undergraduates, 1980.

for the service came from the colleges on a capitation basis, which did not always run smoothly. A basic research effort was introduced to see whether the service might throw up some general problems that could be addressed, such as, for instance, whether there was any faculty more vulnerable than another. Needless to say, English appeared most vulnerable and Veterinary Medicine the more robust. Did a gap year help? On the whole, yes. Was there any difference between state and private education? Both types of school produced a similar proportion of problems, although direct grant schools, as they then were, had a significantly higher proportion of students facing difficulties.

The GPs gradually dropped out of the service and continued to see their student patients in their own surgeries. Their presence in the beginning, however, had helped to emphasize that this was a confidential service. The service continues to flourish, seeing well over 1,000 students and staff members a year, and there are now about ten counsellors who provide a wide range of help, group therapy, etc. It is also recognized as a valuable place for trainee counsellors and the Service provides training sessions for tutors and chaplains.

Jean Ferguson was appointed as the first Medical Counsellor in the newly formed Cambridge University Medical Counselling Service in 1969.

Bradbrook, Girton's new Mistress, returned from her trip to California where she had met the student protest movement. Marcuse, she reported, 'greatly impressed the impressionable, with his unending flow of clichés.' Soon, what she called 'Californian attitudes' were taking hold in Cambridge, and as she wrote, 'reforming the University became an alternative to study.' Chanting undergraduates who threw eggs at Labour ministers and reviled the University's Chancellor, Lord Adrian (discoverer of the D waves in the brain) became an embarrassment. At the same time Rab Butler, Master of Trinity, welcomed a new undergraduate: the Prince of Wales.

HRH knew he had a job to go to afterwards and so did the rest of us, confident and carefree. There was no such thing as student debt, other than one's termly buttery bill. Employers fell over themselves to offer traineeships. Two days after degree-day, I started in Fleet Street.

Valerie Grove (1965)

IN COLLEGE, we had bedders, who were like surrogate mums. They came each morning to make sure that our rooms retained a modicum of order. A lady did our laundry if we wanted. College butteries opened for alcoholic beverages well before the pubs, in those days of restricted licensing hours. For the juvenile and foolhardy, there was the King Street Run, with its eight, seedy little pubs. In order to say you had done the King Street Run, you had to drink a pint in each pub and complete the last one without a pit stop. Childish, of course, and only for the neophyte! Serious drinkers did not have to prove themselves in this way! Also, the beer was awful! It was well before the real ale revolution that has transformed the British ales. It took at least a term to familiarize the palate to the local Greene King bitter. Those who persisted eventually acquired a taste for it, yours truly amongst them.

This was the 1960s, when flower power was all the rage. For boys, brightly coloured, flowery patterned shirts and wide ties were *de*

Climbing

I found that Cambridge at the weekends could feel quite socially claustrophobic, and joined the Cambridge University Climbing Club, partly to get out of town. I held a committee post for a short time, I believe for want of any more talented woman climber, as the number of female mountaineers among members of the University at that time was a handful. A glorious summer meet on the rock ridges of Arolla and Chamonix amid unrivalled scenery; the snow-bound invitation winter meet at the splendid Charles Inglis Clark Hut below the North Face of Ben Nevis at New Year; clambering up to warm rock ledges in Easter sunshine on the University Easter meet in Llanberis Pass: these were fabulous experiences which I treasure to this day. I did not lead climbs much however, and in retrospect I am surprised that this was never overtly addressed, although contemporary climbing books illustrate exactly the sexist assumptions made by both sides at that time. However, the extended mountain days I experienced while at Cambridge led to fine rock-climbing seasons at VS and HVS standard, a splendid further season at Zermatt, and my marriage to an Oxford climbing man the year after graduation. Happy days!

Nicola Jackson (1973)

Clockwise from top left: Arianna Stassinopoulos on the cover of the Varsity Handbook *before becoming President of the Cambridge Union in Michaelmas 1971; List of discos, 1990s; Students' Union poster, October 1970; Gay campaign, 1978.*

rigueur worn with bell-bottomed jeans or trousers and Chelsea boots with zips up the sides. As we all know, the winters are cold in Cambridge. Easterly winds whip up across northern Europe from the Urals, straight to East Anglia, without much in the way to stop them. So we had to have overcoats. The most popular casual coat was an inexpensive, blue, fireman's jacket from the army surplus store. These were half length and made of wool with no collar, had buttons all down the front (à la Beatles jacket) and had a (sic) flaired bottom. On one occasion, with an unpleasant allergic skin reaction I visited a very conservative doctor in the middle of the night in my fireman's jacket.

'Are you with the military?', he asked, in a very posh accent!

'No, I'm from Liverpool', I said!

The girls had straight hair and wore loosely fitting, sack-type dresses with lace trim, flat shoes and beads. They looked scruffy and pretty awful! No wonder the mini skirt era that followed was so successful! Long hair was in vogue for both sexes. Facial hair was fashionable for men, so there were lots of wispy adolescent moustaches and sideburns. Was this inspired by Che Guevara or Sergeant Pepper? Probably both. My sideburns almost joined up with my moustache. When I look at photographs today, I see a Mexican bandit! But it was cool then.

The music was psychedelic with lots of Indian tablas and sitars and hints of transcendental meditation and mind-altering substances. It was all very innocent really. The Beatles were taking drugs at this time (a fact we only really learned later), but happily, drugs were not yet part of the mainstream. Everyone knew someone who had smoked pot or who had tried LSD, but it was not the norm. Suicide was fairly common, because the pressure was so intense. Most people came up to Cambridge (and probably still do) having been at the top or near the top of their school academically, only to find they were pretty average at Cambridge. This happened to me. It was a salutary experience and one of the essential lessons of Cambridge. It was amazing, however, how the tough academic environment and difficult conditions forced individuals to work together. Strong friendships formed quickly, just like in a military combat unit.

Jonathan King (of *Everyone's Gone to the Moon* fame) managed to be an undergraduate and a pop star at one and the same time. Pretty cool we all thought at the time! He could be seen around Cambridge, presumably between his London recording sessions, in his black cape. Did I mention that the *Phantom of the Opera* style capes were popular?

Staircase to a recreation room in Trinity, 1968.

At May Balls, black capes were everywhere, we looked like so many Count Draculas! The Who broke their guitars at Christ's May Ball in 1967, while in the next marquee The Temperance Seven were playing their form of bouncy and popular jazz. Meanwhile, Jethro Tull, complete with working-class inferiority complex, were insulting the audience at Churchill's May Ball. On the subject of insulting, on one occasion I attended a very posh, private, black-tie dinner party. Someone had asked for, and got, the worst stripper that the supplying organization, presumably the local strip joint, had on their books. She was big; really, really big! She brought her own record player with stripper-type music that sounded very scratchy. A skinny undergraduate at the front of the assembled throng shouted out, in traditionally irreverent Cambridge tones, 'You're too fat'. Without hesitation, she glided over to him, gracefully for her size and in time with the music, and knocked him senseless!

David Goodwill (1966)

In 1972, the 1960s party was over; but some of the hosts and guests had not realized. We who arrived after the event were already a confused generation. Everything was still urgently polarized in our adolescent minds; but the world had moved on. Meanwhile, were we to take sherry with the Dean or LSD? Attend the Pitt Club or the Bun Shop? The answer in many cases was both.

There were very few women – the bold measures we took to meet some may have demonstrated the energy of innocence, yet still make me angry, as they probably do some of the women in question. My college, the second oldest in the University, was endowed by a woman and yet was one of the last to admit women.

As a visual person many of my memories are as such: the yellowing face of my landlady, who died of liver cancer in the house above the Penguin Bookshop on Trumpington Street; the double helix on the wall of Francis Crick's house in Portugal Place; charismatic teachers and lecturers: Richard Gooder, George Steiner and a visiting Roland

Night-climbing

I am one of the two who made the first ascent of the University Library Tower, which was completed at 4.30am on the morning of 13 June 1978. My climbing partner, Timothy Jefferson, a brilliant graduate student at Queens' studying for his PhD, was killed in a climbing accident on Artisonraju in the Cordillera Blanca in Peru in 1983.

Tim and I could not have completed the climb were it not for the work that had been done during 1977–8 by four other teams, indeed there was a certain amount of healthy competition within the small world of Cambridge night-climbers (most of us members and officers of CUMC) for the prize of cracking what was the last unclimbed university building in Cambridge. The final attempt was our third, progress having been severely inhibited by the revelation, on our second foray, that the bolts we had placed to protect the climb and had left in situ had been removed by the authorities.

My recollections of that June night are as fresh today as ever: the ease, in the end, with which the final pitch of the climb was completed; the exhilaration of standing on top of the City's highest building: views in the gathering dawn light of the profusion of towers and spires and steeples, the Backs, the glittering lights of the May Balls.

The descent, directly down the front of the building, involved two abseils, the first via one of the corners to decorate a statue with what we hoped would be a lasting sign of the ascent (having run a chair up the flagpole), a T-shirt round its neck. The panic as we stood on the roof above the main entrance, attempting to free the ropes, which had stuck … and the relief that we were able to reach the ground with a second rope and untangle the first, before disappearing under the incredulous eyes of returning May Ball revellers.

Ian Edwards
(1976)

Barthes. Captain Beefheart and Lou Reed playing rock concerts; playing in rock groups at May Balls; publishing and writing my first work; the bizarre approach from the Secret Intelligence Service; and the mandatory and fruitless interview in Brooklands Avenue with the University Disappointments Board.

Jonathan Mantle (1972)

The long hot Easter Term of 1976 and varying the morning break between coffee in the Whim in Trinity Street and tea in the Copper Kettle in King's Parade.

The chap who, naked but for a policeman's helmet, rode his bike down King's Parade during Rag Week in 1977.

Having my own primitive guide to inflation by looking at the price of moussaka at the Eros Restaurant, initially in Petty Cury and later also opposite St John's. It was 45p when I went up and, I think, about 95p when I graduated.

The normality, welcome ordinariness and generally relaxed atmosphere of the Market Place during exam time and the occasional treat from Andy's Record Stall.

Professor Pevsner's packed lectures on Fridays at 5pm, strictly for History of Art and Architecture students but open to all who had paid the Composition Fee, a real extension exercise for the brain and introduction to the appreciation of the beautiful.

Looking down the long stretch of Grange Road for the last time the day before graduation, wondering whether life thereafter would be as straightforward and happy and realizing that Cambridge and its beautiful buildings would be there long after me.

Sarah Hobbs (1974)

I arrived in Cambridge in 1986, in the heyday of Thatcherism, and began to look for two things to satisfy my 18-year-old thirst for life: new friends, and some kind of political expression. Friendships were quickly made and slowly consolidated over countless coffees in the faculty buttery or the University Library café, pints of beer at the Anchor, and the odd cocktail at Browns, to satisfy our more Bridesheadian fantasies of Oxbridge. Political expression for a would-be lefty, however, was more difficult to satisfy. There was a strong Conservative leaning in the University at the time. The first meeting I attended of my college's left-wing society, shortly after Freshers' Week, produced only nine people.

But to look at it another way, Cambridge was a refuge from the pressures of a fast-moving

A Time of Timid Transition

When I went up in October 1971, there was a convention by which undergraduates were meant to wear gowns to supervisions, where they were to be addressed as 'Mr' or 'Miss'. The purpose, I think, was to make the student feel intellectually respectable and independent – an equal in discussion. In fact, few supervisors seemed to require gowns, and all of them addressed the students by their first names. I never discovered what we were meant to call them in return, though I occasionally found myself biting back the word 'sir'.

I was lucky to be there at all, since the housemaster at my school had advised Emmanuel that I was a bad lot. Perhaps he was right. Like all the other freshmen, I had shoulder-length hair and dirty clothes. The senior members of the University, whatever their nominal informality, viewed us warily. I think they were in a state of shock, following the events of the previous five years, which had seen undergraduates sitting in, marching and demonstrating. One or two had ended up in prison. Much of this activism must have seemed counter-educational to older people who had spent their lives at universities. In its extreme form, it placed a desire for equality and non-discrimination above the value of learning. The immediate effect of undergraduate revolt was limited by the short academic terms and the three-year life of the student, but the principles of that Sixties rebellion were widely adopted at secondary-school level and in teacher-training colleges, so that before too long, Cambridge was, for the first time, having to admit freshmen from whom knowledge had been, for political reasons, withheld by their teachers. So the marches and sit-ins did ultimately affect the university, though less directly than their organizers had planned.

In the early 1970s we were the last of the old grammar school children, crammed with learning for its own sake, little interested in exam grades and still less in league tables, the idea of which would have united senior and junior members in distaste. Few of us expected to get first class degrees and few of us did. A first was a mixed blessing, in any case, since it implied that your future lay not in the City, at the racetrack or in Hollywood, but in teaching on a remote campus. A 2:2 was the default degree, which showed you had completed the course but done other things as well; a 2:1 was a bit showy. However, one of the victories of the Soixante-Huitards at Cambridge was to end the 'divisive' – or was it 'discriminatory'? – separation of the seconds into two classes; so everyone I knew in 1974 got an unclassified second, which in later life was referred to as a 2:1.

It was not a glorious period in Cambridge history, but it had a marked character. It was a time of timid transition. We were not only among the last of the old grammar school children, we were the very last of the centuries-old masculine era. King's had admitted a handful of girls – or women as they were always known in this context – but all the other colleges except Girton, Newnham and New Hall were boys only, so that girls were vastly outnumbered. We were a dying gasp, an evolutionary oddity before the Cambridge undergrad mutated into a robust new species. With candidly mixed motives, we boys spent a good deal of our time agitating for co-residence, having 'emergency lunches' in Trinity parlour or marching with torches on St Catharine's; but, like Moses granted his glimpse into the Promised Land, we did not live to enjoy it.

Student life today looks a lot more fun than '73, but you must take your life as you find it. I was well taught in Emmanuel and was directed to other congenial teachers in King's, Sidney Sussex and Magdalene. I remember discussing with my director of studies, John Harvey, whether it was more important to end the war in Vietnam or to preserve a felicitous enjambement in one of Shelley's odes, and I knew then that I had met someone who took literature even more seriously than I did. This wasn't rock'n'roll, but it was typical of something intransigent and puritanical about the University which spoke powerfully to me, and for which in later years I have been grateful.

Sebastian Faulks (1971)

---

consumerist society, and an antidote. It provided a time for reflection and creativity. This for me, at least, was possible through music, theatre productions, and my course. Reading English Literature at this time was in itself a great privilege but also felt somewhat of an anachronism, in a society which increasingly valued profit margins over spiritual and intellectual growth. Studying in the subdued grandeur of the University Library, cycling across Cambridge on frosty mornings with numb fingers to attend lectures on Greek tragedy, discussing the religious imagery of English medieval poetry, writing essays while gazing out of the window to see college Fellows playing bowls on the lawn … all these experiences added up to an existence that was a far cry from the voracious world of capitalism outside, and were probably common to undergraduates over the last couple of hundred years at least. But we didn't spend three years posturing about declaiming T.S. Eliot; there was a core of normality about our life too, as well as a strong streak of hedonism. We were dedicated viewers of *Neighbours*, which I am certain was the most popular TV programme amongst undergraduates at the time. And many an evening which doubtless could have been spent in some career-enhancing way was idled away drinking copious amounts of alcohol and playing endless games of cards.

I had worked in London for a year before 'going up', and had been encouraged by colleagues to give up my university place and stay in London earning 'loads of money', as the popular expression of the time went. I am glad to say I didn't take their advice.

Jo Cholmondley (1986)

I ARRIVED at Cambridge University in the autumn of 1988, at the age of 18, ostensibly in order to begin a three-year history degree, but in reality to pursue two objectives of extraordinary importance: girls (I had in mind ones with glasses and a slightly melancholic air who would be capable of tears during the final movement of the Agnus Dei in Bach's Mass in B Minor) and, more vaguely, creativity.

The official reason for being in Cambridge turned out to be the most disappointing. The history degree required that one study an idiosyncratic selection of subjects in intellectual, economic and political history. But there was no overall conception of what history was for, and there seemed to be no interest in instilling students with a well-rounded knowledge of the past. One term, I studied the agricultural development of Britain in the 19th century, in another, the unification of Italy, in a third, the philosophy of Thomas Hobbes. But this otherwise calamitous history degree did have one immense benefit: it was neither very difficult, nor time-consuming. I was therefore able to educate myself (always the best option), with the help of the University Library and an account at Heffers bookshop, which my parents had, in a fit of generosity they were later to regret, agreed to pay for.

As for the girls, rather like my history course, what I had hoped for did not occur, but huge subsidiary benefits flowed from this disappointment nevertheless. Gustave Flaubert summed these up when he explained to Louise Colet that, had he fallen happily in love with a woman at 18, he would never have become a writer. Or, as Proust put it, 'A woman whom we need and who makes us suffer elicits from us a whole gamut of feelings far more profound and more vital than does a man of genius who interests us.'

It turned out that glasses-wearing, Bach-loving beauties (attractive if they took off their glasses) were either not present in abundance at Cambridge between the years 1988–91, or simply had enough good taste not to look in my direction. There was a succession of fruitless pursuits and much agony, which inspired me to read even more. Literature and unrequited love have deep affinities; it is when we are experiencing the latter (eating chocolate in bed, weeping at 3am), that we are most drawn to the former. Happiness may be good for the body, but unhappiness is better for bookstores and the survival of literature.

Throughout my time at Cambridge, I worried about what would come after. I did not take the view that the time to sort out a career would occur after graduation, partly because I must have sensed that I was not interested in pursuing an ordinary career. My concern throughout was to find the correct literary form, and this project made me more self-involved, more introspective than I might otherwise have been. I look back on my time at Cambridge with a certain pity and humour: they were not easy years, there were high expectations and many insecurities. I have never desired to relive that time, but I can see also that it was a necessary part of that stumbling process one calls self-development.

Alain de Botton (1988)

MY most distinctive memories are the chance meetings with friends from totally different academic backgrounds (one of the great advantages of the college system), who were fundamentally original people. Without, of course, ever having planned it, we could spend hours talking about all sorts of things I never dreamed I would discuss: Belgian 'new beat', the history of Naples, playing the banjo.... It obviously wasn't productive in a strictly academic sense, but it was fun, and also enriching. People were not embarrassed to be fascinated by their subject, and they were also fascinated by others' fascination, and so on. Of course, there was more to Cambridge than that, excessive drinking, arguments, bad food ... but none of it particularly original.

I was at Cambridge during an interesting 'in between' period: the internet was not yet a common feature in most students' lives, essays were still largely handwritten; we were emerging from a period of penury and entering a big economic boom; a kind of sepia Englishness was just on the point of being pollinated by all sorts of foreign influences (you couldn't get a decent espresso then, budget airlines were in their infancy). But whatever Cambridge looks like today, I hope the spirit I encountered during my time there is still going strong.

Eric Woehrling (1989)

Gown fitting in A.E. Clothier.

Descriptions of Cambridge Societies, *Varsity Handbook, 1960s.*

Descriptions of Cambridge Societies, Varsity Handbook, 1960s.

C.U. STAMP CLUB

The Stamp Club offers a focal point for philatelists in the University, avoiding that exhausting search for people with common interests. The main meetings include one or two distinguished speakers, auctions, a competition, discussions on topics of interest, an annual dinner and, of course, general informal meetings.

We run a comprehensive Exchange Packet Scheme, and many members find this ideal for acquisition and disposal of material. The Club caters for a wide range of interest... ...eginner or a serious investor, there'll be a ... ...for 3 years.

Tape Recording Society

Membership is open to all interested in recording, whether they have a recorder or not. The Society was founded in order to bring those so interested together for the exchange of ideas. Both technical and non-technical interests are served.

The Society meets once a week on Thursdays. A lecture is arranged for every other week, the remaining meetings being taken up with the presentation of our own recordings, competitions etc.

Recordings for other dramatic and musical societies are undertaken, and productions of our own include short plays, etc. Membership fee is 15s. a year.
President: D. Robinson (Pembroke); *Secretary:* T. Wade (Selwyn); *Recording Secretary:* S. P. Robinson (Selwyn).

FREEMASONRY

The Isaac Newton University Lodge exists for the benefit of undergraduates and graduate members of the University. **Contact:** N.F. Rix (Sidney Sussex) **Contact:** P.G. Maxwell-Stuart (Queens')

CAMBRIDGE was where Watson and Crick discovered DNA, but for me, it was life outside the classroom where I did most of my learning. There was a language laboratory where we could listen to tapes and watch films, and language classes were held too. There were societies and clubs for just about every activity and interest group imaginable. The Dalai Lama came to speak, as did Amos Oz, the late King Hussein of Jordan, the late Edward Said, and Noam Chomsky. I volunteered at a homeless shelter and listened to the stories of how the men ended up there. There were campaigns urging us to change our bank accounts because of third-world debt, and that was where I learnt that even bank accounts were not innocent. There were accusations of the exploitation of native peoples by multinational companies, including the one that sponsored my scholarship to Cambridge.

Ting Hway Wong (1992)

IT'S NEVER easy to capture a generalised experience. But turn-of-the-millennium Cambridge differed from the hothouse of idealism and political ideology I've been assured it once was. Instead, it felt rather like a holiday resort.

Attending lectures was not always dissimilar from hanging out on the beach. You might pretend to be listening to Thucydides' account of war with Sparta but really you'd be staring at the blonde girl across the lecture hall. You'd spot someone you fancied on the Sidgwick Site and then drunkenly reveal your feelings face to face that night in a club.

There were no more than five Cambridge venues that could, with any hint of seriousness, call themselves clubs. But around these famous five the weekly cycle of university life revolved. Ok, so *plus ça change*, earlier generations of graduates might say. You had clubs, we had all-night parties. No doubt. But you had parties and politics.

Cambridge life in the late Nineties and early Noughties mirrored the Westminster landscape. Now that Blair had dragged the Labour

BRITISH RAILWAYS
B.R. 21711
COACH RESERVED

For *Cambridge University Railway Club* Party
From .... LIVERPOOL STREET .... To *Cambridge*
Train *20.36* Date *17.2.73* Signature ...

Railway Club

Membership of the Cambridge University Railway Club offered weekly meetings addressed by senior railway officers (British Rail at the time seemed to be run by Cambridge graduates). It also organized excursions to railway installations in East Anglia and beyond. Consequently we enjoyed some marvellous experiences, which would be impossible today: travelling, for example, in a brake van behind a freight train over what is now Thameslink from Cricklewood to Hither Green, and waving to surprised passengers awaiting Circle Line trains at Farringdon. But the most memorable were the relatively local trips: to Whitemoor (March) to see the biggest marshalling yard in the country in action, to Harwich, or (again by freight train) from Downham Market to Stoke Ferry and back. On the Stoke Ferry branch we were all allowed to have a turn at driving the class 31 diesel: there was no HSE in the 1960s!

Tony Kirby
(1964)

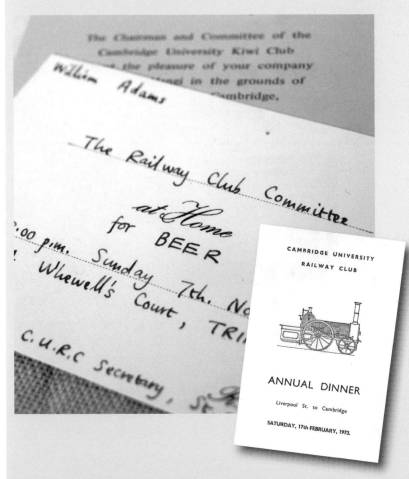

The Chairman and Committee of the Cambridge University Kiwi Club ... the pleasure of your company ... ...tangi in the grounds of ... ...ambridge.

William Adams

The Railway Club Committee
at Home
for BEER
...00 pm. Sunday 7th. No...
Whewell's Court, TRI...
C.U.R.C Secretary, St...

CAMBRIDGE UNIVERSITY RAILWAY CLUB

ANNUAL DINNER

Liverpool St. to Cambridge

SATURDAY, 17th FEBRUARY, 1973.

Ballet Club

I watched proudly from the wings last term as two students, one a geographer and one a linguist, performed a passionate *pas de deux* before a sold-out auditorium in our production of *Alice in Wonderland*. The annual CU Ballet Club show is the predominant event in our calendar and brings the chance for all members to perform, regardless of ability. For some it is the chance to fulfil their childhood dreams of donning a tutu, for others it is the opportunity to feel the excitement and camaraderie of backstage preparations for the first time. Many only decide to experiment with ballet upon arrival at Cambridge, whilst others have been dancing since they were three years old, yet all revel in the chance to bring ballet to the academically minded city.

To watch natural scientists, classicists, physicists and mathematicians pirouetting together is to observe an extraordinary example of how universally accessible ballet remains, and to experience the unity it can bring to a diverse group. Whilst some suggest that ballet is a dying art form, the enthusiastic, 70-plus membership of the Cambridge University Ballet Club suggests otherwise.

Sarah Wilkinson

(2005)

Summer, 1993.

former Chancellor succeeded in doing was making the case for apathy.

Ideology seemed all but dead in the debating chambers of Parliament. And it didn't show many signs of life on the floor of the Cambridge Union. It had become a pale imitation of the catalyst for political exchange it once was. In the years immediately before national and student politics collided in 2004 with the contentious issue of tuition fees, and before the Iraq war of 2003, fox-hunting was one of the few issues that got students out of bed.

Conversation over canteen food rarely turned to a world beyond Cambridge. Gap year stories might be exchanged but beyond that there was little sense that we all fitted into a wider experience. Great fun it certainly was, but we weren't about to change the world. Club Cambridge, in more senses than one.

Matthew Stadlen (1999)

BY the time I got to Cambridge, the access battle was over. We state comprehensive kids swaggered in, not wide-eyed with wonder, but with an air of taking possession of what had always been our birthright. There was little cachet in a foppy floppy forelock. Shaved heads and flat vowels cartwheeled in and ruled over the lawns. Our efforts to out-grit our peers were at times reminiscent of a Monty Python sketch: '35% 5 A* – C?! That's practically Eton compared to where I went to school…'. Deep down, we were a little disappointed at having missed out on a good and bloody class war. So we tried for a bit of a spat over top-up fees; fought and thought we'd won, and then lost again. In a clever, if short-lived PR move, even the University pretended to be against them for a while – but surely breathed a sigh of relief when they scraped through Parliament in early 2004.

We were born in 1980 or just after. We'd heard that Cambridge under the Tories was a fiercely competitive place, everyone clambering over each other onto the corporate ladder to dizzying heights of personal acquisition. But by the time we arrived, third-way teenagers of this neon-bright Britannia, it was a bit different. Postgraduate

party kicking and screaming onto the centre ground, there wasn't much up for debate. Successive Tory leaders tried and failed to persuade us all that there was still a point to the Conservative party.

Ken Clarke, yet to be beaten back into fourth place by David Cameron in his leadership bid, paid a visit to the Cambridge Union. Charismatic he may have been, but all this cigar-toting, jazz-loving affluence was confidently assumed, so we had the luxury of combining it with a social and global conscience. International development and environmentalism became sought-after career paths. And we could be open about the limits of our ambition too. A few girls said out loud that they looked forward to staying at home and having babies. When Cambridge used to be a girl's golden ticket out of all of that, now slogging over your degree might just be to ensure you had something interesting to occupy you in the gaps between goslings. We wanted to get happy, not rich. In SPS we even had lectures on how to be happy

---

38   *Cambridge Slang*

A Dictionary Of Cambridge Slang

A long way: anywhere more than five minutes' walk away.

Backs, *n*: the area between the backs of the colleges and Queens' Road, close to the Cam.

Bedder, *n*: Member of college staff (now always female) who makes students' beds and cleans their rooms.

Boatie, *n*: Rower, usually with same characteristics as a rugger-bugger.

Bop, a.k.a. **Sweaty**, a.k.a. **Event**, *n*: disco, sometimes with food, always with drink.

Ministry of Information or **UL**, *n*: The University Library.

Bumps, *n*: Complicated rowing races in which each college boat tries to catch up with the next.

'Cambridge' (as in 'so Cambridge'), *adj*: used to describe something that is meant to characterise student life, usually with sense of somebody taking something to extremes.

Cindy's: reference to 5th Avenue, nightclub, usually derogatory.

Compsci, *n*: Student reading computer science, usually derogatory. See natsci.

Confie, *n*: conference delegate (usually used in combination with irritation about 'how delegates take over colleges outside term'.)

Desmond (also dezzy), *n*: Lower second in exams, usually finals. From Desmond Tutu (two-two).

Dosser, *n*: Lazy person. (from 'doss-house').

Dweeb (rare), *n*: See narg.

Emma, *n*: Emmanuel College

undergraduate politics or journalism. Also to ~, *verb*.

JCR, *n*: Junior Combination Room. Either an undergraduate common room, or the students elected to look after undergraduate affairs by their peers.

King Street Run, *n*: Tour of the King St pubs in each of which the participants must drink a pint.

Mathmo, *n*: Student reading Mathematics.

May Week, *n*: Week in June (confusingly) when May Balls occur. (f. original month when balls were held.)

Muso, *n*: 1. Student reading music. 2. Musician (often one and the same).

Narg, *n*: A student (usually male) who is hard-working, boring and socially inept; typically physically unattractive and badly-dressed. 2, *v.i.* To ~ (perh. f. imitating narg's manner of speech)

Natsci, *n*: student of natural sciences, usually derogatory, hinting that they are nargs.

Pidge or **P/hole**, *n*: student's mail pigeon-hole (abbrev.)

Plodge, *n*: porters' lodge (abbrev.)

Quiche, *v.i.*: to wimp out, to be cowardly and weak.

Rag, *n*: students' fund-raising charity. Also ~ Week. (f. obs. Rag=jape)

Rugger-bugger, *n*: Rugby-player, esp. one given to rowdy behaviour and drunkenness.

Shark, *v.i.*: to pursue members of the opposite sex unscrupulously.

Spod, *n*: See narg.

Squash, *n*: open meeting at start of year (usually alcoholic) of a college or University ... for the purposes of recruiting new

A Cambridge English Dictionary

A is for Auditions
Cambridge auditions are uniquely deceitful affairs: all but the smallest parts have been handed out well in advance to the director's friends. *See also T for theatre*

B is for Bedders
Bedders are officially employed to preserve the morals of their staircases. Placing a bin outside your door will keep them out but only a fiver concealed within can ensure discretion.

C is for Christianity
Widespread and very, well-organised in Cambridge. Centres on the Round Church for evangelical Anglicans and Fisher House for Catholics. Undoubtedly worthy and dangerous to knock. Cambridge Christianity is relentlessly cheerful. Bring your own tambourine.

D is for Death Van, The
This burger stand appears in Market Square at full moon. Avoid. *See also G for gastro-enteritis.*

E is for Enthusiasm
Social death in Cambridge. The University's turnout point de zèle may mean vegetating for three years, but it's sooh much cooler that way.

F is for Films
Cambridge is, for the moment, ...

H is for Hacks
Found at CUSU, CUCA, the TRG, the Union, Uni-left, indeed wherever there is an acronym. Universally despised but still assumed to have dazzling prospects. Hackery is the talentless vainly trying to borrow the prestige of that old 'Cambridge' myth.

I is for Instant Coffee
You're a fresher, flapping your fledgling wings, yearning to enjoy your new-won independence, throw off the bourgeois shackles of family life... Why then do you feel an urge to bridge colleges as nosy bedders, sarcastic chums to Hob-Nobs, crumpets and jam tarts and to brew horribly weak instant coffee? It's because you are, deep down, your mother. *See also F for Freud.*

J is for James, Clive
It seems a fair guess that kindly relations the length and breadth of the country will have bought Cambridge-bound freshers Clive's latest offering, 'May Week was in June'. Pad out ...

mates with 'Eat the Rich' rallies. He made such an impression on the left that the diminutive don beat him up. *See also R for rôle model.*

L is for Lectures
One in a year is your record to beat (English) or four hundred odd (Medicine). Lectures have regularly been given to one student; Sir Isaac Newton talked to an empty hall.

M is for Misogyny
As much a feature of the older Cambridge colleges as nosy bedders, sarcastic porters and terrible food. Feminists view dons' misogyny as evidence of the University's sexual fascism, cynics wonder if the dons aren't simply jealous of female students for distracting all the boys. Either way, the dons will keep up the outrageous sexism as long as New Hall rises to the bait.

N is for Night Life
Hopefully your tastes are for beer & ABBA, crowded pubs and sweet cocktails. Vomit is a Cambridge favourite ...

P is for Pitt Club
Once a sprawling haven of clubland for Cambridge's public schoolboys, the Pitt Club is now one room grotter than any JCR. The entrance fee of several hundred pounds entitles you to throw bread at the steward and discuss bores both large and small with OTC members, whose mess it also is.

Q is for Queen's Sons, The
Prince Edward and, no doubt, Prince Charles in his day, brought out the worst in Cambridge. Despite having left years ago, Prince Edward's ghost stalks the sad corridors of the Pitt Club, CUCA, and the Union. His presence lent some credibility to the self-delusions of Cambridge's social climbers and, even now, desperate diary writers, hostesses and ball organisers invoke this mythical beast in order to raise circulations, attendances or simply money.

R is for Rugby and for Rowing
One is a painful, pointless, élitist, macho, beer-swilling sport dominated by middle-aged international athletes drafted in to read Land Economy, the other is an increasingly egalitarian, serious, modern, healthy team activity. Which is which, alas, I've forgotten.

S is for Stereotypes
Sloanes & seccies, arties & hearties, medics & mathmos – they're all ...

Top: From A Students' Guide to Cambridge, *1991.*

Above: Varsity Freshers Issue, *1991.*

Juggling

Despite our name, Cambridge University Juggling Association, some of our members cannot even juggle in the classical sense of juggling balls. This is due to our club covering a much larger category of activities: the manipulation of objects (with the addition of your own body) in challenging and visually pleasing ways. These include disciplines such as poi, devil stick, diablo, contact juggling, staff spinning and unicycling.

Juggling offers a method of relaxation, experimentation and self improvement. During periods of high stress, such as exam term, juggling can clear the mind of such worries while you try to perfect a new trick you have just learnt. In which case we provide and lend a host of equipment from juggling balls and clubs to unicycles or spinning plates.

Most of all the association offers a great social scene where people come to exchange tricks, gain inspiration and meet up at the pub after every session. We also have a yearly Varsity competition with Oxford and Imperial College, London, which involves great battles of beer-swilling along with some juggling-related games. Next year's host is Cambridge.

The majority of our members come to us with no juggling skills, but quickly learn from others at our twice-weekly meetings. Here we offer a warm, dry space for people to come, juggle and socialize.

There is also appeal for the pyromaniacs out there with termly fire nights: get togethers at which a large quantity of paraffin, lighter and fire equipment, such as fire poi and staff, provides copious quantities of fun, supervised by the experienced to make sure nothing goes wrong!

Harry Waye

(2004)

Chess

Still going strong after more than a century, Cambridge University Chess Club beat Oxford in most competitions in 2007–8, and naturally, anything we didn't win wasn't important. Well… almost! We did miss out on taking Freshers' Varsity narrowly, by one board, and lost the Town–Gown and Insurance Club matches. But the club has, without a doubt, gone from strength to strength; we won last year's 125th Varsity Match, bringing the running total to Cambridge 65 – Oxford 60, and dominated Seconds' Varsity 8 – 2.

Organising the Chess Club has come with its own distinct little package of quirks and challenges. The CUCC Jacques Cuppers chessboard, stolen from the club in the 1960s, has resurfaced for auction in London, and for the past few months we've been working with Sir Alan Fersht (President 1964–5) to get it back, though there've been problems, since decades' worth of club records were accidentally burnt a few years back. We're looking into establishing a club library, and preparations are in place for several large-scale events, including a top-level, international-standard match between Oxbridge alumni. We've moved towards making the club more open and accessible as well, buying new equipment for loan to college clubs, rebranding our public image, abolishing our membership policy, and targeting our events and publications to cater for a wider audience.

Loren Lam

(2005)

May Ball invitations.

(interesting, I grant you, but made it still harder to convince friends you were doing a serious degree). And God still had a job. Religious faith of all flavours was alive and well, and actively marketed round quadrangles and up staircases.

September 11 happened while I was at Cambridge. Where were you when you heard? I was learning to yodel like a Hungarian shepherd for a fully ancient Greek version of Sophocles' *Electra*. Really, only in Cambridge. But as the nation's young and earnest, did we lead the charge against all the new millennial war-mongering that 9/11 ignited? There was dissent and there was debate. But our fury certainly didn't bring the place to a standstill. I remember a couple of nights' knuckle-gnawing over how I felt about it all, and whether I wanted to join the February 2003 protest against the Iraq war. Friends shot me the 'how could you?' look normally reserved for baby killers when I said I wasn't quite sure if I needed a coach ticket for London that day. 'So how was it?' I asked meekly, emerging from the library straight into the path of my college's chief thumper of anti-war tubs. 'Oh, er, didn't go in the end', she mumbled. 'Essay crisis'. There are geo-political tectonics, and there are essay deadlines. And we knew which took priority.

Staying with the Cambridge students' early Noughties priorities, alcohol deserves a special mention. I spent a few fist-in-mouth weeks as *Varsity* news editor when, encouraged by us, a surprising number of the world's more and less respectable media outlets ran 'Cambridge Students Get Hammered!' stories, followed by 'Cambridge Students Get Hammered! – and this time it's the GIRLS!' and, have mercy upon us all, 'Cambridge Students Get Hammered! – and this time its the POSH GIRLS!' Students have always drunk. Cambridge students have always drunk. But as Britain began to self-define as the binge-drink centre of the universe, IQ was no defence. From matriculation to May Week, and every night in between, it was what kept us awake all night and asleep through lectures. It wasn't very pretty and it wasn't very inclusive. For all those with a little more imagination, or a jolly good reason not to, it was kind of tough. We'd decided, as a generation, that we couldn't have fun without it. And if you thought you could, we told you you were wrong.

Not long ago we went back to Cambridge to pick up our fake MAs. In a speech at the pre-ceremony luncheon (luncheon? who says luncheon? that's Cambridge all over for you) our college bursar noted that many of our year group would have received their Cambridge offer letters in the first few days of the year 2000. So it wasn't impossible, he went on to quip, that our three or four years' stint at this venerable institution had actually been the result of some milennially generated electronic mutation. Perhaps the real braniacs had reluctantly sloped off to Durham or Bristol, and the pretenders that sat before him had been accidentally shoed in by the short-sighted IT moles of their parents' generation. It was a good joke but, however we'd really negotiated the application lottery, we all breathed a quiet sigh of relief at having made it through.

Judith Whitely (2000)

Above: St John's May Ball, 2008.

Left: Fireworks during May Week, 2008.

ganging, so distant from the supposed long-haired eccentricity of Cambridge yesteryear, became familiar. The two student newspapers thrived, bloated with premium-rate colour advertisements urging the University's finest to drop books long enough to board the milk round.

Careerism nevertheless remained a subplot until the first summer vacation, which brought with it the realisation that flimsy notions of future employment required serious structural attention. This was not unique to Cambridge, but a wider undergraduate response to a competitive and fluid job market. Engineers, medics, historians and English students keenly sought placements. I resolved to acquire the holy grail of work experience, aware that Part 1 of the Social and Political Sciences Tripos – a charming blunder through philosophy, child psychology and the breeding patterns of spear-wielding Saharans – was not overly vocational. One week at *The Observer*, 'doorstepping' Soham villagers caught in the murders media circus, proved shocking and helpful to my journalistic ambitions.

The academic burden predictably accumulated thereafter. Having slaved to acquire the requisite A levels, we laboured under the impression (intentionally seeded, perhaps) that our Cambridge supervisors considered us inferior to previous generations, capable of learning by rote and regurgitating texts but often a disappointment when it came to thinking originally. Easter Term began with its customary clatter of lost marbles: heads dropped, conversations conformed to competitive revision, Beta blocker stocks dipped and Sainsbury's sold out of fish. 'Have you got The Fear?' chuckled the still sane to one another. One unwelcome theory suggested that grade inflation had risen through the schools system to universities, heaping pressure to attain at least a 2:1 to enter the job market with chin raised. We need not have flapped so much. Our 131 SPS finalists were graded 48 firsts, 67 2:1s, 11 2:2s and one third, and that bleary last May Week became a celebration rather than a wake.

Oliver Duff (2001)

A NAÏVE Bedfordshire state school lad who hadn't learnt the value of a pronounced 't', I stumbled in to the concrete Cripps Building late September 2001 clutching *Leviathan*, a Playstation and a poster featuring bottled beers of the world. St John's housed a collective of getters-on, savvy young machines primed by exam-centric schooling and supportive parents to Achieve, be it grades, recitals, society memberships or sports clubs. A few arrived fresh from internships at orchestras, powerhouses of international finance and government departments. This guaranteed a vibrant, if initially intimidating, student life.

The big City banks, consultancies and law firms took two days to leave finger marks on our downy arms. Even before a lecture could be delivered or the first barrel changed in the college bar, many dozens of white-collared, freebie-waving recruitment agents descended upon the Freshers' Fair, a flapping gauntlet not dissimilar to taxi drivers at the arrivals gate of an African airport. Take our biro! Our branded bottle opener! Just sign your email here... Such pin-striped press

Investment banking recruitment at the Careers Fair, 2007.

I WENT up to Selwyn in 2003. I was struck by how dynamic and fast-paced this famously old-fashioned town was, and wondered if secretly it always had been. From our arrival hyperactive clubs and societies reps dashed about, competing for our attention and for the right to carry our cases up to our new rooms. This manic recruitment drive continued throughout Michaelmas, often aided by free wine, until everyone had signed away every last minute of spare time, and much of their work time too.

Religious groups seemed to have the most luck (they probably wouldn't call it that) and suddenly hundreds were wearing hooded sweatshirts emblazoned with biblical slogans gently reminding the rest of us that we were damned. Those who still didn't get the message had a whole tiny Bible stuffed into their pigeonhole. Anyone over 5'10" and stockier than Kate Moss was flattered into submission by their Boat Club captain, with delusions of Varsity Race grandeur obscuring the miserable reality of 5am starts, alcohol bans and eating a whole malt loaf at the start of a race before throwing it up at the end.

As well as being essentially post-politics, ours was a post-sexism era; female students had equal opportunity to work, play and drink too much. Female drinking societies, their names generally alluding to sexual acts, dined weekly with male drinking societies, their names generally alluding to acts of raw strength, either in college halls or town curry houses. If the latter, chaos typically ensued, with local couples out for a quiet Indian watching in horror as world-class scholars ate mango chutney off each other's bodies.

One thing of which we were acutely aware was the University's dependence on technology. High-speed internet access was by then standard in every room, and Cambridge's lifeblood was the Hermes email system, a one-stop shop for sending essays, organising supervisions and apologising for not having sent your essay for the

supervision. No one sent actual physical objects any more; we were convinced the last bicycle-riding University postmen were only there to reassure the tourists.

Cambridge students were one of the first British groups allowed on to the social networking website Facebook. This merely meant we were among the first to discover how utterly ruinous to productivity it was. Help groups sprung up with names like 'I'm suing Facebook when I fail my degree' and 'procrastination' became the *malaise du jour*. But it took the pain out of courting. Having spied your target in lectures, a trawl of their Facebook page revealed their favourite author – Joyce, music – the Beatles and political views – left-wing. The next day they would arrive in the lecture hall to find you thumbing *Ulysses*, with 'She Loves You' blaring through your headphones and a red rosette on your lapel. Irresistible.

Jon Swaine (2003)

"*Although as we shall presently see, there were some redeeming features in my life at Cambridge, my time was sadly wasted there, and worse than wasted. From my passion for shooting and for hunting, and, when this failed, for riding across country, I got into a sporting set, including some dissipated, low-minded young men. We used often to dine together in the evening, though these dinners often included men of a higher stamp, and we sometimes drank too much, with jolly singing and playing at cards afterwards. I know that I ought to feel ashamed of days and evenings thus spent, but as some of my friends were very pleasant, and we were all in the highest spirits, I cannot help looking back at those times with much pleasure.*"

Charles Darwin, *His Life Told in an Autobiographical Chapter, and in a Selected Series of his Published Letters*, edited by his son, Francis Darwin, 1902

Right: Clare Bridge illuminated, Summer 2008.

'The Cambridge novel'

JONATHAN SALE

What is Cambridge's answer to *Brideshead Revisited*? Is there a Cam-based version of Evelyn Waugh's iconic saga, published in 1945, of well-heeled Oxford undergraduates? If not, what do Cambridge novels say about the place?

Certainly the University has, over the centuries, thrown up major writers: Milton, Marlow, Wordsworth, Tennyson, Thackeray, E.M. Forster, Hughes and Plath, and a number of authors today work happily within Cambridge postal districts. Its resources make it conducive for creation, according to a literary don in A.S. Byatt's novel *Still Life*: 'Good writers should be good readers.' But the heroine disagrees when she sees the eminent novelist E.M. Forster dozing during a tea party: 'Cambridge was, she thought, not a good place for writers.' The real E.M. Forster shared this critical opinion: 'Not a place in which a writer ought to remain', was his judgement on Cambridge, and he should know: he scarcely wrote a creative word after becoming a resident of King's College. He had produced one of the classic university novels, *The Longest Journey*, much earlier. The hero begins his day in an intellectual Paradise by reading Theocritus, 'the greatest of Greek poets', lunches with a 'merry don', walks with friends and returns to college for a quibbling philosophical discussion, to the strains of Wagner, about whether a cow exists if there is no one to observe it.

'Cambridge has been a bridge to pass over, narrow and one-way', declares Graham Chainey in *A Literary History of Cambridge*, adding that while *Brideshead Revisited* takes Oxford very seriously, Tom Sharpe's *Porterhouse Blue* sends Cambridge up. 'There is little serious fiction set in Cambridge. Most novels are thrillers and comedies, which treat it like a stage set. There is very little fiction that treats Cambridge as a serious place with intellectuals living there.' As long ago as 1898, a critic noted that for every one Cambridge novel, there were 20 set in Oxford. And out of any 100 Cambridge novels written in the post-Waugh period, perhaps five concentrate on actual student life.

Porterhouse Blue is one of the many Cambridge novels which largely ignore students, being concerned with the machinations of the High Table of an imaginary college. Another is *The Masters*, which C.P. Snow wrote after a short stint of teaching at Christ's; the action, if that's the word, is confined to the battle for the top job. *Gargoyles and Port* by

E.M. Forster in King's College in 1964.

Mary Selby includes in its cast list the randy Bursar of 'St Alupert's' and two children but depicts few characters in the age gap between. The heroine of Stephanie Merritt's darker drama, *Gaveston*, is a research student at St Dunstan's and the niece of a press baron. *Cordial and Corrosive* is Sophie Hannah's tale of graduates struggling for the same Fellowship at 'Summerton' College. *Bad Chemistry* by Nora Kelly is a murder yarn set among the academics in the Science Labs, while *Unquiet Spirit* by Derek Wilson features parapsychologist Nathaniel Gye on the track of spooky and criminal goings-on at 'St Thomas's'.

'Crime fiction is a way of giving an impression or reflection of university life', points out Mike Petty, the retired librarian who managed to (speed)read the hundreds of works of local fiction in his care at the Central Library's Cambridgeshire Collection. Certainly the

    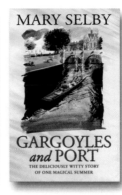 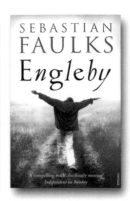

college play in *The Bad Quarto* will bring back memories, embarrassing or otherwise, to former Thespians. One of Jill Paton Walsh's series featuring Imogen Quy, amateur detective and college nurse at 'St Agatha's', this also features some dangerous nocturnal ascents of university buildings, as does another novel with a 2007 vintage, *The Night Climbers* by Ivo Stourton. An aristocrat Spiderman pops into its hero's room at the top of a staircase in 'Tudor College' and embroils him in activities which would be called 'underground' if they weren't taking place at roof-top level.

In *King's Parade* it is the upper echelons of undergraduate life which are caricatured by Simon Sebag Montefiore, whose Thatcherites, real toffs and revolutionaries battle for control of the Union during the greedy 1980s. A prince is in residence; he wonders whether it would be wise to take a high-class girl nicknamed 'Scrubber' to a May Ball.

In the first half of his recent novel *Engleby*, Sebastian Faulks provides what seems a more typical account of the undergraduate experience: the cold student houses, the shower-free rooms in college, the ADC crowd, the live music gigs and the suit bought from Oxfam for the job interviews. But the hero finds himself helping police with their enquiries in a murder investigation, which does not generally happen to those in stat. pup. and the book moves on well beyond the Cambridge borders.

As does *Still Life*. In the Cambridge portion of the novel by 1950s student A.S. Byatt, the heroine luxuriates in 'a garden full of young men', i.e. a university blessed with a ratio of 11 blokes to each female. Some lads are weedier than others: a rejected suitor bursts into tears, while another smashes a teacup with a poker. With the more virile, she plays two kinds of 'dating games'; one involves quizzing each other about the date of an unknown poem, the other features spermicidal jelly.

Byatt's heightened sensibilities and precious perceptions may have been true for a more exquisite minority of 1950s undergraduates, but it is her contemporary Andrew Sinclair whose *My Friend Judas* nails down the zeitgeist in a more recognizable way. This is a lively chronicle of student life: after-hours entry into college by climbing over the wall or appealing to a sympathetic porter; the heightened sensations of May Week; the lowered sensations of exam week. Sinclair's funny, downbeat

story begins with Ben, its gloomy, hip hero, standing on a bridge to pee into the Cam and ends with him being sent down for publishing a blasphemous poem in his student mag. The originals of the characters can also be recognized. The villain of the story (Ben's co-editor, given the boot at the same time) is partly based on the late Mark Boxer, the cartoonist and brilliant first editor of the *Sunday Times Magazine*, who had in fact been sent down for the above blasphemy when editing *Granta*. The 'Judas' of the title has been 'outed' as a famous woman journalist.

Frederick Raphael's *The Glittering Prizes* also includes an emotional May Week: a girl leaves the boyfriend who is horrified at her pregnancy and during the Ball becomes engaged to another student. Like Raphael, the hero is a young Jewish lad from the suburbs who arrives in Cambridge in the early 1950s and leaves as a budding novelist. He and his pushy thespian friends swap bon mots and girlfriends while fiddling the drama club expenses.

Thrusting themselves into the worlds of television, film and education, Raphael's creations enjoy subsequent years which feel like an extension of undergraduate life: Cambridge by other means. This witty novel, which satirized the media so sharply, was turned into a very successful television and, more recently, radio series.

Interesting, beguiling, sometimes amusing and occasionally scary: Cambridge-based fiction is all of these. Yet nothing has had the lasting impact of Waugh's classic, even if 'Brideshead' is sometimes used as a term of abuse. There is still room for The Great Cambridge Novel but, if you are going to write it, remember that Cambridge may not be the place in which to do it.

Jonathan Sale (1962) *is a freelance journalist who writes a weekly interview series and reviews books for the* Independent.

"'So this is the city of dreaming spires', Sheila said.
'Theoretically that's Oxford', Adam said. 'This is the city of perspiring dreams.'"

From *The Glittering Prizes*, Frederick Raphael, 1976

Arts and Humanities

From Sophocles to semiotics

MARY BEARD

In 1888 John Seeley, Professor of Modern History and distinguished classicist, addressed a conference of French teachers in Cambridge. Classicist by training though he was, he believed that 'the needs of modern life were peremptorily demanding very much more devotion to the study of modern languages than had ever been devoted to them.' It is 'absurd', he argued, '… to consider that a youth cannot learn grace from Racine, eloquence from Rousseau, elevation and force from Victor Hugo, not to say from Dante and Goethe.'

In Seeley's day, arts and humanities in Cambridge meant a narrow range of subjects: just classics, moral sciences (or 'philosophy', as we now call it), theology, plus Semitic and Indian languages (later redefined as 'Oriental Studies', and again in 2006 as 'Asian and Middle Eastern Studies'); medieval and modern languages was the most recent appearance on the block, newly created in 1886. It was only in the 20th century that English, Anglo-Saxon, music and the history of art became subjects in their own right. And it is only in the last 50 years that these faculties have gradually clustered around the Sidgwick Site, with dedicated libraries, lecture and seminar rooms and research centres – in effect, an interdisciplinary arts 'campus', with 3,000 undergraduates and almost 300 permanent academic staff, studying everything from Sophocles to surrealism, the *Battle of the Books* to the war on terror.

A forward-looking late-Victorian would, I imagine, be both surprised and gratified by these developments over the last century or so. Surprised, for example, that those classical courses, which – as Seeley was gently hinting – seemed to many in the late 19th century to be standing in the way of intellectual progress, have thrived as a thoroughly modern intellectual discipline. There are now more students studying Latin and Greek at Cambridge than there were in Seeley's time. In fact, barring the occasional bumper year in the early-to-mid 20th century, there are more people studying classics – at undergraduate or postgraduate level – than there have ever been in the 800-year history of the University. And, alongside Latin and Greek, you will find other so-called 'dead' languages being brought back to new life here: Old Norse, Akkadian, Medieval Irish, Ancient Egyptian hieroglyphs and many more.

Left: View across the Sidgwick Avenue site showing the Raised Faculty Building, which houses the Casimir Lewy Philosophy Library.

Cambridge has a long tradition in Middle Eastern and East Asian studies: the Sir Thomas Adams Chair of Arabic, founded in 1643, is the oldest chair of Arabic in the English-speaking world. Illustrated is a page from the Shahnama *of* Firdausi, *the Persian Book of Kings. There are several versions in Cambridge, all of which appear on the Shahnama Project website, a joint initiative by Cambridge and Edinburgh Universities. Harold Bailey, to whom this one belonged, was a Fellow of Queens' College and Professor of Sanskrit. His former home in Brooklands Avenue houses the Ancient India and Iran Trust, where this manuscript is now kept.*

Gratified, because a diversity of disciplines has been achieved beyond what anyone 100 years ago could have hoped. Nowhere more clearly than in the provision of languages. Seeley trailed the virtues of French, German and Italian. There are a dozen others – from Dutch to Japanese (not to mention English) – that make up the tally of tongues currently taught or studied in Cambridge courses, not to mention the 150 available in the dedicated language centre. By my calculations, there are more languages studied at degree level per square metre of the Sidgwick Site than anywhere else in the world.

It is not, of course, that Cambridge is a kind of elevated 'language school'. It is true that some of our intellectual energy continues to be devoted to the technical resources that the study of any language needs. Two separate specialist research teams are, for example, currently at work on a grammar of medieval Greek and a new dictionary of ancient

I was a classicist, with special interest in the languages and literature, and naturally hoped to come into contact with the authors of some of the books I had appreciated at school. The ambition was satisfied to an extent I should never have believed possible, not only by lectures, but also by the many college Classical Society evenings, most of which were open to girls from any college. I specially remember John Chadwick, the iconic figure who, with Michael Ventris, was credited with the decipherment of Linear B. Most years he took over a lecture theatre in the Classical Archaeology building, as this was equipped to show slides, and gave a course of lectures describing the decipherment. I cannot tell you how privileged we felt to attend this. Tension was heightened by his opening, when he put up a photo of Ventris and in an impassioned voice told us how the discovery was all due to him – a fairly rare, but not unprecedented, case of self-deprecation and honesty from our dons. When lecturing to students of his own discipline, philology, he was quite different, much more intense. He lectured on Greek dialects. I do not believe there were any published works at that time which covered the subject in this detail. We had roneoed sheets of inscriptions, and he would run through the points identifying the dialects, hinting at the translation on the way. The only catch was, he started talking as he came in, and rattled on without pausing for breath until the hour was up, when he would sweep out, leaving us dazed. It was those hours (three a week, including Saturdays if I remember correctly) that destroyed my handwriting, which had been quite neat and legible up to then.

Mary Clark
(1996)

I read classics and vividly remember being enthralled by the outstanding series of lectures on Sophocles by Professor Sir Denys Page – Regius Professor of Greek and Master of Jesus College. Sir Denys could hold an audience in the palm of his hand and the lecture was always packed to overflowing when he was on.

He had a very deliberate style of delivery, with pregnant pauses and clearings of the throat – this all added to the drama. We all knew of the professional disagreement between him and Professor Sir Maurice Bowra (at the Other Place!) in their interpretation of the works of Sophocles – and that was quite a personal matter between the two great men. When I attended his series of lectures, he did not mention this disagreement until lecture three (I think it was); but as soon as he brought up the name Bowra for the first time, he paused and cleared his throat and went on: 'Of course you know that he has written a book on this subject …. It is a very large book … a book not without its uses … for pressing flowers, for instance!' The lecture theatre dissolved into roars of laughter, after which Sir Denys swept on with the subject and never mentioned Bowra again in the remaining five lectures.

Robert Perry
(1968)

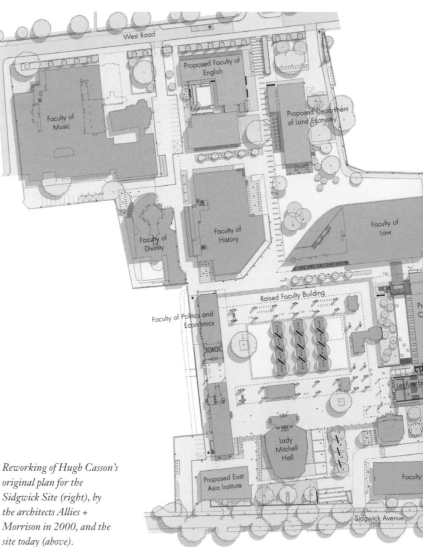

Reworking of Hugh Casson's original plan for the Sidgwick Site (right), by the architects Allies + Morrison in 2000, and the site today (above).

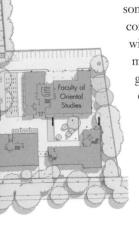

I am one of the many Cambridge students who benefited from the flexibility of the Tripos system. I read classics (with intensive Greek – a subject that had not been on the curriculum at my Lincolnshire state school) for Part I, and English for Part II.

The two years of classics were hard work for me, however. Not only had I no Greek on arrival, I didn't really have much Latin either. My school had been an early convert to the Cambridge Latin Course, and whilst I had hugely enjoyed it, it did result in my Latin skills being well behind those of most of my privately educated peers.

My translation skills certainly did get better, but I don't think I ever really caught up. I hope things have improved since; in the late 1970s, the Cambridge Classics Faculty meant well, but I think weren't really aware of just how behind some of us Cambridge Latin Course graduates were.

I had no problems with the intensive Greek, or the literature, history and philosophy papers, however, especially when the teachers were the younger, more exciting ones, the John Hendersons, M.M. McKenzies and Mary Beards.

Anne Williams
(1977)

I came up in 1959, having learnt Russian during National Service, and was eager to learn more. I spent my time cycling furiously between Station Road for oral classes with Mrs Hackel, a Russian émigré who had swum across a river in escaping from the Soviet Union; to Sidgwick Avenue for lectures; and once a week up the Madingley Road for tutorials with Nikolai Andreyev, the popular and ebullient survivor of years in Soviet prison camps. Lecturers who caught my imagination were Edward Sands, who translated with us texts from the Russian classics – this was for second-year students but his grasp of the language was so compelling that I sneaked in during my third year – and Ian Young, who taught Russian history. I was fortunate in all these mentors, but also in the wider Cambridge intellectual community: I remember Isaiah Berlin (speaking at the speed of a machine gun) giving a notable public lecture on Russian 19th-century thought, while George Steiner's book *Tolstoy or Dostoyevsky* was published opportunely for me to draw on it for my Finals.

Christopher Rundle
(1959)

Greek. Why? Because the existing reference books are either hopelessly inadequate, out-of-date or simply wrong. But for most of us, languages are the means to wider ends in the study of literature, culture, religion, politics and history.

Students are attracted to the humanities courses in Cambridge by the opportunities they offer to engage with the central issues that face *humanity*: questions of cultural and religious difference, of the dangerous inheritance of history, of contested definitions of culture, propriety, art, freedom or good governance. The student experience here is founded on a rigorous and specialist academic education (whether in the complexities of literary, film or gender theory, the use of the pluperfect subjunctive, or the hard core of philosophical logic). But it is an education that is always combined with a sense of the bigger picture – and does not duck the question of why and how these issues might matter outside, as well as inside, the academy.

Inevitably none of this is quite so simple as that grandly confident description may make it sound. How, for example, do we adapt our teaching and learning to changes in the school curriculum? It is not (as some prophets of doom like to suggest) that students now come to us knowing less than they used to; but they do come with different skills and knowing different things. I find myself very pleased that we see no more of those generations of elite boys who had learned precious little else but Latin and Greek since the age of 11. But we are demanding an enormous amount from our students, and from ourselves as teachers, to have them learn sometimes both Latin and Greek from scratch *and* to ensure that within their undergraduate career they have a chance to explore the big issues that those languages open up for them. My hunch is that they work harder than any generation of students ever has before.

I studied modern languages: French and Italian, taking Italian from scratch. I enjoyed my subject and found the Italian teaching for total novices like me excellent.

I remember Professor Pat Boyd giving a 'lecture' in my second year. But it wasn't a lecture. Instead he played his students a recording of Italian poet Giuseppe Ungaretti reading his own poems, which dealt with death, love, war and exile, amongst other things. This was unusual teaching methodology for Cambridge, even in the 1990s. We all sat still, quiet and clearly moved by the poems. The recording made them immediate and accessible, suddenly alive, recent, relevant. It gave me the courage to read those and other poems in a language which at that point I was just beginning to drink from. I enjoyed it so much that I attended the same lecture in my fourth year, just for the pleasure of tuning into it and to our inspirational professor again.

Lena Ruth Brown
(1992)

I remember a wonderful series of lectures on the history of cinema and Dr Natali's classes for those of us taking Latin *ab initio*. I also crossed disciplines and attended a few of Professor Skinner's lectures on the early Florentine republics; these lectures were full of Latin, and I loved being able to keep up with them. In my third year I took a new paper on sexuality and gender in comparative medieval literature which involved studying texts in three languages; I don't think any two students were reading the same combination of languages. This enabled me to compare Chaucer with his French and Italian contemporaries.

Katherine Steele
(1993)

Pei-I Wu teaching Mandarin in the East Asia Institute, 2007.

It goes without saying that the excitement of a Cambridge education, for learners and teachers, has a lot to do with the close connections we foster between teaching and research. It is not just that new research feeds into the student curriculum, but the experience of teaching can feed equally importantly back into research. There is nothing like the challenge of trying out your new ideas on a group of bright students: they can be the most constructive and fearless critics you ever have.

But what is it that drives those new ideas? Sometimes it is the raw excitement of discovery, and humanities in Cambridge have had more

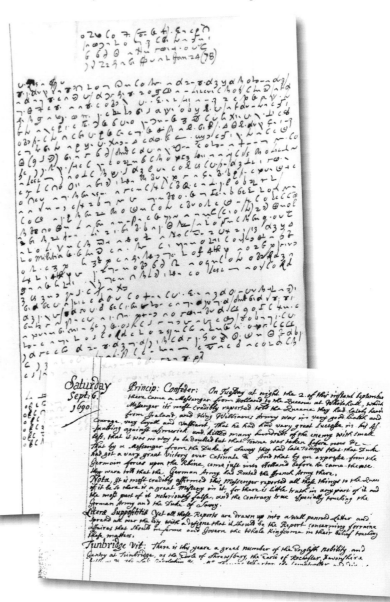
Roger Morrice's index to the Entring Book, *an important record of life in the late 17th century (above, in code; below right, decoded page). The three-volume book is kept in the Dr Williams' Library in London and was published in 2007 by a team under the leadership of historian Mark Goldie of Churchill College.*

James Stirling's History Faculty building. Completed in 1968, it won a RIBA Gold Medal in 1970 but was not universally popular.

than their fair share of that over the last few decades. The Cambridge contribution to the decipherment of the early Greek script of Linear B is well known (and with it came first-hand knowledge of the day-to-day operations of a prehistoric community that are still being studied here). But that is only one of a long list of Cambridge discoveries and decipherments that have brought new documents and new cultures to our attention: from the recent decoding of the language of ancient Caria (in modern Turkey) to the first publication in 2007 of Roger Morrice's *Entring Book* – a 'new', multi-volume 17th-century diary that may turn out to rival even Pepys.

By and large, though, 'discovery' in that sense is not the stock-in-trade of humanities research. Our work aims to be revolutionary in a different guise – by challenging and redefining the way the world, its history, literature and culture are understood. In 1937 a journalist tried to sum up the achievement of J. G. Frazer, Cambridge classicist and anthropologist, and author of that anthropological classic *The Golden Bough*, then over 80. Frazer had, he wrote, 'changed the world': not, he remarked topically, like Hitler or Lenin, not by politics or violence, but 'by altering the chemical composition of the cultural air that all men breathe'. You could say that, too, about many other of our great Cambridge predecessors – about Wittgenstein, or Leavis, or Jane Harrison. Whether you had read them or not, things were never quite the same again.

And similar revolutions are almost certainly in the making as I write. For research in the humanities – even in what might appear from the outside to be the most narrow of scholarly specialisms – is always a risky business. It is exciting, radical, mind-changing and potentially dangerous. And here in Cambridge we are fortunate that it has been bravely and richly resourced. Anyone who imagines that the solitary scholar at work in the University Library comes at little cost is guilty of forgetting the incalculable investment over the last eight centuries in manuscripts, books and the other tools of the humanities trade.

If John Seeley were to return to Cambridge now, he would no doubt be taken aback to find that what he would have known as the Corpus Christi College cricket pitch was now the Sidgwick Site. I think, however, that he would be tickled by the design of 'his' History Faculty. To be sure, it is a controversial building with detractors as well as admirers. But the joke of James Stirling's design lies in the simple fact that he has housed the historians in a structure that might look better suited to the astro-physicists; he has presented 'history' as 'rocket science'.

Reforming modernizer (in University politics, at least), Seeley would have liked that.

Mary Beard is Professor in Classics and a Fellow of Newnham College. She is also Classics Editor of the Times Literary Supplement.

History: transformation and immutability

QUENTIN SKINNER

My credentials for writing about changes in the History Faculty over the past 50 years are embarrassingly good. I sat the Cambridge entrance examination exactly 50 years ago, and came up to read history at Caius in 1959. I took my BA in 1962, and I was elected to a Fellowship at Christ's later in the same year. Although I have sometimes worked elsewhere (France, Australia, the United States), I have basically been teaching in the faculty ever since.

Sometimes I feel that surprisingly little has changed. The main unit of undergraduate teaching in history is still the weekly essay discussed with a supervisor. Nor has the structure of the undergraduate course been greatly modified. There is still a two-year Part I, largely given over to outline papers, followed by a single-year Part II focused on more detailed themes, and students still agree that they much prefer Part II to Part I. Teaching has become more specialised, but even in the 1960s I was already encouraged to base my lecturing largely on my research, a privilege still enjoyed by everyone in the faculty. The size of the undergraduate body has also remained uncannily stable. When I took my Finals in 1962, I was one of 208 students graduating in history; the graduating class in 2006 was exactly the same size. Finally, no one could fail to notice that the ethnic and even the social background of the undergraduate body has likewise remained – to put it as neutrally as possible – astonishingly unaltered.

As often in Cambridge, however, surface similarities mask deep processes of development. I must not speak at excessive length about the transformations that have merely affected the teaching staff, but some of these have been striking enough. Half a century ago, virtually the entire faculty was Cambridge-educated. By contrast, over half the present staff took their first degrees elsewhere. Besides becoming more diverse, we have also become more wholehearted in our dedication to historical scholarship. This is not to say that the faculty had no scholars of international distinction 50 years ago; arguably it contained a higher percentage than it does today. But it also contained a number of colleagues who, whilst generally conscientious in discharging their teaching and administrative duties, scarcely occupied themselves with historical research at all. This breed is now extinct, fatally weakened by the University's imposition of staff appraisal in 1987 and finally killed off by the government's introduction of regular research assessments in 1992.

The Seeley Library, in James Stirling's History Faculty building.

Of recent times a far larger proportion of us have been granted resounding titles by the University. Fifty years ago, the faculty contained nine professors and two senior scholars on whom the title of reader had been conferred. Everyone else was simply a lecturer. It was only after the University instituted systematic procedures for personal promotion in the course of the 1980s that it came to be widely felt that, although everyone begins as a lecturer, it would be a mark of failure to retire with that rank. The faculty now has twice as many professors and four times as many readers as it had when I was an undergraduate, and these proportions are undoubtedly set to rise.

*Herbert Butterfield,
Regius Professor
of Modern History
1963–8 and Master
of Peterhouse
1955–68.*

A yet more striking alteration has been in the gender balance of the teaching staff. If you look at the faculty lists of 50 years ago, you find only two women lecturers out of a total teaching staff of 43. Today the figure is 16 out of 54. This is obviously a big improvement, but if we are talking about *balance* it remains unsatisfactory, a reminder of the obvious fact that women academics still receive too little encouragement at every stage of their careers.

What about changes in the experience of being an undergraduate in history over the past half-century? There is still a weekly essay to be written, but 50 years ago you would have put on your gown and gone to your supervisor's rooms to read it out. Nowadays dress codes among staff and students alike tend to be extremely informal, and the days of reading out essays have long since gone. Students hand in their

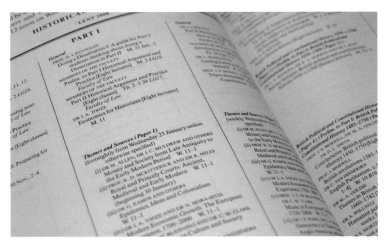

History Tripos lecture list, 2007, from the University Reporter.

When I went up to Cambridge in 1949, I shared lodgings with an agnostic mathematician. 'Read this, it will shake your faith', he said, pointing to *The Origins of Modern Science 1300–1800* (1949) by Herbert Butterfield. I was able to reply: 'This might shake your agnosticism', pointing him to *Christianity and History* (1949). 'Good Lord, the same man!' Amazingly, in that same autumn *George III, Lord North and the People 1779–1780* also appeared from the same pen. Butterfield was approaching the climax of his career as a historian in Cambridge.

John Turner
(1949)

I quickly learned that lectures were dispensable but did get out of bed for John Saltmarsh, who lectured on economic history. He cut a Dickensian figure with a shock of grey hair standing to attention and long sideburns. A famous crowd-pleasing moment was when he demonstrated the sod-turning plough with the aid of a 12-inch ruler. His opening lecture of the year was designed to impress us fresh young things and it did: 'I have myself spoken with a man who spoke to William IV. (*pause*) That, ladies and gentlemen, (pause) is history.'

I had certainly not expected Mr Goulding Brown. He was a cadaverous man of great age as it seemed at the time, who always wore a black jacket, striped trousers, winged collar and black tie. I see Ramsey MacDonald on his deathbed when I think of him. He would refer often to 'this wretched century'. (It was 1962, the Beatles had just arrived and I felt that the 20th century was beginning to get its act together.) 'This country began its decline when they began paying MPs' was another theme. GB lived in a tall, coal-fire warmed house in Brookside. He had rooms in college but was not a Fellow; the reason, we were led to believe, was a slight long ago by one or another party. The room he taught in was on the ground floor in Old Court. Were supervisions always conducted at dusk on a winter's afternoon or do I just remember it so? Certainly we read our essays by the light of a single standard lamp while GB sat in a tall chair, his back to the window so that his face was invisible. Thus it was that when a friend finished his essay he was puzzled by the silence from GB who remained motionless, his face obscured. The undergraduate waited for a response but none came. He coughed in case GB had dozed off, but no movement. After several minutes the student stood up and moved closer to GB to see that his eyes were closed and his head tilted forward. We had often joked that the old fellow was at death's door; perhaps that door had now opened. The student could detect no breathing so he leaned closer, his ear to GB's chest to listen for the heart. He had just begun to unbutton the shirt when GB awoke, not best pleased.

GB's reading lists were idiosyncratic. Few books written since 1920 were recommended. I recall searching out an article from an ancient and obscure journal in the Seeley Library to find a pencil note in the margin, 'only Goulding Brown could have sent you here'.

Will Wyatt
(1962)

Professor Plumb I remember for the massive detail about 18th-century elections and for teaching by making us laugh for a lot of the time, a skill I would love to have been able to emulate; I also remember his declaring on the morning of the 1964 general election that for one more day we would still have a grouse-shooting prime minister.

Other memories that stand out are working in the old Seeley Library (next to the Senate House) and sitting like a broody hen on books on a Friday in order to be able to borrow them over the weekend, and the challenge of trying to find my first book in the UL (which I think is one of those skills that you then master for life like riding a bicycle or controlling a punt!).

John Newman
(1964)

During my first term, when I saw Professor Harry Hinsley most, I was just soldiering through secondary materials, but when he had asked me if I wanted to talk, I instantly replied that I did. Why be able to enjoy the company of a man as interesting as Harry Hinsley, I thought, and not do it? That term we met once a week in his rooms, which made me think of Faust's study. Bookshelves against the walls, of course, as in all academic rooms, but on top of the books standing vertically lay mountains of others plus innumerable papers and miscellaneous publications. He pulled up a chair facing me. 'Well how are you settling in?' he would ask, and I would tell him what I was reading, mostly from the official history of World War II; then we would chat about it, then perhaps about the war generally, or about one of his books, and sometimes about his days at Bletchley reading German naval codes. 'Would you like a glass of sherry?' he always asked after about half-an-hour had passed.

President Truman once said that if you want something done ask the busiest man; the others will never find the time. Harry Hinsley was that man, supervising an astonishing number of dissertations, holding key positions in the University Library and Press, subsequently Master of St John's, and later Vice-Chancellor of the University. Yet whenever I needed to see him, he would almost invariably say, 'Oh, my dear boy, I can't see you today. I am sorry. Will tomorrow be alright?' I thought of my days at Harvard where many professors had office hours once a week, and in fact, rarely showed up. I realize that getting a PhD is a time of enormous anxiety for many people but for me it was a delightful experience for many reasons, not the least being the time spent with Harry Hinsley.

Henry Ryan
(1975)

Alternative Prospectus, 1982

The thing that I regret about my three years studying History is that I opted not to write a dissertation for Part II. At the time, a three-hour exam seemed much more tempting. At least they came up with the question that way. It was only when I was revising for the Part II exams that I realised how much I'd have liked to dig deep into Hobbes and sovereignty.

The Cambridge course was really a course in snapshots. There was a huge menu to choose from. My third year was spent on 20th-century political thought, Japanese economic history and Kenyan nationalism. Friends at Oxford or other universities, by contrast, seemed to be stuck endlessly on slightly tired debates about the English civil war. You couldn't fail to take away the sense that history was so much more than a narrative of political events, and that Europe was not the only stage where the past was played out.

The flipside was that the three years involved a lot of jumping about between different things. You would spend a term doing eight relatively self-contained essays, and it was time to move on to a completely new subject. Looking back, the chance to have given some subjects greater attention, or gaining a greater context surrounding them, by studying a related course in literature or philosophy, say, would have offered a welcome opportunity to cross new boundaries.

I am not sure that one-to-one teaching, still seen as the hallmark of a Cambridge arts education, is as perfect a system as it's said to be. I spent the year after graduating doing a Master's in Chicago. The value of a seminar system was easy to see: the participation and questions of other students made you think about things that you wouldn't have thought to think about, or made you realise things that you didn't know that you hadn't known.

It was only when I had three years of taught courses after Cambridge that I no longer took for granted the excellence of the teaching that I had. Those that jump to my mind include Polly O'Hanlon (the West and the Rest paper in Part I), John Lonsdale (the special subject on Kenyatta) and Martin Ruehl (political thought). The lectures were more hit and miss. But Tim Blanning's lectures on the Enlightenment or Quentin Skinner's revision seminars on political thought stand out as master lessons in communication.

It wasn't all work. The lawyers had their heavy books. The scientists were always in a lab. The one-essay-a-week rhythm gave a pace to life that left a lot of time for friends and a world outside the library.

Fred Hobson
(1999)

Geoffrey Elton

In lectures, Elton was magisterial. Despite his shortness, he had a powerful presence. He would enter, in black gown, and stride rapidly to the lectern and begin straight away. He carried no books or any written material. I heard him lecture on the Tudors for a whole academic year and he never once used notes. This was evidence of the extent of his mastery of his subject. Compared with some of the other lecturers, the attention he received from his audience was remarkable.

There were often moments of humour, particularly when he launched into his favourite target, A.L. Rowse, the Oxford historian who had the temerity to write about Geoffrey's period of Tudor history. Elton dismissed much of Rowse's period as romantic nonsense. In his criticism of Rowse, he was certain of the rectitude of his own interpretation of the Tudors – and almost libellous in his attacks.

Jeremy Bennet (1959)

Geoffrey Elton, Regius Professor of Modern History
1983–8 and Fellow of Clare College. Portrait by Liz Clifford, 1985.

Geoffrey Elton was the scholar as showman; always a polished performance, with a running commentary on the politics of the University alongside those of the Tudor court. He was one of the few outspoken defenders of the new History Faculty building, and would claim that it was the conservatives of the faculty who embraced the daring new building whereas the radicals disliked it. On that subject I had to disagree with him: the Seeley is still the noisiest library I have ever worked in, as well as the coldest in winter and the hottest in summer.

Alison Cawley (1979)

---

work beforehand and expect written comments which are then discussed. More important, the person to whom you give your essay will not necessarily be a Fellow of your college, but will rather be an expert in the relevant field. The fact that supervisions are largely organised by subject rather than college means that it now matters much less which college you belong to when it comes to being satisfactorily taught. There is also more self-consciousness about the need to ensure that the experience of being supervised is not a threatening one. All supervisors receive a code of practice from the University, and long overdue efforts have been made to ensure that no bullying or sexual harassment take place.

While the structure of the Tripos has remained the same, the contents of the syllabus altered greatly with the major reforms of the mid-1960s and early 1970s. When I took Part I, there was a heavy and compulsory emphasis on English history, and more specifically on the history of high politics. Nowadays students are introduced from the outset to broader topics in social, cultural and intellectual history, and the University has allowed the faculty to grow considerably in size to meet these more specialised needs. No less than 11 new lectureships have been added in the years since I graduated. It must be admitted, however, that even our current teaching is by no means as wide-ranging as one might expect. During the 1980s a Professorship in American History was added, but there is still no established chair in Russian or Chinese or Latin American or Middle Eastern history. Of course we cannot do everything, particularly when budgets are so tight, but it is arguable that we still concentrate too much on Europe.

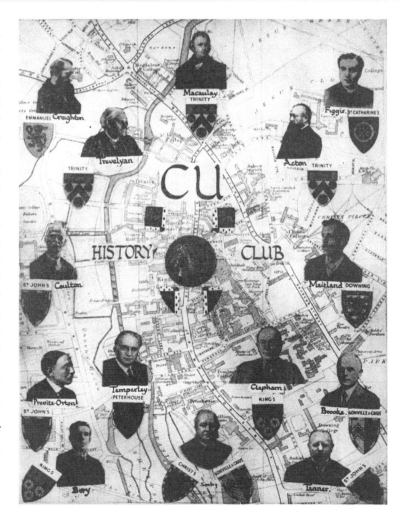

History Club map of Cambridge showing eminent historians and their colleges, c.1950.

Mark Goldie lecturing, 2008.

A further important innovation is that the faculty has increasingly taken over the organisation of teaching, which in turn has required a greatly increased administrative staff. Fifty years ago the faculty was administered by one formidable lady, Miss Box, who worked from a single room behind a pub in Green Street. We now find that to cope not merely with our own needs, but also with the growing bureaucratic burdens heaped on us by successive governments, we have to employ a full-time administrative staff of 14, all of whom work long and hard on our behalf.

This tilting of the balance from colleges to faculty was undoubtedly hastened by the opening of the faculty's own building in 1968. James Stirling won the competition with a highly experimental design, which was awarded the Gold Medal of the Royal Institute of British Architects in 1970. I well remember the meeting at which the faculty resolutely refused to accept the commemorative plaque. We certainly experienced some problems with Stirling's glass-and-steel construction in its early years, and there are colleagues who still love to grumble about it. But after extensive renovation in the early 1980s, including the installation of double-glazing to limit the extravagant thermal gain and loss, it seems to me that the building works pretty well. It provides us with all our lecture and seminar rooms, it houses our entire administrative staff, and it incorporates – in a truly spectacular space – the Seeley Historical Library, itself one of the glories of the faculty, with a collection of over 90,000 books.

One difference that undergraduates may not notice is that nowadays they join a faculty far more heavily committed to postgraduate education. When I first started teaching, research students were relatively few in number, and little special provision was made for them. Now they constitute a large item on the credit side of the University's ledger, and in the History Faculty we currently have nearly 250 students registered for the PhD degree. An associated development is that we also offer a wide range of one-year taught Master's courses. These were unknown until the end of the 1980s, but we currently have six MPhils taken by a total of nearly 100 students every year, and more of these are planned. One highly educative consequence has been that the faculty has become a far more international place. Last year, in my own MPhil seminar, I taught a group in which a majority of the members, in speaking English, were not using their native tongue.

Of all the changes in the faculty since I first joined it, none has been of greater significance than the rise in the number of women students. Fifty years ago, only 26 women graduated in history, less than 12 per cent of the total. Furthermore, this number was in decline, and when I took my degree in 1962 there were only 16 women in the year, less than eight per cent of the graduating class. The situation began to improve only in the 1970s, when the men's colleges finally agreed to admit women undergraduates, beginning with Churchill, Clare and King's in 1972. By 1984, all but the most traditionalist colleges (Peterhouse and Magdalene) were co-educational. The effect on the numbers reading history was not immediate, and even at the end of the 1980s less than 40 per cent of our students were female. But in 1992, for the first time, more women were admitted to read history than men, and since that time the ratio has stabilised at roughly half-and-half. Two years ago 95 women graduated, and last year the number was 100; these were respectively 46 and 51 per cent of the total graduating class.

The academic life of Cambridge undergraduates comes to an end with the posting of their results on the Senate House board. One striking development over the past half-century is that, in history as in all other subjects, the probability of finding that you have been awarded a first class degree has steadily increased. Many explanations have been suggested, including the fact that students work harder, that they are more efficiently taught, and that colleges have become more successful in recruiting only those of outstanding ability. These improvements surely help to explain the virtual disappearance of 2:2 and third class degrees. Fifty years ago, in a total graduating class of 226 in history, there were 96 2:2s and 35 thirds. Last year there were only eight 2:2s and no thirds at all. It might be wondered, however, whether the reasons I have cited fully account for the remarkable rise in the number of first class degrees. When I graduated in 1962, 18 firsts were awarded in a total list of 208. Last year, 42 firsts were awarded (exactly half of them to women) in a total list of 196. In other words, the probability of getting a first has nearly quadrupled, while the probability of being given a 2:1 if you miss your first has become a virtual certainty.

How distinguished is the present Faculty of History? I want to end with a loud blast of the trumpet. One measure worth applying is the official one represented by the Research Assessment Exercise, in which the faculty has never failed to obtain the highest possible grade of excellence. Another measure is provided by the Wolfson History Awards, which have been offered annually since 1972. So far these prizes – munificent as well as prestigious – have been won by nine scholars who were members of the faculty at the time. If one adds the winners who began as undergraduates in the faculty, the number rises by a further 16. No other department in the country can begin to rival these records of scholarly success.

Quentin Skinner *was Regius Professor of Modern History until 2008 and a Fellow of Christ's College. He is now Professor in the Humanities at Queen Mary, University of London.*

English: wider worlds of literature and criticism

Stefan Collini

In the middle decades of the 20th century, the phrase 'Cambridge English' referred to something that was at once broader and more controversial than the existence of a particular academic department, just as, at other times and in other disciplines, 'Chicago economics' or 'Oxford philosophy' have done. These (relatively rare) labellings signalled a general perception that a distinctive and highly influential style of practising the discipline in question was intimately associated with the work of a single university. From its foundation in the 1920s, the Cambridge English Faculty, animated in its early decades by the work of such critics as I.A. Richards, F.R. Leavis and William Empson, departed from the Germanic model of philological and historical scholarship that had largely dominated the earliest courses in 'English Language and Literature' elsewhere in Britain. The special character of 'Cambridge English' in its early days has been summarized as 'critical, comparative, and contemporary'. Criticism, the disciplined discrimination and assessment of value in works of literature, was understood as the defining activity at the heart of both the study and teaching of the subject. The emphasis on 'practical criticism', the close analysis of the detail of the verbal texture of a work of literature – 'the words on the page', taken, for the purposes of the pedagogic exercise, in isolation from any identifying authorial and historical information – was central. But the approach was also comparative in its insistence that English writing be read with a constant awareness of its relations to classical and European traditions

> "For the first time I'm taking a program which should slowly spread pathways and bridges over the whistling voids of my ignorance. My lecture schedule is about 11 hours (morning) during the week with men whose books are beginning to fill my shelves: F.R. Leavis on criticism; a magnificent, acid, malevolently humorous little man who looks exactly like a bandy-legged leprechaun; Basil Willey on the moralists (he's written enormous, readable books on the 17th, 18th and 19th-century background); and, if I have time next term, David Daiches on the Modern English Novel."

Sylvia Plath, writing in 1956, *Letters Home*, 1975

The English Faculty building by architects Allies + Morrison, completed in 2004.

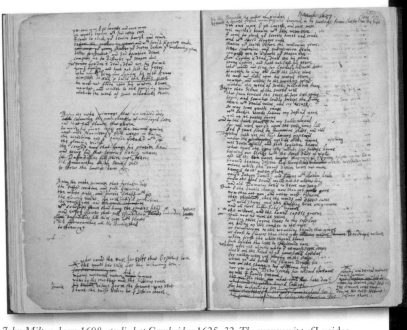

John Milton, born 1608, studied at Cambridge 1625–32. The manuscript of Lycidas
is in Trinity College Library, and the portrait (right), by Sir Peter Lely, in his college, Christ's.

both of literature and of philosophical and moral reflection. And it was contemporary, engaging not just with the established canon of past masterpieces but with newly published work which had yet to undergo the sifting of time and scholarly judgement. (One small practical index of this commitment is to be found in the fact that the most recent period-paper in the English Tripos has never had a terminal date: it has always spanned literature from such-and-such a year 'to the present'.)

These three characteristics were never the whole story, even in Cambridge, and although this conception of the subject was enormously influential not just in Britain but also in other parts of the English-speaking world (albeit more indirectly in the United States), it always provoked fierce resistance. Criticism could seem scarcely an objective, still less a 'scientific', exercise: critical disputes often appeared to outsiders more productive of heat than of light. But part of the excitement attendant upon this conception of the subject came from the way that one's whole personality, one's very identity or being, was engaged in the raw, unmediated encounter with the uncontrollable powers and beauties of great literature (this approach tended to disregard writing not thought to belong in this exalted category). The study of English, understood in these terms, was personal, passionate and polemical.

From the 1960s onwards, the discipline as a whole underwent profound changes. At different moments, members of the English Faculty contributed to, profited from, and stood out against, various of these developments. Along the way, 'Cambridge English' lost some of its earlier distinctiveness, becoming more plural, perhaps more ecumenical, certainly more recognisably professional. The major changes were of three different kinds. First, the assumptions on which the peculiar activity of 'criticism' rests were subjected to fundamental

and systematic analysis: what are the preconditions, intellectual or social, for the act of 'reading'? what are the standards of judgement? what counts as 'literature'? A greater methodological self-consciousness became fashionable, often formulated in idioms derived from culturally more distant philosophical and sociological traditions. 'Literary theory', as this ensemble of enquiries came to be known, left its mark in Cambridge, sometimes in the form of a bruise or a deep scar.

The second change involved a geographical expansion. 'English' had always been an unsteady metonymy: from the earliest beginnings of the subject in the 19th century, literature written in the English language by Welsh, Scottish and Irish writers had been included, often with insufficient acknowledgement of the importance of these national identities. In the course of the 20th century, it became increasingly unsatisfactory simply to ignore (or subsume) American writing, and a separate paper devoted to it first appeared in the Tripos in 1973. Thereafter, the whole exploding world of 'literature in English' more and more made its presence felt. This body of writing was initially classified as 'Commonwealth Literature', though that made a selection on awkwardly, and (soon) datedly, political grounds. Some preferred to call it 'postcolonial literature', though that built another, no less disputable, political story into the definition. In any event, to the study of Melville, Faulkner and Moore were added Naipaul, White, Achebe, Walcott, Coetzee and many others. Again, a separate paper was introduced into the Tripos, in 1994, encouraging connections with writing in non-European languages as well as in the Francophone and Hispanophone traditions. In both cases, new appointments were made to teach the new areas, though the Cambridge preference has been to keep the study of these rich bodies of literature in close and fruitful proximity to English literary history rather than treating them as self-contained specialisms.

I had just left the RAF, where having served in Bomber Command I had become familiar with Cambridge, especially the pubs, and I entered Christ's to read English. My abiding memories are of the lectures by Dadie Rylands. I had only just heard of Donne and certainly knew nothing of 'Revenge Tragedies' and the like. This was 1946 and at the time we didn't seem to be as preoccupied with people's sexual preferences.

In any case, I just thought of George Rylands as being a marvellous lecturer with a magnetic personality. He made it all come alive.

Godfrey Dann
(1946)

"I was invited to tea with the Leavises yesterday. The other guests were Marius Bewley, H.A. Mason, John Coleman, Reg Jinks and three others. Queenie is a terrific talker – a dark little woman in horn-rimmed spectacles, plainly dressed, talking incessantly. Even when other people are talking, she can be heard shooting out her rapid sentences to someone across the room. But the curious thing is she was always worth listening to. She was talking about Henry James, Hawthorne, *Partisan Review*, George Orwell, Huxley, Gide, Mauriac, E.M. Forster, Peggy Guggenheim, home-made cakes (which were excellent), her refusal to wear a hat ('I've only bought one since I was married and that was to return a call from a Master's wife. I bought gloves, handbag, hat, all new, and when I called she was out')."

David Matthews in a letter of the time to his parents
(1948)

I attended his lectures during Part I of the Tripos, and, in the second year, his almost alone, preferring to row. Nobody seemed to mind or, if they did, bother to say anything. My sharpest memory is of him lecturing beside the skeleton of a large horse in one of the laboratories near Downing. He wore a gown that looked as if he had borrowed it from his gyp. Beside the horse he was a slight figure. He had a monotonous and rather metallic voice and made no attempt at histrionics. His lectures were popular but not really packed. One was aware that his was a voice crying in the wilderness.

J.S. Dodge
(1948)

For myself, there is no question but that Leavis was and is the great doctor. One didn't have to imitate his embattled belligerence, his at times unnecessary aggression, or ultimately accept his critical conclusions, though I would maintain that where one disagreed, one could only do so by submitting a more finely argued critical conclusion, and these are not always at one's beck and call. But his method, or rather the way he developed it, was unique, and greatly affected the study of English literature in our time. What he implicitly claimed to be dealing with was art, and he demanded that it be recognised as such. Criticism for him was not the negative act that it is often taken to be: it was essentially positive, the *recreation* of a text, with optimum relevance to the words on the page: it was *appreciation* of an art form, requiring an active participation of the reader, where reading is not the passive intake that it so easily becomes. But these are all generalisations. The test is to see him in action.

David Wilkinson
(1954)

Two members of the English Faculty discuss recent trends in contemporary criticism

Cambridge Students Alternative Prospectus, 1983

F.R. Leavis, lecturing in 1962. The controversial literary critic taught at Downing College between 1931 and 1964.

NO SMO

From supervisions at dons' houses or flats on leafy streets to lectures at the starkly modern Sidgwick Site, from research in the cavernous University Library to fledgling politics at the Union Society building, I rode my aging Triumph bicycle to so many new intellectual and spiritual experiences and some real inspirations. In English literature, I remember Raymond Williams's lectures: strange chewed-up accent, socialist views and Stalin-style suit with long brown boots. Then, Colin McCabe supervisions: flowing hair, early deconstructionalist, highly opinionated but brilliant. And George Steiner, guest speaker at Lady Mitchell Hall: massive audience, arms sweeping inside his voluminous gown, no need for a microphone. Big personalities and intellects, not always agreed with.

Over three years the bike deteriorated. The brakes wore down, the Sturmey Archer 3-Speed truck stuck in third, and the dynamo driven headlamp shed less and less light. But it carried me to the amazing scope of Cambridge University.

Brian Weight
(1969)

During Part I, Leavis's legacy was undiminished, and practical criticism tutorials with John Newton loom large in my memory. I still have my second-year lectures notes: from John Holloway and John Beer on poetry and criticism; Frank Kermode on the 20th-century novel; John Casey on aesthetics and criticism; and Jeremy Prynne on poetry. Then there were the young Turks: Stephen Heath on Victorian social criticism; Roger Scruton on aesthetics; and Colin McCabe on – James Joyce? I customised my Tripos requirements and was granted a faculty 'grace' allowing me to ditch the compulsory 18th century in favour of early French. In John Stevens's beautiful rooms at Magdalene we read Chrétien de Troyes's Arthurian tales and the *Lais* of Marie de France. Men in gowns also read out long essays; I was gownless and my essays short, but Dr Stevens was encouraging. I enjoyed tutorials on American literature with the specialist Richard Gooder, also my Director of Studies in Clare. In Part II, I attended tutorials for the compulsory tragedy paper with Harold Mason, an eccentric humanist and former colleague of the Leavises. He also held special evening meetings for us to read Dante's *Inferno* in Italian, to learn to 'feel' what it meant without knowing the language. These tutorials contrasted sharply with those for the Joyce paper with Stephen Heath. Having recently translated the work of post-structuralist Roland Barthes, Stephen encouraged me to apply semiotic and psychoanalytic theories to *Finnegans Wake*. I read this several times, and pored over concordances to establish the frequency of the word 'chocolate'. Later Colin McCabe became the focus of the famous schism in the English Department between the humanists/Leavisites and the structuralists, but for me Stephen Heath was the true radical of the faculty who taught us to approach language as a set of relationships dependent on time and place, rather than as natural and perennial.

Felicia Hughes-Freeland
(1973)

English Faculty library, West Road.

The third change was more diffuse, since it involved multiple expansions of the types of material studied, including the extension (and sometimes the repudiation) of 'the canon' of great authors, and the pursuit of interpretatively relevant material into the byways of non-literary history. The most striking example of the first kind of expansion has been the increased attention directed to writing by women (linked to a greater alertness to questions of gender in general). These concerns made a cautious appearance in the English Tripos in 1982 with the introduction of a paper on 'The Literary Representation of Women', to be succeeded in 1988 by one on 'Gender and Writing'.

Evidence of the second kind of expansion is pervasive in the work done in contemporary literary studies, in Cambridge as elsewhere: Jacobean drama may be studied in the light of court records bearing on such common themes as marriage and inheritance, just as Victorian novels may be set among the sermons and books of spiritual

Tragedy questions in the English Tripos examinations, 2001.

*Gillian Beer,
King Edward VII
Professor of
English Literature
(1994–2002), a
Fellow of Girton
College (1965–94)
and President
of Clare Hall
(1994–2001).*

When I chose to go up to Girton in 1978 I could not have anticipated that cycling miles along the Huntingdon Road would shape my legs for the rest of my life. Neither could I have picked a more interesting period to be at Cambridge, due to the so-called structuralism debate that convulsed the English Department. Colin McCabe had, allegedly, been denied tenure because of his espousal of French critical theory. Suddenly we all wanted to read Barthes, Saussure and Derrida. I remember attending a debate on the issue in the Senate House, in which my hero, Professor Raymond Williams, spoke. We felt important in our gowns and very excited by European literary theory.

Gwyneth Lewis
(1978)

It started badly. Waiting for the interview, crouched behind a large oak door, straining to hear what the preceding candidate was being asked. All I could hear were her sobs. I later found out why: 'Read the sonnet in front of you and tell me about its structure and syntax!' Syntax?! Alliteration was all you needed at A level! Now what was a sonnet again? I ventured that it might be 'er, by Shakespeare'. Apparently that was a given.

The first two years were a chronological cross-country run from Langland to the modernists: a different author every week; a test of stamina as much as sparkle. I enjoyed it once I had been taught how to write. Week two's essay on *Gawain* was covered in Dr Axton's scrawl: 'far too impressionistic to pass as literary criticism'. I winced but liked the fact that he didn't pull his punches. We all learnt fast that English at Cambridge was about 'practical criticism': close analysis of the text; words on the page; 'structure and syntax'. None of that thematic, imagery, lit-crit nonsense.

The third year was 'time to knuckle down' and I relished the chance to specialise, studying Dante with the inspirational Robin Kirkpatrick; and Samuel Johnson with brilliant, erudite Freya Johnston. The tragedy paper is still going strong too; but perhaps the modern tragedy in the faculty is the decline in the popularity of the orthodox canon and the growing predilection for less worthy, thematic papers (Post-1970s Literature; Post-Colonial literature etc). As one great old don put it to me when I was deciding what to take: why come to Cambridge and study books you could read on the beach?

English was a luxurious degree: we never went to lectures; we were variously thespy, pretentious, cultured, quirky. But never let it be said that we didn't work hard. Along with the scientists and the lawyers, we traipsed into the college library (replete with its own shower facilities) at 3am and would search in vain for a spare desk. Keen beans reserved their library desks in February, pinning family photos to the hessian above the desks: makeshift reservation signs.

Every English student I ever knew found the subject a joy and a privilege. And even if I don't get asked very often to translate 14th-century poetry or to analyse a Renaissance ballad, at least I had the chance, once upon a time, to contemplate higher minds and to learn what are Great Works.

Jeremy Brier
(1999)

guidance addressed to their earliest readers. Although such styles of work do eventually reshape teaching, they also highlight the increasing gap between the detailed, novelty-driven imperatives of 'research' (in some ways an inappropriate term for some of the best work in English) and the duty to introduce each new undergraduate generation to the landmarks of their literary inheritance. Part I of the Tripos still tries to acquaint students with some of the range of writing from the Middle Ages to the present, teaching that is informed and refreshed by the fact that recent publications by members of the faculty have ranged across topics as disparate as medieval plainsong, Renaissance forestry, 18th-century political economy, Victorian physics and 20th-century film-making.

One way to summarise these changes would be to say that 'English Literature' has been displaced by 'writing in English', but that would be too simple. It was noticeable that when the faculty undertook a large-scale revision of Part I of the Tripos at the beginning of the 21st century, the 'core texts' specified for the various period papers were mostly the familiar names of Spenser, Milton, Wordsworth, Dickens, Woolf, Eliot and company. Moreover, recent publications by members of the faculty have amply illustrated a more general renewal of interest in the aesthetic, in the role of the imagination, in prosody and versification, and in 'literariness'. For some time, the faculty has been characterized by intellectual pluralism rather than the dominance of any one critical orthodoxy or approach, and in this respect it has been faithful to the legacy of its most distinguished members from this period, including Raymond Williams, Frank Kermode, Christopher Ricks, Marilyn Butler and Gillian Beer, among many others.

English Faculty seminar on Seamus Heaney.

English had traditionally been thought of as a college-based teaching subject in Cambridge, focussed on work for the individual supervision or small practical criticism class. While this remains at the heart of the undergraduate experience (and it has to be remembered that in addition to 39 University-appointed teaching staff there are also some 35 college-supported lecturers in English, more than in any other subject in the University), the various activities of the faculty have become more centrally organized in recent decades – a shift both symbolised and furthered by the new faculty building. This period has also seen a marked expansion of graduate numbers, partly consequent upon the establishment of MPhil courses (including most recently an inter-faculty collaboration in setting up an MPhil in 'Screen Media and Cultures'). The digital revolution has also been embraced: notable online projects include 'The Medieval Imaginations', 'English Handwriting 1500–1700: an online course', and 'The Virtual Classroom'.

There have, nonetheless, been some recent developments in the discipline that Cambridge has not embraced. English at undergraduate level remains, quite properly, a general humane education, not a form of pre-professional training. The faculty does not, for example, teach 'Theatre Studies', which has grown up as a practice-oriented programme in many universities, though drama is studied throughout the Tripos, including in recent years Part II options such as 'Shakespeare in Performance'. The budding Thespian does not lack for stimulus or opportunity in Cambridge, and our graduates remain prominent in the nation's theatrical life. Similarly, the English Tripos does not include 'Creative Writing' as a taught element, though a lot of it, of high quality, goes on in Cambridge. In recent decades, the faculty has been able to boast a number of notable poets and novelists among its teachers, including Geoffrey Hill and J.H. Prynne, while several of the faculty's graduates have, over the same period, gone on to be among the leading writers of their generation, from Graham Swift to Zadie Smith.

No doubt each 'discipline' can, on occasion, exhibit a prickly self-consciousness about its own distinctiveness, but English – certainly that partly real, partly idealised activity still known as 'Cambridge English' – has had some good grounds for thinking that it is unlike any other subject. The chartless voyage involved in every exercise in 'practical criticism', the mixture of strangeness and recognition in each encounter with an imagined world, the challenges to assumptions about how words mean, how people function, how life might be lived – these experiences are, and should be, intense, personal and not wholly resolvable. While the faculty has contributed with some distinction to the international transformation of the subject over the past three or four decades, central elements in the study and teaching of English at Cambridge would continue to be recognisable to its founding generations.

Stefan Collini is Professor of Intellectual History and English Literature and a Fellow of Clare Hall.

Cambridge English in the 1950s

I begin with two remembered essay titles from those years. When we arrived at Newnham a subject was posted on a notice board – we were to write an essay for our first supervision. It was 'Paradoxically, Donne's poetry is too simple to satisfy. Its complexity is all on the surface.' (C.S. Lewis) There was no guidance or bibliography that I remember. I believed, innocently, that I was required to read all the poems of John Donne before I set about the essay. I did so, with great excitement. The second subject was one of the choices for a three-hour essay in our Part II English Tripos. 'The novel is the highest form of human expression yet attained.' (D.H. Lawrence)

Taken together those two topics sum up most of my Cambridge experience. The expectation that we could write an essay in a week, in our first week, on a difficult poet was typical of the way in which we were expected to be able to direct our own studies. Fortunately for me I had read a lot of Donne for the now long-abolished entrance examination – I had anxiously wildly over-prepared for that – and that reading stood me in good stead for at least two years. I believed that studying 'English' was to do with reading and writing, and after sampling a few lectures came to the conclusion that it was more profitable to spend uninterrupted hours in the University Library, which, in memory, is the place and institution I most loved in Cambridge. No other copyright library allows students access to the stacks and lets them borrow books. The shelves were wonderful.

The lectures were mixed. Several lecturers were, it seemed, still reciting texts they had already published in book form. What they lectured on was only loosely connected to what we were meant to be reading and writing about. I went to Elizabeth Zeeman's illuminating lectures on medieval literature, and A.P. Rossiter on Shakespeare (even though he made it clear he didn't think women should be present). He was killed (on his motor-bike) at the end of my first year. There were no seminars, or class discussions, and much of a supervision was taken up with the reading of essays. Reading English was a solitary pursuit. In my third year I developed an obsession with Cambridge Platonism and Plato in general and simply read deeply in the Library. I was also writing a novel, about which the Newnham dons were surprisingly sympathetic. They said 'take a day a fortnight and write'. I wrote on, in lectures, when I went to them.

'English' in those days was profoundly influenced by F.R. Leavis, who had both precise ideas about how to read closely and well, and a belief that the English Department was the centre of any university. My mother had been taught by both Leavis and I.A. Richards in the 1920s, when Richards invented the idea of practical criticism. There was something wonderfully exciting about the close attention to words (and rhythms, and contexts and sentence structure) that these ways of reading required. But I was also uneasy about the whole semi-religious aura Leavis cast about literature. I thought constantly of T.S. Eliot's dictum 'Our literature is a substitute for a religion, and so is our religion.' I went to two of Leavis's discussion classes in Downing – he was famous for saying scholarship consisted in saying 'Yes, but…' Nobody else, in practice, appeared to be allowed to say either 'Yes' or 'No'. He stated that none of us had read Meredith's *Modern Love*, and when I said I had, he stated 'Well, you didn't like it', and went on to disparage it.

That exam question about Lawrence was probably set by Leavis who was examining in 1957. Precisely because I wanted to write a novel I needed to argue against Lawrence – literature is a craft, not a religion. Our literary perspective was intolerably *narrow*. I knew my essay would be ill-received. Leavis's morality was, I think, very good for school English – dedicated teachers went out from Cambridge and taught classes with true passion. But the idealism was dangerous. I knew a man who had a novel accepted by a publisher and took it back, in case Leavis might read and dislike it. I am almost the only English graduate of my generation who dared to write a novel. The faculty *boasted* that only three PhDs in English had been awarded since the war. They did not seem to question the teaching and supervision of all the failed students.

When I later taught the wonderful degree course at UCL devised by Frank Kermode and Randolph Quirk, with its tiered teaching – lectures, seminars and tutorials (one to one) all deepening a subject and looking at it from different angles, I saw what Cambridge had not given me. At UCL we went to each other's lectures – we discussed the same things at the same times with our groups – with two teachers to a group to avoid autocracy. We did *think together* as I now think a university should. Cambridge suited me, partly because of my over-preparation for the entrance exam (I had read a lot already), partly because I am a natural library solitary. And the English teaching did centre on reading accurately what was on the page.

A.S. Byatt (1954) has written short stories and novels, most notably *Possession*, which won the Booker Prize in 1990. She was made a DBE in 1999, and is an Honorary Fellow of Newnham College.

The old English Department building on West Road, where the faculty was based until 2002.

Philosophy: imagination and precision

Simon Blackburn

In many people's minds philosophy in Cambridge is identified with the great trio of G.E. Moore, Bertrand Russell and Ludwig Wittgenstein. These three certainly dominated the subject, albeit in slightly different ways, in the last decade of the 19th century and the first half of the 20th. The approach with which they are identified, known as 'analytic(al) philosophy', is usually described in terms of a revolution overthrowing misty Hegelianism and idealism, which lingered on in other more benighted parts of Britain well after it had been banished from Cambridge. But as usual with simple stories of revolutions, the picture is actually much more complicated. Analytical philosophy was supposed to be new in its concentration on meaning, and in the self-image of the philosopher as a kind of analytical chemist, only breaking concepts into their constituents rather than substances. But others before Moore, for example the doughty Victorian Henry Sidgwick, had visibly done philosophy in very much the same way as Moore and Russell, and indeed some of the arguments of each of these men find an ancestry still further back. For example, Moore advanced what became his most famous single contribution, the 'Open Question' argument against supposing that there could be any analysis of ethical qualities, such as goodness, in terms of scientific or psychological properties. But the argument is also found almost verbatim in Richard Price, in the 18th century. Russell's writing on induction and on religion, and much of his philosophy of perception, was substantially a replay of David Hume. What was genuinely new was the deployment of new forms of logic, essentially due to the great German writer Gottlob Frege, and the hope that new logical tools could open a way through old and intractable philosophical thickets. It was to this modern logic that Russell and Whitehead made their monumental contribution, *Principia Mathematica*, of which the last volume came out in 1912.

Cambridge of course had nurtured philosophers before the great trio appeared. Perhaps we can claim Francis Bacon, the philosophizing Lord Chancellor and prophet of the scientific revolution of the 17th century, although he was a law student while in Cambridge. We might even claim a little piece of the great humanist Erasmus who visited from the Netherlands. More certainly, in the 17th century there was the group known as the Cambridge Platonists, a group of relatively optimistic divines who hoped to challenge the dreary pessimism of Calvinism, low-church 'enthusiasm' in general, and the rising

> "Cambridge was important in my life through the fact that it gave me friends, and experience of intellectual discussion, but it was not important through the actual academic instruction … Most of what I learned in philosophy has come to seem to me erroneous, and I spent many subsequent years in gradually unlearning the habits of thought I had there acquired. The only habit of thought of real value that I acquired there was intellectual honesty."
>
> Bertrand Russell, *Autobiography*, 1967

PRINCIPIA MATHEMATICA TO ∗56

BY
ALFRED NORTH WHITEHEAD
AND
BERTRAND RUSSELL, F.R.S.

CAMBRIDGE
UNIVERSITY PRESS

Above right: Principia Mathematica, *published from 1910.*

Right: Bertrand Russell as a BA in mathematics, Trinity College, 1893.

philosophical classic because, while it is easy to dislike the conclusion, it is fiendishly hard to say what is wrong with the argument. Broad, by contrast, worked not with flashes of brilliance so much as dogged persistence, distinguishing, for instance, 17 different theories about the relation between mind and body, and proceeding to list in great detail their strengths and weaknesses. Like Moore himself, Broad may have ground slow, but his strength lay in grinding exceeding small. If there was grit in the machinery, Broad would find it. He also had a pronounced sense of mischief, perhaps illustrated in his remark that when Philosophy, or Moral Sciences, as the Tripos was then called, started up at the end of the Second World War, 'never in the history of human thought have so few been taught so little by so many'.

The only Cambridge philosopher with the confidence and brilliance to stand up to Wittgenstein was Frank Ramsey (the economist Piero Sraffa was also no punchbag). In the few years between graduation and his early death at the age of 27, Ramsey made seminal contributions in economics, mathematics, philosophy of science, logic and the philosophy of language. 'Ramsey sentences' are a

The Moral Sciences Club, 1910. Russell is seated fifth from the left. G.E. Moore and J.M.E. McTaggart are standing in the middle row third from the right and at the end of the row respectively.

materialism and atheism of Hobbes. They included Ralph Cudworth, Nathaniel Culverwell, Henry More and Benjamin Whichcote.

It is no use trying to disguise the 18th-century slump in Cambridge's philosophical fortunes, as the Enlightenment broke out elsewhere, in Edinburgh, Paris and the Netherlands, but went largely unnoticed in East Anglia. However, the 19th century saw the great polymath and philosopher of science, William Whewell, enthroned in Trinity. Whewell deserves credit for being the first thinker to stress the importance of falsification as the method of scientific progress, a century before Karl Popper rode to fame on the same idea. He perhaps deserves less credit for arguing, against Darwin, that the presence of a benevolent designer in the universe was shown by the fact that the period of the diurnal rotation of the earth gives human beings exactly the amount of time that they need to sleep. Of course, if we use the term philosophy in its widest sense, Darwin himself is one of the glories of Cambridge natural philosophy, along with Newton, Maxwell, Rutherford, or Watson and Crick.

Henry Sidgwick, who gave up a substantial proportion of his salary in order to fund a second Chair in Philosophy in the University – an example I urge alumni to follow – is another great Victorian philosopher. Keynes's unkind comment that 'he never did anything but wonder whether Christianity was true and prove it wasn't and hope that it was' is now regarded as pretty wide of the mark, and Sidgwick's monumental work on ethics is again on mainstream agendas.

Two contemporaries of Moore, Russell and Wittgenstein who are also enjoying something of a resurgence are the magnificently named John McTaggart Ellis McTaggart and C.D. Broad. The former, an idealist who owed more to Hegel than Frege, is remembered for his tantalizing, not wholly believable, proof of the unreality of time, a

Frank Ramsey, mathematician, economist and philosopher, who translated Wittgenstein's Tractatus *at the age of 19 and became a Fellow of King's College in 1924. He died of jaundice in 1930.*

My recollections of Ludwig Wittgenstein remain unforgettable. I never had a one-to-one relationship with him, but I 'sat at his feet' – quite literally! – at the occasional meetings of the Moral Science Club at which from time to time he took the chair. Although reputed to be 'difficult' and even potentially ferocious, I never found him anything but courteous, welcoming and good-humoured. He had an extraordinary radiance and to this day I remain convinced that he was a mystic.

Intellectually, I never understood a word of what Wittgenstein said, and I was relieved to hear later that one of my lecturers, Dr Ewing, had confessed to the same! But the few hours I was privileged to pass in Wittgenstein's presence were, to me, something to be treasured for a lifetime.

Edward Hain, formerly E.H. Bullivant
(1938)

In addition to my research work in the laboratory I took up the opportunity to attend various courses of lectures. Some of these, such as those by Eméleus and Lennard-Jones, were chemical but there was also a tempting variety of other lectures on offer. In my first year I went to Bertrand Russell's series entitled 'Introduction to Philosophy', a riveting performance by the perennially challenging doyen of English philosophers. The lectures were held on Thursday afternoons during the Michaelmas and Lent Terms in the Large Examination Hall which was packed to capacity. At 5pm precisely Russell entered the Hall, a slightly built man with a shock of silver hair.

There was instant silence and he began: 'I have called this series of lectures "Introduction to Philosophy". Perhaps I should have called it "Introduction to my Philosophy". I shall make no attempt to give an impartial survey of what used to be called philosophy up to now. I am concerned mainly to discuss…' and so on. In his characteristically thin, high-pitched, almost rasping voice he spoke simply and forcefully, and with complete conviction that he was on a plane with previous great philosophers. It was a bravura performance and a masterly exposition which was all the more remarkable for being given by a person who was already in his 77th year. Not everyone stayed the whole course but for those of us who did the experience was enormously rewarding.

Norman Greenwood
(1948)

standard part of the philosopher's toolkit, and the 'Ramsey test' for conditionals has a similar status in logic. Ramsey was probably the first philosopher to build a bridge from the formal, logical concerns of Cambridge to the philosophy of American pragmatism, and this is a bridge which today sees large crowds going both ways.

Philosophy did not stop with these heroes. Post-war professors included the gnomic John Wisdom, and the contrastingly larger-than-life Richard Braithwaite. Bernard Williams and Elizabeth Anscombe, the former Britain's most eminent moral philosopher, and the latter Wittgenstein's most eminent translator and pupil, each enriched the tradition in different ways. The former in particular edged Cambridge back towards appreciating a more historical dimension to previous thinkers, which the analytic tradition had tended to ignore, rather as the analytical chemist does not need to know the history of discovery of the rock he is investigating. By sheer brilliance and force of example Williams also placed moral and political philosophy, cold-shouldered in the analytical heyday, firmly back into the centre of the subject, where they belong.

And so we come to the present generation, contemporaries about whom the historian talks at peril. Perhaps it suffices to say that anyone coming to work at Cambridge is conscious of the gaze of our ancestors and the standards and traditions of thought they have passed on to us. It is certainly an honour, but whether it is an inspiration or a burden probably depends on how well we think our own work is going. What is undeniable is that generations of students are grateful for the rigour and precision they come to appreciate at Cambridge, and it is encouraging to report that in recent years more and more, from every part of the world, have been knocking at our door. Broad's quip would be completely out of place applied to today's bursting lecture rooms, and crowded syllabus.

Simon Blackburn is Professor of Philosophy and a Fellow of Trinity College.

Philosopher Jonathan Barnes addresses a meeting of the Moral Sciences Club, 2006.

Ludwig Wittgenstein

Wittgenstein was trained as an engineer, and became interested in the foundations of mathematics as a result. Advised to do so by Frege, he arrived in Cambridge in 1911, to work with Bertrand Russell. Initially Russell could not decide if he was a genius or mad, and it is easy to sympathize. Wittgenstein was solipsistic, obsessive and something of a bully but he was also charismatic, and a genius. He is now a natural subject for biographers, as well as poets and musicians. He published almost nothing apart from the *Tractatus Logico-Philosophicus* (right), written during the First World War and published in 1921. Directly afterwards, convinced that he had solved all soluble philosophical and logical problems, he gave up the subject and became a schoolteacher in rural Austria. He was only persuaded that there was work still to do by Frank Ramsey, who engineered his return to Cambridge in 1929. Wittgenstein decided that he needed a Cambridge degree, and submitted the *Tractatus*, by then widely acknowledged a philosophical classic, as his thesis. Moore and Russell were the examiners, with Moore famously commenting: 'It is my personal opinion that Mr Wittgenstein's thesis is a work of genius; but be that as it may, it is certainly well up to the standard required for the

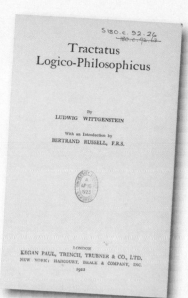

Cambridge degree of doctor of philosophy.'

From this time on, during his 'later period', he wrote no books, but his lectures and notes were collected into the famous *Philosophical Investigations*, which appeared in 1953, two years after his death, and into many subsequent collections. As a general remark, while in his early work Wittgenstein thought in terms of a direct, almost pictorial relationship between sentences and facts, in the later work he turned to think about sayings as doings, concentrating on what is done with language. He came to think that the vice of concentrating on logical form, as the early work did, suppressed the motley, divergent, messy everyday facts of meaning and thinking. One of his favourite quotations was from Goethe: 'in the beginning was the deed', and it is recorded that he thought of giving his later work as a motto Kent's remark in *King Lear*: 'I'll teach you differences.'

Wittgenstein's writing has a pithy, direct quality. It immediately impresses the reader as urgent, and central, and utterly committed to going straight to the heart of things. It has also proved surprisingly indeterminate, appearing in different ways to different readers, and therefore generating mountains of commentary and indeed mutually hostile schools of interpretation. But times move on, and it is now a while since he monopolized Cambridge philosophy.

Simon Blackburn

Wittgenstein (right) with his friend, the mathematician Francis Skinner.

Correspondence between Russell and Lady Ottoline Morrell, describing Wittgenstein, 1912.

Archaeology: moving beyond prehistory

Graeme Barker

ambridge University has one of the longest histories of teaching and researching archaeology of any British university, indeed of any university. The subject was first recognised as a discipline here through the Disney Professorship. John Disney was a Midlands-born barrister who inherited the family's collection of antiquities on the death of his father in 1816, developed a passion for collecting, and endowed a Disney Professorship of Archaeology at the University in 1851 with a gift of £1,000. The first full-time Disney Professor, not until 1927, was the classicist Sir Ellis Minns. With the establishment of the Laurence Professorship in Classical Archaeology in 1930 (held first by Arthur Bernard Cook), the Disney Professorship has been held ever since by prehistorians: Dorothy Garrod (1939–52), Grahame Clark (1952–74), Glyn Daniel (1974–81), Colin Renfrew (1981–2004), and myself (2004–).

Cambridge's archaeologists today are based not just in the Department of Archaeology but also in the Cambridge Archaeological Unit, the Faculties of Classics and Continuing Education, the Fitzwilliam Museum, the Leverhulme Centre for Human Evolutionary Studies, the McDonald Institute for Archaeological Research, and the Museum of Archaeology and Anthropology, as well as in several colleges. What links this community, and makes Cambridge a world-class centre of excellence for the subject, is the shared philosophy that archaeology is the material-based study of the human past applicable to all regions of the world, to all peoples, and to the entire human career from its most remote beginnings to yesterday. The establishment in 1990 of the McDonald Institute through the generosity of the industrialist Dr D. McDonald and the vision of Colin Renfrew created a marvellous umbrella institution that supports the work of this rich and diverse archaeological community through its laboratories, project space, seminar facilities, research grants and publications.

Many of the world's most influential prehistorians have held positions in the Department of Archaeology, beginning with the palaeolithic archaeologist Miles Burkitt, who introduced the teaching of prehistory in 1915. Dorothy Garrod, Cambridge's first female professor, found evidence for Neanderthal people occupying caves in Mount Carmel, Israel, not just before but also after the arrival there of anatomically modern humans. Her evidence was dismissed by some at the time but is centre-stage today in debates about when, how and why Neanderthals were replaced by modern humans. She also set up the structure of the present Tripos Part II, which offers students unparalleled opportunities for the comparative study of ancient societies of different degrees of complexity and in different parts of the world.

Grahame Clark pioneered the study of relations between prehistoric societies and their environment, his 1949–51 investigations of an encampment of pre-agricultural hunter-fisher-gatherers at Star Carr near Scarborough (c.7,500 BC) still being regarded as the most

Left: Dorothy Garrod, Cambridge's first woman professor, became Disney Professor of Archaeology in 1939. She specialised in the prehistory of the Levant and contributed greatly to the present understanding of the evolution of human settlement in the region.

Colin Renfrew, Disney Professor from 1981 to 2004 and founding Director of the McDonald Institute for Archaeological Research.

Leslie Cram with a donkey skeleton.

important mesolithic excavation anywhere in Europe. Other members of his department also made profound contributions to prehistoric archaeology. Charles McBurney, for example, discovered the most important deep archaeological sequence in North Africa at the Haua Fteah cave (now being reinvestigated by a Cambridge team). Eric Higgs, a former sheep-farmer from the Shropshire hills and my own PhD supervisor, directed an influential if iconoclastic research project on the origins and early history of agriculture. Glyn Daniel, the great populariser of the *Animal, Vegetable, or Mineral?* radio show, wrote with equal style and erudition on neolithic megalith-builders, the history of archaeology, and French cuisine. John Coles laid the foundations for a modern understanding of the European Bronze Age, combining immaculate excavations in the Somerset Levels, experimental archaeology and, now in active retirement, cutting-edge studies of Scandinavian rock art.

David Clarke, who died tragically early in 1976, revolutionised theoretical debates about the nature, purpose and *modus operandi* of the subject. His legacy was a generation of students led by Ian Hodder through the 1970s and 1980s that was profoundly critical of the perceived emphasis of Clark and Higgs on the subsistence activities of prehistoric societies (*Homo economicus* in their phrase), and their failure to think about the social norms and ideologies structuring societies. The impact of these 'post-processual' archaeologists on archaeological theory and practice worldwide has been just as profound as that of the 'processualists' who taught them.

Summer vacation 1963, Nea Nikomedeia in northern Greece, Grahame Clark's early neolithic site excavated jointly with Harvard University, at the end of my second year studying the palaeolithic in the Faculty of Archaeology and Anthropology. My job was twofold under Eric Higgs: firstly to catalogue and assemble the excavated animal remains for study back at Cambridge; secondly to collect modern comparative osteological material for the department. I procured skeletons of sheep and goat from the local butchers, then boiled away any remaining flesh on the edge of the excavation site in my ex-army field water heater. Where possible, I acquired skeletons like the donkey (above) which I found while swimming in the local river, washed up on the beach. All these bones were of interest to the half-starved local cats despite quantities of washing powder added to the water in the maceration process. So I stored the bones in food safes on the balcony in the photo in the half-finished museum which was the finds office and the male dormitory.

The Easter vacation in my first year had been spent digging for Neanderthal man in Jersey under Charles McBurney. In my first summer vacation I was looking after the animal bones on Peter Salway's Roman dig at Hockwold in Norfolk.

Leslie Cram
(1961)

Tutorials with Glyn Daniel were memorable. He had rooms at St John's, overlooking the river and the Bridge of Sighs. The ante-room was a library: books on the floor, on tables, on shelves and in cases. Some were unopened and others had been left as if a breeze had turned the pages to emphasise some salient point. Instead of bookends Glyn used archaeological artefacts. There was an Acheulian flint hand axe, made by one of our ancestors, perhaps half a million years ago, propping up an excavation report by Sir Mortimer Wheeler. The exam questions he set me were difficult unless, of course, you had travelled as far and wide as himself: 'The Celts, civilisation or barbarism?', and 'Skeuomorphs – discuss their significance in archaeology'.

Duncan Smith
(1969)

Chris Stimpson, a PhD student, examines a leopard skull in the Grahame Clark Laboratory for Zooarchaeology in the McDonald Institute for Archaeological Research.

Top left: Emma Pomeroy, an archaeology undergraduate undertaking her excavation training in Pupićina cave, Croatia, 2001.

Left: Tamsin O'Connell, Wellcome Trust Research Fellow in Bioarchaeology, in the Dorothy Garrod Laboratory for Isotopic Analysis, using a mass spectrometer.

Since his arrival in 1981 Colin Renfrew has presided over this hothouse of debate, energising it still more with his commitment to use material culture to study the early history of those most intangible attributes of our species (and earlier species?): language and cognition. Alongside his theoretical projects, he also revolutionised the scientific basis of Cambridge archaeology, combining the McDonald endowment and another from the Pitt-Rivers family to establish a suite of laboratories for studying animal bones, plant remains, soils and sediments, and 'archaeogenetics', the study of ancient and modern DNA to track human migrations. Another innovation was his establishment of the Illicit Antiquities Research Centre (IARC), which was a significant influence in persuading the UK government to accede to the 1970 UNESCO Convention on the Means of Prohibiting and Preventing the Illicit Import, Export and Transfer of Ownership of Cultural Property, the primary international legislation in this area. The IARC was awarded the European Archaeological Heritage Prize (2004) in recognition of its 'internationally unique' contribution to European and world heritage protection, and the Archaeological Institute of America's Outstanding Public Service Award in 2006.

And the future? We intend to maintain Cambridge's commitment to the study of the entirety of the human career as a global project, fostering a broad spectrum of theoretical approaches, integrating humanities- and science-based methods, and putting them together in innovative field projects that continue to set new agendas for the subject. Archaeology is a team subject *par excellence*, and the involvement of our students in our excavation and survey projects all over the world – this summer's menu was typical, from the Cambridgeshire fens and the Orkneys to Afghanistan, Australia, Borneo, China, Egypt, Siberia, South Africa, Syria, Uruguay and Vietnam – involves them in cutting-edge research alongside their teachers 'at the coal face'. It is an inspiring way to learn, and to teach. It should continue to produce future generations of outstanding Cambridge archaeologists who will question what we taught them, as we did our own teachers, and inspire them to head off into the field themselves with the same passion to try to piece together and understand the human career.

Graeme Barker is Disney Professor of Archaeology, Director of the McDonald Institute for Archaeological Research and a Fellow of St John's College.

Architecture

Diane Haigh

Architecture has reached the centenary of its first toehold in the University. In May 1908 the Senate approved the introduction of an architecture exam as part of existing degree courses for students who might want to pursue a career in the profession. This tentative start was consolidated when the Arts & Crafts architect E.S. Prior became Slade Professor of Fine Art in 1912 and offered the first practical instruction in architectural design. He acknowledged the difficulty of teaching architecture in an academic context: 'Neither classical scholarship nor mathematical acumen means of itself anything in the science of building. But the desire to make and learn what *making* is – that is the gist of it' (Prior, inaugural lecture, *Journal of the RIBA*, 1912). This tension between academic scholarship and the practice of design is still a live issue.

The architecture degree was established in 1922 and the School of Architecture moved into no.1 Scroope Terrace in 1924, where it remains to this day. Behind this sober façade life has been anything but quiet. The transforming event was the arrival of Sir Leslie Martin as the first Professor of Architecture in 1956. The University wanted to appoint a successful practitioner to the new chair, and Martin had unequalled credentials as head of the LCC Architects' Department and leader of the design team for the Royal Festival Hall. Under Martin the status and confidence of the school took off. The existing three-year degree course in architecture was supplemented by a two-year diploma course, to complete the academic training required by students who decide to enter the architectural profession.

(Left) Leslie Martin, first incumbent of the Chair of Architecture from 1956 to 1972 and Fellow of Jesus College. As well as the Royal Festival Hall in London, he was responsible for many new buildings in Cambridge including halls of residence for Gonville & Caius and Peterhouse, the Faculty of Music and the new extension to Kettle's Yard.

Scroope Terrace, home of the Faculty of Architecture and History of Art.

The school expanded into no.5 Scroope Terrace and a brooding brick extension was built behind no.1.

Martin's gentlemanly architectural practice in Little Shelford produced beautiful, hand-crafted buildings in Cambridge, Oxford and elsewhere, and his assistants provided a regular supply of stimulating teachers. To further his vision of university-based architectural education and research, Martin founded the Centre for Land Use and Built Form Studies in 1967. The initial impetus was mathematical modelling of buildings and urban systems, made possible by the rapidly increasing power of computers. A huge amount was achieved in a burst of energy and enthusiasm in the first few years of research.

Martin's professorship, we now realise, coincided with the high point of post-war technocratic optimism that collapsed so comprehensively in the 1970s. Martin was succeeded as professor by Bill Howell, who was tragically killed in a car crash after barely a year, and then by Sandy Wilson in 1976. Wilson had been a protégé of Leslie Martin in the 1950s and 1960s – he designed the 1950s brick extension at Scroope Terrace – but had lost faith in modernism. He brought in new teachers who also rejected modernist conventions, provoking

The Department of Architecture's new undergraduate studios to the rear of Scroope Terrace.

heated debate with those who continued to pursue Martin's agenda. The Martin Centre, as LUBFS was renamed in 1974, moved to Chaucer Road, where it formed a separate entity from the teaching in Scroope Terrace. The worlds did intersect, but most undergraduates and many teachers never ventured to Chaucer Road.

The teaching of architecture has always been focused on the design studio; this is the feature of the department that is most exceptional within the University. The architecture course involves a full range of lectures on the technical, theoretical and historical context of architecture, but its heart is the design studio where all these elements are synthesised in the individual student's pursuit of a design project. It is an extraordinarily demanding process, requiring the widest breadth of understanding to be focused on a specific design proposal. Architectural students are trained to explore problems and solutions creatively, to question the brief and to make informed judgements – all this has immediate application in the world of practice. Design is different from analysis and criticism, and is a crucial component of effective action and decision-making; it seems curious that the University is so reticent about supporting this type of creative teaching.

The design studio is simultaneously an activity and a place, and both are resource-intensive. Nurturing the development of each and every student's individual design ideas takes enormous time and commitment from the studio teachers; and, uniquely in the University, the department provides its undergraduates with a workplace, generating a studio culture of teamwork and perpetual cross-fertilisation of ideas. In 2007 the design studio moved into a new, light-filled extension behind no.5 Scroope Terrace, making room for the Martin Centre to move into Scroope Terrace from Chaucer Road, with the hope that physical proximity will foster communication and exchange.

The consolidation of teaching and research on the Scroope Terrace site is part of the restructuring that followed the 2002 research assessment exercise, when architecture's disappointing grade provoked a crisis and even the threat of closure. One of the greatest casualties was the two-year diploma. Happily, the post-first degree course is being relaunched in an innovative format comprising a one-year MPhil followed by a year in affiliated architectural practices.

Recent academic appointments in the department have reflected the greater emphasis on research. Whereas the department used to be dominated by lecturers who combined a successful architectural practice with teaching in the design studio, this model has all but disappeared. Research is now thriving with new funded projects and rapid growth in the number of researchers. To ensure that the design studio remains fully resourced, the department has received support from architectural practices, who are funding visiting design Fellows.

Throughout the recent period of restructuring the undergraduate architecture course has remained one of the most popular in the University, measured by the number of applicants per place. Being a small department with only 40–45 places in each year, the result is an intake of high-achieving and hugely motivated students. As architecture is a subject which impacts on the built environment that surrounds everyone, it is surely crucial that Cambridge should continue to play a top-level role in teaching, research and debate. Evidence of the impact of architecture at Cambridge was revealed by the phenomenal range and strength of support attracted by the successful campaign against the threat of closure in 2004 – a disturbing but also an encouraging and rejuvenating episode, from which the department has now emerged with renewed confidence.

Diane Haigh *is Director of Architecture and Design Review at the Commission for Architecture and the Built Environment. She was formerly a member of the Department of Architecture and a Fellow of Trinity Hall.*

Architecture students on the Senate House lawn, November 2004, protesting at a plan to close the department, later withdrawn.

I knew that Cambridge was where I needed to be. I sent for the College Handbook, applied to half a dozen colleges and was summarily refused by each: I had not taken A levels; or the quotas for foreign students had already been met; or in spite of my four years of higher education, two years in Columbia College plus two years at the School of Architecture, I did not have the degree required of all research students.

I learned through Peter Eisenman, then teaching at Cambridge and working on his doctorate, that for every rule within the University there was a prescribed way of breaking the rule. If the professor wished, he could break the rules. The Director of Columbia's school of Architecture signed a glowing letter of recommendation written by me, I packed my bags and portfolio, and left for London.

Within a few days I had an appointment in Cambridge with Sir Leslie Martin. He looked at my portfolio. I told him how much I admired his work. He called the Senior Tutor at King's. He said there was a young man in his office, all the way from New York, who would be a positive addition to the student body. In a minute I was accepted. I entered King's and the third year of the School of Architecture to read Part II, the first foreigner without an undergraduate degree to do so.

I spent two glorious years in Cambridge. Giants such as Nikolaus Pevsner, Ernst Gombrich and Henry-Russell Hitchcock were in residence at that time. The biggest guns, British and European, in the architecture profession passed through regularly, and the quality of student work was far superior to that which I had experienced in the US. The Department of Architecture, quite small by today's standards, had the well-deserved reputation of being among the best in the world. Le Corbusier was God and the eight volumes of his *Oeuvres complètes* were my bible.

The rigour and passion that I still bring to my work was nourished and allowed to blossom in Cambridge. I take great pride and feel extraordinarily fortunate to have been a part of that great institution. The bulldogs may be gone, along with half-crowns and tuppence, but nothing in my life has served me better.

Peter Berman
(1962)

For me, the most valuable part of the architecture course was the weekly meeting with my design supervisor, as the teaching centred around projects with a 'crit' at the end of each term.

'Crits' were highly charged occasions when students presented their designs to internal and invited critics. It was a brutal system and students were sometimes reduced to despair by scathing comments. Tears were not uncommon, among male as well as female students, partly due to exhaustion after being up all night. Many found it hard to thrive in this intense atmosphere.

The critics could be unpredictable, even baffling at times, as when they praised an open-plan glass-walled music school, even though it lacked sound insulation which was the most basic requirement of the brief! On another occasion, a Chinese professor described at length, and with eloquent arm waving, how designing a building was like making love to woman.

I never had a very bad crit myself and, the one time I had a poor one, I felt elated because it meant my work was being taken seriously at last. I was very touched when my fellow students gathered around to commiserate with me.

Yvonne Jerrold
(1974)

Among the privileges of being an architectural student at Cambridge was having a workspace in Scroope Terrace. Some disciplined individuals used this within sensible hours and maintained a social life and sporting commitments in college. Others, like me, made this workspace our primary focus and the department our college. We succumbed to architectural addiction and were subsumed by possibility – social, formal, endless. Many of the long hours we kept were spent enjoyably wasting time together, like naughty children trusted with our own front door keys and left without supervision. I made excellent friends. A cool, creative buzz pervaded the landscape of sticky scraps of card and blunt scalpel blades, fuelled by the mix of post- and undergraduate students. Steve, the live-in caretaker with the patience of a saint, kept a discreet eye on things and prevented catastrophe.

At the very beginning we started on the same back foot. On our first excruciating studio day we were challenged to present drawings of our favourite space to our new classmates. Sparkier presentations were of sweet jars or rucksacks, not local churches, and we glimpsed a broader meaning of space. Rare flashes of lucidity became gradually more frequent in subsequent years, helped by second and third year students learning together. For the diploma, old hands like me were joined by a number of talented students from other schools. The fresh blood was imperative for a school that had a propensity to stagnate. At the end of each of the five years, portfolio hand-in compounded our late night habits into sequential 'all-nighters'. We usually fell asleep in our celebratory pints. In undergraduate years we woke from this to find that we had about 24 hours to revise the year's lectures for the exams. God knows how we passed these but it was unusual to fail.

Deadlines and crits were the aspects of our training most resonant with the realities of practice. It should come as a surprise that I left undergraduate study not knowing the dimensions of a standard brick. Such inexcusable ignorance is not unusual amongst architecture graduates. Although construction and structures were introduced in weekly lectures, these seemed dry and abstract concerns to me. Snapshots of the reality of the profession were injected with visits to local sites with pale-faced job architects but the most effective inspiration was the act of building and 1:1 constructions were among the most successful student projects.

Sally Rendel
(1992)

The gentle muse

LEO MELLOR

In the 16th century Edmund Spenser believed there was something special in the Cambridge water. After praising the nobility of the River Ouse, he found the reason for this flowed from one of its tributaries – the Cam. For in Cambridge the river was 'adorned' by 'many a gentle Muse and many a learned wit.' It is perhaps only too plausible to assume that as long as there have been students at Cambridge they have written poetry. A recent rhyme of 'Fen Ditton' with 'to sit on' was a contemporary nadir, but it is part of a tradition. For poetry by the Cam has not only meant Milton, Wordsworth, Byron, Brooke and Empson, all of whom wrote while they were undergraduates, but also doggerel, pathos and regular epitaphs for college cats. Yet throughout the 20th century Cambridge undergraduate poetry was where many experiments – including the magazine *Experiment* in the 1920s – occurred and new ideas from Surrealism to L=A=N=G=U=A=G=E writing were introduced to

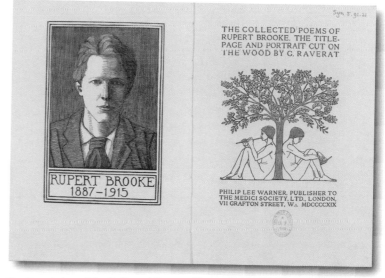

Top: Frontispiece to The Collected Poems *of Rupert Brooke (1919).*

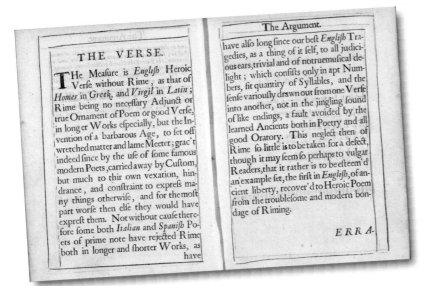

Above: Milton's justification of the blank verse of Paradise Lost, *produced at the request of the poem's publisher, 1690.*

Left: The fields beside the Cam on the path up to Grantchester, known as Grantchester Meadow.

Britain. In the 1970s Perfect Bound lived up to its name by proving that not all poetry magazines have to be spineless in form or content, and in the 1980s *Equofinality* gave rise to Equipage, a small press still run from Jesus College. In the 1990s Rem-Press and Barque both emerged from student groupings, and currently Arehouse, Bad Press and Landfill fly the flag.

For Cambridge students, from the day they arrive, are exposed to new writers, theories and intellectual horizons. A natural response is the inevitable groupings, friendships, rivalries and discipleships: all these act to stimulate writing. Then comes the difficulty of showing it to the world… Tiny magazines flower and wither every year, but a hint of their excitement comes in the titles: *Phrasis*, *MEAT*, *word-up*, *Tresspassers will be* and *bottle-top*. Steadier landmarks include *The Mays*, formerly *The May Anthologies*, a yearly Oxbridge round-up that brings together poetry and prose. Administered and edited by students, with a guest editor making the final choices, this has ranged from haikus to poems festooned with footnotes. There is (thankfully) no 'creative writing' course as part of the University, and the interlacing of academic study and poetry has always been problematic as well as pleasurable; an undergraduate recently lamented 'I can't read Eliot all

Small poetry magazines, mostly shortlived.

day and then write…' But within the English Faculty, where many of the senior members are themselves poets, students can still submit an 'original composition' as part of the Tripos; such work has the glorious effect of only being used to elevate a student's marks – and discounted otherwise. Moreover, recognition can also come through accolades such as the Brewer-Hall Award and the Kinsella-Ryan Prize, with the latter preserving the names of two successful Judith E. Wilson Fellows who ran inspirational workshops. The Harper-Wood Studentship gives a young writer subsistence for a year and allows them to venture abroad; recent poets have travelled to Welsh-speaking Patagonia and Svalbard.

Graduate students have recently been especially active in writing and promoting poetry – with the crypt-like Drama Studio, deep below the new English Faculty building, hosting the Cambridge Series readings and performances such as the Experimental Women Poetry Festival. At these events current students have read alongside invited poets, many of whom also studied here. But beyond such showcases and journals there will always be those who just want to scribble something in a college room late at night to try to capture a fraction of a feeling. There is, after all, the Cam to return to as a perpetual subject for even the most uncertain first verse. It is a strangely forgiving river: everything thrown in it will eventually come out in the Wash.

Leo Mellor *is a poet and Fellow in English at New Hall.*

First instituted in 1813, the Chancellor's Medal, is awarded annually for the best poem in English written by a student. This particular medal was won by David William Alun Llewellyn of St John's College in 1923.

I arrived at Cambridge in the autumn of 2000 to read English. I had chosen Cambridge over Oxford because Cambridge offered the option of submitting a portfolio of 'creative writing' as part of one's final degree. My chosen college, Queens', had Stephen Fry and Graham Swift as recent alumni, as well as Desiderius Erasmus and T.H. White, the author of *The Sword in the Stone* series. A year above me, Mark Watson was already making his name as a talented comic writer. And I wanted to be a writer. In fact, I wanted to be a *poet*: a dream that I was forced to relinquish a term or two in when it became clear even to me that my 'poems' were rather more like a series of Alan Bennett-style *Talking Heads* monologues than the taut, flinty, abstruse verses I'd wanted them to be.

But, even if my dream-life as a poet was short-lived, there were plenty of other prospects for a wannabe writer at Cambridge. There were comedy sketches and revues, one-act play competitions, new writing 'festivals' and events like the annual *Smorgasbord*, held at the Corpus Playroom – where my first ever playlet was performed. There were college magazines and newspapers, there were the University publications, *Varsity* and *TCS*, there were countless occasional or one-off collections of fiction, and there were, of course, the famous *May Anthologies*, or *The Mays*, as they were referred to by those in the know. Zadie Smith, whose novel *White Teeth* was published the year I matriculated, had famously been 'discovered' through a short story in the anthology. When the call went out for submissions, I decided to try writing a short story: 20,000 words later I realised, to my horror, that I was actually mid-way through a novel. I sent the first self-contained-*ish* section in, but it didn't even get long-listed, let alone selected for publication. I wobbled for a day or so, but the compulsion to continue over-rode my chagrin and wounded pride, and the 'story' eventually became my first novel, *Where They Were Missed*.

Cambridge was a heightened and rarefied atmosphere for an eager young writer to be in. One of my tutors was a novelist, and a number of others, including my Director of Studies, were esteemed poets. I still remember the flutter of excitement on opening a literary magazine for the first time to see pieces written by people I *knew*, or the delight of coming across a stack of books at a second-hand stall that had belonged to Bill Buford, the founding editor of *Granta*. But thrilling as it was to be surrounded by such brilliant writers, I don't think I really 'found my voice' – or my confidence in writing as a feasible career – until after I'd left Cambridge: it's deeply dispiriting, if not downright impossible, to be slogging away at one's own clunky, old-chestnutty prose whilst reading and writing on Joyce, or discussing Flaubert and Woolf and W.S. Graham. In many ways, and I have heard many people say this, it is only possible to appreciate Cambridge, and the opportunities it offered, in retrospect.

However, the single most important episode in my career to date has been, without a doubt, participating in a series of masterclasses taken by the Scottish playwright Chris Hannan. Chris was the Judith E. Wilson Fellow during my second year at university, and he held

Woodcut of the Mill Pond c.1950, by the artist and author Gwen Raverat, a granddaughter of Charles Darwin.

workshops every week for two terms, introducing ideas and aspects of playwriting and then, in the final term, inviting professional directors to come up for a weekend and facilitate rehearsed readings of our plays. There was a core group of three, myself, Ben Musgrave and Jack Thorne, all of whom are now professional playwrights, and we all agree how deeply indebted we are to Chris's enthusiasm, encouragement and dedication beyond the call of duty. I can honestly say that I would not be where I am now – if a playwright at all – if it wasn't for Chris's classes.

In my final year of university, I lived in a little attic room with a sloping ceiling and a gas fire, four floors up a winding stone staircase, looking out over the rooftops of King's and John's and Trinity. As the cliché goes – and the relics of my early attempts at fiction from those days bear all too blatant witness to my hapless familiarity with clichés – it could have come straight out of a Merchant Ivory film. I used to write last thing at night after my essays had been dashed off (or abandoned in despair), sitting at my antique roll-top desk overlooking the spires, and it felt like Writing with a capital letter. These days, now that I'm writing for a living, I have to be up and at my desk – overlooking a massive industrial building site in the East End of London – first thing in the morning, and it isn't by any stretch of the imagination half as romantic.

I recently went back to Cambridge to have supper with an old friend who has just completed a PhD. He showed me some creased, annotated pages he'd found, dated in the autumn of 2001 – the first sketches of what became my first novel. They were printed in royal-blue, ten-point Courier New, the fake typewriter font – the closest I could get to Ezra Pound and his violet typewriter ribbon. I always used to promise myself that if ever I was a 'proper' writer I'd write on an antique typewriter with expensive ribbon. I still write on my old laptop, however: but I've graduated to the much more elegant Garamond (black, size twelve): the font I used to use for essays, in the vain hope that it would somehow make their arguments look more sophisticated.

I was wary that, looking back, I might get sentimental or idealise the writing life at Cambridge. And much of what I've written does indeed sound like a fantasy. But it was – is – more than that, too. Some of the friends I met as an unrealistic and idealistic student are among my closest artistic collaborators today. And these days, I can in all conscience go back during the summer months and lie by the river sipping gin and tonics and reciting Romantic poetry, which I always used to think was what writers at Cambridge were supposed, nay obliged, to do but which, due to the looming spectre of the University Library and impending Finals, was the one thing I didn't do enough of when I was there.

Lucy Caldwell
(2000)

I found studying English totally inhibiting as a writer, though it's made me a fearless reader, which has been a lasting legacy. I wrote nothing until I'd left Cambridge and the English canon behind. It didn't help that a young woman was hailed in the national press as 'the new Shakespeare' while we were up. I believe there was some scandal involving a ménage à trois with a lecturer. We haven't heard from her in a while, though, which secretly pleases me.

I could see that it was, in principle, possible to combine writing with scholarship, and I was lucky enough to study for my Milton paper with poet Geoffrey Hill. I'm ashamed to confess that I only made it to his 9am lectures once; the spirit was willing but the flesh was sleepy first thing in the morning. Geoffrey Hill himself was a delight, though a hard taskmaster. I've kept my essays with his comments on them. He would answer the door looking glum and formidable but we'd end up giggling.

The physical geography of the city has left its mark on me. I still dream about cycling down the Huntingdon Road after dark and I'm often worrying about being prosecuted for not having lights, though this never actually happened to me. Another recurring nightmare is turning up at college and finding that I hate my room. I think I moved more often than anybody else in Cambridge. One summer I lived in Girton Tower which was invaded by thunder bugs from the harvest and had to move again while the exterminators did their work.

I fell in love, caught glandular fever, had a nervous breakdown, took time out, came back up and somehow got a double first, which seemed like a good revenge, I'm not sure on what. The best thing, though, has been the long and rewarding process of recovering from the intensely inhibiting conditions of being young, creatively inhibited but permanently fired up by the landscape of English literature and theory.

Gwyneth Lewis
(1978)

The life and disappearance of *Granta*

John Simpson

As the times and the University changed, so did *Granta*, Cambridge's pre-eminent undergraduate magazine. Founded in 1889 as 'A College Joke To Cure The Dumps', it was for long years a rip-off of *Punch*, yet it was always inventive and well-written. Contributors included A.A. Milne, E.M. Forster, Cecil Beaton, William Empson, Thom Gunn, Ted Hughes, Sylvia Plath and Peter Cook. Its editors were often in trouble. The writer and cartoonist Mark Boxer was sent down in the 1950s for printing a poem about God which ended 'You son of a bitch, you snotty old sod'. David Frost produced some brilliant editions and almost ran the magazine into the ground. By 1965 the distinguished poet J.H. Prynne was the don in charge, and the editors were Reg Gadney, an action painter who later became a successful novelist, and Jim Philip, another poet. One of their associates was a pioneer of concrete poetry, Mike Weaver, who taught me at Magdalene. Mike recommended me to them as the next editor; partly, I think, because I happened to be passing while they were discussing who to appoint.

Nicholas Snowman came with me as co-editor, and Ridley Burnett and Norman Hammond ran the business and sales sides. There was no office, just an in-tray at a Silver Street bookshop. The money problems never went away. Once we had a showdown with someone who had been pocketing *Granta*'s cash. He turned up with a gun, and fired it in my face, though it turned out to be a replica. Our art editor, the weirdly imaginative and talented Richard Yeend, put an Aubrey Beardsley drawing on the cover of my first edition and as a result has been credited by at least one cultural historian with having started the Beardsley-*Yellow*

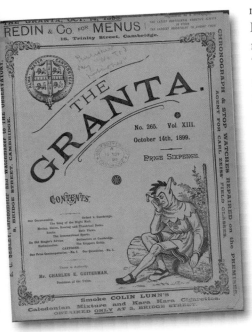

Christopher Angeloglou

Above: David Frost, editor of Granta, *at the printers, 1962.*
Left: An early edition of Granta, *1899.*

historian with having started the Beardsley-*Yellow Book* revival of the 1960s. Another edition was less successful; the cover featured a photograph of a Chinese restaurant, the Pagoda, cropped so that only the letters 'GOD' appeared. Fearing a religious theme, Cambridge students shunned it, and one night Norman Hammond and I dropped 2,000 unsold copies into the Cam off Magdalene bridge. *Granta*'s financial survival was always in doubt, though Nicholas Snowman produced an opera edition which sold out completely, copies changing hands in London for remarkable prices.

The magazine's later life was strange. A tough-minded American called Bill Buford turned it into a highly successful literary magazine.

Off the back of it, he created a publishing house. Both throve, but when Buford left Cambridge the connection withered away. Now you have to be in your forties to remember *Granta* as the University's best known site for good prose and poetry.

Back in 1967 Snowman, Jim Philip and I edited an anthology of *Granta*, as part of the endless effort to keep it afloat. The book did well, and occasionally, even now, I see a tatty copy for sale in the five-pence bin outside some second-hand bookshop. But it isn't much, alas, to show for a century of Cambridge writing.

John Simpson read English at Magdalene, where he is now an Honorary Fellow, from 1963 to 1966. He joined the BBC on leaving, and has remained there ever since.

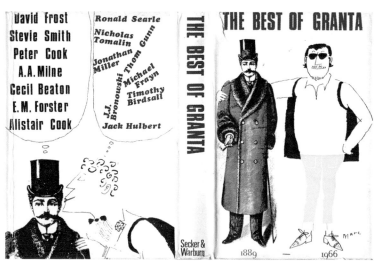
Granta anthology, 1967, edited by John Simpson and Jim Philip.

Varsity

Mark Weatherall

'A good newspaper', wrote Arthur Miller, 'is a nation talking to itself.' From 1947 to the present day, Cambridge students have talked to themselves through the medium of *Varsity*, the Cambridge student newspaper, founded by the exuberant Harry Newman. The name had belonged to a pre-war publication, and was chosen so that Newman could get an allocation of paper from the Board of Trade. The paper sold 5,000 copies at a price of 3d on the first day. Its early success continued throughout the 1950s and 1960s, repeatedly winning the National Union of Students' competition for the best student newspaper, and earning itself a reputation for smugness. The entrepreneurial spirit of the age was exemplified by Michael Winner, editor in 1955, who briefly, though ultimately unsuccessfully, tried to conquer the Dark Blue market by establishing an Oxford edition of the paper. By the early 1960s *Varsity* considered itself a mini-Fleet Street production, 250 copies being sent down to London each week for distribution to the news desks of the national papers. Despite this, Suzy Menkes, appointed *Varsity*'s first female editor in 1966, recalled that her tutor looked on student journalism as a 'frivolous and unworthy occupation'.

In the late 1960s, however, the paper was hit hard by the effect on advertising revenue of tax changes on national industries. It also had competition. *Stop Press* began as a radical campaigning newspaper, founded in 1972 by the Cambridge Students' Union (CSU). Despite going bust after only five issues, it

Arthur Pottersman and Peter Hill working with the lead type of Varsity *as it went to press in 1961, when it was still printed in Bury St Edmunds.*

VARSITY
The Cambridge University Newspaper

HUGE NEW SCIENCE CENTRE PLANNED

Front page of the first regular issue of Varsity *after the war, 1947.*

soon reappeared, this time being distributed for free. Guaranteed distribution was crucial in attracting advertising away from *Varsity*. By 1973 *Varsity* was losing over £1,000 a year and was in the red, despite maintaining high journalistic standards under the editorship of Jeremy Paxman. The issue of 27 February 1973 was its last.

It seems strange that it was at this moment that two perilously insecure titles should merge, but in retrospect pooling their

Varsity *was subsumed in* Stop Press *in 1973, resuming its proper name in 1987.*

complementary resources was the only way for them to survive. *Stop Press with Varsity* inherited the financial insecurities of its predecessors and the style of *Stop Press*, though its *Varsity* heritage gradually reasserted itself. Sport and arts reappeared; investigative journalism replaced propaganda and polemic; when in 1979 the NUS resurrected its annual student journalism awards, Michael Sheridan and Andrew Gowers were named student journalists of the year, an honour repeated over the following decade by Andrew Rawnsley, Sarah Green and James Wood. By 1987 it seemed natural to revert to the name which had served the paper for the first 26 years of its existence.

In the late 1980s and 1990s, much of the energies of the *Varsity* teams were diverted into the new technologies of the desktop publishing revolution. For nearly 20 years paste-up took place in the basement of the CSU (later CUSU) offices in Round Church Street, the Herculean labours being boosted by the '*Varsity* lunch': £5 worth of food bought out of editorial funds by one of the members of the team. When I first dabbled in *Varsity* in 1988, the 'lunch' could consist entirely of smarties and coke, or of taramasalata and pitta bread, depending on the tastes of the person responsible. In

Daily Varsity, *1992.*

Editorial team of Varsity, *1972.*

When my ten-year-old son first saw this picture he wondered why there were only three women in it. So perfect that it was taken outside the local Gents. In fact there is only one – one of the people who was to sit in the editor's chair, Laura Sparkes.

Why did we all – apart from Nick Garthwaite, who's holding the sign – affect such studied seriousness? I guess it was to do with being cool (which, as you can see from the photograph, was an effort in which we failed). But it was also because, in the way of all Cambridge undertakings, we took ourselves ludicrously seriously.

We didn't think ourselves as bad as the boobies who stood up in the Union, interjecting on Points of Order, and who reappeared a few years later as members of the Cabinet. But we held earnest editorial conferences and discussed what ex-cathedra statement ought to thunder out of the leader column as if it made the slightest difference.

I was the editor when this picture was taken. But the most important figure is the man front right, the business manager. *Varsity* ran on a permanent overdraft, with an ever-present debt to the printers, on whom we descended en masse each week, to supervise the chiselling on the hot metal to make our rather prolix words fit the available space. The debt had supposedly been run up in the 1960s when a previous generation had decided that what the University newspaper really needed was *a colour supplement*. We were still paying for it a decade later. In fact, I don't think it was ever paid for.

A few of us went on to make careers in the media. But most of the *Varsity* crowd got proper jobs and, rightly, treated the paper as just a bit of student fun. That was the right approach. But it could only have been decent fun if we had genuinely cared about what we were doing.

(Footnote: My ten-year-old also had no idea what the machine was sitting on the ground at my feet.)

Jeremy Paxman
(1969)

I was *Varsity*'s news editor under Michael Winner's editorship. After the first edition of the term had hit the shops, some of the staff were having a beer in a spirit of mutual congratulation. We thought it a pity that Oxford didn't have a newspaper as good as *Varsity*. Winner suddenly got up, collected some loose change and left. He returned about ten minutes later and said he had telephoned *The Times* to tell them that *Varsity* was going to publish in Oxford.

Our team set off to Oxford in a fleet of taxis (much to the horror of our budget-conscious business manager) to recruit a network of Oxford correspondents, start news-gathering, sell advertising and set up a distribution system. Winner was apprehensive about student violence and recruited, I don't know how, members of the Cambridge water-polo team as minders.

The Oxford edition duly appeared and sold over 3,000 copies – far more than *Cherwell* – on top of the regular 6,000 Cambridge copies. The reaction was mixed – basically that we'd shown *Cherwell* a thing or two, but we hadn't really got deeply into the Oxford scene. We took this as a compliment, given the immensity of the task. As a postscript, the following week the editor of the Manchester University student newspaper came to see us. He was fed up with being tightly controlled by the Students' Union and wanted us to publish a Manchester *Varsity*. We politely declined.

Peter Dulton
(1953)

As a reporter on *Varsity*, I took the opportunity one day to write a short piece about a reading by E.M. Forster from his unfinished novel, *Arctic Summer*. It gave me the excuse to knock on the door of the famous figure who used to shuffle round the college, and to seek the momentary contact with fame that Cambridge offered from time to time. Since I took a *Varsity* photographer, Colin Godman, with me, I thought it would be a good idea to have a photograph taken with the great man. I stood casually by the mantelpiece and tried to look as if I was discussing aspects of the novel. In fact, because I forgot to take off my raincoat I always feel now that I look as if I am the man (or boy) from the gas board discussing where the leak might be.

Karl Sabbagh
(1961)

In the years before I came up to Cambridge I harboured a burning desire – to edit *Varsity*. I'd edited the school rag but never thought I'd get my hands on the *Varsity* reins. How many school newspaper editors must there be at Cambridge? I'd thought. They can't all get a bite of the cherry. And what of the illustrious past editors? I had heard how people like Richard Whiteley, Michael Winner and Jeremy Paxman had all edited the University newspaper and their accounts sounded so glamorous – I wanted to live the student editor's dream!

Progressing through the ranks from visual arts editor to news editor I applied to become editor in the penultimate term of my third and final year at Cambridge. I applied alongside my friend and fellow *Varsity* stalwart Reji and we were thrilled when the call came to offer us co-editorship.

The Christmas vacation before we began was spent, almost constantly, on the phone to each other, agonising over our new design and vision for the newspaper. Back in Cambridge in January we had a big team meeting in Emmanuel College so that all the section editors could meet one another. Of course the reason why two non–Emmanuel editors chose such a place to host this meeting was the sub-standard premises we occupied. Our offices in a Victorian terrace on Trumpington Street, which were shared with both CUSU and our rival newspaper *The Cambridge Student* (*TCS*), were very small and could barely accommodate the editors and deputy editors let alone our full editorial team which numbered over 30. The offices themselves were grim beyond belief. Old pizza boxes and mouldy cups of tea littered the surfaces whilst one could never tuck one's legs under the tables due to the overflowing back issues of *Varsity* that were piled up there.

Our glamorous lifestyle consisted of our hotly anticipated lunch-time board meetings (free sandwiches courtesy of *Varsity* Publication ltd) and Thursday evenings (free pizza and Thai food courtesy of our advertisers). How we lived it up!

We had an old TV fixed to the wall which brought me much comfort on a Thursday night ('putting the paper to bed night') until my enjoyment of EastEnders was cruelly curtailed when the business manager remembered that he had not renewed the licence as a cost-cutting

E.M. Forster with Karl Sabbagh, 1962.

The Cambridge Student *(TCS). was launched in 1999, and is published by Cambridge University Students' Union, with both on-line and print editions.*

measure. Thursday evening was always a no-go for my friends. They knew the horror hours we used to work on *Varsity*. Occasionally I'd meet them coming in from various nightclubs but usually I returned with sunlight breaking through and my college friends fast asleep.

Thursday evenings were not without amusement, however. We'd always have CUSU officers popping in to see what propaganda they could get into the newspaper and to try and get a preview look at our front page. It amuses me so much to remember how important people thought *Varsity* was – me included. I remember an ex-Union President telling me grim-faced, 'We were really worried about what damage you could do to us'. With a readership of about 2,000 probably not very much!

Front pages were always difficult. Invariably they would be written on the final day – and would take into consideration *TCS*'s front page. On the night of the 2004 CUSU election we stayed up later than ever. Going along to the count – even counting a few ballot papers myself – we got back to the office and had to write up pronto. Giddiness, however, got the better of us in that terrible way it can afflict people who really don't have the time to spare. Never have I laughed so much as we tried to think up a snappy headline for our front page which carried a large photo of the incoming CUSU President. I couldn't possibly repeat some of the suggestions and the actual headline – 'Close Call' accompanying the new President on his mobile phone – seems quite lame in comparison to some of the flighty alternatives we considered!

I did enjoy my time with *Varsity* – so much in fact that I did it all over again in a Winner-esque move when I went over to Oxford for my Master's, editing *Isis* for a term. But it wasn't half as exciting and glamorous as my time amongst the pizza boxes in Trumpington Street!

Laura-Jane Foley
(2001)

1990, one year after *Varsity*'s move to new premises in Trumpington Street, a considerable investment was made in an Apple Mac-based DTP system. This allowed innovations such as *Daily Varsity*, first published in May Week 1992, and ultimately *Varsity Online*. I became editor in 1992, having served time as 'Apostle' (ghost-writing the notorious gossip column for my friend Kingsmill Bond, whose contacts among the upper echelons of Cambridge society kept us in copy, and the lawyers busy), sports editor and editor of the final incarnation of the *Varsity Yearbook*. I loved it all. I didn't want to become a journalist – though lots around me did – and in fact I'd have been hard pushed to explain exactly what I was doing there. Looking back now I can understand: it was the buzz of being at the centre of things, knowing (or at least thinking I knew) exactly what was going on.

What then do Cambridge students hear when they talk to themselves through *Varsity*? Through all its ups and downs, disasters, resurrections, renaming and revamping, *Varsity* has mirrored the concerns, preoccupations and prejudices of Cambridge students. By turns *Varsity*, like the student body itself, has been left-wing, right-wing, moderate, radical, highbrow, lowbrow, boring and even fascinating. At times it has modelled itself on Ivy League campus newspapers, the *Daily Mirror*, the underground press of the 1960s, or the *Independent*. Often it has been content simply to be itself. Whatever its outward appearance, there is at the core of the paper's long survival a tradition of independence, collaboration and co-operation – and perhaps a slight bolshieness – that Cambridge students recognise, enjoy, and come to treasure.

Mark Weatherall *(1986) edited* Varsity *in 1992. He read medical sciences before completing an MPhil and PhD. He is now a consultant neurologist.*

Both university newspapers are now distributed free.

Research

12

A story of explosive growth

William Brown

Research has always been a central part of Cambridge academic life, going hand-in-hand with teaching. Whether it was a matter of discovering electrons, decoding ancient texts, or analysing economies, academic staff have traditionally arranged their research around the teaching of their students. The reason is not just that teachers who are themselves aware of the doubts and excitements of current research provide the most challenging teaching for lively young minds. It is also that the naïve questions of those lively minds are themselves a fine stimulus for research. Cambridge is deeply committed to maintaining this symbiosis. But, paradoxically, the University's growing success at research is making it harder to sustain. Why is this? And how is the University keeping the link alive?

Part of the challenge comes from the fact that government funding of universities has, over the past 20 years, increasingly separated out teaching from research. Core research funding is now based on a periodic rating process that compares British universities, discipline by discipline, called the Research Assessment Exercise. No university has performed better under this than Cambridge. But the separate funding of research has increased the challenge of upholding the salience of teaching in academic priorities.

Besides this, the scale of research has grown enormously, especially in the sciences. International research success increasingly demands bigger teams, many of whose members carry out little or no teaching. These are backed up by growing numbers of trainee researchers working for their doctoral degrees. You get some impression of how things have changed by looking at the proportion of Cambridge's budget that is tied to specific research projects. Up until the mid-1980s research accounted for only a quarter of all spending – by 2006 it had risen to over a half.

Reflecting this is the recent shift in the balance between academic staff in tenured jobs on the one hand, and those in purely research jobs on the other. Up until the mid-1980s there were always more than twice as many tenured staff as full-time research staff. But then the research staff numbers started to grow, and they have since grown three times as fast. The numbers drew equal in 1997 and by 2006 tenured staff were outnumbered by research staff by half as many again.

There has been as big a change among students. While undergraduate numbers have only grown very slowly in recent decades, numbers of graduate students, mainly receiving research training, have surged ahead to double since the mid-1980s. By 2006, there was one graduate for every two undergraduates and their share of the Cambridge student population continues to grow. Although a quarter of these graduates are studying one-year Master's degrees, many of them hope to do well enough to proceed on to study for research doctorates.

This remarkable growth in the number of graduate students, mostly being trained in research, has had two notable characteristics. First, an increasing proportion of them are women. Women graduate students have advanced from comprising a minimal percentage in their

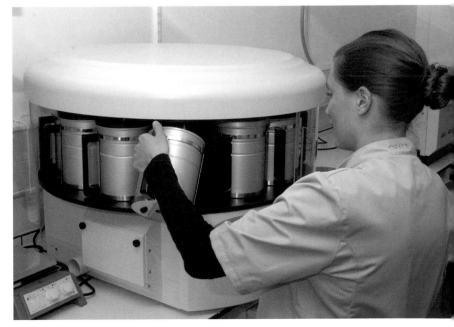

Above: Laboratory work at Cancer Research UK/Hutchinson Institute.

Opposite: Darwin College, founded in 1964 as the first Cambridge college exclusively for graduate research students, is housed in buildings bordering the Cam, including Newnham Grange, the home of Sir George Darwin, second son of Charles Darwin and Plumian Professor of Astronomy.

I turned up at Cambridge having just finished my undergraduate studies at Yale. Graduate student life in Cambridge, by virtue of the colleges, was much friendlier than I had expected. Being affiliated with both a college and a department was good for our intellects as well as for our social lives. Our days may have been spent in tissue culture, writing code, debating philosophy, solving proofs, or learning law but by the evening there was always time for tea and a chat, or a pick-up game of Scrabble in the MCR bar. Indeed, we spent a lot of time commiserating about the trials and tribulations of each other's research over a pint at the Castle Inn.

Jennifer Su Thompson
(2000)

Research was the core reason I came to Cambridge. I spent most days in the first-floor dog lab doing kidney experiments. At the end of the experiments we would snap-freeze kidney slices in liquid nitrogen and then repair to the Addenbrooke's canteen where we would have steak and kidney pie. That didn't last long as the food eventually conjured up visions of urine collections and kidney slices and canisters of liquid nitrogen that made steak and kidney pie unpalatable. The lab day would be interrupted by coffee break in the morning, lunch, and then tea break in the afternoon.

The other enjoyable part about working at Downing Site was that it was locked down tight at a relatively early hour. When abstracts for meetings were due I was given a key by the Prof, walked onto the site by squeezing through the gate of adjoining Downing College at a point where it was missing a post, and by the end of the evening needed to scale the small gate at Downing Site because everything else was locked. Obtaining data by this means gave me the impression I was doing something vaguely illegal, and it was exciting.

Gordon L. Klein
(1970)

POSTGRADUATE STUDENT NUMBERS

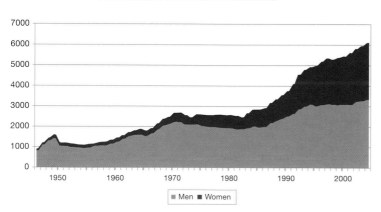

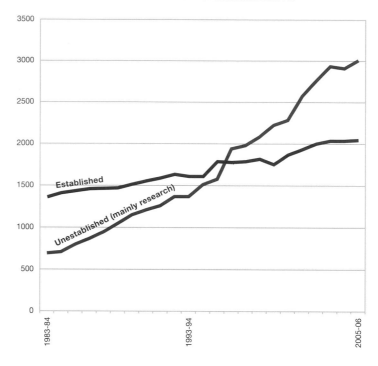

How research staff have come to outnumber tenured staff
Approximate annual growth rates since 1983-84 are as follows:
Established staff: 2%   Unestablished staff: 7%

parents' generation to nearly half of graduate students by 2006. Second, a growing proportion of them come to Cambridge from other countries. In 1980 under a third of all graduate students were from outside the UK; by 2006 that had risen to a half and was continuing to rise. Indeed, the number of British-born graduate students in Cambridge has been fairly steady for a decade; the recent growth has largely comprised arrivals from abroad, currently from about a hundred different nationalities. At the graduate level, Cambridge has become one of the most international universities in the world.

What lies behind this internationalising of our graduate students? In part it reflects the global nature of research, and of Cambridge's reputation. But that alone is not enough, because however much the brightest young people worldwide might want to come to Cambridge to work at the frontiers of research, they cannot do so without massive support for their fees and living costs, far beyond the reach of any normal family.

All major universities know that their research success depends in large part upon the quality of the research students they attract. These are the foot-soldiers and future leaders of their universities' research achievements. As a result, there is intense international competition among the leading universities for the most promising new graduates from anywhere in the world who aspire to do research degrees. Many universities, especially in the US, offer these outstanding young people teaching opportunities to earn their keep during their degree, in addition to bursaries and scholarships to cover their costs. But Cambridge has always eschewed making research students too dependent on tutorial and other earnings. The University's view has been that a full-time research student should indeed be full-time, in order to complete a solid research training at a relatively early age. This throws a heavy burden on to the financial support of graduate students by other means.

Cambridge has met this challenge by creating a series of trust funds. These started in 1980, when a change in government policy required overseas students to pay much higher fees than home students. The Cambridge Commonwealth Trust and the Cambridge Overseas Trust were established, with early help from, among others, Trinity College and what is now Cambridge Assessment. Energetic campaigning, and the sustained support of distinguished alumni from all over the world, have achieved a steady accumulation of gifts for both underlying endowment and current finance. In 1993 the Cambridge European Trust was created and in 2000 an unprecedentedly generous endowment from the Gates Foundation added substantially to available funds. In recognition of their great strategic importance, both the University and

Trinity College now contribute to these trust funds on a regular basis.

The scale of their achievement is formidable. Since 1980, a total of over 12,000 Cambridge overseas students have relied on these trust funds. In 2006 over 2,500 overseas students were supported by them, wholly or in part. This is a major reason why Cambridge's overseas graduate numbers have continued to expand despite a steady reduction of government support since the mid-1990s. About two-thirds of these were graduates, comprising about half of the University's overseas graduate students. For some students the financial support is total, but for others it is partial, sufficient to make it possible for them to come to Cambridge when added to funds available from other sources, such as scholarships from the student's own country, or from departmental funds. This system of student support, on a scale unsurpassed in Britain and, for that matter, by almost any other university in the world, has been crucial to Cambridge's continuing international research success.

In general, the University has adapted to this rapid growth in the proportion of staff and students committed to full-time research

Biomedical research students from the New Addenbrooke's site on the Darwin Bridge.

remarkably smoothly. New colleges have been established since the 1960s, wholly or largely dedicated to graduate students: Darwin, Wolfson, Clare Hall, St Edmunds and Hughes Hall. But all the colleges have been happy to build up their graduate student communities. Some have chosen to make a special place for students on some of the more vocational graduate courses such as medicine, management and teaching. But those studying for research degrees are distributed across all the colleges. And they are all members of colleges, even if their workplaces are themselves not part of the University, such as the MRC's Laboratory of Molecular Biology, or the British Antarctic Survey.

As head of a graduate college, I never cease to marvel at the diversity of research through which our students get their training. A social anthropology student studying how villagers cope with minefields in her native Cambodia may have a room next door to a molecular biologist shedding light on the causes of Alzheimer's disease by studying genetic correlates of aberrations in fruit flies. An historian looking at the funding of public works in medieval Norfolk may run the football team with a computer scientist developing protocols for quantum encryption. The long, tough, and in many ways lonely route to a PhD is for many made bearable by the fact that the Cambridge graduate community is so large, and bound together socially and intellectually through its colleges, and by so many sporting, musical, national and diverse other networks.

Research at the new Cancer Research UK/Cambridge Institute ranges from cell biology to imaging and experimental medicine.

One challenge facing the University, as a very consciously collegiate community, is that, for the growing numbers of full-time research staff, the colleges are not a part of life. Many research staff undertake some college teaching and some win hotly contested college research fellowships. But the majority of them have little interaction with the college life that, traditionally, has epitomised Cambridge. Their world is increasingly that of the new sites, such as those at West Cambridge or around the new Addenbrooke's Hospital, where so much of the University's research is now burgeoning. For research students, collegiate Cambridge is an important reality. But for many of the full-time research staff from whom students may receive their training, it is not.

The importance of including the University's growing research community in its collegiate communities takes us back to where we started. The symbiosis between teaching and research is central to Cambridge's long-term success. The constant flux of able young people, at both undergraduate and graduate levels, refreshes the University's research life as the tide refreshes a beach. Teaching, training, and providing fresh minds with the means to tackle fundamental research problems are essential to the advancement of understanding. Maintaining the University as a coherent intellectual community will be central to its keeping its international pre-eminence.

Wolfson College, founded in 1965, was the first college established for both men and women and admits graduate students and a limited number of mature students studying for a first degree.

William Brown *is Master of Darwin College and Montague Burton Professor of Industrial Relations.*

CRASSH: a humanities initiative

MARY JACOBUS

Ten years ago, humanities researchers in Cambridge lacked a way to talk to each other across the boundaries of Cambridge's powerful faculties and schools. Despite the wealth of individual research, there was no framework for interdisciplinary collaboration such as had long existed in major US universities. The Centre for Research in the Arts, Social Sciences and Humanities (immediately known by its acronym CRASSH) came into being as a response. Set up in 2001, and originally intended to occupy a new building on the Sidgwick Site, it eventually found a niche behind the Old Cambridge University Press in the former Printer's House, symbolically placed mid-way between the main humanities and social science sites, in the middle of Cambridge.

The centre's current home, already bursting at the seams, signals access of all kinds (to the public as well as its overlapping constituencies), along with a necessary degree of autonomy. The Centre's aim of promoting interdisciplinary dialogue has gone hand in hand with responsiveness to the two schools it straddles. At the heart of its activities lies the belief that the disciplines need to talk to each other in order to stay at the cutting edge. Spanning traditional divides, and energised by human interaction, the centre provides a testing-ground for new ideas. To lend coherence, its programmes and activities – fellowships, conferences and research groups – are clustered under a common thematic umbrella. CRASSH themes have included the Organisation of Knowledge, Evidence, Cultural Transmission and Disciplinary Change, and (from 2009 to 2011) The Future University.

As the centre has evolved, the challenge has been to adapt its activities to Cambridge structures and local needs, and to make their impact felt more widely across the humanities. The centre now supports upward of 25 conferences a year, many of them convened by early career researchers. Alongside its visiting fellowships, CRASSH now includes an Early Career fellowship programme to nurture young Cambridge academics at a critical point in their careers. Funded by the Newton Trust and the Mellon Foundation, collaborative graduate groups work together on issues as different as the city, China and reproduction, cutting their teeth on new ventures and organisational challenges. Most recently, as part of a Mellon-funded international consortium of Centres of Disciplinary Innovation, the centre has begun to forge a link between forward-facing research and curricular innovation by way of collaborative teaching fellowships.

A research centre offers a site for critical reflection – for both withdrawal and re-engagement. When visiting Fellows are asked what they most value in their time at CRASSH, they often say: 'space to think'. The centre's oblique angle to its constituencies and to the University provides both a space–time model for intensive work and a meeting-place: the solitary researcher meets the collaborative project. During their life-span at CRASSH, individual and joint research projects come together and draw apart in a movement choreographed by the ways in which ideas gestate, percolate and cross-fertilise one another. This human process is what makes the humanities (as well as CRASSH) host to humanistic thought in its broadest sense.

No account of a research centre would be complete without practicalities. True research centres are not simply virtual spaces. When two or three directors get together, they are as likely to find themselves talking about space and funding as about the ideas that drive their differing agendas and

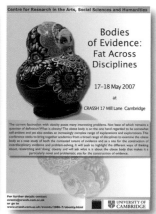

Seminars at CRASSH.

The University Centre, opened in 1967 on Granta Place, was built following the Bridges Report with a grant from the Wolfson Foundation to provide collegiate services to graduate students without colleges. It is now open to all members of the University and hosts the Gates Scholars as well as careers fairs and other events.

The day I arrived in Cambridge to begin my PhD, 1 October 1961, I found a handwritten note at my lodgings. It began 'Dear Steinberg', and came from Mr F.H. – later Sir Harry – Hinsley, my supervisor. The St John's Fellow in American history had become Vice-Chancellor of the new University of East Anglia. Could I teach American history to 13 'pupils'? Mr Hinsley never asked if I knew any American history. That seemed not to matter. A clever chap could supervise anything; he just 'mugged it up'.

I began my research in an equally vague way. I had to learn how to take notes and file information, how to organise my research, how to use footnotes, how to construct arguments, by myself. Nobody asked me to compile a bibliography or submit a research proposal. My supervisor read drafts very conscientiously but never discussed the nuts-and-bolts of historical research. One just 'got on with it' somehow.

By contrast the US graduate school, then and now, showed its origins in German *Wissenschaft*: three years of courses, formal apprenticeship as 'Teaching Assistants' and a professional comprehensive examination before research could begin. Ruthless graduate schools regularly culled students after their first year.

Cambridge has moved towards that model. By 1999 the History Faculty had attracted hundreds of students to PhD and MPhil programmes. The faculty gave them classes in research practice and assessed their progress as in America, but never adopted the obligatory three years of course work and examination before starting research.

When in 1999 I accepted a job at an American university, I had suddenly to serve on PhD 'committees', examine students in generals and work with teaching assistants. As an American who went 'home' after more than 30 years in Cambridge, I could see both systems with some perspective. Course work in the first two years certainly helps to fill gaps and obligatory semesters as teaching assistants introduce students to class preparation and the stress of giving marks. The year leading to general examinations forces the American graduate student to design huge reading lists and somehow get through them. Students leave graduate school with a knowledge of the relevant literature in three or four fields which my desultory course never gave me.

Cambridge 'examines' ('grades' in American) better than any American university. Cambridge 'double marking' requires two examiners to mark written work 'blind' and only compare notes to agree marks once they have done so. In an American university, TAs mark their students in lecture courses by themselves with neither guidance nor supervision. Professors may see difficult cases but often not even that. TAs scarcely older than their students confront unaided the haggling by which spoiled, privileged undergraduates try to extort better grades.

The American history department takes more time than Cambridge to train graduate students but the students seem to enjoy it less. They resent their professors ('we "are serfs"', said one bitter graduate student to me) and despise their students. The typical American department observes strict, unwritten rules of seniority. Graduate students come bottom and know it.

The Cambridge History Faculty relies on colleges to offer their graduate students social lives and housing that no American university can match. They go to formal halls and have 'Middle Combination Rooms'. They mix mainly with students not in their own fields. During my three decades in Cambridge I certainly heard complaints but not the systemic bitterness that I met in the US. More than 40 years have passed since I started my graduate study. Had I the chance to do it again, I would still choose Cambridge.

Jonathan Steinberg
(1961)

Blue Sky Research

Radio waves, X-rays, radioactivity and DNA: 200 years ago we had no idea they existed, but they were all around us, invisible, waiting to be discovered, and capable of transforming our lives; and all with a strong Cambridge connection. Like many discoveries, they have had a major impact on society but resulted from the curiosity of small groups of individuals pursuing their own interests. Their subjects mattered to them alone, and no government committee or company executive had identified the area as being of future importance. How can Cambridge ensure that it is able to discover those things that are currently unimaginable but will be part of everyday life in 200 years' time?

Charles Darwin's microscope.

Mankind faces major environmental challenges such as climate change and loss of natural resources. Health problems in the developed world due to over-eating or longer lives will occupy us as much as starvation and epidemics elsewhere. Governments, charities and the private sector will identify research targets and fund interdisciplinary research groups that need to be co-ordinated and managed in a top-down fashion. In future, ever more research cash will be channelled in this way. Cambridge has a tradition of brilliant individuals who follow their own instincts rather than the instructions of management committees, but it is clear that if we are to maintain a flow of major research funds then the University will have to learn how to set out and manage ambitious projects while its members set aside personal agendas for the common good. Newer institutions lacking our traditions and resources have learned this lesson earlier than we have.

However, although top-down strategic programmes might be a good way of turning science into applicable technology, they don't necessarily lead to major breakthroughs, which are often made in accidental discoveries and wrongly conceived experiments or by maverick individuals pursuing an unpopular idea. Original discoveries often have to be accidental because the experts in the field 'know' the experiment must fail, so nobody can get a grant to do the experiment, and committees trying to foresee the future miss the key advances. So, we have to make room in managed projects for individuality and unpredictability, even if they don't lead to the desired outcome.

This problem is universal, not restricted to Cambridge, but we are better placed to deal with it than most: through the freedom provided by endowments, and courageous intellectual leadership, we can support people as well as projects, and trust their personal scientific judgements. This is risky – it will lead to many failures judged by utilitarian criteria. The best discoveries are often made by scientists working just outside their own field (Crick was a physicist): knowing the literature in one field can close your mind to revolution in that area, but can prepare you for a productive jump into another. We need to be broad and deep, but not know too much about the problem, so really outstanding individuals change fields every few years.

In 2002 Donald Rumsfeld, then US Secretary for Defense, famously said: 'As we know … there are things we know we know. We also know … there are some things we do not know. But there are also unknown unknowns, the ones we don't know we don't know.' He was ridiculed by the press, I think unfairly. Though no fan of Rumsfeld, I believe what he said was profound. If Cambridge can support those looking for the unknown unknowns, then we will continue to transform the future as we have in the past.

Jeremy Sanders is Professor of Chemistry and a Deputy Vice-Chancellor.

---

initiatives. Space, in this sense, means privacy to read and write (offices), along with public space for intellectual and social interaction (seminar rooms, a place to make coffee). Some of the best discussions in CRASSH happen in the kitchen or over sandwiches. Eating together, like the work-in-progress seminar, is a weekly ritual that distinguishes the real research centre from the virtual 'centre of centres' beloved of administrators looking for economies of scale or space. The digital collaboratory may be the distinctive model for new humanities research, but it can only thrive with face-to-face interaction.

And funding? CRASSH was launched thanks to the generosity of two colleges, St John's and Trinity, along with continuing support from the University. Called on to justify its existence, CRASSH can confidently point to its enrichment of humanities research culture, its support of new initiatives and the magnet it provides for researchers at all levels. But this is only a small part of its value to the University. Visiting lecturers, artists, poets, novelists and film-makers revitalise the arts; controversial and urgent topical issues (the environment, human rights) prompt public and political figures into dialogue and reach out to wider audiences. The humanities at Cambridge, often perceived as an overwhelmingly scientific and technological university, are appropriately showcased. But most of all, CRASSH offers Cambridge a glimpse of the future – the future university – that keeps an ancient university in continuous and dynamic tension with its past.

Mary Jacobus is Director of CRASSH, Grace 2 Professor of English and a Fellow of Churchill College.

Social Sciences

13

Studying the human world

GEOFFREY HAWTHORN

'Social sciences first appeared in the list of subjects for examination in Cambridge in 1969. It had been a contentious arrival. To the more parochial and extreme, it had been seen to invite youthful rage and slack standards; to the more informed, an unappetising mixture of American scientism and European theory and a wilful disregard for the past. Yet it was far from new.

The idea of a 'science' of the human had been implanted in the University by William Whewell in the Moral Sciences Tripos that he introduced, with a parallel scheme for the natural sciences, in 1848. That included almost all the kinds of human enquiry and worldly concern then current. Each soon asserted itself, and in what proved to be an almost regular series of upheavals every quarter-century or so, separate Triposes broke away. History, moved by J.R. Seeley, who had practical purposes and wanted to call it 'politics', began in 1872; economics, moved by Alfred Marshall, appeared (with 'associated branches of political science') in 1903; and an endowment provided a Chair of Political Science, assigned to history, in 1927. From the natural sciences, A.C. Haddon achieved an examination in anthropology in 1913, combined with non-classical archaeology in a new Tripos in 1922, and W.H.G. Rivers had been appointed director of a new Psychological Laboratory, which stayed within natural sciences, in 1907. Sociology also had been suggested by the fund that endowed the Professorship of Political Science; the University hesitated, and the offer was withdrawn. The subject was talked about again in the 1950s and slipped quietly into economics in 1960. In the same year, in law, the small Department of Criminal Science that had been set up under the distinguished Leon Radzinowicz in 1949 became the country's first Institute of Criminology.

By the 1960s, therefore, many of the human or social sciences in Cambridge, if not all, were successful but scattered, and still not formally so described. In response to a demand that was being attractively met elsewhere for teaching them, a committee was in 1968 charged with deciding what to do. It unavoidably and, as it now can seem, wisely left what existed as it was and embraced change, and the name, by recommending a Tripos in Social and Political Sciences (a collective description first used by Seeley); it also agreed, for one tenure only, to a Professorship of Sociology. Modern politics and a more social, less experimental psychology, which had crept into the teaching of management in Engineering, were to be given places of their own; social anthropology was to be added (as it turned out, briefly) as 'comparative sociology', and a separate, modernist sociology also. History, economics and linguistics were also to be represented. There was much debate, and the proposals were but narrowly approved by the Regent House – 'Ah yes, I voted against you', people would say to me when I arrived to teach for the Tripos, more drearily 'is it a science?'. John Barnes was elected to the new chair, and moral sciences was renamed philosophy. On Barnes's retirement in the 1980s, his chair was established, Anthony Giddens was elected to it, and the Tripos was given a faculty. Established chairs in social and developmental psychology (Antony Manstead in 2002 together with a personal professorship for Martin Richards for his Centre for Family Research) and modern politics (Andrew Gamble in 2007) were to follow. Meanwhile, after a further quarter-century, politics, restive under another institutional subordination, had led each of the subjects to

UNIVERSITY OF CAMBRIDGE
17 MILL LANE

School of Arts and Humanities
School of the Biological Sciences
            and Faculty Office
Department of Plant Sciences (PGF)
School of the Humanities and Social Sciences
Centre of International Studies
Centre of Latin American Studies
Department of Politics
Development Studies
Mongolia and Inner Asia Studies Unit
Social Anthropology Research
School of the Physical Sciences
School of Technology
Centre for Gender Studies
Centre for Research in the Arts, Social Sciences and Humanities (CRASSH)
Graduate Union / Cafe - Entrance ➡
University Card Office

Old Press Site 1 Car Park
No Unauthorised Parking

Opposite: The Mond Building, once part of the Cavendish Laboratory built for Piotr Kapitza, is now the Centre for African Studies and also home to the Mongolia and Inner Asia Studies Unit. It retains its connection with the past in the form of the Eric Gill crocodile carved on the outside and the bas-relief cameo of Rutherford in the foyer. 'Crocodile' was Kapitza's nickname for Rutherford.

form their own department, and international studies had floated free from history and acquired its own chair, first held by James Mayall, in 1997. Several of the social sciences had also begun in a more applied way to flourish in Education, Land Economy and what is now the Judge Business School.

To those committed to professional reason, the outcome can verge on the absurd. To the more cautious, it can seem wisely reactive. To those who care about intellectual life, it has been productive. The disciplines of the social sciences are more than usually subject to worldly engagement, ideological contest and methodological dispute. In a university that by the late 20th century valued research as highly as teaching, their gradual accumulation across a proliferating number of separate institutions that defied rational ordering was allowing curiosities that coherent planning could, and probably would, have stifled. In some cases, in resolving insecurities in new kinds of international conflict, modelling economic uncertainty, thinking about the governance of the European Union, the effects of debt on states, early childhood, families, social capital, employment, the causes of crime and responses to it, curiosities have been satisfied and advances made within one or more of the social sciences themselves. In others, in political theory, in questions about how to approach the past, modern foreign parts, music and the other arts, about how to understand the self and its identities, not least those of gender and faith, and how to read texts, connections have been made across the social sciences and humanities. Bernard Williams, a moral philosopher, actively encouraged the social and political sciences and profoundly enlivened thinking about these and the arts; Moses Finley and Keith Hopkins, Professors of Ancient History, brought earlier work in sociology to their post; W.G. Runciman has offered a sociological account of the evolution of the modern from the ancient; Jack Goody and Alan Macfarlane, Professors of Anthropology, have between them reflected on literacy and the visual, the culture of flowers and cuisine, social history, comparative sociology and historiography, as well as their more particularly ethnographic interests in Africa and South Asia; John Dunn, a Professor of Politics, has written on the history and philosophical foundations of political theory, modern revolutions, West Africa and East Asia; Partha Dasgupta, a Professor of Economics who has worked on central issues in human well-being as well as game theory and other technical questions in economic theory, has the rare distinction of having been elected Fellow of the British Academy and the Royal Society. Interdisciplinary centres for the study of Africa, Latin America and South Asia had appeared in the 1960s, and in 2001, a more general Centre of Research in the Arts, Social Sciences and Humanities was instituted to extend adventures across the fields. In yet other cases, in the work of the anthropologist Marilyn Strathern and of a new centre for the Study of Human Evolution on issues of genetics, in research on autism, in developmental psychology, in neuroscience, and in what has come to be called environmental change, social sciences have been combining with the natural.

The old Addenbrooke's Hospital building, now the Judge Business School.

The social sciences are modernity's response to itself. An anxious world is keen to use them, and temptations in the agendas of the research councils, foundations and public bodies on which they depend for funds to reach short-sightedly for the future are strong. But these subjects also have their own dynamics, are loosely bounded and rarely stable. How they fit, intellectually and institutionally, with themselves and other disciplines will continue to be contentious. An incorrigibly plural university, in which those who practise them are free to defend what they already do as well as to change it, and in which they have constantly to explain themselves to the non-professional young, is essential to enable them to go on arguing about the world that wants them. And with it.

Geoffrey Hawthorn is a Fellow of Clare Hall and was Professor of International Politics until 2007.

W.H.R. Rivers and Psychology

Cambridge had the first Department of Psychology in Britain, founded in 1897, and since then psychology has been studied there as an experimental and medical science, as well as in a social science context. The polymath W.H.R. Rivers combined all of these strands in his own work. He remains famous for his research, both as an anthropologist and as a clinician, discovering the 'shell-shock syndrome' from observations of soldiers recuperating from their experiences in the First World War, so memorably depicted in the Booker-prize-winning *Regeneration Trilogy* by Pat Barker. He also played a major part in the origins of the Department of Experimental Psychology at Cambridge. In 1897 the University had still not taken the bold step of many universities in Germany and the US of founding such a department, despite the earlier efforts of the psychophysicist and philosopher J. Ward. However, in that year they created a Lectureship in Physiological and Experimental Psychology to which Rivers was appointed, housed initially in the Department of Physiology. Rivers had already been teaching sensory physiology to medical students at Cambridge, following his graduation from University College London in medicine at the exceptionally young age of 22. His postgraduate medical training in the early 1890s had taken him to the National Hospital, Queen Square, London for neurology and brain surgery under Hughlings, Jackson and Horsley; and for psychiatry, to the Bethlem Hospital and to Heidelberg to work with the later discoverer of schizophrenia, Emile Kraepelin.

As an anthropologist, on his pioneering expeditions to the Torres Straits Islands and to India, Rivers was to employ for one of his investigations psychophysical methods for comparing the senses of the natives with Europeans (finding not very much in the way of differences). On his return, he collaborated with the neurologist Henry Head on far-sighted studies, though in a rather grisly experiment, in which he measured the return of sensation to a patch of skin on Head's arm following its denervation by severing the cutaneous nerve. This famous experiment, performed at rooms in St John's College, was to presage some of the themes running through the work of the department over the next 100 years, ranging from psychophysics to neuropsychology, and even to the transplantation of neural tissues into the brain and the subsequent influence on behaviour in experimental animals.

The Psychological Laboratory was emancipated by its move in 1903 to a single room at Mill Lane. Rivers was joined in 1909 by C.S. Myers as a lecturer, and in 1912 the Psychological Laboratory was finally opened, just before the outbreak of the hostilities of the Great War. Rivers was to make his initial discoveries on shell-shock

Rivers and Henry Head performing neurological experiments on themselves.

W.H.R. Rivers conducting anthropological research on Torres Straits islanders.

syndrome at a Medical Research Council (MRC)-sponsored hospital near Liverpool. The MRC has always had a close link with Cambridge experimental psychology and later opened the Applied Psychology Unit (now the Brain and Cognitive Sciences Unit) in Cambridge under Kenneth Craik. In more recent times it has funded the Behavioural and Clinical Neuroscience Institute, thus sustaining the research interests of the department in psychopathology, experimental psychology and the brain.

Rivers died unexpectedly in his college rooms in 1922, the year in which F. Bartlett took over from Myers as Head of Department. The subsequent history of the department can be briefly summarized. It was assigned by Royal Commission to a new Faculty of Biological Sciences in 1926. The first Chair of Experimental Psychology was founded in 1931, to be occupied so far by only four individuals: the cognitive psychologist F. Bartlett (1951–2), the neuropsychologist O.L. Zangwill (1952–82), the animal-learning theorist N.J. Mackintosh (1982–2002) and the behavioural neuroscientist T.W. Robbins (2002–). These developments underline the strong interdisciplinary, but essentially biological, underpinnings of experimental psychology in Cambridge, which have complemented the later and separate development of the subject here as a social science. However, despite their distinct origins, the polymath Rivers can be said to have contributed to both of these strands of psychology in Cambridge.

Trevor Robbins is Professor of Experimental Psychology and Director of the MRC Centre in Behavioural and Clinical Neuroscience.

Experimental Psychology

Alternative Prospectus, 1989

Politics: the sceptical and inquisitive spirit

DAVID RUNCIMAN

Enoch Powell, the former Tory minister and pre-eminently controversial figure of post-war British politics, was once at a party in Cambridge when he found himself talking to a local professor. The academic knew all about the politician but the politician knew nothing about the academic. 'What do you do?' Powell asked. 'I teach politics', came the reply. Powell fixed him with a gimlet-eyed stare. 'You can't *teach* politics', he announced emphatically. Then he marched off.

For someone of Powell's generation, educated at Cambridge in the 1920s, this was a statement of fact. The traditional Cambridge view had always been that politics was not a subject in its own right, but only something you could learn about through something else. Originally, that something else was 'the moral sciences', a grand amalgam of history, philosophy, economics and classics, but as the different subjects moved apart at the beginning of the 20th century, politics had to be studied in one or other of these faculties. If you were interested in power, you could read history; if you were interested in justice, you could read philosophy; if you were interested in distribution, you could read economics. But if you wanted to study politics, you had better go to Oxford, or Essex, or Aberystwyth; failing that, you had better go abroad.

This wasn't just an institutional accident. It also reflected a well-established temperamental outlook, one that viewed politics as an empty technocratic exercise when it was studied for its own sake. The quintessential voice of this view of the world belonged to Michael Oakeshott, who was also educated at Cambridge in the 1920s, and who constructed an entire philosophy around the idea that politics was not something you could treat as a rational enterprise, to be written about in academic journals. Politics was something you *did*; writing about it was best left to the historians.

Times change, however. Cambridge now has its own Politics Department, established in 2003 (before then, Cambridge was almost certainly the last major university in the world without one, though it did, and still does, have the Faculty of Social and Political Sciences, where the Politics Department is housed). It also now has an established Chair of Politics, which has been occupied since 2007 by Andrew Gamble, one of the world's leading political economists. It is

Andrew Gamble giving the inaugural lecture for the new Chair of Politics, 2008.

Michael Derringer

still a tiny department by worldwide standards – there are currently ten of us, compared to 30 or 40 in many British universities and nearly 100 at Oxford. But it is growing, and it has the buzz some of these other places must have had 50 or 100 years ago – the buzz of a subject that is finally free to do its own thing.

Yet something that hasn't changed is the idea that politics in Cambridge is a subject that only makes sense as part of a wider intellectual framework, and not simply as a technical discipline in its own right. This doesn't mean that Oakeshott's spirit is still lingering about the place (Oakeshott is pretty fashionable these days – doubtless to his own amazement, were he still alive – but not in Cambridge; his vogue is among post-modernists in the US). Certainly it doesn't mean that Enoch Powell's withering contempt for the collision between academics and real politicians has any place in what we do (I don't think Powell is fashionable anywhere anymore, not even in Northern Ireland). But what it does mean is that we teach politics as a subject for which all other subjects are relevant, and which cannot be understood without what some politicians still like to call a hinterland.

The politics stream for undergraduates is now one of the most popular in the University, and a large part of its attraction both for students and the people who teach them is that politics is a way of studying everything else – history, philosophy, economics, even classics – just as it was once thought that everything else was a way of studying politics. We don't expect students to have any particular qualifications in these subjects before they start – politics within SPS probably has the most diverse intake of any subject in the University – but we do expect them to have picked up a sceptical, inquisitive spirit by the time they leave, one that sees the politics behind things that purport to be apolitical, as well as the absence of political understanding behind much of what purports to be at the cutting edge.

One thing that we still don't have, yet, is a stream of Cambridge graduates taking this sceptical spirit out into the world of professional politics. As I write this, Britain (or rather the Labour Party) has just got rid of one Oxford-educated Prime Minister (the eighth since 1945, during which time there have been none from Cambridge), and replaced him with someone who learned his politics in Scotland. The next generation of British politicians, who look set to dominate for a decade or more, is made up of a raft of 30- and 40-somethings who all studied PPE at Oxford, from David Miliband and Ed Balls for Labour to David Cameron and William Hague for the Tories. The chances of the next British Prime Minister having been educated at Oxford still look pretty high.

As a 40-something who studied philosophy and history at Cambridge, this is my generation of politicians. It seems churlish to complain about their astonishingly narrow educational provenance – Oxford must be doing something right if it keeps producing people willing to give politics a go. So I look forward to teaching the next generation of Cambridge students how this group of politicians gets on, and trying to encourage them to be sceptical about the idea that politics should be limited to the activities of people like these. But we don't want Cambridge students to be sceptical about the idea that politics matters, nor do we want them to doubt that it is worth doing as well as studying. It would be nice if more of them tried to have a go themselves.

David Runciman *is University Senior Lecturer in Political Theory, and a Fellow at Trinity Hall.*

Bust of William Pitt in Pembroke College, where he matriculated in 1773, aged 14.

Cambridge Prime Ministers

Name	Years	Party	College
Robert Walpole	1721–42	Whig	King's
Duke of Newcastle	1754–6	Whig	Clare
Marquess of Rockingham	1765–6 1782	Whig	St John's
Duke of Grafton	1768–70	Whig	Peterhouse
William Pitt	1783–1801	Whig	Pembroke
Spencer Perceval	1809–1812	Tory	Trinity
Viscount Goderich	1827–8	Tory	St John's
Earl Grey	1830–4	Whig	Trinity
Viscount Melbourne	1834	Whig	Trinity
Earl of Aberdeen	1852–5	Tory	St John's
Viscount Palmerston	1855–8	Whig	St John's
Arthur Balfour	1902–5	Tory	Trinity
Henry Campbell-Bannerman	1905–8	Liberal	Trinity
Stanley Baldwin	1923–4 1924–9 1935–7	Tory	Trinity

Economics: from moral sciences to game theory

Geoffrey Harcourt

Keynes called Malthus 'the first of the Cambridge economists', praising his philosophical, moral, historical, theoretical and observational approach to economic problems, and his ability to 'penetrate these events [with understanding] by a mixture of intuitive selection and formal principle and thus … interpret the problem and propose the remedy'. This approach characterises Cambridge economics at its best ever since.

In an era of globalisation and the pursuit of economic solutions to climate change, Arthur Pigou's legacy of concern with social welfare issues is reflected today in the writings of Amartya Sen, one of Cambridge's Nobel Laureates (1998), and Partha Dasgupta, and in models of optimum taxation and saving (derived from Frank Ramsey's 1920s articles) to which are married the effects of asymmetric economic information and principal–agent relationships (here, governments and tax payers) which are the concerns of James

Mirrlees, another Nobel Laureate (1996). David Newbery, the last Director of the Department of Applied Economics, works within this tradition; he is interested in applied microeconomic problems, especially in developing and transitional economies.

This focus can be traced back to the origins of the Economics Tripos, started in 1903 by Alfred Marshall, Professor of Political Economy (1885–1908), which grew out of the Moral Sciences Tripos and Marshall himself. He stressed the philosophy that economics should have practical use by understanding and improving economic systems within constraints imposed by liberal political and economic traditions. His two major theoretical developments were the theory of value and distribution, which he analysed using partial equilibrium analysis, and the theory of money and monetary policy set within the Cambridge version of the quantity theory of money.

The old Marshall Library of Economics on the Downing site. The Economics Faculty moved to Sidgwick Avenue in 1960 and the building now houses the Haddon Library and the Museum of Archaeology and Anthropology.

John Maynard Keynes

Just above the main entrance to the Cambridge Arts Theatre there is a blue plaque celebrating the life of its founder, John Maynard Keynes (1883–1946). In a few short words it states that Keynes was a Fellow and Bursar of King's College, an economist, philosopher, businessman, civil servant and diplomat. The plaque is easy to miss, but those who do notice it are no doubt left wondering how this famous son of Cambridge could have packed so much into a life spanning just 62 years.

Keynes was born in Cambridge and, after Eton, entered King's as an undergraduate studying mathematics. His academic brilliance ensured entry into the secretive Apostles where he rubbed shoulders with the likes of Lytton Strachey and Bertrand Russell. Russell, for one, was well aware of the power of Keynes's intellect, later claiming that Keynes had the sharpest mind that he had ever known. Despite securing a first class degree, Keynes's interests turned to economics and he quickly became a leading light on the Cambridge economics scene.

Outside Cambridge, Keynes first made his name with *The Economic Consequences of the Peace* (1919), a strongly worded attack on the First World War peace settlement. Over subsequent years, he developed revolutionary ideas about how the economy works, culminating in *The General Theory of Employment, Interest and Money*, which appeared on 4 February 1936, the day after the formal opening of the Arts Theatre. The remaining years of Keynes's life were largely spent defending his magnum opus and serving in the British government during the Second World War, where he played a key role in changing the way in which politicians and civil servants construct, implement and manage fiscal policy. The publication of the Beveridge Report in 1942 and its assumption that the government could run the economy along Keynesian lines after the war provided further evidence of Keynes's influence within British political and economic circles. His death in 1946 was marked by memorial services in Washington and in London at Westminster Abbey. There was also a service at King's College Chapel, although Keynes's wish to have his ashes interred there was either forgotten or ignored by his brother Geoffrey, who instead scattered them on the hills above Keynes's country home in Sussex.

Despite his passing, Keynes's ideas were taken up rapidly, not only in Britain but also in the US. By 1971, President Nixon could confidently declare that 'We are all Keynesians now'. However, the 'Age of Keynes' – characterised by strong economic growth and low

Above: John Maynard Keynes writing his King's fellowship dissertation. Portrait by Duncan Grant, 1908.

Left: Manuscript outline of The General Theory of Employment, Interest and Money, *published in 1936.*

inflation – was brought to an abrupt end by the 1973 oil crisis. The Keynesian model could not cope with the ensuing upturn in inflation and increased unemployment. Milton Friedman and his brand of monetarism stepped into the breach, receiving a stamp of approval from the Reagan and Thatcher governments. But although the high point of Keynesian orthodoxy may have passed, it was by no means the end of Keynes. In what sociologists of science refer to as 'obliteration by incorporation', the theories associated with his name (correctly or incorrectly) have become a fundamental part of economists' toolboxes across the world, whether they know it or not. Although Keynes died young, his ideas live on.

Robert Cord is a research student in the history and philosophy of science at St Edmund's and author of *Keynes: Life and Times* (London, 2007).

During the 1950s, one of the rooms on the top floor of the old Marshall Library in Cambridge University held a most unusual apparatus: an engine (sic) used to teach macroeconomics. It was a large metal chest, taller than a man and three times as broad. Its front face was a maze of interconnected transparent tubes containing coloured liquid, with a wide, vertical, central tube and a number of side tubes feeding into it. The liquid in the side tubes was controlled by taps. The main tube fed by the others represented the national income, and the side tubes demonstrated the various influences on it: the rate of interest, money supply, consumer prices etc.

The most interesting feature of the machine was that it described a dynamic world, by showing how some inputs influenced all the others positively or negatively, and how the end result of varying quantities of inputs determined national income.

The National Income Machine must have been the only multivariate model that had been constructed by a plumber! But like all mathematical models, everything depended on the judgement of the person who controlled the taps to alter the volume of the inputs. All the machine could do was to illustrate the outcomes, and in doing this the degree of influence of each input had of course been determined by the person who gave the plumber his instructions about the diameter of the tubes.

John Jones
(1950)

Cambridge has always been concerned with the practical applications of economics. Keynes and Kaldor were the most prominent of many government advisors from Cambridge. The Department of Applied Economics, a brainchild of Keynes, was started in 1945 with Richard Stone as its first Director. Under his direction its officers made innovative advances in many areas of applied economics. Stone himself, with James Meade, pioneered a national accounting framework for the British economy during the Second World War. Stone's subsequent developments at the international level led to his Nobel Prize in 1984.

Stone's successor, Brian Reddaway (1953–70) inspired common-sense, down-to-earth applied projects with policy applications. His successor, Wynne Godley (1970–85), after a career as a professional oboe player and then in the Treasury, drew on Marshall's concept of the long period and Keynes's analysis of the processes at work in modern capitalism to provide a framework of relationships incorporating double entry concepts, resulting after many years in a quantum jump in our understanding of national and international dynamic monetary macroeconomic processes.

The Keynesian revolution, which produced *The General Theory of Employment, Interest and Money* (1936), marked Keynes's move away from the Marshallian tradition, especially the dichotomy between the real and the monetary in the workings of the economy and concentration on the long period, and defined Cambridge economics for much of the 20th century. There was a basic inconsistency within

Marshall's approach in that his view of economies as organic evolving systems did not sit well with the static partial equilibrium analysis using the *ceteris paribus* pound, which he pioneered. Breaking out of the latter and forming theories within the former characterises the best Cambridge contributions ever since.

Keynes's younger colleagues, Kahn, Meade, Dennis Robertson, Austin and Joan Robinson, Piero Sraffa, played important roles in bringing about the transition in Keyne's approach from the Marshallian tradition to *The General Theory*. Keynes was the innovator, changing us, as Meade put it, from looking at the world as a saving dog wagging an investment tail to an investment dog wagging a saving tail. He provided an original theory of a monetary production economy. Meade's writings on international economics within a Keynesian (and Pigovian) framework led to him receiving the Nobel Prize in 1977.

Especially significant are the contributions of Piero Sraffa who was the first to suggest, in a series of papers in the 1920s and 1930s, that Marshall's theory should be discarded. Brought to Cambridge through Keynes's influence, Sraffa was a left-wing Italian. He worked for many years on editing Ricardo's works and correspondence (1951–73), in later years closely with Maurice Dobb. He wrote a profound critique of the conceptual foundations of neoclassical economics, simultaneously rehabilitating the classical and Marxian approach to theorising.

Inspired by the work of the Polish economist Michal Kalecki, who independently discovered the principal propositions of *The General Theory* within a framework derived from Marx, Joan Robinson was also concerned with a re-evaluation of Marx as an economist. In the post-war period, Joan Robinson, perhaps the personification of the Cambridge school, along with Kahn, Kaldor and later Pasinetti, worked on Cambridge post-Keynesian growth theory, 'the generalisation of *The General Theory* to the long period', using as the foundation for their arguments the concept of steady growth or 'Golden Age' growth paths. Kalecki provided a two-sided relationship between profitability and accumulation. He (and Richard Goodwin independently) argued that trend and cycle are indissolubly mixed, so providing a theory of cyclical growth. Together with Sraffa, Joan Robinson simultaneously led the Cambridge attack on the conceptual foundations of the mainstream theory of value and

Right: Alfred Marshall, Professor of Political Economy from 1884 to 1908 and creator of the Economics Tripos.

distribution. This was set within the context of the heated exchanges of the 1950s–1970s that became known as the Cambridge vs Cambridge controversies in capital theory. Most of the figures on this side of the Atlantic are now dead. Pasinetti is the senior living heir, the last great system builder, combining the insights of the classicals, Marx, Keynes and the post-Keynesians.

The most important infusion of modern approaches to economic theory into Cambridge came with Frank Hahn's appointment in the early 1960s and subsequent chair in the 1970s. The faculty in the 1960s read like a *Who's Who* of economists. Factionalism (always a characteristic of Cambridge economics) and the creation of new

Left: Partha Dasgupta, Frank Ramsay Professor of Economics and a Fellow of St John's, is a specialist in the economics of development and the environment.

universities played their part in the subsequent loss of ground to the Americans and to the practices of leading US departments, with differentiated products, comparative advantage and historical traditions increasingly discounted.

Hahn and Robin Matthews wrote a survey of growth theory in 1964, a role model for survey articles ever since. Hahn also wrote with Kenneth Arrow (Stanford) the definitive monograph on general equilibrium theory. In the 1980s and 1990s Hahn, Kaldor and other Cambridge economists were in the vanguard of those attacking the theoretical propositions and policy recommendations of the monetarists and new classical macroeconomists. Cambridge economic historians – Deane, Feinstein, Matthews, Mitchell – used Keynesian national income constructions to analyse the developments of advanced and developing economies.

Leadership in world economics has now passed to the US. Nevertheless, Cambridge economists continue to make significant contributions in many areas – econometrics, game theory, labour economics – and to work on the key problems of our time: climate change, developing economies, exhaustible resources and social capital. And a Cambridge economist, Partha Dasgupta, wrote *Economics: A Very Short Introduction* (2007) in Oxford University Press's influential series of 'very short introductions'. By comparing the present and future lots of two ten-year-old girls, one in a comfortable US suburb, the other in a poor African village, he discusses the 'urgent problems humanity faces today' combined with 'an account of the *reasoning* [modern] economists apply'.

Geoffrey Harcourt *is a Distinguished Fellow of the History of Economics Society. He is Emeritus Reader in the History of Economic Theory at Cambridge, Emeritus Fellow of Jesus College, and Professor Emeritus at the University of Adelaide.*

Left: The new Marshall Library at the Faculty of Economics.

Joan Robinson

One of the more famous sights of Cambridge in the 1950s was of a hatless middle-aged woman wearing a faded MA gown, prematurely white hair parted in the middle and pulled back into a bun from a noble forehead, sedately riding a ladies' bicycle of antique appearance across Coe Fen to the Mill Lane lecture rooms. One young man would whisper to another, 'That was Joan Robinson'.

Though everyone knew her as 'Joan' she was invariably addressed and usually referred to as 'Mrs Robinson'. That was long before 1965 when she acceded to a chair after the retirement of her husband and began to be called 'Professor'.

It is evident from this account that the 'teaching' Joan Robinson offered her undergraduate pupils, those like me at any rate, was moral rather than narrowly academic. She always treated us as her intellectual equals, demanding from us the same standards of rigour, clarity and honesty as she expected of her academic colleagues. Bracing – not to say flattering – as this was, it did not really help most of us; indeed, like many of her academic colleagues we were not her equals. With one possible exception (an eminent American economist still living) Joan Robinson was the most intelligent person I have ever met. She instantly grasped the implications of a set of assumptions, followed them through to a degree of complexity far beyond the grasp of any ordinary mind, saw at once the weakness in any line of argument, and was incapable of understanding why the rest of us were unable to follow.

At the time John Chown and I were her pupils, Mrs Robinson had just written her famous 1954 *Review of Economic Studies* article on 'The Production Function and the Theory of Capital', which seems to have inaugurated her sustained campaign against neoclassical theories of production, distribution and growth. Of course she expected that we would immediately see the point and become her allies in a godly crusade against the dragon of neoclassical orthodoxy, which she saw as ideological tear gas, blinding us all to the worst features of a capitalism she hated with the enthusiastic zeal of a true believer...

Neither Chown nor I shared Joan Robinson's patrician disdain for capitalist acts between consenting adults. We were active members of the University Conservative Association. We were sharply critical of the dismal experiment in socialism inflicted on a long-suffering British public by the post-war Labour government which she, like many of her Cambridge colleagues, had fervently supported. We had read *1984* and *The Road to Serfdom*. And we had been invited to luncheon at Caius College by Peter Bauer, a lonely advocate of liberal values and the free market who, with one or two others of like mind, was regarded as untouchable by most of his colleagues in the Faculty of Economics and Politics. Looking back, it seems now that we were

Joan Robinson, Fellow of Newnham College and Professor of Economics from 1965, was the first female Fellow of King's College and author of The Accumulation of Capital.

Thatcherites avant la lettre. We regarded Mrs Robinson's romantic infatuation with Communist China as richly comic.

Yet even where politics were concerned, her tough-minded fairness was never really in doubt. John Chown recalls an incident I had forgotten and which may have taken place before my return to Cambridge. 'I once had a major row with her on some politically loaded point,' he reports. 'But fearing assault I said, "Well, perhaps you have a point." Her face fell. "It's a waste of time coming to supervisions if you are going to agree with me." After that, no quarter asked or given.'

A.M.C. Waterman, excerpted from the *Review of Political Economy*, Vol. 15, No. 4, October 2003

Business: a Cambridge start-up

Sandra Dawson

'A great business school at the heart of Cambridge, advancing knowledge and leadership through people who will leave a mark on the world.'

Friends greeted the news that I was leaving Imperial College for Cambridge to head its nascent business school with surprise for me and doubt for Cambridge. Perhaps naïve; I never doubted that Cambridge was fertile soil and the harvest was ours to be lost. Failure or mediocrity never seemed an option. In the University we had remarkable strength in the core disciplines which underlie scholarship in management and business: mathematics, economics, law, engineering, social and political sciences. From engineering, we inherited a small group of core faculty and students who moved across under the generous sponsorship of Alec Broers, then Head of Department, whose unremitting certainty that successful development would follow was captured later in a chance remark: 'Successful children have the proudest parents.' In location we had, on our doorstep, a chaotic network creating successful technology-based businesses, and, just 60 minutes away, the City of London which was fast becoming the capital market of the world. In global reach we had a university name renowned for excellence in original scholarship and its application.

Back in 1995, we opened an iconic building which was the talk of the town; now all we needed was to make the place hum and sing with scholarship, learning and application so that in every way we sat in the heart of the University. Not that I thought it would be easy. Internally, Cambridge was not universally convinced that what some saw as a 'trade school' could or should be encouraged. Cast your mind back to the debates over the introduction of engineering, law or medicine, I would say and now see what lustre and strength they add to the University. Externally, we were a late entrant into the excessively tough international market of business education in which the main competitors were already household words. And we were unknown. Indeed, if I had secured £100 for every time my introduction was greeted with the remark 'I did not know that Cambridge had a business school', I would have quickly

satisfied our endowment needs. But the question for me was never, 'Could we build a business school worthy of the name of Cambridge?' but 'Could we build a business school quickly enough to enhance the name of Cambridge?'

The full story is yet to be created, but the plot is clear. Excellent academics have been recruited from all corners of the globe, matching the strength and diversity of our applicant pool of graduates. Generous benefactors have provided money for endowment and for current use. Alumni give their talents, time and money to develop their school as better than any other. An advisory board with an international membership of astounding reach and depth is helpfully involved in questioning, supporting, suggesting and advising.

Every student in the Judge Business School is rigorously schooled in the underlying intellectual foundations and at the same time tastes their application through practical project experience with companies and social enterprises, as well as immersing themselves in wider collegiate Cambridge. They come as graduate students, the best from every continent, to read for the MBA, MPhil and PhD; and, just as we go to press, for a brand new degree of Master in Finance. A highly selective group of Cambridge undergraduates, having completed a Part I in another subject, apply internally for one of the 70 places on the Part II Management Studies Tripos.

What highlights would I pick? Being a great business school is all about people, their knowledge and its application, and the achievements and contributions of faculty, students, alumni, collaborators, sponsors and benefactors provide many highlights. Every academic or corporate prize, every top student evaluation, every endowed chair, every research paper published, every curriculum innovation and enhanced learning experience are all highlights. So too was the moment of agreement on our new short name (from Judge Institute of Management Studies to Judge Business School), our shared strategy and robust business model. Make no mistake, vision and identity, strategy and planning, income and expenditure, reserves and investment are as important to a business

Management Studies lecture list, University Reporter, *2007.*

school as they are to a business. These are all clear milestones, but more fluid, yet equally important to achieve, was a developing culture, with a rejection of fixed choices between two stereotypically conflicting forces. We have a passionate commitment to encourage collaboration as well as competition, to nurture interdisciplinary developments as well as core disciplines, and above all an inclination to respect, rather than seek to crush, difference. There are several dimensions to this. At a fundamental intellectual level there is the difference between the quantitatively based natural scientific methodologies and approaches in social science and humanities. Stereotypes would say (but with different assignations), one was hard, the other soft, one was critical, the other unquestioning and overfull of assumptions; one was demanding, the other was easy. A business school should not choose between the two; the Judge has both, as witnessed by the depth and reach of interdisciplinary collaboration, and in the managerial capacity of alumni.

Beyond respect for intellectual and personality differences, there are different sectors of management experience. Most of our work reflects the concerns of commercial business in global markets; our research, case studies, student projects and graduate employment are predominantly in leading financial institutions, transnational utility companies, big name consultancies, multinational producers of goods and services and entrepreneurial start-ups in the major established and emerging economies of the world. Yet we are also hugely aware of the challenges faced in the world of social and public enterprise, where the complexity of stakeholders, traditional cultures and uncertain business models requires management skills of the highest calibre if performance is to be improved. But how could we finance developments and student admissions in this third sector where our tuition fees would seem prohibitive, and where there was a natural suspicion of business? Having co-funded the building with Sir Paul Judge, Simon Sainsbury provided that support through the Monument Trust with two critically important consequences. One was to create a window for the majority who would be for ever in the commercial world to see the challenges and opportunities for partnership and learning across sectors, as well as better insight into the subject of corporate responsibility. The second was to create more skilled capacity within the third sector, to show the fundamental importance of good management for achieving social as well as commercial purposes, and to create better understanding of the corporate world, not least because cross-sector partnerships are likely to become more, not less, likely. The stories of the investment bankers, senior executives, consultants and entrepreneurs who have graduated from the Judge are all unique and important; they are also better known than those from the third sector who have been supported as Sainsbury scholars on the MBA and are now managing hugely significant social enterprises and public projects in Afghanistan, Sudan, India, Jordan, Israel and the UK.

Sandra Dawson is Master of Sidney Sussex College, and KPMG Professor of Management Studies and was, until recently, Director of the Judge Business School.

The Judge MBA does not change personal competencies but it elevates one's game to new heights, providing the confidence to tackle any issue at any level. Since graduating I have worked with UN agencies to turn around and build the Afghanistan Information Management Services in ministries that previously had no computers; established the first full census in Afghanistan (to be conducted in 2008) with support from countries as diverse as Turkey, much of the EU, USA, Iran, China and India; most recently led a humanitarian team scattered across southern Sudan fighting biweekly disease outbreaks and extensive flooding.

In brief, the Judge MBA enables one to lead with confidence in uncharted waters, plotting out the course, marking the reefs and blazing a trail where others can follow.

David Saunders
(MBA 1996)

I came from working with displaced and migrant workers in urban slums. At Judge I was able to apply my learning to the sector I love; I researched microfinance institutions for risk management in global banking, and worked on the consulting project for the World Health Organisation. I even wrote a paper about a Fair Trade company's IPO decision for Capital Markets! I'm currently working at the Oxfam International Secretariat, and have been amazed to see that I can apply my learning to Oxfam's work every single day, from marketing and knowledge management to the microfinance programme in the post-Tsunami context. I am very pleased that I could develop critical tools to achieve social goals in more effective ways through my year in Cambridge.

Anna Kim
(MBA 2006)

I recall my time in the Judge Institute of Management Studies in 1995 with an absurd degree of exaggerated sentimentality, unbridled joy and rose-tinted memories of everything associated with Cambridge University. We were only the second set of guinea pigs on the MPhil in Management Studies, with newly planted scraggly trees on the Judge's lawn, no library to speak of and the Lycos search engine as our only concept of the World Wide Web. I was a young person from a small island in the West Indies.

Indra Marajh
1995 (MPhil Management Studies 1996)

Right: Inside the Judge Business School. The old Addenbrooke's Hospital building was refurbished and extended to accommodate a school of management studies by architect John Outram in 1995 with a gift from Sir Paul and Lady Judge.

Law: adjusting to new needs

DAVID FELDMAN

Law faculties serve an important social function by encouraging societies to think in a rational, principled way about how and why they coerce people, and reminding us of the dangers as well as the potential benefits of using law to achieve change or secure social stability. Cambridge scholars have been doing this for centuries. Legal studies were flourishing by 1250, initially focussing on Roman Catholic Canon law (dropped after the Reformation) and Roman law, and increasingly accommodating comparative law, the law of nations (international law), legal history and jurisprudence (philosophy of law). English law (common and statute), mainly taught by and for practitioners in Inns of Court, was not significantly studied in universities until the 18th century (in Oxford) and the 19th century (in Cambridge and London).

Law Faculty building, designed by Norman Foster and Partners and completed in 1995.

The old Law School, from Ackerman's History of the University of Cambridge, *1815.*

English law and its study have had to respond to rapid changes in technology, public administration, social structures and expectations since the 19th century. But two contrasting recent phenomena have reinforced the value of the medieval practice of approaching law from perspectives rising above national boundaries: firstly, a desire to make decisions as close as possible to the level of the people affected by them; secondly, globalisation in trade, commerce, communications and politics, with regional systems like the European Union and the Council of Europe and worldwide institutions such as the United Nations and the World Trade Organisation affecting and being affected by national legal systems. We use history, international studies, philosophy, comparative law and social sciences to understand the nature of law and of the societies in which it operates, how it works, and its effects.

Global changes have also spawned new fields of law and enforcement mechanisms. Human-rights and humanitarian law now regularly come before national and international legal tribunals. The power of governments and non-governmental agencies and the diminishing capacity of politics to secure accountability and remedy injustice have stimulated the growth of legal and administrative institutions to serve those purposes, including ombudsmen and administrative courts and tribunals. As the commercial importance of patents and copyrights has grown, intellectual property law has become more important and more sophisticated.

Law schools have both reacted to and driven these changes. The Tripos and LLM curricula have expanded accordingly. In 1907 the Tripos consisted of papers in Roman law, constitutional law and

The Law Faculty contained very few good lecturers in 1948. They may have been good academic lawyers, but their delivery was abysmal. (Possibly that accounted for the contempt amounting to hatred that practising lawyers showed them in those days. It has certainly got better now, but it is still nowhere near the reverence that is shown to professors on the Continent.) In fact, it got so bad that I nearly proposed that the faculty hire some out-of-work actors to deliver the lectures, but I doubted if that would have improved my career prospects.

The only one that was excellent was Dr Ellis Lewis, who lectured on advanced legal theory quite brilliantly. However, the one that was fun was Henry Barnes, as you could never tell what he was going to say next. There was a splendid legend that he had been President of Mexico for a short time. This allegedly occurred when he had been taken on as Minister for Justice, there was a revolution, and all the ministers senior to him rapidly resigned, leaving him in lonely, and unexpected, eminence. But then that was what one expected of dons in those days: they did extraordinary things.

Brian Russell
(1948)

My first encounter with the Law Faculty came when I was studying Japanese. A group of us had been kicked out of the Oriental Studies library in the early evening, but with exams looming we decided it would be sensible to work a little longer. So we went round the corner to the Squire Law Library, which seemed to be forever open. The glass building was, and is, a magnificent place to work, even if on that first foray amongst the lawyers we did get some dirty looks from those who clearly thought of us as intruders.

But two years later I was sitting in the same Faculty, this time as a law student who just about knew how to navigate the library to find the articles, books and cases which were named on endless reading lists. The volume of work was in some ways much greater than in Japanese, but in other ways law was easier – everything was written in English, for example. My lecture classes increased in size from 8 students to about 250, and there was an incessant patter of laptops which the acoustics of the lecture halls did well to drown out. But listening to the lecturers was worth the effort, and not only when they launched into animated rants about the state of the law. Learning that our lecturers struggled with grey areas of the law was reassuring; appreciating that clear reasoning is far more important than any 'right' answer was invaluable.

Paul Davies
(2002)

The working area of the new Squire Law Library in the faculty building on the Sidgwick site.

history, general jurisprudence and international law in Part I, and real and personal property, contract and tort, and criminal law in Part II. By 2007 there were more than two dozen papers on offer across the Tripos, and 28 on the LLM.

The academic legal community has become similarly diversified. The Cambridge Law Faculty has benefited from this, maintaining its core historical strengths while undertaking new initiatives in many other fields. For example, international law has flourished: the Lauterpacht Centre for International Law is an international forum for scholars from all over the world, and current faculty expertise encompasses the WTO, formation of states, cultural property and many other fields. Researchers in the Institute of Criminology and criminal lawyers have made major contributions to law and public policy. In public law (my own field) the faculty addresses pressing problems for modern states: the relationship between state security and human rights in the face of terrorist threats; the roles of constitutions in nation-building, national security and recovery from war; parliamentary and common-law foundations of judicial review of administrative and legislative action; and the extra-territorial extent of state power. Our intellectual property lawyers investigate everything from the place of confidentiality in medical research to means of offering legal protection against counterfeiting to distinctive aromas in perfumes. Our corporate specialists grapple with vital issues of corporate governance and social responsibility, examining the effects of different legal doctrines, organisational models and regulatory schemes. Our property lawyers consider the relationship between property rights and other human rights, such as a right to respect for a person's home or other people's rights to express themselves by campaigning on our land. In family law, a strong social-scientific element guides scholars' work on the law affecting child-care, financial provision on the end of relationships, and many other topical subjects.

Behind these specific examples lie fundamental questions. Do societies or economic structures such as national or globalised markets dictate the shape of a nation's law, or does law dictate the shape of societies and markets (or neither)? Can there be said to be a right answer to any or every question of law? How rational can judicial reasoning be? Our theorists encompass a wide range of philosophical positions, from a strict separation of law from other systems and values to those who believe that morality or social usefulness is a necessary element in all legal systems. There is no Cambridge 'school' or orthodoxy on these or other questions.

There are, however, two elements that unite the faculty. First, as law has to produce results in society if it is to be useful, we seek to ensure that our scholarship contributes to public life. Our members regularly contribute to law reform, serving as members of and advisers to the Law Commission and advising government departments. The first Whewell Professor, Sir William Harcourt, combined his tenure of the chair (1869–87) with being successively Solicitor General,

Leon Radzinowicz: Criminology

Leon Radzinowicz was instrumental in establishing the first Institute of Criminology in any English university. In the immediate post-war years, criminology was unknown as an academic discipline in England. There were three 'English' criminologists: Mannheim in London, Grunhut in Oxford and Radzinowicz in Cambridge, all émigrés from pre-war Europe. Radzinowicz was known as a legal historian – he had just published the first two volumes of his painstakingly researched *History of English Criminal Law*. Together with J.W.C. Turner, he established the Department of Criminal Science and began the publication of a series of research monographs which became the English Studies in Criminal Science.

In the late 1950s, R.A. Butler, then Home Secretary, decided that the country needed an Institute of Criminology to provide a centre of research, and Radzinowicz seized the opportunity to establish the new institute in Cambridge. He was appointed first Wolfson Professor of Criminology in 1959. He gathered a small team of researchers around him and they embarked on a series of ambitious research projects. At the same time the first postgraduate course in criminology was offered. The institute, at first based in Scroope Terrace, was later moved to temporary accommodation in West Road, where it remained for 40 years. Radzinowicz himself did not engage in criminological research; he saw his role as promoting research by others and increasing awareness of the newly established discipline. He travelled widely, lecturing in many countries. His lectures inspired many overseas students to come to Cambridge to study criminology under him, but they were sometimes disappointed to see little of him, as he was abroad on other lecture tours.

Left: Leon Radzinowicz. Portrait by Juliet Pannett, 1967.

Radzinowicz played a significant part in public life, serving as a member of the Royal Commission on Capital Punishment in the 1950s and later on the unsuccessful Royal Commission on the Penal System. His enquiry into prison security in 1968 had a powerful influence on subsequent prison policy. His personality had many facets. As Director of the institute, his behaviour could be controversial. He got his way by a combination of political skill and personal charm. On one occasion a colleague, determined to vent his anger over some issue, went to Radzinowicz's house (Radzinowicz preferred to work at home and was rarely present in the institute) to confront him. Radzinowicz answered the door with the words: 'My old friend! What a pleasure to see you. I have just received a bottle of very fine old Scotch whisky and I need your opinion of it.' The colleague's anger was dissipated immediately. Every Cambridge taxi driver had a different Radzinowicz story, usually about a demand to drive him to a particular destination in an impossibly short time. On one occasion he succeeded in persuading British Railways to delay the departure of the prestigious Fenman (the 8.48 from Cambridge to London) so that he would be able to catch it.

He lived a long life, moving to the US in retirement, and was academically active until the end of his life, publishing an autobiography shortly before his death at the age of 93.

David Thomas is an Emeritus Fellow of Trinity Hall and was a researcher, lecturer and then Reader in Criminal Justice at the Institute of Criminology 1971–2001.

Home Secretary and Chancellor of the Exchequer. The current incumbent, Professor James Crawford, is much in demand as an adviser to states, advocate before national and international tribunals, international arbitrator, and participant in the work of the International Law Commission. My career included several years as legal adviser to the Parliamentary Joint Select Committee on Human Rights, and I sit as an international judge of the Constitutional Court of Bosnia and Herzegovina. Our European Community and comparative lawyers help to guide the development of Europe and states far beyond it. Secondly, we share a commitment to rigorous research and analysis, and willingness to learn from other legal systems, societies and periods. These elements are as important to us and to society now as they were in the 13th century.

David Feldman *is Rouse Ball Professor of English Law, Chairman of the Faculty Board of Law and a Fellow of Downing College.*

Julian Andrews

The Radzinowicz Library in the Institute of Criminology.

Radicalism and activism

Tim Stanley

Whenever in the bar of King's College drinking with my old comrades, I always take a moment to ponder the hammer and sickle hidden in a corner on the wall facing the Front Court. It is a reminder of a more exciting, if not better, age. Every year the JCR gives the hammer and sickle a fresh coat of red paint, but every year the act becomes a little more anachronistic and a lot more ironic. Now a distant memory, political radicalism in 21st-century Cambridge is little more than decoration and whimsy.

On occasion, I have seen Cambridge students flirt with issues bigger than themselves. There was an impressive showing of Cantabrians at the anti-Iraq war demonstrations in 2003 and the small community of Muslim students has become commendably noisy of late, campaigning against various 'wars for oil' and the slow erosion of civil liberties. During the Make Poverty History crusade wristbands were in great evidence and college JCRs are increasingly 'right-on' on issues of recycling, minority representation, disabled access and investment in the arms industry. When the government considered allowing universities to set unlimited top-up fees CUSU organised an effective campaign of private lobbying and public disobedience. Some 4,000 of us jeered and screamed like feral beasts outside the Senate House in protest, banging drums and blowing whistles. Several colleges arrived with red banners and I even grew a beard for the occasion. Our aim was to disturb a University Council meeting at 9.30am and, although few of us had ever been awake so early, we were surprisingly effective. The Council was duly unnerved, bowed to pressure, took no decision that day and only raised fees after putting in place a bursary system.

Also, activism within the parties is undergoing something of a renaissance. The Trotskyites are as insidious as ever and several students have run as Green candidates in local elections. The most popular and best-read party is probably the Liberal Democrats, although the Labour Club is more ethnically and socially diverse. It drinks more, too, and has a reputation for radicalism. Last year it broke from the national student Labour Party in opposition to its lack of opposition to the war. In 2007 it even elected a woman chair, which makes it very unusual indeed among student groups.

But these are exceptions. CUSU is passionately apolitical and 'services not politics' has consistently beaten 'the revolution starts here' as a campaign slogan for the presidency. Turn-out in student body elections is pitiful, as is attendance at its council meetings. Activists complain that students will take part if something is of headline importance, but return to their books if long-term commitment is threatened.

Perhaps the funk and desperate isolation of early 21st-century activism was best illustrated when an alliance of hardboiled leftists occupied an abandoned Cambridge curry house in 2005 and turned it into a squat. The goal was to provide a meeting space of ideas and activism and to offer day-care services to locals. It was raided by the police within a week and rightly so. We had turned it into a sordid paradise of drugs, alcohol and poorly executed sex. The spirit of the 1960s is there, but the flesh is very weak.

Tim Stanley is a historian, political theorist and former chair of the Cambridge University Labour Club. He is co-author of The End of Politics *(2006).*

Above: Students taking part in the national anti-fees demonstration, London, October 2003.
Opposite: Cambridge CND protestor, 1962.

Occupation of the Old Schools, October 1968:

Giles Oliver (1966) writes: 'That is me in the centre turning the crank on the Gestetner machine, in the Council Room. The main aim was to show "solidarity" with countless other students and assorted movements in the UK and abroad. We wanted to shock people by taking over a University building right in the heart of things, so everyone could see flags and posters hanging out of the elegant first-floor windows. I recall there was a sense of frustration – and we didn't want to be left behind as radical wallflowers as occupations swept the campuses. It went on for two or three days, we had not prepared, and it was uncomfortable dozing in the wooden window alcoves, but we thought we were heroes.'

Nicholas Roberts (1966), who took this picture for the Shilling Paper, *writes: 'I remember walking out of the building when it was over. It was a bitterly cold night with frost or snow on the ground. We had to run a gauntlet of right-wing hearties jeering, scuffling, spitting, who were kept separated from us by police and Proctors. Dispersing into the streets I think we all felt a let-down, as though we had returned from the precipice of revolutionary action to the quiet domesticity of a winter night in Cambridge.'*

1968

When I arrived at Cambridge in autumn 1968, the student mood contrasted sharply with Manchester, where I had spent the previous four years. Left-wing politics, of course, had always been a strictly minority pastime, with the activists invariably a tiny minority. From the early summer of 1968, though, this was no longer the case. Left-wing politics, now of the revolutionary brand, inspired by the May events in France and the Tet offensive in Vietnam, came to command, seemingly overnight, the active support of an extremely large cross-section of students. Not in Cambridge, however. When I arrived it felt like a quaint backwater, far removed from what was happening to students elsewhere or in the world outside. Relatively few were engaged on the left, and those that were found themselves spectators in an unappetising contest between the Trotskyist left and the Situationists, a small and obscure group who spent their time trying to take over meetings of the Socialist Society and whose revolutionary agenda consisted of persuading students to walk across college greens and other such revolutionary acts. Not surprisingly, the left was small and isolated, never able even vaguely to fill the Lady Mitchell Hall.

On reflection, there were probably two reasons why Cambridge lagged behind other places. Firstly, it was a seat of privilege, which helps to explain such a patently self-indulgent and frivolous group as the Situationists, who were non-existent at most universities. Secondly, the college structure conspired against a University-wide student politics that had been the theatre of activity elsewhere. But Cambridge was not only a seat of privilege, it was also an enormously stimulating centre of scholarship, a place where many students were manifestly serious about the world. Cambridge, for this reason, also has a longer and richer history of student left-wing politics than any other UK university.

In Cambridge, 1968 saw no great student demonstrations or sit-ins, but an arcane and esoteric left that existed on the distant margins of student life. But 1968, along with 1969, proved a

Nicholas Roberts

Arrival in Cambridge in 1972 was clouded by the feeling that the era of pop culture and student radicalism had come to an end and we had missed the party. So when one evening after hall, word spread that there was a riot in progress on the Sidgwick Site, excitement was intense. Perhaps the 1960s lived on. As groups streamed towards the site, I found myself in company with an American postgrad. He had been in Chicago during the Democratic Convention riots of 1968 and was keen to compare that experience with the local version. First impressions were not promising. About 30 activists were clustered around the glass entrance of the Lady Mitchell Hall and their leaders were rattling the doors in a half-hearted attempt to gain entry and stage a sit-in. My new friend started to mutter about the ineffectual nature of this protest. At that moment authority re-asserted itself. The imposing figure of a proctor in full academic dress strode through the crowd, accompanied by his two bulldogs. The fact that he was swinging a bound copy of the *Statutes and Ordinances* from a length of metal chain only added to the unreality of the scene. After a brief stand-off, the demonstrators started to rattle the doors again. The effect was instantaneous. The demonstrators leapt backwards as if they had received an electric shock and after a few minutes everyone drifted away. A voice from Illinois could be heard muttering in disbelief, 'Call that a riot?'

John Adams
(1972)

A teach-in on university governance at Lady Mitchell Hall, when demands included greater representation of students on University Council and the abolition of gate hours, 1968.

transitional period during which the Situationists were isolated, the Socialist Society became the focus of the university's left – with a far bigger following than that of the Labour Club which, during these years, was a relatively isolated and unappealing group – and at the same time began to reach out to the wider student body. The left also spawned a student newspaper, the *Shilling Paper*, which was rather more influential than *Varsity*, and attracted some of the most interesting students around as well as a significant group of dons. In 1970 the Garden House demonstration against the Greek junta captured the national headlines and indirectly led to the formation of the Cambridge Students' Union, the first representative student body, thereby overcoming the fragmentation of the student body, and mirroring wider changes in the University. It is also noteworthy that by far the most influential group within a left which by now commanded the support of, I would guess, a thousand or more students, was the Communist Party branch. This, in itself, was an oddity, because elsewhere the Communist Party was marginal amongst students during the period 1968–71: it was a distant echo of the 1930s, when the CP was similarly influential in Cambridge. Interestingly, the local Communist Party branch proved the birthplace of Euro-Communism within the British CP, and indirectly went on to have a significant impact on the Labour Party from the late 1970s to the 1990s.

Martin Jacques (1968) is a former editor of Marxism Today, *author of* When China Rules the World *(to be published in 2009), and political columnist for the* Guardian, *the* Sunday Times *and* The Times.

I found myself involved in a Shakespeare reading society, which met once a month in one of our rooms to read a Shakespeare play, and I became secretary of it, responsible for choosing the play and also casting parts. One member was called Guy Burgess. He was, I believe, an old Etonian, and evidently intelligent and intellectual, but his tastes were different from other people's. He would be described as 'louche' today. In his room he kept a Buddha on a table, and found pleasure in blowing cigarette smoke into its mouth so that the smoke came out of its navel; we others found it rather vulgar. But we had no notion of his other political activities, which later brought him such notoriety.

Another familiar figure was Anthony Blunt. He was a tall, elegant man with blonde hair, who hobnobbed with some of the Fellows, but treated with disdain ordinary mortals who played football and cricket. He was already becoming known as an artistic type.

A third man later notorious (Philby) was one of the same year as myself, playing a relatively undistinguished part in the public school set, but known to be the son of a famous explorer, which gave him a cachet of his own.

Gervase Markham
(1929)

There were three Communist Party of Great Britain branches in Cambridge at in my time: the students' branch for undergrads, the staff branch for other members of the University, and the city branch. As far as I could see, and I was secretary of the students' branch, for nearly three years, there was little contact between the three branches.

Burgess and MacLean, Philby and Blunt, Cairncross. The names of the Cambridge Communist traitors are well known to nearly all of us now. I am confident that the Burgess and MacLean affair was only of the vaguest interest to me in 1960–3; in fact, I hardly would have known any of the details. I had zero interest in passing on secrets to the USSR even had it occurred to me that I might ever be in a position to have access to such. To me the international working-class revolution was everything I worked towards, but spying played no part in it whatsoever. This was the Krushchev period of 1956–66 when it seemed to the ill-informed, at least, that the socialist world would outperform the capitalist one, not only economically, but also (and above all) morally. In the creation of Socialist/Communist man, forms of cheating like espionage would not, it seemed to me, play a part.

I certainly believed what we were told in the CPGB: that we were expected to act in a way such that those with whom we worked and associated would have cause to respect us for our integrity, hard work and dedication to the interests of working people. We were also told that our main task as students was not political work, but to excel at our studies so that later we might achieve as influential a position as possible, in society and the world of work. This in itself was our chief political job.

I had gone up to Cambridge as, already, a CPGB member, having joined the Hull Young Communist League on 1 March 1959. I was interested to find, as members of the Cambridge students' branch in October 1960, the young offspring of well-known CPGB members (to us, 'comrades'). Brian Pollitt at King's was the son of General Secretary Harry Pollitt. Mark Dunman, also at King's, of Jack Dunman; Margaret Thomson at Newnham, daughter of George Thomson, Professor of Greek at Birmingham.

Each branch member was asked to volunteer to 'work' in a University club of his own choice. One was to promote our (Party's) influence through our membership of the selected club. I, on the basis of an interest in Asia, chose the Asian Club. I neglected to attend their meetings. Brian Pollitt chose the Cambridge Union Society, in which he made a name for himself. Since the Union's membership fees were high, the Party branch stumped up for Brian's fees. His membership of the Cambridge Union made the national press in, I think, 1962 when he took his Finals. If I remember, the story went that 'hearties' broke into his bedroom the night before his Finals started and trampled on him. Brian was standing for the post of President of the Union at the time. He succeeded.

Conrad Wood
(1960)

The Cambridge Evening News *reports the demonstration against the Greek Junta outside the Garden House Hotel, which turned into a riot, 13 February 1970.*

A False Dawn

As a political and social commentator I've found my undergraduate days at Cambridge an invaluable resource – but of a most perverse kind. Let me explain. We students saw ourselves as living through a transitional time in the culture and politics of our nation. The old, we believed, was giving way to the new. But what we were all convinced was happening was not happening at all. The transition was a mirage. The imagined dawn of a new world order was a false dawn. In retrospect the early 1970s were the end of a dream, not the beginning.

'Student unrest' was the buzz-headline of the era. Elsewhere in Britain it had been more spectacular. In France it had been heralded as the start of a revolution. In America it was big news. At Cambridge the Master of my college, Clare, the then Sir Eric Ashby, had just handed over the vice-chancellorship after a tenure distinguished by his wily, liberal-minded willingness to bend a little in the gale, and the whiff of revolution was fainter: only a whiff. But the Students' Union was flexing its left-wing muscles, colleges like mine were forming their own unions, there were talks of boycotts of this lecturer or that on account of their reactionary views, everyone was taking their bank accounts out of Barclays because of South Africa, there were excited rumours (unfounded) in my college that our Senior Tutor was a Stalinist – and then, in 1970, Cambridge's own contribution to world revolution: the Garden House Riots.

These had been inspired by a tourist promotion called 'Greek Week', involving the expensive Garden House Hotel. The student riots around the hotel were directed against the right-wing regime of the Greek Colonels. The situation got out of hand, violence erupted, a token handful of students was arrested (causing great resentment against the University proctors) and one of my fellow-undergraduates at Clare was charged, convicted, and sent (to general shock) to borstal. The more overheated imaginations among us could even speculate that this was the beginning of what we thought was occurring in France. Not much later came the Red Brigade in Germany – all somehow part, we would assume, of the break-up of the old order. Capitalism was over, we thought. The free market was over. Price controls were in; wage controls were coming in; and inevitably Britain would move towards a mixed social-market economy run by the trade unions, the CBI and a left-of-centre government.

To be smart or cool at Cambridge then was to listen to Joni Mitchell, Leonard Cohen, Janis Jopling and, of course, Dylan. Asked what you wanted to do after graduating, you talked earnestly of social work, the relief of poverty, helping out for no pay at a law centre somewhere, or – if you were a more establishment figure – joining the public sector. Business and finance were thought contemptible. When I ran for office in our college students' union I had to pretend to be an independent.

Did we even notice the Conservative Party winning the 1970 General Election? If we did, it was dismissed as a doomed, attempted counter-revolution – which of course at first it was.

But the world was changing, Britain was changing. Changing, however, in precisely the opposite direction from what we all assumed. The revolution up there in the stratosphere where the high clouds fly above the Fenland mists was a counter-revolution. Keith Joseph, that John-the-Baptist of Thatcherism, was making speeches about the end of compromise and a new, hard-edged Conservative fightback. The Red Brigade would go nowhere. Student unrest would peter out. Chairman Mao was not the future. Soviet Communism had (in retrospect) already over-reached itself. The battle for Vietnam would be lost, yes, but the battle against world Communism would be won. And most of my fellow-students would move into conventional jobs, many in the private sector, reverting to type.

Varsity cartoonist Robin Webster depicts the undergraduate politician, 1962.

Alex Allen with his afro hair and his huge Afghan coat was to end up as John Major's private secretary, fighting to keep the parade ground of St James's Palace as a civil service car-park; and after that as British High Commissioner in Canberra. Freaky James Lefanu was to end up writing as a doctor for the readers of the *Daily Telegraph*. Peter Stothard, shorn of his wild curls and de-shod of his daring little grey shoes, was to end up as editor of *The Times*, and ride the jet-stream with war-leader Tony Blair.

I said at the outset that my Cambridge days taught me something big. It is this: when people tell me that the War on Terror will last for 30 years; that China is the new Russia, Russia the new Germany or neo-Conservatism the new Marxism; that the latest drugs are set to overwhelm the younger generation (whither cannabis 1972? whither LSD?)... or that, in short, the hopes and terrors that loom largest among the cleverest people in the best universities during the keenest years of their lives are pointers to what is to come, I remember Cambridge, 1969–72. It was all a dead end.

Matthew Parris (1968)

I WENT up to King's in 1965, though things didn't start to get interesting until the following year. It was a time of immense change, though perhaps not as much as we imagined then. The Summer of Love was 1967, and while nobody from Cambridge – not even the women – went round with flowers in their hair, we did wear some pretty extraordinary garments under the gowns which were still obligatory for hall. Each new Beatles single was listened to time and again, culminating in *Sergeant Pepper* which kept us occupied for hours a day during May and June 1967. We bopped frenziedly to each Rolling Stones record, and some people even tried to get the 'poetry' of Bob Dylan onto the English Faculty syllabus.

I joined *Varsity* in my first week. As disillusion set in, with the Labour government and with Vietnam, politics became less respectable, and few from my generation were heading for Parliament. A whole generation of nearly men, Ken Clarke and Michael Howard, had already gone, and were languishing between the days of student glory and national fame. Journalism was becoming more respectable, and almost anyone from *Varsity* who chose to could find a job in Fleet Street. Our heroes were star reporters such as Nicholas Tomalin, not long graduated but already famously brave and possessed, as he said, of 'a plausible manner and rat-like cunning'.

The Labour Club changed its name to the Socialist Society, and having abandoned boring old leafleting outside factory gates, and passing resolutions against Vietnam (how they must have trembled in the White House!) we decided on direct action. Perhaps they did notice in Washington; it was a time of demonstrations, leading up to the *événements* of 1968. Maybe our mass protest outside the Senate House against Denis Healey – Defence Secretary at the time – helped in some small way to prove to Harold Wilson that there was far too much strife and political capital to be lost by sending the troops Lyndon Johnson wanted. The *Daily Express* sent an excitable reporter to interview these revolutionaries, before we left to become lawyers, accountants, public relations officers, television executives, hacks and, in some cases, to do useful jobs such as teaching.

Simon Hoggart (1965)

STUDENTS at Cambridge University in 1969, when I arrived, were very much caught up in the swirl of student activism which spread across much of the world. Paris 1968 and the Prague Spring were recent memories. There was deep feeling about the dictatorships in Greece, Spain and Portugal. We wanted to contest apartheid by urging universities and colleges to refuse to invest in South Africa. The Labour government was coming to a desultory end. Edward Heath's Tory government, which arrived in June 1970, seemed millions of miles from our concerns, a perception reinforced by their decision to expel from Britain Rudi Dutschke, the German student leader who had been shot and seriously wounded by a right-wing extremist.

It came closer to home too. University admissions policies, notably the general refusal to admit women, student finance, and student representation in relevant decisions on the curriculum and government of the University were just part of the policy cocktail which a wide range of opinion contested vigorously in just about every arena. We felt that change was needed and that it was down to us to make it happen.

This sometimes exhilarating mix led directly to the campaign to create in Cambridge a Students' Union through which representation could be made to the University and more widely.

This idea of a genuine students' union was commonplace elsewhere, powerful and popular since its existence depended upon regular affiliation votes by the colleges – often a nail-biting process.

Its meetings, often large and passionate, were accompanied by a wide range of political actions, including demonstrations, petitions, 'occupations' of University buildings, 'rent strikes' and the like which

Cambridge Students Union also suffers from being in a collegiate university. Although it is funded by college student unions, interest in C.S.U. remains low, as most students look to their colleges for their social life and to college J.C.R.s to deal with 'political' problems such as guest rules and room prices. Although the central union does run services and co-ordiate campaigns, it can not overcome the parochialism that a collegiate university inevitably suffers from. The dons encourage it. Parochialism is a sure safeguard against demands for any kind of radical change.

we are always ready to listen to students' views

Alternative Prospectus, 1979

Above: CUCA Committee, 1978:

Guy Brew writes: 'This photograph was taken after the "formal" one, which had included "Rab" Butler, then Master of Trinity, and President of CUCA at the time, which is why we were in Great Court. I am second from the left in the second row. James Callaghan was still Prime Minister, but in less than a year the "Winter of Discontent" and a General Election would bring the change in government we were working for, and put Margaret Thatcher in Number 10. Though most of us had a sincere interest in politics, and a number would go on to play an active role in the party, we also had a good time, enjoying our CUCA garden parties and annual champagne boat trips.

There are two current Conservative MPs in this group – David Lidington (Aylesbury), half way up the fountain on the right, and Andrew Mitchell (Sutton Coldfield) on the bottom row talking to Caroline Sargent. Top left, hands on hips, is Adair Turner, who became Director General of the CBI and then Chairman of the Pensions Commission.'

were at that time relatively commonplace across the country, though shocking in conservative Cambridge. Some of these led to University disciplinary proceedings, such as the enquiry into an occupation presided over by the legendary Lord Devlin. The University's counsel was Bob (later Lord, now sadly deceased) Alexander. I recall sacking the Students' Union's QC after the first day because I thought he wasn't putting our case strongly enough, and taking on the brief myself – a character-forming experience!

But these student actions did lead to many changes, now mostly unremarkable, which brought the University into the contemporary world. Our final and unsuccessful effort was to try and find a Student Union headquarters and social centre, in the form of a modernised Cambridge Union Debating Society. This change required success in a complicated sequence of votes, and finally we just failed, so that the Cambridge Union remains today unreformed and Cambridge still lacks a central students' union.

John Newbigin was the first President of the Cambridge Students Union, I the second and Mike Grabiner the third. There was an enormous constellation of participants, many of whom have found substantial fame or notoriety in later life. But I for one do not regret our efforts to promote change in the University and to try and give students more of a voice in the institutions of which they are a part.

Charles Clarke (1969)

1997

Had I been in search of historical ironies – as opposed to free food and drink – I might have noticed one on the day in 1996 that I attended a presentation, given by some investment bank or other, at the Garden House Hotel on Mill Lane. (I had no intention of working in investment banking, but as joint editor of *Varsity*, I'd published plenty of stories about the graduate recruitment 'milk round', and wanted to see it at first hand.) Those with memories of February 1970 will better remember the Garden House as the scene of violent protests against the Greek government; several Cambridge students ended up in jail. Twenty-six years later, we showed up not to riot, but to have dangled in front of us the kind of starting salaries we'd barely dreamed of. My only act of rebellion was not to accept – which doesn't count, because they never made me an offer.

It wasn't that professional concerns had replaced student politics, though; rather, student politics had become professionalised. The coming Blair landslide was a certainty; the next year, the *New Statesman* would publish a triumphalist book of interviews with Labour politicians, entitled *Preparing for Power*. To be involved

Varsity, 1996

A girl clad in a t-shirt with Che Guevara's face emblazoned across it recently cornered me at a party. She asked me whether I was a member of the Cambridge University Conservative Association. Yes, I said – I was. Suddenly, she erupted in a burst of hemp and long, uncombed hair. All students, she stated, should be radical by default. Anyone who deviated from the party line was nothing less than a traitor.

'Don't you want to save the world?' she exclaimed. I took a hefty swig of my drink.

'What, right now?' I asked. It was barely 10.30.

Walking unsteadily home at the end of the evening, I realised that she had a point. Consensus dictates that it is the sworn duty of every student to sit in a field smoking roll-ups whilst making low-budget films about homeless polar bears for the duration of their time at university. In a city whose political scene is dominated by soap-dodging eco-warriors and ferociously smug anarcho-pessimists, there is an undeniably reactionary element to what we do in the Cambridge University Conservative Association. We get dressed up in black tie on flimsy pretexts. We host parties during which cheese gets ground into carpets and port ends up staining the ceiling. We occasionally turn out en masse to oppose left-wing motions at the Cambridge Union.

However, the fact remains that Cambridge is not, and never has been, a hotbed of activism. CUCA has fought long and hard against a rising tide of political apathy for each one of its members. Last year, we resorted to shock tactics in a desperate attempt to boost our numbers. Two of our female committee members bravely volunteered to pose by our stand at the University Freshers' Fair wearing naught but Union Jack bikinis and inviting smiles. Their efforts were rewarded with a truly spectacular boom in membership.

Far be it from me to suggest that we present a united front. This is politics, and factional intrigues (the like of which have not been seen since Cardinal Wolsey put up a few backs in the court of Henry VIII) dominate the proceedings. Back after back is routinely stabbed during election season, and the minutes of CUCA committee meetings read like a transcript of an all-in wrestling match. The casual observer must wonder what it is that keeps us together in one piece. Sometimes I wonder too. Of course, the career prospects for members are excellent. The eight consecutive CUCA chairmen who served during the Golden Age of the late 1960s that were subsequently elected to Parliament need no introduction. But beyond this is the incontestable truth behind the cliché – that the closest friendships are those forged in times of adversity. Canvassing in a city without a single Conservative councillor to its name binds every single member of CUCA in linkages that last. I believe that there will always be a table in the corner at Cambridge weddings packed with former members of the association, all of whom will be fondly reminiscing about the time that an elderly man with an Alsatian and a string vest chased them half-way around Cherry Hinton for pushing a leaflet through his letterbox.

Emma Hughes

(2004)

Sit-down rent protest on Trumpington Street, 1999.

Stop the War demonstrators in the corridors of the Gordon Laboratory, Department of Materials Science, which carries out defence research, October 2002.

Then, at 6am, in my capacity as student journalist, I staggered down St Andrew's Street to be interviewed at BBC Radio Cambridge, where I bumped into the city's newly-elected MP, Anne Campbell. Then I went back to my room and fell asleep, to the sound of the *Today* programme announcing the dawn of a new era.

Oliver Burkman (1994)

Protests as French Front National leader Jean-Marie Le Pen arrives to address the Union Society, April 2003.

with student politics in any serious way meant establishing yourself as a major player in Cambridge Labour Students. And, sure enough, within a year or so of graduating, the names I'd written about in *Varsity* started cropping up as special advisers in Downing Street.

The atmosphere was heady with anticipation of the end of the sclerotic old guard, and the start of something new. But one strange side-effect was the way it rendered some Cambridge Tories endearing, even to those of my political leanings. I'd arrived at Christ's College from a northern comprehensive (although not, to be honest, a very gritty one) and the port-drinking student traditionalists I encountered were somehow immensely appealing. With the way things were going, few of them held hopes of political careers. It would be almost a decade before the Conservatives looked remotely electable again. That laid-back lack of ambition was something I needed to imbibe, if only as an antidote to my own overwrought approach to essays and exams. And so, in May 1997, I toasted the dawn of the Blair years – this was before George Bush came along to complicate matters, of course – but I did so with a glass of port, in a smart set of rooms in Christ's, in the company of a number of people who'd voted for John Major.

Counting ballot papers after CUSU elections, 2007.

Debating and the Union Society

STEPHEN PARKINSON

Older than 14 colleges, the Boat Race, and Trinity May Ball, the Cambridge Union has long been an important part of Cambridge life. It is, first and foremost, a debating society – though the style of its weekly debates has changed over the generations. Guest speakers were first invited in the 1880s and, whereas the debates of the 1950s and 1960s were still predominantly between student debaters, with one invited speaker on each side, those of the last 20 years have tended to include a larger number of guests, with students relegated to the opening speeches (or filling in for the inevitable last-minute cancellations). Purists lament the preponderance of Big Brother 'stars' who have visited the Union in recent years, but then the man who brought the programme to British screens, Peter Bazalgette, is an ex-President himself.

In fact, today's motions are just as serious as those of earlier generations. Many motions debated 40 years ago are re-run today with little variation. The Union has regularly considered whether the American Dream is the world's nightmare (firmly deciding, under Bush, that it is), and motions on Israel and Palestine still guarantee the most lively and divided Houses. The motion of 'No Confidence' in Her Majesty's Government remains an annual tradition: the New Labour governments have held the confidence of the present generation with very few exceptions – and did so again by 236 to 205 votes last year. Even the invasion of Iraq, which the Union opposed from the outset, has done little to shake its support.

But other universities have debating societies; what makes the Union different is that it has always been much more besides. It is a private members' club, a bolt-hole

Varsity 1955

Left: Debating Chamber of the all-male Union Society, 1962.

Christopher Angeloglou

Right: Stained-glass window from the Union Society building.

from college, and still the only central student venue. Even in its earliest days, members joined the Union for reasons other than debating. In the 19th century, its clubhouse facilities were the main draw. Out of the first Union ball in 1954 grew Union 'Ents', now a thriving part of the Union's activities. The bar, not pictured in pre-war recruitment leaflets sent to freshmen for fear of concerning their parents, now hosts regular 'club nights'.

Some of the Union's activities have withered, of course: the kitchens which once employed four staff to provide lunches and teas for members have stood empty for a decade. But the decline started long before; daily meals began to tail off from the mid-1960s as undergraduates were lured away by new snack bars and hang-outs, both in colleges and around the city.

Union membership today includes some 5,000 resident members of the University. The best year for recruitment was in 1978–9, when 2,278 new members (72 per cent of freshmen) signed up. The Labour Students organised an anti-Union campaign throughout the 1980s, but never seriously dented the Union's figures.

Because of its restricted membership, the Union has never pretended to be representative of the student body, though there has often been considerable outside interest in its deliberations. In 1939, when it debated conscription, pictures of the debate were wired to London for the following day's *Daily Express*, which described it as Cambridge's 'Parliament'. But the Union has rarely presumed to act as

Union Committee, Easter 1963, including three future Conservative Cabinet ministers: Kenneth Clarke (centre, seated), Michael Howard (centre, standing) and Norman Lamont (far right, standing). Mani Ayar (far left, seated), became a minister in the government of India.

There were some of our contemporaries in the early 1970s who argued that the Union was a busted flush, that it no longer represented serious political debate and discussion, but was a place where silly undergraduates dressed up and spouted on and tried to avoid seeming too ambitious. I like to think we proved them wrong. My recollections of the Union are of a place where there was intense debate, where serious positions were argued out, where political ideals were turned over and over and matched against reality, and where some of the most inspiring and engaging political figures of the day came to speak and to be questioned. Yes, of course there was some silliness along the way. We were students, having fun. But I can think of no better preparation for the serious world of politics and public life.

Germaine Greer came to debate against William Buckley on women's liberation, to a packed Chamber where you could have heard a pin drop. Judith Todd and Trevor Huddleston swept their audience of its feet with their passion about what was happening to what was then Rhodesia. John Mortimer inveighed against censorship; Hugh MacDiarmid argued for Scottish independence; Harold Wilson talked about his first period of government; Donald Soper lifted our moral sights; Eugene McCarthy spoke of his presidential campaign that had transformed American politics. My own final 'Presidential Debate' was on the motion 'Liberty is meaningless outside the context of Equality'; and I'd table the same motion again today if I had half the chance. These were some of the great issues of the day, and here was an opportunity to hear about them, learn about them, speak out about them, and test our own views and advocacy against both our peers and those who had a lifetime of experience behind them. No busted flush here.

And at the same time as we were exploring these great national and global themes we were also engaged in our own internal Cambridge crusade – to create what was called 'the Open Union', our attempt to throw open the social facilities and activities of the Union to the whole student body and to establish a real social centre for the University. Passions ran high. Standing Committee elections were determined by whether you were for or against the Open Union. And we nearly succeeded: we won the argument amongst the Union's own membership, we won over the University authorities, we won the popular vote amongst students as a whole, and we even won in every single college bar one. But because we failed in that one college we couldn't make the change. One of the great 'what-nearly-happened' moments of student history.

I wouldn't have missed any of it for the world. The internal battles, the great debates, the issues and ideas and lessons learned. And when I eventually ended up in the Commons, I found that the place was very different, but that the issues, the ideas and the lessons were to stand me in very good stead.

Chris Smith (Lord Smith of Finsbury)
(1969)

Above: Anne Mallalieu, first woman to be elected President of the Union Society, in Michaelmas Term 1967. Her final, Presidential, debate was on the motion that 'The game is more important than the score'. This led, appropriately, to a career in law and politics, when she became a QC and then a Labour peer.

The Union was an all-male society until 1963, but those who deprecate the slow pace of change should remember that the Union opened its doors to both sexes before any of the colleges did. There have been 21 female Presidents since Ann Mallalieu became the first in 1967. The 2005–6 academic year was the first with three successive women in the chair.

Yet the Union retains something of a traditionalist image, and a reputation for a pro-Tory bias. The so-called 'Cambridge Mafia' of Leon Brittan, John Gummer, Michael Howard, Ken Clarke and Norman Lamont – all Presidents in 1960–4 and later Cabinet ministers – certainly does much to sustain this. But there have been strong periods for the Left too: two of the last Presidents before the Second World War (and one in the midst of the 'Mafia') were Communists, and there was a strong period of Labour involvement in the late 1960s and early 1970s. Chris Smith and Hélène Hayman, both ex-Presidents, are now in the Lords; Patricia Hewitt was on the Union's Standing Committee; and Hugh Anderson would very likely have risen to prominence had he not died of cancer shortly after his presidency in 1969.

such. While its subjects for debate have long included hot topics within the University, the Union only really captures the attention of Cambridge as a whole when the society itself is the story – usually for upholding the principles of free speech. There was a sit-in at the Union to try to stop Enoch Powell speaking in 1969, but this – alongside the Garden House Riot – was the closest Cambridge came to the spirit of the *soixante-huitards*. More recently, protesters tried to disrupt a meeting with Jean-Marie Le Pen in 2003, but a packed Chamber showed its disdain for him more effectively: with searching questions and free debate.

A prime reason for the under-representation of left-leaning undergraduates since the 1970s has probably been the establishment of a separate students' union, which has created a rival political sphere for those so inclined. Anyone wanting to boycott Nestlé, impose a corporate view about abortion, or offer 'no platform' to those they disagree with, now have another vehicle in the shape of CUSU, while the Union continues to hold debates purely for the sake of debating. A campaign in the early 1980s sought to persuade the Union to move its bank account and cancel speakers as a stance against apartheid, but rows today tend to be restricted to the Union's perpetually arcane electoral rules, or whether speakers should continue to wear black tie. (It was most recently abolished by an incoming President in 2002, but brought back immediately by his successor.)

Whatever their politics, the Union has acquired, and perhaps nurtured, a reputation for being a stepping-stone towards a political career. Twenty-four Presidents since the Second World War have become MPs; 17 (with some overlap) have entered the House of Lords. But for all their successes, and despite the record of its younger sister at

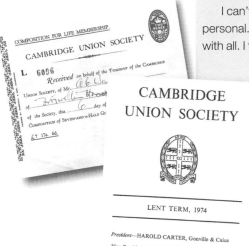

Left: Union debate, 28 November 2007. Speakers debating the motion 'This House believes the comprehensive system is failing Britain's poor' included Anthony Seldon, Master of Wellington College, journalist Peter Hitchens and David Chaytnor, Labour MP for Bury North.

CAMBRIDGE
UNION SOCIETY

LENT TERM, 1974

President—HAROLD CARTER, Gonville & Caius

Vice-President—TOBY HARRIS, Trinity

Secretary—STEPHEN WEIL, Jesus

*Standing
Committee*—DAVID HOLDER, Corpus Christi
TALMAI MORGAN, Emmanuel
DAVID BEAN, Trinity Hall
SUSAN PACK, Lucy Cavendish
SHEILA BRIGGS, Newnham
SANDY WALKINGTON, Trinity Hall

Junior Treasurer—BRADOC GALLANT, Pembroke

Director of Entertainments—ALAN LARKMAN, Selwyn

Treasurer—R. C. ANDREW, M.A., Sidney Sussex

Librarian—D. McKITTERICK, M.A., St. John's

Steward—S. M. SCHAMA, M.A., Christ's

Chief Clerk—ROLAND THOMPSON

Assistant Clerk—BARRY THODAY

I have to admit I only joined the Union by accident. Before coming up I hadn't the faintest idea what it was. Indeed, it was only when a fellow freshman, who I assumed was less sophisticated, announced he had joined that I rushed to do so. But it was a gamble.

As I was shown around, in the awed company of hushed undergraduates, I heard an announcement about a freshmen's debating competition. It whetted my appetite. I decided to enter. In the final round, the motion was: 'This House prefers Marks and Spencer to Spencer and Marx'. I weighed in on the side of the latter, exuding all the deliberate learning of an expensive Indian education. What I lacked in rhetoric – and it was quite a bit – I made up for with erudition. And I won.

Two months later a second accident added to my fortunes. The undergraduate opposing the sixth debate of term fortuitously fell ill. Stephen Weil, the Union President, perhaps inspired by my freshman victory, asked if I would take his place. The motion was 'This House reaffirms its faith in America'. The other guests were Charles Wheeler of the BBC, Anthony Howard of the *New Statesmen* and Birch Bayh, a US Senator. I decided to be witty. 'America,' I pronounced, 'is a Coca-Cola culture, swamped by Ginger Ale, Seven Up and Canada Dry.' It wasn't really funny but it had the House in stitches.

By the end of my first term I had attracted enough attention to risk an act of audacious temerity: I stood for election to the Union Standing Committee. The combination of an English-speaking wog, whose name led many to believe he was a girl, with a talent for daringly speaking out, resulted in a collection of votes – no doubt some mistaken – that proved hard to beat.

I can't say the Union career that followed was political. It was personal. I sought to be independent, hoping that would find favour with all. I tried to be striking, even outrageous, convinced that if I stood out I would be remembered. And, without being provincial, I was determined to be Indian.

I was elected President for the Lent Term of 1977. Determined to be different, my first event was not a debate but a concert: Ravi Shankar playing at King's College Chapel. It ended with my presidential debate, just days before the 1977 elections in India, and the end of the Emergency. Perhaps I had sensed change in the air. Or perhaps I was risking my luck. But instead of handing over to my successor I staged a mock coup, declared my own emergency and announced I would continue in office!

Alas, I spent so much time on this gimmick I was poorly prepared for the debate that followed. I fear I was a disappointment. That the motion 'Equality should be the first principle' was carried is a tribute to the generosity of the House and the large-heartedness of Union tradition that always ensures the retiring President wins.

Karan Thapar
(1974)

Maybe I was naïve or ignorant, or indeed both, but I did not quite realise what I was getting involved in when I stood to be a member of the Committee at the Union. I was 'fast-tracked' by an ambitious and sharp co-member who saw an opportunity to challenge for Vice-President and wanted me on his ticket as Secretary.

He had some vision of us being a 'dream team' and it seemed to work. I was then elected as V-P without too much trouble but when it came to the election for President, things were very different. It seems I was making progress too quickly and too easily and as I was only in my second year, quite rightly a very strong challenger decided to oppose me. This is when I became aware that politics can be a dirty business. I was accused of having no plans, no vision and no real interest in the Union. It was not unlike the usual barrage during a General Election. I was the target of a very focused and clever campaign.

Luckily, I had friends who were much more streetwise than me. I shamelessly deployed the talents of Matthew Gould, a friend with great intellect and a marketing skill from which I would learn. He designed my manifesto and, beating Tony Blair to the post by a good few years, we went for style over substance. The photograph of me was as glamorous as we could manage, the debate topics were light and fun, as befits an Easter Term when everyone has exams to worry about.

'This House Believes it's the Winning, not the Taking Part that Counts' was an early sign of my inclination towards sport while the presidential debate, 'This House Believes that Blondes Have More Fun' was deliberately daft. It worked, but only just. The election result was incredibly close and for the first time I realised that I cared about it. As President, I don't think I changed the world but I'm not sure that many people have ever been able to exert much influence over the permanent staff, who viewed any suggestions of change as if it was the work of dangerous revolutionaries.

I think the Union experience taught me more about the real world than almost anything else in my formative years. I learnt to think on my feet, to argue persuasively for things I believed in and for things I did not, to trust some people but not all. I practised oral acrobatics on a weekly basis, which proved to be invaluable training for my life as a broadcaster.

I would also like to thank the Union for allowing me to sit between two Tory MPs – one who was a current Cabinet minister and the other who had recently been 'moved sideways'. In the space of an hour, the previously attractive idea of working in politics became an anathema. What a blessing, for everyone. I am pleased to say that Matthew, the brains behind my election success, went on to write speeches for Robin Cook, among others. We both ended up in careers that suited our skills.

Clare Balding
(1990)

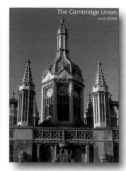

Oxford, the Union has never produced a Prime Minister. In fact, none of the Cantabrigian premiers since the Union's foundation in 1815 spoke there as undergraduates.

Plenty of Union officers have achieved great things in fields other than politics, however; they include an Olympic medallist, an Oscar nominee, and two winners of the Nobel Peace Prize. Probably the most famous ex-President is one who was only peripherally political: John Maynard Keynes in 1905. Fewer alumni seem to go into politics now; of the 24 post-war Presidents to enter the Commons, only four were Presidents since 1970. But perhaps this is unfair: recent vintages take time to mature. Plenty of ex-Presidents lurk below the surface in the same professions as their predecessors – principally law, politics and journalism. Only the numbers going into the Church have declined. Whether the Union creates the leaders of future generations or is merely a magnet for them in their ambitious early years is a subject for debate itself. But one thing is certain: those whose names you hear in its Chamber are among those you are most likely to hear again long after Cambridge.

Stephen Parkinson was President of the Union, Lent 2004. *His book* Recollections of the Cambridge Union 1939–1990 *will be published in 2009.*

On Ambition

If you go look in that cupboard, or on your wardrobe top shelf, you'll find that now sepia-riddled matriculation photo purchased all those many years ago. Take it out, dust it off and peer at the fading tableau of times past.

Though some of those present that day will still be in your life now – the life-long friends in whose pockets you lived throughout your time by the Cam – there are others which are familiar, but were known only from a distance then and, if they remain known now, it is only from the television, the newspaper or the occasional West End trip. They are the Union hack, the *Varsity* scribe, the ADC dilettante, the CUSU politician and those who dabbled in CUCA or the Labour Club. For some of them Cambridge was the place where they would seek Warhol's 15 minutes; for others, that limelight now stretches into years, if not decades. These were Cambridge's celebrities, those who decided that the greasy pole was to be their home for their three-year stretch, those the rest of the University looked on sometimes with adoration, contempt or mild amusement.

However, the reality is that this is something that is somewhere in all of us, just more obvious in some than others. To have ended up here in the first place, ambition in some guise must be a part of one's make-up: why otherwise would you put yourself through the rigmarole of actually getting into this place? Having 15,000 intelligent, aspirational people living in each other's pockets for three years is never going to result in a feast of apathy and sloth. Hence it is no surprise that 'hackery', a word that appears only to be used in this manner here and in the Other Place, is an unchanging constant in Cambridge life.

However, there are two things that should temper any grudging respect to those who let their ambition run untamed during their time in the Fens. The first is that prominence and position, if that is what you seek for your university life, is not a difficult thing to achieve. Cambridge is a small town, naturally introspective, and there are innumerable societies of which you can become treasurer, secretary or president. Only a limited number of these require any real talent to climb upwards, and even then the pool is small and some always slip through the net, as a bad night at the Corpus Playroom would show only too soon. Even when the filter does actually work, really talentless little Napoleons can always console themselves that the world of college economics societies and departmental yoga clubs is there for the taking. Cynics would say the Union would be the purest representation of this. Cynics would probably be right.

The second, and many would say worse, problem is that of seeking prominence for its own sake alone. The Varsity 100 is today the ultimate representation of all that is wrong with Cambridge's priorities. In it the hundred 'most powerful' students are listed, pictured and lauded. Having morphed into an annual event of shameless self-aggrandisement it is a monster that feeds the cult of the Cambridge celebrity.

The Varsity 100 list. Celebrity journalism comes to Cambridge.

However, not all do it for fame or out of pure ambition, and those who do it because they believe that what they're doing is good/right are by no means guaranteed to do a better job. A clumsy assessment of my random-sample three years of CUSU would be that whilst all three presidents had talent, two appeared to care as much for the trappings of the position and what it offered for the future as for the job itself, whilst another cared nothing for his public profile, kept his head down, and worked hard. He was, as it turned out, the most ineffective of the three. The other two negotiated their year well, made good use of the springboard, and made great use of their talents after leaving the Fens.

And in reality all this manoeuvring, elections and seemingly annual Union presidential scandals are utterly harmless and meaningless in all but the most exceptional cases. The safe learning environment of Cambridge allows you to make mistakes while it doesn't cost the earth to do so, and while leading the Union or the ADC is hardly akin to running the country, or the National Theatre, at least some practice in managing something meaningless is likely to mean there are fewer mistakes to make when you are finally in charge of running something that matters. And for those who come to ambition later in life all is far from lost. Although when Michael Howard faced Jeremy Paxman in the run-up to the 2005 General Election it was the same set-up as it had been in their student days, many other key players in the approach to the ballot box – Alistair Campbell, the *Guardian*'s Alan Rushbridger notable among them – had passed through Cambridge with barely a ripple. Though student hackery is a good training ground, it is hardly the only way to the top.

Tom Ebbutt was editor of *Varsity* in Michaelmas 2002 and inventor of the annual 'Varsity 100'.

Extending access in a digital age

P ETER F OX

A post-doctoral research Fellow arrives in Cambridge to embark on a new project to investigate the psychological impact of exposure to battlefield stress. She is interested not only in the current state of knowledge about Post-Traumatic Stress Disorder (PTSD) also but in historical manifestations of the condition. From her laboratory she carries out a literature search on the University Library's *Newton* online catalogue, its electronic resources and the e-journals@cambridge website. These direct her to books and journals on current medical research as well as providing her with online access to electronic journals and a range of online abstracting services and databases.

In order to enlarge the scope of her study on the historical aspects of PTSD she walks over to the University Library, where the Reading Room staff show her the subject bibliographies and direct her to the open-access parts of the Library where she can browse the psychology and medicine sections. Psychiatry and psychology are one of the Library's many areas of strength, and she finds books not only in English but also in other languages, especially German, which she reads fluently.

She is keen to consult primary sources, and in the Rare Books Reading Room the specialist staff suggest that she looks at the books in the Hunter Collection, a private library on the history of psychiatric treatment, acquired by the University Library in 1982. For PTSD as experienced by soldiers during and after the First World War she is thrilled to discover the First World War collection, a treasure-trove of ephemera and pamphlets collected at the time. In the Manuscripts

Opposite: The Reading Room, 2008.

Left: West Room and Dome Room, in the Old University Library, *1800, by Thomas Rowlandson.*

I came up to Emma in 1954 from National Service. During lectures and labs at the Cavendish I fell under the spell of a charming Newnham undergraduate. Having read a pirated copy of *Lady Chatterley's Lover* in Paris, with its refreshing treatment of human sexuality, I thought it might be nice for her to read it. So I pedalled up to the University Library, wrote out the reference slip, and gave it to the young woman at the desk. She read it, paled and reached under the counter and pressed what must have been some sort of bank robbery alarm bell. Instantly an older man appeared, and, after hearing what I wanted, told the clerk to leave and that he would handle this.

He explained to me that the book I wanted was forbidden by the Lord Chancellor of England and locked, with similar books, in a glass case behind the Chief Librarian's desk. However, if I really wanted to read it I could make arrangements to do so, sitting in a special room while watched by some sort of invigilator. He was horrified when I explained that I only wanted to lend the novel to a student at Newnham. That is completely out of the question, he ruled, and I returned to my college rather upset. I decided to write a letter of protest to the Chief Librarian, and did so, finishing up with the sentence: 'Mrs Grundy might have been delighted with these arrangements but as an ex-National Service commissioned officer, I am appalled.'

Two weeks later the college porter handed me a card from the Master inviting me for sherry at the Lodge. My friends immediately sensed trouble. I arrived at the Lodge next afternoon to find the Senior Tutor and my own tutor waiting with the Master all trying to keep straight faces. My tutor handed me back my letter to the Librarian and asked if I had written it. I admitted that I had. The Master said: 'Well, Lee, you've really gone and done it now. You are going to have to make arrangements to apologise to this eminent man of letters or it looks as though we might have to send you down!'

I was enjoying Emmanuel far too much to make an issue and quickly made arrangements to meet with the man I had so impetuously compared to Mrs Grundy. Wearing my best suit and gown I entered his office. He suggested that my agenda in wishing to borrow the book was one of lechery and seduction, and he made it clear that it was totally unacceptable to him and the University. I wasn't in a position to argue and returned to my rooms in North Court with the apology grudgingly accepted. Five years later, Penguin Books won its famous case and the book is now to be found in every public library in the western world.

Ken Lee
(1954)

"*The sight of such a building would effectually deter a student from paying it a visit. I do not know whether it is too late, or if we are irrevocably bound to this motor factory, or steam laundry, or whatever the model is; but if not, some physician ought to administer an emetic to the Buildings Syndicate.*"

Letter to the *Cambridge Review*, October 1929, from W.H.D. Rouse, Headmaster of the Perse School

Topping out the tower of the new University Library in 1930.

The low building across the courtyard houses the Newton Catalogue room.

Bliss in North Front 4

There is only one thing better than having the Information Superhighway on your doorstep and that is being able to borrow vehicles to whizz along it. The Cambridge University Library provides the first boon to all members of the University (plus others) and the second to MAs (Cantab). Once through those massive portals, readers have access not only to a vast array of manuscript material and electronic information but *mirabile dictu* to books … on open shelves. They can thus employ to the full that incomparable tool of academic research, serendipity. And graduates can take home the fruits of their browsing for perusal at leisure.

These two boons, unique in a British legal deposit library, have kept me in Cambridge for nearly half a century. As an undergraduate I quickly learned to love the UL, which was so much greater than the Seeley (then adjoining St Mary's Passage) in amplitude and abundance. I was delighted to do my PhD on the Oxford Movement in Cambridge, for I came across innumerable calf-bound volumes in the stacks, occasionally with their pages uncut, that did not appear in bibliographies. Some were anonymous collections of Victorian divinity simply entitled *Tracts*, which gave my thesis an entirely fortuitous (not to say spurious) erudition. I would never have discovered such items in the Bodleian, where you have to know what you are looking for in order to request it and it takes time to arrive – some Oxford dons find it easier to drive over to Cambridge to pursue their studies.

Later, whether writing lectures or doing book reviews or earning my bread as a jobbing author, I found the UL a priceless resource. In fact, it's hard to understand how historians and others can produce books without having access to such a treasury of knowledge. The London Library is excellent, of course, but its holdings are dwarfed by those of the UL and distant readers have to get their books by post, a laborious and costly process. The British Library and, still more, the Library of Congress, eclipse the UL in size but you have to be on the spot to use them.

Certainly the Cambridge University Library has gaps – when writing recently about the British Empire I found a particular paucity of foreign publications – and it needs the resources to fill them. It is not perfect in other respects. Over the years it has inevitably become busier and more bureaucratic. The computerised catalogue remains temperamental. New books are slow to arrive and missing ones are slower to be replaced. A few readers take advantage of the UL's liberal regime to treat it as a club. Despite injunctions against its use, the mobile phone remains a menace, filling the stacks with a maddening susurrus.

Yet these are insignificant blemishes on an institution which not only provides the University with the sinews of scholarship but affords individuals the unutterable thrill of intellectual discovery. Most of my life has been devoted to reading and writing; and both activities have been marvellously facilitated by the UL, which I regard as a blissful home from home. If there is an afterlife, I hope to spend it haunting the place; you may encounter me in the region of North Front 4.

Piers Brendon (1960) is a Fellow of Churchill College and author of *The Dark Valley* and *The Decline and Fall of the British Empire*.

Reading Room she finds several collections of war diaries and letters written home by officers and men serving on the Western Front. These include the correspondence of Edward Dent, Professor of Music at Cambridge, with graduates serving in France including the poet Siegfried Sassoon, and, of particular relevance to her current interests, the diary of Lieutenant Colonel Herbert Crocker, commander of the Cheshire Regiment in Iraq in 1917–18, which came to the Library with the Royal Commonwealth Society collections.

She becomes a regular user of the Library.

This is a scene played out daily by scholars and students in all subjects finding new ways to exploit the UL's collections to support their current research needs. For the last 600 years, the Library has been at the heart of the teaching and learning process in the University, providing its members with access to one of the world's great collections of books, manuscripts and journals.

That collection was housed for most of its existence in the Old Schools, in the centre of the city, a range of buildings now occupied mainly by the University's administrators. In the 1920s, when the site had become so crowded that it could no longer accommodate the Library, a new location was found in what was then the outskirts of the University. Though greeted at the time with consternation by those who felt that having to cross the river to get to their library marked the beginning of the end of civilisation, the move proved to be a decision of remarkable foresight. It facilitated a rethinking of the role of the university library in the early 20th century, with the result that, following the North American, rather than the European, model, the new building was constructed with a range of specialist reading rooms, but, most importantly it had large areas of open-access shelving. Still today the UL is believed to have the largest collection of books in Europe to which readers have direct access – around two million. The

Left: A fragment of a Genizah manuscript, a rich source of evidence relating to the medieval world of the Mediterranean area, which came from a collection of synagogue records in Cairo and is one of the treasures of the University Library.

variety of working spaces, so that the needs of readers who like to study in proximity to others or who like to hide themselves away in corners are equally provided for. The ethos among the staff is to facilitate the research of their readers – indeed the scenario above shows how the specialist knowledge of Library staff can not only support it but actually help to shape a research project. The scenario also demonstrates how a great library is more than just the sum of its parts. The collections may have come from disparate sources and at different times, but it is the links between them – often links that are identified through the knowledge of the Library staff – that enable new connections to be made and new insights gained.

The scenario also shows how the electronic revolution has transformed, and complicated, the work and services of the Library in the last decade. Users' information needs are far from homogeneous. At one end of the spectrum is the 'information consumer' of the Google generation, who expects seamless online access to all the information he or she needs. At the other end is the traditional scholar, usually in a humanities discipline, for whom paper-based documents and books are still the predominant research resource. For the majority at present, a 'hybrid' library service is what is needed, offering a combination of online and traditional resources, supplemented by the assistance of expert staff, either working online or in reading rooms.

The Library's approach to these 21st-century challenges is to continue to provide physical access to the collections whilst at the same time making more and more of them accessible via the internet. The first stage of this process is to provide access to the finding aids – the catalogues – from anywhere in the world. Records for most of the

site was much larger than the building placed upon it but that space was reserved for future expansion. In the last decade the Library building has grown considerably, and once the final phase of the current development is completed, the physical needs of readers, the collections and the staff will be met well into the 21st century. Though less extensive than the British Library or the Bodleian, the UL's collection is still enormous – if all the shelves were placed end-to-end, they would stretch from Cambridge to Brighton.

But size is not everything, and what makes the UL such a special place is a combination of its 'user-friendliness' and its collections. As well as the facility to browse among the open-access stacks and (for members of the University) to borrow from them, the building has a

For me, one of the most delicious aspects of studying at Cambridge was using the University Library. As a student of social and political sciences, access to books was a constant issue. The Tripos had expanded massively in the years preceding my arrival and the faculty library was under constant pressure. So I often found myself popping over the road to the sinister colossus that was the University Library. I loved it. The rabbit warrens of open-access stacks felt womb-like: a secure cocoon of scholarship. The idea that one could find nearly anything either on the shelves or by completing an order slip was intoxicating. One day I found myself flicking through a *Who's Who* of the former East Germany, just because I could. The Library was full of characters. The 'wolfman' (so-called by my contemporaries for his extravagant mutton-chop sideburns) stalked the corridors in plus-fours, mumbling to himself. I loved to spy on the venerable old dons, squinting through their reading glasses at some important tome. Whereas I diligently produced reams of notes, I watched in awe at how aged scholars merely wrote down the odd word on an index card. The best thing of all? The tea room to which one could repair to discuss lofty matters over cake. How eminently civilised.

Keith Kahn-Harris
(1991)

Above: One of the Library's many treasured medieval manuscripts: the 'Mass of St Gregory' *from a* 15th-century Book of Hours.

Legal Deposit

Every Thursday afternoon a van arrives at the University Library loaded with around 1,500 books and 2,000 issues of periodicals, together with hundreds of maps and pieces of sheet music. This is the Library's intake of materials received by legal deposit, a right that it shares with the British Library, the university libraries of Oxford and Dublin (Trinity College), and the national libraries of Scotland and Wales. Cambridge University Library became a legal deposit library as a result of the Copyright Act of 1710 and because legal deposit and copyright provisions were enshrined in the same acts until the 20th century, the libraries are still popularly referred to as 'copyright libraries'. The Legal Deposit Libraries Act of 2003 reiterated the right of the legal deposit libraries to receive a copy of all publications printed in the UK and Ireland and also laid the foundations for extending this right to electronic publications.

Each year Cambridge receives some 70,000 monographs by legal deposit and 100,000 journal issues, in addition to items purchased from around the world. The great majority are delivered in multiple copies to the London-based Agent for the Legal Deposit Libraries which acts for and distributes to five of the six libraries (the British Library receives its deposited copies directly). Cambridge's weekly consignment ranges from popular magazines to learned journals, from encyclopaedias and scholarly monographs to the latest Jeffrey Archer novel. On arrival, books, periodicals, maps and sheet music are sent to the specialist departments for processing. Books are divided into categories representing primary or secondary academic importance and the former are prioritised for cataloguing. Reference books and items of interest to specialist reading rooms or to dependent libraries such as the Medical Library or the Squire Law Library are identified and distributed. Books specifically requested by readers are made immediately available in the Reading Room.

To facilitate co-operation, most libraries follow international standards which determine how a book is described, what elements are indexed in catalogues, how its subject is consistently expressed, what standardised form is used for an author's name and how this information is coded for a computer to process. Cambridge expects to be able to find and use catalogue records for many of its books from external sources but also makes available its own original cataloguing for the reciprocal benefit of libraries worldwide. Even when records can be found, the consistency of their relationship to the existing local catalogue needs to be checked – does a book about Trinity College Cambridge appear in the catalogue under 'Trinity College Cambridge', 'Cambridge. Trinity College', 'Cambridge. University. Trinity College', 'University of Cambridge. Trinity College'? In a catalogue of several million records, it is essential to maintain consistency if books on the same topic or by the same author are to be found by one search.

Cambridge uses its own classification system for the subject arrangement of books on open shelves and has its own criteria for determining whether books are to be borrowable or restricted for use in particular reading rooms. Implementation of these decisions will often involve the need to bind or laminate paperbacks, processes which are carried out in the Library. Books then receive a unique classmark. A barcode, similarly unique, links the bibliographic description to the physical item or items it represents, allowing the catalogue to tell when a book is on loan. Finally, spine labels are produced and, in the case of borrowable books, the week's output emerges in the new books display near the Library entrance every Friday morning.

Stephen Hills is Head of English Cataloguing and Cataloguing Policy.

Library's printed books can now be searched online through the Newton catalogue, and a growing proportion of the records for manuscripts and archives can be found through the Janus website. More and more full-text services are being offered, with readers now able to consult over 20,000 electronic journals and over a quarter of a million e-books. The Library's own collections are also being digitised and made available over the internet, with special emphasis being placed on the unique items, such as the papers of the great Cambridge scientists Newton and Darwin, photographs of the Empire from the Royal Commonwealth Society collections, the immensely important collection of Jewish documents in the Genizah collection, and medieval manuscript treasures such as the 13th-century Anglo-Norman verse life of St Edward the Confessor.

The University Library has been described in a national newspaper as 'the nearest thing to Paradise that this world has to offer'. For many scholars it is the reason they stay in Cambridge. We intend to keep it as relevant to the scholars and students of the future as it has been for much of the University's past.

Peter Fox has been University Librarian since 1994 and is a Fellow of Selwyn College.

Right: Working in the library stacks.

A SPECIMEN of the Letters belonging to the University of CAMBRIDGE.

A B C D
A B C D E
A B C D E F
A B C D E F

Two Lines English.

Quousque tandem a-butere, Catilina, pati-
O dii immortales! ubi

Double Pica.

Atque super vitâ plaudere, morte queri.   mmoda vixit
Tros Tyriusque   Britannis

Paragon.

Death only now appears to ease their Grief,   Death, the
Jove'sOsiers Woods, Floods. Powers

Best Great Primmer.

Manner of Yard-Wide Stuffs what-soever all Black Durants, and Rashes
Features of Him here, tho' true, but

Old Great Primmer.

is now compelled by his great Losses, to implore the Relief of Charitable
Anno Dom. 1730. *December, Novem-*

Oldest Great Primmer very much used.

mention'd in a Statute made in the first Year of the Reign of our most gracious
Prince of Wales, and his Open and Se-

Best English.

Old English N. 3. very much used.

ACCA AUREUS videbir sic tamenduas
Baccalaureus in actum per se vel quàm ju

Best Pica much used.

956 Cicero de Divinatione a Davisio   Cant. 1721
91 *Lucien de la Traduction de N. P. Sieur D'Ablan-*

Old Pica very much used.

Homas Edwards Arm. Ballivus Libertat' Epis' *Ee*
de ssign. ad om' pred' tenend. *Om' G* ad respontn

Best Long Primmer.

nus; quare legit, *ille in infinita*-II. pag. 17. Sane, quod mo
nuit *tem omnem peregrinabatur.* Viro*Velleius Paterculus* lib. I

Old Long Primmer N. 1. much used

valente *dialectico magna luctatio est.* In coelo autem crasso &
Et valentes] Robusti, fortes.   Infra: *In qua tibi cum*

Old Long Primmer N. 2. very much used.

Ex his intelligi potest Arist. sub *Propositione* arrnationem
tanquam Probatıoni *subjectam,* Hæc enim est qua constituit,

New Brevier.

Dtu, inaugura illa vetus Zenonis Istum enim.Agedum, inquit, sermo
CAPUT I.   RINCIPIO creavit   2 Quum autem esset

Old Brevier.

nPsirama.roo&equosu.ijsand   ia,ecasiuivAirucbst.istiuvigb uucxrir.tsno
um utpeisim,son nbiomadon rtœpniar,,detonnuslnrceuisbmc & dr,sevxsm

Minion.

V. 1. Act. 1, 15.'Psal. 1lc4c.35, 6, .8E11.   J V.2. Hebr. 21, 3.   J V. 6.sal.11.3
5, 10; .12. Psal. 148, 5. I. Psal. 32, 6. Job. 38, 11, & 30, 7.   V.13 1714. Psal. 135,

Paragon Greek.

Ὅκκα κεν ἀγγελίας καζακύσεις τᾶς ἀλ
εγεινᾶς· Κάτθανεν ἁ ΚΑΡΟΛΙΝΑ·

English Geeek much used.

γὰρ ἀπήγγειλέ μοι, ὃν σὺ τῷ δεγατίῳ διελάσας
μεταξὺ δειπνεῖλα ἐφόνευσας, ὅτι μὲ πρὸς τὰς

Long Primmer Greek much used.

τύφου αὐτὸν ὑπεπλήσουν καὶ ὅτι ἆρα ἢ ὥησε μὲν 'ΟΥΔΠΟ μὴ κỳ
εἴποιε, παρλόίῳ ὑδερφοροῦντες, αὐτοῦ π ψιυριοαιεν. ὑπὲρ τοῦ,

Brevier Greek.

Πρόδικος ὁ σοφὸς ἐν τῷ συγγράμματι τῷ περὶ τὰ Ηεκιλέες ὅπερ ἢ κỳ
πλείσοις ἐπιδείκνυται ὅτας περὶ τῆς ἀρετῆς ἀποφαίνεται ἆρε πως λέ

Long Primmer Hebrew.

תְּנֻשָּׁנָה תְּנֻשָּׁנָה תְּנֻשָּׁנָה תְּנֻשָּׁנָה אֲנֻשֵׁי
נֻגַּשׁ יְנֻגַּשׁ נֻגַּשׁ נֻגַּשׁ תְּנֻשֵׁי

English Arabick.

نسل مهاف ياسيف للاينم

Cambridge University Press

JEREMY MYNOTT

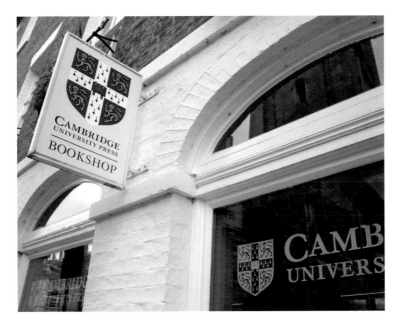

The Press Bookshop at 1 Trinity St is a thriving modern bookshop, operating on the oldest bookshop site in the country and in the middle of the University and the city. It carries large stocks – all 30,000 Press titles currently in print – and it also carries a large symbolic loading. The Press of Cambridge University is one ancient body operating within another, both of them independent charitable corporations with a shared constitutional commitment to education and learning but different and complementary ways of promoting this: the University largely through teaching and research and the Press through printing and publishing. The story of the relationship over nearly five centuries is the story of how these similarities and differences have evolved and been negotiated. The Press has been variously managed as a commercial venture operating under the University's licence (the original relationship with the first printers); an operation managed directly by the University itself (Bentley's reform of 1696, whereby the 'Curators' supervised both the publishing and the business operations – even to the point of sharing personally in the financial risks); a business partnership (with the Clay family from 1854 to 1916); and a separate

charitable foundation operating under ultimate University control (as finally codified in the 1981 statutes).

The Press is therefore difficult to classify – sometimes an alarming status to have – and in all these and other variant forms there has been scope for different degrees of tension and collaboration, though in this respect the relationship between Press and University has surely been no less intimate and no more anomalous than that between the colleges and the University. Collaboration has most fruitfully taken the form of the publication under the Press's imprint of leading figures associated with the University – the roll-call in the early centuries including such authors as Milton, Harvey, Bentley, Porson and, outstandingly, Newton, even if the Press has never achieved quite the degree of penetration envisaged in the University's Grace of June 1622, which required any graduate of the University who wrote a book to offer it to the Press and any teacher to use only Cambridge-printed books! In the early 20th century, as the publishing expanded, the list of great Cambridge authors continued with Moore, Whitehead and Russell in philosophy (though a catch was dropped with Wittgenstein), Maitland (still in print), Acton (founder of the Cambridge Histories), Oakeshott and Housman, and there was the further growth of a serious scientific list (unusual even now for a university press) through Rutherford, Hardy, Thomson, Eddington and Jeans. And the more recent successors of these have included Joseph Needham, Geoffrey Elton, Moses Finley,

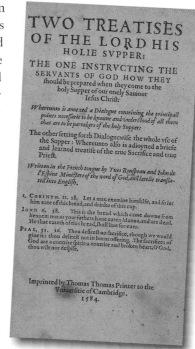

Right: The title page of the first book published by Cambridge University Press, Two Treatises of the Lord His Holie Supper, *1584, printed by Thomas Thomas.*

Opposite: A specimen of type letters used by the University Press, 1740.

Bernard Williams, Jack Goody, Amartya Sen, Quentin Skinner and Steven Hawking.

The Press is now a leading publisher in many academic fields, *the* leader in some. But there have been enormous structural changes in the output and operations that have had their own consequences for its present status internationally and within the University. First, by some point in the mid-20th century the Press had moved irrevocably away from its traditional dependence on the printing business. Even during my own career that declined from being 35 per cent of turnover to the ten per cent or so it is today. Directly associated with that went a reduced dependence on the Bible, once the mainstay of the Press but now less than one per cent of turnover, even though it is still widely assumed to be its best-seller, an honour which actually passed long ago to two decidedly secular textbooks: first Godfrey and Siddons's *Four-figure Tables* and then Murphy's *English Grammar in Use* (with over 16 million sales to date, and rising).

The really transformative changes, however, came from the Press's enterprise in exploiting a piece of historical luck, that we were publishing in what became the world language, or at any rate the world language for science, scholarship, business and communications. That meant there were world markets, particularly in the USA, for the Press's prestigious academic output of monographs, textbooks, professional and reference books and journals, and later its growing list of electronic publications; there was a schools market in Commonwealth countries for customised or locally originated texts, linked where possible with the activities of the examinations boards; and there was a vast and burgeoning market in the non-English-speaking world for English Language Teaching publications. ELT was effectively launched in the 1970s, gathered pace with a burst of very successful publishing through the 1980s and 1990s and now accounts for over a third of the Press's worldwide turnover. This expansion in turn required the development of a large international network of branches and offices, so a high proportion of the map of the inhabited world became coloured pale blue.

I used to tease a former Vice-Chancellor that most of the world's population knew about Cambridge only from the Boat Race or from the Press's publications – we were by then publishing over 2,000 new titles a year and selling some 20 million units into over 200 countries – so the University should be paying us for the use of the name rather than *vice versa* (as was regularly proposed). This rhetorical gambit was always unsuccessful but it did make a point. The Press is now more important to the University in terms of its size, influence and revenues than it has ever been, but also more distant from it in its daily preoccupations. There are still strong and very productive links with its local base of world-class authors and institutions, but that is generally because they are world-class and not because they are local. There is scope here for new forms of the old tensions and a need for new forms of understanding and collaboration, which are generally better expressed and achieved in terms of a shared culture and shared values and standards than through the narrow requirements of governance, audit, scrutiny and procedure.

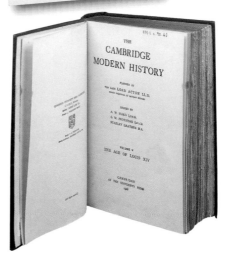

Left: Letter from Lord Acton concerning the proposed Cambridge Modern History *series, of which he was to be the first editor.*

Above: Cambridge Modern History *was published in 12 volumes under three co-editors between 1902 and 1912 after Acton became ill in 1901.*

Right: The Pitt Building, home of the Cambridge University Press from 1833. Printing was moved to Shaftesbury Road in 1963, and the publishing departments followed in 1980. It is now used for conferences.

The University as a whole is a federation of different institutions, each with its own needs and purposes within the overall project of 'education and research' and each with very different relationships with the outside world. The Press needs the freedom to behave as the complex entrepreneurial enterprise it has become and must be. But its centre is still firmly in Cambridge. It is governed by Syndics appointed by the University, its surpluses are shared with the University and its overall responsibilities are unchanged: it still exists to disseminate 'education and research' by applying the highest possible standards – the University's standards – to its worldwide programme of publications and so give the University itself a global reach, prominence and standing it may not achieve by other means.

Jeremy Mynott *worked at Cambridge University Press from 1968 to 2002 and was successively editorial director, managing director and chief executive.*

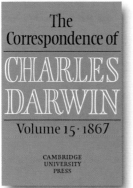

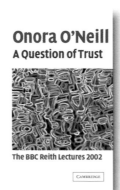

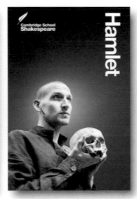

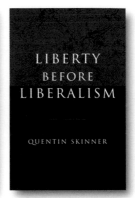

Recent CUP publications from Cambridge academics: The Correspondence of Charles Darwin, *Volume 15, edited by Frederick Burkhardt, published in 2006. Joseph Needham, Master of Gonville & Caius, biochemist and sinologist, wrote the series* Science and Civilisation in China *over almost 50 years, the most recent volume published posthumously in 2004. Former Professor of Philosophy and Principal of Newnham College, Onora O'Neill's* Reith Lectures *published in 2002. The Cambridge School Shakespeare series* Hamlet, *edited by Richard Andrews and Rex Gibson, published in 2005. Historian Quentin Skinner has been published by CUP since 1978.*

Fitzwilliam's munificent bequest

DUNCAN ROBINSON

In 2004 the Fitzwilliam Museum opened its new courtyard development which provides almost 3,000 square metres of additional space for the collections and their users. The architects, John Miller + Partners, responded imaginatively to the challenge they were given, to create a building within a building and thereby to accommodate a whole range of visitor services, in addition to a new gallery for temporary exhibitions, conservation studios and curatorial offices. By remodelling the southern entrance, it became possible to offer an attractive, accessible alternative to the main entrance hall, a *tour-de-force* of high Victorian Baroque which is sadly deficient in amenity.

It is hard to imagine what the Museum's founder, Richard, Viscount Fitzwilliam, had in mind when he specified in his will that the University should 'cause to be erected and built a good substantial Museum Repository' for his collection. There were few precedents in Britain, except for the Ashmolean Museum at Oxford, which mainly comprised Tradescant's cabinet of curiosities, not yet housed in C.R. Cockerell's elegant building. There was, of course, the British Museum, established by Act of Parliament in 1753, but that too was kept temporarily at Montagu House, pending the approval of designs for a purpose-built museum. That took place seven years after Fitzwilliam's death in 1816, when Robert Smirke set the standard for the 19th century's temple for the arts. For all its erudite Roman and Italianate references, George Basevi's building on Trumpington Street, which opened to the public in 1848, clearly reflects the prototype then nearing completion in Bloomsbury.

What is undeniable is the synergy between the founder's building, with its giant portico and pediment from which the nine Muses look down, and the Grand Tourist's collection it was designed to house. For Fitzwilliam belonged to that favoured generation of Englishmen whose tastes were informed by their travels abroad, in his case frequently to Paris, at least twice to Italy and once to Spain. Those habits of a lifetime

came to an abrupt end with the French Revolution and the Napoleonic wars; ironically, the very events which led to the dispersal of art collections from the mainland of Europe and the establishment of London as the centre of the international art market. Towards the end of his life, Fitzwilliam was given the opportunity to acquire paintings by Titian, Veronese and Palma Vecchio: paintings he could only have admired at a distance in his youth, when they were securely in the possession of the dukes of Orléans. By the time he wrote his will, he must have been deeply conscious of the mutability of worldly goods, and all the more determined to entrust his collections to the safe-keeping of his old University, where he clearly hoped that they would be protected from the kind of political and social pressures to which individuals are so vulnerable. But his motives were not purely precautionary; he also believed that the Museum and its contents would contribute, in his own words, to 'the increase of learning and the other great objects of that Noble Foundation.'

Opposite: The Courtauld gallery showing two of the founder's original bequests. Veronese's Hermes, Herse and Aglauros *(left, above table) and Palma Vecchio's* Venus and Cupid *(centre).*

Right: The Hamilton Kerr Institute. As a department of the Fitzwilliam, the institute not only undertakes the conservation and restoration of easel paintings but also trains painting conservators and engages in scientific, technical and art historical research.

In the two hundred years that have elapsed since the *Country News* reported, on 13 April 1816, that 'two wagons loaded with part of the munificent and valuable bequest of the late Lord Viscount Fitzwilliam to this University, arrived here', the Museum's collections have grown in breadth and depth, to comprise today many thousands of objects reflecting cultures from East and West, from antiquity to the present day. The Fitzwilliam is widely recognised as one of the world's leading museums, and as one of the most innovative and resourceful. Its founder's affirmation of 'the increase of learning' has lost none of its relevance today for an institution that attracts hundreds of thousands of visitors every year from all over the world. As one of the two most important university museums in Britain, it is committed to encouraging the use of the collections for research and teaching. Its own direct provision includes an ongoing programme of research and publication by members of the curatorial staff into the collections and their conservation; the Hamilton Kerr Institute, a department of the Museum located six miles out of Cambridge in dedicated premises, is one of a handful of internationally recognised research institutes which provides practice-based training for conservators.

But the Fitzwilliam is also one of the University's most visible and proactive interfaces with the city and the region. A member of the East of England's 'Hub', an organised constituency of regional museums, its involvement in learning is by no means limited to higher education. It was the first university museum in this country to have a full-time head of education on its permanent, academic staff. Over the past 20 years, the Museum's education service has developed a series of interdisciplinary programmes for children and adults, for special interest groups and for those with special needs. One of the first, 'MAGIC', standing for Museums and Galleries in Cambridge, led participants on an information trail around a sequence of museums, including the Botanic Garden. More recently, 'Transformers' explored the interrelationships between art and science, looking in particular at how artists use colour and light to convey invisible ideas, while 'Art and Wellbeing' covers a wide range of activities for patients in and out of hospitals. Not everything is so structured; the Department of Antiquities organises drop-in sessions for visitors to 'meet the antiquities', while 'Fitzkits' are available at the entrances to the Museum for curious young visitors who want to explore for themselves at weekends or during the holidays.

Above: Ginger jar and cover, English, London, 1673–4, Maker's mark of Jacob Bodendeich.

Above: Guan jar, Chinese, Yuan dynasty, c.1330–68.

Left: The courtyard extension at the Fitzwilliam Museum.

Rachel Sinfield, Museum education officer, leads a session for schoolchildren.

I discovered the Fitzwilliam when I was an undergraduate at Cambridge. It is a wonderful treasure. There are some fabulous things there and I have continued to visit the Museum ever since.

In the early days of Duncan Robinson's directorship, he organised a show of colour field paintings: Morris Louis, Kenneth Noland and Jules Olitski. The Fitzwilliam really went out on a limb and showed things that were not well known at that time and people loved it. Later a larger show spotlighted Helen Frankenthaler, Noland, Olitski and Larry Poons. These exhibitions, compiled against a backdrop of medieval works and old masters, show the breadth of the Fitzwilliam's interests and remit.

It is a great size for a museum: not overwhelming, but big enough to have a very rich permanent collection. I really have seen some wonderful art there.

Anthony Caro
(2007)

In 2004 the Museum launched 'Pharos', a web-based information resource which uses works of art in the collection to access information in different fields of knowledge and includes video clips to explain techniques such as bronze-casting and manuscript illumination. At the same time, a new generation of portable e-guides was introduced as a pilot scheme, designed to enable visitors to find out more about individual works of art while standing in front of them. With the rapid evolution of information and communication technology, it is difficult to predict what will come next, but the Museum operates on two guiding principles: that the visitor's experience in the galleries may be enhanced but must not be impaired by gadgetry, and that the maintenance and development of a user-friendly website is a key to success, as millions of users now turn to that source for information, knowledge and, increasingly, the enjoyment of being virtual visitors.

There is, of course, no substitute for the real thing, for direct, personal encounters with works of art, some but not all of which are on permanent display in the primary galleries. Others, for a variety of reasons, can be seen only occasionally, under carefully controlled conditions. The exhibition *The Cambridge Illuminations*, which took place in 2005, was one such occasion. Organised jointly with the University Library, it brought to light some 215 of the most important medieval and Renaissance illustrated manuscripts and early printed books from college and University holdings all over Cambridge. Some of the earliest, including the famous Gospels of St Augustine from Corpus Christi College, were rescued from the Dissolution of the Monasteries in the 16th century. Others were acquired more recently including, famously, the 14th-century Macclesfield Psalter from Shirburn Castle, which was obtained after a public appeal by the Art Fund, with a massive grant from the Heritage Lottery Fund, only months before the exhibition opened. Just as Richard Fitzwilliam's faith in his university as an institutional custodian of treasures from the past was well founded, so

…almost my favourite museum is the Fitzwilliam at Cambridge. It has too much on the walls and there is furniture besides, but it adds up to just the kind of inspired clutter that has always appealed to me. When I was stationed in Cambridge in the 1950s I used to go there on Saturday afternoons out of term, when the Museum (and the town) was virtually empty.

The first room I would head for was on the right at the head of the stairs. There were some grand pictures but they were mostly English paintings then: a portrait of Thomas Hardy by Augustus John, some Constable sketches and paintings by Camden Town artists and, presiding over them all, another Augustus John, a portrait of Sir William Nicholson, painted in 1909. He's in a long thin black overcoat, hand outstretched resting on his stick, urbane, disdainful and looking not unlike George Zucco, the actor who played Professor Moriarty to Basil Rathbone's Sherlock Holmes in the 1939 film. I didn't even know then that William Nicholson was himself a painter; what it was I admired was his detachment and his urbanity, to the extent that the first chance I got I bought a thin secondhand black overcoat which made me look as spidery as he did.

Alan Bennett, *Art, Architecture and Authors: Untold Stories,* **2005**

it continues to live up to its responsibilities. To quote from a recent report to the University, 'Like the University itself, the Fitzwilliam Museum is part of the national heritage, but, much more, it is part of a living and continuing culture it is our statutory duty to transmit.'

Duncan Robinson was Director of the Fitzwilliam Museum 1995–2007 and is Master of Magdalene College.

The Inheritance

Classical collections

PAUL CARTLEDGE

The founder of the Fitzwilliam Museum had, almost inevitably for one of his age and station, been a Grand Tourist. When it came to translating his bequest to the University into concrete – or rather stone – reality, the museum designed by George Basevi (1794–1845) was, again almost inevitably, neoclassical in style. Fittingly therefore the architect called upon in 1848 to complete Basevi's original plan, C.R. Cockerell (1788–1863), had himself been a pioneer of archaeological exploration in Greece, and a member of the committee established in 1836 to determine whether the Bassae frieze and other such statuary in the British Museum, most notably the Parthenon marbles, acquired by the seventh Lord Elgin, had originally been coloured.

Viscount Fitzwilliam (d. 1816) left a vast sum of money (£100,000), in addition to his books, manuscripts, paintings and prints, for the endowment and embellishment of his museum. As early as 1823, the scholar-adventurer Giovanni Battista Belzoni presented the lid from the granite sarcophagus of Ramesses III (1184–53 BC), a far-from-humble start to what has become the Museum's fine Egyptian collection, now magnificently redisplayed thanks to public as well as private munificence. Another private gift, by John Disney in 1850, added substantial Roman sculpture to the Museum's holdings, and in 1864 the purchase of the Leake collection complemented that with Greek terracottas, coins, gems and, not least, vases.

It was entirely apt, therefore, that the first Director of the Museum (appointed 1876) was the University's distinguished Slade Professor of Fine Art, Sidney Colvin. Further donations, both public and private, bequests and purchases have left the Museum's Department of Antiquities in rude health. A recent selection of 'treasures', published for a wide readership, effortlessly filled 20 glossy pages with handsome images and scholarly descriptions of some 100 artefacts, ranging in date from c.12,000 BC to the ninth century AD, and in space from France and Italy to Iraq and Pakistan.

In one vital respect the growth of the classical antiquities collections proved too much for the Fitzwilliam to handle. In 1850 a Fellow of Trinity donated 40 or so plaster casts to the University for its Cast Collection, but in 1877 the Museum's Syndicate, at Director Colvin's behest, allocated all of £200 (then still a very large sum indeed) for the purchase of further casts of ancient sculpture, to include whole friezes and pediments as well as

individual statues or statue-groups. The guiding thought was that at least the portable or mobile examples should serve as visual teaching aids, being wheeled into lectures as required. So great was the take-up, at a time when cast-collecting by museums and individuals alike was something of a rage, that a new, purpose-built home had to be found for them. Hence the Museum of Classical Archaeology was created in 1884, by the architect Basil Champneys, in Little St Mary's Lane. The opening ceremony was attended by a grandson of Queen Victoria and the famous history painters (Lord) Frederic Leighton and Lawrence Alma Tadema.

The Peplos Kore, dating from the sixth century BC. The polychrome version was an initiative of Laurence Professor Robert Cook to reconstruct the statue as it would have looked in ancient Greece, where, it was known, statues were painted.

Left: The Museum of Classical Archaeology, Sidgwick Avenue, which houses one of the most complete cast collections in the world and offers a valuable teaching resource.

Below: The Newton Hall Athena, which arrived in the Fitzwilliam Museum in 2006, belonged to Sir Charles Walston, Director of the Fitzwilliam Museum 1883–9, who was also a Reader in Classical Art and Archaeology and originator of the Cambridge Greek play.

Colvin's drive was supported by the Fitzwilliam's second Director, the wealthy American scholar Charles Waldstein, later Sir Charles Walston, and the collection was soon expanded to roughly its present size of 600-odd pieces. In 1982, on expiry of its lease from Peterhouse, the 'Ark' as it was known was relocated to its present position on the top floor of the new Faculty of Classics building on Sidgwick Avenue. It is estimated that there are now some 150 cast collections in the world, but as recently as 50 years ago there were many more. An unholy trinity of factors – the rise of photography, decline of devotion to a Western artistic canon, and development of a counter-orthodoxy of modernist aesthetics – has been held responsible for their widespread destruction and dispersal. Cambridge's Cast Collection is now one of the most complete there is.

And it's still a living thing, far from an old fossil. Visitors, including many groups of schoolchildren, are often shocked to see the gaudily painted cast of the Peplos Kore, a major Athenian sculpture from the sixth century BC. But the painted scheme, an initiative of the late Laurence Professor, Robert Cook (1909–2000), is thought to be more than just a wild fantasy. It is a generous, £20,000 legacy of Cook's, too, that has made possible the purchase of casts that either fill gaps in the collection, such as the Prima Porta Augustus and the Tetrarchs group, or move the collection forward in tandem with discoveries in the field, such as the 15-foot high kouros, or nude youth, discovered in 1980 on the Aegean island of Samos, the original home of Pythagoras.

Paul Cartledge *is Professor of Greek History and a Fellow of Clare College.*

Above: Silver tetradrachm from Syracuse, c.485-479 BC, McClean Collection in the Fitzwilliam Museum.

Kettle's Yard: the Louvre of the Pebble

MICHAEL HARRISON

In 1995 I asked Ian Hamilton Finlay, the Scottish concrete poet, to contribute a work, in response to the house at Kettle's Yard, to a celebration of Jim Ede's centenary. The parcel I unpacked revealed a large, flat pebble inscribed with the words: *KETTLE'S YARD, CAMBRIDGE, ENGLAND IS THE LOUVRE OF THE PEBBLE.*

A few years later, I found myself talking in the Louvre about Kettle's Yard and describing myself as something of an impostor, a curator of shadows and reflections, as much as a curator of works of art, and conscious that Ede would have preferred my job to be 'Resident' rather than Director. Pebbles, geodes, shells, fossils all find their place amid the china and glass, the books and the furniture and, of course, his remarkable collection of 20th-century works of art, all touched by the changing light of each afternoon when the blinds are opened and the house is open to visitors.

Ede had been brought up in the Fitzwilliam Museum, as he played truant from the Leys School, and in the Louvre, guided by his kindly aunt Maude. And 16 years at the Tate Gallery had taught him how people relate, or fail to relate, to art in great museums. At the same time, he was acutely aware that the art made by his friends – Ben and Winifred Nicholson and David Jones – belonged to everyday life and hung more naturally in a home than in the porticoed art gallery.

Kettle's Yard was conceived as an antidote to stuffy museums, and to art being valued as a commercial commodity or as illustrations to the history of art. But also, in Cambridge, it was an offering to students and academics, steeped in their specialist subjects, suggesting that there are other needs that have to be met if human beings are to reach their full potential. For 16 years Ede opened the door to those curious to find out more, who then might leave with a borrowed picture under their arm.

Now Kettle's Yard is known the world over for the Brancusi *Head of Prometheus*, set famously on the piano, its exquisite Miró painting and its

> "… *in a world rocked by greed, misunderstanding and fear, with the imminence of collapse into unbelievable horrors, it is still possible and justifiable to find important the exact placing of two pebbles.*"
> **Jim Ede in 1957**

Left: Jim Ede (1895–1990), creator of Kettle's Yard (above), which he gave to the University in 1966.

Opposite page: The Dancer, *Henri Gaudier-Brzeska, 1913.*

Kettle's Yard – this is probably what I remember most about my four years at Cambridge, apart from the astonishing architectural setting through which one moved every day. Jim Ede was setting up Kettle's Yard in my matriculation year and I heard about it when he gave a talk to the student arts society, but I never organized myself to visit. One day, as I was walking past Trinity, I saw Jim coming the other way. He stopped me and said, 'I know you, don't I? Have you been to Kettle's Yard?'

'Er, no, but I'm going to.'

'What are you doing this afternoon?'

'Er…'

'Right, come at 2 o'clock and stay for tea.'

I never did discover what it was about me that prompted this invitation to tea. Only a sort of inner circle of students were invited to tea and I was completely ignorant about all the arts. Whatever the reason, it was the start of one of the most enriching friendships in my life.

Alan Shrimpton
(1957)

The thing is, it took some years for the point of Kettle's Yard to sink in properly. I may have been inhabited by more contradictions than most undergraduates were in the late 1960s, but not I think hugely so. I was certainly torn between possible selves, or at least activities, a lot of the time, but that's part of growing up. One of the first things I'd abandoned when I got to Cambridge was the idea that I might be a painter — by the time of my first visit to Kettle's Yard I was already clear about that. Then I stopped acting. I changed the kind of clothes I wore, and the people I hung out with. I never lost my interest in grand intellectual systems, cultural history, patterns of influence and all that sort of thing, but my encounters with Kettle's Yard eventually shifted the focus of that interest on to the materials themselves and their forms. I continued to read Ruskin and Pater as well as Herbert Marcuse and Guy Debord, and continued to puzzle over the relation of art to things and to history and politics, and to worry about what poetry was really for. But always now with a closer reference to the process of production itself. I began to think about these things in terms of ideas that had got into my mind in Kettle's Yard, ideas about matter, materials, permanence and ephemerality, and how looking relates to seeing. In fact that was when I started to get some distant sense of the extraordinary complexity of the whole simple business of casting light on things.

Ian Patterson
(1966)

unrivalled holdings of Gaudier-Brzeska, but also as an exemplar of how we all might like to live, in modest but beautiful surroundings where objects converse with each other and with us, and where we can take time to reflect.

What of Kettle's Yard in the 21st century? Ede's time has surely passed. Having given Kettle's Yard to the University in 1966, he left in

Kettle's Yard runs lunchtime student concerts, a chamber music series and a new music programme led by a New Music Fellow.

1973 and died, aged 94 in 1990. His claims to contemporaneity for what he called his 'quixotic' scheme had already been challenged by Ben Nicholson. How now to keep Ede's purpose alive?

The house and its collection are much as Ede had them. Worn-out rugs and upholstery – you can still sit in the chairs – are restored or replaced, but the spiral of pebbles remains and the Venetian mirror still sends its rainbows into the upstairs lounge; artists continue to respond and new work is commissioned to come and go, to open new conversations. Jim Ede's ambitious chamber music series still flourishes, now alongside lunchtime student concerts and a New Music programme, with more commissions, led by a New Music Fellow. And next door, a gallery which has grown three times, stage-by-stage, presents the very latest international work, alternating with exhibitions which explore connections with the recent past and with other disciplines.

Fifty years on, 'the imminence of collapse into unbelievable horrors' seems not to have left us, and the frenzy of modern life extends even into our great museums as a signal of their success. Jim Ede hoped that every university would have its own Kettle's Yard, but his creation has remained unique, while the need to pause and contemplate is ever more pressing.

At the time of this publication there are plans to build an education wing to extend an already vibrant programme of lifelong learning, and to open up creative opportunities for students and children. A café to encourage longer and more frequent visits, an extended art library to allow it to keep up-to-date, a properly appointed collection store, and a new gallery space to develop the conversation between the contemporary and the modern historical are all part of the next 'quixotic scheme'.

Visitors still come and pull the bell and Jim Ede's message still rings true – and students continue to borrow a picture for their wall.

Michael Harrison has been the Director of Kettle's Yard since 1992, and was previously head of the Arts Council touring exhibitions programme.

The Kettle's Yard pebble spiral, formed from 87 spherical pebbles picked up on Norfolk beaches by Jim Ede.

Seven Visits

I ring the bell of the house, sign in and go straight upstairs. The house is full, as usual, of happy-looking visitors. You can tell the new from the old. The new ones wander about in a wide-eyed exclamatory ecstasy of disbelief. The ones who're returning either wander through the house with the kind of pride that means they think it belongs to them, or, if they're with someone, make straight for their favourite places and artefacts, saying things like Come and see! or Wait till you see it! In each of the rooms there's a polite and friendly – I'm trying to think of the right word, warden? watcher? keeper? – I mean the kind people who keep an eye on the art and help the visitors with information, I meet one of these ladies on the way upstairs and as I pass her I say. The Gaudier-Brzeska room's still in the loft, isn't it? (I say it rhetorically, really, because I know the room'll still be there, of course it'll still be there, and partly because I'm one of those returning visitors proud to be going back to something I already know and love and keen to let others know that's what I am.) Yes it is, she says, and then she adds. You know, it's the one room I felt least comfortable

about in the whole house in the first little while of my working here. No, I say, it's not comforting, is it, it's the opposite of comforting, it's properly modern in its brightness and its energy, it'll never date. Exactly, she says, and I go off up the stairs of this most comforting house to the unsettling nature of things sprung just under its roof, like a trap for a wild creature, a room full of exactly that uncomforting wildness Gaudier-Brzeska catches in the jaw of the fox, or the arrogant point of the little bearded jaw on the Head of Ezra Pound, or the triangular, genital nothing-but-mouth on the girl whose whole face is a joyful modernist double-entendre. I'm there for about ten minutes, thinking about the title of one of the most naturalist of the works, Grace and Speed, the careful, naturalist rendition of the wing of a big bird of prey, when I notice for the first time, in a small picture of a line-up of tenement buildings at the other end of the room, an unexpected streak of bright blue running right through the picture's centre.

Ali Smith (1985), *A Room to Live In; A Kettle's Yard Anthology*, 2007

Science museums: great expeditions preserved

LIBA TAUB

The scientific collections and museums of the University of Cambridge are amongst the most important and exciting in the world: their range of subjects and holdings is outstanding. These collections are dynamic: new acquisitions are constantly added, including a range of objects from ancient fossils to ethnographic material of distant cultures to living plant specimens. The University's scientific museums offer unsurpassed resources for the research and teaching activities of their associated departments, while simultaneously providing special windows for the public to view closely the work of the University.

The holdings of many of these scientific collections are closely related; for example, important material relating to Charles Darwin's research is held by several university institutions. Darwin was an undergraduate at Cambridge; while on the *Beagle* voyage, he regularly sent back specimens to his former teacher, John Stevens Henslow, Professor of Botany. Recognising the value of studying plants, Henslow founded the University Botanic Garden in 1846, as a teaching and research resource; the 10,000 species currently in the garden are there for scientific purposes. Specimens collected by Darwin are in the University Herbarium, begun in 1761 and today home to an internationally famous collection of over a million pressed plant specimens; professional and amateur researchers use the collections in their taxonomic and ecological investigations.

Other specimens collected by Darwin, including some of the famous Galapagos finches, found their way to the University Museum of Zoology. After his return, Darwin lodged in Cambridge arranging for specimens to be studied and described for publication by the experts of the day. Many of the fish specimens were subsequently transferred to the Museum of Zoology. After Darwin's death, his family donated some invertebrate specimens from the voyage, as well as the microscope slides that Darwin prepared during his study of barnacles, the work which helped establish his scientific credentials. Darwin's specimens are not only of historical interest: many continue to be the subject of research enquiries today.

Cambridge has maintained a policy of acquisition and care for zoological specimens since the Cambridge Philosophical Society founded its collection in 1814. The Museum of Zoology now holds over

a million specimens. Many derive from the great expeditions of the 19th century. Others were sent by colonial administrators passionate about natural history, or purchased from professional collectors like Alfred Wallace, who were themselves great naturalists. The collections are worldwide in scope, and exceptional in the range and diversity of animals that they represent. The curators proudly maintain the tradition of teaching in front of specimens in the gallery. Often, students will be examining the very specimens that are featured in textbooks and lectures. This rare experience of Cambridge students may explain why the Zoology Department's alumni occupy so many senior positions in evolutionary biology.

Scientific expeditions and active collecting activities provided much of the material in the University's museums. Opened in 1904, the Sedgwick Museum of Earth Sciences has its origins in the early 18th century, and also includes specimens from Darwin, as well as many other important figures. John Woodward (1665–1728) was Doctor of Physic (Medicine) and a collector of rock, mineral, fossil and archaeological specimens from around the world. When he died, he bequeathed half of

The Museum of the Department of Zoology, which holds many specimens collected by Charles Darwin during his expedition on HMS Beagle.

The main gallery of the Whipple Museum of the History of Science.

his collection to the University, which later purchased the rest. During his lifetime Woodward paid people to collect on his behalf and, as a result, amassed more than 9,000 specimens. The collecting activities of 'amateurs' remains important to the Sedgwick. In 2001 significant fossilised remains of a crocodile (an incomplete mandible preliminarily identified as *Steneosaurus* sp.) and an ichthyosaur (*Brachypterygius* sp.) were discovered by two local amateur collectors in the Cambridgeshire fens at Mepal, near Ely. The fossils were donated to the Sedgwick Museum by the owners of the land.

The Scott Polar Institute, founded in 1920 as the national memorial to Captain R.F. Scott and his companions, who perished on their return from the South Pole, has a museum which houses collections on all aspects of polar exploration, polar history and modern polar science and technology, including outstanding objects made by the indigenous peoples of northern Canada, Greenland and Alaska, dating from the 18th century to the 1980s. These objects attest to the skill and ingenuity of these groups, while also documenting cultural change as access to European materials and technology has altered traditional economy and lifestyle.

Several of the University's museums have played an important role in discipline-building. The Museum of Archaeology and Anthropology developed out of the University's Museum of General and Local Archaeology, established in 1884. The founding collections included the holdings of the Cambridge Antiquarian Society – primarily local antiquities – and outstanding Polynesian material donated by Alfred Maudslay and Sir Arthur Gordon, who had recently returned from colonial posts in Fiji. While anthropology was not yet taught in the University, and archaeology was largely restricted to Classics, research interest in these fields was developing apace. In 1898 the Cambridge Expedition to the Torres Strait (between Australia and Papua New Guinea) laid the foundations for the development of anthropology as a modern, field-based discipline, and contributed many artefacts and photographs to the Museum.

Similarly, the founding of the Whipple Museum of the History of Science predates the creation of the Department of History and Philosophy of Science. Robert Stewart Whipple presented his collection of 1,000 scientific instruments, and a similar number of rare books, to the University in 1944. Whipple came to Cambridge in 1898 as personal assistant to Horace Darwin (youngest son of Charles), the founder of the Cambridge Scientific Instrument Company; he rose to become chairman of the firm. The Museum was founded with the support of Whipple and a number of Cambridge academics committed to the study of the history of science. Today, in keeping with the wishes of the founders, the Whipple Museum and its collections play an active role in the teaching of the history and philosophy of science. The collection includes Darwin's microscope, as well as his notes regarding its use, and the handkerchief he used as a dust-cover to protect the instrument.

Liba Taub is Director and Curator of the Whipple Museum of the History of Science and Director of Studies in the History and Philosophy of Science at Newnham College.

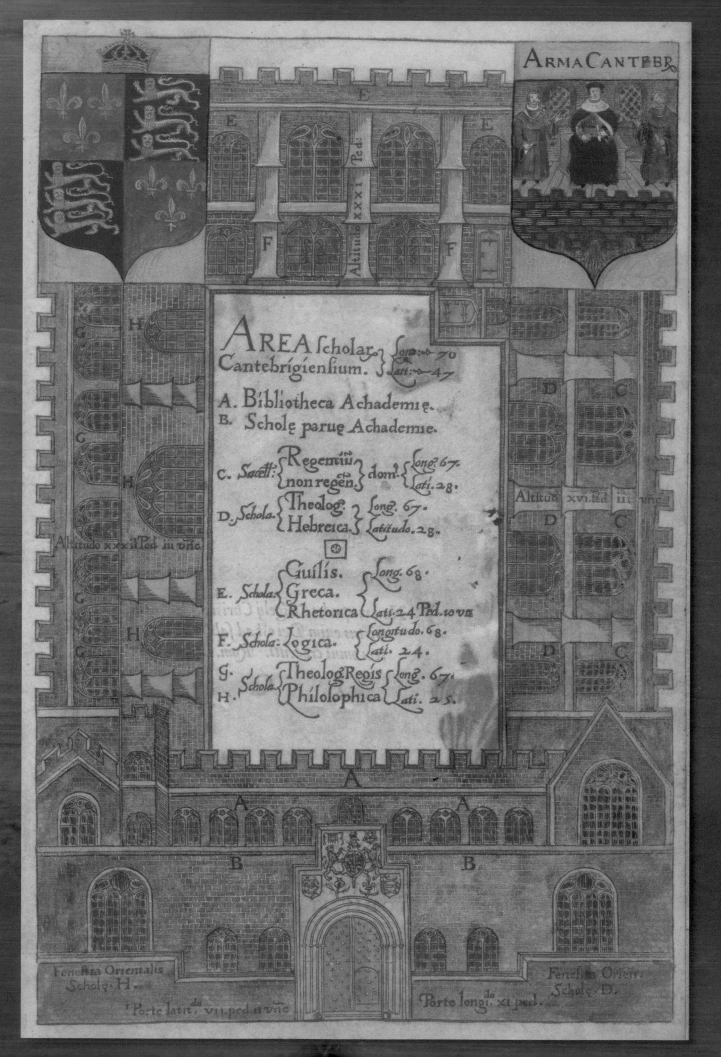

ARMA CANTEBR

AREA Scholar. {Long: 70
Cantebrigiensium. {Lati: 47

A. Bibliotheca Achademiæ.
B. Scholæ paruæ Achademiæ.

C. Sacell: {Regentiü {dom: {Long. 67.
           {non regen {   {Lati. 28.

D. Schola {Theolog. {Long. 67.
          {Hebreica. {Latitudo. 28.

E. Schola {Guilis. {Long. 68.
          {Greca.
          {Rhetorica {Lati. 24 Ped. 10 vñ

F. Schola. Logica. {Longitudo. 68.
                   {Lati. 24.

G. {Schola {Theolog Regis {Long. 67.
H. {   {Philolophica {Lati. 25.

Altitudo XVI. fed III vñc

Altitudo XXX II Ped. III vñc

Fenestra Orientalis
Scholæ H.

Fenestra Orient:
Scholæ D.

Porte latit: VII ped. II vñc   Porte longi: XI ped.

The Inheritance

University buildings before 1900

DEBORAH HOWARD

The last half century has seen a dramatic explosion in the University's architectural patronage, with major new buildings for teaching and research and the construction of complete new sites. Yet in the early centuries of its history the University had few resources for building, for both space and capital endowments were in chronically short supply.

As any tourist knows, the centre of Cambridge is strewn with colleges, but where is the University? The iconic landmarks on the visitor's itinerary all belong to the colleges: King's College Chapel, Trinity Great Court, the Mathematical Bridge of Queens', the Gates of Caius and so on. Until the early 18th century, the University itself was squeezed into a small quadrangular court built between 1370 and 1475, surrounded on three sides by buildings belonging to King's College and on the east side by a dense mass of townhouses. This so-called Schools Quadrangle contained the Regent House, the Library and all the teaching rooms. At this point the University was almost invisible, and even Great St Mary's, the so-called 'university church', was the town's main parish church.

Graduates of Cambridge, of course, cherish memories, whether good or bad, of the Senate House from the nervous scrutiny of examination results and the subsequent graduation ceremony. Despite its prominent position, however, the Senate House itself is just a fragment of a more ambitious scheme. By the time that David Loggan recorded the Schools Quadrangle in his famous volume of engravings of Cambridge in 1688 (see over, top left), the University of Oxford already boasted the Bodleian Library and Wren's Sheldonian Theatre. Not surprisingly, Cambridge began to sense impending inferiority. In 1712–13 Wren's former pupil, Nicholas Hawksmoor, devised a bold plan for redesigning the centre of Cambridge, but this was prompted by a commission for a new court for King's, not by any University initiative. The scheme included a sweeping vista from the gate of Christ's to King's College Chapel, across a spacious forum (the Market Place) to be created between the churches of Great St Mary's and St Edward's.

Left: The Schools Quadrangle, from Matthew Parker's Catalogus cancellariorum, *1574, presented to the Chancellor, Lord Burleigh.*

Right: Entrance to the Old Schools, 2008.

That Hawksmoor's grandiose plan remained on paper brings us to the crucial difficulty faced by the University in establishing its identity in the townscape. The appropriation of public space needs political and financial power. Whereas a pope, a monarch or a mercantile elite could acquire private land for new urban developments, the clout of a small group of University professors depended on endowments and the occasional generosity of the colleges. In the classic town–gown rivalry in Cambridge, the colleges played a more vigorous part than the University, who could hardly compete with the prosperous citizens of the town, loth to sacrifice their commercial hub.

Soon after Hawksmoor's abortive visit, the architect James Gibbs was invited to Cambridge where he designed the Senate House in 1722, and

Hiroshi Shimura

Above: The Old Schools Quadrangle, from David Loggan's Cantabrigia illustrata, *1688. This complex of buildings, erected piecemeal between 1370 and 1475, was then, as now, closely surrounded by other buildings and scarcely visible from the rest of the city. It is still the heart of the University's administration.*

Below: James Gibbs's plan for the University of Cambridge, 1722, from his Book of Architecture, *1728. Only the Senate House (on the right) was ever constructed. The central wing was to contain the Library, and the south side (on the left) the Registry and meeting rooms, with the University Press above.*

the Fellows' building at King's in the following year. Gibbs's project for the University involved a three-sided court facing Great St Mary's (below). The west side was to contain the Library, and the south side the Registry and meeting rooms, with the University Press above. At this point the townhouses on the site were finally swept away, an idea originally mooted in the 1670s. As a former pupil of Carlo Fontana in Rome, Gibbs designed the Senate House as a stately classical *palazzo* with Baroque flourishes, decorated inside by the Italian plasterworkers who also adorned Gibbs's St Martin's-in-the-Fields. The importation of Portland stone ensured that the Senate House exerted its authority, for its gleaming whiteness contrasted sharply with the more crumbly, yellowish Ketton stone of King's College Chapel.

In the end the buildings on the other two sides of the court were never built. Opposition came in part from Dr Gooch, the Master of Caius, who complained that the south wing would 'shut out all View of that noble Fabrick King's Chapell.' Here, as on many other occasions, the colleges had the power to block University initiatives. The new Library wing was built in 1745–8 by the lesser architect Stephen Wright, and the small lawn in front remains the only significant open space belonging to the University in the centre of Cambridge (opposite page).

At this point – even after the age of Newton – there were still almost no facilities for science teaching. What is now the New Museums Site was given to the University for the Botanic Garden in 1762, and in 1786 a building was erected there for the teaching of botany and natural

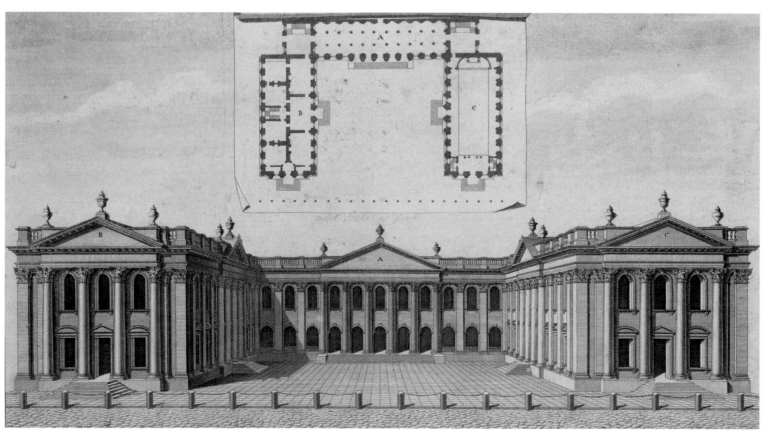

A view of the Public Library, the Senate House and St Mary's Church, *by P.S. Lamborn, 1769. The new Library wing on the left was built in 1745–8. The engraving shows rubble from the recent demolition of the houses on the site of Senate House Yard.*

philosophy. It soon became clear, however, that science teaching was seriously handicapped, and in 1846–52 the Botanic Garden was moved to its present site to vacate building land in the town. As well as lecture theatres, the seven Professors of Science needed museums and storerooms for experimental apparatus, including (for the Jacksonian Professor) 'machinery and steam engines … and a forge, and furnace for melting minerals etc.' A new teaching building was designed by the architect Anthony Salvin, but the University had only £5,000 in hand towards the estimated cost of £23,166, soon rising to £27,000. The colleges were not inclined towards generosity, and the fund-raising proved long, drawn-out and painful. Salvin's building was eventually begun in 1863, and soon afterwards a donation from the Duke of Devonshire allowed the construction of the first Cavendish Laboratory.

During this period, of course, the University did achieve several notable building projects, in particular the Observatory, the Pitt Building for the University Press and the Fitzwilliam Museum. But apart from the Cockerell Library behind the Senate House, these contributed only marginally to the teaching and administration of the University, and did not lend the University a well-defined architectural identity in the city of Cambridge. Nevertheless, even today, the Old Schools remains the powerhouse of the University and the seat of the Vice-Chancellor's authority. More than doubled in size by the acquisition of the Old Court of King's on its west side in 1829, it preserves both the memory and the fabric of the University's ancient origins.

Deborah Howard is Professor of Architectural History and a Fellow of St John's College.

Overleaf: Autumn in Cambridge, Clare College bridge. Photograph by Hiroshi Shimura.

Court, campus and city

PETER CAROLIN

Not so long ago, everything within the University (Girton famously excepted) used to be within an easy bike ride. No longer. It is Stagecoach's Uni 4 bus, running (every 20 minutes) from the University's West Cambridge Site off Madingley Road down to the Medical School on the new Addenbrooke's Hospital site that currently defines the geographical extent of the University. Within the past 50 years, the area occupied by the University and colleges has almost doubled. And if, as seems possible, work on the huge North-West Cambridge Site begins around 2012, the area will increase again. In both the University and the college estates, change and expansion are taking place at an awe-inspiring rate.

It took 25 years to build – with staged construction – Cambridge's earliest surviving court, Old Court at Corpus, completed in 1377. The latest, Magdalene's Cripps Court, part of the great college building boom of the past 20 years, was built in 15 months. It is one of several new college courts which have, since the demise of the Cambridge landlady, enabled colleges to house more undergraduates in college accommodation. New libraries have responded to the need for improved study and computing facilities. New assembly spaces have reflected the demands of the vacation conference market and the introduction of non-curricular college lecture programmes.

And, of course, there are the new colleges. Fifty years ago, the Churchill College competition provided architects and their academic clients with an opportunity to recast the collegiate form into something appropriate for the 20th century. The selected design – once described as the Blenheim of the Welfare State – retained the court form, more or less. That example was followed, on less generous budgets, by its near-neighbours, Fitzwilliam and New Hall. Fitzwilliam has recently been totally reordered: its new entrance, a brilliant reinvention of the traditional college gatehouse, is placed on Storey's Way. New Hall, formerly marooned like an albino whale by the side of Huntingdon Road, has been skilfully restored and expanded.

Opposite: Architect Hugh Casson's sketch proposal for the Sidgwick Avenue Arts and Humanities site viewed from West Road, 1957.

Right: Fitzwilliam College, the traditional gatehouse reinvented by architects Allies + Morrison, 2004.

However, as the University increases its emphasis on research and, with it, the postgraduate intake, a question mark hangs over the universal application of the court form. Ever since the late 1960s, postgraduate students – many with partners, some with children – have displayed a preference for living in 'houses' rather than courts. In response to this, Corpus acquired a group of houses in Cranmer Road, Trinity built individual 'tower houses' in Burrell's Field and Churchill recently constructed three 'houses' in an orchard behind Wolfson Court.

Colleges tend to build well and respond to change because the 'commissioning client' is also the 'user client'. For the University, it is far more difficult. Nowhere are the consequences more evident than on the New Museums and Downing sites. Both have their origins in the late 19th and early 20th century science building boom and today resemble typical metropolitan hospital sites filled with ad hoc extensions, temporary buildings and parked cars.

As seen from Trumpington Street, the University's one genuine old hospital site, the Judge Business School's Old Addenbrooke's Site, appears to have fared much better. Although somewhat densely and disjointedly developed at the rear (for Biotechnology, Biochemistry and others), lawns have replaced parked cars at the front. It looks impressive but the enclosing high railings are a reminder of the missed

Peter Cook

The new fume extract funnels on the roof of the Department of Chemistry, designed by Nicholas Ray Associates, 2001.

opportunity to create a new public space (related to the Fitzwilliam Museum) where the University might have presented itself to the visiting public.

To the south, on Lensfield Road, lies Chemistry. Here, the biggest challenge was not so much how to expand it, but how to upgrade the laboratories and accommodate the greatly heightened fume extracts. Against all the odds, the outcome – Nicholas Ray Associates' six highly visible raking copper-covered funnels set in a counterpoint to Cambridge's tallest spire – is seen by many as an enhancement to the Cambridge skyline.

Over to the west and across the Backs, off Sidgwick Avenue, lies the first of the University's campus sites. Its designer, Hugh Casson, held on to the court form and, to a degree, to the principle of continuous building ranges – of which the Raised Faculty Building is, as built, the

Institute of Criminology on the Sidgwick Site, designed by Allies + Morrison, 2004.

sole example. But the ordering ideas behind his 1956 plan were subverted by both James Stirling's 1964 History Faculty and Norman Foster's 1995 Law Faculty. Together with the 1997 Faculty of Divinity, these three distinctive buildings march across the centre of the site like a family of elephants. In 2000, with pressure for new buildings on the site and a prejudice from the planning authority against further development, the University faced a seemingly intractable problem.

What was needed was a more modest approach to building design and place-making. The appointment of Allies and Morrison as both master-planners and architects of the new buildings secured the necessary planning consents. So far, two buildings have been completed. English, planned around a small three-sided court, sets a new scale for West Road and clearly identifies the route from the University Library through the Sidgwick Site and on towards Newnham. Criminology is an elegantly crafted building whose clever organisation and beautiful landscaping have maximised the potential of what had been regarded as a too-small, unbuildable site. Another two buildings are planned.

Further north, adjacent to Clarkson and Wilberforce Roads, lies the new Maths Campus. Here, a highly effective partnership between the head of the Department of Applied Mathematics and Theoretical

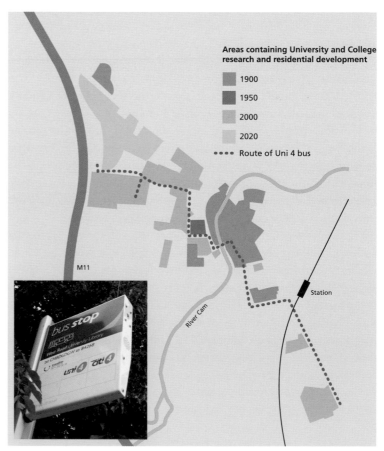

Above: The route of the Uni 4 bus defines the University's extent.

Opposite: The William Gates Building was the first to be completed on the West Cambridge campus in 2001. The architects were RMJM London.

Physics (DAMTP) and Edward Cullinan Architects resulted, despite some articulate local opposition, in raising funds and completing eight new research pavilions, a large communal space, a library and gatehouse, in record time. The new buildings are highly energy-efficient and, thanks to the selection and quality of materials, will require minimal external maintenance.

Further to the west, between Madingley Road and the Coton footpath, is the University's vast West Cambridge Site. At the time of its proposal as a major area for science and engineering expansion, it was occupied by the Vet School, the Cavendish Laboratory, Engineering's Whittle Laboratory and various private units such as Schlumberger's large research building and the British Antarctic Survey. Incorporating these disparate elements and the Vet School's huge paddocks and, at the same time, overcoming the city's antagonism towards any further University expansion was a huge challenge.

The appointed master-planners, Sir Richard MacCormac and his colleagues, have used the paddocks as the basis for a giant version of the Cambridge 'Backs' – where the colleges are seen from Queen's Road across meadow and lawn. Here, the greatest concentration of buildings, looking south over the fields, will nudge up to a great south-facing colonnade aligned with the principal pedestrian and cycle link back to the colleges and city centre. This inspired solution answered the planning authority's strong preference for a suburban approach.

In a way, it is unfair to criticise West Cambridge just now. RMJM's new Computer and Microsoft Research Laboratories are impressive but the road system is incomplete, the postgraduate flats are temporarily somewhat isolated, and two new buildings have just started construction. Elements which will bring the site to life – such as the café, Cambridge Enterprise building, shops and sports centre – have yet to be built.

There are, nevertheless, causes for real concern. The only sheltered small-scale pedestrian space on the entire site has had an unnecessary road driven through it, some totally undistinguished and pretentious corporate architecture has appeared and there is every indication that the coherence of the site is, on the client side, no-one's business. One

senses that a skilled master-planner has been hampered by political circumstance and, crucially, by the absence of a design champion within the University.

As it continues to develop West Cambridge and plans the huge North-West Cambridge Site, it is becoming abundantly clear that the University's greatest challenge is not the design of independent buildings – important as that is – but the coherence of entire sites. This is a matter not just of appearance but of enabling social and intellectual discourse, ensuring sustainability and securing economic value. Our predecessors successfully evolved the college form. Can we, within a far shorter time-frame, now evolve a University equivalent?

Few bodies can be less well suited to the challenging role of the modern client than academia. Initial decision-making can be both difficult and painfully slow. Trying later, often over a space of several years, to make the time to provide the necessary support and championing of a project can impose awful strains. Despite this, over the past 20 years, the University and colleges have built more than ever before. And, on the whole, they've done it well – and even, on occasion, brilliantly.

Peter Carolin is Professor Emeritus of Architecture and a Fellow of Corpus Christi College.

Above: West Cambridge Site aerial view, 2008.

Right: Competition-winning entry for West Cambridge colonnade with solar panels, 2002. Not currently programmed for construction. Marks Barfield, architects.

Cambridge Futures

With the West and North-West Cambridge sites, the University is deeply involved in the process of city-making and of developing and articulating an exemplary vision for the uncertain future we face. It was a sense of this responsibility that led the Department of Architecture to initiate and lead the groundbreaking Cambridge Futures project of 1997–9. Collaborating with the local government and business communities and engaging in non-confrontational discussions, a department research team developed and evaluated seven alternative visions for the future form of the Cambridge region. This enabled an informed public debate and formed the basis for the new County Structure Plan, thus helping to break the planning logjam and replace the lack of vision that was seriously affecting the city and region's prosperity and quality of life.

Cambridge Futures, 1999.

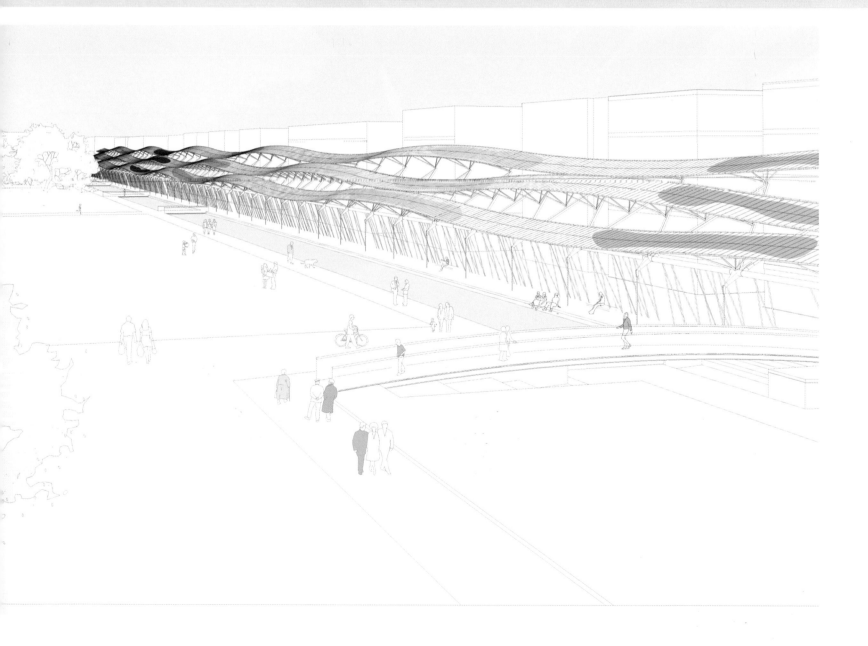

Biological and Medical Sciences

Unravelling the secrets of life

RON LASKEY AND JEAN THOMAS

The 20th century saw an explosion in our knowledge of living organisms and especially of the molecules that make up all living things. There were major advances in our understanding of heredity, how embryos develop, how cells divide and interact, how brains control behaviour, how animals and plant species have evolved and how communities of plants and animals interact with each other and with their environments. We now know far more about biodiversity and the urgent task of preserving it. We know far more about the biological basis of diseases such as cancer, diabetes, obesity and dementias and are far better equipped to seek new treatments. Cambridge was at the heart of this biological revolution, which has thrived on partnerships between the University and surrounding institutes, exemplified by the MRC Laboratory of Molecular Biology on the New Addenbrooke's Site in Hills Road. Staff of that laboratory have won more Nobel Prizes than most countries and their work has had a profound and growing impact on human health. Institutes like this and, of course, the core of the University itself have served as magnets to attract further investment by research councils and major medical charities such as the Wellcome Trust and Cancer Research UK, resulting in a proliferation of world-class research institutes. These are not just ivory towers; many staff have dual affiliations between the University and research institutes and many play active roles in teaching, either through the college supervision system or through undergraduate lectures and practical classes. Together they have created a vibrant and exciting critical mass in this area of rapidly advancing discovery.

The growing interaction between biological and physical sciences calls for scientists with a broad understanding of many fields. The Natural Sciences Tripos is designed to deliver scientists who have this breadth of knowledge and understanding. It encourages undergraduates to study a wide range of subjects in their first year, including both biological and physical sciences, and then to specialise progressively until they usually study a single subject in their final year. This diverse start provides a broad foundation for their subsequent education, but also exposes them to exciting areas of scientific progress that they may not have encountered before.

One of the most important biological breakthroughs of the 20th century was made in Cambridge in 1953 when James Watson and Francis Crick discovered the double helical structure of DNA. A plaque on the Austin Building on the New Museums Site now marks the location of this crucial discovery. A former Cambridge University undergraduate, Rosalind Franklin, performed the X-ray diffraction experiments on DNA at King's College London that led Watson and Crick to propose their model. This was a true breakthrough, triggering immediate advances in our understanding of heredity. It suggested ways in which genetic information could be encoded and it explained how this coded information could be passed from one generation to the next.

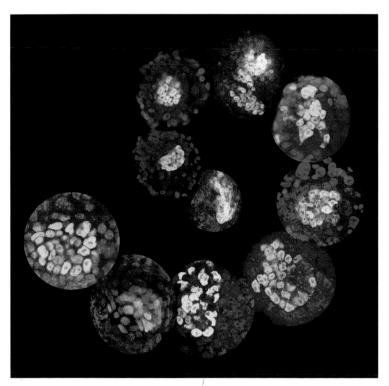

Opposite: The double-helix structure of DNA in a sculpture by Charles Jencks in the garden of Memorial Court, Clare College, which was unveiled by James Watson in 2005.

Left: Stem cells (green) derived from mouse embryos. Image supplied by Joanne Maldonado-Saldivia and Azim Surani.

Reading the information encoded in DNA required further advances, namely methods for determining the sequence of nucleotides in DNA. For this and his earlier work, Fred Sanger became the first man to win the same Nobel Prize twice. The first was in 1958 for determining the sequence of proteins at the Department of Biochemistry, and the second in 1980 for determining the sequence of DNA at the Medical Research Council Laboratory of Molecular Biology.

If DNA is the information software of living things, proteins are the hardware. First they have structural roles, and second, they are catalysts that perform most of the chemical reactions of life. Max Perutz and John Kendrew shared the Nobel Prize for Chemistry in 1962 for solving the three-dimensional structure of proteins, in particular haemoglobin and myoglobin. The influence of Max Perutz on molecular biology in Cambridge has been extraordinary. Not only did he found and chair the MRC Laboratory of Molecular Biology here, but, remarkably, three former members of his own research group (Crick, Watson and Kendrew) and Perutz himself shared two Nobel Prizes between them in the same year, 1962, for work performed in an MRC Unit in the Cavendish Laboratory of the University.

The double helix structure of DNA proposed by Watson and Crick suggested that the DNA molecule might duplicate by unwinding the two helical strands so that each would become a template for assembly of the new strand. Work in the Cambridge Department of Biochemistry by Tim Hunt (now Sir Tim) identified molecules called cyclins that determine when DNA is duplicated and when cells divide to form two cells. For this he shared the Nobel Prize for Medicine in 2001.

A small minority of cells in the body divide only rarely. These are the stem cells, versatile precursors of the many specialised cells in our bodies

Francis Crick and James Watson, 1953.

and one of the most exciting areas of current biological research. They offer the tantalising potential for renewal and replacement of damaged or diseased cells in the body. Cambridge scientists have played preeminent roles in their discovery and characterisation and in 2006 a new

Sanger and Sulston

Fred Sanger determined the amino acid sequence of the protein insulin in the Department of Biochemistry, demonstrating for the first time that proteins have unique amino acid sequences. It is hard to overstate the importance of this discovery; it showed for the first time that each protein has a unique, defined sequence of amino acids, a fact that had previously been disputed. For this he received the first of his two Nobel Prizes for Chemistry in 1958. He subsequently moved to the MRC Laboratory of Molecular Biology, where he discovered how to read the sequence of DNA itself. This study has spawned whole institutes. The best known of these is appropriately called the Wellcome Trust Sanger Institute and it played a major part in determining the DNA sequence of the human genome under the leadership of John Sulston, just outside Cambridge.

John Sulston was an undergraduate and graduate student in Cambridge University and before leading the Human Genome Project he spent most of his career at the MRC Laboratory of Molecular Biology studying nematode worms. Indeed, the sequencing infrastructure that led to the determination of the sequence of the

human genome was first set up to determine the sequence of the nematode worm genome. John Sulston (now Sir John) shared the Nobel Prize for Medicine in 2002 with Sydney Brenner and Bob Horvitz who had all worked together at the MRC Laboratory of Molecular Biology in Cambridge.

Fred Sanger. Portrait by Liam Woon.   *Sir John Sulston. Portrait by Tom Phillips, RA.*

Cambridge Nobel Prize winners Max Perutz, John Kendrew, Francis Crick and James Watson at the prize-giving ceremony in 1962.

Wellcome Trust Centre for Stem Cell Research opened in the University. Embryonic stem cells and methods of propagating them were discovered in the Department of Genetics by Martin Evans (now Sir Martin), who shared the Nobel Prize for Medicine in 2007. Earlier, the concept that cells could be reprogrammed to alternative fates had been pioneered by John Gurdon (now Sir John), more than justifying the naming of the Wellcome Trust/Cancer Research UK Gurdon Institute after him. There has been another enormous benefit from Cambridge studies of very early development, namely the invention of *in vitro* fertilisation by Bob Edwards in the former Department of Physiology.

Antibodies are the protein molecules that protect us from invading micro-organisms such as bacteria and viruses and they play an essential role in our health and survival. Mistakes in their production by our bodies lie at the heart of several crucial diseases, including some forms of diabetes and allergic reactions. Cesar Milstein (MRC Laboratory of Molecular Biology and Darwin College) and George Köhler invented a method of producing essentially endless amounts of purified, highly specific antibodies from cultured cells. These 'monoclonal antibodies' make up about a third of all new drugs that are currently reaching the market and they have opened up an enormous range of clinical applications from diagnostics to cancer therapy. The highly publicised breast cancer treatment Herceptin is an example. Another Cambridge scientist, Greg Winter (Trinity College), developed methods of engineering antibodies to minimise their rejection by the patient's body. Not only has this delivered immediate and tangible health benefits, but it has also generated a multi-million pound industry through companies such as Cambridge Antibody Technology and Domantis. Other spin-off companies that have arisen from exploitation of biomedical research discoveries within the University include KuDOS, Cantab Pharmaceuticals, Astex, Chroma and Abcam, amongst many others.

As illustrated in the pages that follow, Cambridge's strengths in biology go far beyond cells and molecules into such areas as behaviour,

My era was an amazing period, with so many areas of science 'taking off'. Watson and Crick had elucidated the structure of DNA with the help of X-ray crystallography, and Sir Lawrence Bragg was in the habit of wandering into our crystallography and metallurgy practical classes. Max Perutz lectured to our first year 'biology of cells' students. One such lecture began along the lines of: 'there are currently three known RNA structures – no, I tell a lie, the fourth arrived on my desk this morning'. No doubt he was gilding the lily for dramatic effect but such words certainly reflected the excitement and speed of advances of that era.

In my first term, my supervisor, radio astronomer Dr Ann Gower, took me up rickety stairs to her office under the eaves of the old Cavendish and showed me some lines and blips on a chart – early evidence of pulsars. In the new Cavendish I attended Professor Pippard's physics lectures and found them completely incomprehensible.

In my second year I studied experimental psychology as well as physics. This began a personal move towards the biological sciences. I was fascinated by Professor Zangwill's lectures on brain structure and function and by the links between psychology and physiology. These two departments shared a corridor and Sue Iverson lectured to us on physiological psychology at one end while her husband Les was identifying dopamine as the crucial missing neurotransmitter in Parkinson's disease at the other. This was truly a heady atmosphere in which to be a science undergraduate, and I believe that only in Cambridge, with its broadly based Tripos, could one have experienced such a stimulating and exhilarating three years in such an exciting decade.

Katherine Bradnock
(1966)

I originally matriculated in the physical sciences, but the first year lectures in biology of cells were too powerful to ignore, particularly those of Dr ap Rees, and the magic of Tennis Court Road and the romance of the Cavendish labs drew me in. I quickly switched from physics to physiology, despite the pleas of my advisers that we needed women in the physical sciences. (As I recall, there were 400 or so people in my first year physics class, and approximately four of us were women, although I'm sure that my memory exaggerates.)

I can still remember how it felt to sit in lectures by Profs Perham, Thomas, Northcote and my adviser, Professor Tipton. The lectures were never long enough, although my aching wrist attested to their pace and density. Jean Thomas was particularly inspiring, and most of the women in the audience simply wanted to 'be' her. Once she got started, however, we didn't have time to admire her shoes, or her hair, as we flew through the various modifications one could make to a protein.

Judith A. Owen
(1969)

I completed a laboratory-based Master's in molecular genetics at the Wellcome Trust/CRC Institute, and there became fluent in the language of basic science with more depth than after years of biology training in college and summer internships – it was truly after all the lunchtime lectures and conversations with my mentors in the lab that I came to understand genetics, in the birthplace of the double helix and so many great predecessors.

Leslie Manace
(2000)

The research environment in biological and medical science offers exciting future possibilities.

evolution and conservation of biodiversity. These strengths befit the University that educated Charles Darwin and houses many of his specimen collections. In addition to the Departments of Zoology, Genetics and Plant Sciences, the Department of Earth Sciences has made major contributions to the study of evolution too, from Sedgwick in Darwin's time to Simon Conway-Morris now. Recent University highlights in the field of evolution include discoveries of how limbs and digits evolved in land vertebrates, for which Jenny Clack of the Department of Zoology received the Girauld Elliott Medal from the US National Academy of Sciences.

The exciting research environment in biological and medical sciences has provided a fertile background for undergraduate teaching and for training of the many research students who populate the departments and research institutes. Furthermore, the current excitement in biological sciences is spilling over into many of the physical science departments, resulting in the forging of close links between disciplines that were once far apart. A recent meeting to co-ordinate cancer research across Cambridge invited additional speakers from Chemistry, Engineering, Physics and Mathematics and benefited enormously from the pooling of

2001 Nobel Prize for Medicine laureate Tim Hunt (right), serving as Junior Proctor in 1982.

various perspectives and insights. Indeed, one of the most exciting aspects of teaching and research in biomedical sciences in Cambridge today is the collapse of historical barriers between subjects and their replacement by new waves of interaction, communication and collaboration.

Ron Laskey is Charles Darwin Professor of Animal Embryology, Fellow of Darwin College and Honorary Director of the MRC Cancer Cell Unit in the Hutchison/MRC Cancer Research Centre.

Jean Thomas is Professor of Macromolecular Biochemistry and Master of St Catharine's College.

Clinical medicine: teaching, training and trials

PATRICK SISSONS

Thankfully decision-making in Cambridge University has improved since the full century of debate that preceded the decision to open a School of Clinical Medicine (SCM) in 1975. Medical teaching for the Cambridge MB degree was well established by the late 19th century, but unfortunately nearly all students had to move elsewhere for their clinical training. This finally changed when Addenbrooke's Hospital moved from the site where it opened in 1766 in Trumpington Street, to the new site on Hills Road. The Clinical School now comprises 12 University departments, which span the clinical disciplines, participating in teaching, research and clinical care within Cambridge University Hospitals (Addenbrooke's and the Rosie Maternity Hospital) and the SCM's other partner hospitals (including Papworth Hospital and the Mental Health Trust). Since 1540 Cambridge medicine has been led by the Regius Professors of Physic. Two of them were key to the development of the Clinical School, namely Lord Butterfield (1975–87), who guided its establishment, and Sir Keith Peters (1987–2005) who developed it into the thriving research cauldron it is today.

Planning of the new site was farsighted, establishing partnerships between the major regional hospital for the East of England, the University Clinical School, the Medical Research Council and medical charities on a single campus in Cambridge. It creates an exceptional environment for the highest international quality of collaborative biomedical research, and its translation into benefit for patients.

One hundred and fifty new doctors graduate from the Clinical School each year. About half the students who enter Cambridge to read medicine complete their training here: the others continue their clinical studies elsewhere, mainly in London. The clinical course was initially the shortest in the UK, but it was lengthened in 2005 to allow students more time for their studies. In 1990 the first MB PhD programme in the UK was established, enrolling eight to ten students a year into a three-year PhD integrated with their clinical course. This has been highly successful and many of its early graduates are now emerging as promising biomedical researchers. In 2001 a new graduate entry course opened, allowing students who hold first degrees in other subjects to study medicine. Much of the clinical teaching for the Cambridge Graduate Course is based at the West Suffolk Hospital, reflecting the partnership between the SCM and the regional hospitals involved in its teaching.

Research strengths in the SCM include cancer, metabolic diseases such as obesity and diabetes (see next section), neurosciences and mental health, cardiovascular disease, genetic medicine, transplantation, immunity, infection, epidemiology, public health and primary care. There are a number of cross-departmental research institutes on the campus under the aegis of the SCM. The Cambridge Institute for Medical Research (CIMR) exemplifies the spirit of the SCM's research,

The Theatre of Anatomy, the old Anatomical School in Queen's Lane, 1815.

I enjoyed 'Meaters', the irreverent name given to the anatomy hall with its 50 white porcelain tables, on each of which lay a corpse embalmed and preserved with formalin, covered with a cloth smeared with vaseline and a thin white rubber sheet to prevent the tissues from becoming desiccated. Each cadaver was dissected by eight students – one pair at the head and neck, another pair working on the chest and abdomen, a third on an arm and the fourth on a leg. Contrary to lay-people's expectations, this is not a distasteful or disturbing undertaking. The bodies bear as little relationship to a living person as a joint of meat hanging in a butcher's shop does to a fleecy lamb baa-ing for its mother in a field.

Richard Bayliss
(1938)

I remember vividly the dissection room in the Anatomy Department, mainly through its smell of formalin. We sat round our designated bodies, up to eight students for each body, trying desperately to find some vital anatomical structure. There was a strong chance that in our enthusiasm and ignorance we had severed or mutilated the relevant part. Milo Keynes, and other demonstrators who seemed to live in the dissection room, would wander round and offer help to find the particularly elusive body parts.

In physiology the end-of-term light relief, instead of a lecture, was to watch the 1940s film of Hodgkin and Huxley, both Nobel Prize winners, collecting giant squid off Plymouth. They were fully equipped with sou'westers, waders etc, and having caught their squid they then performed their world-famous experiments which showed how nerve impulses were transmitted.

Dr Hickson, physiologist, would wear wonderful white gum boots when demonstrating an animal experiment on stage, while supervisions with Dr Gordon Wright in his room in Clare Memorial Court frequently ended with wine or sherry. I am not sure who needed the drinks more, Dr Wright or the students. He has a superb memory for names and faces and I still bump into him on his bike in Cambridge.

Dr Grundy, a pharmacologist from my own college, Trinity Hall, invented marvellous mnemonics for drugs, some with rather complex associations. There was certainly one which contained Sophia Loren. He also had his list of ten Desert Island Drugs. He even laid on tutorials for us after we had moved on to London as clinical students, to help us get through Finals.

Fiona Cornish
(1978)

Medical students learning to take blood from plastic arms.

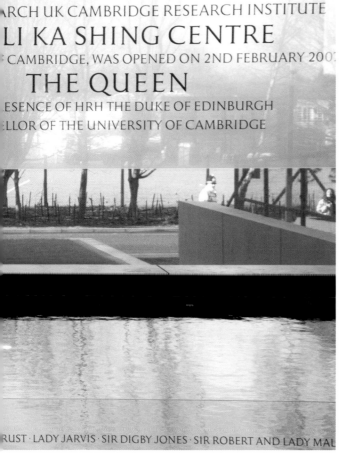

ARCH UK CAMBRIDGE RESEARCH INSTITUTE

LI KA SHING CENTRE

CAMBRIDGE, WAS OPENED ON 2ND FEBRUARY 200

THE QUEEN

ESENCE OF HRH THE DUKE OF EDINBURGH

LLOR OF THE UNIVERSITY OF CAMBRIDGE

RUST · LADY JARVIS · SIR DIGBY JONES · SIR ROBERT AND LADY MAL

Opening of the Cancer Research UK Cambridge Research Institute, 2007.

Reading medical sciences at Cambridge in the early 1980s was a lot of fun but not much use for doctoring. The first patient I met was a dead one (start as you mean to go on) and there was no preparation for the initiation rites of the dissection room. No-one warned me of the smell of formalin and the sound of a jig-saw taking off the top of the skull. And let's not forget the unfeasibly large genitals, swollen in the preservation process.

My dissection partner was called Jocky, a Scottish woman only marginally less ham-fisted than me. We shared a body with two scholars from Trinity, who meticulously dissected out the smallest of nerve roots while we hacked our way through fat. The arrangement worked well for organs of which there were two (kidneys, lungs, testicles) but the heart, brain and bladder were destined to end in tears.

Biochemistry, pharmacology, embryology and immunology were intellectually challenging and not always comprehensible. Physiology was easier to understand but had at that time a heavy reliance on animal experiments. We had one cat between two of us as we probed its brain to see which leg moved, and I turned up early to one practical to find a large number of chicks being extinguished. This was to give us the chance to dissect out a tiny neck muscle called the *biventer cervicis*, which I think contained both smooth and striated fibres. At the time, it seemed like a waste of a good chick.

My tutorials were made easier by a lack of scholars. We jousted a bit with the odd exhibitioner, but we quickly divided into those who were going to take it all very seriously and rid the world of all known diseases, and those (particularly the ginger, freckly ones) who couldn't believe their luck, washing up in a college that was 80 per cent female. Twenty-five years ago, you didn't have to work too hard. You could skip a few lectures and still fluke a 2:2 by question-spotting. I learnt the anatomy of the arm but not the leg, the abdomen but not the pelvis or perineum.

I had three wonderful years but learnt very little about being a doctor. In retrospect, it was perfect. We train doctors far too young. You can qualify at 23 and be landed with huge expectation and responsibility that you lack the maturity and happy memories to handle. Students need three years relatively free from pressure to discover themselves, dye their hair pink and gain a bit of emotional ballast before hitting the NHS full on.

Phil Hammond
(1981)

providing an interface between basic and clinical science, which is crucial to its objective of understanding the molecular mechanisms of disease. Currently, CIMR comprises some 250 scientists. One quarter are graduate students and 40 per cent of the principal investigators are active clinicians. There is exceptional strength in 'experimental medicine' in the SCM, focussed through the Wellcome Trust Clinical Research Facility in the hospital, which enables 'near patient' research to be conducted in a dedicated clinical research environment. Early highlights of research in the SCM included the pioneering work of Roy Calne in organ transplantation and Nick Hales in introducing radio-immuno-assay to the study of diabetes.

Cancer research in Cambridge exemplifies the recent growth, with two new institutes constructed through benefactions from Sir Ka Shing Li: the Hutchison/MRC Research Centre and the Cancer Research UK Cambridge Research Institute, opened by Her Majesty The Queen in February 2007. Highlights include co-discovery of the breast cancer susceptibility gene BRCA2, recognition of how BRCA2 works to protect chromosomes and how stem cells divide to replace worn-out tissues. Communication between institutes is co-ordinated by a newly formed Cambridge Cancer Centre, to integrate Cambridge's exceptional critical mass of expertise on this crucial disease that kills one quarter of the UK population.

The partnership between Cambridge University Hospitals and the University of Cambridge has been chosen as one of five NHS Comprehensive Biomedical Research Centres in England to allow leading biomedical and clinical scientists to work together for translation of research into patient benefit. Starting in 2008 the '2020 Vision' plans to double the size of the campus through the development of an additional 70 acres, allowing the relocation of Papworth Hospital and development of a new Cardiothoracic Research Institute and a new building for the MRC Laboratory of Molecular Biology. The future of Cambridge medicine in the 21st century looks bright indeed!

Patrick Sissons is Regius Professor of Physic, Head of the School of Clinical Medicine and a Fellow of Darwin College.

Understanding Nutrition and Metabolism

Nutrition and how we use the food we consume (metabolism) has sprung to public attention because obesity has become one of the most important public health issues of today. Discoveries originating in Cambridge have changed scientific thinking in this field. Gowland Hopkins pioneered research on vitamins; McCance and Widdowson defined minimal daily intakes of many nutrients; Kodicek unravelled the complex way in which vitamin D acts and Sanger determined the structure of insulin, for which he was awarded the first of his two Nobel Prizes for Chemistry, in 1958.

Cambridge has also been at the centre of fundamental studies of cellular metabolism to produce energy-rich compounds such as ATP, which is the universal currency for energy transactions in the cell. These include muscle contraction, heat generation and cellular movement amongst many other examples. The Cambridge biologist David Keilin developed the concept of the respiratory chain that generates ATP within cells. Ultimately the energy from food is harnessed by the action of an enzyme complex called the F1 ATPase, located in sub-cellular structures called mitochondria. The structure of this crucial enzyme complex was determined by Sir John Walker and colleagues after 20 years' work at the MRC Laboratory of Molecular Biology (LMB), resulting in the Nobel Prize for Chemistry in 1997.

A new purpose-built Institute of Metabolic Science brings together the metabolic research and clinical activities of the University, the MRC and the Hospital Trust. Highlights of current research in this area include studies by Stephen O'Rahilly and Sadaf Farooqi, John Todd, Krishna Chatterjee, Nick Wareham, Tim Cox and others which aim to elucidate the molecular basis for inherited disorders of human metabolism and use that knowledge to improve patient care. John Todd's pioneering work in the genetics of Type 1 diabetes has played a key role in bringing our understanding of the complex genetics of diabetes to its current exciting and highly productive phase.

Cambridge has led the world in the discovery of genetic defects underlying childhood obesity. Studies in twins and adopted children suggest that there is a strong genetic component to obesity, in addition to the more obvious lifestyle factors. Sadaf Farooqi and Stephen O'Rahilly have identified several genetic defects causing severe childhood obesity. Children who were found to lack a protein called leptin, because of mutations in both copies of the leptin gene, were severely obese with uncontrollable appetites. Daily injection of the leptin protein completely normalised the appetite and weight of these children and restored them to good health. This research showed that leptin is absolutely required for normal appetite control in humans. Several of the other genetic defects found in obese children interfere with the normal function of leptin in the brain. Not only do these studies cast valuable light on the regulation of human appetite and body weight, but they also identify potential approaches to treatment for the range of disorders that are contributing to the global epidemic of obesity.

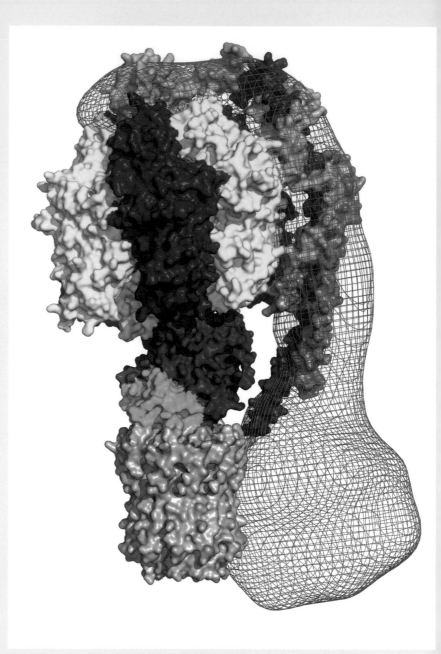

The structure of the ATP synthase from mitochondria, the central enzyme in converting energy in foods into ATP, the energy currency of biology. Image provided by Sir John Walker.

The tradition of fundamental and applied biological research in the University and its affiliated institutes thrives in Cambridge. It has enhanced our understanding of nutrition and energy transfer in living organisms, and of the composition and function of the living cell. Most importantly, it has had profound consequences for understanding the dynamic chemistry of the body and for improved diagnosis and treatment of human diseases such as obesity.

Tim Cox is Professor of Medicine and Honorary Consultant Physician at Addenbrooke's Hospital, and a Fellow of Sidney Sussex College.

Neuroscience: mysteries of the brain

CHRISTINE HOLT AND ROGER KEYNES

There are few greater challenges in biology than understanding the human brain and how its billions of nerve cells co-operate and communicate. The subject of neuroscience addresses the vast spectrum of issues that underlie these challenges, including how nerve cells send and receive messages, how their patterns of selective communication develop, the cellular basis of memory and understanding, and how these can be modelled computationally.

Early studies of nerve cells produced a cascade of Nobel Prizes for Cambridge-educated physiologists. Lord Adrian made the first recordings of electrical impulses in single nerve fibres in the living animal, and shared the Nobel Prize with Sir Charles Sherrington, who also coined the word 'synapse' for nerve cell junctions. Sir Henry Dale identified the first transmitter from nerve cells, namely acetylcholine, and in 1963 Sir Alan Hodgkin and Sir Andrew Huxley shared the Nobel Prize for determining the physical basis of the nerve impulse and its propagation,

using squid giant nerve fibres. They then reconstructed the shape of the impulse using model mathematical equations – a heroic effort using the hand-cranked calculators of the time, and the dawn of the now-burgeoning field of computational neuroscience.

This tradition established a certain *style* of neuroscience in Cambridge, notably rooted in experiment. Successes that followed nearer the end of the 20th century include deeper insights into the biophysics of cell membranes, and the development of 'psychophysics' as an approach to studying the links between physical stimuli and their propagation. Experiments involving impaling single nerve cells with a minute needle (microelectrode) and recording changes in voltage potential across the membrane have revealed the workings of hair cells in the ear and photoreceptors in the eye in extraordinary detail. The 1960s also saw the beginning of developmental and genetic neuroscience in Cambridge, with Sydney Brenner's ambition at the MRC Laboratory of Molecular

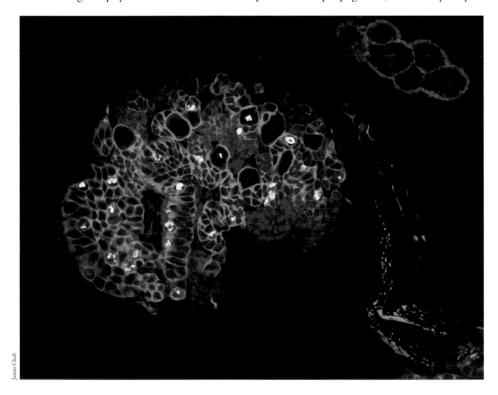

James Chell

Above: Andrea Brand, Herchel Professor of Molecular Biology, with her laboratory team at the Wellcome Trust/ Cancer Research UK Gurdon Institute, which was founded in 1989 to promote research into developmental biology and cancer biology.

Left: A brain lobe from a drosophila larva, showing cells outlined in green, cell nuclei in red, neuronal nuclei in blue, and dividing cells in yellow/orange.

It was during my more conventional studies that I first became aware of what was going on in neurophysiology. In the earlier years of the 20th century Professor Adrian had already discovered the way in which nerves registered the intensity of sensory input by increasing the frequency with which they transmitted impulses of the same size. In other words, there appeared to be something about the structure and function of nerves which prevented them from increasing the magnitude of a particular impulse, so that the only way they could register intensity was by multiplying the number of identical impulses generated per second. Although he had, as yet, no reason to express his findings in such terms, Adrian's frequency/intensity law anticipated the now widely accepted concept of digital representation. It wasn't until after the Second World War that anyone knew how nerves generated their distinctive traffic of information, but by the time I arrived in Cambridge Alan Hodgkin and Andrew Huxley had begun to solve the problem by analysing the peculiar properties of the nerve membrane and the way in which selective changes in its ionic permeability created the succession of impulses whose invariable size Adrian had already identified.

Meanwhile Horace Barlow and his colleagues were investigating the electro-physiology of the retina and I was lucky enough to persuade Horace to give me a first-hand account of work which would transform the scientific understanding of vision.

For some reason, though, I was almost entirely unaware of the revolution which was about to ensue in the Cavendish Laboratory where Francis Crick and James Watson finally cracked the genetic code, revealing, without their expressing it in so many words, the fundamentally digital basis of hereditary information. Although I occasionally frequented the pub in which it happened, I was not there when Crick and Watson burst into the Eagle announcing that they had solved the mystery of life and it wasn't until some years later that I became acquainted with another Cambridge microbiologist, Sidney Brenner, whose own work on the subject was to win him the Nobel Prize.

Jonathan Miller
(1953)

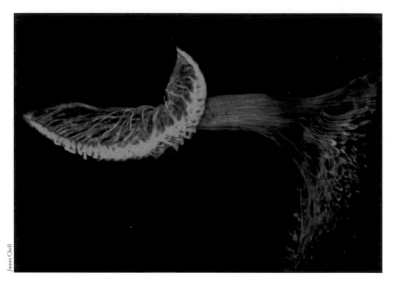

Axons of the developing drosophila visual system, stained for Fasciclin II.

arise. This knowledge will help to build an understanding of how the brain is put together and, by yielding information about how nerves grow, may help in the quest for treating human developmental disorders and brain injury. Indeed, the inability of the central nervous system to repair itself after injury is a leading challenge for medical science. Researchers at the Department of Clinical Neurosciences and the Brain Repair Centre on the Addenbrooke's site are tackling this with a combination of approaches, including the use of stem cells. They are also investigating the causes and treatment of disabling illnesses such as Alzheimer's disease, Parkinson's disease and multiple sclerosis.

Trying to understand the higher cognitive functioning of the brain in humans and other model systems is an exciting area of neuroscience that has recently come of age. Imaging techniques such as MRI (magnetic resonance imaging) are being used to identify which areas of the human brain are active at a particular time, and so to begin to uncover the wiring circuits that underlie cognition and behaviour. Work in the Department of Experimental Psychology and the MRC Cognition and Brain Sciences Unit, one of the largest international centres of cognitive neuroscientists, is studying the fundamental brain processes of memory, attention, emotion and communication. A related and fascinating area concerns how we make complex decisions in our everyday lives, and how this is linked behaviourally to motivation and reward.

We still know very little about the detailed neural circuits that generate the sophisticated functions of the brain: how they arise, how they work, and why they might malfunction. These are questions that are certain to keep neuroscientists occupied in Cambridge for many years to come.

Christine Holt *is Professor of Developmental Neuroscience and a Fellow of Gonville & Caius College.*

Biology to understand how genes generate the wiring and function of the nervous system of the nematode worm. His collaboration with John Sulston and Robert Horvitz, which included a cell-by-cell analysis of the developing nervous system, simultaneously established the molecular basis of cell death, and they shared the Nobel Prize for this work in 2002.

Neuroscience in Cambridge has expanded remarkably in recent years. Alongside the biological and clinical sciences, it now embraces subjects as diverse as mathematics, economics, linguistics and engineering. Indeed, the recently launched Cambridge Neuroscience Initiative lists some 300 investigators spread over 30 different departments and institutes in the city.

One area of particular strength is developmental neuroscience. This asks fundamental questions about brain development, such as how stem cells decide to become different nerve cells, how the brain is patterned into specialised areas and how complex nerve connections

Roger Keynes *is Professor of Neuroscience and a Fellow of Trinity College.*

Animal behaviour: chaffinches, meerkats and man

NICHOLAS DAVIES

Studies of animal behaviour can sometimes take unexpected turns. Observations by Robert Hinde on the behaviour of a captive colony of rhesus monkeys near Cambridge helped to change regulations on parental visits to children in hospital. He had attended discussions at the Tavistock Institute, led by the London psychiatrist John Bowlby (a Cambridge graduate), who had clinical evidence that the strict rules then limiting parental visits to children in hospitals had adverse effects on personality development. Hinde's experiments on early social experience in monkeys showed that brief mother–infant separations produced effects detectable a year later, and his studies helped to change hospital practices. Hinde also encouraged rigorous scientific studies of primates in the field. He supervised the PhDs of

Jane Goodall (chimpanzees) and Diane Fossey (gorillas), whose pioneering work has changed the way we think of our great ape cousins and ourselves. Jane Goodall's chimpanzee discoveries inspired Hinde and his wife Joan Stevenson-Hinde to study individual differences in behaviour, first in rhesus monkeys, and then in children.

Hinde worked in the Sub-Department of Animal Behaviour, set up at Madingley in 1950 by W.H. Thorpe. It was the first laboratory in the UK to be devoted to the study of behavioural biology and has influenced research worldwide. Thorpe pioneered studies of bird song with hand-raised chaffinches, keeping them in aviaries made partly from metal left over from beach defences in the war, with bird food stored in a Nissen hut bought for £1 from the old Home Guard. He analysed the chaffinches' song using a machine, the sound spectrograph, which had been developed by Bell Telephone Laboratories for analysing human speech. His experiments showed that learning was important for normal song development, but chaffinches would not copy any song they heard: rather, they were predisposed to learn chaffinch-like song. This and subsequent

Above: Patrick Bateson, now Emeritus Professor of Ethology, studying the early behaviour of chicks.

Left: Robert Hinde, Master of St John's College (1989–94) and now Emeritus Professor in the Sub-Department of Animal Behaviour, with his former PhD student Jane Goodall at Gombe Stream Reserve, Tanzania, on one of his visits between 1967 and 1972.

Tim Clutton-Brock, Prince Philip Professor of Ecology and Evolutionary Biology, studying meerkats in the field in the Kalahari.

work by Thorpe's distinguished student, Peter Marler, helped to blur the boundaries between instinct and learning by showing that different species are genetically predisposed to learn different things.

Patrick Bateson (Now Sir Patrick, director of the Madingley Laboratory, 1978–88) and Gabriel Horn (now Sir Gabriel) studied how young precocial birds (such as domestic chicks) develop a strong social preference for the first conspicuous object they see after hatching. They discovered that a particular area of the brain was concerned with imprinting, and analysed the cellular and molecular processes involved in memory formation. Bateson also showed how early experience in birds influenced mate choice and promoted outbreeding. Subsequent work by Barry Keverne has revealed some surprising and subtle ways by which fathers can enhance the development of their offspring, even before birth. In mice, certain genes are expressed only when they originate from the father. By controlling placental hormone production, these genes increase the resources the mother provides to the foetus, and also affect foetal brain development so that daughters will be generous mothers in the future.

In recent years, studies in the Department of Experimental Psychology and at Madingley have focused on features of cognition once claimed to be unique to humans. In the 1980s Nicholas Mackintosh discovered that members of the crow family could learn rules and

concepts beyond the capabilities of many animals. Following this lead, Nicola Clayton, Anthony Dickinson and Nathan Emery are studying food storing by captive scrub jays. Their elegant experiments reveal that these birds have remarkable memory, not only for where they store, but also for what they store, and when, so they can retrieve particular items before they have perished (memory feats equivalent to a human remembering the exact locations in a fridge of hundreds of items, together with all their individual sell-by dates). Furthermore, the scrub jays plan their storing in relation to future needs and keep track of potential thieves, relocating stores others have observed them catching.

In the Department of Zoology, Tim Clutton-Brock's studies of red deer on the Isle of Rum (Scotland) and meerkats in the Kalahari (South Africa) have attracted public attention through their extensive television coverage. He has shown how individual differences in male and female behaviour influence their lifetime reproductive success, and have consequences, too, for population dynamics. With increasing concerns for the future of wild populations, field studies will be important not only for understanding how behaviour evolves but for ensuring appropriate ecological conditions for nature to thrive.

Nick Davies is Professor of Behavioural Ecology in the Department of Zoology and a Fellow of Pembroke College.

Plant sciences: the vital importance of plants

John Gray and Peter Grubb

The world is waking up to the twin threats of climate change and the loss of whole species of animals and plants. The University's strengths in plant sciences equip it well to meet these challenges. These strengths range from plant ecology and conservation to the cutting edge of cellular and molecular biology. There are exciting new developments in these areas, including a donation from the Gatsby Charitable Foundation of approximately £90 million for the establishment of a new Sainsbury Laboratory for the study of plant diversity and development and the appointment of Professor David Baulcombe as the new Professor of Botany. His pioneering work with plants established the role of small RNA molecules in controlling many aspects of gene expression, a mechanism that is now known to apply universally, even though his work in plants was the first to establish it.

There is a long tradition of plant sciences in Cambridge. The Chair of Botany was established in 1728, the Botanic Garden moved to its present site in 1846 and the Botany School, which houses the Department of Plant Sciences and the University Herbarium, was opened in 1904. The Botanic Garden and the Herbarium house a remarkable collection of plant diversity, including a living collection of over 1,000 trees and 10,000 other plants and a collection of over 1 million herbarium specimens, including those collected by Charles Darwin during the voyage of the *Beagle* and 50,000 type specimens, which form the basis of species descriptions. These collections will be reunited when the Herbarium moves to the new Sainsbury Laboratory in 2010.

The specimen collections have helped sustain the department's strengths in plant systematics, ecology and conservation. Cambridge provided the driving force for the publication of the *Flora of the British Isles*, *Flora Europaea* and *European Garden Flora*, and Peter Sell and Gina Murrell, both assistant curators of the Herbarium, have nearly completed the five-volume *Flora of Great Britain and Ireland*. Strong foundations in plant ecology were laid by Arthur Tansley, one of the

The lake at the Botanic Garden.

great pioneers of the subject in Europe, and by Harry Godwin, who established one of the first carbon-dating laboratories in the world dedicated to studies on past vegetation. They were also leaders in establishing the conservation movement, and both were rewarded with knighthoods for their services to conservation. They were both heavily involved with the Nature Conservancy, which was established in 1947 following pressure from Tansley. Plans to create a Conservation Campus on the North-West Cambridge Site will enhance interactions between the University and conservation organisations, and provide new generations of informed students.

Cambridge's current strength in cellular and molecular aspects of plant science can be traced back to F.F. Blackman, who introduced the concept of limiting factors in biology and suggested that photosynthesis must involve separate light and dark reactions, and to his student George Briggs, who introduced mathematical rigour into many aspects of plant science, including enzyme kinetics (with J.B.S. Haldane), growth analysis and ion transport. Cambridge has been hugely influential in the field of ion transport in plants, most recently through Enid MacRobbie's group, working on giant algal cells and on stomatal guard cells.

Cambridge has embraced molecular and cellular technologies and a majority of current members of the Department of Plant Sciences work, at least in part, with *Arabidopsis thaliana*, the little weed that has revolutionised studies in plant biology. With easily accessible genetic tools and a complete genome sequence, *Arabidopsis* is currently used for studies in root development, circadian rhythms, chloroplast formation, gene expression, virology, regulation of metabolic pathways and much more. However, crop plants, such as potato, tomato and barley, are not forgotten, nor are specialised plants such as *Antirrhinum* and *Cleome*, which are being used to study plant–insect interactions affecting pollination and the evolution of C4 photosynthesis. In addition, the biology of algae has had a renaissance, with studies on biosynthesis, metabolic control, carbon dioxide fixation and cell division patterns. These studies will be enhanced by the appointment of David Baulcombe, who has developed artificial small RNA systems for manipulating gene expression in *Chlamydomonas*, a unicellular green alga.

The gift from the Gatsby Foundation and the appointment of David Baulcombe will ensure that the future of plant sciences in Cambridge is even stronger than its outstanding past. The world is becoming increasingly aware of the importance and fragility of plant biodiversity and Cambridge will be uniquely placed to make major future contributions to this vitally important area of science.

John Gray is Professor of Plant Molecular Biology, Head of the Department of Plant Science and a Fellow of Robinson College.

Peter Grubb is Emeritus Professor of Investigative Plant Ecology and a Fellow of Magdalene College.

Above: 'The University Botanic Garden', from Ackerman's History of the University of Cambridge, *1815. At that time, the gardens and herbarium were located on what is now the New Museums Site.*

Left: Arabidopsis thaliana, *whose easily accessible genetic tools have revolutionised studies in plant biology.*

One of the perks of reading botany was the occasional excursions to view the local flora. These began modestly with gentle cycle rides into the surrounding countryside. A stubble field might appear uncompromising, but we found a surprising number of small weeds, some with beautiful flowers when examined closely. Max Walters identified them all with ease, and often had an anecdote for each one, which helped to fix them in our minds.

In the summer term we graduated to Saturday afternoon field trips taking us further afield. The ancient double-decker bus used on such occasions gave up the ghost on Croydon Hill. We all descended and walked up the hill, while the engine was restarted and the bus crawled to the top. We finally arrived at Buff Wood, which is exceptional in having both primroses and oxlips growing together. They freely interbreed giving all sorts of hybrids, which are a challenge to sort out. Fortunately this wood is owned by the University, ensuring that its botanical treasures will be preserved.

For me the ultimate excursion was a European tour hunting for wild perennial flax, as part of my PhD research. This plant with its pale blue flowers might well be considered a Cambridge emblem. Its British headquarters are on the Gog Magog hills, where it was first recorded in 1660 by John Ray.

David Ockendon
(1960)

Conserving Biodiversity

Global development is having devastating effects on natural populations of living organisms and on their interdependent communities. This challenge is one that Cambridge is well placed to address, with strong teaching and research programmes in conservation and biodiversity spanning animal and plant sciences, conservation science, political ecology, economics and policy. We are now building on these foundations to create major new strategic initiatives in understanding and conserving biodiversity.

The University is developing a new Sainsbury Laboratory for Plant Biodiversity and Development. This laboratory, funded by the Gatsby Foundation, will provide Cambridge with the largest plant science research facility in Europe, housing over 120 scientists. Located in the University's Botanic Garden, the laboratory will be dedicated to understanding the origin and nature of plant diversity. It will house the University Herbarium, a collection of over one million plant specimens, enhancing the value of the collection by bringing it into intimate contact with the relevant science and scientists.

Generous benefactions have recently enabled the University to establish new chairs in conservation. These chairs span a range of disciplines: Tim Clutton-Brock is the Prince Philip Professor of Ecology and Evolutionary Biology; Bill Sutherland is the Miriam Rothschild Professor of Conservation Biology; and Bill Adams is the Moran Professor of Conservation and Development.

The challenge for universities in contributing to the conservation of biodiversity was recently laid down in an editorial in *Nature*:

The distance between [academic scientists and practitioners in conservation] creates a sometimes-yawning 'implementation gap' between theory and practice ... What is needed is a concerted effort by both academic scientists and practitioners to get out of their respective ruts, open up paths of communication, share information and seek ever more efficient means to a common end.

– Nature, *8 November 2007*

For decades the Cambridge area has attracted world-renowned conservation organisations to establish offices in the region, and in recent years the synergies between the University and these organisations have been growing. A new partnership, the Cambridge Conservation Initiative, has recently been launched to ensure that conservation research, education, policy and practice are interconnected. Our work to integrate these organisational activities has already led to the creation of a new Master's course in Conservation Leadership, generously funded by the Mava Foundation, and the participating bodies are collaborating in horizon-scanning programmes to facilitate future collaborative projects.

More ambitiously, we are collectively developing plans for a conservation campus on the North-West Cambridge Site. This campus will see a new multidisciplinary University centre for research and training (including the Master's programme) co-located with a number of conservation institutions to create the largest conservation cluster in the world. The campus will provide shared facilities to enhance the serendipitous interactions that are key to breaking down the barriers between theory and practice.

We believe that the Cambridge conservation community has a unique opportunity to establish a global centre of excellence in biodiversity conservation research and education, and to develop a new structure of collaboration and knowledge exchange with conservation strategists, policy-makers and practitioners.

Ian Leslie *is Professor of Computer Science, former head of the Computer Laboratory, and Pro-Vice-Chancellor for Research and Sustainability.*

Left: Biodiversity in central Cambridge.

Charles Darwin

At the end of his life, Charles Darwin (1809–82) looked back to his time at Cambridge as 'worse than wasted', filled with singing, card-playing, drinking and shooting. But he also knew that Cambridge was where he formed new interests in science, honed skills in argument and debate, and made the contacts that proved essential to his future. Science was not yet a subject that could be studied for a degree, but he learned much from the botanist John Stevens Henslow and the geologist Adam Sedgwick. The young Darwin, who matriculated at Christ's College in 1828, was keenly interested in natural history. He searched the Fens for rare insects, brought unusual specimens into Sedgwick's lectures, and learned about the variability of plant species from the University's remarkable collections of dried and living plants.

Through the Cambridge network, Darwin was offered a place on the *Beagle* voyage around the world, the journey that changed him from an aspiring parson naturalist to an accomplished man of science. During the next five years he observed carefully, developed new theories in geology, and collected everything from squids in jars to hunks of solid silver. Many of these unique specimens occupy pride of place in Cambridge science collections today. After his return, Darwin published his *Beagle* findings and a lively account of the places he had seen, and then turned his attention to the 'mystery of mysteries', the evolution of new species. His theory of natural selection, as outlined in *On the Origin of Species* (1859), *The Descent of Man* (1871) and other books, transformed the debate about the place of humans in the natural world. He defended and developed his ideas in a remarkable international correspondence: discussing theology with Harvard professors, enquiring about depictions of animals in archaeological digs in the ancient Near East, asking for bird-skins from West Africa. These remarkable letters, some 14,500 in all, are now in the course of complete publication to the highest editorial standards by the Darwin Correspondence Project, which is based in the University Library and linked to the Department of History and Philosophy of Science. The Library holds the main collection of his papers and is the major centre for research in this field. The correspondence, published by Cambridge University Press, provides a remarkable window not only on Darwin himself but on the intellectual and cultural history of the 19th century as a whole.

Darwin's writings contributed to the evolutionary foundations of science even as the research enterprise became increasingly oriented around university laboratories of the kind that blossomed in Cambridge in the late Victorian era. His sons played a vital role in this process: George became a leading mathematical geophysicist, Francis was a botanist, and Horace founded the Cambridge Scientific Instrument Company – which later, through the Whipple bequest, led to the establishment of the Whipple Museum of the History of Science. By 1909, when the University celebrated the centennial of his birth, Darwin had become a national icon and a local hero, symbolising the University's leading role in international scientific research – a position that has continued to the present day.

Jim Secord is Director of the Darwin Correspondence Project and Professor of History and Philosophy of Science.

Left: Darwin beetling in his student days, drawn by his friend and contemporary Albert Way.

Above: The full collection of Charles Darwin's correspondence is now available online.

Scientists and venture capital

RICHARD FRIEND

The development of Cambridge as a centre for high technology is much documented and maybe over-analysed. However, from the creation of the Trinity Science Park in the 1970s to the present day, what was a 'cottage industry' has grown to become a very significant source of activity and employment (of the order of 1,000 high-tech companies with 'CB' postcodes with more than 30,000 employees). Though there is often criticism that Cambridge has not grown any very 'large' companies, the accumulated employment is very significant, and the diversity and breadth within the cluster may provide Cambridge with a structure that is more robust to cyclical downturns in the economy (the cluster was not very much affected by the 'dotcom' crash in 2000/2001). The role of the University in the growth of this is indirect. Trinity and, later, other colleges, have offered well-branded accommodation that has often been intelligently targeted at new companies, but few of these have been set up to take direct advantage of science and technology created within the University.

I am not proposing to add further to the discussion of what caused the Cambridge high technology economy to develop as it has. However, this remarkable development on our doorstep has come to be a very valuable resource for the University. Over this period the business of making basic research useful and exploitable has moved from being an unregulated 'minority sport' to a mainstream part of the delivery of academic research in science and technology.

My own research in the late 1980s was concerned with the possibility that carbon-based molecular materials might show semiconducting properties similar to those of silicon. This area had been accessible to experimental physicists because there was also interest in the organic chemistry community, and we had been fortunate to set up a collaboration with Andrew Holmes in the Department of Chemistry, whose group was among the first to produce semiconducting polymers that could be processed to form the thin films we needed for our experiments. We had set out to make working devices, and had successfully made a range of transistors and these provided excellent test-beds for the experimental determination of the semiconducting behaviour of these materials. These transistors were not then of any great practical significance, but we found, unexpectedly, that we could produce visible (initially green) light emission when driving an electrical current through simple diode structures. This was clearly important, and we (Donal Bradley and Jeremy Burroughes) worked very quickly to establish why this was happening. We thought it was worth filing a patent, and went off to the University's technology transfer office (then named the Wolfson Industrial Liaison Office), which was a very small affair at that time. What we needed and what we got was encouragement and networking. Resourcing was another matter, and although we were put in contact with excellent patent agents, we picked up the costs of the initial patent filing ourselves.

Patents are like small babies: to prosper they need expensive and time-consuming nurture. I think I had always known the former though not the latter, but it was soon clear that getting value from the patent required a lot of work, and that we would have to drive it along.

Opposite: Aerial view of the first Science Park on the northern edge of Cambridge beside the A14.

Michael Derringer

With a lot of support from the Wolfson Office and a growing group of supporters outside the University but in Cambridge, we had by 1992 formed a company, Cambridge Display Technology, CDT, to carry out the development work that would convert exciting research into manufacturable technology. Seed funding to cover patent costs was raised from Cambridge Research and Innovation, and networking of a range of business angels was driven by Hermann Hauser. As the pressure on my time built up I finally realised what real freedoms we enjoy in the University – not only was I free to take time and energy to do all this away from the ordinary run of academic work, but the University provided positive encouragement to do so. CDT was set up with the University as a significant shareholder and with Board representation. CDT has prospered, and has maintained a 100 or so jobs at its sites in Cambridge, Cambourne and Godmanchester. CDT became a public company, listed on Nasdaq, before being wholly acquired by the Sumitomo Chemical Company in late 2007.

By early 2000 our research on polymer transistors had reached the point at which commercialisation was realistic, and Henning Sirringhaus and I in the Cavendish set out to form a second company, Plastic Logic. We were helped considerably by Hermann Hauser and were lucky enough to bring Stuart Evans in as CEO as we formed the company. Perhaps because we were now seasoned hands, we made rather less use of the University's technology transfer support system, but were aware that we continued to enjoy their support. The Cambridge high technology landscape had changed a lot in the intervening decade, and both business advice and support, and also access to substantial venture capital funding had changed beyond recognition. Very importantly, a position in a start-up company had

Shankar Balasubramanian with his research group examining the role of quadruplex DNA and RNA structures. His company, Solexa (now part of Illumina), developed a low-cost approach to DNA sequencing.

become a respectable career choice both for PhDs graduating from the University and for those already in jobs elsewhere in the Cambridge high-tech cluster, so that it was now relatively easy to take on really excellent scientists and engineers with the range of skills needed to create an engineering company. Plastic Logic (as of spring 2008) is now building a manufacturing plant to produce flexible electronic-paper displays in Germany (Dresden) and is set to become a significant manufacturing company.

These two companies sit alongside a growing number of spin-off companies that the University has produced. Early-stage funding is always problematic but matters have improved considerably, through, for example, the University's Challenge Fund. Direct University participation as a shareholder (CDT was the first) is now commonplace. I have always been pleased to have the University very clearly aware of what I have been doing and there is no better way to achieve this than to have them as a shareholder.

My commercial and industrial involvement with CDT and Plastic Logic has forced me to re-examine my understanding of the relationship between science and technology. I had presumed that the two companies would move gracefully away from contact with university research. However, technology has often enabled scientific discovery, and indeed access to the best technology is the best competitive advantage that a university experimental science group can get. We have sustained a close working relationship between the University group and the two companies, and our continuing research programme in the Cavendish

Plastic Logic eReader.

has had real advantage through the access we have been able to get to better materials and better device processing. I think we have achieved a very positive net return in 'research output' on the time spent getting the companies going. Another important lesson learned for me is the futility of attempting to do 'applied research' in the University – it is done so much better in a commercial context, whereas we can do 'basic research' very well indeed.

The growing scale of commercial involvement has put the University's very liberal and laissez-faire intellectual property regime into the spotlight. The University, in its collective wisdom, had been careful not to create prescriptive rules, and the inventors, not the University, had been de facto owners of patents and other intellectual property emerging from research. Pressure has come both externally (the government requires evidence that the University is proactive in

making technology transfer happen) and internally (the incessant creep of the accountability culture). The University set about producing a 'policy' to provide a defensible and workable structure, but any change to the 'free for all' that had served us well in the past drew very strong criticism from some quarters in the University, which, of course, as is the way in Cambridge, was colourfully covered in the press. Early draft regulations were in my view not well thought through, but the version that the Regent House supported in 2005 does get things right. It requires that the University know what we are up to, but does leave us (the inventors) in the driving seat. Given that the hard work still needs to be done by the inventors, this is absolutely as it has to be.

Richard Friend *is Cavendish Professor of Physics and co-founder of Cambridge Display Technology and Plastic Logic.*

The Napp Pharmaceutical Company, one of the earliest tenants on the Trinity Science Park.

Faith resurgent

DAVID F. FORD

Perhaps the most reliable generalisation about spiritual Cambridge in the past 50 years is that the significance of the spiritual and religious, and the complexity of their interplay with the secular, are now acknowledged more openly and adequately. Put crudely, in the 1960s it was widely taken for granted by those educated in both the West and the Communist East that Christianity, together with other religions, was in irreversible decline, and that there would be an increasingly non-religious, secularised future. By the first decade of the 21st century the perception had changed. Communism appeared to be in decline and it seemed unlikely that the estimated two billion Christians around the world would disappear soon. It was even clearer that the billion or so Muslims were a presence to be reckoned with, not least in the public sphere. In addition, some other religions had increased in prominence and there had been a flourishing of new religious movements and of many phenomena loosely labelled 'spiritual'.

The impact of all this on Cambridge has been considerable. The University has become far more fully international – it now draws students and academics from around the world. This has made it a meeting-place of the world's spiritual traditions, beliefs and practices. The main effect of this is often remarked upon by students. Given the pervasive collegiality of the University – especially in colleges and small-group teaching, but also in departments, clubs and societies, and all sorts of informal groupings – for most the experience of Cambridge includes getting to know quite well several people of different faiths and commitments. The result is a great deal of conversation and discussion that touches on religion and the spiritual directly or indirectly. The international character also tends to change the perception of one's own faith tradition – Muslims from Malaysia meet with those from Egypt, Nigeria, Pakistan or London, and it is brought home to Christians from Britain that most of their fellow-believers are in the global south.

All of this has been reflected in more formalised ways across the University. There are now chaplains for the range of faiths represented in the University, and often also for denominations within faiths. Some colleges, such as Robinson and Fitzwilliam, have developed ecumenical Christian chaplaincies; some with more secular traditions do not employ chaplains; most have Anglican chaplains or deans,

Above: The Khmer Buddha at Kettle's Yard.

Opposite: The lectern and organ in King's College Chapel.

The Revd Dr Ramsey, as he was then in 1952, was the Regius Professor of Divinity, connected with Magdalene College. Knowing that he had trained for the ministry at what was then Cuddeson Theological College near Oxford, where my uncle had been, and where I was due to go that autumn, I invited him to tea in my rooms, hoping to gather something more about the place.

I can still hear his heavy tread approaching up the winding stairs to my door. In Michael comes, 'Simon, how lovely to come back into my rooms!' Little had I imagined that he had been an undergraduate at the college, still less that he had my very rooms. After a tea with, I remember, an immense choice of spreads, Michael Ramsey put my fears to rest with such words as, 'You don't have to genuflect if you don't want…' spoken in that loving voice of his, his grandfatherly eyebrows working up and down above that broad reassuring smile.

He knew he was to be Bishop of Durham, and in due course, Archbishop of York, and thence to Canterbury.

Simon Willink
(1949)

Sir Cam

There were two ministers at Cambridge Wesley Church in my time, Donald Rose and Whitfield Foy, and I liked them both. Donald Rose took the Sunday morning services in my first two years, and he did so with quiet dignity, leading a large and lively congregation in acts of worship which were always seemly and sometimes inspiring. Whitfield Foy, who succeeded him, brought different talents to the task. He had a highly intelligent and somewhat troubled mind, with a knack for delivering short, pithy sermons which set his congregations thinking.

And think we did. Chris and I would chew over the sermons each week, and carry on our analysis. The Methodist group was the epitome of the Cambridge Methodist experience. It was an ingenious device going back, like itinerancy, to the 18th-century teaching of John Wesley. Meth Soc set up a dozen or more of these cells, every one with an appointed Leader but otherwise enjoying complete autonomy to pursue its activities in the rooms of its members as they chose. Study outlines were recommended and normally the groups kept to these, reporting back to the large and jolly tea-parties held by the Society on Sunday afternoons. But essentially every group developed its own corporate and intellectual life, with its own agenda. Many successful matches were made in the groups, and many men and women received calls to the ministry of the Church or to the mission-field in far-flung parts of the world. I received no such call, but my group nevertheless exercised a powerful influence on my Cambridge years.

Angus Buchanan
(1950)

whose roles vary greatly. One of the striking things about chaplaincy has been its dynamism in responding to new situations and people both by innovating and by adapting traditional patterns. It has continued to be an attractive option for some of the most academically and pastorally gifted ministers (and, increasingly, lay people and those from faith traditions without 'clergy') to serve as chaplains in the University for some years.

Among students, University-wide faith-based societies have multiplied, such as the Jewish Society, the Islamic Society and the Hindu Cultural Society. These have been responsible for imaginative initiatives such as Islamic Awareness Week and an increasingly successful variety show called Mastana, held at the Cambridge Arts Theatre to celebrate the cultural heritage of the Indian sub-continent. A recent addition is the energetic Cambridge University Faiths Forum, dedicated to inter-faith understanding and collaboration. CUFF has representatives from the main student faith societies and has been recognised by the award of a government grant for its work.

The main faith constituency has continued to be Christianity, and its student landscape has changed considerably. The most active 'student churches' are St Andrew the Great (formerly the Round Church), Eden Baptist and Holy Trinity, with Great St Mary's renovation of Michaelhouse into a chapel, restaurant and meeting place adding a new centre. Many college chapels are thriving more than in the late 20th century, as is Fisher House, the base for the Roman Catholic chaplaincy. Perhaps the most striking difference from 50 years ago is the decline of the Student Christian Movement. SCM had a mixture of mainstream, open faith combined with strong intellectual,

Mervyn Stockwood

Cambridge in the autumn of 1956 was in a total ferment over the invasion of the Suez Canal. I was an 18-year-old undergraduate and went to a protest rally on Parker's Piece. There was virtually no green grass to be seen, so packed was it with people. One of the most striking speeches came from a clergyman called Mervyn Stockwood. Then in Great St Mary's Church at 11am on Sunday, 4 November 1956 I heard him preach. It was an unforgettable moment. The church was packed to overflowing – the galleries full all around. Queues outside unable to get in. Referring to Prime Minister Anthony Eden's television broadcast of the previous evening, he said: 'A man does not easily court unpopularity, risk political suicide, divide the nation as it has not been divided for years, estrange our allies and hurt our friends, unless he is absolutely convinced in his conscience that he must do what he is doing, and that ultimately the world will believe that he is right.'

He went on: 'What of the other side? The basic charge of the critics is that the British, by taking the law into their own hands, by acting as their own judge, by disregarding their covenanted word, have committed a crime against the whole edifice of international law.'

Mervyn ended that remarkable sermon by saying we should say together the General Confession, and to say it, not just for ourselves, not just for our country, but for the tragic disorder that rebellious man has brought to this world. Two days later Soviet tanks rolled into Budapest. The Western democracies protested but Suez had destroyed our authority. The nakedness, the sheer oppressive nature of Soviet Communism was revealed for all to see and I, for one, never forgot it.

So controversial was the sermon, and the Conservative-controlled City Council so outraged, that they declined to attend the traditional Remembrance Day service a few weeks later. Perhaps because of the boycott by the Mayor, Great St Mary's was packed with 1,500 people and there were long queues down King's Parade to Corpus Christi and another queue around the market place.

What about Mervyn the man who became a lifelong friend? Flamboyant, relishing controversy, while quietly wrestling with his homosexuality of which I was totally unaware, until some years later.

Mervyn Stockwood, vicar of Great St Mary's 1955–9, after a Sunday service. Great St Mary's almost certainly predates the foundation of the University and was used as its first Senate House, treasury and archive, although the present building dates from the 15th century.

Mervyn was, on the one hand, a strangely gregarious showman, apparently super-confident; and a convinced socialist, but also a man who spent hours on his knees, who was strangely humble, and a loner who agonised over his religion and who wanted in a way to live a more simple life. The *bon viveur* who was also happy to come regularly to a cheese lunch in my rooms in college. The man who argued against wearing a dog collar but as a bishop wore a purple cassock, earning the memorable put-down from the Bishop of London: 'Ah Mervyn, incognito I presume?'

Harold Macmillan, the Conservative Prime Minister, spent time persuading Mervyn to leave Cambridge and become Bishop of Southwark. It proved to be an enlightened appointment.

Mervyn Stockwood brought something unique to a generation of undergraduates. His incumbency was in the highest traditions of Great St Mary's.

David Owen (Lord Owen of Plymouth) (1956)

ethical and political commitments, and played the leading role in student Christian and political life for many years. The Christian Union, which numerically replaced it, was in a conservative evangelical tradition; but since the turn of the century it has in turn been outnumbered by Fusion groups – charismatic, moderately evangelical and linked to independent churches in Cambridge.

Yet to focus on faith communities misses a great deal. Spiritual energies are also expressed in a vast number of other ways by those who identify with traditions of faith and those who do not.

Right: The Cambridge University Buddhist Society is the second oldest Buddhist society in Britain, and its Honorary President is the Dalai Lama.

Monsignor Gilbey

Few Cambridge figures made such a spectacular impression on so wide a range of those at the University over such a long period as Father (later Monsignor) Alfred Newman Gilbey, who had been at Trinity just after the Great War and who served as the Roman Catholic chaplain at the University 1932–65. Described by a friend of his later life as 'a vision of a quintessentially happier Cambridge now all but lost', he exuded the elegance of the privileged Edwardian world in which he had been brought up and to whose social manners and values he clung tenaciously. He echoed a feeling widespread in some circles that we were living in the aftermath of a bygone golden age, especially in the ancient universities. He spoke of the 'electric telephone' and of the 'motoring car'. He had a baroque quality which, like his Catholicism, may have derived from his beloved Spanish mother. Dressed immaculately in a frock coat and topper or alternatively in a cassock and broad-brimmed clerical hat, Monsignor Gilbey cut an arresting figure moving about Cambridge. He hunted with the Trinity Foot Beagles and founded a fashionable dining club called the Strafford. He made no secret of his distaste for 20th-century egalitarianism and its vision of universal social mobility. He had a well-stocked mind in matters of history (especially that of the University), literature and architecture as well as religion, and he expressed himself with clarity and fluency in an ornate voice. His deep spirituality inspired others.

Loyal and charitable to a fault, he was always on hand to answer a call for help from any of his flock (his phrase). He had many devoted admirers, not all, by any means, from privileged backgrounds or co-religionists, who kept up with him long after they had gone down. He subsidised the chaplaincy at Fisher House from his own patrimony and was often to be seen at the Bath Hotel entertaining members of his flock or others. Drawing on considerable goodwill towards him in high places in the land, he fought a long, and ultimately successful, battle to prevent Fisher House being taken over in the redevelopment of Petty Cury and its environs. Following a campaign by some disenchanted members of the Catholic Fisher Society against his refusal to admit to the chaplaincy female Catholic undergraduates (of which there were then only a handful), Monsignor Gilbey was forced to resign in 1965. He moved to the Travellers Club in Pall Mall but was often still to be seen visiting old haunts and old friends in Cambridge. He lived in good health until 1998 when he died at the age of 97. He had become a minor national institution, featured periodically in the press. Much mourned, he lies buried in the courtyard of Fisher House.

Charles Lysaght (1962)

Music is probably a more pervasive and noticeable mark of spiritual Cambridge than anything else. The choir of King's College is best known, but that is just the most obvious musical feature. The richness and depth of choral Cambridge is astonishing. In an area of less than a square mile are to be found some of the world's great choirs singing the sacred music of the West – besides King's there are St John's, Trinity, Clare, Jesus, Gonville & Caius and others. The Anglican choral tradition has flourished here as never before, with new music continually commissioned and performed, and listeners vastly multiplied through mass media, compact discs, and growing numbers of visitors to Cambridge. Musical Cambridge is of course far broader than this. It performs other forms of explicitly religious music (one of the Muslim chaplains to the University at present is a composer of Islamic hymns and songs; a recent Jewish fellow of Newnham was noted for her liturgical chanting) and also a great deal of other music.

"If you are a Jew or a Buddhist, you will have to make an effort to find out about the relevant religions' groups and societies. If you are a Moslem you will find your needs badly catered for in Cambridge, and will have to work especially hard. Whether you're a Christian or not, you won't have to wait more than a few days before CICCU—the Cambridge Inter-Collegiate Christian Union—catches up with you."

Varsity Handbook, 1980–1

Music raises fascinating issues about the very nature of the 'spiritual' and its relation to the 'religious', and indeed encourages us to be cautious about drawing clear defining lines. Music is a good symbol of the spiritual as ranging from God-centred joy, praise, thanks, lament, confession and other expressions located firmly within a specific religious tradition (St Augustine said: 'Whoever sings prays twice') through to forms with no explicit religious associations at all. Do most people attending the best-known chapels come 'for the music' or to worship? That questionable 'either/or' underlines the complexity of the relationship between the spiritual, the religious and the secular; and the lack of simple defining lines is appropriate to the character of spiritual Cambridge.

Besides music there are literature, drama and all the arts, including flourishing dance groups. Many societies and clubs are concerned to serve justice, peace and other good causes. A striking feature of the University as a whole over the past 50 years has been an increasing number of initiatives that take on responsibilities beyond the University at local, national and international levels. Groups such as Student Action for Refugees, the Cambridge Stop AIDS Society, the CU Fund for South African Education, the CU Kenya Project and Sakhya (Cambridge Friends of India) are just the tip of the iceberg, and beyond such groups members of the University are involved in an extraordinary array of other public responsibilities.

Most pervasive is the core concern of the University for academic disciplines. All subjects require spiritual virtues and disciplines in the

Entrance to the Faculty of Divinity displaying quotations from sacred texts in eight different languages, including English, Arabic, Hebrew and Sanskrit.

When I left school in 1950 the idea of university was out of the question. So imagine my surprise at the age of 35 when Newnham and my Director of Studies to be, John Bowker, in his words decided to 'take the risk' of admitting this woman who did not have an A level to her name to read for the Theological Tripos.

It was a great time to be studying theology. Lectures were stimulating and fun, one remembers with affection Professor 'Charlie' Moule dealing with pompous first years who disagreed with something he had said in a lecture. In his inimitable way this great New Testament scholar would address the young (usually!) man, 'With great respect…'

I remember the excitement of discovering philosophy and, while waiting for a supervision, listening to Don Cupitt (Emmanuel) negotiating for leniency for an undergraduate who had been involved in the riots – I think it was the time of the disastrous visit of the then Prime Minister Harold Wilson. This was a very different side to the author of *The Myth of God Incarnate* and *The Sea of Faith*.

I treasure the memory of the shambling figure of Professor Donald MacKinnon, the packed lecture room in the Old Divinity School for his occasional lectures, and the same figure deep in conversation with one of the homeless for whom he always had time.

Supervisions with Bishop John Robinson (Trinity). The introduction into the Tripos of comparative religion and being sent off into the UL to research the topic of John Bowker's next lecture, to see if I came up with anything different. The path I began on then led me to be one of the first 32 women of the Church of England to be ordained to the priesthood in Bristol Cathedral in 1994. The tools we were given during our undergraduate years have enabled me to think radically but rationally, and to converse in depth with people using very different expressions and language about the meaning and challenge of life and faith.

Rosemary Dawn Watling
(1967)

I well remember sitting in the Divinity School Library in the mid-1970s and occasionally hearing Professor MacKinnon lumbering about the room. He always had a pencil in his mouth while in the library, and as he searched you could hear crunching sounds as he completely devoured it. Some of the bits fell on the floor, but quite a lot of it seemed to be eaten!

One day I met the janitor of the Divinity School, a man called Mr Root, coming into the building carrying a little bag. He transferred from the bag to a plate a small currant bun. I asked him what he was doing. In a slightly despairing tone he explained that every morning he had to go up to the 'Whim' in Trinity Street, queue up to buy the bun on a plate, then take it back for Professor MacKinnon's elevenses.

Stephen Pattison
(1973)

Cambridge was a time of deep uncertainty and insecurity in my journey of faith. I arrived with a largely unexamined, highly experiential Christian faith that combined contemplative mysticism with charismatic fervour. It had withstood the depredations of a damp, public school Anglicanism and the regimented civil religion of a year in the army. However, in studying history my belief was tipped into the seething cauldron of the hermeneutics of suspicion. In the midst of this faith-quake I immersed myself in the paganism of my fellow students.

Cambridge was not a secular place then. Everyone I knew possessed a faith that Sophocles, Cicero and Augustine would have easily recognised and whose ancient gods now go by the name of 'competition', 'drivenness' and 'achievement'. So, along with everyone else I tried to make a name for myself, turning theatre, sports, even social life itself into a quest for honour and glory. My rediscovery of humility came by a strange, uniquely Cantabrian route.

I was invited to join the Roof Climbing Society after abseiling down the side of Queens' College to deliver a nocturnal Valentine's Day message. The recipient of this message recounted the tale to a neighbour at her orchestra. The next evening I received a knock on my door and an invitation to come on a night-climb up the side of Clare College. And so I was initiated into a secret sect that had been going for over 100 years.

My catechesis consisted of climbs over the Wren Library and forays across the roofs of St John's and Pembroke. It was on these that I found a form of exhilaration, a central point of which was that no one else could see it. Half its joy lay in keeping one's light under a bushel rather than appearing before the gaze of others.

The apogee of this cult was the Senate House leap: a standing jump over Senate House Passage from a ledge on Caius onto a wider ledge on the Senate House opposite. Failure meant severe injury or even death. In contemplating whether or not to undertake this ritual test I came to terms with my fear, particularly my fear of failure. I discovered a sense of limit and realised the futility of such worldly endeavour. In short, being scared is a great tonic for an arrogant soul. In turning away from the Senate House leap I recovered my vision for an altogether different kind of leap.

Luke Bretherton
(1988)

pursuit of meaning, understanding, knowledge, ethics and the wisdom needed to relate a field to other fields and to human life more widely. Perhaps the chief sign that the University has in fact been taking this dimension seriously is the way it deals with the field where spiritual questions are most explicit. Since the early 1990s the Faculty of Divinity has undergone the greatest transformation in its history. It has a new Edward Cullinan building on the Sidgwick Site, student numbers have increased ahead of the University average, it has expanded through four endowed posts and an array of projects based in its new Centre for Advanced Religious and Theological Studies, and its Theology and Religious Studies Tripos has been reformed to do justice both to traditional strengths in Christianity and also to other areas such as Judaism, Islam, Indian religions and the human and natural sciences.

In June 2007 the Pro-Vice-Chancellor Kate Pretty opened an event in Lancaster House, London, during the last weeks of the premiership of Tony Blair. The Cambridge Inter-Faith Programme was hosting on behalf of the University a conference on 'Islam and Muslims in the World Today', attended by Muslims and others from over 30 countries. Speakers included the Prince of Wales, the Prime Minister, Chancellor of the Exchequer Gordon Brown, the Leader of the Opposition, the Grand Mufti of Egypt, the Bishop of London and a range of religious and civil society leaders and academics. Fifty years ago such an event is hard to imagine; it is a fitting symbol of the complex interplay of the religious and the secular that marks spiritual Cambridge in the 21st century.

David F. Ford *is Regius Professor of Divinity and a Fellow of Selwyn College.*

Clare College Choir, 2007.

Michael Derringer

Jewish Cambridge

I arrived having had a fairly traditional, though by no means orthodox, Jewish upbringing. My father was a pillar of the West London Synagogue, the first Reform synagogue in Britain, and I had had my bat mitzvah there and had been close to the extraordinarily charismatic senior rabbi there, Hugo Gryn. My father had been a warden there, wandering around the West End of London in full morning dress, to my acute embarrassment. But by my late teens I was breaking away. I had a non-Jewish boyfriend – at least, his father was Jewish but he had no interest. I was fiercely left wing. I was ready to be an archaeologist, a social reformer, a music lover, a Hebraist, but I was not ready to do much Jewishly. So in my first year I did not even go home for the most solemn day of the year, Yom Kippur, the Day of Atonement, to my parents' horror, but wandered around feeling very strange and lost.

Eighteen months later, I was coming to the end of the relationship with my boyfriend, whom I had met before going up to Cambridge. My anger at Judaism – and at my somewhat traditional north-west London upbringing – had abated somewhat, and my father, whom I adored, had had a serious heart problem. How all that fits together I neither knew then nor know now, but I began to be interested again.

I went to the Jewish Society a couple of times, but it was too orthodox for me, and the food was truly terrible. But at the beginning of my third year, Nicholas de Lange arrived in Cambridge, as a new Schechter lecturer in Jewish studies. He introduced me to the Progressive Jewish Group, which I then started going to fairly regularly. I loved it. It was a bit chaotic, not very knowledgeable, the services were fun, we ate together or went out to drink together afterwards, and the people were great. Sometimes we would go and eat with the more orthodox Jewish students at the synagogue in Thompson's Lane, but I never really forgave them for the poor quality of the food – it was disgusting, and I have always been a foodie. But I began to get more interested in things Jewish. Nicholas was a profound influence. He introduced me to my next boyfriend – now my husband of 34 years – and he also got me thinking about becoming a rabbi. I had started Cambridge ambivalent about my Judaism. As a result of Nicholas de Lange, my cousin Erwin Rosenthal, who taught Hebrew and Arabic and had invited me round for supper time and again, and Sebastian Brock, who is not Jewish but thought I was being pathetic in not learning more about my religion and heritage, I left Cambridge committed, a good deal more knowledgeable, and convinced that being Jewish, and teaching Judaism, could be fun.

This was not a time of huge Jewish activity at Cambridge. But there were strengths to the various Jewish groups, and something of an awareness that there were lots of Jewish students at Cambridge, most of whom paid their Judaism no attention unless they went home. But during that four-year period, Jewish studies, hitherto unknown as such in Cambridge, became a real academic possibility. What had been rabbinics, or Biblical Hebrew, or a bit of modern Hebrew, became

something you could study in a different way. So I learned about Jews in medieval southern France and the cross-faith relationships that were commonplace at the time. I studied Biblical commentators with wonderful professors from the Hebrew University in Jerusalem, and I learned that you could – and should – think differently about Judaism, that it is living, breathing, and very very book-based – and that Jews like nothing better than a good argument. I've been hooked ever since, and I think nothing gave my father greater joy than my returning from Cambridge at the end of my second year a committed Jew once again, but this time as a result of my own decision.

Julia Neuberger (1969) is a rabbi and a Liberal Democrat member of the House of Lords.

Freshers' Fair, 2006.

Julian Andrews

As a student at another university in the early 1990s, my experience of Cambridge revolved mainly around titanic struggles on the basketball court, some won some lost! There were also, inevitably, some books by Cambridge's finest that I did actually read between important games.

Unexpectedly, in 1994, I was given the opportunity to meet these luminaries 'face to face' when I arrived at Westcott House Theological College to begin training as an Anglican priest. I had felt a call to the priesthood since about the age of 13 and after four years of basketball and studies in history it was now time for me to amaze my university friends and prepare for life as a priest. That didn't mean sport was no longer a passion. I played basketball for Jesus College and my fellow Westcott ordinands said this was extremely appropriate because from now on I should be doing 'everything for Jesus' anyway!

The three years I spent in Cambridge studying theology and preparing for ordained ministry made a lasting impression. So much so that I returned in 2006 to become the Chaplain to University Staff at Great St Mary's, the University Church. In the meantime I had been a parish priest in North Wales and then a chaplain with the Royal Navy and Royal Marines Commandos.

I was ordained at the age of 25, a youngster in church terms, and from that perspective I have always had an affinity with young people and my chosen paths in ministry have often reflected this.

Great St Mary's has a long history of engaging with young minds, students and staff alike, from the great Sunday evening services of Mervyn Stockwood's day through to the multi-faith encounters of today's chaplaincy work. The most impressive aspect of this university is and always has been its young people, and from a spiritual point of view, their capacity to search for God with honesty and integrity. Today that means in a truly ecumenical and multi-faith way.

As an ordinand and a chaplain in Cambridge I have witnessed first-hand the great contribution that young people have made to this historic institution and to the city. They have an appetite for knowledge and understanding that helps them look for God in places that others have often long forgotten about. They can see beyond the constraints of institutions and through tribal allegiances.

As a member of the student community and as a member of staff, this university has taught me many things over the years but perhaps the greatest gift it has given to me is the privilege of being with young, enquiring, exploring minds who can meet in a spirit of mutual respect and friendship seeking learning and knowledge above all else. My ministry has been enhanced and continues to benefit immensely from being part of this experience and I thank God for the challenges and insight that I have been afforded by this institution's young people as they continue to explore 'spirituality and faith' together in new and exciting ways.

Christian Heycocks
Chaplain to University Staff

Cambridge bishops: Archbishop of Canterbury, Rowan Williams, who studied at Christ's and was Dean and Chaplain of Clare 1984–6 and the Archbishop of York, John Sentamu, who read theology at Selwyn before training for the priesthood at Ridley Hall.

Muslim Cambridge

Cambridge has attracted Muslim students for over a hundred years now, and some of them have made a considerable impact on the world. Muhammad Iqbal was perhaps the best known, while Abdallah Yusuf Ali (St John's, 1891–5) was famous as one of the first 'natives' in the Indian Civil Service; later he published a translation of the Koran which has outsold all others.

Today most of the University's 800 or so Muslim students are native Britons, from a wide range of ethnic backgrounds. The University Islamic Society has become one of the largest University societies, with over 700 members. In partnership with the Oxbridge Muslim Alumni Association it maintains contacts with a growing network of graduates, who work in the full range of professions, although medicine and law are especially well represented. An annual alumni dinner at the Guildhall attracts several hundred high-flyers, and confirms Cambridge's reputation as a nursery for new Muslim talent.

The Islamic Society organises a wide range of activities, including Koran circles, prayer groups, football tournaments and an annual Islam Awareness Week. Some colleges also have their own fledgling Islamic Societies. But Cambridge's religious infrastructure has struggled to keep up with this new demography. There is not a single mosque in the city centre, and students and University staff have to make their way to mosques in the suburbs, or to a dozen informal venues across the city to observe the Friday congregational prayer, the main event of the Muslim week. This number grows during the Muslim fasting month of Ramadan, which culminates in a festival prayer which attracts upwards of 3,000 people.

There are prayer facilities on the West Cambridge Site, but the Muslim chaplaincy has its office in the Muslim prayer room on the Sidgwick Site. Here students may meet the chaplain, John Butt. Educated at Stoneyhurst by Jesuits, he later, after travelling in Afghanistan and converting to Islam, graduated from India's leading Islamic university, Dar al-Ulum (Deoband). He is assisted by myself (under my Islamic name Abdal Hakim Murad). Neighbouring Anglia Ruskin University boasts one of the UK's first female Muslim chaplains, Sheridan James, a Cambridge graduate in theology. Together this team tries to cope with a bewilderingly diverse range of student issues and problems.

The most common problem seems to be work-related stress. The chaplaincy and the various Muslim pastoral organisations working in Cambridge hence try to provide means of relaxation. One result has been a male-voice choir, 'Harmonia Alcorani', which has performed at Wembley Arena and other major venues. The songs are in English, Turkish or Arabic, using either British folk tunes, or the subtle quarter-tones and complex syncopations of traditional Islamic music.

Left: Sir Muhammad Iqbal (1873–1938). Born in the Punjab, Iqbal studied law at Trinity, graduating in 1906. On returning to India he practised as a successful barrister, served as head of the Muslim League, and became the 20th century's best-known Urdu poet. His idea of a separate homeland for India's Muslims, developed during his student days in Cambridge, ensured his immortalisation as the 'Father of Pakistan', where his birthday is a national holiday.

Following this success, a lively women's choir has also been established. Islamic crafts are encouraged wherever local expertise permits, and courses in Arabic calligraphy with a visiting teacher from Istanbul have proved popular. There is a Koranic study circle, and also, most recently, a very highbrow all-female group that meets to discuss religious novels.

Other issues tackled by the chaplaincy team range from mundane questions of explaining Muslim dietary rules to college chefs, or channelling requests for time off for religious holidays, to more searching, personal questions. Students unexpectedly falling in love across religious boundaries need careful guidance on how to break news to friends and parents. Seriously ill students require sensitive attention, and may need help with running errands and communicating with supervisors, colleges and examiners. Most of the bright young Muslim people at Cambridge need no help in defining their identity, but at times, experiencing the full richness of the city while maintaining a strong religious commitment can produce strains and raise questions about a student's self-understanding.

Tim Winter is Sheikh Zayed Lecturer in Islamic Studies and a Fellow of Wolfson College.

Harmonia Alcorani, the Muslim male-voice choir, 2007.

Science and religion

JOHN POLKINGHORNE

The university of Isaac Newton – scientific genius and a deeply, if unorthodoxly, religious man – is an institution in which one would expect there to be serious intellectual discussion concerning how the scientific and religious world views relate to each other. This has indeed been the case and the last 50 years saw a vigorous engagement with these issues.

Some contributors to the debate have been Cambridge alumni who pursued their mature academic careers elsewhere. One such was Eric Mascall, Pembroke mathematician and Anglican priest, who became a Student of Christ Church, Oxford. There he delivered an important series of Bampton lectures, anticipating many of the issues that would dominate the discussion in the following half-century. They were subsequently published as *Christian Theology and Natural Science* (1956). Mascall wrote in the Thomist tradition stemming from Aquinas, for which the unrestricted search for truth is seen ultimately as the search for God. A less academic writer on these matters, but an influential public speaker, was the distinguished theoretical chemist, Charles Coulson. He emphasised what he saw as the complementary relationship between science and religion.

I chose to stay in Cambridge, eventually as Professor of Mathematical Physics (1968–79) and later Dean of Trinity Hall and President of Queens'. Much of the science and religion discussion in the second half of the 20th century centred on the physical sciences. The deep intelligibility and rational beauty revealed in fundamental physics, together with the fine-tuning of natural law necessary for a universe to be capable of developing carbon-based life, were held to encourage the belief that a divine mind and creatorly purpose lay behind cosmic history. I developed a revised version of natural theology along these lines, claiming the achievement of enhanced insight rather than proof, and seeking to complement rather than rival science's description of natural processes.

The Oxford physical biochemist, Arthur Peacocke, spent the years 1973–84 in Cambridge as Dean of Clare. He interpreted the role of chance in evolutionary process not as a sign of meaninglessness, but as a method for the exploration of potentiality, expressed through a process of continuing creation. In a phrase coined by the Cambridge author Charles Kingsley shortly after the publication of *On the Origin of Species*, evolution was to be understood theologically as the divine allowing of creatures to 'make themselves'. Peacocke delighted in musical metaphors and he saw creation as a grand improvisation, rather than the performance of a fixed score. He also pioneered a course on science and theology which has become a permanent part of the Theology and Religious Studies Tripos.

Peacocke and I both contributed to two topics that have proved important in the recent science and religion debate. One was the claim that science and theology are intellectual cousins under the skin, in that both are seeking understanding attained through motivated beliefs, even if the appropriate sources of motivation differ. We believed that a philosophy of critical realism applied to both disciplines. The other topic was one that dominated discussion in the 1990s: how to reconcile scientific insight with theological belief in divine providential action. Careful analysis of the intrinsic unpredictabilities present in nature, together with recognition that science's account of causal process is actually rather patchy, showed that science has failed to establish the causal closure of the world on its own reductionist terms.

The Golden Helix,
19 Portugal Place,
Cambridge.

12th October, 1961.

cheque returned with comps.

(229)

Dear Sir Winston,

It was kind of you to write.   I am sorry you do not understand why I resigned.

To make my position a little clearer I enclose a cheque for ten guineas to open the Churchill College Hetairae fund.   My hope is that eventually it will be possible to build permanent accommodation within the College, to house a carefully chosen selection of young ladies in the charge of a suitable Madam who, once the institution has become traditional, will doubtless be provided, without offence, with dining rights at the high table.

Such a building will, I feel confident, be an amenity which many who live in the college will enjoy very much, and yet the instruction need not be compulsory and none need enter it unless they wish. Moreover it would be open (conscience permitting) not merely to members of the Church of England, but also to Catholics, Non-Conformists, Jews, Moslems, Hindus, Zen Buddhists and even to atheists and agnostics such as myself.

And yet I cannot help feeling that when you pass on my offer to the other Trustees - as I hope you will - they may not share my enthusiasms for such a truly educational project.   They may feel, being men of the world, that to house such an Establishment, however great the need and however correctly conducted, within the actual College would not command universal respect.   They may even feel my offer of ten guineas to be a joke in rather poor taste.

Continued.......

W.S.C.

- 2 -

But that is exactly my view of the proposal of the Trustees to build a chapel, after the middle of the 20th century, in a new College and in particular in one with a special emphasis on science. Naturally some members of the College will be Christian, at least for the next decade or so, but I do not see why the College should tacitly endorse their beliefs by providing them with special facilities. The churches in the town, it has been said, are half empty. Let them go there.   It will be no further than they have to go to their lectures.

Even a joke in poor taste can be enjoyed, but I regret that my enjoyment of it has entailed my resignation from the College which bears your illustrious name.

Understandably I shall not be present on Saturday.   I hope it all goes off well.

Yours sincerely,

Francis Crick

F.H.C. Crick.

Sir Winston Churchill, K.G., M.P.,
Chartwell,
Westerham,
KENT.

W.D.C.

Nobel laureate Francis Crick writes to Sir Winston Churchill in 1961, protesting at the proposal to provide a chapel for the new Churchill College.

A significant but relatively unexplored interface between science and religion relates to the border with the human sciences. It was therefore an important development in 1993 when Susan Howatch endowed at Cambridge the first permanent university post in science and theology in the United Kingdom, a position whose holder, Fraser Watts, has a scientific background in psychology. Through his leadership, Cambridge has become a major international centre in which these issues are explored.

Of course, by no means all Cambridge scientists have been sympathetic to religious belief. Francis Crick, arguably the greatest Cambridge scientist of the second half of the 20th century, was a trenchant opponent of religion. He resigned his fellowship at Churchill in protest at the college's accepting the private benefaction of a chapel. Hoyle, Bondi and Gold, who developed the interesting but now abandoned steady state theory of cosmology, were not motivated solely by scientific considerations, but also by the hope that the removal of a 'moment of creation' would be a blow to religious belief. Stephen Hawking thought something similar when his speculative quantum cosmology seemed to indicate that the universe might have a finite age but no identifiable beginning. A theologian, however, would say that creation is not primarily about how things began but why things exist.

Herman Bondi became Master of Churchill and supported the Humanist Society in its continuing role of speaking for atheism in the University. Cambridge atheists have been staunch and articulate in defending their position, but their discourse has been free from the kind of shrill polemic that has characterised recent Oxford atheist authors.

A university that did not take seriously a careful and critical evaluation of the claims of science and of religion would not be wholly fulfilling its academic task. There has been no danger of this default in Cambridge.

John Polkinghorne is a Fellow of Queens' College. Until 1979 he was Professor of Mathematical Physics but resigned to become an ordained Anglican minister.

Hiroshi Shimura

Left: The chapel at Churchill, which was the subject of bitter controversy when the college was founded. The building is on a plot of land leased to a Chapel Trust composed of Christian Fellows of the college and is, thus, not officially the college chapel. It was not constructed until this compromise was reached in 1967. The architect was Richard Sheppard and it features stained glass by John Piper.

A question of balance

SOPHIE PICKFORD

The Cambridge sporting scene is perhaps best known for its bastions of Britishness – the Boat Race, the Varsity Match, the Hawks' Club and the Bumps, for example. Ruffians (that's 'alumni' to you and me) will, at the slightest whiff of a good match, don their old club tie, break open the Pimm's and cheer fanatically for the youth of today, custodians of all they hold dear in their alma mater. As a recent graduate and committed sportswoman, I can confirm that there are few sights more encouraging on the sidelines than some elderly supporters reminding you of your place in the grand scheme of things: one day I'll be there too, draped in a slightly faded lion-clad banner and tottering along the touchline. But, nostalgia aside, what are the true issues that underlie Cambridge's sporting scene today? What 21st-century concerns are student athletes facing and what direction are we moving in?

In 1892 the *Cambridge Review* observed that 'a swimming bath is now beginning to be considered as a necessity in most of our large public schools … consequently, it seems strange that we are still without one'. This astute commentator of 113 years ago could, sadly, just as well have been writing this week, for the travesty continues – Cambridge University has no pool. In fact, Cambridge University has, overall, very poor centralised sporting facilities indeed. To be fair, plans for a multi-million-pound sports centre including a sports hall, squash and tennis courts, 50m pool and sports science centre are underway; architectural models have been built, a site chosen and fund-raising has begun. But, as with the fabled Cambridge rowing lake or the ice rink, this has all been going on for rather a long time and a new injection of enthusiasm, publicity or, perhaps more importantly, money, is the order of the day. In the meantime, the University swimming and water polo clubs continue to use the Leys School pool for the majority of their training, one of the University's less fine traditions stretching back to 1906.

Opposite: The Men's Hockey Blues come out at the start of the 2008 Varsity Hockey Match at Southgate Hockey Club in north London. Cambridge beat Oxford 3:1.

Gentlemen could learn the art of balancing on a Penny Farthing in the pioneer days of the University Bicycle Club. Founded in 1874, the club organised races against Oxford and London, this one in 1879.

The sports complex envisaged by the powers that be would place Cambridge at the very top of its field in the country in terms of sporting facilities. The current and prolonged absence of such a provision suggests to the wider world that Cambridge takes little interest in the well-rounded scholar, something that we know not to be true. The lack of truly competitive facilities to rival other elite establishments will ultimately only increase the rate of the 'brain drain' to the US and to other UK universities, a very real problem in today's academic meat market. Perhaps it is this

This was possibly the high time for Cambridge sport. Peter May was collecting an impossible number of Blues, and a Welsh international hockey forward didn't get a Blue because the England one was in the team already. We also beat the Other Place a satisfactory number of times. I put the shot and chucked the discus in the vague hope of a little Half Blue, but no luck. However, Peterhouse did come second in the whole University my second year in the athletics Cuppers, having won the Second Division in my first. Pretty good for the smallest college.

To mention how unbelievably amateur it was in those days, in my second year the University took on their first ever professional coach (Harvard had three for field sports alone). All coaching before that was from dons who were also athletes. For example, in the shot we had Bonzo Howland, who had been the first-string for England. But most of the time we were left on our own.

It was also enjoyable to go sailing at St Ives, even if it meant quite a long bike ride there and back. The Cruising Club had an immensely cosy club room in Ram Yard, which contained an impressive array of silverware, for these were the years when Stewart Morris and the other Cambridge dinghy sailors were winning just about everything. We still had the old Cambridge One-Designs (built by Uffa Fox, F2-5, Fee, Fie, Fo and Fum). These were immensely precious and sailed only by the best sailors! (Fireflies were the single-handed boat in the 1948 Olympics).

B.S. Russell
(1948)

argument that the University will finally respond to, for without such a sports complex, Cambridge will soon lag behind on the national sporting scene. Sooner or later, the money for the long-awaited West Cambridge development will have to appear.

This raises the thorny problem of money. The corporatisation of academia is a hot topic at the moment. Voices throughout our fine establishment can be heard lamenting or extolling the increased reliance of the University on big business, yet supporter or detractor, we all know that financial viability is fundamental to research. Where the money comes from, some would argue, isn't as important as the fact it is coming at all. The same process is being struggled with on the playing fields, in the swimming pools and boathouses of Cambridge: to what extent should we rely on corporate sponsorship? What is it that forces clubs down this route? And what alternatives do we have? Almost every major sports team representing the University has some level of corporate cash sponsorship, yet even this corporate money is not enough for clubs to balance their books. The sports syndicate subsidises the deficit, but their contribution does not plug the hole entirely. This is where student subs come in, and where the lottery begins. A comparison of the cost of trialling in different sports highlights a shocking imbalance in the level of student contributions, with sports such as women's rowing proving particularly draining on student coffers. Perhaps a

more centralised effort to accrue funds for clubs would be the long-term answer, at least in order to streamline the process.

On the upside (and despite Cambridge's various financial woes), the University continues to produce an impressive array of sporting stars. The 'Talented Athlete Scholarship Scheme' (TASS), a government-led initiative that aims to bridge the gaping hole in funding for elite athletes while they are students, is a case in point. The list of achievements to date by Cambridge's TASS athletes is truly impressive. The majority have represented either England or Great Britain in their chosen sport, and some have already had considerable success at international level. Each has been individually nominated by their National Governing Body. The students on the scheme are 'scholar-athletes' in the true sense of the term, and the delicate balance between sport and work is an issue that frequently rears its head. Karen Pearce, who has run the scheme in Cambridge in recent years, stresses that the main goal of TASS is 'to give athletes the chance to go to university whilst not jeopardising their sporting chances by doing so', but maintaining their dual lives is a constant struggle, which requires them to be 'very determined and focussed'.

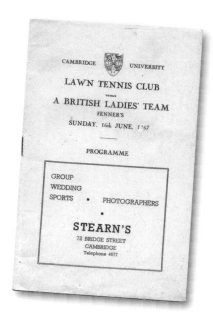

The University Lawn Tennis Club was founded in 1881.

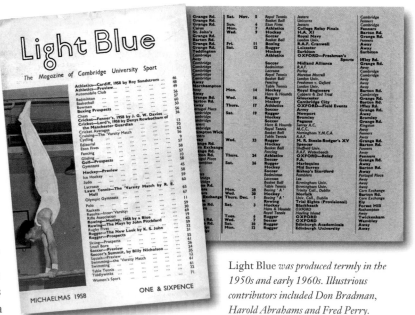

Light Blue *was produced termly in the 1950s and early 1960s. Illustrious contributors included Don Bradman, Harold Abrahams and Fred Perry.*

women's, and it is men's sport that on average attracts more funding. Yet it seems that a sea-change in attitude is needed as much as an injection of cash or facilities. People have to start really caring about women's sport, attending friends' matches and demanding that women's sport is given the prominence it deserves. Perhaps a grass-roots revolution such as this will prompt the bigger changes that women's sport needs, levelling the more important sporting disparities between the sexes in Cambridge? In any case, the increased financial stability and prominence of the Ospreys can only help in this endeavour.

Varsity Ice Hockey.

Only the briefest of overviews of the challenges and delights facing Cambridge sportsmen and women today, some of them age-old in character, some more modern, this article is just the beginning of the Cambridge sporting story. Perhaps Juvenal's oft-quoted phrase, *mens sana in corpore sano* ('a healthy mind in a healthy body'), still finds its apotheosis in seats of higher learning such as Cambridge. Perhaps, just maybe, it will also still apply to the old lady you'll see wielding a zimmer-frame on the side-lines in 50 years' time.

Sophie Pickford (1998) is a former sports editor of Varsity *and was Vice-Captain of the Women's water polo team, 2002, and has two half blues. She is a Research Fellow in Art History at St Edmund's.*

The balance of work and sport at university is an age-old problem still very much present today. The average Cambridge undergraduate is expected to spend around 40 hours per week on their degree, though according to one Head of Department in the arts and humanities 'reading time may well take it above that'. That's over six-and-a-half hours a day, six days a week. Trialling for a University sport can add anything from seven hours a week to this, peaking with the Herculean efforts of rowers, whose weekly schedule involves 16 hours of training, plus significant time spent travelling to and from Ely. The resultant 70-hour marathon faced by rowers leaves little time for illness, a social life, or anything else. CUBC coach Duncan Holland believes in the importance of academic studies: 'Our members are scholar athletes. Their priority is education, rowing is a recreation.' Some students thrive under the pressure, others don't, and there seems to be little or no correlation between Tripos results and sporting obsession. Hugh Laurie, rowing Blue and President of Footlights, got a third in his Arch. and Anth. Finals, whilst Oscar winner Sam Mendes, University cricketer and director of numerous plays during his Cambridge years, was awarded a first in English.

Aside from this balance between work and sport, what can be said of the equally important balance between the sexes? The opening of the Ospreys' new clubhouse on Jesus Lane in recent years is a giant step forward in recognition for elite sportswomen at the University, yet few would deny that there is still a gender bias in Cambridge sport. It is the men's Boat Race and the men's rugby Varsity Match that are televised, spectator numbers at men's matches in general are much higher than at

The new University Sports Centre, planned for the West Cambridge Site: the centre is designed to sit beside a lake and to include a swimming pool, six squash courts and four clay tennis courts, and a multipurpose sports hall suitable for badminton, netball, five-a-side football, martial arts and fencing. On the first floor, there will be a spectator viewing gallery, a lakeside café as well as a Sports Science Centre which will concentrate on rehabilitation, performance testing and research. The building will feature a sedum roof covering so that it will blend into the surrounding landscape. As of 2008, the centre has still to be funded.

On the river

Sunset over a crowded river at Jesus Green.

I f there is one sport that a Cambridge undergraduate or postgraduate is likely to try, then that sport must be rowing. In any given year, a conservative estimate would be that at least 2,000 of the year's students actively participate in a crew in one of the more than 30 college boat clubs. The May Bumps alone consist of ten divisions of 17 Eights, or over 1,500 people, and that's before you include the coaches, supporters and hangers-on. Over the year, at least 2,000–2,500 students row on the River Cam.

Compared with a 'normal' local rowing club, student rowing will always have some differences. Most important is the short lifespan of their members as they pass through their academic degrees. This means that every year there is a new influx of eager new members, and a burst of activity in each college in early October as their boat club tries to tempt them into trying rowing. Many do... Around 1,000 take to the water in their early weeks at Cambridge and, although at least half of them may only try it for a term or so, many do become hooked. This in itself seems strange to today's observers: most novice rowing now takes place in the 'early morning', after first light and before lectures, and it can be hard to see why all these people would voluntarily subject themselves to freezing pre-breakfast exercise, especially as the river has become so overcrowded that all they often do is sit in a long queue surrounded by similarly frozen people! This is a major change over the last 10–20 years, driven largely by the increasing academic pressures on students. When I was a student at Jesus College in the 1980s, in six years of rowing I experienced only two early morning outings!

This level of trial and take-up of rowing means that Cambridge could be one of the most significant nursery grounds for rowing in the country, and certainly has one of the highest participation rates. The Cam is undoubtedly one of the busiest (and smallest) rivers in the country for rowing activity. However, an impartial observer would have to say that college rowing today is far behind the heady heights of the middle of last century, when college crews regularly featured in Henley finals and on occasion made up significant proportions of national crews. Resolving this decline continues to be the single greatest challenge facing Cambridge rowing today. College rowing is still the breeding ground for the University rowers of CUWBC and

After the University Fours and the Colquhoun and Bushe-Fox Sculls, the Fairbairn Cup is one of the main fixtures in winter. The race consists of staggered time trials and the fastest boat in each class wins its pennant. Over a four-day period successive crews would row along winding Stations of the Cross, down the river, past the Pike and Eel, the Glass Houses and the crooked tree. Each crew member focused on the shoulder of the man in front, and for an eternity each of us would be locked onto the rhythmic, dipping movement of that shoulder. Squaring, feathering, taking the catch, going up and down the slide, pulling the handle of the oar into one's gut, guided by the shrill voice of the cox.

Then came the dreaded Long Reach, which never seemed to end, and, still suffering, the crew would eventually pull past Ditton and Grassy Corner, all the way to the Railway Bridge, this side of Bait's Bite Lock. It took about 25 minutes of heart-stopping effort, until you heard a train rumbling above your head and knew that two more strokes would take you beyond the bridge and past the pole of the finishing point.

However humble, a cold but psyched-up crew can become edgy, if not irascible, when their rhythm is interrupted by things like other crews cutting across your bows or locking blades with you. Or seizing precedence on the river. One morning, our crew had just come to the end of Plough Reach when a cyclist from CUBC came down the banks of the river. The Blue Boat was on a course, coming down The Gut and heading around Grassy Corner towards us.

'Bloody hell…' we muttered.

Reluctantly we pushed for the bank, grabbed tufts of grass and pulled ourselves to the side. On the opposite bank two other crews had also pulled across. We sat bobbing at the sedge, irritated and impatient.

And suddenly, without further warning, there they were.

The cox looked like a wax doll in a cap and jacket. He was hunched up against the prow and speaking into a throat mike.

I think everyone's jaw went a little slack. Eight blades disappeared soundlessly into the water and came out again wet, flashing in the morning sunlight. A single, sinuous arc; one movement. Eight oarsmen, fixated and unseeing, shot past us in total silence. The overwhelming impression was one of magnificence. It was as stunning as the wave of spontaneous applause that erupted from both sides of the river banks. I thought: 'What am I doing?' I found myself, a grown man and a cynic to boot, applauding hysterically.

François Theron
(1981)

Trying to row for both college and university is like trying to satisfy a wife and a mistress. You can't. There could be only one winner, and for me it was the CUBC. Nothing wrong with rowing for Jesus, quite the opposite: it was much more fun. But there is nothing to beat the raw heat of competition, and that's just to get in the Blue Boat in the first place.

I did three Boat Races, and lost all of them by a total of 11½ lengths. In 1982 we led by a length, went wide under Hammersmith, and got rowed past. In 1983 we were awful and didn't see Oxford till the Ball that night. In 1984 tragedy struck: Pete Hobson, coxing, was not told that a big barge had been moored at the start, and on our final warm-up burst we smacked right into it at full tilt. The sharp loud crack as the bows snapped and bent up, the weirdly rapid deceleration as we slowed to a drift, and the panic as we realised we were sinking in the middle of a rapid flood tide all came in a surreal blur. We madly and centipede-like rowed to the Putney wall as the boat went under the surface. We didn't know how deep the water was so someone dived in, and found it to be about two feet deep. Oh. On Sunday we raced in the hastily borrowed GB squad boat and lost. Both crews beat the race record, Oxford by 12 seconds more than us. On the finishing line someone swore, which the microphones on Chiswick Bridge picked up, and I suddenly realised that it was all over. For ever. Losing crews don't tend to have reunions, and the only one we've had was a 19-year one for a TV programme about the sinking. Eight of the nine came, but there was a sadness under the surface; we all knew we had lost that race. Alf Twinn, the charismatic and ancient boatman, cheered me up no end afterwards with 'You're alright, you know-nothing Canterbury git, Sir', and he heaved off to get a top-up of 'jungle juice', as his 'blood corporals' were running a bit low. He had leukaemia, but would claim after every transfusion to feel like a frisky 20-year-old, and be able to take on and beat any (possibly even all) of us in a boxing match. I don't know whose blood he was getting, but we never risked it, because he just might have.

My jilted lover was Jesus, the best rowing college long-term, though near its nadir when I was there. Rowing runs deep and emotively in the ancient cement of its three-sided courts; the only college that can see its (or any) boathouse. Steve Fairbairn was the great inspiration 100 or so years ago, and even in the 1980s, when you talked of 'Steve', no-one thought you meant Mr (now Sir Steve) Redgrave, as Fairbairn's little ditties like 'miles makes champions' created generations of disciples. Jesus used to pace the Blue Boat, as I was regularly reminded at breakfast after 5am training sessions (one-hour run before dawn, then 90 mins weights). I tried my best to honour the Jesus boat club for its generosity in not ostracising me, by coaching men and women right from my first to my last term, peddling along that diabolical towpath, getting into single sculls to win the Bushe-Fox and Colquhoun Sculls, the Double Sculls, and to coach Fours and Eights. In my final year, with a rush of guilt-ridden blood to the head, I told the CUBC I'd be stroking the Jesus Light Four in the Michaelmas races. CUBC threw me out and we lost the final. Despite having two Blues, I had to trial in the 'Dung Barges' with all the other hopefuls and hopelesses, and with two weeks of penance paid, I was allowed back in, suitably chastened. Strangely, I still feel that I did not put enough into college to make up for not being available for the Bumps.

Ewan Pearson
(1981)

CULRC, whose profile the University is keen to exploit to their advantage. Even within the more professional setup of CUBC, the potential development ground of the colleges is recognised, and considerable energy given to an annual development squad bringing on both future University and current college rowers.

As with many things about Cambridge, the way organised student rowing has developed over time has been through ad hoc evolution. Intercollegiate rowing competitions have been going on almost as long as rowing in Cambridge itself, with Bumps records going back to 1827. When these events started, at least apocryphally, the idea was that crews from one college hid in the reeds and leapt out and chased their opponents by surprise! There was not even consistency in boat size, with crews having between six and ten members.

The Bumps (and Cambridge) remained a male preserve until the 1970s saw increasing numbers of colleges admitting women. Before this, the fledgling CUWBC crew had been given a place in the 'men's' Bumps, racing in one of the lower divisions. However, the advent of women's college rowing led inevitably to the creation of women's racing divisions. As the numbers of women were initially quite small, these divisions differed from those of the men, as they raced in Fours rather than Eights. More significant in terms of organisation, the men's and women's events, although they happened on the same days, with alternating divisions, were run separately by the two University Clubs (CUBC and CUWBC), each with slightly different rules. This also meant that, as numbers increased, there was no single forum in which they could agree how to accommodate this growth. This resulted in unsustainable increases in both the number of divisions and number of boats in a division. In 1990 the women's Bumps divisions finally moved into Eights (ending the amusing site of Bumps marshals rushing to change starting chains from Fours to Eights divisions as they alternated!). Reflecting the changing gender balance in the University, there has also been a progressive reduction in the number of men's divisions and an increase for women – not quite equal yet, but there are now five-and-a-half men's and four-and-a-half women's divisions in the Mays, a reasonably accurate reflection of current demand.

During the latter part of the 1980s, it became increasingly clear that the main University rowing clubs had to focus their efforts on their Boat Race campaigns, and simply did not have the resources or inclination to continue administering college rowing. CUBC made its move towards professionalism, and also shifted its training base to Ely. CUWBC, whilst also (and, unfathomably, still) living from hand to mouth and relying virtually completely on committed volunteers for its support, started to train more professionally, increased its squad size, and eventually moved for most of the year out to Ely. At the same time, the demands for coordination on the Cam itself continued to grow, taking an ever-increasing amount of time for those trying to do it.

Eventually, and largely through the drive and vision of Dr John Marks (then CUBC and CUWBC Senior Treasurer), it became clear that the college clubs needed the creation of a new body to oversee the regulation of student rowing on the Cam, and hence in 1994 came the creation of the Cambridge University Combined Boat Clubs

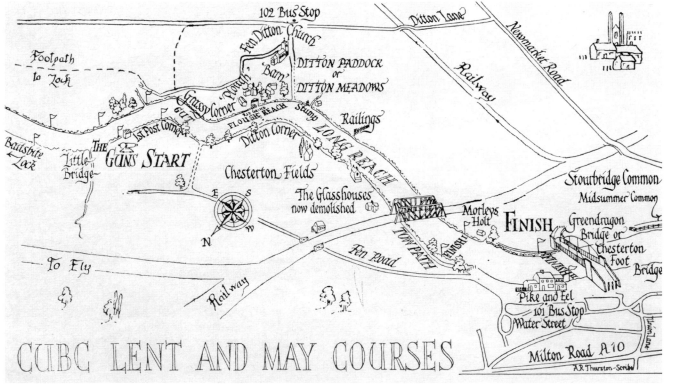

Map of the Bumps course.

The May Bumps, 2007.

Hiroshi Shimura

(CUCBC). This has taken responsibility for organising the major University rowing events in Cambridge (Lent and May Bumps, University Fours, Small Boats Regatta), for regulating day-to-day rowing activities on the river and also the college-run events and, increasingly, the strategic interactions that are required with the University itself, and the various local authorities, other user groups, River Cam Conservancy, police, the ARA and the 'town' Cambridgeshire Rowing Association. Although often unseen by the rowers themselves, these activities take considerable (and entirely voluntary) time and energy from a permanent student executive committee (with five–six members) and Senior Committee.

Looking to the future, Cambridge student rowing faces several difficult challenges. On a tiny, and these days multi-user, stretch of water such as the Cam, balancing the desire to encourage participation and provide enough time and water to allow useful learning and training is currently insurmountable; in stark terms, there are far too many clubs (both town and gown) and participants (maybe even by a factor of four or more) all trying inevitably ineffectively to use the same short time slots on the river. Given a genuine desire from the University for Cambridge to produce truly rounded graduates, that is, to develop both the academic and non-academic skills required for life after university, there needs to be a more balanced approach that would better allow spreading the training load through the day. In the longer term, there is some light at the end of the tunnel in the twin forms of the Cambridge Sports Lakes and the CamToo proposal. However, although both would make a vital contribution to securing the future of Cambridge student rowing, neither are 'magic bullet' solutions, while any such developments that do eventually take place will only be available in the middle-distance future.

Peter Convey (1980) is Chairman of Cambridge University Combined Boat Clubs.

When I came up to New Hall, then only seven years old, I joined Val Goldsborough as the second New Hall woman engineer. At the time there were no engineers in Newnham or Girton and we studied with men from other colleges, many of whom rowed with their college clubs.

We both liked the idea of rowing although we had no previous experience. We obtained permission to restart CUWBC and advertised for others to join us. Here we were blessed by the presence in St Chad's of the artist Carola Brotherton, who drew us eye-catching posters for all three women's colleges.

We were viewed as something of a novelty and were televised on our second outing in an unsteady Eight full of absolute beginners. In our first University novices race we received compliments on our style from the masses of spectators who clapped and cheered us. By the second term, in the Lent Bumps, we had our enthusiastic supporters supplemented by national journalists and photographers.

However, the rowing politics of the time took us completely by surprise. We totally failed to appreciate the novelty of women rowing against men and entered University races as the only events available to our inexperienced crew. Our fellow students were glad to support us: our presence brought attention to rowing for enjoyment, instead of being confined to the serious business of the University trials and the chosen Eight.

Canon Duckworth was chaplain and coach at the new Churchill College and chairman of the Coxes' Society. As 'our beady-eyed brother', he gleefully included 'his sturdy sisters' in mixed crews, mainly with Churchill men. At the last minute he included me as no. 2 in the successful 1963 Coxes' Eight in the Fairbairn races, as I both rowed and coxed by then. With his bubbling enthusiasm, he was known as Chumpha, addressing me as 'Tyranness' and inspiring us to 'hit 'em hard', 'with fire in our belly'!

At this time, the politics became serious as senior members of CUBC, under pressure from the ARA, wanted to exclude CUWBC from membership as a university boat club. An attempt was made to limit membership to clubs only from individual colleges. Long evening arguments ensued but were familiar territory for us because of our engineering experience: we were used to being outnumbered. A compromise was reached, removing the right of each club to have a boat on the river. To outsiders this looked like the end of our time in University races but we knew that sufficient crews withdrew each year for us to keep the place we already had. The University Boat Club could keep face with the ARA and women would continue to row in the Bumps.

Jean Anscombe
(1961)

NINE GIRLS LAND UP THE CREEK

AS THEIR BOAT RIVALS BUMP BY

Letter from Canon 'Jimmy' Noel Duckworth in support of the women's boat during the campaign to have them banned from the Bumps, 1963.

The Oxford and Cambridge Boat Race

What is the Boat Race? The Boat Race is one, albeit the most prestigious, of a series of sporting events held each year between the universities of Oxford and Cambridge, having their origins in a combination of the then primacy of the two universities and the growth of amateur sport in Victorian England. At root, therefore, the Boat Race is an adjunct to the primary academic purposes of the universities, especially since, at least thus far, neither university has expressed any interest in sports scholarships on the US model.

Unlike any other Varsity sport the Boat Race remains a national, indeed international, phenomenon. This can be attributed to several disparate factors which combine in a unique combination of sporting excellence and national heritage, including the gladiatorial simplicity of a winner and a loser, the disproportionate effort for no reward (even for the successful crew) and the neutral venue of the river Thames as it winds through London: the Boat Race is a great London event.

But sporting excellence is at the heart of the phenomenon; in an age where world class in whatever sport is constantly available, Boat Race crews must be able to demonstrate that they are top quality crews judged by the highest national and international standards. This is why the gap between college rowing and Varsity rowing will remain forever unbridgeable: the days when the best college crews could claim to be of national let alone international standard ended more than 50 years ago.

The first race was rowed in 1829 at Henley-on-Thames, the second in London in 1836. It was not until 1845 that the now traditional Putney to Mortlake course was first raced. Races have been held every year (except during the two world wars in the last century) since 1856. The current score (after the 2007 race) is 79 wins to Cambridge and 73 to Oxford, with one dead heat in 1877. The race record is held by the 1998 Cambridge crew and stands at 16 mins 19 seconds.

For years, the Boat Race was run on a very informal basis by the London Representative of the two university clubs, himself an old Blue, with help from a few volunteers. The London Representative is now the Chief Executive of the Boat Race Company Limited, the management company which organizes the Boat Race. This development reflects the amount of time and effort required to stage what is one of the largest sporting events in the country. Sponsorship, which has been a part of the race since the 1970s, has helped offset the increasing costs enormously.

What was once a private race is now a major public event, albeit with a private race still at the heart of it!

Howard Jacobs (1971) is Chief Executive of the Boat Race Company Ltd.

Cambridge claim victory in the 150th Boat Race in 2004.

Julian Andrews

Gates Scholar Kris Coventry, who rowed at no.2 in the 150th Boat Race, in the Captain's Room, the CUBC club room in the Goldie Boathouse, where the names of all CUBC crews are painted on wall panels.

CUBC and the Boat Race

In the last 20 years the CUBC has metamorphosed from an amateur, student-run club to a professional centre of excellence, creating and attracting international-level athletes on a regular basis. Testament to the club's strength is apparent in the composition of recent crews – of the 17 different athletes competing in the last three Blue Boats seven were Olympians, including an Olympic Champion and three World Champions.

Within rowing circles the draw of the Boat Race is such that there is a significant annual influx of international calibre oarsmen keen to compete in this prestigious event. Reflecting the changing nature of the University, where postgraduate admissions now constitute a greater portion of the annual intake, the original domination of the British undergraduate has given way to a greater proportion of foreign postgraduates in the modern crews.

For athletes the attraction of the race is twofold: its distinctive combination of tradition and high profile within the sporting world sets it apart from other rowing events, while the gruelling nature of the 4 ¼ mile course, over three times the length of Olympic races, makes it a challenge in itself. Though copied by universities in Britain and the US, the Oxford–Cambridge Boat Race is still universally recognised as one of the highlights of any career.

Despite the hype surrounding the race, the CUBC remains true to its origins. Although it employs two full-time professional coaches and a boatman, the club is still run by the student President, elected internally and ratified by the college boat club captains. It also looks to the colleges to provide the majority of trialists at the start of every year

and strongly encourages its members to return to their college boat clubs for the May Bumps.

There is no easy way into the two University crews. International and college oarsmen need to have academically qualified for their places at the University and must stay ahead of their studies while attending 11 training sessions a week, a commitment of some 32 hours, including weights sessions and around 200km on the water. The athletes are continually tested and assessed throughout the six-month training process, with the Blue Boat and Goldie (reserve) crews formed in February, around eight weeks before the race.

The club exists for one purpose, to beat Oxford; to do so means racing at the limit of one's stamina for 17 minutes alongside a crew of equally fit athletes. It is both an endurance event and a sprint as the crews try to get the vital boat length in front from which they can control the race. This is a high-pressure but gradual process, trying to move steadily away and holding form until the opposition breaks. To win is to justify the whole year's sacrifice and create a bond between the athletes that is never forgotten; to lose is one of the worst possible experiences in sport. Regardless of the result, the commitment to the club and the race lasts a lifetime and every year the old Blues will get nervous around Easter, knowing that Oxford will occasionally win but saying the old CUBC prayer, 'Lord, let it not be this year'.

Kieran West (1995) rowed in the Blue Boat in 1999, 2001, 2006 and 2007. He was CUBC President in 2001. He won a gold medal in the Men's Eight at the Sydney Olympics and the World Championship in the Coxed Fours in 2002. He is studying for a PhD at Pembroke College.

Although I studied at Cambridge, went on to pursue a Master's and then a PhD at other universities, I would have to say that the training and education I most remember is that which came from being a member of CUWBC.

The professionalism of CUWBC without any material support or obvious facilities impressed me from the start. The overriding goal – to win the Boat Race - was always the guiding factor. The importance of that goal, and the implicit need to do everything you could and leave no stone unturned in its pursuit, was evident from my first introduction to CUWBC when I joined the Development Squad during my first summer in Cambridge in 1990.

My first taste of six-lane racing at the National Championships that year and the excitement of making it into the final left me with no doubts about the technical, physical and mental standards required to take on the challenge of getting eight oarswomen and one coxswain to work in close harmony over 2,000m and win.

I can remember watching videos of the other crews, looking at the speed of entry of the blade each time it entered the water and comparing it with that of my crew… with no inkling that 14 years later I would be studying the entry of the blade of the Romanians and Belarussians, my main competitors in the Athens Olympics, days ahead of racing them to win silver in 2004.

For I could have had no better training ground than CUWBC for my campaign to win an Olympic medal that led me through two Boat Races, six World Championships and three Olympic Games. I could not have had better mentors than Roger Silk and Ron Needs, whose combined wisdom and inspiration I soaked up avidly and referred to constantly through my rowing career. Their concentration on detail combined with a feel for the tiny movements necessary for a crew to move in synchrony taught me the complex but fascinating art and science of rowing. They taught me how it could lead to that magical sensation of the rowing boat 'flying' over the water, seemingly effortlessly, yet powered by maximum human effort. They also taught me the unavoidable need to train hard, put in the hours, cut no corners, and persist through the uncomfortable outings where the boat had to be worked and prepared for potential flying at a later date! These were lessons not just for rowing, but for anything taken on in life.

I lost my first Boat Race in 1991. It is still one of the most painful moments of my sporting career, but in retrospect it was a defining moment. I realized the pain of losing, and the importance of doing everything possible to avoid that. And I appreciated the joy of winning in 1993, all the more sweet for having tasted defeat.

The coaches and the professional system that Ron and Roger ran whilst I was in Cambridge were the best basis I could have ever had on which to build an Olympic rowing career. My first taste of international rowing came a year after I graduated when I competed in Canada in the 1994 Commonwealth Games and won a bronze medal in the England Women's Eight. An impressive three rowers out of this Eight came from CUWBC. Ten years later, an even more impressive three rowers out of eight who won medals for Great Britain in women's rowing came from CUWBC. It is only tragic that this is not recognized, supported and celebrated as it deserves to be.

Catherine Bishop
(1989)

Catherine Bishop with her Pairs partner, Katherine Grainger, winning a silver medal at the Athens Olympics, 2004.

Women's Rowing: CUWBC

As it took centuries for the University of Cambridge to allow women to undertake study there like men, and decades after that before they were admitted to degrees – who will forget the sight of octogenarians climbing out of coaches in 1999 to be allowed to matriculate 50 years late? – so it is with sport.

The University of Cambridge Women's Boat Club, despite having alumnae who have represented their country at the Olympic Games, still lives from hand to mouth as it did when I was rowing. It seems to fall between stools and miss out on the generous sponsorship and support which the well-established CUBC receives.

The second-class status could be understood when I rowed for CUWBC in the late 1960s. At that point the ratio of women to men was about one to ten. Our crews were formed from undergraduates from the three women's colleges plus some members from the graduate colleges. We changed in a tiny cloakroom in Trinity boathouse, were coached by other undergraduate oarsmen who gave up their time to support the women, rowed against men's crews in the lower divisions of the Bumps – and occasionally bumped some of them, which did not go down too well. We had no training facilities or schedules. But we won year after year when rowing against Oxford on either the Cam or the Isis. We won gold medals at BUSAF, once memorably on the Thames in flood, later at the (then) new rowing course at Holme Pierrepont, near Nottingham. We hoped to make international status. The experiences I had rowing and training on the Cam were the most rewarding and formative of the time I spent at Cambridge: early morning outings whether it was calm summer mornings or battling through hail or breaking the ice on the Cam in winter; the exhilaration of completing a race however exhausted one felt; the bonding with fellow athletes. These I have not forgotten long after things academic have faded.

I am sure the present crews would say the same about their rowing. But, despite the fact that since the early 1970s female undergraduates have been admitted to the men's colleges and gained academic equality

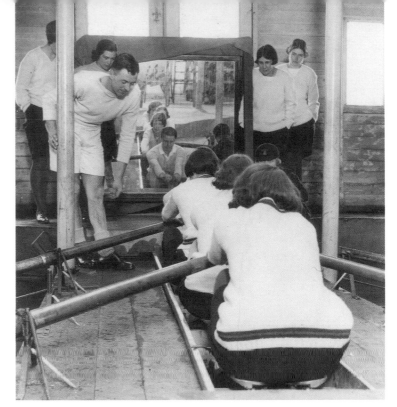

Cambridge University Women's Boat Club training, 1928. The first women's Boat Race was rowed in 1927.

with their male counterparts, not much has changed for the members of CUWBC. The three crews of oarswomen who represent Cambridge University today still have no changing facilities or boathouse. They pay a large amount to row out of their own pockets. They have devoted, but unpaid, coaches and perhaps better represent the spirit of the Boat Race than is evident in the present CUBC televised event. But they, too, have no proper training facilities. They get up at crack of dawn to get the train to Ely. They have to keep their boats on the grass beside Churchill boathouse. Not for them a Goldie boathouse, or the joint facilities specially built for all crews who represent Oxford, which their counterparts there enjoy.

In the words of the immortal Cambridge joke:

'How many Fellows does it take to change a light bulb?'

'*Change…?*'

***Jane Kingsbury** rowed in the Women's Blue Boat in 1971, 1972 and 1973. She is a committee member of CUWBC.*

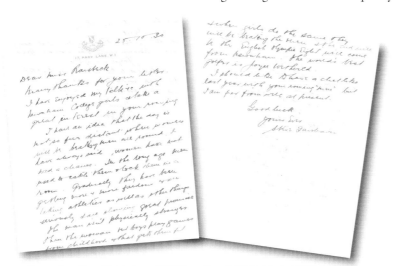

Letter from Steve Fairbairn to NCBC president Edith Raisbeck, 1930.

On dry land

Rugby Union

Undergraduates from the leading public schools introduced rugby to Cambridge as early as 1839, when a match is first recorded on Parker's Piece. The game was played casually in the University over the next 30 years, until the formal record of the University Rugby Union Club (CURUFC) joining the newly created Rugby Football Union (1873). In February 1872 the first Inter-Varsity match was held at the Parks, Oxford, less than a year after the first international between England and Scotland, and by 1884 Blues were awarded to participants in the match.

By the 1890s the Varsity Match had transferred to the Queen's Club in London, when it was attracting around 10,000 spectators. This strengthened the club's financial base, enabling it to purchase in 1896 its present ground on Grange Road. The Varsity Match transferred to Twickenham in 1921, and by the late 1930s the journalist E.H.D. Sewell reckoned the fixture to be the second most important match in the calendar of the British rugby follower (after England versus Scotland).

Casual fixtures between colleges were known as early as the 1880s, and in the 1920s collegiate competition was established on a sound and regular basis, and a University second XV, the LX Club, was formed. In the 1940s and 1950s around half of the Blues side were, or would become, internationals: although the quantity of internationals declined thereafter, the quality did not. Between the 1960s and 1980s, the club produced some of the most capped players in the history of Ireland (Mike Gibson), Wales (Gerald Davies), Scotland (Gavin Hastings) and England (Rob Andrew). Fluctuating attendances at Varsity Matches revived in the late 1980s and peaked in 1995 at nearly 70,000, a world record for a midweek club fixture.

The contribution of CURUFC to the wider development of rugby has been significant. First, it has been innovative in ways that subsequently changed the laws of the game. The Varsity Match of 1875 was the first match to feature a 'try' as a scoring opportunity in its own right and to fix upon a team of 15 players (international matches followed suit two years later). In 1892 the referee took sole charge of the game, replacing the captains as adjudicators. In the 1990s the colleges participated in a 'Laws Clinic' under the scrutiny of the Rugby Football Union, monitoring the impact of changes to the laws of the game.

Second, Cambridge rugby has contributed disproportionately to the spread of the sport around the globe. In the 1880s and 1890s various undergraduates returned to their native South Africa, New Zealand and Australia having played rugby at Cambridge, spreading the word to the far reaches of the Empire. In 1899 Edward Bramwell Clarke of Corpus Christi introduced rugby to his students at Keio University, thus sowing a seed which has flowered throughout Japan. CURUFC has long pioneered a tradition of touring to countries where

The 60th anniversary Steele-Bodger Match, November 2007, at Grange Road. Captained by former Ireland international Kevin Maggs, the Steele-Bodgers were defeated 43:24 by the Blues.

The Steele-Bodger Match

In January 1948, quite out of the blue, Dr Windsor Lewis, who for so many years had been the guiding force of Cambridge rugby, telephoned me to ask if I would be interested in raising a team to play against the University. The idea was for the match to be regarded as a final test for the University team which was due to play Oxford. Ideally, therefore, the game was to take place at the end of November, by which time the selection process for the Blues XV would hopefully have been completed.

For several years in the 1930s, Jenny Greenwood, President of the Rugby Football Union, had brought a team to Cambridge with similar intent but the fixture had ceased before the Second World War.

Naturally I was delighted, but ensured it was accepted that there would be a dinner afterwards so that the relatively inexperienced University players would be able to pick the brains of the international players, an opportunity that had not been available when I played in the corresponding fixture at Oxford for Major Stanley's XV.

In the early days, the invitation side needed to be very strong merely to hold their own with the University XV, who were of course physically bolstered by the more mature undergraduates returning from War Service. In 1948 I included 12 current internationals, amongst them Haydn Tanner and Bleddyn Williams, the two outstanding players of that era, and then only won the match 13:9. The following year 13 internationals played and the final score was 12:6. These were hard matches and just what was needed before playing Oxford.

During the following years, and particularly from the mid-1950s, Cambridge rugby flourished with a steady stream of young players who made up for their lack of experience and physicality by their youth and fitness. There were two matches every week and with daily training both Oxford and Cambridge were a match for any club in the land. By the end of most games they were running the opposition ragged, as clubs only trained twice weekly in the evening after their players had done a full day's work. This was a golden period with overseas tours in the autumn almost every year, the top rugby writers at every game prior to the Varsity Match, London clubs vying with each other to get a fixture and hopefully enrol a promising player or two for their own club at the end of term. This period seemed too good to last, and it was.

Changes in University procedures and also in the game had a considerable impact. The University broadened its intake and tightened its admissions policy. The increase in the number of postgraduates, many from overseas, was generally positive for rugby football. Then came the National Leagues which meant fewer Saturday fixtures and fewer matches and that was followed in 1995 by professionalism and still fewer fixtures – all of them midweek and most under floodlights.

The matches with my side have always been competitive encounters but played in the best of spirits, for nothing really is at stake except pride in one's own performance. Because of the quality of rugby played and the lively dinner that followed, it used to be unusual for an invitation to play to be turned down. Nowadays leagues and professionalism have made the collection of an invitation team much more difficult as clubs have become ultra-protective and more reluctant to release players.

It would seem that the match has fulfilled its original purpose of providing the chosen XV with a stiff test. Sixty matches have been played and the Varsity has won 27 and two have been drawn. The visiting team has been captained 19 times by a former Cambridge captain, 28 times by a player who has captained his country and six times by a captain of the British Lions – so no doubt about the quality. Then there was Andy Ripley who was playing junior rugby when invited by telephone and he thought at first the invitation was from a store's team called 'Steele and Bodger'. Andy was a successful athlete who came to rugby football late but still won all the honours possible. As captain, on no fewer than six occasions, he was quite unpredictable, but the crowd always enjoyed it. The legendary businessman Tony O'Reilly accepted an invitation but on the morning of the match an emergency board meeting became essential and he asked for approval to land on the pitch in his helicopter. That was refused on safety grounds so he hired a stretch limousine and apparently had his board meeting en route from London to Cambridge.

On one occasion in the 1950s the fog was so thick that no play was possible but it was agreed to reassemble and play on the following Monday. Fourteen of the original team returned and played. The 15th was Dr Norman Davidson, Scotland's out half who sadly had to decline but with very good reason as that was the actual day he was due to emigrate to New Zealand! I can recall the great Welsh half-backs, Cliff Morgan and Rex Willis, coming six years on the trot, travelling in the Bentley owned by Rex's father, and they packed the car with four other Cardiff players. During those years several Cambridge captains in their turn told me which players were in doubt for their Blue and needed testing out. I would tell Cliff who quickly tested them and, once he had found them wanting or good enough, strolled to the touchline and asked me if he might now get on and enjoy his own game.

Having once played my team are entitled to wear the distinctive tie with its maroon background, matching the colour of the original club jersey, also featuring diagonal Cambridge Blue stripes with lions courant in gold in between the stripes – very smart.

Michael Steele-Bodger (1946) was Captain of CURUFC. He is President of the Barbarians and a former President of the RFU.

The Varsity Match, 1946, when Cambridge were captained by Micky Steele-Bodger. Oxford won 15:5. L to r: M.R. Steele-Bodger (captain) and E. Bole (both hidden), H.J.H.Gatford, W.G. Davies, J.M. Hunter, S.V. Perry, H.H. Campbell, T.S. MacRoberts, A.P. Henderson.

the game is in its infancy, notably the US in 1934 and Argentina in 1948. The latter was certainly linked to the appearance of an Argentinian, Barry Holmes, in the 1947 Varsity Match: Holmes was capped for Argentina against France in 1949, but tragically died of typhoid fever soon after.

Third, hardly any clubs in the world have produced as many international players, or as many administrators of, and commentators upon, the sport. At the latest count, Cambridge has produced 320 internationals representing nine senior countries. Not all of these managed to obtain Blues. Malcolm Young played for the LXs in the 1960s and was scrum half for England in the 1970s, while his LX Club team-mate, Mike Lamb, enjoyed a lengthy and successful career in rugby league with Bradford Northern and Leeds. A succession of council members of the Rugby Football Union were led by Presidents such as Wavell Wakefield, J.V. Smith and Ian Beer, while Paul Ackford, Steve James (*Sunday Telegraph*), Eddie Butler, Alistair Hignell, Ian Robertson (BBC), and David Hands (*The Times*) are just a few of the journalists.

The contribution of CURUFC to other aspects of sport in Cambridge is also notable, although less well known. In the 1980s and 1990s, the club provided funds and expertise to nurture the development of women's rugby within the University. Even more remarkable, a Loans Book, kept by club treasurers in the 1920s and 1930s, reveals that the club provided generous financial support to the University athletics, cricket, hockey, lawn tennis, boxing, racquets, swimming, rifle, and fives clubs: in many cases, the loans were subsequently cancelled.

CURUFC might claim, with its counterpart at Oxford, to be the most influential rugby club in the history of the game. In the 19th century its undergraduates helped to spread the game far beyond the English public schools, and its Blues teams shaped the modern laws. In the 20th century, it proselytised in unlikely corners of the globe while producing scores of international players for the home countries; it did so right up until the advent of professionalism in 1995.

The immense influence of Cambridge over 175 years of amateur rugby owed much to the quality of its students and the international reach of the University. Scholastic life created more time and flexibility for leading players to hone their skills and fitness than was available to most amateurs elsewhere, who were burdened by work and domestic commitments; Cambridge players were consequently among the most 'professional' players of the amateur age.

It follows that professional rugby dealt a terminal blow to the influence of Cambridge on the rugby world: an academically selective university with no means or remit to admit, or to remunerate, the best rugby players cannot compete with a professional infrastructure. The semi-professionalism of the ranks below the professional elite in England has also posed severe challenges by contributing to the declining strength and variety of the club's fixture list. Even the Varsity Match now hangs upon a thread of tradition.

THE CAMBRIDGE UNIVERSITY RUGBY UNION CENTENARY
To celebrate the centenary of the Cambridge University Rugby Union a match was played against the Barbarians which was followed by a dinner held at Trinity College. Mac went along and sketched many old Blues, former Captains and Internationals, as well as the President and Vice President of Cambridge and the Barbarians.

Rugby at Cambridge still attracts some high quality young players from across the globe, because it exemplifies both fine tradition and the ideal of the academic all-rounder. These attributes continue to strike a chord within the City of London, which remains a source of vital financial support. Similarly, women rugby players still have the opportunity to influence the women's game for as long as it remains amateur. If it responds to such challenges with its customary flexibility and innovation, Cambridge rugby can still play a worthwhile role in the wider game.

Mark Bailey *was Captain of CURUFC in 1983 and 1984, and a CURUFC Committee Member 1983–2000. He is Headmaster of Leeds Grammar School.*

On 11 December 2001, 14 of the Cambridge rugby team who played 40 years previously against Oxford walked out onto the turf at Twickenham. We took up our positions for a team photograph, before returning to the stand to watch the latest encounter between the two old rivals. All of us could pause to reflect on our achievement of 1961: we were members of the only team in the long history of the Varsity match to go to Twickenham having won every game. But now we had to take on Oxford. Would we falter at the last and most vital step?

At the start of the Michaelmas Term, I had taken the long walk down King's Parade to Ryder and Amies, hoping against hope that, after the seniors trials, I had, perhaps, at least been selected for the LX, the second University XV.

I looked over the shoulders of the group of others seeing who had made it into the two teams, and felt a pang of disappointment when my name was not in the list for the LX. So I glanced across to the next sheet of paper, and was shocked to see that I had been selected for the Varsity team to play Guy's Hospital at Grange Road two days hence. In those days, the players selected had their school and

The CURUFC Japanese tour, 1953, which was the first foreign tour after the war.

college against their name. I was such an unknown that the secretary did not know my initials, or my school.

Whereas the University team today plays only seven or so games before Twickenham and Oxford, we played 14 matches, two a week, in the build-up to the trial of strength in December. I recall a sense of awe and nerves as I walked down to Grange Road for my first match. I was joining players I had only known as a spectator: the 1961 team was a remarkable and fortunate mix of talent. We had nine international caps, from Scotland, England and Wales. Our fly half, Gordon Waddell, was captain of Scotland and a British Lion. The second row was a powerhouse with Brian Thomas of Wales and John Owen of England. My tight head prop played for England, our scrum half and both centres were also England caps. In the back row we had Roger Michaelson of Wales and John Brash of Scotland. Most of the rest of us were to play in international trials.

The progress of this team towards Twickenham took on a momentum of its own. We defeated Cardiff, Coventry and London Scottish in the space of seven days. Newport were the only side to attain over ten points against us, but we still beat them. Micky Steele Bodger selected a virtual British Lions team to take us on, including the Lions front row, and we beat them too. That evening, our captain Mike Wade announced his team: I was offered my Blue. Rituals followed; port and nuts with our President, Windsor Lewis, in Pembroke, outfitting for the Blue blazer, the team photograph, the train down to London the day before the match, and checking into the hotel on Richmond Hill.

We never underestimated Oxford. They, too, had a very strong team that centred on Richard Sharp, their brilliant fly-half, John Willcox, the England fullback, and Peter Stagg, the tallest man yet to play international rugby. And both sides were as fit as the opposition and equally determined to win.

We played before a packed Twickenham which was said to contain a record crowd of 68,000 people. They saw a very hard fought first half, with no score until ten minutes from half time. I wrote these words in my diary that evening: 'About 30 minutes into the Varsity match, occurred the greatest moment of my life.' I can still hear the roar of the crowd as I touched down and etched on my memory are the ecstatic faces of the nearest spectators as I looked up. My first thought was the hope that the pass back to me was not judged forward. It wasn't and we were 3:0 up at half time.

And so the score remained until deep into the second half, when Richard Sharp dropped a spectacular goal to level at 3:3. For 11 minutes, there was an arm wrestle until he tried another drop kick. We charged it, our centre, Geoff Frankcom, kicked it on and on, and then touched down his try as the ball was nearly over the dead ball line. It was now 6:3, with time nearly up. Then, well into injury time, Gordon Waddell from our line-out managed his own drop kick and we were safe. The final whistle saw us winners 9:3, the only undefeated side in the history of the Varsity Match.

Charles Higham
(1959)

The 23-year-old environmental engineer steps from the sideline. His west-country accent barely discernible above the din of the crowd, he asks the call be repeated. Satisfied as to the response, he sets himself briefly, before rifling a throw between two pairs of grasping opposition hands. Elevated by the combined power of a 27-year-old South African doctor and a 24-year-old Welsh economist, a 20-year-old engineer from Kent arcs gracefully toward the centre of the line-out. Plucking the ball mid-flight, he directs it expertly toward his waiting scrum half, a political scientist from Northern Ireland.

Immediately, the scrum half fires a long pass infield, hitting his inside centre square in the chest. The New Zealander slows, struggling to gain control of the ball. The defence almost upon him, he applies all his 33 years' experience, and feints to his left. Onrushing tacklers are momentarily distracted by the lightning-fast 21-year-old English physicist angling in from the blindside wing. Several seconds gained, the New Zealander dummies right to his Scottish fullback, buying yet more time. With pinpoint accuracy, he finally sends a flat ball across the chest of his outside centre, a 27-year-old Italian lawyer, to reach the drifting open-side winger. With startling ease, the winger changes angle and accelerates, the combination of agility and pace ensuring his path to the try-line remains clear. Planting the ball, the 19-year-old historian jogs back to halfway, his broad smile reflected on the faces of his 14 waiting team-mates.

From this snapshot of the Blues at the start of the new millennium it will be evident to those with even a passing interest in CURUFC that the demography of its members is markedly different from that of 20 years ago. Age, nationality and fields of study have become increasingly diverse, reflective of several fundamental issues influencing the club in the past decade.

Of these, rugby's entry to the ranks of professional sport has been perhaps the greatest challenge. The sport now provides a realistic short-term career option for many promising young rugby players, and it is not unusual for university education to be placed 'on hold', as rugby goals are pursued within the remunerated realms of Premiership club structures. Cambridge and Oxford rugby clubs now face foes more formidable than those questioning the relevance of the December match: the number and quality of autumn internationals, the length of the Premiership season, and the commercial realities of media coverage have all combined to adversely affect the profile of the Varsity Match.

The surrounding tertiary environment has also influenced the club. Cambridge University's continued development of both undergraduate and postgraduate course options, and the global awareness of the value of a Cambridge education, have resulted in an international student body of varying ages and interests. In terms of participation and spectator appeal, allegiance to the sport of rugby in general, and to CURUFC in particular, cannot be taken for granted. In addition, students face increasing financial constraints, specific performance targets and wider commercial expectations of academic excellence. As a consequence, extracurricular activity, whilst not forsaken, may understandably slip down the list of priorities.

Thankfully, certain aspects of the club continue unaltered. At the time of writing Tony Rodgers was striding manfully toward his 27th year as coach of the Light Blues. He is best likened to the old pair of rugby boots, pulled from the bottom of a rugby bag at the start of each season: battered and beaten, slightly frayed at the edges, sporting a missing stud and with the faint whiff of six-month-old mud. While thoughts of upgrading may flicker briefly, they are quickly extinguished by memories of what you and this ancient piece of equipment have achieved together. In true Dorothy-esque fashion, you put them on, click the heels and hope for one more bit of magic.

Another core component remains unchanged, binding the 19-year-old three-time Blue of the 1920s to the 29-year-old LX's reserve of the 1990s, the Australian broking Japanese equities in London to the Englishman tracking elephants in Kenya. It is, of course, the pride a player feels when he pulls on the light blue and white hoops of Cambridge, and the desire of each to do justice to those who have done so in the past. Whilst this remains true, I hold no fears for the future of CURUFC.

Duncan Blaikie
(2001)

The Blues, captained by Duncan Blaikie, celebrate victory in the 2002 Varsity Match.

Football

If the days of Cambridge making a mark at the highest level of England's national sport are long gone, the University will forever have an important place in the history of the game. For when the Football Association was founded in 1863 – the first of more than 200 national associations around the world – it was the Cambridge Rules, as initially drawn up in a Trinity College room 17 years earlier and modified to something more like the present-day version, that were adopted as 'the most desirable code'. Thus, as Colin Weir wrote in his *History of Cambridge University Association Football Club*: 'It would be hard to exaggerate the influence that the University footballers of Cambridge have had on the game in England and subsequently all over the world.' Indeed, when Melvyn Bragg compiled *Twelve Books That Have Changed The World* in 2006, he included this first published rule-book as one of them.

Like rugby union, from which the Cambridge Rules effectively divorced it, football in those earliest days was very much the preserve of the public schools and universities, so it was not surprising that Oxbridge should be among the most enthusiastic and successful practitioners. There is even evidence to suggest that CUAFC is the oldest football club in the world, a claim contested by Sheffield. The first Varsity Match took place in 1874, when Cambridge, fielding eight Trinity men, were beaten 1:0. Three years later, the teams might even have met in one of the first FA Cup finals; both reached the last four of the competition but whereas Oxford received a bye, the Light Blues lost by a single goal to the Wanderers, a team of old Harrovians, who then defeated Oxford in the final.

Until the turn of the century (and in one or two cases much later), Cambridge players regularly represented the full England international team, forebears of David Beckham and Wayne Rooney, but even before the end of the Victorian era, football had changed irrevocably following the introduction of professionalism. A simple chronological list of FA Cup winners illustrates the transformation; from 1884 onwards, every winning team is a recognisable current professional club.

The universities effectively became part of the amateur game, Cambridge providing amateur internationals for England as late as the 1960s when one of them, the goalkeeper Mike Pinner, played for seven League clubs, including Manchester United. Another, Peter Phillips, was a centre forward for Cambridge United in the early 1970s, and a decade later Steve Palmer played for Ipswich Town and Watford in the Premier League in a career of almost 600 matches.

The Varsity Match was played at Wembley from 1953 until 1987, attendances peaking at 23,000 in 1969. It continues to be staged at a professional stadium, often at Fulham's riverside home, Craven Cottage, on Boat Race day, and although playing standards have proved difficult to maintain, for 1,000 male and some 400 female students regularly playing at Cambridge these days, the game is the thing.

***Steve Tongue** (1970) is football correspondent for the* Independent on Sunday.

Varsity Match 2006. Cambridge beat Oxford 1:0.

I learned to play sport in the north of England where there wasn't a lot of grass around. The football and rugby pitches were heaps of mud in the winter and brown, arid, grassless wastelands in the spring and summer. The tennis courts were made of either hard concrete or red shale. The cricket pitches tended to nestle in the shade of looming factory chimneys or railway bridges rather than Norman churches or rolling downs. No flashy off drives or delicate late cuts or we got punched in the face by the coach, a gnarled old pro from the Lancashire League. Then I got to Cambridge and I was overwhelmed with the sight of so much green grass.

Wherever you looked there were beautifully kept sports grounds with their immaculate lawns and charming pavilions. In the summer, and particularly after Tripos was over, college grounds were filled with cricketers and tennis players revelling in the grass courts. It fulfilled all my fantasies which had been fuelled by boarding school stories of boys who played sport every afternoon. Those deadly dull mornings in the Mill Lane Lecture Rooms or the UL were only made bearable by the prospect of sport at Barton Road after lunch.

The football we played still retained echoes of its Corinthian past, a spirit far removed from the hacking and cheating which had been integral to the Manchester Jewish Soccer League. The three cheers for the opposition at the end of each game surprised me every time I heard it. Caius had a pretty good team in the late 1960s and I was glad to be part of it. The photograph of the team I eventually captained is on the wall as I write, fading into nothingness with each passing summer. How appallingly symbolic!

Colin Shindler
(1967)

Lacrosse

The only sport I excelled at at university level was lacrosse. But, by sharing a room in my second year with the marvellously gifted footballer Ralph Cowan, I was able to meet cricketers such as Peter May, Doug Insole and Hubert Doggart. No one who was at Fenners one Saturday in 1949 will ever forget the opening partnership by Hubert Doggart and John Dawes of 415 not out against Essex. We skipped lectures on the following Monday morning expecting to see the world record being broken. But Doug Insole had declared over the weekend, saying that the game was greater than records.

G. Walter Wilde

(1948)

Judo

In 1958 our captain, Richard Lock, transformed the fortunes of the CUJC when he secured the services of Kenshiro Abbe to instruct the club. Sensei Abbe was a small, kind and exquisitely courteous Japanese. He was a 7th Dan, so we in our turn were exquisitely courteous to him. Sensei Abbe was able to combine the gentlest of natures with a steely determination to win, and he set about teaching us to do the same. In the 1950s judo valued skill above strength, and dirty tricks were unknown. Except, of course, to ambitious top-dogs. The arrival in Britain of the outstandingly talented Abbe was not well received by a jealous judo establishment. It sought to undermine him by spreading unpleasant rumours. Sad proof that judo was yet another sport in which sporting spirit is too easily eclipsed by the personal vanities of its administrators.

In the CUJC a new *lingua franca* emerged. 'Necessary must win', 'necessary more turn', 'bye and bye neck strongle' were building blocks in our new language. And before the University match: necessary no smoking, necessary no drinking, necessary much sleeping; to Richard Lock's reasonable question 'What about women?' the answer was equally reasonable: 'Aaah. Women sometimes necessary'. If memory serves me correctly, 8:0 to us in 1958, and in 1959 under another excellent captain, Quintin Chambers, 7:1.

Sadly Kenshiro Abbe was later seriously injured in a motor accident and returned to Japan, where he died. To his grateful protégés his memorial is the long-lasting uplift he gave to the CUJC, and the affection with which we remember his gentleness and skill. And also his lasting impact on the English language.

Omar Malik

(1956)

Cricket

By general consensus, University cricket at Cambridge peaked with the 1950 side that contained five players of Test quality: Peter May, John Dewes, David Sheppard, Hubert Doggart and J.J. Warr all represented England around that time. Over the years, other Cambridge men like Ted Dexter, Mike Brearley and Michael Atherton have followed their example, but the number of Light Blues going on to play for their country has been in steady decline ever since that impressive quintet.

The scrapping of National Service in 1960, and later, of sports-loving admissions tutors, has contributed to the decline, eroding the quality and quantity of cricketing talent entering the University. Nowadays, the club has been forced to merge with neighbouring Anglia Ruskin University in order to retain its first-class status, a privilege cherished by previous generations.

This new hybrid, known as the Cambridge University Cricket Centre of Excellence (CUCCE), contests the majority of the fixtures each season, though not the Varsity Matches against Oxford (now played over one and three-day formats). Maintaining their tradition and singularity, these remain as contests between the students of the two great universities.

Being a summer sport that clashed with important exams, cricket was long seen as the villain of the piece by tutors convinced that all non-academic activity must be treated with suspicion. Yet for those who did play at Fenners, the chance to escape the tension building in libraries all around Cambridge during the summer term was a godsend.

It also offered an experience not granted to many: to play first-class cricket against professional county sides without the added expectation of having to win. Although victories were not unknown, such as the one during my time against Lancashire (a result that saw the Lancashire captain promptly hauled before the county's cricket committee), draws were the more realistic measure of success. Provided the defeats weren't too humiliating, it was mostly great fun, and the healthy combination of exercise and fresh air was further enhanced by the salad lunches, served unfailingly on match days throughout the 1970s and 1980s. Yet not everyone enjoyed the piles of lettuce and tomato and when the West Indies touring team played a two-day match at Fenners in 1980, they ignored the greenery and sent out for Kentucky Fried Chicken instead.

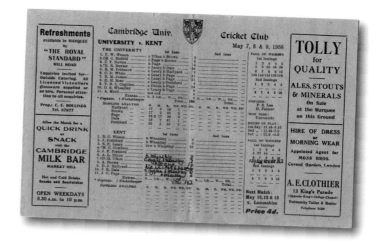

The Cambridge team, 1950, which featured David Sheppard (second from left, standing), Peter May (far right, standing) and Hubert Doggart (centre, sitting).

That particular game brought a big crowd and a big innings from Aziz Mubarak, a research chemist and opening bat from Sri Lanka. A man of few words, Aziz flayed the West Indies' much vaunted pace attack, taking a particular fancy to the fearsome Colin Croft. At lunch, Croft forewent his Kentucky drumsticks to psyche out his nemesis by staring at him in the pavilion. It worked too, and he dismissed Aziz for 86 soon after the break.

Batsmen were favoured at Fenners. The pitches, especially the featherbeds prepared by the legendary groundsman, Cyril Coote, offered little to bowlers of any denomination and were full of runs. Little surprise then that Cambridge's best players tended to be batsmen like May, Dexter, Atherton and the suave Pakistani, Majid Khan.

Conditions were not totally disheartening for bowlers. As more than one coach intoned: 'If you can trouble batsmen at Fenners you can trouble them anywhere.' Trouble was, it didn't happen very often, and over the decades spectators have applauded many more hundreds than five-wicket hauls.

Playing against county sides offered a rigorous yardstick for those considering a career in cricket, which, during my time, was about half the team. This posed a dilemma though. Did we try to ape the pros, or rise above the warm-ups and practice to lord it like amateurs sitting on a big inheritance?

Both were tried, though it mostly depended on the ambition of the captain. In my first year, the skipper, Ian Greig, would stress the need to make good our modest batting and bowling with ferocious displays in the field. 'See these,' he'd say pointing to his freshly laundered whites, 'if anyone leaves this field with fewer grass stains than me, they'll be fined five quid.' Fortunately, he had a dicky knee and didn't dive much, though it took us a season before we realised it.

Our coach, Brian 'Tonker' Taylor, a former captain of Essex, was also on hand to dispense useful advice, though his dressing-room tips were certainly not based on the science taught in the lecture rooms of Free School Lane. When one batsman turned up a little queasy after a late-night mixture of cocktail parties and curry, Tonker was quick to offer a cure. 'Stay off the exotic grub and drink some port and brandy,' the latter duly administered by the Fenners barman.

Tonker was quick to encourage and whenever counties arrived with bowlers fast and nasty enough to cause widespread anxiety among the batsmen, he'd say: 'The only thing you need to worry about him is that he won't let the ball go.' Unfortunately he never let on whether this homily was meant to soothe or confuse and by the time batsmen had worked out what he meant, the said fast bowler had often sent them packing.

My days at Fenners were among the most enjoyable of my cricket career and the friendships made with team mates during those times remain strong. I still see Aziz Mubarak every time I visit Sri Lanka, which in my job as cricket correspondent of the *Daily Telegraph* is about every four years. He, as with most of the Blues I meet up with, is immensely proud of his time at Cambridge, and a team photo of the 1979 team that beat Oxford by an innings and 52 runs at Lord's has pride of place in his house.

Derek Pringle (1978) *is cricket correspondent for the* Daily Telegraph, *a former Captain of CUCC and England international.*

Cambridge celebrate taking a wicket on day 2 of the four-day Varsity Match, 2007.

Hockey

Hockey has always been something of a poor relation on the national sporting scene. Happily it continues to enjoy a much greater prominence at university level, where it is the largest of the Full Blue sports. Over the course of the season almost 100 students will represent one of the University's six teams in 130 matches. Another 800 students will play hockey in the college leagues. Its sheer size gives CUHC the enviable status of being the most vibrant Cambridge club off the pitch, as well as one of the most successful on it.

Since the men's and women's clubs were amalgamated in 2000, CUHC has gone from strength to strength. The men's Blues currently compete in the South Division of the English Hockey League – the Coca-Cola League 1 of the hockey world! – while the women's Blues are in the top division of the East League. The men's second team won the National Second XI trophy in 2007, while the women reached the semi-finals of BUSA in 2000. The magic of the cup has also brought some top clubs to Wilberforce Road, including Surbiton in 2003, one of the top English sides, fresh from their bronze medal in the European Cup Winners' Cup.

Meanwhile the Varsity Match continues to provide a focus for the season, though it has moved from the National Hockey Stadium to Southgate Hockey Club in north London, after the former succumbed to the clutches of football. The day has grown into a festival of hockey,

Mens Hockey second XI Varsity Match, 2005. Cambridge Wanderers beat Oxford Infrequents 6:0.

"*Eccentrics have always held a memorable place in the Senior Common Rooms of Oxford and Cambridge and have been a source of fascination for dons and undergraduates alike. In the 1870s and 1880s, such a one brought enormous gaiety to the university life of Cambridge and his influence even spilled over into hockey in its infancy. Oscar Browning was a Fellow of King's from 1875 to 1909 after many years teaching at Eton. E.F. Benson in his book* As We Were *wrote of Browning that 'his snobbishness was of a really remarkable order: it was impossible not to respect a quality of such fire and purity, for, although waddling with obesity, he took to playing hockey for the pleasure of being wiped over the shins by HRH Prince Edward of Wales.'*

18 October 1883 must have been a golden day for Oscar Browning as it was then that the Prince of Wales (later Edward VII) took his elder son, Prince 'Eddy' (Albert Victor, Duke of Clarence and Avondale) to Trinity and left him there as a Cambridge undergraduate. It is reported that he had been crammed for the Cambridge entrance throughout the summer of 1883, though his tutors were sceptical about the use of his attending lectures as 'he hardly knows the meaning of the words "to read".' It may well be that, to keep him from the rigours of the lecture hall, Prince Eddy asked if a hockey club could be started in his first year. He had learnt to play, probably at Teddington, before he went up.

A Club was formed of carefully selected dons and undergraduates at Trinity; Clare, King's, and Gonville & Caius closely followed. The sides consisted of eight men, the grounds were bumpy and the hockey sticks thin.

It was this group that Browning, portly as he was, joined in order to have the irresistible pleasure of being on the same field as a member of the Royal Family.

In spite of this royal interest, the game had a hard struggle to get established in the two universities. Few came up with any experience of the game from school; Marlborough and Rossall were a couple of major exceptions. Suitable grounds were hard to find. Colleges were unhelpful and Parker's Piece was only available irregularly. ... With no lack of determination, in 1890 CUHC was founded by E.G. Gallop (Gonville & Caius), who was elected president; G. Lewis (Marlborough and Trinity), a keen supporter, was elected captain with the main object of inaugurating a match with their friends in Oxford. After Lewis sent off a 'challenge' to Oxford the organisers had great difficulty in selecting and finding a ground that was acceptable to both sides. Eventually they were allowed the use of the outfield of the cricket ground in the Parks, Oxford, which itself had only been used for cricket since 1881 after a protracted filibuster by Revd C. Dodgson (better known as Lewis Carroll), a mathematics don at Christ Church. So Cambridge, a little reluctantly, made the long railway journey to Oxford. Though Cambridge were some six years ahead of Oxford in the hockey world, the first match on 3 March 1890 resulted in an unlooked-for 2:1 victory for Oxford."

Extract from the introduction to the programme for the 100th match written by I.A. Hayward, archivist for the Oxford and Cambridge Hockey Match

Athletics

Founded in 1857, CUAC is one of the oldest university athletics clubs in the world. Today's successors to international sporting alumni such as Harold Abrahams, Chris Brasher and Jon Ridgeon include Steve Green and Ben Carne (below)

competing in the 400 metre hurdles in 2005. Steve was selected to represent Great Britain at the European Indoor Championships in 2007. Ben competed in the World University Games in 2007.

The first women's Varsity athletics match took place in 1975. The first women's captain, Sarah Bull, went on to compete in the Commonwealth Games and has been followed by many other world-class athletes. Charlotte Roach (right), who is studying natural sciences at Trinity, competed for Great Britain as part of the gold-medal-winning team in the Junior Women's European Cross Country Championships in 2007. Phyllis Agbo, who was also at Trinity, is an international heptathlete.

featuring eight matches between schools, colleges and alumni as well as the Blues games themselves. It continues to attract hundreds of supporters and provides a fitting pinnacle for many of the players' careers. Some, of course, go on to greater things. Richard Dodds captained Cambridge in 1981, before leading out the Great Britain team seven years later at the Seoul Olympics, where they beat Germany 3:1 to take the gold medal.

Running the club is very much a student effort, and it is this as much as anything that causes it to be so fondly remembered by thousands of alumni around the world. Unfortunately the rapid turnover of people brings persistent challenges. Coaches and structures come and go on an annual basis, with little sense of progression or a long-term plan. This is an inevitable consequence of the University's lack of systemic support for sport. Hockey suffers as much as anyone from a chronic lack of investment in facilities for sport and extra-curricular activities.

In spite of these frustrations hockey has been insulated from the difficulties that have confronted some clubs, struggling to maintain an identity in a professional age which has stretched the gap between the universities and the top levels. It is fortunate that the club is able to train as much as any club in the country, since we pick our players from the smallest pool. Nevertheless it is still possible for CUHC to compete towards the top levels of the game. Like all university clubs it is subject to frustrating inconsistencies which see top sides get a deserved promotion before being broken up into a team that crashes right back down again. Such is the lottery of the annual intake. Once this is accepted as a fact of life the club can continue to do what it does best: providing a huge number of students with the opportunity to benefit from all aspects of training, playing and living in high level sport.

Matthew Richardson was CUHC President 2007–8.

The Cambridge Blue

There is no record of any colour being worn at the first-ever sporting match between Oxford and Cambridge, which was at cricket, held on 4 June 1827. In the first Boat Race on 10 June 1829 at Henley, the Cambridge crew wore white, with a scarlet or pink sash, honouring their captain, W Snow, from St John's. The second Boat Race, in 1836, is the event associated with the origin of the 'Blue'. Just before the race, R.N. Phipps of Eton and Christ's is said to have called at a haberdasher's and asked for a piece of ribbon or silk to decorate the Cambridge bow. The colour of the ribbon was light blue, perhaps because it was Eton's colour, or possibly because it was that of Gonville & Caius as there were three Caians in the boat, or simply because it was the nearest bit of ribbon to hand. For whatever reason, the choice of light blue stuck and became the official colour of the Cambridge University Boat Club.

These early Varsity Matches did not become regular fixtures immediately, the cricket match becoming annual only from 1838 and the Boat Race from 1856. As University clubs were established and organised regular matches against Oxford, they were free to choose any colour but most preferred to continue in an established tradition and picked light blue. Out of courtesy, clubs would seek permission from CUBC before awarding light blue colours to their members, as a result of which the President of CUBC became the arbiter of affairs for over 40 years, accepting and rejecting petitions for Blue and Half Blue status, usually in consultation with the Presidents of the other two senior clubs: cricket and athletics.

The hegemony of CUBC was broken by the rugby and soccer clubs which had been established for some time before their first Varsity Matches in 1872 and 1874 respectively. Both clubs attracted large crowds at their matches and included international players in their membership, but when they sought Full Blues in 1883, the CUBC President, together with the athletics and cricket club captains, was only prepared to offer a

Basketball

Playing for the Cambridge basketball team in 1969-71 was distinguished not by the facilities for playing the sport (the University had none in those days) but by the team members and opponents one rubbed shoulders with.

Training took place in such dubious black holes as the Howard Mallet Centre and Fenners gym. Fenners may have been the stomping ground of many an England cricket immortal but for basketball players in the unbelievably cramped gym with the erratically bouncing floor it served only as an easy means of dislocating fingers.

The real memories are of teaming up with the likes of Roger Haydock, currently Professor of Physics at Oregon University, the only basketball playmaker who was able to apply the laws of quantum physics to shooting free-throws; Hashem Pesaran, currently Professor of Economics, Trinity College Cambridge; Zdenek Drabek, then a refugee from the Russian invasion of Czechoslovakia, now Senior Advisor at WTO and a former minister in the Czech government; along with other assorted US draft dodgers (those were the days of the Vietnam war), against an Oxford team made up almost entirely of Bill Bradley, later NBA star and US presidential candidate. The experience was memorable not for the standard of basketball played but for the intellectual level of conversations, the highlight being the Cambridge captain Bill Sheasgreen (Director of Ithaca College, London Center) writing the names of the team members on a beer-mat in Egyptian hieroglyphics. The star of the basketball team 1969-71 was Zdenek Drabek. In those days he was somewhat moody and temperamental, presumably the result of his exile from his homeland. On one occasion the team was playing a club in Birmingham; all our games were away as the University had no facilities for minority sports in those days, basketball being only the second most popular sport in the world. After a decision of one of the referees that went against him, Stan (as he was known) let out a stream of incomprehensible Czech phrases, only to discover to his great amazement and shame that the referee was also Czech, and he was given a severe warning for whatever it was he said. Presumably his description of the ref's mother was not complimentary.

Chris Daniels
(1968)

Boxing

In February 2007 the 100th Varsity Boxing Match took place at Bethnal Green, the first time it had been held in London for 70 years. It is now the oldest annual inter-club amateur boxing match in the world but it could so easily have been different. In January 1969, the Oxford boxing club disbanded just weeks before the Varsity Match, citing financial problems. Cambridge were left with a Corn Exchange booking and no opponents – and, more seriously, no Blues. The captain, Charles Rooney, told the *Daily Telegraph* correspondent that CUABC, which had held its first bout in 1897, would 'make every effort to survive' but admitted that the future of the Cambridge club was now uncertain.

Emma Hagan of St Edmund's and the US Marines after winning her bout at the 100th Varsity Boxing Match in March 2007 at Bethnal Green.

Fortunately, a Lincoln College freshman, Robert Nairac, who was later to be killed in Northern Ireland, decided to take matters into his own hands. He managed to produce the necessary team of nine boxers, ranging from featherweight to heavyweight, and, although the Blue status of the contest was still undecided, the match was on. There followed one of the closest contests in Varsity history with Cambridge winning 5:4 as a result of a walkover in the heavyweight division.

In a year that saw riots erupt at universities throughout Europe, the *Evening Standard* summed up the match appropriately: 'Oxford v. Cambridge, in fact, turned out to be the finest and friendliest university riot of the season.' Those fortunate enough to receive their Blues and Half Blues at Bethnal Green and in previous contests – since 2001 this has included at least two women, CUABC President 2006–7, Cat Tubb, and US Marine, Emma Hagan – might like to raise a glass to the man whose efforts rescued both clubs, Captain Robert Nairac GC.

Charles Garraway
(1968)

---

limited number of Full Blues to be shared between the two sports. Mutiny ensued with the rugby players awarding themselves Blues in December 1884 and the soccer players following suit in spring 1885. A major debate at the Union before a huge audience saw the football supporters triumphant and CUBC forced to concede.

By the early 20th century it seems to have been agreed that it was inappropriate for the Boat Club to determine the status of all other sports, so the first official Blues Committee was established in 1912. Only the Full Blue sports were represented and CUBC maintained its dominance by holding two seats, chairing the committee and retaining a casting vote. To the original core, which now also included hockey, were added new members as their sports gained Full Blue status: lawn tennis (1922), golf (1938), boxing (1948), squash (1960), swimming (1966), cross country (1977) and basketball (1996); so the current Blues Committee has 14 members. The permanent, but non-voting, Secretary to the committee has always been a don and there have only been seven of these in the 95 years of the committee's existence, so a degree of continuity is assured.

The work of the committee is taken up with judging requests for Full or Half Blues, mindful of the need to maintain standards and not devalue the Blue. It first decides on the appropriate status for the sport. This raises the perpetual knotty question of what is a sport. Chess, for example, has jealously guarded its Half Blue status, gained in the pre-Blues Committee

Cambridge rugby Blues, 2007.

era – it was an extremely popular spectator sport in the 1870s; while dance sport, one of the University's most popular activities, has only recently, and then after heated debate on the committee, received Half Blue status. Whilst steeped in tradition, the committee is always prepared to move with the times if evidence of permanence can be shown. This means an applicant sport must have played at least five successive Varsity Matches. Once status is determined, the club captains in perpetuity are given leave to award Full Blues or Half Blues as appropriate; while the Blues Committee itself decides on discretionary and extraordinary cases.

The Blues Committee has no jurisdiction over the women's clubs and does not award Blues to women. This is the province of the independent Women's Blues Committee, which means that female coxes of the Blue Boat, such as Rebecca Dowbiggin in 2007 and 2008, must be proposed by the men's committee but ratified by the women's. The women's committee was established in the 1960s; its function closely parallels the men's and is serviced by a don, in this case as Senior Treasurer. The women's committee membership is much wider than that of the men's, including as it does the captains of every women's sport of at least Half Blue status. The differences in size and make-up mean that occasionally the two committees reach different decisions for a single sport; this creates some interesting situations! Nevertheless the two committees liaise closely and both are represented on the Joint Blues Committee of Oxford and Cambridge, which oversees the rules for Varsity Matches.

At present, a Full Blue in a major sport is probably regarded as highly as ever, both in Cambridge and beyond. Although other universities, with higher sporting standards, may now produce better sportsmen and women, their 'colours', for instance the 'purple', have never gained the cachet of an Oxbridge Blue.

***Christopher Thorne**, Emeritus Senior Tutor of St Catharine's College, was Secretary of the Blues Committee from 1977 to 1997.*

> *"While it is acknowledged that sporting standards overall still do not match those of the balmy middle-fifties, the value of a Blue has paradoxically never been greater. 'Graduate unemployment crises' hold no fears for Oxbridge sportsmen, secure in the knowledge that you never see a Blue at the Labour Exchange."*
>
> **Varsity Handbook, 1971–2**

Overleaf: Cambridge in winter. Photograph by Hiroshi Shimura.

Hawks and Ospreys

When members of the newly formed CURUFC wanted to join the St John's Eagles, a social club principally for St John's cricketers, it was decided in 1872 to found the Hawks' Club as a social club for all Blue sportsmen in all colleges. Membership was and continues to be by election only and for men only. There have, however, been major changes in recent years. The connection with St John's was finally broken when the lease on premises owned by the college in All Saints Passage expired in 1966. There followed an unsuccessful experiment in sharing premises with the Pitt Club, which ended when old Hawks Douglas Calder and Colin Kolbert persuaded Rocco Forte to sell them the elegant townhouse in Portugal Place, which is now the club's headquarters. After a huge fund-raising effort and a major refurbishment, 18 Portugal Place opened in 1992. The generosity of the widow of James Van Alon, a lawn tennis Blue, allowed the club to buy out the mortgage on the clubhouse and now the resident membership using it each year starts at about 60, rising, as Varsity Matches are played, to about 200 by the end of the year. The clubhouse also generates income and provides a useful link with the professional life of Cambridge by hosting a dining rights club for local business people. The most significant event of the year for many alumni Hawks is the London Dinner, which has been held annually since 1936 and allows Hawks of all generations to gather together on the eve of the Varsity Rugby Match. In 1996 the club established the Hawks Charitable Trust, which awards grants to anyone, male or female, in the University who is at or near the top of their sport and in need of funds. It is now the biggest single source of sporting funds in the University and recent recipients have included Natalie McGoldrick, who represents Great Britain in equestrian events, Phyllis Agbo, heptathlete, and middle distance runner, Andy Baddeley.

In 1985 the Hawks were joined by a sister organisation, the Ospreys, founded to promote opportunities, recognition and support for sportswomen, who now compete in 41 sports in the University. With over 1,000 current and alumni members, the club attracts significant corporate sponsorship to provide bursaries to its members.

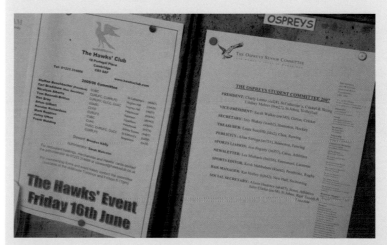

Modern management in a medieval framework

Martin Daunton

When a team of Japanese academics was appointed to advise their government on reform of their universities, it was natural for them to visit Cambridge. Their reasoning was impeccable: here was one of the world's greatest universities, and it was obvious that its system of governance must be a model to follow. Logic soon gave way to puzzlement as we tried to explain how the University is run, until all was clear: the Senate House is a building and Regent House is people. They had every reason to be puzzled, for the governance of the University of Cambridge is entirely unlike any other university, corporation or charity.

Critics argue that the success of Cambridge comes despite a system of governance that is castigated as medieval and sorely in need of modernising to allow swifter action in response to rapidly changing circumstances. To these critics, stronger executive power and managerial authority would allow greater effectiveness, a more efficient use of resources, and would free academics to teach and research. Defenders of the Cambridge system respond that a university cannot be run in the same way as a business corporation where success is easily measured in output or the bottom line. Success is much more intangible, depending on leading academics pushing the boundaries of knowledge by questioning received wisdom, and teaching students to be critical and precise, original and creative. Will they do this more effectively in a more managerial system, or by preserving the medieval sense of a university as a self-governing community of scholars? Universities depend on the commitment of the academics who work in them, on their freedom to think in new ways – and systems of governance should be judged by this measure of effectiveness. The logic of our Japanese visitors might be sound and the success of Cambridge over such a long period might after all arise from its unique way of running its affairs.

The issue facing Cambridge as it enters its ninth century is: how can the greatest possible efficiency in the use of scarce resources, entirely reasonably expected by the government, charities and benefactors, be combined with the greatest possible participation by academics whose enthusiasm, ideas and questioning intelligence are so vital to success? The Vice-Chancellor cannot be a chief executive of a business corporation telling everyone what to do; neither can academics act irresponsibly in their use of their constitutional power. At the heart of present debates is where exactly the balance should be drawn between efficiency and democratic self-rule.

One analogy for the governance of Cambridge is Athenian or participatory democracy: all University officers and Fellows of colleges constitute Regent House to which any business that requires approval is submitted as a Grace. In most cases, this is a mere formality, though members of Regent House may raise items of concern at a 'discussion' held in Senate House, and a ballot may be called if requested by 25 members. The operation of Regent House is not without its critics: the rhetoric at discussions often falls below the standard of Demosthenes; larger strategic issues may be overlooked and attendance is frequently low. Eager reformers complain that the prospect of a discussion or ballot hinders much-needed change and provides an outlet for special pleading. As a result, Regent House seems irrelevant to many of its members so

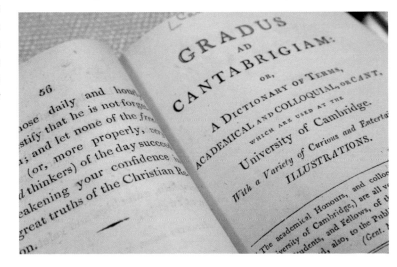

Opposite: The Esquire Bedells, of whom there are now two, carry silver maces presented to the University by the first Duke of Buckingham when accompanying the Vice-Chancellor at formal occasions, such as honorary degree ceremonies. The University Marshal carries a mahogany mace tipped with silver, which was originally made for the Yeoman Bedell, an office which was abolished in 1858.

Right: Gradus ad Cantabrigiam, *a dictionary of terms used at the University of Cambridge, published in 1807.*

Detail from Senate House Hill on Degree Day Morning, *1863, by Robert Farren. Recognisable in the crowd are Leslie Stephen, Thomas Geldart, Henry Fawcett and Henry Latham, all Fellows of Trinity Hall, where the painting hangs. One of the graduands has already received a wooden spoon for the worst pass in the Mathematics Tripos.*

PROCTOR, an academical officer, whose business it is, περιπολεισθαι, to *walk the round*, and see that there is no chambering and wantonness, no rioting and drunkenness. PROCTORS had need be Masters of ARTS, for they are exposed to many scrapes.

DEAN—Udorum tetricus censor et asper.
                                          Mart.

The principal business of a *Dean* is to inflict impositions for irregularities, &c. Old Holingshed, in his Chronicle, describing Cambridge, speaks of 'certeine censors, or DEANES, appointed to looke to the behaviour, and maner of the Studentes there, whom they punish *very severely*, if they make any default, according to the quantitye and qualitye of their trespasses.'

ESQUIRE BEDELS; Gentlemen-ushers to the Vice-Chancellor, who walk before him on all public occasions, bearing each (there are three of them) a silver staff, or mace, on his shoulders, and habited in the dress of his degree, which is usually that of A. M. One of the 'Squire Bedels, likewise, walks before the preacher at St. Mary's, and sees him ... into the pulpit! The present Bishop of London, Dr. Porteus, was an Esquire Bedel at Cam-

Cambridge definitions from 1807 (see previous page).

that participatory democracy becomes an illusion. Nevertheless, at their best the discussions are a safety valve and a way of raising genuine concerns, providing a sense of academic autonomy. The solution is not to abolish or trammel Regent House, but rather to ensure that more people know about the crucial issues of the University through green or white papers, and web-based discussions, so that Regent House can regain a real sense of involvement with the wider University.

The participatory democracy of Regent House is complemented by the representative democracy of Council. Policies and proposals from the many committees and faculties of the University are considered by the Council and then presented as Reports and Graces to Regent House. The Council is chaired by the Vice-Chancellor who is no longer, as in the recent past, drawn in rotation from the heads of colleges for a short term of two years. Rather the vice-chancellorship is now a full-time post with a longer term of at least five but no more than seven years, offering a greater sense of continuity and professionalism. At present, the Council has 19 elected members of whom 16 are elected by Regent House. Those elected by Regent House are four from among the heads of colleges, four from among the professors and readers and eight from among the other members of Regent House. The students elect three of their number, of whom one must be a graduate student. Recently, a new category of external member has been introduced; there are currently two such members, nominated by the Council and appointed by Regent House.

Here are two major topics of debate: should the Vice-Chancellor chair a body to which she reports, or should there be an independent chairman as in most organisations; and how many external members should sit on Council? The introduction of an independent chairman is more widely accepted than the recommendation of the Committee of University Chairmen that the majority of any governing body should be made up of external members – a proposition that collides with Regent House's commitment to the model of a self-governing community of scholars. The recent report on 'The Good Governance of Cambridge University' steered a cautious middle path, reflecting the difficulties encountered at Oxford where the attempt to increase the number of external members led to very public dissent. The report argued that a majority of external members would threaten a loss of internal confidence, and proposed that external membership should be increased to four in order to demonstrate to the outside world that the University is run in an efficient way. The change has recently been accepted, and it now remains to be seen whether further change will be required by outside pressures. Certainly, the existing Council will only work effectively if its members act in the general interests of the wider community by dealing with major strategic issues in a constructive way. Participatory and representative democracies are both in their ways excellent systems of government, offering a sense of autonomy and empowerment – always provided that members of the University engage in a responsible and constructive way and avoid destructive criticism.

Of course, Cambridge is a collegiate university and the colleges are directly represented on the Council. In practice, the four heads of house include the chairman and secretary of the Colleges' Committee, the assembly of all 31 heads of house which discusses issues of common concern. The Vice-Chancellor and other senior officers of the University attend the Colleges' Committee, and the exchange of information and co-ordination of activities are now effective and constructive. These discussions are facilitated by the Colleges' Standing Committee whose members include representatives of the Bursars' and Senior Tutors' Committees. The Standing Committee mutates into the University and Colleges Joint Committee with the addition of representatives of the University. The result is that the colleges and the University can reach a common understanding on matters such as fund-raising, admissions and teaching – as well as agreeing on how to handle the many external challenges faced by the University. Allegations that colleges abuse their independence to block sensible reforms are now misplaced. Although the colleges rightly remain competitive on the river and in academic league tables, rivalry is compatible with a co-operative pursuit of common goals.

The Council has general responsibility for the management of the University and its resources, but most policy is fed up from a plethora of other committees, syndics and above all the General Board of the Faculties. The General Board has charge of academic and educational policy, and has representatives from the six schools of the University, as well as cross-membership from Council. The General Board receives direct reports from the Education and Research Policy Committees; other committees such as Personnel, Planning and Resources, Resource Management and Buildings are joint bodies of General Board and Council. By now, the diary of an academic politician is overwhelmed and midnight oil is being consumed to read piles of papers, some of which become too familiar as they migrate from one committee to another. Attempting to explain the relationship between Council and General Board is not easy even for the initiated, and the report on good governance made the radical suggestion that their roles and responsibilities should be set out in a short document! A more revolutionary suggestion is that Council and General Board should merge in order to create a more focussed and coherent system. This proposal was rejected on grounds understandable to a US politician: that checks and balances are important in order to prevent a concentration of power with its threat to academic freedom from 'centralisation' and an over-mighty executive. As our politician might also point out, checks and balances can lead to stand-offs.

The General Board, as well as the committees dealing with resources, offer a platform for an increasingly powerful group of individuals: the Chairs of the Councils of the Schools of Humanities and Social Sciences, Arts and Humanities, Technology, Biological Sciences, Physical Sciences and Medicine. The clumsy title of the post reflects past practice when the heads of departments and faculties would meet as a council of the school under a chairman who had no real power and no control of resources. In those days, faculties received their funding directly from the University Chest in a sort of planned economy. Now, resources are allocated to the schools in something like an internal market through the Resource Allocation Model which assigns costs and revenues for activities. The Chairs of the Councils of the Schools have acquired considerable financial power and hold virtually full-time jobs, raising fears in the minds of some members of Regent House that they are evolving into Deans – precisely the sort of management cadre that causes such alarm to proponents of academic freedom and self-rule. The decision to retain the old name proved wise, for the role of chairman has evolved through accepted custom and practice, allowing a major reform of administrative procedures with remarkable ease. Concern that the schools threaten the independence of faculties by inserting a new layer of bureaucracy has been minimised though not removed by carefully portraying them as devolving power away from the centre rather than accruing it from below. The Chairs of the Councils are still elected by the council of the individual school and not appointed by the Vice-Chancellor. A balance between managerial efficiency and academic autonomy has been achieved with some success.

At the same time as the Chairs have gained financial oversight of the schools, a new team of Pro-Vice-Chancellors has taken responsibility for functions such as Human Resources, Research, Planning and Resources, Education and International Relations. The PVCs now chair many committees of the Council and General Board, and attend the meetings of both bodies. Although there is still room for improvement in the structure, the PVCs do now oversee strategic developments and drive change – always through the committee structure and not through managerial fiat. As a result, the Vice-Chancellor can focus more effectively on her own priorities and responsibilities. Evolution will doubtless continue, perhaps on the lines of great US universities where the role of the Vice-Chancellor is divided into the President who deals with external relations and fund-raising, and the Provost who deals with internal issues. The Vice-Chancellor spends about half her time on matters internal to the University, and half on the tasks more traditionally associated with a university President, engaging with the government and donors. At the moment, there is no formally designated senior PVC or Provost, though the PVC for Planning and Resources is evolving in that direction. Should this role be more clearly specified, and would it be more

Right: The University Council, the principal executive and policy-making body, meeting at the Old Schools, 2008.

Michael Derringer

Town and gown

Relations between the city of Cambridge and the University, town and gown, have, over the centuries, caused more or less tension, not always straightforwardly between the one corporation and the other. The last explosive undergraduate celebration of Guy Fawkes Night was probably that of 1954: that was certainly a nuisance to the police, but should be interpreted not as an anti-town manifestation so much as an unseemly continuation of a perceived tradition. The Cambridge police kept a store of old uniforms for use on such occasions so that showers of soot and flour were of little concern — and most police helmets were returned the next day.

Earlier events of a similar kind involved bouts of fisticuffs between undergraduates and bargees, most of whom were not from Cambridge.

In fact the very first charter surviving in the University Archives is concerned with relations between the University and the town: it dates from 1266 and establishes a panel of representatives of the two corporations to fix rents of houses every five years, there being, of course, no university or college premises at that date.

The town, denied its claim to city status by the University in James I's reign, has historically had an ambivalent view. For the Mayor and Corporation it was a cuckoo in the nest; for tradesmen, a golden goose, so long as they did not get discommuned (put out of bounds to students) for allowing too much credit.

While the University could well have been said to have dominated the city since at least the 14th century, when, as a result of royal

Gown! Gown! – Town! Town! – or the Battle of Peas Hill from Gradus ad Cantabrigiam, *1824.*

retribution for the Peasants' Revolt, the University's control of the market, among other things, was vastly increased, this domination has long since faded into oblivion. Vice-Chancellors no longer excommunicate mayors for the sin of insubordination, the Proctors no longer imprison ladies suspected, usually with good reason, of being 'of easy virtue'. As these 'rights' were, usually willingly, relinquished, arrangements were made for the University to be represented on the town/city council — a regulation long since abandoned as plenty have been found more than happy to stand for election.

Elisabeth Leedham-Green

Stephen Fleet, Registrary, Deputy Vice-Chancellor and Master of Downing College from 2000 to 2003, who was instrumental in the establishment of a permanent vice-chancellorship and other administrative reforms associated with WASS. Painted by Ophelia Redpath.

sensible to associate it with education and research, which are the central objectives of the University?

The governance and management of the University of Cambridge is immensely complex and highly distinctive. It can often seem frustratingly slow and cumbersome. But it also has great virtues, allowing engagement at all levels in order to create the sense of responsibility and liberty which contribute so powerfully to the success of Cambridge. The University's academic reputation is extremely high, despite a lower level of resource than its international competitors. Doubtless there is room for improvement and simplification as the roles of the Chairs of the Councils of the Schools and Pro-Vice-Chancellors continue to evolve. The strongest supporters of self-government are guilty of obscurantism which can play into the hands of their opponents who are eager for sweeping (and divisive) reform; the advocates of tighter managerial controls threaten to undermine the academic autonomy which is central to success. Gradual evolution in governance has steered a middle course between an atavistic clinging to the past and a leap into the unknown, between smug satisfaction and destructive change. We might not recommend that our Japanese colleagues copy the details of Cambridge's governance; we would recommend that they adopt its spirit.

Martin Daunton *is Professor of Economic History and Master of Trinity Hall.*

Running the University

Income and spending

TONY MINSON

In 1976, when I joined the Department of Pathology, the University had recently issued a discussion document which concluded that Cambridge had reached an optimum size. Further growth, it was argued, would threaten the collegiate style of education and would lead to an imbalance in the relationship between the University and the small town of Cambridge. The University had apparently reached 'steady-state'. During the next 30 years I watched the University expand: new buildings for Law, Divinity, English, Criminology and Music on the Sidgwick Site; the largest Maths Campus in the world at Clarkson Road; Computer Science, Electrical Engineering and Nanoscience at West Cambridge; Biochemistry, the Judge Business School, Developmental Biology and Pharmacology in the city centre, and a thriving new Medical School at the Old Addenbrooke's Site. This did not feel like 'steady-state'! The fears expressed 30 years ago have not, however, materialised. Undergraduate numbers *have* increased – from about 8,500 to 11,000 – but we have managed to absorb this modest increase and the collegiate style of education has not changed. The city of Cambridge has grown to include 'Silicon Fen', the largest high-tech bio-tech cluster in Europe, and has more than kept pace with the growth of the University.

The new buildings provided greatly improved teaching facilities but they were also needed to accommodate a growing amount of research activity, and it is that research that has kept us in the Premier League of world universities. Back in 1976 the University's operating budget amounted to £27 million per year. Now (in 2007) it is £600 million per year. And where it comes from has changed too. In the early 1970s more than two-thirds of the University's income came as an annual block grant from the government and we had little idea how the actual figure was derived. Research grants and contracts were barely significant as a source of income – I remember that in the Pathology Department, the research grant accounts were kept in a notebook! Today the University is running thousands of individual research projects contracted by charities, research councils, industry or government agencies, and the total value is about £200 million per year – more than a third of our total income. We still receive an annual 'Block Grant' from the government but now it comprises less than one-third of our income and, importantly, the figure is calculated by a precise formula: so much for each student (the 'teaching' element) and so much for the volume and quality of research (the 'research' element).

In 2003 I moved from the Pathology Department to the inner sanctums of the Old Schools as Pro-Vice-Chancellor for Planning and Resources with responsibility for integrating academic planning with financial planning. By that time the income sources of the University were looking as they do in the graphic overleaf, making the point that more than half our total income derives directly or indirectly from research activity, whereas all forms of undergraduate and postgraduate teaching attract less than a quarter. Indeed, our determination to maintain the quality of undergraduate education in Cambridge means that we spend far more per undergraduate than we receive in income.

Right: The University Chest, which is the responsibility of the Registrary and was used for keeping University monies and, until the 14th century, all the University's books. This one has 17 locks and dates from the 15th century, its predecessor having been burned during the Peasants' Revolt of 1381. It is kept in the Old Schools.

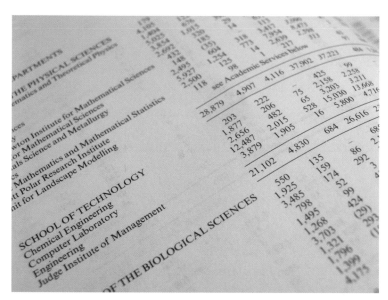

University accounts, University Reporter, *2007.*

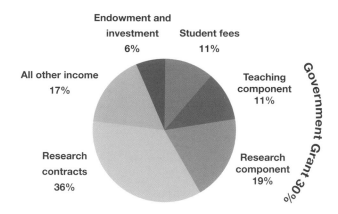

University Income — 2007 (Total £600m)

- Endowment and investment 6%
- Student fees 11%
- All other income 17%
- Teaching component 11%
- Research contracts 36%
- Research component 19%
- Government Grant 30%

These changes in the sources and mechanisms of funding have had a number of consequences. The first is the complexity of funding: we receive many thousands of research grants and in nearly all cases the sponsor demands specific accounting for the expenditure incurred. And since the government Block Grant is based on a formula, we must maintain precise records of student numbers by subject, gender, race, socioeconomic class etc., as well as precise records of research activity and performance. Add 'Freedom of Information' and 'Data Protection' and it is apparent that the administrative burden has grown substantially. Our records must be accountable and auditable. We have invested tens of millions in secure information systems to cover finance, student records, staff, payroll and research grants management. The notebook will no longer do!

Of course, this administrative effort is not primarily about accountability and audit. Good information management systems have given us a much clearer understanding of our costs, both direct and indirect, and of how we earn our income. We have developed a model (a Resource Allocation Model) that describes the income and expenditure associated with different activities, and allows any department to calculate how much it earns and how much its activity costs. We do not allocate funds 'as earned' because this would seriously distort the balance of academic activity in the University, but the existence of a robust model allows departments to assess the financial consequences of their academic plans. The amalgamated plans of all parts of the University are scrutinised to ensure that they are academically consistent with the University's mission, and the impact of these plans on income and expenditure leads to a long-term financial forecast – then we can decide whether the plans can be afforded!

One big question hangs over this whole area of the University's finances and occupies a lot of our time. Are our sources of income sufficiently diverse and are we too dependent on government? Our two big sources of income are government (the 'Block Grant') and research grants (many of which also come from government agencies). A downturn in the economy, a change in government Higher Education policy or a reduced UK commitment to research and development could reduce our income substantially. Cambridge is less dependent on government funding than it was 30 years ago, but in those days government took a more 'hands-off' approach to Higher Education whereas today we are more exposed to political trends. We need to spread the risk by diversifying: by maximising the return we get from the University's £1 billion endowment fund, and by building the fund itself to levels a little more like those of our international competitors, perhaps by charging more realistic tuition fees supported by generous bursaries. These are long-term policy goals but much has been done: an impressive investment office has been set up; we are building a generous bursary system and we are beginning to engage more effectively with alumni and other potential benefactors.

Tony Minson *is Professor of Virology and, until 2006, was Pro-Vice-Chancellor with special responsibility for issues concerned with Planning and Resources.*

Sir Cam

Benefactors and Financial Support

My recollection of my time as an undergraduate at Cambridge is, I imagine, very similar to that of many others of my generation. We studied, played, lived and grew in our wonderful collegiate university with only the most cursory understanding of how it came to be. In particular, growing up in a generation where education was regarded as something to be stewarded by the government, and funded largely by the taxpayer, I have no doubt that I was among many of that time who regarded such an arrangement as the norm.

But even a brief review of the financial history of collegiate Cambridge shows that this experience was very much the exception, for over most of its 800-year life the success of Cambridge has depended not on subvention from the state but on the support of many benefactors. Visionary philanthropists from all walks of life have helped make Cambridge what it is, dating back to the earliest moments of its existence. The first Cambridge college, Peterhouse, was founded in 1284 by the generosity of Hugo de Balsham, Bishop of Ely. More than 250 years later, Henry VIII founded Trinity College, further endowing five Regius Professorships in Divinity, Hebrew, Greek, Physic and Civil Law with a cumulative gift of £200.

Succeeding generations built on these great foundations. In 1704 a legacy from Thomas Plume founded an observatory and endowed a Professorship of Astronomy and Experimental Philosophy. In 1816 Richard, seventh Viscount Fitzwilliam of Merrion, left £100,000 and his collections of paintings, prints, books and manuscripts to further 'the Increase of Learning and other great Objects of that Noble Foundation'. This led to the establishment of the Fitzwilliam Museum. Other benefactions have been no less transformational. In the 1870s, the seventh Duke of Devonshire endowed the Cavendish Laboratory for the study of physics. Sir Ernest Rutherford, who won the Nobel Prize for Chemistry in 1908 for his investigations into the disintegration of the elements and the chemistry of radioactive substances, is one of the laboratory's best-known students.

In the latter part of the last and the beginning of the current centuries, generous and far-sighted benefactors have continued to support the evolution of Cambridge to help keep its capability abreast of changing needs. The Wolfson Foundation funded the building of the University Centre, established the Institute of Criminology, and refounded Wolfson College, subsequently named in its honour. Sir David Robinson founded Robinson College, formally opening in 1981, and the Bill and Melinda Gates Foundation made an exceptional gift to the University to establish the Gates Cambridge Trust, which created in perpetuity an international scholarship programme for outstanding international graduate students.

As Co-Chairman of the 800th Anniversary Campaign, it is very gratifying for me to see the stimulating effect that benefactions from the current generation of donors to Cambridge have on the University. Seeing newly recruited academics, watching staff as they undertake world-changing research in refitted labs, and meeting bright young undergraduates full of energy and enthusiasm for their first term in

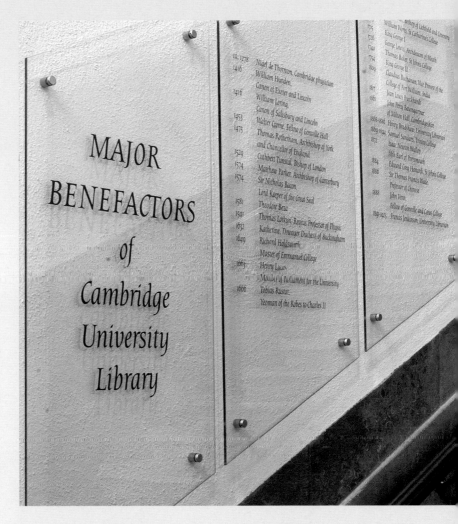

college, have underlined for me that the 800th Anniversary is very much more than an exercise in nostalgia.

As we reach 2009, close attention to the need and opportunity for renewal, safeguarding all that is best while adapting to a fast-changing environment, will be critical. The assumptions about finance which my generation took for granted in our youth no longer hold good. If we are to continue to do the things we want to do, establish a comprehensive bursary scheme, and maintain academic and research standards in a competitive world, we must be ambitious and creative. With the leadership of an outstanding Vice-Chancellor, collegiate Cambridge is rising to these challenges in a determined and strategic way.

The campaign to raise £1 billion raises the bar University-wide. Donors are equipping this great university for current and future generations, just as their forebears did with their own benefactions. This is an immensely exciting time and gives us excellent cause to celebrate our history so far, and to look forward to the great contribution that collegiate Cambridge should continue to make in changing the future.

David Walker (1958) is a former chairman of Morgan Stanley and Co-Chairman of the Cambridge University 800th Anniversary Campaign

comedy

adc theatre

advance booking

Student Drama

Talent and temerity

BENEDICT NIGHTINGALE

Since Cambridge has produced no fewer than four of the five artistic directors who have so far run the National Theatre, and none of them had any formal training after they went down, there must be something right with the University's undergraduate theatre. Since it has also produced two of the current batch of theatrical knights – and, again, the only two to have gone straight into the profession without a stopover at RADA or any acting academy – there must be something very right with the University's student theatre.

Peter Hall, who was at St Catharine's 1950–3, went on to found the Royal Shakespeare Company before taking over from Laurence Olivier as the National's supremo. Nicholas Hytner, at Trinity Hall 1974–7, is the latest of his successors on the South Bank. But if there was a golden age in Cambridge theatre it was between (roughly) 1957 and (roughly) 1962, when Trevor Nunn, Richard Eyre, Ian McKellen and Derek Jacobi overlapped, along with Michael Pennington, Corin Redgrave, John Shrapnel, Miriam Margolyes and several others who have helped make British theatre the creative force it is now.

Hytner thinks that a well-equipped theatre run and largely financed by undergraduates was a key factor. True, the University Players, the Mummers, the Marlowe Society and other groups have also staged their work in the Arts Theatre, the Corn Exchange and even Great St Mary's Church; but it's the Amateur Dramatic Club or ADC that has really mattered. That's the theatre in which Peter Hall, following the example of his friends and contemporaries John Barton and Peter Wood, launched his career by directing a version of Anouilh's *Eurydice* – and where just about every Cambridge Thespian, from John Bird to Tilda Swinton, has acted since.

Though Pennington and others acknowledge the encouragement of George 'Dadie' Rylands, and Hytner was much helped by Graham Storey and Peter Holland, Cambridge dons seem often to have been unhelpful or positively hostile to undergraduate performers. I myself recall a Senior

Fellow at Magdalene bluntly declaring that 'gentlemen don't act' and, in an academic atmosphere where drama was seen as literature only, the less snobbish tended to regard the theatre as a hindrance to serious study. Playing a long succession of major roles, including Anouilh's *Antigone* and Giraudoux's *Ondine*, didn't of course prevent Margaret Drabble getting a starred first; but maybe she was a special case.

No, what drove those undergraduate actors was a combination of opportunity (Pennington played 30 parts in three years before leaving to become a mainstay of the RSC) and a single-minded sense of purpose. Eyre, who was eventually to take over from Hall at the National, describes Cambridge actors of his generation as 'cocky, immodest, self-regarding, ostentatious, vain and self-important', with 'intrigues, jealousies, stars and careers conceived on the lines of what were imagined to be the real thing', and Pennington feels he and his contemporaries were 'horrible little professionals before our time'. As Michael Frayn, who wrote a Footlights revue, once put it: 'You're never so famous as when you're at Cambridge.'

But that yearning for fame, that quasi-professionalism meant that the able and ambitious left rich in experience. Flip through *Varsity*, reading reviews of Tim Brooke-Taylor's Trigorin in *The Seagull*, or of David Frost's Actor-Manager in *Six Characters in Search of an Author*, or of productions by John Tusa, Stephen Frears or the future principal of RADA, Nick Barter. You'll be astonished by the range of work attempted: Miller, Williams, Betti, Wesker, Ayme, Camus,

Left: Façade of the ADC Theatre on Park Street.

Right: Derek Jacobi rehearsing a Mummers production of Christopher Fry's A Sleep of Prisoners *with Michael Burrell and Richard Kay in Great St Mary's directed by Waris Habibullah (now Hussein).*

David Thomas

The second-ever Cambridge Greek play, Aristophanes' The Birds (1883), which featured incidental music by Hubert Parry. The Cambridge Greek play is now performed every three years at the Arts Theatre.

Sergeant Musgrave's Dance at the ADC, 1962. Produced by Trevor Nunn with (l to r) Stephen Frears, Michael Apted and Chris Kelly.

Cocteau, Sartre, Beckett, Ionesco, Pinter, Whiting, Arden, Kops, Dennis, Brecht, Gorky, Strindberg, Hauptmann, Lorca, Webster, Sheridan, Wycherley as well as Anouilh, Giraudoux, Chekhov, Pirandello and, of course, every variety of Shakespeare. All this, in a university without the theatre department and directing and acting courses you find in even minor US colleges.

Moreover, some work was bold by any standards. Hytner and a friend, John Till, formed their own company, calling it Cambridge Music Theatre, and staged Brecht and Weill's *Rise and Fall of the City of Mahagonny* in a massive piece of scaffolding they'd built in the Corn Exchange. Nunn took both a Footlights revue, complete with Cleese, Chapman, Brooke-Taylor and Margolyes, and Ibsen's unwieldy *Brand*, this time with Margolyes as 'a wild mountain girl', to a cabaret space on the Edinburgh Fringe that immediately afterwards became the city's principal repertory theatre, the Traverse. Griff Rhys Jones's ambitious production of Jonson's *Bartholomew Fair* for the Marlowe Society seems to have impressed everyone, as did Sam Mendes's revival of *Cyrano de Bergerac*, with Tom Hollander as the Breton with the improbable nose.

Almost as importantly, undergraduates learnt what they couldn't do. Eyre was praised for his 'silent detachment' as the alienated title character in Osborne's *Epitaph for George Dillon*, but still remembers with embarrassment wearing a gold lamé suit and singing bad songs in a musical about the pop industry called *Expresso Bongo*. Frears, who was directing the show, sent him to a hypnotist in hopes of improving his performance, but it was all too clear that Eyre wasn't born to be an actor. Likewise with Hytner, who reduced his audiences to unwanted hilarity with his playing of a tyrannical general in Betti's *Queen and the Rebels*.

Somewhat similarly, Nunn must have learned something from the overlong *Macbeth* – Eyre both a feverish Seyton and an unwittingly comical monk in the England scene – that he staged at Cambridge in 1962, for his subsequent production of the play for the RSC, with McKellen and Judi Dench, was the strongest of our era. Incidentally, Nunn answers the accusation that there's a Cambridge network or mafia in the British theatre by pointing out that it was his work at the Belgrade, Coventry, and not at the University which impressed Peter Hall enough to invite him to Stratford, thus launching a career that was to see him running first the RSC, then the National. Others have felt that being at Cambridge was an actual obstacle to professional acceptance. 'People wanted recent graduates to get their hands dirty,' says Hytner, 'to temper their cleverness and self-confidence with real experience.'

Indeed, Cambridge probably left its theatrical undergraduates with plenty to unlearn. Yes, they acquired drive, seriousness and the chance to explore the world's drama on stage. If they performed for the Marlowe Society, with its interest in Elizabethan drama, they were also encouraged to speak verse with a care and articulacy now often missing in the professional theatre. But Eyre is among those who feel that there's something called 'university acting' which is 'all architecture and no heart, assembled by an intelligent mind over-conscious of meanings, of content, of style, of history'. Maybe that helps explain why some successful Cambridge actors didn't make it in the real world.

Oedipus the King

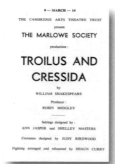

9 — MARCH — 14
THE CAMBRIDGE ARTS THEATRE TRUST
present
THE MARLOWE SOCIETY
production:

TROILUS AND CRESSIDA
by
WILLIAM SHAKESPEARE

Producer:
ROBIN MIDGLEY

Settings designed by:
ANN JASPER and SHELLEY MASTERS
Costumes designed by JUDY BIRDWOOD
Fighting arranged and rehearsed by SHAUN CURRY

But many did: not only McKellen and Jacobi, but Stephen Fry, Rachel Weisz, Emma Thompson, Sacha Baron Cohen and the man now regarded by many as the finest actor of his generation, Simon Russell Beale, who was at Caius 1979–82. He didn't act as often at Cambridge as he would have wished, because he was a choral scholar and was obliged to sing when other undergraduates were rehearsing plays. But he still managed to play the sinister title character in an adapation of Conrad's *Secret Agent*, intepreted Sir Epicure Mammon as an 'innocent child' in *The Alchemist* and, staying with Ben Jonson, was Sir Politic Would-Be to Fry's *Volpone*. He himself has particularly strong memories of his contemporary, Tilda Swinton, who took leading roles in several plays, including Athol Fugard's *Statements After an Arrest Under the Immorality Act* – 'I can't tell you how glamorous she was.'

Moreover, the top echelons of the British theatre are crammed with directors who honed their skills at Camridge: not only Hall, Nunn and Hytner, but Stephen Unwin, founder of English Touring Theatre; Sam Mendes, who turned London's tiny Donmar into the pacemaker in the moribund heart of the West End and went on to win an Oscar for *American Beauty*; Tim Supple, ex-director of the Young Vic and, recently, the director of a much-praised, multi-language *Midsummer Night's Dream*; Dominic Dromgoole, now the artistic director of Shakespeare's Globe; Nicholas Kent, who runs London's Tricycle Theatre and, when at Cambridge, directed many productions, among them the premiere of *Nadir of Fools* by his fellow-undergraduate, Howard Brenton; and Rupert Goold, who has won rave reviews for directing Patrick Stewart in *Macbeth* and *The Tempest*.

What fun it would be to time-warp back to some of those undergraduate productions. Who wouldn't want to see Stephen Fry as the comic pedant Holofernes in the Marlowe Society's revival of *Love's Labour's Lost*, or Sacha Cohen as the Turkish emperor Bajazeth in Supple's production of Marlowe's own *Tamburlaine*, or an undergraduate David Hare's staging of *Oh, What a Lovely War!*? Or, back in the golden age, Redgrave and McKellen giving what *Varsity* called 'respectively confident and highly intelligent and extravagant, blustery, virtuoso performances' in Wycherley's *Country Wife*? Or one 'Ian McKellan' as Hjalmar Ekdal in Ibsen's *Wild Duck*, 'his voice following carefully all the necessary variations of pomposity and self-apology'? Or even Ian McKellen himself as a sour and selfish artist in John Whiting's *Saint's Day*, 'showing deep feeling and considerable sincerity, though hopelessly miscast'? Or a certain 'Derek Jakobi' in Christopher Fry's *Sleep of Prisoners*, playing a private soldier who dreamed of himself as a series of Biblical figures – and proved 'frightening as Cain, nobly pathetic as David and deeply moving as Abraham'?

Benedict Nightingale (1959) *is a writer and journalist and has been theatre critic of* The Times *since 1990.*

I BELONG to the generation whose time at Cambridge was interrupted by War Service. I managed two terms at Peterhouse in 1943 before being called up into the Navy, and returned after the war from 1946 to 1948, when I became much involved in theatre.

It was a lively scene, though not many of my contemporaries went on to careers in the professional theatre. Quite a few, like me, were diverted into the BBC.

An exception was Stephen Joseph, son of the revue star Hermione Gingold, who ruled the Footlights at that time. He was a great champion of theatre-in-the-round and founded the Playhouse in Scarborough which became Alan Ayckbourn's base. The ADC was flourishing. We took Bernard Shaw's *You Never Can Tell* to Sweden, and students of Uppsala University responded by performing Strindberg's infinitely gloomy *Easter* in Cambridge – in Swedish. The Marlowe Society paid a memorable visit to Berlin during the Airlift of 1948 with Shakespeare's *Measure for Measure* and Webster's *The White Devil*. The society was dominated at that time by the legendary George 'Dadie' Rylands from King's whose obsession with good verse speaking led him at times to audition actors with his back to the stage, the better to assess the balance of voices. Dadie often reserved leading roles for himself and his fellow Kingsman Donald Beves, who was a brilliant Shakespearan clown. Another leading figure during collaborations with the Cambridge Musical Society was Camille Prior, a diminutive dynamo known universally as 'Pop'. In my time she produced a spectacular version of Purcell's *Dioclesian*.

There was a considerable crop of smaller theatrical companies which grew up around one or two leading figures and relied on them for their success. The Cambridge Theatre Group and University Actors are just two that come to mind. And of course many colleges, incuding my own, staged their own theatrical entertainments. At Peterhouse I wanted to produced Vanbrugh's *The Provoked Wife* but the Master had loftier ideas. We did the *Oedipus at Colonus* of Sophocles in the college garden.

Richard Baker (1943)

Right: Signed programme from the 1951 production by Dadie Rylands of Coriolanus, *featuring John Barton, Peter Hall, Roger Jenkins, Peter Wood and John Wilder.*

THE CAMBRIDGE ARTS THEATRE

By arrangement with
THE CAMBRIDGE
ARTS THEATRE TRUST

THE MARLOWE SOCIETY
AND
THE A.D.C.

present their

1951 ANNUAL LENT TERM PRODUCTION

CORIOLANUS

BY

WILLIAM SHAKESPEARE

1951

MONDAY 5 MARCH   FOR SIX DAYS
Evenings at 8.   Matinees Thursday and Saturday at 2.30

I read natural sciences, though I really wanted to act and swim. I swam against Oxford my first year and was in the Footlights revue. I had a horrible object lesson during the run of *A Flash in the Cam* as it was naïvely called. I had been to a party at my tutor's and was slightly drunk, on sherry. It showed slightly on stage but not much. The directors, Ian Kellie and Peter Jeffrey, gave me a bollocking. Two nights later, someone else was seriously pissed and rolling about on the stage. Peter said: 'Right, you and Chris Pym get on and ad-lib for three minutes to cover the scene change.' We did, and somehow managed to make them laugh. A more professional audience would have howled us down. The revue was unbearably exciting but we were all studiedly cool about it. I was not a great success as an actor. I was too awkward and shy. I still have nightmares where I find myself standing on the stage, tongue-tied and with hands as big as hams. In one-act plays, giving the new members of the Amateur Dramatic Club the chance to shine before an audience, I played Master Salathiel Pavey in *Spring 1600* with Sasha Moorsom, with whom I instantly fell in love. John Barton played a walk-through part as Mr Shakespeare and Peter Hall was in a gloomy Strindberg piece called *After the Fire*.

James Cellan Jones (1949)

I WAS awarded an exhibition in English to St Catharine's College in 1950. On my first day, I stood on Clare bridge and looked at the misty river. I felt inadequate. Obviously you needed a private income to enjoy this place, mutual friends from the right school and a confidence bred of your class which I, the grammar school-educated son of a country stationmaster, simply didn't have. Though things didn't of course turn out like that…

A figure crossed the bridge in the mist and came towards me. Like me, he carried his gown, new and untorn; like me he looked anxious. He introduced himself. His voice was reassuringly cockney. His name was Tony Church and he was bent on being an actor. We fell upon each other's enthusiasm for the theatre, his for acting, mine for directing, as if it were a secret religion in a pagan land; and began a working friendship which has lasted over the years.

At Cambridge I was to meet many people who have remained colleagues for all my professional life in the theatre … none more so than John Barton who in the early 1950s was almost single-handedly responsible for setting the drama standards at Cambridge. As a freshman, I was in awe of him, but he soon became the close friend and colleague I have admired throughout my life. He was already at that time a fiercely professional director, expert at staging and lighting. He dominated the ADC and Marlowe committees with his rigorous demands and would have no truck with amateurism. Without John, I don't think my Cambridge theatre generation would have achieved so much. He not only set standards himself, he expected others to do the same. His influence in Cambridge lasted for many years, even after he had left – from Peter Wood to Jonathan Miller and from Trevor Nunn to Richard Eyre.

I studied hard during my first year at Cambridge, keeping drama to a minimum, though I was seen in one or two productions, including playing the First Citizen in the Marlowe Society's *Coriolanus* and watching, fascinated, as George 'Dadie' Rylands directed…

I gradually, though, became more and more involved with University theatre, particularly the Marlowe. I dug deeper into Shakespeare, studying the text in depth, and acting in, among other things, a production of *Julius Caesar* directed by Dadie Rylands and John Barton in which we all attempted to speak Elizabethan (something which I can still do as a party piece!). John and I also acted together – as Mercutio and Tybalt – in a production of *Romeo and Juliet*. We devised the most impossibly dangerous (and long) rapier and dagger fight. It stole all the notices and was much praised but I suspect that it brought the play to a complete halt. As the Prince of Cats I wore too much chrome make-up and had a very flat voice … but the performance worked.

Even better, I started to direct, co-staging Rattigan's *The Browning Version* with John Barton. At last I found myself analysing the acting process …. It was, though, not until my final year that, with financial help from friends, I mounted my first independent production. I had somewhat optimistically booked the ADC for such a project on arrival

1948 production by Donald Beves of The White Devil. *Kneeling on the left, Dadie Rylands as Brachiano, in the middle, Gillian Webb as Vittoria and on the right, Donald Beves as Flamineo.*

1952 production by John Barton of Julius Caesar, *showing Peter Hall, Peter Orr, Tony Church, Michael Bakewell.*

at Cambridge three years earlier. My chosen play was Anouilh's *Point of Departure*. Becoming a director was a deeply pleasurable physical experience – like being dropped into a warm pool and finding I could swim. I had never felt that life was so easy, so relaxed, so assured. I knew I had much to learn, but the practised amateur actors in the large cast supported me and seemed pleased at the help I could offer. I quickly forged the group into a company. The play was a success with the public and the University reviewers and my supporters got their money back.

I discovered at last that I could direct … and I remember precisely the moment that I knew: we were rehearsing in a large room in the Bull Hostel, an annexe of St Catharine's which had formerly been a seedy hotel. The gas fire popped and the traffic on King's Parade went by the windows. We were in our third day of work and were trying to define a particular scene's purpose in the pattern of the play. The analytical training I had received in the English Faculty was proving useful – I was asking the right questions. In addition, I now understood something about actors, something about teaching and something about leading a group. I was on my way…

Peter Hall (1950)

I'M AT a Footlights concert in Falcon Yard deep in the Lent Term freeze of 1963, watching Bill Oddie, John Cleese, Tony Buffery, Graham Chapman – many more comic talents, in full spate. The small clubroom is a fug, packed to the rafters with members and guests, howling with laughter. A serious fire would have altered the course of comedy in Britain for the next three decades. On my right is a spare crew-cut man I recognise – Herb Elliott, world mile and 1,500 metre record-holder and, to an ex-schoolboy athlete just about the most awesome figure one could possibly find oneself crammed next to. A guest? A visitor? Possibly doing some course – here he is squashed into a roomful of eager undergraduates, and he's loving it. Will he be around next week to see the *Miss Julie* I'm about to open in? I don't think I'm about to ask him.

STUDENT theatre in Cambridge (at the genial, scruffy ADC or sometimes at the Arts Theatre) often overlapped with the Footlights in terms of personnel and camaraderie; undergrads frequently had a foot in both camps. I can't help thinking, though, that comedy was at a slightly more advanced stage on the evolutionary scale. These nascent Pythons and Goodies were operating at a pretty sophisticated level – some were already writing professional material for the media.

Undergraduate theatre works (or doesn't) in a different way from that simple, rapturous talent to amuse. During my three years I was very lucky; I was around and worked with some extremely talented people – as subsequent careers have proved. There were no barriers: one performed in everything – Sophocles, O'Neill, Shakespeare, Pinter. We were fearless, competitive, energetic. But were we any good?

Unlike drama school, university theatre contains little critical authority; your audiences and your critics are, by and large, your peers.

John Shrapnel as Creon in 'Antigone' at the A.D.C.

Varsity, 1962

It tends to be hermetic, there's not much symbiosis – I didn't see many plays beyond Cambridge. The Jazz Club, on the other hand, would regularly play host to top-flight London musicians. Reading *Encore* magazine (the original one) and debating the Future of the Theatre wasn't necessarily going to equip you for contributing to it: only experience was going to do that. You wouldn't expect an undergraduate law student to be able to stand up and fight a case in court.

So, there was a lot to learn and only a two-year generational authority to learn from and then, perhaps, impart. Most of those productions are hazy now – their quality, uncertain. It's the sociality that stays in the memory. We won the Edinburgh Fringe Trophy with *Waiting For Godot* which Stephen Frears directed; I don't recall a huge amount about the production, but I do remember him handing me a book during rehearsal – *Catch 22*: 'You've got to read this.'

As we busied away at our productions, larger dramas were going on around us. I watched F.R. Leavis deliver his final lecture in Mill Lane. He was reading from *Little Dorrit* to a packed audience, simply and without inflection. Finally, he glanced at his watch, checked the lecture-room clock and said: 'Well, this is goodbye. And I think it *is* goodbye…'

And he strode down the aisle, away from Mill Lane, and Cambridge (the scene of his triumphs and humiliations) forever.

John Shrapnel (1961)

Nicholas Hytner's production of Love's Labours Lost *in the Trinity Hall Fellows' Garden, 1975.*

'The words of Mercury are harsh after the songs of Apollo. You that way, we this way.'

The last speech of *Love's Labour's Lost* is probably its most famous, but it didn't suit whatever it was I thought I was doing to the play for the ADC's 1975 May Week show in Trinity Hall Fellows' Garden, so I cut it. I genuinely can't remember why. There was, I think, some elaborately staged musical farewell for the four couples whose betrothals are cut short by news of the King of France's death, and I suppose I couldn't work out what Mercury and Apollo had to do with it.

Self-confidence is the hallmark of undergraduate directors, so it barely occurred to me that the problem was less with the play than with my understanding of it. But I got stuck on the opening night behind a very old man shuffling furiously out of the garden. 'The words of Mercury', he was saying, repeatedly, to anyone who'd listen, 'are harsh after the songs of Apollo. You that way, we this way.' I was within an inch of tapping him on the shoulder and telling him to get over it, when I recognised him. It was I.A. Richards, the founding father of modern literary criticism and the inventor of close reading, and I'd ruined his evening.

But I didn't care. I do now, but then I was impervious. It was impossible for me to imagine *Love's Labour's Lost* being done better than it was done there, on the lawn beneath the willow tree. No matter that it was interrupted constantly by the sound of punts lurching up the river carrying the pissed survivors of the afternoon's parties. Or that it was completely obliterated one night by some glam rock wannabes warming up for the Clare May Ball. It was, or so I thought, unimprovable.

In reality, the production was full of the kind of stuff I'd seen the RSC do with Shakespeare's comedies. It was set in the long hot summer of 1914, which I thought was a stroke of genius: the play as an anthem for a doomed generation. It was an idea so

obvious that I've seen it done three times since, and I probably ripped it off from some previous production that I'd read about. But however short they are on originality, undergraduate theatre people are long on energy. Cambridge has been a cauldron of theatrical ambition since at least the 16th century, when the so-called University Wits descended on the London theatre, having decided that playwriting was too important a business to be left to mere actors. The Cambridge crowd included Christopher Marlowe, Thomas Lodge and Robert Greene; amongst those who somehow managed without a degree was Shakespeare. More recently, Cambridge can boast of having produced four out of five directors of the National Theatre. It's worth recording that the one who got away was Laurence Olivier, who – like his Elizabethan actor forebears – rather puts the achievements of us university wits into perspective.

Those of us who have thrived in the professional theatre have long since realised that there's as much to be learned from an actor who knows from experience how to play a scene as there is from any amount of close reading. But nothing seems impossible in the Cambridge theatre, no play too ambitious, no scheme too crazy. There are always friends who are ready to help, and rivals eager to prophesy disaster – which is an irresistible spur to success. The arrogance dribbles remorselessly away during a life in the theatre, but the determination survives.

And it's the blissful self-belief that I remember most fondly. *Love's Labour's Lost* was almost certainly as terrible as I.A. Richards thought it was, but as daylight gave way every night to the precariously slung floodlights, it was possible to imagine that we were breathing the very essence of romantic comedy. Cocooned by the darkness and buoyed up by the audience's unshakeable determination to enjoy itself, a determination that rose as the temperature fell, we thought we had a hotline to Shakespeare.

Nicholas Hytner (1974)

I OFTEN recall Dr Goldie's reaction to my poor Finals result in the summer of 1994. I can't quite quote him (I never quite could – that's the problem with studying for a history degree when you're involved in 21 theatre productions in three short years) but the general gist was: 'Well, Rick, let's be honest …. If your degree had been in acting you'd have got a first!' He wasn't talking about quality, I hasten to add, just giving a very honest judgement on what my work had really gone into, and that was Cambridge University theatre: the Marlowe, the Mummers (I was President of both – what do you mean, I took on too much?), the Footlights, Edinburgh, even a cheeky London run during the Michaelmas Term of my second year which we won't go into here … principally acting but also directing, and even writing. You name it, I had

1969 productions.

*Left: Dominic Dromgoole's 1997
production of* Peribanez.

a go. And those three years essentially self-training remain very close to my heart, along with plenty of the personalities I shared them with.

You can seriously immerse yourself in drama at Cambridge. Playing Humbert Humbert in *Lolita* at the ADC crystallized this in my first year, and directing *Macbeth* with Sacha Grunpeter in the title role (a rare actor … very sadly missed) was the highlight of my second, along with *Function of the Orgasm* winning the Guardian Award for the Mummers at the Edinburgh Festival in the summer of 1993. In my final year I was determined to let my hair down a bit, and duly played a Footlights Dame (ducky!) before rounding off my time playing the Doctor in a promenade production of *Frankenstein* for the Marlowe. THEN I decided to do some studying…

But I like to think I've paid my dues to that sidelined history degree in some small way: Lt Harry Welsh in *Band of Brothers*, Bosun John Vincent in *Shackleton*, Major Philip Newman in *Dunkirk*, 'real' men who lived through 'real' drama from the past, who I've tried to bring to life as characters in a modern strand of historical document called television drama.

Rick Warden (1991)

ARRIVING in Cambridge during Freshers' Week, I remember being overwhelmed by the sheer number of leaflets crammed into my pigeon-hole. Like a pioneer stepping off the boat into the New World, I thrilled at the concept of reinventing myself through membership of glamorous and exotic-sounding clubs. The fact that I had no experience and even less an idea of what these societies were actually about, didn't seem that great a hurdle. And so, after three days spent

tearing across town for meetings with the Model United Nations Society, the Revelation Rock Gospel Choir and the Mountaineering Club, I realised I was either going to have to narrow my field of interest or join a Nervous Breakdown Society.

One of the new passions I did continue to indulge during this period of expanding horizons, however, was dance. And, with a growing confidence, only very loosely based in reality, I decided to share my talent with the general public and choreograph a number in a dance show at the ADC. Jauntily named *Mick's Bar*, the show charted the evolution of dance from the shimmying of the speakeasies through to the leg-warmered scissor kicks of the 1980s, culminating in an explosive, kids-from-Fame type finale. Having learned the Charleston some years before and thereafter proceeded to do it with annoying regularity at parties in an attempt to appear interesting, I decided this was my genre. I cast my number with a line-up of highly talented dancers and taught them everything I could glean off a bad VHS of *The Boyfriend*. I was quite pleased with the result. So was my cast.

Although I acted in 18 productions at Cambridge over the course of my three years, followed by a year at drama school and a variety of productions since, I have never received a review quite like the one I did for *Mick's Bar*. The *Varsity* critic shot us down from a great height: 'The Charleston has never looked so awkward', he mused, 'as a group of females with rather low centres of gravity clumped indelicately round the stage.' With a final cut and thrust, he wrote off the whole show with the most casually devastating of put-downs: 'The cast enjoyed themselves tremendously.' Actually, he was right.

Amy Shindler (1994)

I DIDN'T go to Cambridge to act – having grown up in a predictably professional, Anglo-Indian family in Singapore (mother and brother: doctors; father: actuary; sister: teacher) the slot of family lawyer needed to be filled so I read English at Jesus en route to doing a law conversion course. Acting had always been the extra-curricular activity of choice and by the Lent Term of my first year at Cambridge I was doing as much theatre as work on my degree, if not more. I was never really part of the big establishments – I didn't do a play at the ADC till my second year and never did a Footlights show. I cut my teeth in a production of *A Day in the Death of Joe Egg* at the Playroom and I credit that week as the time that changed my life. Nothing had ever felt as good as being in that play and, although I wasn't aware of it at the time, from that point on I was never going to be a lawyer. I remained good to my family's expectations, however, and in my third year I applied to law schools and drama schools at the same time. I was routinely doing three plays a term but at the end of Michaelmas in my third year, I idiotically turned down playing Gertrude in the ETG tour of *Hamlet*; instead, I went back to Singapore for Christmas and didn't tell my mother about the drama school auditions I was doing the following term. I don't think I was ready to face her disapproval.

Extraordinarily, I got an offer of a scholarship on the three-year course at LAMDA and a place at the College of Law in London on the same day. I was in the middle of rehearsing what was probably, if I had to rate them, my favourite theatre experience at Cambridge: the Marlowe Society's production of a sharp and brilliant new version of *Electra* at the newly refurbished Arts Theatre. There were five of us playing Electra and the Chorus (two of whom were my closest friends), the Arts had been in a temporary home for a few years and we were the first University show back in there – I was so proud to be in it. I was shocked at the offer from LAMDA (as were a few others – I'll never forget an ADC luminary saying to me, 'But you're not good enough for that!' I had never really been part of The Gang and I think he was genuinely surprised), and I knew that I couldn't turn it down.

I came to realise that I had done my mother a terrible disservice – although bemused by the idea of acting professionally, she has been unfailingly supportive of me. I think it helps that she's seen me on the TV. My training at LAMDA made me the actor I am but there is no way I would be an actor had it not been for Cambridge and that week at the Playroom.

Stephanie Street (1995)

ADC committee, 1993.

Matt Atwood writes: "I'm the one taped to the chair. I was the treasurer that year. Although I still wonder what possessed us to create this scene, it was born out of the close bond that we had developed: a large, and somewhat dysfunctional family. Looking at it now, with all that has gone on in the world in the last 13 years, I can't help but find the image of being bound and gagged rather distasteful. At the time the world seemed a less aggressive place.

The ADC Theatre is remarkable. Run and maintained entirely by students who learn on the job: no drama department, no formal teaching. I still haven't come across anything like it. It had more than a hint of Neverland. I spent so many hours in that theatre, often working in the dark, frequently throughout the night, and I loved every minute of it. At least half of us in the photo dabbled in professional theatre after leaving Cambridge. I got a job with the English National Opera on the strength of the experience I had gained."

Right: Stephen Sondheim's Sweeney Todd, *ADC, November 2000.*

Michael Derringer

ADC 2008 productions.

Oxygen *by Carl Djerassi and Roald Hoffmann at the ADC, October 2004.*

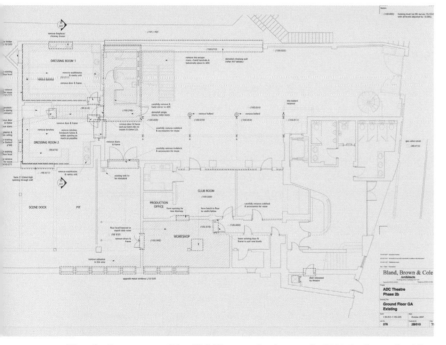

Plans for the next stage of the ADC Theatre redevelopment. In 2008 the theatre closed for six months for a major overhaul of the dressing room, stage and rehearsal spaces.

ABOUT a year ago, I ran into a friend from Cambridge, now a successful comedian, at a party following the recording of a TV sitcom in which he stars. He spotted me and I watched as there played across his face cartoon frames of uncertainty, recognition and horror. 'Josie, hello, it's been…' he said… 'Nine years?' I offered. 'Listen', he drew me from the hearing of TV executives, 'Can I just say, I am so sorry about the Footlights Pantomime.'

I HAVE almost no idea what he was talking about. There is a hazy recollection of being traduced by the cruel and unusual foreshortening of a technical rehearsal. My friend was then Footlights President and I was the Director on the ADC Committee. In Cambridge terms we were Olympians and, in the great and shameful tradition of Cambridge drama, I must, during that incident, have occupied enough moral high ground that he still felt guilty about it nine years later.

It would have been my fault for attempting (as I did for three years) some theatrical feat that lay far beyond the bounds of our capabilities but unnervingly within the limits of our endurance. You could convince anyone of anything. And get the money for it. My most infamous scheme was borrowing, from the timber company where my father then worked, the wooden frame of a Barratt home and enlisting our company of *Twelfth Night* actors to erect five rooms and two staircases in the middle of Sheep's Green. My best friend from that time still uses my then-quite-visionary, now-clearly-insane cry: 'It will be as if a house fell from the sky' to check me in any present-day excess.

Before I bluffed my way into directing the ADC freshers' show, I had never directed a play in my life. Having broken away from my Catholic Salford state school to attend the dangerously secular Eccles College, I found myself on stage one night thinking, 'She's standing in the wrong place; I'm awful, he's really bad and that light certainly shouldn't be green.' The rude instinct was there, although I would never have learnt the confidence without Cambridge drama's exceptional opportunities for hubris. We never, ever questioned – as I now do almost daily – whether or not we had the clout or the right to direct huge classical plays, run theatres and demand money to make our work. Given this, is it a surprise that every single artistic director of the National Theatre has been a Cambridge graduate? We shimmered with confidence. And, my God, we took ourselves seriously. My over-reaching student days started me on my present path but, in many ways, the ten years following Cambridge have been a gradual process of lightening-up.

Josie Rourke (1995)

Footlights

DANIEL MORGENSTERN

The Cambridge Footlights: to some, a name synonymous with the crème de la crème of up-and-coming comedy talent; to others, the embodiment of all that's wrong with the world and another example of why students shouldn't be allowed to perform in public. As *Scotland on Sunday* put it in 1995 in one of their more vitriolic reviews: 'These students, like most students, should shut up until they grow up…' The renowned history of the Footlights Dramatic Club is perhaps the club's greatest asset and perpetual curse. For the current student membership of Footlights, the opportunities and publicity afforded by the Footlights name are invaluable; yet, at the same time, trying to live up to the standards set by previous generations can be difficult – particularly when audiences are wont to compare current productions with the output of alumni who may have been working professionally for many years.

Fortunately for me, my performing with Footlights never got further than a very brief appearance during a committee 'Smoker', when I was dragged onto stage to make up the numbers for a sketch, and I have therefore managed to avoid the unkind eye of the critics. Instead, my involvement in the club has been on the producing and financial side, trying to bring some order to areas of the club's activity that have traditionally been ignored by a club dominated – as one may argue it should be – by writer-performers. It has been an eye-opening experience seeing several generations of students coming through the club and then finding their way into the professional world (be that in comedy or in management consultancy).

Revue programmes from 1955, 1963 and 1978.

Someone who was witness to more generations than most was Dr Harry Porter, who first became Footlights Senior Treasurer in 1962. After retiring from this role, supposedly after VAT inspectors investigating the club raided his house, Dr Porter became Senior Archivist, liberating the club's archives from the University Library and meticulously cataloguing and expanding them in the basement of his house. This was a role that Dr Porter held until his death in 2003, with many generations of Footlights members benefiting from his discreet influence and the opportunity to explore the club's history and previous creative output – usually whilst sitting in a small cold basement room with a cup of tea.

Footlights proudly traces its beginnings all the way back to 1883 and an infamous cricket match at the Fulbourn Pauper Lunatic, but it is really over the last 50 years that the club has made its name, producing a stream of influential writers and performers – which Footlights never fails to mention in its publicity materials. In the 1950s, Julian Slade and Jonathan Miller found their feet on the Footlights stage, although it is telling that even then the critics were liable to be unkind. On the 1955 production, *Between The Lines*, the *Daily Sketch* asked: 'What has happened to the Footlights who once fed new ideas and new style to the West End stage? … Jonathan Miller wants to be a chemist and not a theatrical cult. I back his judgement.'

The 1960s was one of the club's most successful periods with many Footlights performers of the time going on to be household names. Peter Cook, Eleanor Bron, David Frost, John Cleese, Graham Chapman,

FOOTLIGHTS
DRAMATIC CLUB
"Probably the best known of all the Dramatic Club"
— *Varsity Handbook.*

☆ ☆ ☆

The President and Committee invite those interested in auditioning or submitting material to discuss the possibilities of membership over a glass of sherry.

TOMORROW, SUNDAY 14th,
at noon
in
THE CLUBROOM at 5 FALCON YARD
(off Petty Cury)

Harry Porter, Senior Treasurer and Archivist of Footlights for 40 years.

Footlights revue, Pop Goes Mrs Jessop, with Peter Cook (centre) and David Frost (third from right), 1960.

Graeme Garden, Tim Brooke-Taylor, Bill Oddie, Miriam Margolyes, Eric Idle, Germaine Greer, Julie Covington and Clive James all performed with Footlights and their names have graced Footlights programmes and press releases ever since. The 1963 show *Cambridge Circus* (originally entitled *A Clump of Plinths*) even transferred to London, running for three months at the Lyric Theatre on Shaftesbury Avenue before transferring, rather bizarrely, to New Zealand and then, less bizarrely but more lucratively, to Broadway. Again, the critics were not always kind, inevitably comparing the current Footlights crop unfavourably with their predecessors. The *Daily Mail* asked: 'Have they got a new Jonathan Miller among them? I may as well get the answer over right away. No.'

The 1970s saw a new batch of future celebrities: Clive Anderson, Griff Rhys Jones, Rory McGrath and Douglas Adams, who directed the 1976 revue *A Kick in the Stalls*. This was also the period when the club began regularly to tour its May Week revue during the summer holiday, the focus being a run at the Edinburgh Festival Fringe. Today Footlights remains probably the only student group to

Left: The Cellar Tapes, *1981.*

Right: The Footlights summer show of 1962 joined forces with the Cambridge Theatre Company in a tour to the Edinburgh Festival, both productions directed by Trevor Nunn (seated at front with Marion McNaughton). Well-known Footlights members involved included Graham Chapman (with pipe), Tim Brooke-Taylor, John Cleese, Hugh McDonald, Ian (now Lord) Lang and Tony Hendra. The Footlights show was called Double Take, *while the CTC production was Ibsen's* Brand.

Members of the Cambridge Footlights Revue can be seen on BBC 1 on Bank Holiday Monday in extracts from their performance at last year's Edinburgh Festival. The actors are (from back to front), Stephen Fry, Hugh Laurie, Paul Shearer, Tony Slattery, Emma Thompson and Penny Dwyer.

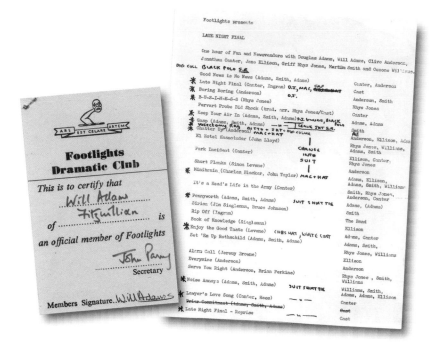

Rainbow Stranglers, *1996, with David Mitchell, Matthew Holness and Lucy Montgomery.*

undertake an annual UK tour. In 1981, Footlights won the first ever Perrier Award for Comedy with *The Cellar Tapes*, directed by Jan Ravens (the club's first female President) and starring Stephen Fry, Hugh Laurie, Tony Slattery and Emma Thompson. The following years saw a continued stream of future household names start their careers with Footlights, including Sandi Toksvig, Neil Mullarkey, Nick Hancock, as well as Steve Punt, Peter (now Hugh) Dennis and David Baddiel who all went on to create *The Mary Whitehouse Experience*.

The club continues to attract many students hoping to establish careers in the professional comedy world, whilst at the same time providing a range of opportunities for those who just want to have a go at writing and performing a sketch or two. My own first encounter with Footlights was in 1993 with a single, failed attempt to audition for the joint Footlights/ADC Pantomime. Sadly, I therefore missed out on the opportunity – afforded instead to two future lawyers – to perform for two weeks wearing nothing more than a pair of gold lamé underpants. Instead, I became involved a few years later, filling the role of Junior Treasurer and helping to arrange and manage the club's annual summer tour. For me, it has always been one of the joys of Cambridge drama that those destined for a career in medicine, engineering, business or perhaps the Catholic Church had the chance to create productions with those destined for 'celebrity' status.

Hugh Dennis with Steve Punt and Nick Hancock, 1984.

The roll call of names continues to the present day. Richard Ayoade and Matthew Holness (winners of the 2001 Perrier Award with Garth Marenghi's *Netherhead*) performed with the club in the 1990s, as did John Oliver, who now regularly appears on the American satirical television programme *The Daily Show with Jon Stewart*. Back in the UK, Robert Webb and David Mitchell (Footlights President in 1996) have had numerous successes on radio and television, including winning a BAFTA for *That Mitchell and Webb Look*. More recent alumni continue the trend with Mark Watson (who directed the 2003 tour show *Non-Sexual Kissing*) winning the first 'If.comeddies' Panel Prize at the Edinburgh Fringe in 2006.

At the core of Footlights there remains each year a group of writer/performers committed to forging a career in comedy. Competition for places in the cast of the annual summer tour show can be particularly fierce and is commonly a focus for Machiavellian political manoeuvring between the show's director, the club President and the committee. Resignations and threats of retaliation have certainly featured over the years. Nevertheless, the club also provides opportunities for anyone who wants to try performing to do so.

The rather oddly titled 'Smokers' (the name being a contraction of 'Smoking Concerts', having its origins in the days of post-prandial cigars and gentlemanly entertainment) are impromptu collections of sketches, comedy songs and stand-up, usually held late in the evening once the (mainly student) audience has had the chance to reach an adequate level of inebriation. Smokers were originally held in the Footlights clubroom, when a black-tie dress code was rigorously enforced. Since the demolition of the original clubroom in Falcon Yard to make way for a shopping centre and the more recent abandonment of the clubroom in the rather less salubrious surroundings of the basement of the Union Society building, the club no longer has premises of its own and Smokers take place at the ADC Theatre. They remain incredibly popular and regularly play to sell-out houses.

The ADC Theatre is also now the focus for the club's three other major annual productions: the Christmas Pantomime, Spring Revue and summer tour show. Traditionally, the club's summer production – its May Week Revue – took place at the Arts Theatre, was produced by the Arts Theatre Trust and filled a central role in the University May Week.

The Footlights production returned to the Arts Theatre for a few years when it reopened in 1997 following redevelopment, but commercial pressures made the arrangement unsustainable and the production now has its home at the ADC Theatre.

The summer tour show remains the artistic highlight of the club's year and provides an opportunity for each year's committee to stamp their mark. The club has no overall artistic policy and the style of productions often changes dramatically from one year to the next, as each committee responds either favourably or not to what has gone before. In 1998, the club brought in a professional director in the form of Cal McCrystal to direct *Between a Rock and a Hard Place*. Cal brought a new style of clowning and physical comedy to the club that persisted for a number of years before a later return to a more sketch-based form. Subsequent years have seen experimentation with more dramatic and emotionally challenging content, moving Footlights away from the stereotype of jolly songs about student life in Cambridge towards something darker and perhaps more sinister. One such production, the 2001 tour show *Far Too Happy* (directed by Phil Breen and Owen Powell), was nominated for a Perrier Best Newcomer award.

Inevitably, the comedy produced by Footlights is influenced by wider trends; nevertheless, as each year's committee takes ownership of the Footlights brand they have the opportunity to practise and to experiment. There is no doubt that Footlights faces much more competition than it once did, with TV and radio comedy, plus an increasing number of groups in Cambridge, competing for attention. Nevertheless, the club's illustrious history helps to ensure a steady stream of new members and a regular audience for its productions. For those wanting to pursue a career in comedy – or those, like me, wanting to spend a few enjoyable years pretending to be a theatre impresario – there is no better foundation than the Cambridge Footlights.

Daniel Morgenstern was Junior Treasurer of the Footlights Dramatic Club 1996–2000 and has been Senior Treasurer ever since.

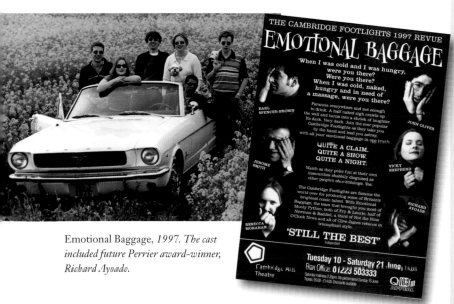

Emotional Baggage, 1997. The cast included future Perrier award-winner, Richard Ayoade.

I had never heard of Footlights before I arrived in Cambridge, which now strikes me as rather odd. I suppose the truth is that I was only vaguely interested in comedy and it had never crossed my mind that I might end up earning my living doing something quite so ridiculous.

It wasn't until the end of my second year that the bug caught me. A friend from Churchill asked if I would write some sketches with him for a 'Smoker'. These were 'try-out' evenings held once or twice a term in the Footlights clubroom, for which all the material was auditioned the day before in front of established Footlights. The afternoon is never a good time to make people laugh, and a rather damp, smelly and empty basement under the Union isn't the ideal place to try but for some reason when it came to my turn someone laughed – I think for roughly the right reasons – and I was hooked.

Of the Smoker itself I don't remember a great deal except that everyone wore dinner jackets, which was bizarro when elsewhere proper comedians were railing against the Thatcher government and mine closures, but in Cambridge such formality seemed completely normal. Earlier that term I had attended a college 'dessert' club at which we were required to open and eat walnuts with a knife and fork – a skill which once acquired will never ever be used again.

As comedians Footlights liked to poke fun at the proper dramatic societies who seemed to take themselves far too seriously, but the truth is that the club took itself very seriously indeed. It put on three shows a year including a May Week Revue which started at the Arts Theatre, and then went on a 30-day tour ending at the Edinburgh Festival. It was the only University society that paid corporation tax, was registered for VAT and owned its own car, a red Ford Cortina, used, so the tax man thought, to ferry cast and props to gigs.

Many members had applied to Cambridge not for the degree course but so they could join Footlights, as a first step to a professional career, and for them it was the most important aspect of their Cambridge life. One friend was very upset to get a 2:2 in Finals not because he could have done better but because with a whole grade between him and failure he realised he could have worked less hard.

Why Footlights has such a good track record I am not entirely sure. In some ways having been to Cambridge is a drawback in the outside world – a dinner jacket and songs about punting certainly don't work terribly well at the Comedy Store – but I guess the advantages outweigh the drawbacks. Footlights gave us confidence, a feeling that we were following a well-trodden path – with Cleese, Chapman, Rhys Jones, Anderson, Fry and Laurie ahead of us. It taught us to write for other people which may not have been in vogue in a world dominated by stand-up, but essential to work on sit-coms and sketch shows. Most importantly, though, it made us usefully unrealistic. If you could sell out the Arts Theatre for two weeks, professional comedy couldn't be that difficult, could it?

(Peter) Hugh Dennis
(1981)

SADLY, I was never a member of the Cambridge Footlights. Instead, like all fellow alumni of the 1989 tour *Absurd Persons Plural*, the comedy club that I joined was the newly rebranded Holsten Pils Footlights. Quite what the terms of the deal were I'm not sure – suffice it to say that all posters, programmes and tour t-shirts sported the Holsten Pils logo, and that the tour was 'launched' upon a rag-tag of uninterested hacks in some rather swanky offices above the ICA in Pall Mall. For Footlights in the late 1980s was a club that had fallen upon hard times.

The membership was low. There was no clubroom to speak of, just an oversized broom cupboard in the bowels of the Cambridge Union. The aspirant's first visit was a crushing blow from which he seldom recovered. There were no lovingly curated links with a glorious past, no knick-knacks handed down from the greats, no comedic runes immortalised in tablets of stone; just a few fading photographs of Clive James in a shoebox and a torn poster for *The Cellar Tapes* that looked like it had been rescued from a house fire.

The tour began at the Arts Theatre to some acclaim, then proceeded to get a thorough kicking in every other venue throughout the country. Some audiences seemed to tolerate it, some even to enjoy it, but local critics were unanimously scathing concerning our breathtaking fall from grace, often singling individual cast members out for what can only be described as personal abuse. Where were the Graham Chapmans and John Cleeses of tomorrow? Certainly not here. By the time we reached the Edinburgh Fringe and the decidedly unglamorous surroundings of Marco's Leisure Centre for our final performances, morale was at a very low ebb indeed.

I don't know who it was that found the review that turned our ship around. I do remember we devoured it backstage. It was written, I think, about the 1961 tour, *Double Take*. At any rate, it consisted of a scathing treatise on how Footlights today wasn't a patch on its former glory, and singled out two members of the cast in particular for what can only be described as personal abuse: Graham Chapman and John Cleese.

And that was the moment, I think, that I took my first step away from comedy novice towards comedy initiate. Footlights is, and was, dire. It is meant to be dire. It has no respect for its past, nor should it have, because its past is nearly always ignominious. It is a place, simply, to take your first steps, whether they be the steps of an enthusiast, a journeyman or a genius. It is a place to fail. Long may it continue to be so.

Ben Miller (1984)

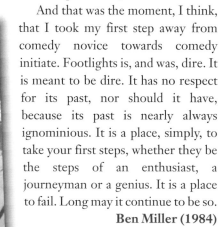
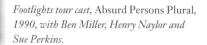

Footlights tour cast, Absurd Persons Plural, *1990, with Ben Miller, Henry Naylor and Sue Perkins.*

Backstage at the Footlights Pantomime, 2007.

IT's a rule of thumb that whilst theatre is best viewed in a grand, vaulted building, as tiered and sparkling as a wedding cake, comedy is best experienced in a cellar – a subterranean hellhole with no recourse to air or light, whose denizens wander the endless corridors, skin as pale as Nosferatu, making puns and practising their arsenal of exaggerated regional accents.

I have no idea why total darkness and the fug of stale beer act as our favoured environment for joke-telling, but you could not get more of a quintessential gag-pit than the (now abandoned) Footlights clubroom. I visited it again recently, and age has not withered it – mainly because it has always been withered. It comes withered as standard.

It's a bunker, maybe four metres deep and five metres long. The smell remains in your nostrils for weeks. Peter Cook's sweat still lingers on the ceiling. In the far corner a sorry curtain hangs limply across a raised platform. The walls hold the wonky, clip-framed mugshots of the great and good: Eleanor Bron, Fry, Laurie, Thompson et al. To the side sits a cardboard box of props, with wigs, fake arms and plastic chickens spilling from it.

That box sums it all up for me. Many people are hostile towards the Footlights, and, in part, I can see why. We had the luxury of trying things out. We would fail, and then have the opportunity to tour nationally with those failures. However, the notion of Footlights as a cohesive machine, pumping out comedians like some kind of media sausage factory doesn't quite cut it for me either. The reality is in that cardboard box – we were a group of half-cut kids trying on costumes. We gravitated towards the club in the same way you'd gravitate towards the Extreme Needlepoint or Chinchilla Appreciation Societies, if that was your bag.

This Way Up, *1999.*

My personal memories are somewhat hazy. I was a shy kid and found alcohol to be a splendid substitute for personal confidence. I remember how dry my mouth felt when I first got on a stage, but also how strangely still I felt inside. I remember watching the fall of Thatcher on television that November, and how we all cheered and smoked and cheered again. But we never thought about making jokes about it. This was the dawn of the Nineties; the resurgence of zane, of character comedy, the physical, the surreal. I don't remember political bravura, or satire, or contemporary relevance of any description. Perhaps we could be kind and say that Thatcher's children found it hard to get any perspective on that era. Or we could be harsher and admit that none of us were very switched on to the real world at that time.

I do know that the friendships forged in that dirty little room and beyond, during that heady period of protracted adolescence, remain some of the greatest of my life.

And surely that's what any decent university club should give you.

Sue Perkins (1988)

Revue programmes from 2000, 2006 and 2007.

I was way too shy to audition for anything in my first term, let alone Footlights. I had too much to lose – after being the funny one for so long at school, rejection would have struck at my very definition – being told I wasn't funny would be like hearing I didn't have brown eyes. But at the end of my second term, I found myself outside the dank, murky clubroom, lurking in the basement of the Union. I really wouldn't have been there at all if I hadn't had a massive crush on a painfully beautiful man who thought me a comic genius. And I would definitely have run away if he hadn't been waiting outside for me to finish.

I did my audition in front of Robert Webb and James Bachman. They laughed in all the right places, in spite of the fact that they can't possibly have found it funny, and gave me a slot in the show. I don't think I breathed once during the five-minute audition, and I know I didn't during the show. Unlike most stand-ups, who do their first few gigs to a handful of people in a pub function room, I played my first gig to a sell-out ADC. It felt like I imagine the first hit of heroin must feel: complete, compelling and necessary. Six weeks later, the beautiful man broke up with me. But 14 years later, I still make my living telling jokes.

In my second year, I performed at every Smoker: in the ADC; in the clubroom; if they'd asked me, I'd have cheerfully done stand-up in the car park. I never auditioned for the big shows, the summer tour, the Spring Revue or the Christmas panto. I knew I wasn't an actor – I was basically a writer, who only performed because I couldn't stand to let someone else get all the credit. I always felt like an oddity, because I didn't do the whole sketch-comedy thing, and conversely, Footlights didn't turn out many stand-ups. I was then, and may still be now, the only female stand-up they've ever produced.

Although I may not have fitted in especially well with a largely male, public school comedy establishment, I was never left out. Footlights had an unspoken rule: if you were funny, you were in. In my third year, I was asked to serve on committee, with David Mitchell as our much-harassed President. The clubroom became my second home, which probably explains why I spent so much of my twenties living in dingy basements. We had a welcoming party for Freshers there, where vats of lurid red and green punch were drunk, spilled, and occasionally thrown, only some of it by the committee. We met every week in that clubroom, we put on writing workshops there, held auditions, arranged performances. It is gone now, I hear, so the current generation won't forever associate comedy with the slight, pervasive aroma of damp emanating from a sticky brown carpet. I think it's their loss.

**Natalie Haynes
(1993)**

Inspiration, refuge and recreation

CHRISTOPHER HOGWOOD

The sight of the choristers of King's College processing from the Chapel after singing an evening service or anthem by Orlando Gibbons always carries (for me, at least) an extra historical frisson, realising that 400 years earlier Gibbons himself at the age of 13 had been one of those choristers and had sung in this very same building (he was listed 1596–9).

The presence of the past used to strike many an undergraduate of my generation in their final summer term while listening to the fading strains of 'Sweet Suffolk Owl' or 'The Silver Swan' as the punts of the Madrigal Society (founded 1928, regrettably dissolved 1968) disappeared into the distance downriver. It still grips millions each year worldwide who tune in to the broadcast service of Nine Lessons and Carols, now entering its second century. Continuity is implicit in this *frisson*, but the atmosphere within the institution diverges increasingly from the pressures of the world outside, where the arts become more a refuge, less a recreation.

Chapel and chapel choirs remain the most permanent feature of Cambridge's active music-making, in the process training many later professional voices, organ scholars and periodically producing close-harmony groups hoping to hit it as rich as the King's Singers.

A second strand of continuity is the University's recognition of composition and living composers. I remember Britten, Tippett and Lutoslawski receiving their honorary doctorates, just as earlier members of the University might have remembered Dvořák, Tchaikovsky, Saint-Saens or Ravel, their careers rotundly summarised in a Latin oration. The post of Professor of Music was created in 1684 when Charles II demanded that Nicholas Staggins, his Master of Music, be awarded a MusD; the University retaliated by appointing him 'public professor' without salary. Since then the majority of appointments have also been composers (Maurice Greene, Thomas Walmisley, William Sterndale Bennet, Charles Villiers Stanford and, most recently, Alexander Goehr). This tradition was first broken in 1926 by the musicologist E.J. Dent and later by Thurston Dart (1962), both of whom overflowed academic barriers and busied themselves in 'extra-mural' events: Dent with the ISCM and opera (at the same time presiding in 1926 over the first Music School 'since the foundation of the University'), Thurston Dart with editing early music, international performance and recording.

In the first years it was not obligatory for the Professor of Music to be resident in the University. Even Stanford, who as organist of Trinity had worked so hard to encourage student performances, later fell out with the authorities and took to giving his harmony classes at the station before making the speediest possible return to London. Originally there had been no formal tuition, and a candidate for the MusB came to Cambridge solely to present his composition (an 'exercise'), and usually paid for its performance as well. Until full-time music courses were initiated as recently as 1947, students could only come to music after several preparatory years in another discipline. Vaughan Williams (Trinity, 1892–4) had to read history before he could proceed to music.

The Music Faculty now offers studies in history, analysis and compositional techniques as a springboard for diversifying into fields such as performance practice, early music, film music, jazz, the

Above: A concert at Christ's in 1767 showing the virtuoso Georg Noëlli playing the pantaleon with local professionals.

Opposite: Verdi's Requiem in King's College Chapel, January 2008. Under the direction of Stephen Cleobury, choral scholars from six college choirs joined with CUMS 1 to perform the monumental work for the first time in the society's 165-year history.

Alternative music-making: the Sandpaper Sessions in Keynes Hall, King's College, 2004.

psychology of music and ethnomusicology. Not everyone reading music intends to become a professional; the prospectus mentions 'financial and/or management careers' as other possible occupations, but the diplomatic service and deep-sea diving have also benefited.

It is the live music of Cambridge which occupies and entertains the majority of students – and here the word is change rather than continuity, a flurry of maximum bravado (and usually minimum rehearsal) crammed into the few weeks of term and dependent on the time and talents of the natural impresarios. The most long-standing organisations are the Musical Society (CUMS, with symphony and chamber orchestras, wind ensemble and chorus), the Music Club (CUMC, with regular recitals by and for its members), the University Opera Society (formerly Group) and the very British Gilbert & Sullivan Society. Other ventures have proved more transitory: the Cambridge Little Opera Group (possibly doomed by its unfortunate initials), the Decadent Music Union, the In Nomine Singers, the Purcell Society…

Some 50 associations are currently listed, including the Brass Band Society, the Chinese Orchestra Society, the Hip-Hop Society and

Benjamin Britten visiting Cambridge, 1950s.

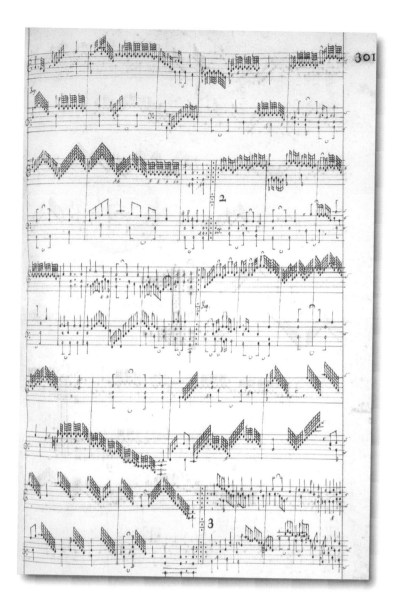

The Fitzwilliam Virginal Book. Known by this name because it was part of Viscount Fitzwilliam's bequest in 1816, the early 17th-century manuscript collection of keyboard music includes 297 separate pieces by composers of the Elizabethan and Jacobean age.

Ethnomusicology

In spring 1983, the Javanese gamelan 'Duta Laras' (Ambassador of Harmony), an orchestra of some 40 bronze metallophones, gongs, gong-chimes and xylophones, encased in red and gilded wooden frames, arrived unexpectedly in the Music Faculty, gift of the Ambassador of Indonesia. Later that year, Ruth Davis was appointed to the University's first designated position in ethnomusicology. Since then, the faculty has incorporated the study of music from throughout the world into all three years of the Music Tripos and it has attracted an international array of graduate and post-doctoral students in ethnomusicology. Recent collaborative research includes digital restoration with the Department of Engineering of Robert Lachmann's comprehensive collection of field recordings from mandatory Palestine (the earliest of its kind in the Middle East). An international conference on Intercultural Encounters in Jewish Music was hosted by Corpus Christi College in July 2008, sponsored by the Rothschild Foundation.

Ruth Davis is Senior Lecturer in Ethnomusicology and a Fellow of Corpus Christi College.

Homerton College Pandemonium Steel Pan Band. The common features are that they are open to all, vulnerable to the variable state of college music-making and financing, yet constantly producing natural leaders, who learn by trial and discordant error to control and mould the input of their peer musicians for whom music is not a chosen discipline, but simply a part of cultural life.

Energy and resourcefulness are the hallmarks of college music: Wagner with 11 players and four singers, a full performance of Purcell's *Fairy Queen* or Satie's *Vexations*. My first hearing of the final scenes of *Don Giovanni* was at a college musical evening, when the entry of the Commendatore (now a distinguished Law Lord) from the Dean's bathroom nearly brought the piano accompaniment to a halt.

Other University musicians achieved extra-mural fame: Raymond Leppard (Monteverdi operas), David Munrow (Early Music Consort and BBC) and now Christopher Page (Gothic Voices carried on to become 'popularisers', doing for music what Glyn Daniels did for archaeology or Stephen Hawking continues to do for cosmology). But it was never obligatory to be a member of the Music Faculty in order to take part in the practical music-making of Cambridge (some indeed have naughtily proposed that the reverse is true), just as it often turns out that a graduate in maths, classics or Eng. Lit. may go on to a career as a professional musician. Of recent names such as John Eliot Gardiner, Andrew Davis, Anthony Pay, David Munrow, Roger Norrington, Emma Johnson, Robin Ticciati and Andrew Manze, fewer than half read music.

Cambridge music has always mixed town with gown. A famous caricature of a concert at Christ's in 1767 shows the virtuoso Georg Noëlli playing the pantaleon with local professionals; the town music club organised performances in the Black Bear in the 18th and 19th centuries; the Cambridge Philharmonic was founded in 1833 and continues today; there were Thursday Concerts in the Guildhall where we regularly heard the Amadeus Quartet or Julius Katchen; and the annual Folk Festival has been going strong since 1965. Much was

Bernhard (Boris) Ord, organist and choirmaster at King's College from 1929 to 1957.

At a CUMS rehearsal in the Music School in Downing, Boris Ord stopped us angrily and shouted: 'This is not Ancient and Modern Hymn Singing; this is JAZZ!' We were rehearsing Constant Lambert's 'Rio Grande'!

Margaret Hartree
(1944)

At my first tutorial with Boris Ord, for which I had carefully prepared a piano accompaniment to a given vocal line, Boris sat in silence, though smoking noisily for what seemed an eternity. At last, the oracle spoke: 'When you write the accompaniment to a song, it is usual to make it fit the tune. Good afternoon, Mr Crickmore.' This was not the kind of pedagogic style which I was later to look for when inspecting the conservatoires as HM Staff Inspector of Music. But it was effective, maybe…

Leon Crickmore
(1950)

Singing with the University Madrigal Society, under Boris Ord, was a special delight. An annual event took place on the river one evening during May Week. The singers sat on six punts lashed together and fastened to the bank underneath King's bridge. The banks each side would be crowded with lecturers, many of whom had made their way there by punt. At about 10pm the six punts were loosened from the side, to allow them to float down the river, the choir singing John Wilbye's lovely madrigal 'Draw on sweet night'.

In 1938 this May Week concert was broadcast by the BBC. A microphone was hung from the bridge above the singers' heads, and an announcer was seated in a cabin nearby. And then, as 10pm drew nigh, a friend of mine, who had been 'listening in', told me that the announcer, speaking into his microphone, told his audience: 'No more words from me now. I will let you listen to the singers float down the river singing "Draw on sweet night" until they can be heard no more.'

But it was not to be. A group of undergraduates from Queens' College, the other side of the bridge, had assembled a fleet of chamber-pots, and into each one they had placed a lighted candle. These they placed on the water, to follow after the madrigal singers. The 'sweet night' suddenly became a very noisy one. The audience on the banks exploded with angry shouts, or else loud laughter, as they tried to sink the chamber-pots with their punt poles. The broadcast came to an untimely end.

Hugh Blenkin
(1935)

Cambridge University Symphony Orchestra performing in Prague during their tour of the Czech Republic, 2006.

changed by the creation of a dedicated concert hall as part of the new faculty buildings on the West Road site (1977), now home to professional series, regular opera and countless undergraduate ventures, with a range of musicians in residence (at the moment the Endellion String Quartet, the Britten Sinfonia and the Academy of Ancient Music). It has noticeably helped the rise of opera productions here; in addition to regular Handel operas, a recent student production of *The Turn of the Screw* showed how finely tuned high tension can be generated on a low-voltage budget.

In this (like most academics) I have omitted mention of the pop world, although it is probable that the names of Cambridge town products such as Syd Barrett and Pink Floyd carry more resonance in the world than several centuries of University musicians combined. Similarly the name of the Fitzwilliam Museum is probably familiar to many musicians (for the Fitzwilliam Virginal Book, only one of its many important holdings), unaware that it is in Cambridge and a splendid location for lunchtime recitals.

From sublime chapel singing down to the scrawniest college quartet, Cambridge demonstrates that effective and rewarding music-making is here the province of the amateur. As a Fellow of Trinity so modestly put it in the 17th century:

We have good *Musick* and *Musicians* here,
If not the best, as good as any where

(Nicholas Hookes, 'To Mr. Lilly, Musick-Master in Cambridge', in *Amanda*, 1653)

Christopher Hogwood *(1960) is Honorary Professor of Music and Fellow of Jesus and Pembroke Colleges. He is a conductor, harpsichordist and scholar of early music.*

A musical never-never land

John Eliot Gardiner

ambridge has traditionally fostered the self-image of being the centre of the universe – never more so than with music. While it is impossible to be totally objective about the Cambridge musical scene in the early 1960s, there is hard evidence of serious musical accomplishment, diversity and the coincidence of a quite exceptional roster of musical talent – of contrasted provenance and aspiration. Forty years on, I am amazed at the astonishing range of music that received an airing. It was performed, admittedly not always well, by as glittering an array of talents as you could have assembled even by amalgamating the very best students of the day attending the music conservatories of the land. Judged by the subsequent careers of its musical luminaries (among them Simon Preston, Andrew Davis, Christopher Hogwood, David Atherton, Christopher Seaman, David Munrow, Simon Standage, Anthony Pay, Christopher van Kampen, Robin Holloway and members of the original King's Singers) you might easily conclude that Cambridge in these years produced a quirky but near-ideal environment for music-making, at times profligate and sometimes undiscriminating, but above all one providing a priceless opportunity to flex creative wings and a testing-ground for subsequent initiatives.

But even that is misleading. Music at Cambridge was not the exclusive preserve of future professionals. In its better orchestras you were as likely to find yourself sharing a desk with a mathematician, a social anthropologist or a nuclear physicist as with a future member of the LSO. Music is a great leveller in that respect, and there was little sense then of an imminent bifurcation between hobby and profession. I, for instance, was reading history and classical Arabic at King's, and it wasn't clear to me until well into my third year where my passion for music, whether as violinist, singer or conductor, would lead. At

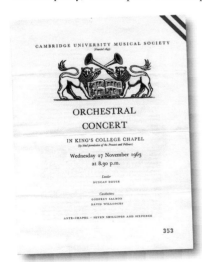

Right: CUMS orchestra trumpet player, 2008.

I couldn't afford the sub and cost of music for CUMS and probably escaped Boris Ord's acidities by joining the 'Clare Canaries', run by the Clare organ scholar. We sang Brahms's *Requiem* not uncreditably in the college chapel. Saturday evening concerts in the Music School were a high point, with Ray Leppard, or perhaps Anne Keynes singing *lieder*.

When Britten's *Let's make an opera!* came to the Arts Theatre I was in the audience as an owl. My Cambridgiest experience was listening to the St Matthew Passion in King's College Chapel with the (borrowed) score balanced on the hot-water bottle on my knees.

Ellaine Mabbutt
(1948)

I came up as a teenager in 1959 to read music and determined to try out all the musical societies. Cambridge Ballet Club was one of these, and at a meeting we were regaled with tales of woe, how the bank balance needed restoring. Someone suggested a stall in the market place. My suggestion to 'put on a ballet' was received with shocked silence. Yet a few months later I had made contact through a mutual friend with a dancer at Girton, Jill Meadows, who had reputedly turned down a scholarship to the Sadlers Wells Ballet to read modern languages. And so Cambridge Modern Ballet was born. Our intermediary Margaret Bassington (later Bent) played the piano, and I later worked the tape recorder, playing Duke Ellington's 'Such Sweet Thunder'. In our third year we commissioned works from student composers, I put together an orchestra and we took over the ADC. The London press came, and I believe this was the start of modern dance in Cambridge, a tradition still alive.

Alan Tongue
(1959)

CAMBRIDGE UNIVERSITY MUSIC CLUB

Cambridge University Chamber Orchestra

Tamás Vásáry **Director/Soloist**
CHARLES PEEBLES Leader

Concert Hall, West Road
Saturday, 27th January 1979
8·30 pm

Programme
10p

CAMBRIDGE UNIVERSITY
CHAMBER ORCHESTRA

Anne Manson
Conductor

Bartok
Rumanian Folk Dances

Martin Butler
Suite from Craig's Progress
With an introduction

Stravinsky **Apollo**

8pm, Saturday 10th May 1997
West Road Concert Hall, Cambridge

Tickets: £8, £6 members/concessions, £4 students) from the Arts
Cinema Box Office, 8 Market Passage, Cambridge, tel: 01223 504444

I read music from 1991 to 1994 and learnt a lot from the Music Tripos, in particular from Dean Sutcliffe, whose lectures and seminars on analysis were eye-opening, but I always considered myself a composer and player, rather than a musicologist.

The viola was my worst instrument, but somehow I still crept inexorably up the ranks towards the front desk in CUMS 1. When I arrived there I realised how absurd the situation was and resigned, leaving my desk-partner in the lurch; but where were all the hundreds of better viola players who should have been in my place? Once I achieved Nirvana and got to play piano with CUCO, but I was so in awe of the other players and the situation that I fudged my solo chromatic scales every time, leading to awkward damage-limitation by the conductor. On the other hand I'm very proud to have played Shostakovich's Piano Concerto no. 1 with the KCMS orchestra, conducted by Ben Finn, who subsequently achieved fame and fortune as one of the twin founding fathers of 'Sibelius' software. My proudest ever musical moment, without a doubt, occurred on tour with CUMS 1 to Ely Cathedral. Between rehearsal and concert (which included the world premiere of Thomas Adès's '…but all shall be well'), most members of the orchestra were quietly hanging around the murky corners of the cathedral, snacking, reading, etc., while Gregorian chant from the service in progress at the far end of the cathedral provided background music. To impress a girl, I went up to the large tam-tam hanging invitingly in the orchestra and struck it as loudly as I could. It was a wonderful sound, beautiful music. Moments later angry priests wielding crooks and censers came hunting for the culprit – by which time I was safe, innocently immersed in a novel. The tam-tam is still one of my favourite instruments. Catastrophe and euphoria were close friends on one other occasion: moments after a disciplinary hearing (the consequence of some memorable behaviour), in which I was presented with a large bill, I ran across the courtyard to conduct the college orchestra in my own piece, *Geissellieder* (Songs of Flagellation) in King's Chapel.

Edward Rushton
(1991)

Cambridge, music – like undergraduate life in general – was taken earnestly, desperately so at times. Not that it was joyless: particularly during May Week there were musical high jinks to be savoured in individual colleges and mad festive miscellanies of under-rehearsed celebration. Nothing, however, quite lived up to the promise of a printer's typo for one scheduled performance of Handel's *Acis and Galatea*: it came out as *Ices and Gala Tea*.

It always struck me as a little strange that performances by the CUMS first orchestra, spearheaded, or so it seemed, by an elite of National Youth Orchestra graduates, should so often add up to a lot less than the sum of its parts. Here was individual talent to burn, yet the concerts seemed often a little insipid and uninspired. Exceptions to this that I recall included a memorable *War Requiem* in King's Chapel, a pairing of Stravinsky's *Les Noces* and Bartok's *Music for Strings, Percussion and Celeste* and a revelatory reading of Schubert's 'Great' Symphony conducted by Christopher Seaman when I and my

CAMBRIDGE UNIVERSITY MADRIGAL SOCIETY

SINGING ON THE RIVER
ON TRINITY COLLEGE BACKS

Tuesday 6 June 1967 at 8.30 p.m.
CONDUCTOR RAYMOND LEPPARD

Thurston Dart, Professor of Music, playing a Dutch chamber organ, 1957. He found the instrument in a cottage in Cambridge and restored it himself.

desk partner could hardly put bow to string for pent-up excitement. Generally more rewarding were the opportunities to take part as singer or player in the revelatory Chelsea Opera Group performances of Berlioz operas conducted by Colin Davis.

The CUMC, ostensibly a chamber music society and located in dingy quarters next to the Music Faculty Library in Downing Place, was in practice a hive of sectarian intrigue: committed evangelists of contemporary music vying for platform space with zealous beard-and-sandals advocates of the lesser baroque. You were as likely to encounter *Pierrot Lunaire* or a new offering from Cambridge's most distinguished composer-resident, Roberto Gerhard, as rare quartets by Hummel, Arriaga or Boccherini, or a consort of crumhorns playing Praetorius. In every case it exposed and helped to fill the gruyère-like holes in one's musical knowledge. Heard at so impressionable an age, these offerings gave one an inkling (not quite a prejudice) that Vivaldi is habitually over-rated, that Telemann is often dull and that the recorder along with the organ, the harmonium and the tuba barely qualify as musical instruments. (I've since revised my opinion about the recorder.)

Then there was a further layer of variable music-making centred around the colleges and their individual music societies. To be asked to take part in their concerts was a wonderful way to make legitimised, non-touristic acquaintance with the various medieval college halls and chapels. I remember emerging one evening from a Pembroke concert with Simon Standage, who had just delivered a vivacious account of a

Mozart violin concerto, turning to me in the street. 'I'm sure I'm due to play another concerto elsewhere this evening,' he said, 'but I can't remember quite where.'

Seen from this distance it was a dream world, one where anything could happen, in which risks were minimal and the fearsome burden of financial dependence scarcely impinged. Risky ambitious ventures could be undertaken with relative impunity. Yet just below the genial surface of Cambridge music there were intense rivalries and distinct factions. These were most pronounced in the world of college choirs. An almost tribal animosity had grown between King's and John's, and their joint supremacy at that stage had not yet been challenged by the creation of brilliant mixed choirs – at Clare, Trinity, and Gonville & Caius. Indeed, for many aficionados the King's Chapel Choir represented a *ne plus ultra* of unsurpassed excellence and a sure route to spiritual ecstasy. Yet as a non-choral scholar and coming from a very different musical background, I found the choir's singing puzzling and disquieting. Audibly comprising so many fine musicians, one could but admire their perfect blend and honed delivery, their homogeneity of sound and the way it was cleverly adjusted to the peculiar magic of the chapel's acoustic in which even the most robust music-making can turn to slush with all the bite of overcooked pasta. More troubling still was an apparent lack of historical awareness and an undifferentiated approach to expression, phrasing, texture and tuning across the entire repertoire, from Taverner to Britten, with the motets of Bach suffering the most. The sentimental, lachrymose style of Victorian church music oozed out in both directions tending to enfeeble Renaissance polyphony and to devitalise the astringent harmonies of the 20th century.

A colossus, towering over these coteries and cliques, was Thurston Dart, that brilliant maverick – part Sherlock Holmes, part expert keyboard player and at that time Professor of Music. I can never forget the encouragement he gave in March 1964 to my greenhorn attempts to tackle Monteverdi's *Vespers of 1610*. 'Make your *own* edition', was his first advice. He even graced several of the early rehearsals, witnessing my desperate quest to elicit passion and Italianate vowel colours from a choir comprising bemused choral scholars drawn from the rival colleges, leavened with sopranos recruited from the London conservatories. From the back of King's Hall, his voice would boom out, 'Mr Gardiner, remind your singers, there is no "r" in 'Lau-da-te'!' The eventual performance was an epiphany of a very personal sort. I owe a huge debt to Cambridge in general and to King's in particular for allowing me such wonderful opportunities for experimental music-making. Up to that point I had been floundering, confused by the abundance of future avenues that kept opening up. But now it was clear. Dart left to open a new Music Faculty at King's College, London. He beckoned and I followed.

John Eliot Gardiner *(1961) is a conductor and founder of the Monteverdi Choir, the Monteverdi Orchestra, the English Baroque Soloists and the Orchestre Révolutionnaire et Romantique.*

I read music at Caius from 1994 to 1997, during the dawning of Cool Britannia, the era which spawned Brit pop and the inescapable strains of 'Wonderwall' and 'Zig-a-zig-ahh'. Halliwell's Union Jack dress became an emblem for a new sensationalist Britain glorying in a status-driven climate fuelled by anthems from Blur and Oasis. Music was also integral to the merchandising of the glossy 'street-friendly' New Labour, who chanted The Farm's 'things can only get better' with their hands in the air as Blair shimmied his way to victory.

It felt slightly odd being inside the cocoon of the Cambridge Music Faculty writing 16th-century polyphony whilst all this was going on, although college club nights, or 'bops' as they were stylishly termed, could offer a glimpse of the action. The degree course itself was rather dry and academic, with college events based around the choir, and faculty events around orchestral performances. However, the student theatre world was buzzing, with many productions being staged in several theatres every term. This scene looked much more exciting and seemed like an opportunity to meet folk from other colleges and possibly the genius auteur-directors of the future. I wrote music for several productions ranging from Marlow to Caryl Churchill, often playing live on a piano in the pit, and really began to enjoy scoring to a narrative. Music theatre was also a happening scene. In my second term I conducted *A House Divided,* a cheery show about McCarthyism by Randall Eng, a visiting Harvard graduate. Having had no previous conducting experience, this was my baptism of fire. I had to coach a cast of ten singers and find and rehearse 15 musicians to play a score ranging from experimental classical to freeform jazz. Luckily for me, most musicians had previously played in the National Youth Orchestra or a conservatoire and were keen to get involved. Dubbed *A House Vacated* due to the scarcity of intrepid audience members, my debut was an exclusive experience, but it did lead to more MD-ing work at the ADC Theatre and other Cambridge venues including *My Fair Lady* and *The Jungle Book*, and performing work in shows at the Edinburgh Festival.

Post-Cambridge I made for the capital's brutal and uncompromising media world, setting up a music production company, Rubykon, in 2000, and I have since scored several TV documentaries and dramas. Writing and performing theatre music at college certainly helped my confidence when I started scoring for picture. The intimate atmosphere in the pit and personality-driven sound of the small ensembles I worked with has inspired my writing and undoubtedly had an impact on my style. And although the course had its turgid moments (writing a fugue a week may have been a doddle for Bach but it gave me a headache that even two paracetemol and a kebab couldn't cure), I don't think I would have had such a bizarre, entertaining and challenging experience elsewhere.

Ruth Barrett
(1994)

Undergraduate musicians of all talents make a recording to raise funds for famine relief, inspired by BandAid, in the Clare Cellars, 2004.

Michael Derringer

Cambridge University Jazz Band, 1956.

Jazz

On a warm summer evening in 1954 I was sitting on the Mill Bridge, enjoying a drink. Suddenly, above the rush of the millstream, came an extraordinary noise, across the water from the direction of Silver Street. For a moment I thought someone must be playing a record by the great jazz saxophonist Sidney Bechet, but then the sound stopped, to be followed by voices and laughter. Going to investigate, I climbed some stairs to a room above the Anchor, to find I had stumbled into a rehearsal by the Cambridge University Jazz Band. The friends I made that evening, and the music they played, would change my life.

Like most undergraduates of the period I had hitherto heard jazz music almost exclusively from records. Now I learned that the CUJB, and other satellite groups, played regularly in pubs and other places around the city. Sometimes town and gown came together to make up groups which played at parties and at the Jazz Band Balls held regularly at the Rex Ballroom. Important visiting bands, like Humphrey Lyttelton and Sandy Brown, were also featured at these events.

The music they played quickly reflected changes and trends in jazz taking place across the country, with 'traditional' music, rooted in the New Orleans style, giving way to 'mainstream' even within the CUJB itself. At one extreme the fiercely 'trad' Joe Lyde Jazzmen held court in the main saloon bar of the Criterion, just off Market Square, while at the top of a staircase in Trinity's Whewell Court a nest of modernists listened religiously to the music of Gerry Mulligan and the 'cool' West Coast school. At Trinity Hall,

a quiet, bespectacled organ scholar named Colin Purbrook revealed himself to be not only a brilliant jazz pianist but a multi-instrumentalist, filling in for different groups on flugel-horn, trombone, clarinet or guitar as required.

The CUJB held regular rehearsals in the Brunswick Schools, when aspiring players were invited to join in. Between 1954 and 1957 the personnel of the band became fairly well established, with a front-line of Peter Robarts-Arnold on trumpet, Derek Moore on clarinet and the remarkable Dick Heckstall-Smith on soprano sax, backed up by a varied rhythm section. This was the group that returned triumphantly from Leeds in March 1956 after winning the Inter-University Jazz contest outright. Derek Moore won the prize for best clarinettist, while the judges voted Dick Heckstall-Smith best instrumentalist of the entire event.

In the 1950s the attraction of jazz was that it was seen partly as a 'subversive' music, a reaction to the rather formal dance music of the time. But Cambridge jazz was always musically inventive and forward-looking. With new personnel, including the great Art Themen on tenor sax, the CUJB went on to further successes at the dawn of 'the Sixties', that seminal period in British popular music. Themen, Purbrook and Heckstall-Smith all became professional jazz musicians, while Cambridge today remains an active and vital centre for all kinds of jazz.

Julian Andrews (1954)

Cambridge and the World

Anne Lonsdale

Cambridge belongs to the 900-year-old tradition of European universities. The very structure of the University indicates, from its outset, the presence of students from different 'nations', while colleges often began with their own regional affiliations. Cambridge was never just an East Anglian institution, but always embodied the range of 'international' expectations of its age. In the past 50 years, this European tradition has revived with the creation of the European Union and, since 1976, Europe has played an increasingly active role in Higher Education. Though Cambridge has not embraced new European exchange programmes wholeheartedly, the University did join one of the earliest European university networks, the Coimbra Group, in 1991, five years after Oxford, and the Cambridge European Trust followed in 1995. Today, ERASMUS students do travel to and from Cambridge in handpicked numbers, but it is hard to persuade British students that it is at least as rewarding to study abroad as to hitchhike to Timbuktu.

The 'year abroad' has long been standard practice in Modern Languages and Oriental Studies but only one other Cambridge degree has a required period of study in a university abroad, the MPhil in Chinese Studies, with equal periods in Cambridge and Beijing Universities. Links with Chinese universities, a major part of the University's international strategy, began under Deng Xiaoping from 1982, were cooled by the events of Tiananmen Square in 1989, and have grown at an astonishing pace since the mid-1990s. Of all students registered in 2007 the Chinese numbered 478, outstripping the US contingent of 435, while special leadership training programmes have been undertaken for top officials and business executives from China. Chinese are well represented, too, among post-doctoral scholars and academic staff, especially in the sciences, and faculties and departments have their own relationships with opposite numbers in most leading universities in China. It is exciting to see the challenges which Indian students and Indian universities are now posing their Chinese colleagues.

The University prefers to see its contacts develop, as mutually advantageous, easily sustainable research ties at departmental level, rather than the fashionable inter-university agreements between Rectors and Presidents which cannot guarantee any worthwhile outcome, particularly in Cambridge, where very independent scientists and scholars prefer to choose research partners. Indeed, Cambridge had until recently only five 'institutional' links: Beijing University and Tsinghua in China, Tokyo and Kyoto Universities in Japan (all dating back to the 20th century), and the creation in 2000, with MIT, of the Cambridge-MIT Institute (CMI), the brainchild of Gordon Brown when Chancellor of the Exchequer.

CMI was established 'to explore how academics, industrialists and educators might work together to stimulate competitiveness, productivity and entrepreneurship'. It is supported by the UK government, with matching industrial and commercial sponsors, its scale and complexity depending on significant resources: some £65 million over the last six years. Most University collaborations barely cover their costs, leaving little leeway for the exploration of shared research and joint courses which CMI has promoted.

Over the last ten years, as fashions shift from 'internationalisation' to 'globalisation', other approaches have come thick and fast, with requests to establish branches both real and 'virtual', even whole e-universities, overseas and to create joint programmes in almost every continent. Since

Right: Duke Zaize, grandson of the Jiaqing Chinese emperor, visits Cambridge to receive an honorary degree in May 1906. He is accompanied by the Vice-Chancellor, Henry Montagu Butler.

Opposite: A Cambridge-inspired view of the world, 1681. The 'English globe', now in the Whipple Museum, was designed by the Earl of Castlemaine, who developed his interest in mathematics and astronomy while an undergraduate at King's. Based on the Ptolemaic system, the earth is stable and cannot be moved, while the original pedestal contained a celestial planisphere which could be rotated to show the movement of the stars. It was made by Joseph Moxon.

the early 1990s, when pressures were mainly European, the level and scope of international activity has probably quadrupled. While in the early 1990s the Vice-Chancellor received one or two invitations a month to attend a key anniversary (such as the Bicentenary of the State University of St Petersburg, where I treasure the memory of two very senior bemedalled Army officers coyly offering a huge basket of flowers to the University Rector, the formidable Mme Verbitskaya), there is now at least one a week, sometimes one or two a day.

One result of this international pressure, which threatened to overwhelm the Vice-Chancellor's Office, was the creation of a Pro-Vice-Chancellor for International Affairs, an office I held from its inauguration in 1998 till 2003, and another, to set up the University's first International Office in 2004. The University has at last been able to put into effect its first agreed international strategy based on its essential values, such as the necessary link between teaching and research, the importance of colleges which make us, as the Vice-Chancellor says, 'small for our size', the richness of educational fare in our libraries and museums, and the opportunities for the interdisciplinary and multidisciplinary approaches available in a large research university with Medical, Veterinary and Architecture Schools. This experience cannot be replicated 'offshore'.

Two vitally important arms of this international strategy, the Cambridge University Press and Cambridge Assessment (formerly the University of Cambridge Local Examinations Syndicate) have long given the University unique global range and scope. Cambridge University Press has been described elsewhere; Cambridge Assessment is responsible for examinations and assessments globally, from Computing Studies online to Business English and English Language testing (including IELTS and 'Cambridge Proficiency') from China to Peru. Its UK-based operations include OCR, which provides GCSE, AS and A2 level examinations. Millions of people across the world feel they have a personal relationship with Cambridge: they, too, have a Cambridge qualification, some with a certificate carrying the Vice-Chancellor's own signature. In 2007 Cambridge Assessment had offices or representatives in 150 countries. Indeed, these two outposts of Cambridge University are active in every continent except Antarctica.

So Cambridge has its own very effective global presence. But it has also accepted as part of its international strategy that great universities

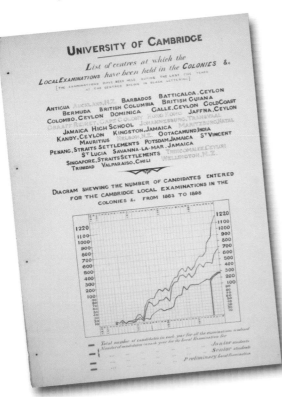

Innovations in Telecommunications meeting held by the Cambridge-MIT Institute, 2005.

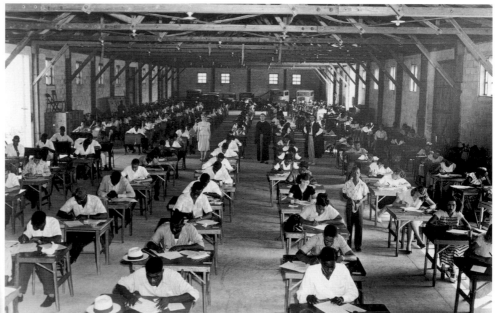

Above: Students taking University of Cambridge Local Examinations Syndicate exams in the Bahamas, 1948.

Left: An exhibition board submitted by the Cambridge Examinations Syndicate to the Paris Exhibition of 1900, showing examination centres around the Empire.

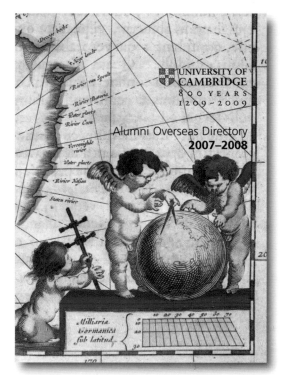

Degree Day, 2007.

Today there are flourishing Cambridge alumni associations in more than 90 countries worldwide. One of the largest is the New York-based Cambridge in America, an independent foundation which promotes interest in and support for Cambridge and its constituent colleges among alumni (around 14,000) and friends in the United States, via a wide-ranging programme of publications and events.

will need to do much of their work through networks – no one institution will be able to cover everything itself. One step in this direction has been LERU, the League of European Research Universities, created in 2002 as a lobby to influence European Commission thinking when devising new EU research programmes. Another, IARU – the International Association of Research Universities – is truly global in character and explores research initiatives between subsets of its members. It remains to be seen, in a world increasingly digital, which of the experiments in international university co-operation will last. Meanwhile, Cambridge attracts more foreign students and recruits more foreign academics than ever before, hugely encouraged by the gift of $250 million from the Bill and Melinda Gates Foundation to set up the Gates Cambridge Scholarships for outstanding graduate students in any field, and from any country except Britain. In the first seven years some 535 students have come to Cambridge for almost every variety of Master's course or PhD. Their academic merit goes without saying, but they must also have 'Gates' qualities – applying their knowledge to the greater good. These scholars will become an increasingly important part of the Cambridge world, adding their achievements to the extraordinary contribution of Cambridge alumni worldwide. Cambridge is a place where friendships are made which last a lifetime and reach around the world. The networks

they form are also a powerful support, and through the new Cambridge Alumni Relations Office, CARO, formed in 2007, the many far-flung and more or less formal Cambridge Societies and Oxford and Cambridge Societies will be able to build on their links and contacts with the University.

So where next? I see two immediate areas where steps need to be taken. First, having created the Cambridge Trusts over 30 years ago to fund brilliant but impecunious international students, we will squander that advantage unless we can admit students and confirm their funding simultaneously, as is done elsewhere. This means integrating the role of University and trusts with colleges as sources of scholarships and bursaries, to ensure that together we can compete in securing the best graduates worldwide.

Our international character also bears on the work of colleges. Cambridge recruits the best academics worldwide so, increasingly, new University and college lecturers have been trained not just outside Oxbridge but outside the UK and have no expectations of the value and potential of the supervision and tutorial systems. Many will choose to opt out of a college fellowship, and concentrate on research, while those who do relish college life will need support to explore this unique pedagogical model. This is just another way in which the increasingly international role and focus of the University has come to bear on every aspect of its life, enriching us immeasurably as it does do.

Anne Lonsdale *is Deputy Vice-Chancellor and President of New Hall.*
Between 1998 and 2003 she was Pro-Vice-Chancellor for External Relations.

'Remaining ferociously engaged'

ALISON RICHARD, VICE-CHANCELLOR OF THE UNIVERSITY

The University does not see far into the future. It flourishes by holding fast to certain values, while helping shape and adapting to changes in the world around it. Such is my view of the simultaneous timelessness and timeliness of University life. It leaves me sceptical of the value of visionary statements about the Cambridge of the future.

So what should be the subject matter of my Epilogue, on this momentous occasion in the life of a great university?

I decided to start with the *Reporter* – the University's official record – as it appeared a century ago. How do the preoccupations of those times reflect or depart from our own? Were any of the transformational changes that have since swept Cambridge anticipated then? Are there insights into our future to be gained from contemplating the past? It turned out to be an instructive exercise, and also reinforced my view of the way universities persist, change and flourish. In this essay, I will certainly make a brief foray into the future, but I will take as my point of departure what I have learned from reading about the past.

In 1909 King Edward VII was still alive but an era was ending. A decade later, there would be few young men of means left alive to apply to Cambridge or Oxford, and both universities would start to run up deficits. The government of the day stepped in to plug the hole and the plug never went away. After the Second World War, the funding of Higher Education by government was transformed from a stop-gap measure into a positive political commitment. Today, the financing and freedoms of Higher Education are once again matters of lively debate.

That is but one of several threads in the history of the last century not foreseen by our predecessors – and not foreseeable. Indeed, they seem to have indulged little in reflections on the past or the future. I found no mention at all of 1909 as a centenary year for the University in the pages of the *Reporter* for that year, and I wonder if they were less willing than we are to overlook uncertainties about the date of the University's foundation. The only anniversaries celebrated were the centenary of Charles Darwin's birth, coupled with the 50th anniversary of the publication of *On the Origin of Species*.

Overwhelmingly, discussions in 1909 focused on the particularities of the present and immediate future. In his address to the Senate on 1 October 1909, the Vice-Chancellor spoke mostly of deaths and departures, philanthropic gifts received, and the importance of not building 'without laying aside a good proportion of the money for the purposes of upkeep'. About a book urging internal reform just published by the Chancellor of the University of Oxford, Cambridge's Vice-Chancellor noted: 'Perhaps to us one of the most interesting things in that book was the revelation how much more urgent the need of reforms is at Oxford than at Cambridge.' Civility and fairness prevailed, however, and he concluded by urging Cambridge not to tarry with its own reforms.

The pages of the *Reporter* echoed and amplified the Vice-Chancellor's preoccupations, with reports on gift stewardship, the purpose and value of scholarships, debates about academic standards, the introduction of new subjects, and the place of languages (including English) in the curriculum. Some entries read as amusing period pieces, like the tussle over the installation of electric lighting in the Library. But alongside them are reports with a distinct ring of the

1642 sun and moon dial in Queens' Old Court.

Opposite: Senate House Passage, Degree Day, 2008.

present, exhibiting care and thought with respect to academic matters, accompanied by passionate and occasionally vituperative discussion. From the perspective of 2009, some of the issues discussed really mattered, and others just seemed to matter at the time. The quality of intelligent and stubborn attentiveness, notwithstanding a certain accompanying grand inefficiency, persists in Cambridge to this day – to its great benefit.

Whatever the resonances with the past, Cambridge in 2009 is a university transformed. The massively expanded role of women is one such transformation. Today there are as many women undergraduates as men, they make up a growing proportion of Cambridge's 6,000 or so graduate students – there were no graduate students at all, as we know them, a century ago – and they are present in increasing numbers among our post-doctoral and academic staff.

Other changes are equally profound. The explosive growth of science has transformed the academic and physical landscape. This has enhanced the University's stature and impact, established the region as an international centre of innovation, and helped dissolve the 'town–gown' divide. Within collegiate Cambridge, 13 colleges have been founded or achieved full collegiate status since 1909. Responsive to growth in the size and the diversity of the student body, they have created new ways of imagining Cambridge colleges. The century has seen incremental changes in Cambridge's organisational arrangements, without losing the idea of the University as a community of scholars and students. In just the last 30 years, the University's accountability to government has increased substantially, even as the proportion of direct public funding has declined.

For much of its history, Cambridge was very exclusive, one of a small handful of universities of significance in the world. For 250 years, it rode on the coat-tails of Empire. Exclusivity and Empire both crumbled during the last century. The contribution of universities to society is now widely recognised, and that has fostered rapid growth in their number. Today, we compete and co-operate with universities all over the world. And we are successful, considered among the finest universities in the world. But what about the future?

National decisions assuredly have a critical bearing on Cambridge's future. The high quality of this country's splendid and diverse university system is clear, and the excellence of Cambridge is integral to the system as a whole. British society and successive British governments have to muster the will to sustain universities, and to allow them greater independence. The alternative is steady decline of the system in the face of intense global competition. Cambridge contributes mightily to the UK's strength in Higher Education, but it also, importantly, benefits greatly. We have a strong interest in assuring not simply the future of our own institution, but the continued vitality of the system as a whole.

Overleaf: High-resolution image of Cambridge kindly supplied by The GeoInformation Group. © The GeoInformation Group. All rights reserved.

Much that lies ahead transcends national borders, however. Innovations in technology are making international travel and global communication faster and easier than ever before. Information flows in a torrent. The world's population continues to grow, and the natural resources that support human life and well-being are used unsustainably. An assault on the health of the planet is under way, with grave potential for human conflict in its wake. These global and societal transformations and challenges are already driving change at Cambridge – in teaching and learning, the composition of our staff and student bodies, and the configuration of research activities and priorities. The changes come in ways that are evident, and ways that we see dimly yet, if at all.

I am certain that the past has little to offer by way of guidance about the course of future change here. But it does offer reassurance, and perhaps one lesson. The reassurance is that our predecessors did *not* anticipate the great changes of the 20th century, and yet modern Cambridge flourishes, timeless and timely. The lesson, I submit, is that the Cambridge community must find ways of remaining ferociously engaged and yet more fleet of foot in a rapidly changing world. If we can do that – and we will – Cambridge will surely keep its flags flying far into the future.

Professor Alison Richard graduated from Newnham in 1969 before gaining a PhD at the University of London. She taught anthropology at Yale, chairing the department from 1986 to 1990, and was Provost from 1994. In 2003 she became the first female Vice-Chancellor of Cambridge since the post became executive. She is a Fellow of Newnham College.

Timeline

1209 Groups of scholars from Oxford reach the ancient Roman trading post of Cambridge to carry on their studies, the earliest record of the University.

1284 Peterhouse, the first college, founded by the Bishop of Ely.

1326 Clare College founded.

1347 Mary, Countess of Pembroke, establishes Pembroke College.

1348 Gonville Hall. In 1577 it was refounded as Gonville & Caius.

1350 Trinity Hall.

1352 Corpus Christi College.

1428 Magdalene College.

1441 King's College is endowed by Henry VI.

1446 Henry VI lays the foundation stone of King's College Chapel.

1448 Queens' College.

1473 St Catharine's College.

1496 Jesus College.

1505 Christ's College.

1511 Lady Margaret Beaufort, mother of Henry VII, founds St John's College.

1546 Henry VIII founds Trinity College.

1570 New statutes issued to the University by Elizabeth I (in force until the 1850s).

1583 The Cambridge University Press, the world's oldest extant established press, begins publishing.

1584 Emmanuel College.

1596 Sidney Sussex.

1730 Senate House built.

1748 Mathematical Tripos established.

1762 The original Botanic Garden endowed by Richard Walker.

1800 Downing College.

1815 Union Society founded.

1816 Fitzwilliam Museum founded.

1824 Classical Tripos established.

1829 First Boat Race between Cambridge and Oxford, won by Oxford.

1851 Moral Sciences Tripos (to 1969, thereafter Philosophy), Natural Sciences Tripos.

1856 Council (of the Senate) established.

1858 Law Tripos
First school examinations organised by the Local Examinations Syndicate (now Cambridge Assessment).

1869 Girton College, the first residential university-level institution for women, opened.

1870   William Cavendish, seventh Duke of Devonshire, endows the new Cavendish Laboratory for the study of experimental physics.

1871   Newnham College.

1875   Historical Tripos.

1882   Selwyn College.

1885   Hughes Hall.

1894   Mechanical Sciences (to 1970, now Engineering).

1896   St Edmund's College.

1905   Economics Tripos.

1918   First festival of Nine Lessons and Carols held in King's Chapel.

1919   English Tripos
        PhD degree introduced (first awarded in 1921).

1921   Anthropology Tripos.

1926   New statutes granted.

1928   Archaeology and Anthropology Tripos.

1934   University Library moves to its new site across the Cam.

1948   Music Tripos
        Women admitted to full membership of the University.

1952   Casson and Condor plans for Sidgwick Site approved.

1954   New Hall.

1958   Oriental Studies Tripos.

1960   Churchill College.

1961   Architecture and Fine Arts Tripos (to 1970).

1964   Darwin College.

1965   Clare Hall, Lucy Cavendish, and Wolfson College.

1966   Fitzwilliam College is formally constituted, having existed since 1869 as Fitzwilliam House, as a hostel for 'Non-Collegiate students'.

1970   Philosophical Tripos (previously Moral Sciences), Engineering (previously Mechanical Sciences).

1972   Computer Sciences Tripos
        Churchill, Clare and King's admit first mixed undergraduate intake.

1975   Trinity College launches Britain's first Science Park.

1976   Homerton College formally adopted by the University, having been established originally in London in 1731.

1979   Robinson College.

1982   Cambridge Commonwealth Trust established.

1987   Management Studies Tripos.

1988   Magdalene becomes last of the former men's colleges to admit women undergraduates.
        Sir Paul Judge endows Judge Institute of Management (Judge Business School from 2005).

1989   WASS Syndicate Report, leading to appointment of first 5–7-year Vice-Chancellor, no longer a college head, and to restructuring of the central administration.

2000   Gates Scholarships are introduced with a $210 million endowment to provide international scholarships in perpetuity.

2002   The University's major new science and technology site at West Cambridge opens with the William Gates Building.

2003   Centre for Mathematical Studies opens on Wilberforce Road.

2008   Alwaleed Bin Talal Centre for Islamic Studies endowed.
        New Hall becomes Murray Edwards College.

2009   Cambridge celebrates its 800th Anniversary.

Note: Discrepancies in dates commonly given for the beginnings of certain Triposes represent the passing of time betwen the decision to establish a Tripos and the year in which the examination was first sat.

Nobel Prize Winners

Nobel Prize for Physics

1904 Lord Rayleigh, Trinity College
Discovering argon

1906 J. J. Thomson, Trinity College
Investigating the electrical conductivity
of gases

1915 William Bragg, Trinity College
Analysing crystal structure using X-rays

1915 Lawrence Bragg, Trinity College
Analysing crystal structure using X-rays

1917 Charles Barkla, Trinity College
Discovering the characteristics of
X-radiation

1922 Niels Bohr, Trinity College
Investigating atomic structure and
radiation

1927 Charles Wilson, Sidney Sussex College
Inventing the cloud chamber

1927 Arthur Holly Compton
Discovering wavelength change in
diffused X-rays

1928 Owen Richardson, Trinity College
Creating Richardson's Law

1933 Paul Dirac, St John's College
Quantum mechanics

1935 James Chadwick,
Gonville & Caius College
Discovering the neutron

1937 George Thomson, Trinity College
Interference in crystals irradiated by
electrons

1947 Edward Appleton, St John's College
Discovering the Appleton Layer

1948 Patrick Blackett, Magdalene /
King's Colleges
Nuclear physics and cosmic radiation

1950 Cecil Powell, Sidney Sussex College
Photography of nuclear processes

1951 John Cockcroft, St John's /
Churchill Colleges
Using accelerated particles to study
atomic nuclei

1951 Ernest Walton, Trinity College
Using accelerated particles to study
atomic nuclei

1954 Max Born
Fundamental research into quantum
mechanics

1973 Brian Josephson, Trinity College
Tunnelling in superconductors and
semiconductors

1974 Martin Ryle, Trinity College
Invention of aperture synthesis

1974 Antony Hewish, Gonville & Caius /
Churchill Colleges
Discovery of pulsars

1977 Nevill Mott, Gonville & Caius /
St John's Colleges
The behaviour of electrons in magnetic
solids

1977 Philip Anderson, Churchill College
The behaviour of electrons in magnetic
solids

1978 Pyotr Kapitsa, Trinity College
Inventing the helium liquefier

1979 Abdus Salam, St John's College
Electromagnetic and weak particle
interactions

1979 Steven Weinberg
Electromagnetic and weak particle
interactions

1983 Subrahmanyan Chandrasekhar,
Trinity College
The evolution and devolution of stars

1983 William Fowler, Pembroke College
The evolution and devolution of stars

1989 Norman Ramsey, Clare College
Developing the separated field method

Nobel Prize for Chemistry

1908 Ernest Rutherford, Trinity College
Atomic structure and radioactivity

1922 Francis Aston, Trinity College
Work on mass spectroscopy

1952 Richard Synge, Trinity College
Developing partition chromatography

1952 Archer Martin, Peterhouse
Developing partition chromatography

1957 Alexander Todd, Christ's College
Work on nucleotides

1958 Frederick Sanger, St John's /
King's Colleges
The structure of the insulin molecule

1962 John Kendrew, Trinity College
Determining the structure of
haemoproteins

1962 Max Perutz, Peterhouse
Determining the structure of
haemoproteins

1964 Dorothy Hodgkin, Newnham / Girton Colleges
The structure of compounds used to fight anaemia

1967 Ronald Norrish, Emmanuel College
The study of fast chemical reactions

1967 George Porter, Emmanuel College
The study of fast chemical reactions

1978 Peter Mitchell, Jesus College
The energy transfer processes in biological systems

1980 Walter Gilbert, Trinity College
The theory of nucleotide links in nucleic acids

1980 Frederick Sanger, St John's College and a Fellow of King's College
The theory of nucleotide links in nucleic acids

1982 Aaron Klug, Trinity College
The structure of biologically active substances

1997 John Walker, Sidney Sussex College
Studying how a spinning enzyme creates the molecule that powers cells in muscles

1998 John Pople, Trinity College
The development of computational methods in quantum chemistry

2000 Alan McDiarmid, Sidney Sussex College
The discovery and development of conductive polymers

2005 Richard R. Schrock
The development of the metathesis method in organic synthesis

Nobel Prize for Medicine

1922 Archibald Hill, Trinity College
Work on heat production in the muscles

1929 Frederick Hopkins, Trinity / Emmanuel Colleges
Discovering growth-stimulating vitamins

1932 Lord Adrian, Trinity College
Work on the function of neurons

1932 Charles Sherrington, Gonville & Caius College
Work on the function of neurons

1936 Henry Dale, Trinity College
The chemical transmission of nerve impulses

1937 Albert Szent-Gyorgyi, Fitzwilliam College
Combustion in biology

1945 Ernst Chain, Fitzwilliam College
The discovery of penicillin

1945 Howard Florey, Gonville & Caius College
The discovery of penicillin

1953 Hans Krebs
Discovering the citric acid cycle

1962 Francis Crick, Gonville & Caius / Churchill Colleges
Determining the structure of DNA

1962 James Watson, Clare College
Determining the structure of DNA

1962 Maurice Wilkins, St John's College
Determining the structure of DNA

1963 Alan Hodgkin, Trinity College
The transmission of impulses along a nerve fibre

1963 Andrew Huxley, Trinity College
The transmission of impulses along a nerve fibre

1972 Rodney Porter, Pembroke College
The chemical structure of antibodies

1979 Allan Cormack, St John's College
Developing CAT scans

1984 Cesar Milstein, Darwin / Fitzwilliam Colleges
Developing a technique for the production of monoclonal antibodies

1984 Georges Kohler
Developing a technique for the production of monoclonal antibodies

2000 Paul Greengard
Discoveries concerning signal transduction in the nervous system

2001 Tim Hunt, Clare College
Discoveries of key regulators of the cell cycle

2002 John Sulston, Pembroke College
Discoveries concerning genetic regulation of organ development and programmed cell death

2002 Sydney Brenner, King's College
Discoveries concerning genetic regulation of organ development and programmed cell death

2007 Martin Evans
Discoveries of principles for introducing specific gene modifications in mice by the use of embryonic stem cells

Nobel Prize for Economics

1972 John Hicks, Gonville & Caius College
The equilibrium theory

1977 James Meade, Trinity College
Contributions to the theory of international trade

1983 Gerard Debreu, Churchill College
Reforming the theory of general equilibrium

1984 Richard Stone, Gonville & Caius College and a Fellow of King's College
Developing a national income accounting system

1996 James Mirrlees, Trinity College
Studying behaviour in the absence of complete information

1998 Amartya Sen, Trinity College
Contributions to welfare economics

2001 Joseph Stiglitz, Gonville & Caius College
Analyses of markets with asymmetric information

Nobel Prize for Literature

1950 Bertrand Russell, Trinity College
For *A History of Western Philosophy*, 1946

1974 Patrick White, King's College
For an epic and psychological narrative art

Nobel Prize for Peace

1925 Austen Chamberlain, Trinity College
Work on the Locarno Pact, 1925

1959 Philip Noel-Baker, King's College
Work towards global disarmament

Index of Names

Page references in *italics* refer to captions to illustrations; references in **bold** are to articles and features

List of Subscribers

Christ's	CHR	Fitzwilliam	F	Magdalene	M	Sidney Sussex	SID
Churchill	CHU	Girton	G	New Hall*	NH	St Catharine's	CTH
Clare	CL	Gonville & Caius	CAI	Newnham	N	St Edmund's	ED
Clare Hall	CLH	Homerton	HO	Pembroke	PEM	St John's	JN
Corpus Christi	CC	Hughes Hall	HH	Peterhouse	PET	Trinity Hall	TH
Darwin	DAR	Jesus	JE	Queens'	Q	Trinity	T
Downing	DOW	King's	K	Robinson	R	Wolfson	W
Emmanuel	EM	Lucy Cavendish	LC	Selwyn	SE		

*Renamed Murray Edwards, 2008

This book has been made possible through the generosity of the following subscribers:
[The matriculation year and college with which each individual is affiliated is listed as supplied by the subscribers.]

Mr Frank Abbey	SE 1951	
Redwood M.A.		
(Cantabrigiensis) Abbot	CTH 1960	
Bernard Abramson	Q 1966	
Dr Moses Acquaah	HH 1988	
Prof. David Adams OBE	CL 1951	
John Adams	SE 1972	
P.I.F. Adams	CHR 1961	
Canon Peter Adams	T 1970	
Will Adams	F 1971	
Gavin Adda	M 1996	
Dr Jaime Adeane	T 2004	
Dr Tess Adkins	K 1972	
Mr Raymond Adlam	Q 1946	
Lee A. Adlerstein	CL 1973	
Beze A. Adogu PhD	DOW 1987	
Chinelo N. Adogu-Eruchalu LLM	LC 1983	
Ijenma U. Adogu-Okwu LLM	ED 1989	
Prof. S.N. Afriat	PEM 1943	
Peter Agar	DOW 1968	
Dr Georgios B. Agelopoulos	W 1994	
Dr Neeraj Aggarwal	CHU 1993	
Siamak Agha-Mohammadi	K 1993	
Edin Agic	W	
Heather Agnew	G 2003	
Jesus Aguirre-Hernandez		
Thomas N. Ahlborn MD	CL 1975	
S.A. Ahmadullah	T 1959	
Mahmood Ahmed		
Thomas Ahnert	JN 1991	
Michael A. Ainslie	DAR 1982	
Nicole Alcott	HO 2003	
G.L.H. Alderson CBE	SE 1959	
Dr Thomas St. John Alderson	TH 1980	
Lucy Alexander		
Dr Shazeeda Ali	DAR 1994	
Dr Patricia Lebre Alireza	LC 1999	
John W. Allam OBE	CHR 1942	
Alastair Allan	DOW 1948	
Laura E. Allan	Q 2004	
R.R. Allan	JN 1951	
Richard Allan	EM 1973	
David J. Allen		
Graham P. Allen	W 1983	
Paul Allen	CHR 1987	
Peter R. Allen	Q 1962	
Mrs Rosemary E. Allen	G 1955	
Eve Allderidge (née Collyer)	NH 1954	
M.G. Allderidge	JN 1954	
Roy C. Allison	F 1957	
Prof. Marcio Almeida	CHU 1980	
Dr Silverio P. Almeida	F 1964	

Michael Alpers	CAI 1954	
B.L. Althoff	PEM 1967	
Paul Ambler	CL 1965	
Mohammed Amin	CL 1969	
Yaa Serwaah Amoah	CLH 2005	
Tony Amor	CL 1964	
Alasdair R. Amos	CHR 2005	
J. Amos	N 1943	
Dr Russell M. Anderson	PEM	
Dr Simon George Anderson	DAR 1995	
Stefan Anderson	EM 1981	
Emily Andrews	PEM 2007	
Julian Andrews	CAI 1954	
Nick Andrews	PEM 1978	
Emma-Kate Angell	R 1991	
Dr Chris Angus	TH 1967	
Henry Annan DSc (Hons) MA Cantab		
MB BChir FFFP FICS FGCS FRCOG		
	SE 1966	
John A. Anning	CL 1957	
Michael Anson	Q 1975	
John Anthony	CAI 2003	
Matt Applewhite	CTH 1998	
Dr Mary Archer		
Julian Arkell	K 1956	
James P. Armitage	JN 2007	
Canon John M. Armson	SE 1959	
D.J.M. Armstrong	SE 1957	
Rebecca Arnfield	JN 1999	
Miss Catherine Arnold	M 1996	
W. Arnold	K 1971	
Amindra S. Arora	CAI 1989	
Andrew Arthur	CAI 1994	
Charles Arthur	M 1971	
Dr Michael Arthur	CAI 1988	
Vincent F. Arthur	PEM 1989	
Dr Endel Aruja	F 1939	
Sarah Ascough (née Harding)	HH 2000	
David (Bill) Asdell	CTH 1945	
Godfrey Ash	CAI 1950	
Dr J.M.A. Ashbourn	CLH	
Michael Louis Ashby		
Nicholas Ashby	TH	
N.W. Ashcroft	CHU 1961	
Mr L.J. Ashford	SID 1931	
The Rt Revd Jeremy C. Ashton	T 1950	
Alex Ashworth	JN 1995	
Sir Bryan Askew	F 1949	
Ms A.M. Askin		
Christina Asprer-Zaballero Frine	NH 1965	
Julian Astbury	JN 1958	
Sumudu Atapattu (née Vithanage)	N 1987	

A.K.H. Atkinson		
Matthew Atkinson	SID 2002	
A.P. Attree (née Chapman)	G 1953	
Conrad Aub-Robinson		
Colin Aubury	SE 1961	
Henry (Jimmy) Aubury	SE 1933	
Kate Aubury	JN 1992	
Mr Jeff Aughton	CAI 1970	
Prof. Colin Austin		
Robert Austin	Q 1946	
Valerie Austin (née Chiverton)	N 1946	
Rachel Jane Avery	T 1998	
Kenneth Stuart Axon	CTH 1958	
Jonathan Zinzi Ayitey	HH 2003	
Jonathan Ayres	R 1989	
Azra Maxwell Azaham	SE 1994	
J.A. de Azcárraga		
David Babington-Smith	T 1986	
Prof. Dr Ulrich Bach	W 1970	
Roland Backhouse	CHU 1966	
Andrew Bacon	CAI 1953	
John Baden	CC 1948	
Dr Chris Bagnall	F 1964	
Hilary Bagshaw	N 1974	
Dr Peter G. Baines		
Jeremy D.I. Baker	R 1989	
Matthew P.J. Baker	M 1992	
Rex Baker	PET 1953	
Stephen J. Baker	EM 1975	
Dr P.J. Bakewell	T 1962	
Dr David Ball	F 1948	
The Rt Revd Michael Ball	Q 1952	
J. Balls		
Karen F. Balmer		
Dr Richard Balasubramaniam	JN 2001	
Prof. Les Balzer	T 1970	
John Bamford		
Sujit Banerji	1965	
Dr Stephen K. Bangert	CHR 1974	
C.N. Banks	F 1957	
Tony Bannard-Smith	CHU 2001	
Jeffrey Bannister	T 1972	
Prof. John A.J. Barbara	T 1965	
Dr Barry Barber	CHR 1951	
Richard Barclay	1946	
J. Norman Bardsley	CHR 1958	
Dr Matthew G. Baring	T 1984	
Daryl Barker	JN 1973	
David Barker AM	JE 1986	
Desmond Lowther Barker		
Peter A. Barker	CTH 1953	
Canon Tim Barker	Q 1975	

Adrian Peter Barlow	CL 1982	
Richard Barlow-Poole	CHR 1938	
Prof. Lawrence Barmann	EM 1968	
Phil Barnard	F 1960	
William S. Barnard	JN 1962	
Anita Barnes	JN 2001	
Revd Anthony Barnes	F 1970	
Dr John J. Barnes	W 1992	
Mr Simon A. Barnett	SE 1980	
Tony Barnett	TH 1963	
Ms M.J. Barraclough	R 1984	
Dr David R. Barrett	CAI 1972	
Michael D. Barrett	CTH 1956	
Prof. John Barsby		
Dr Denis J. Bartlett	JN 1944	
Mr B. David Barton	T 1947	
Dr George Barton	JN 1948	
Revd Canon J.C. Peter Barton	T 1949	
Margaret H. Barton	K 1974	
Stephen Barton	JE 1965	
Jane Barwick-Nesbit (née Nicholson)	G 1979	
Paul Batchelor	JN 1965	
C.D.J. Bathurst	T 1968	
Christopher Batten		
Richard A. Bawden	JE 1947	
Brigadier A.E. Baxter	T 1951	
D.L. Baxter	CL 1965	
Lawrence G. Baxter	CL 1976	
Angela M. Hill (née Bayford)	N 1976	
Adam L.S. Baylis-West	CC 2002	
Simon Baynes	M 1982	
R.A. Beale	PEM	
Prof. D.W. Beard	CHR	
Yuki Beardmore-Gray (née Kidani)	SE 1983	
Julian Beare		
Mrs Caroline Beasley-Murray	G 1964	
Revd Dr Paul Beasley-Murray	JE 1963	
Andrea P. Beatty	CAI 1990	
John R. Beaumont	JN 1949	
Dr Andrew S. Becker	M 1982	
Benjamin Patrick Bedard	DAR 2001	
David A. Baer	CC 1994	
Ian D.S. Beer	CTH 1951	
Bruce A. Beharrell	T 1962	
Michael Belknap	JE 1963	
Nikolay Irina Yury Belkov	ED 2002	
Mr G. Bell		
Mr Graham R. Bell	M 1991	
James Bell	TH 1997	
John Bell	CTH 1950	
Keith Bell	CC 1960	
Prof. Peter R. Bell	CHR 1938	

Robin Bell	F	1965
Tony Bell	W	1995
Dr Dominic Bellenger	JE	1969
Dr James Bellingham	EM	1982
Mr Ben Bennett	JN	1988
Geoffrey L. Bennett		1944
Mr Jeremy Bennett	CL	1959
Mr John Carey Bennett	F	1964
Mark Bennett	JE	1991
Mrs F. Bennetts		
Timothy Mark Benseman	CAI	2003
Dr John S. Benson	PEM	1966
David Berdinner	SE	1968
Annabelle Berenzweig (née Sidhu)	TH	1991
Robert S. Beresford	PET	1951
Ralph J. Berger	JE	1957
Martyn D. Berkin	DOW	1962
Andrew Berkley	CL	1988
Carlos Bernal		
Miss Anneli S.C. Berntsson	M	1996
Sir Nicholas Barrington KCMG CVO	CL	1954
Charles G. Berry		
Ellie Berry	TH	2002
M.J.W. Berry	M	2004
Ingrid Ness Berzins	NH	1972
F. Bettelheim	N	1944
Mrs Felicity Beuchamp (née Money)	G	1943
Gwyn A.J. Bevan	DOW	1948
John Caldwell Beveridge QC	JE	1959
Mr Bhupendra Nath Bhagat	T	1951
Dr Ajit Bhalla	SID	1997
Sandeep Bhargava	T	1984
Rajat Bhatnagar	TH	1997
Peter Bibby	CL	1966
Dr Robert Bigg	CL	1975
John Biggs	CL	1960
Dr Nicola Bignell	JN	1986
Lord Bilimoria CBE DL	SID	1986
Dr David Billett FRSC	TH	1968
Clyde Binfield	EM	1958
The Hon. Mr Justice Ian Binnie	PEM	1960
Hugh J.A. Bird	EM	1937
Mr Jos Bird	DOW	1954
Patrick B. Bird	Q	1953
Mr R.H. Bird		
John Birkett	CTH	1961
Dr Christopher A. Birt	K	1960
D.K. Bisatt	SE	1956
Dr W.A.M. Black	CTH	1959
Robert H. Blackadder		
Mrs Jocelyn Blackburn (née Cockcroft)	N	1953
Malcolm Blackburn	EM	1959
Christopher Blackstone	CL	1960
Prof. Barry Blackwell	Q	1954
Anthony Blaiklock	JN	1974
John C. Blakeley	CAI	1962
Richard Blanchard	CL	1957
Andrew Blane	F	1955
Michael Blank		
Edvard G. Blankenship	DOW	1968
Stephen M.B. Blasdale	CAI	1972
Christopher Blaum	JE	2006
Revd Hugh Blenkin	T	1938
Dr Neil Bliss	JN	1953
Dr D.C.M. Blomberg	NH	1970
Dr John E. Blundell	CAI	1940
Kofi E. Boayke	ED	2005
Mr Richard P. Boggon	CL	1954
In memory of Major W.M.G. Bompa	JN	1939

Richard G.A. Bone	CL	1985
Ralph Bonnett	PEM	1949
Lloyd Straughan Bookless	CHU	1964
Tan Boon Seng	M	1974
Michael Charles McMillan Boon	CC	2001
Philippa Alice Borton	NH	2005
Jay Bosanquet	T	1967
Charles Botsford	CHR	1978
Peter Bottomley MP	T	1963
Prebendary Roger Bould	SE	1951
Mr Ian C. Boulton	JN	1971
Thomas B. Boulton MD	EM	1943
Nicholas Bourne AM		
Christopher Bovell		
Francis W. Bowden	CHR	1961
Dr Kenneth Bowen	JN	
J.V. Bowman	PEM	1973
The Revd Dr Robert W. Bowman		
Mr Anthony E. Bowring	CL	1960
The Edgar Bowring Fund		
Philip Bowring	CTH	1960
M.A.L. Bowyer	PEM	1942
Mr Timothy Boycott		
Dr Thomas A. Boyd	DAR	1972
Revd Martin Boyns		
S.W. Boys Smith		
Christine Brack	G	1961
Terence Brack	CAI	1958
Prof. Adrian J. Bradbrook	Q	1966
Rob Bradbury	R	1983
Prof. D.A. Brading	PEM	1957
Nick Bradley	PEM	1976
Dr Katherine Bradnock (née Ryder)	NH	1966
Dr John E. Bradshaw	F	1968
Dr R.H. Bradshaw	TH	1986
Ben Brafman	DOW	2000
Guilherme Brafman	DOW	1973
Adam Brand	CL	1960
Dr Boris Peter Brand	JN	1943
S. Jonathan Milo Brand	CHR	1974
Mr Michael Brandon		
Dr John H. Brandt	CL	1962
Mr Robert Brash CMG	T	1942
The Revd Tim Bravington	T	1953
Douglas Brear	CHR	1962
Michael Brear	TH	2002
Mark Breeze	EM	1997
Dr Mark Brennan	DOW	1976
Jonathan Brent	DOW	1989
Dr Thomas P. Brent	M	1962
Michael Brett	T	1953
L. Guy Brew	CAI	1976
Hugh V. Brewerton	EM	1956
Revd John William Bridgen	K	1959
Patrick E. Bridgwater	PEM	1944
Dr Lawson W. Brigham	DAR	1997
Miss Helen Bright		
Mr D. Britton		
Sylvia Broadfoot	HO	1967
Ian Brockington		
Mr Kay Henning Brodersen		
J.A. Brooks	CAI	1959
Prof. Donald M. Broom	CTH	1961
Mr Ivor W. Broomhead MChir FRCS	JN	1942
The Venerable J. Michael Brotherton	JN	1956
Abbe L. Brown (née Lockhart)	NH	1989
Mrs Adrienne Brown		
C.W. Brown	F	1964
Christopher Brown	CTH	1967

Dr Jason P. Brown	W	1992
K.F.C. Brown	TH	1935
Dr Keith Brown	SID	1973
Nigel C. Brown	T	1960
Philip Brown	EM	1964
Tim Brown	EM	1961
Helen Broxap	R	
Major Alisdair Bruce	SE	1963
Mr P.A. Bruce	Q	1979
Mrs R.E. Bruce	EM	1980
Paul B. Brudenell	EM	1954
Michael Brufal de Melgarejo, Marqués de Lendinez	CHR	1958
Richard Bruin	CTH	2003
Mr Malcolm H. Brummer	DOW	1966
Steve Brumpton	JN	1995
Stephen Brushett	CL	1973
John Bryant	CTH	1962
Dr James H. Bryce	CHU	1979
G.L. Buchanan	T	1959
David and Jenny Buck	EM/N	1954
Prof. Matthias Buck	F	1987
Kenneth H. Buckley	K	1943
David Buckton	JN	1954
H. Boyce Budd	T	1962
Michael Bullivant		
Elaine M. Bullock (née Pomeroy)	G	1949
Laura Fay Bullock	G	1999
Mr Jeremy J. Bunting	CTH	1953
Dr Mark J. Burby	M	1992
J.A. Burdon-Cooper	JN	1958
Richard Burger	K	1989
Hugh Burkitt	PEM	1963
Mrs Diana Burnett (née Hargreaves)	G	1957
Lewis Burnett	F	1997
Jean Burnham	G	1972
Nicholas Burns		
Deborah J. Burrell (née Andrews)	SID	1994
James D. Burrell	PEM	1992
Nigel Burrell	EM	1978
Amelia Burrett	K	2001
Kevin A. Burrows	CHU	1997
Simon Burrows	JN	2000
Claude Bursill	JN	1945
Mr Warwick R. Burton	JN	1973
Elsie Butcher (née Parry)	HO	1942
Peter Butenschon	T	1963
Douglas N. Byrne	JN	1942
Prof. Richard Byrne	JN	1969
Peter T. Bysouth	CC	1999
Mr Julian Cable	SE	1989
Sir Adrian Cadbury	K	1949
James A. Caesar	CTH	1965
Alice Cairns	N	2007
Alex Callander	JN	1979
John Campbell Callow	CHR	1952
Cambridge Thai Foundation		
Alan J. Cameron		
Donald William Cameron	CHU	1960
Peter Camilletti	T	1984
Sharon Camilletti	TH	1999
Dr A.J.P. Campbell	JN	1952
Colin Campbell	JN	1960
Mr Howard H. Campbell MC	M	1940
Tony Canham	CL	1951
G.R. (Charles) Canner	Q	1947
Dr Jack R. Cannon	EM	1951
Neil J. Cantile	Q	1991
Dr Raphael Cantor	TH	1958
Carlos Alberto Carbajo-Martinez	DAR	1995
Philippa Carbutt	N	1991
Dr Michael Carlile	TH	1951

Jane Carmichael	NH	2002
J. David Carr	CHR	1956
John A. Carrington		
Dr Bertrand C. Carissimo	HH	1982
J.A. Carruthers	TH	1956
Prof. E. Jane Carruthers	CLH	
Peter Carruthers	CHU	1971
Mr Ian C. Carter	PEM	1982
Patrick R.N. Carter	SE	1991
Sir Bryan Cartledge	JN	1951
Vikki R. Cartwright	N	1995
J.M. Casement	SID	1985
Dr Allan T. Casey	SID	1954
Mr Tim Cashman	PET	1980
Christopher Caseley	CC	1994
Mr Sebastian Cassel	PEM	2002
Dr Bruce R. Cassell	Q	1978
Peter C. Caswell	Q	1955
Peter Cave	K	1972
R.C. Cave	CC	1985
Robert Cawthorn	T	1959
Lewis T. Chadderton	CAI	1959
Rosalie Challis (née Hughes Jones)	G	1957
Sir John Chalstrey	Q	1951
Mr Hugh R. Chambers	CC	1973
Dr Dominic C.B. Chan	T	1988
Ka Keung Chan	R	1986
M.L. Chan		
Nicholas Kei Cheong Chan	PEM	1988
Robert H.Y. Chan	HH	1984
Sommarat Chantarat	SID	2001
Gary A. Chapman		
Emeritus Prof. N.B. Chapman	M	1935
Dr Richard L. Chapman	CC	1954
Michael Charlesworth	T	1949
Ross N. Charlton	CL	1951
David Chart	T	1990
R.V. Chartener	M	1982
Prof. Philip Chatwin	TH	1960
Dr Ioannis Chatzigeorgiou	CLH	2002
Christopher (Kim) Cheetham	TH	1956
Eleanor Cheetham	Q	1993
Koh Chen Chen	CHR	2001
Dr Robert Chen	K	1983
Soo Kien Chen	HH	2003
Xi Chen	N	2002
Derek Chetwin	JE	1949
Dr Kim Cheung		
Seow-Ping Chew	N	1995
Martin Child	CC	1964
Sharon Chin	N	1996
Candy Ching Ho	M	1997
Thomas S.Y. Choong	M	1996
Anup-Sing Choudry	CC	1980
Dr Chan Kam Chow	W	1982
David Chrisp	F	1956
Lapadrada Chujinda	TH	2006
Chan Ka Chun	CHU	2001
Esther K. Chung	TH	1985
Kah Seng Chung	CHU	1974
N.B.M. Clack	JN	1949
Nicole D. Clarke	N	1995
John Andrew Clare	CL	1963
Alan Clark	CTH/F	1965/84
Brian F.C. Clark	K	1955
Chris Clark	PEM	1964
David P. Clark	CHR	1973
Dr George P.M. Clark		1965
John Clark	SE	1958
Judith Clark	HO	1967
Dr Michael Clark	JN	1957
Paul Clark	Q	1966

Paul Richard Clark	SID	2002
Barry D. Clarke	PEM	1981
Dr Geoffrey Clarke	SE	1956
Dr John Nathaniel Clarke	CLH	1995
Dr John S. Clarke	K	1948
Laura Clarke	CAI	2002
Tim Clarke	M	1994
William R. Clarke	F	1953
Alan Clarkson	CHR	1954
Prof. John Clarkson	TH	1981
Revd Canon Colin Clay	CHR	1952
Henry Clay	PEM	1973
Murray Clayson	SID	1979
Alexander Clayton	Q	2007
Prof. James L. Clayton		
Dr J.R.A. Cleaver	JE	1966
Neil Richard Clement	HH	1985
Prof. Kenneth J. Clemetson	CHR	1965
Simon Clephan	F	1977
A.N. Cliffe	EM	1977
Terence Clifford	JN	1960
Henry T. Clifton	JN	1946
Prof. G.J.H. Clingham	CTH	1975
David Clipsham	SE	1964
Robert J. Clover-Brown	SE	1965
Denis Coan	DAR	2004
David Coatsworth MA Cantab	ED	2001
Mike Cobb	F	1970
Dr Alan B. Cobban	T	1961
A.H. Cockayne		
Mr Neil E. Cockroft	JN	1980
Colin Cohen		
Harlan K. Cohen	DAR	1971
Richard James Lee Coleman	CC	1987
Ian R. Coles	CHU	1975
John P. Colfer	Q	1989
Mr James R. Colgate	JN	2005
Dr Peter Collecott	JN	1969
Kenneth W. Collier	PET	1952
Robert Collin	T	1937
Dr Alison Collins	NH	1988
David R.B. Collins		1964
Peter Collins	JN	1962
Richard J. Collins	DOW	1963
Ruaidhri Collins	PEM	1988
Sean A. Collins	M	1969
John R. Collis	SID	1958
Prof. Howard M. Colquhoun	CTH	1969
John Colquhoun	CTH	1964
Alexander Francis Lionel Colson		
Stephanie Colver	N	1964
Alan J. Colvill	TH	1975
Vince Colvin		
Nicholas Comfort	T	1964
Quentin Compton-Bishop	JN	1977
Stuart Condie	CTH	1975
George F. Connelly	JN	1940
Dr C.K. Connolly TD MA FRCP	CAI	1955
Dr Robert F. Conti	W	1990
J.R. Coody		
Anthony Crook	CL	1979
Jonathan Harry Cook	JE	2005
Steven Cook		
H.G.W. Cooke	T	1941
Helen Cooke	CTH	1998
Dr John A. Cooke	T	1972
Lisa Cooke	LC	1984
Dr F.B. Cookson	JN	1955
Mr Eric H. Cooley	CL	1945
D.R. Cooling	JN	1957
Simon Coombs	PET	1983
B.A. Cooper	JN	1966

Dr Brian F. Cooper	CTH	1965
David J. Cooper	CTH	1957
Dr M.B.S. Cooper	DOW	1943
Mr Mark G. Cooper	SE	2001
M.E. Coops	JN	1950
Christopher Cope		
Michael Copp	CTH	2000
Claudio Corbetta	R	1994
Sir Brian Corby	JN	1949
Peter Cordingley	PEM	1997
Gilbert Corke		
Robert S. Cornish	JE	1950
Javier Corominas	SID	2000
Jessica Corsi	JN	1990
Ronald H. Cosford	K	1954
Mr Christopher Costa	K	1989
George Cotsikis	HH	1995
The Revd James E. Cotter	CAI	1960
Beverley Cottrell	LC	1979
Mark H. Couchman	SE	1943
Philip A. Coucke	HH	2001
Mr Robert V. Court		
Wilfred Court	CAI	1946
Dr Philip Cowdall	F	
James A.F. Cowderoy	JE	1978
Eleanor Cowie	N	1961
Peter Cowie		
Michael L. Cowper	TH	1949
Nigel Cox	SID	1969
Prof. Noel Cox		
Stephen R. Coxford	CAI	1980
Mr Leon Crickmore	K	1950
Anthea Craighead	DOW	2001
Adrian Crampton	T	1978
Paul Craven	JN	1983
Giles P.V. Creagh	CL	1945
Christopher Greening	CL	1960
Prof. Ian Creese	Q	1967
Julian M. Crick (née Boness)	G	1979
Timothy J. Crist	K	1973
Alfred G. Crocker	Q	1947
Malcolm Crockford	CL	1962
Dr Nigel H. Croft	CAI	1974
Adrian J. Cronje	CL	1995
Terrence Crooks	K	1968
Richard Crosby	JN	
E.F. Malcolm Cross	SID	1943
Geoffrey W. Cross	F	1954
J. Anthony Cross	CL	1987
Dr Philip H. Crosskey	PEM	1944
Peter M. Crossley		
Robert M. Croucher	CHR	1959
Rob Crow	JN	1961
J.G.P. Crowden CVO		
Shane Redmond Crowe	ED	1997
Mr Philip Stephen Crowther	DOW	1978
Charles Cruden	JN	1993
David Cruttenden	CTH	1967
Nigel J. Cumberland	Q	1986
Peter Cunich	M	1987
Revd Aidan Michael Cunningham		
	DOW	1961
Laura M.C. Cunningham LLM	HH	2007
Dr Tom Cunningham	Q	1964
William John Curry	PEM	2002
David W. Curtis	EM	1947
K.C. Curtis	JN	1979
P.J. Curtis	K	1957
Dr Rodney A.P. Curtis	SE	1956
Dr W.D. Cussins		
Graham A. Cutting	F	1976
Prof. B.A. Dadson		

Michael Dale	K	1955
Mr J. Martin Dalgleish	CAI	1964
Dr Peter Dallas Ross	K	1940
A.G. Daltry	JN	1952
Geoffrey Darby	SID	1948
John Darbyshire	DOW	1953
Michael L. Darling	JE	1950
Dr Gour K. Das	Q	1966
Revd Guenter Daum	W	2001
Dr Anthony P. Davenport	CTH	1995
Dr Anthony Davey	T	1955
David Wilson David	K	1968
Rosemary Davidson	TH	1980
Mrs Euphan D. Davies	N	1966
Gary G.H. Davies		
Mr G.B. Davies		
J. Owen Davies	JE	1939
John G.W.D. Davies	EM	1979
Laura Davies (née Cooper)	JN	1976
M.C. Davies	PEM	1970
Morys Davies	CAI	1957
Neil Davies	JN	1976
P.T. Davies	JN	1948
Tim Davies	CHR	1981
Robert J. Davis	CAI	1976
Thomas A. Davis	TH	1958
Alistair Davison	JN	1978
Laura Davison	Q	2006
Elliot W. Dawson	T	1955
John Dawson	K	1963
Keith and Pam Dawson	CC/HO	1959
Shenaiya N. Day (née Khurody)	HO	1986
Enrique de Alba	DOW	1982
Dr G.F.C. de Bruyn	PET	1962
Margaret A. de C. Hartree	N	1944
M. De La F. Ford	T	1950
Vicomte Roland de Rosiere	M	1978
Mr D. Richard de Silva	JN	2005
M.E. Dean		
Dr John R. Deane	PEM	1970
Dr G. De L. Dear	T	1973
K.R. Deasley	F	1965
Robert J. Dee	JN	1949
Christopher Deeks	PET	1979
Julie Dendle Jones	CAI	1987
D.B. Dennis	Q	1965
Dr Christopher M. Dent	JE	1970
Michael Derringer	CC	2000
Dr Gabriel des Rosiers	DAR	1994
Prof. Don E. Detmer	CLH	
N.P.H. Dewes	DOW	1948
Adrian C. Dewey	JN	1979
John Dewhurst	EM	1950
Sumant Dhamija		
Dr Susanna di Feliciantonio	JN	1997
Dr Mark Dickens	CLH	2003
Martin J. Dickinson	SE	1963
J. Dickins		
W. Ian Dickinson	CTH	1953
Dr J.P. Dickinson	JN	1957
Simon L.C. Diggins		
R. Dingle		
Dr Adam L. Dinham	SE	1993
Roger Dix	JN	1974
Malcolm Dixon	CHU	1964
Stanley Dixon	K	1953
Thomas H. Dixon	SE	1943
Dr Wendy L. Dixon		
Olga E.C. Dixon-Brown MPhil MRICS		
	PET	2001
Kevin Dobson	G	1983
Anthony R.F. Dodd	M	1954

J.S. Dodge	CTH	1948
Phil Doherty	SID	1980
Chris Dolby	JN	1980
Dr Ray Dolby	PEM	1957
The Revd Dr P.H. Donald	CAI	1980
Luke Donnan	TH	2003
Suzanne A.L. Donnellan	JE	1999
John Donnelly	SID	1988
Molly Clare Donohue	ED	2002
Kathryn Dooks	CHR	1998
Prof. Tony Dorey	PEM	1957
Margaret Double	G	1950
Mr Andrew P. Dowden	TH	1983
G. Graham Down	CAI	1952
Dr John E. Downes	EM	1953
Prof. Grenville Draper	CL	1970
Dr Manuel Dries	G	2007
Dr Scott Drimie	DAR	2000
Dr Alexander A.G. Driskill-Smith	CAI	1992
Paul Drohan	M	1985
P.M.E. Drury		
Prof. C.G. du Toit	EM	1977
Jitander Dudee	M	1983
D.M. Dudley		
Amb. Robert W. Duemling	JN	1950
David J. Duffy	TH	1963
H.J.A. (Tim) Dugan	CAI	1952
Dr J. Keith Dugdale	PET	1958
Elizabeth Sibthorp Duignan	W/M	1976
Dr R. Duke		
K.L. Duliba	CTH	1980
Reginald Dumas	TH	1954
Michael F. Dumont	CTH	1963
Archie Dunbar	PEM	1948
Ruth Dundas	N	1946
Dr John Dunderdale	CHR	1943
Stuart J. Dunlop	CC	1992
Prof. Peter M. Dunn	JN	1950
Patricia Dunnett	JN	1988
Raymond Dunnett	Q	1965
Denis Dunstone	CL	1956
Dr D. Joe Dunthorn	CL	1961
Kathleen M. Duparc	G	1939
Srinivasan Dwarakanath	DAR	1991
Mr Richard Dyer	CHU	1979
Dr P. de K. Dykes	K	1946
D.S.M. Eadie	T	1935
Michael C.A. Eaton	JE	1961
Stephen D. Eccles	T	1956
Kristen A. Eckert	EM	2004
Trent Eddy	T	1990
Robert Steel Edgar	EM	1949
Dr W.M. Edgar	CAI	1941
Dr Philip Edmondson	CHR	1957
Ian M.D. Edwards	EM	1976
Dr Robert M. Edwards	K	1999
Suzi Edwards	SE	1993
Dr James Eedle	DOW	1949
Margaret Eedle (née Hooson)	HO	1949
Dr Holger Eick	T	1998
Dr Vernon W. Eldred	CTH	1943
Michael Elliott	Q	1966
Steven Elliott	TH	1973
Tania Elliott	DAR	1974
Andrea S. Ellis	CTH	1980
Keith Ellis	JN	1952
Mr Peter R. Ellis	SID	1945
Emma L. Ellison	HO	2001
Dr Sohier Elneil	LC	1997
Dr Clive Elphick	Q	1975
Sue Eltringham		
Bob Ely	TH	1950

Name	College	Year
Prof. John Wilton-Ely	JE	1958
Kenneth G. Elzinga	DOW	
Clyde K. Emery Jr	F	1957
Pissi Emilia	G	1995
R.E. Emms	Q	1956
James F. English Jr	CL	1949
Dr Michael C. English	PEM	1982
Dr Mary-Anne Enoch (née Newton)	K	1972
David Ensor	JN	1975
Dr Liora Malki-Epshtein	T	2000
Prof. David W. Erbach	K	1972
Sol Garcia Estrada	CLH	2002
Dr John E. Etherton	F	1974
Dr Andrew L. Evans	CAI	1972
Mr Denys Evans	TH	1949
Mr Gordon H. Evans	CL	1945
J. Wynford Evans CBE	JN	1952
John C. Evans	CAI	1974
Martin Evans	CHR	1971
Dr Martin C. Evans		
Dr Nerys Evans (née Davies)	N	1955
Paul Evans	I	1980
The Rt Revd R.J. Evans	CAI	1959
Daniel Simon Faas	CLH	2002
R.W. Fair	EM	1962
Peter F. Falstrup	T	1941
Anthony V. Falzon	TH	1989
Mr J.F. Fane		
N.H. Fanshawe	CAI	1929
Alan R. Farquhar	CC	1971
S.A. Farr	Q	1975
Prof. Paddy Farrell	PEM	1965
G.R. Farren	CHU	1966
Bruce Farthing	CTH	1948
M.N. Farwell	JN	1979
David Fassbender	ED	1999
Albert Fawcett		
C.B. d'A. Fearn	CAI	1952
John and Anna Fearnall	SE	1984
H.A. Fenn	T	1961
Elizabeth Fenwick	G	1957
J.J. Fenwick	PEM	1952
Brian Fenwick-Smith	JN	1959
Lewis H. Ferguson	K	1966
Anil P. Fernando	F	1955
Wimalsen H. Fernando	EM	1953
T.A. Anne-Celia Feutrie	K	2006
Maximillian Fevers	W	1998
Helen Field	N	1980
Dr Kim R. Field	TH	2002
Mr John de Figueiredo	TH	1962
Debbie Finucane	PEM	2001
Dr Maria T. Fiorini	CHU	1995
Geoffrey M. Firth	Q	1941
Margaret M. Firth (née Gatehouse)	G	1944
Peter M. Firth	PET	2002
Anne Dorsey Fiske	DAR	1971
Lorraine G. Fiset PhD	N	1952
Colin D.T. Fitch	CTH	1953
Dr Gillian FitzGerald (née Dennis)	NH	1972
John Fitzpatrick-Nash	JN	1963
Adrian E. Flatt	CAI	1945
Alan F. Fleming	CL	1950
G.J. Fletcher	T	1947
Kate Fletcher	M	1994
C.J. Flower	CAI	1951
Richard Fluck	TH	1979
Robert E. Flynn	F	1957
Michael J. Fogg	JN	1967
Dennis B. Forbes	JN	
Prof. Duncan A. Forbes	W	1992
Dr Malcolm H. Forbes	SE	1960
Adriana Elizabeth Sian Ford	PET	2000
Philip Ford	CL	1968
Dr Peter Forder	T	1968
Dr Roger Forder	T	1965
Forero-Velez Family		
Sean Forester	CAI/W	2000
M.L.N. Forrest		
Dr Jack D. Forrester	CC	1953
Ian J. Forsyth	Q	1954
Revd E.J.G. Foster		
Paul Foulkes	CHU	1986
Paul James Fox	JE	2003
Peter Fox	SE	1976
Guy Francis	T	1957
Jeremy I. Francis	Q	1969
Dr Sarah Francis	NH	1960
Donald M. Francke	CTH	1950
Dr Blas Frangione	K	1969
Dr Wendy Frank	R	1981
Revd Cortland Fransella	TH	1967
Dr Paul J. Fray		
Dr Murray C. Frazer	CAI	1967
Cicely Frances Freeman		
John Freeth	SE	1959
Laurent Frideres	G	1997
J.H. Frings		
David G. Frodin	CL	1967
David R. Fryatt		
Redwood Fryxell		
Dr Heinz Fuchs	SID	1997
Mr Peter Fuchs	JN	1959
Luis Arturo Fuentes	EM	1999
Mr F. Fuentes Ostos	F	1992
Martin Fuller	CAI	1986
William Fullerton	Q	1952
Eugene Fung	JE	1991
Dr Wai Lun Alan Fung	DAR	2001
Dr Mark H. Fussell	SID	1953
Mrs Agapi Fylaktou Cattaneo	M	1998
Valentina Gagliardi	TH	1998
F. Galantini		
Dr Alan W. Galbraith	SE	1954
Dr Charles H. Gallimore	CAI	1960
Prof. Thomas P. Gallanis	JN	1992
Francesca Galli	PEM	2006
Warren R.J.D. Galloway	F	2000
David Galvin	PET	1992
John Gamlin	F	1958
Tina Gandhi	SID	2000
Barrie C. Gane		
Dr Christine Gardiner (née Boettcher)	F	1995
Paul Gardiner	TH	1980
Peter Gardner	TH	1953
Robert J.M. Gardner	PEM	1958
Andrew Garety	CL	1968
Angela Garner (née Beckett)	HO	1983
John F. Garrood	JN	1944
Charles H.B. Garraway		
Dr Tom Garrett	CAI	1962
His Hon. Judge Gaskell	CL	1966
Dr George B. Gasson	Q	1949
Paul A. Gatenby	CLH	1988
Mr John Gavin	DOW	1949
Dr Irina Gavrilenko	W	2007
Julian Gee		
Michael I. Gee	PEM	1946
Mr J. Gent		
Graham George	DOW	1964
Mr P.W. George		
Tony George	CHR	1957
Annie Georgitseas	Q	1983
Sir Peter Gershon	CHU	1966
Mr Alexandre F.J.P. Geulette	SID	2003
Dr Abdollah Ghavami	Q	2000
Dr Elizabeth R. Gibb	JN	2002
Dr Stuart L. Gibb	CHU	1999
John Gibbon	SID	1964
Anthony Gibbs	T	1956
Martyn Gibbs	M	1960
Dr Russell Gibbs	CAI	1948
I.G. Gibson	DOW	1949
Mr John M. Gibson	CHR	1955
Dr Talat M. Giddings	DAR	1972
John Gilchrist	T	1953
Dr Robert Gilchrist	TH	1951
Geoffrey J. Giles	ED	1969
Dr Denise Gilgen	LC	1991
Dr Ralph J. Gillis	JE	1976
David E.E. Gillman		
Prof. J. Gittins		
Magnus R.E. Gittins	TH	2002
Dr Peter Gittins	JN	1943
Mark Gizejewski	SE	1995
G.S. Gladstone		
Michael Glasby	NH	1983
Mirela I. (Ivan) and Bryan S. Glass	W	2000
Fiona Gledhill	G	1975
Dr Leda Agapi Glyptis	K	1997
Prof. Sunthara Gnanalingam	T	1946
Mr K.J.M. Godlewski	F	1945
D.H. Golby	JN	1958
Stanley P. Gold		
Mel Goldberg	JN	1960
Neville C. Goldrein CBE		1942
Prof. Margaret Ann Goldstein	CLH	2001
Andrew G. Goldston	PET	1993
Siân Goldthorpe Stein	N	1984
Li Gong	JE	1987
A.W.T. Gooch		
George Edwin Goodall	TH	1969
Amanda J. Gooddie	SE	1981
Howard R. Gooddie	EM	1951
Timothy J.R. Goode	SE	1969
F.R. Goodenough	M	1948
Mr Anthony Goodfellow	M	1959
Davis P. Goodman Esq.	JN	1978
Brigadier H.J. Goodson OBE	JN	1952
Dr David J. Goodwill	CHR	1966
Michael Goodwin	PEM	1967
The Revd Christopher W.H. Goodwins	JN	1955
Sir Jack Goody	JN	
Dorothy C. Gordon	W	1976
Michael Gorman	K	1963
Julian Gornall-Thode	CTH	1998
Prof. Richard Goss	K	1955
Tony Gosse	TH	1962
Dr Graham Gould	K	1980
Katerina Gould		
Theodore Gouliouris	T	1996
Nelson H.H. Graburn		1955
Markus Graebig	DAR	2006
Kevin Grafton	TH	1971
David M. Graham	PEM	1966
Prof. Nigel J.D. Graham	CTH	1972
Roderick R. Graham	M	1983
Dr Timothy C. Graham	Q	1973
Beric Graham-Smith	F	1949
Dr Clive Grant	HO	1979
Gregory M. Grant MD	CAI	1987
D.H. Gray		
Sir Denis Pereira Gray		
Mr Peter H. Gray	CAI	1956
Dr Ron Gray	EM	1938
Steven Gray	CTH	1986
Stewart Gray	CHU	1987
Dr Ivor Grayson-Smith	JN	1961
Diane Graziano	CHU	1979
Prof. Norman N. Greenwood	SID	1948
Alan Gregory	CHR	1978
Mike Gregson	TH	1952
The Revd Prof. Robert Gribben	F	1966
Trevor Grigg	TH	1955
A. Gregory Grimsal	HH	1980
Dr Guy L. Gronquist	CL	1980
Richard B. Gross	T	1973
Peter J. Grove	T	1967
Deborah Grubbe		
A.R. Gubbay	JE	1953
Mrs Hazel Guest (née Rider)	N	1946
Simon Guest	CC	1987
Richard S. Guha	T	1966
C. Michael Guilford	Q	1949
Mr Inderpal Sing Gujral	F	1998
Andrea Gumucio		2007
Miss Suhasini Gunasena	W	1999
Dr Jan B. Gutowski		
Michael Gwinnell	CC	1964
Sven Haake	TH	
Anthony Habgood	CAI	1968
The Rt Hon. the Lord Hacking	CL	1958
Ben Hadden	CC	2001
Mrs Jane Carson Bon Hadden		
John Alexander Hadden	CC	2001
Nigel Hadfield		
Mr Bernard Hadley	CL	1969
Dr and Mrs J.W. Hadley		
Jonathan H.R. Hadley	TH	1990
Peter Hadley	JN	1986
Dr Reinmar Hager	T	1999
P. Haggett		
Richard Hagon	SE	1966
Donald Haigh FSA	CTH	1944
Gary Haigh	JN	1983
Prof. Thomas Haine	CTH	1985
Alfred W. Hales	K	1962
Ian Hall	JN	1982
Jean A. Hall	HH	1975
J.J. Hall	T	1959
Dr Jennifer Hall	G	1954
Martin Hall	TH	1978
Prof. Michael B. Hall	CLH	1982
Rebecca Anne Hall	W	2001
In Memoriam Ross Hume Hall Ph	CHR	1953
Stephen Hall	CHR	1953
John Hall-Craggs		
S. Halliday	PEM	1961
Dr Rosemary Halliwell (née Wyatt-Millington)	Q	1993
Dr John H. Halton	JE	1950
Mr William S. Ham	K	1942
Dr Hamad A.A. Hamad-Elneil	SID	1962
A.G.K. Hamilton	PEM	1964
Dundas Hamilton	CL	1939
F.E.M.C. Hamilton	N	1966
Kim Hammer	N	1989
Paul C. Hammer	JN	1998
Dr Allen W. Hancock II	JN	1966
G.T. Hancock	Q	1956
Dr Peter R. Handford		
Gillian Hankey	N	1962
Martin Hankey	T	1962
Dr John Hannah	CHR	1958

Heidi Elisa Kalloo-Hosein	T	1994
Toshiaki Kamijo	TH	2000
Alex D. Kanarek		
Sheila Kaplow	G	1949
Prof. Karega-Munene	DAR	1986
Mrs Jill Kashap (née Brumfitt)	SID	1979
Mr Prabhu Kashap	F	1980
Chieko Kato	W	1993
Dr Dominic Henley Katter	ED	1998
Dr Horst Gunter Kausch	SID	1987
Dr Daniel A.W. Kaute	CHU	1991
Jolyon Kay		
Dr Richard Kay	CHU	1970
Leong Weng Kee	PET	1979
David Keeling	JN	1960
Ruth Keeling	PEM	2001
James M. Kelley		
Sir David Kelly CBE	JN	1956
Godfrey K. Kelly	F	1948
Prof. Michael J. Kelly		
Dr Roy Kelly	F	1963
Francis Kemausuor	DAR	2005
David Kent	PEM	1943
William Edward Kenyon	CAI	1966
Robert Ker	PET	1959
Michael J. Kerr	CL	1969
Dr Philip J. Kerry	DOW	1973
Dr Maha M.O. Khayyat	ED	2001
Shaista E. Khilji	Q	1994
Nawshir D. Khurody	T	1955
Winston P. Kiang		
Graeme Kidd	CL	1945
Mr Tanil R. Kilachand	Q	1956
Dr Robert Lee Kilpatrick		1981
Prof. Hiroshi Kimura	HH	1984
Christopher King		
Revd Peter King	F	1972
Richard A. King	DAR	1986
Dr Mervin Kingston	M	1945
Col Richard Kinsella-Bevan	K	1962
Linda J. Kirk	CAI	
Christopher Kirker	JE	1969
Mrs Jane Carson Kirkland	CC	2001
Bill Kirkman	W	1968
S.G. Kirsch	T	1949
Christopher Kirwin	Q	1961
Dr Marwan Kishek	SE	1979
John Kitching	CHR	1971
M.R. Sarisdiguna Kitiyakara	M	1957
Anita J. Klaus MA MD	NH	1986
Prof. Gordon L. Klein	W	1970
Dr H.W. Klein	F	1967
Jonathan D. Klein	TH	1979
Jason P. Kliewer	CTH	2003
Stephen John Klimczuk	EM	2004
Enrique E. Klix	CLH	1997
K.A. Knaggs		
A.M. Kneen	SE	1970
Matthew S. Knight	CAI	2004
Miss M.A. Knott	N	1932
Dr Geoffrey Knowles		
J.E.A. Knowles	M	1955
Prof. Huxley H.M. Knox-Macaulay	F	1955
Ryuzo Kodama	JN	1973
Winston Koh T.H.	CHU	1982
Anna M. Kosicka		1974
Chaiwat Kositkhun	PET	1997
Stephanie Kozakowski	DAR	2004
Peter A. Kreisky	DOW	1965
Dr Niels Krüger	CTH	1995
Dr Praveen Kumar	CLH	1996
J. Kenneth Kuntz		

Li Kwan-Hung	G	2006
Philip Kwee	CC	
Jimmy Sin Hang Kwong	Q	2003
Prof. W.K. (Patrick) Lacey	CTH	1940
Anton Lach	CLH	1969
Michael Lacovara	PEM	1984
Christopher Lacy	Q	1965
Prof. Radoslaw J. Ladzinski	M	1959
Dr Joseph J. Lagowski	SID	1959
Caroline Lai Tung	DOW	1982
Edith and T.W. Lai	CAI	2006
Ying Ying Lai	SID	2007
Prof. Robert A. Lamb PhD ScD	W	1974
Andrew Lambert	W	1997
John C. Lambert	CHR	1942
John M. Lambert		
Dr Alison J. Lamming	G	1960
Dr M. Peter Lance	JE	1965
Rex Lanham	JE	1956
Robert P.D. Laniak	HH	1983
Dr Gaye T. Lansdell	TH	1992
Bryan Larkin		
Mr Richard G. Larkin	CHU	1971
Kenneth V. Larman	Q	1943
Christopher Latham	CL	1952
Sir Michael Latham	K	1961
Chin-Hin Lau	W	1995
Queenie Lau		
Jeanne M. Lavin	NH	1979
Prof. Roderick J. Lawrence	JN	
Katherine Lawther (née Cameron)	G	1959
Alexandra Lawton	CC	1996
Tristram Lawton	CC	1999
Stanley E. Lazic	K	2002
Dr John A. Leake	JN	1958
E.H. Leaton	JN	1948
Mrs J.E. Leaver		
David Ledingham	F	2008
Vincent Lee Hong Fay	F	1999
Dr Albert S. Lee	T	1997
Carline A. Lee	EM	1988
Dr Cheol Ju Lee	F	
Elizbeth Lee Fuh Yen	W	1984
Gerald Lee	CTH	1995
Hoi Yee (Diana) Lee	DAR	2007
Ho-Joon Lee	W	1998
Dr Jason T.C. Lee	CC	1994
Dr Jonathan L.C. Lee	CL	1997
Ming San Lee	R	1983
Patrick Fook Yau Lee	T	1990
Dr S.T. Lee		
Dr Trevor Lee	JE	1995
Dr Trevor W.R. Lee	W	2004
Dr Mark S. Leeson	SID	1986
Anthony Lees-Smith	SE	1995
Dr George Lefroy	CL	
John Lehman		
Wendy E. Leich Vet MB	CHU	1983
Eugene E. Lemcio	T	
Robert J. Lenardon	CC	
Don Lennard	JN	1961
Andrew Lennon	TH	1998
David Leonard		
Yves Leservoisier	JN	1952
W. Bruce Leslie		
Ivan A.D. Lessard	F	1991
Alex Lesser	CTH	2006
Guy Lesser	CTH	1978
Mrs Jill Letherland		
Howard Letty	Q	1943
C.W. Leung	JN	1999
Hilary Levey	LC	2002

Dr John J. Lewandowski	CHU	2004
Dr Andrew Lewis	SID	1985
J. Brian Lewis	K	1964
Dr John Scott Lewis	JN	1946
Maggie Lewis	G	1979
Sir David K.P. Li	SE	1968
Mann Ken Li	Q	1987
Martin Li	M	1982
T.-S. Li	ED	2000
R.A. Lidwell		
Monica Lightburne	G	1956
Sylvia Lightburne	G	1946
Brian Lightowler	PET	1950
Dr C.T. Lim	JE	1996
K.T. Lim	T	1997
Dr May G.B. Lim	N	1958
Lin Lin	G	2006
Lin Yong		
Garth Lindrup	JN	1977
Dr Ian M. Ling	PEM	1967
John Liquorish		
Henry R.W. Little	DOW	2005
David Liu	W	1983
David Livermore	JN	1958
Mr Brian J. Livingston	Q	1955
Mr L.M.B. Livingstone-Learmonth		
	JN	1997
Mrs L.M.B. Livingstone-Learmonth		
	JE	1996
Michael Llewellyn-Smith	PEM	1962
Dr Antony Lloyd	CL	1957
Catherine Lloyd	Q	1986
D.G. Lloyd	CHR	1952
Mark Lloyd-Price	T	1964
Richard Mandle Lloyd-Roberts	PEM	1975
Mrs J. Morag Loader	N	1983
Dr Samuel Logan	CHR	1988
Nicolas Lois		
Mrs A. Long		
C.E.C. Long	CAI	1949
James B. Longley		
Peter Hovenden Longley	CTH	1963
Tan Shun Loong	PEM	1995
Barry Ian Lord	JN	1974
George de Forest Lord		
Ronald J. Lorimer	F	1952
Dr Elena Loukoianova	Q	2000
Maria Lourdes Lising Baylon MCD MPhil		
	LC	1999
Amanda Lovell	F	1985
Zoe Lovett	CHR	1995
Edward Low		
David Loy	CC	1948
Jacky Lui	CAI	1992
Brian Luker	SID	1955
Michael Lumley	JN	1957
Dr John K. Lundy	CLH	2002
Maris Lusis		
E.B. Lynch	M	1959
Mrs L.A. Lyne (née Rees)	G	1963
Dr Anne Lyon	N	1967
Johnny Lyons	DAR	1991
Charles Lysaght	CHR	1962
Dr Colin Ma	CAI	1976
Dr Ronald Ma	SID	1988
Douglas B. MacAdam	SID	1955
David MacBryde	PEM	1958
Kimberley Macdonald	EM	2002
Stephen MacDonell	CL	1990
Prof. Neil W. MacGill	T	1953
Dr James Mackay	T	1977
Alastair MacKenzie Ross	CL	

Bernadette MacKenzie Ross	G	1959
David MacKenzie Ross	CL	1956
Jen Yee MacKenzie Ross (née Chan)	Q	2000
Robert MacKenzie Ross	R	
Duncan Mackenzie	PEM	1952
J.G. Mackley BA	EM	1947
Dr Richard L. Mackman	JE	1985
Scott K. MacLennan	JN	2006
J.M. Macleod		
Sir Richard Macombe	DOW	1971
Upali G. Madanayake	EM	1955
Mr David G. Madden		
Malcolm Maddock	JN	1967
Mr George Magnus		
Sabrina Fiaschè Magro	DAR	2001
Mrs Mair du Plooy	CC	1996
Donon Daniel Mak		
Donald Hindley Makinson		
Kyla Malcolm	JE	1993
Golnar Malek	W	2006
In memory of Elsa Care Malik (née Barker)		
	G	1924
In memory of Jalal D. Malik	T	1926
Sudeep Malik	ED	1999
Colin Mallet	TH	1965
Meena S. Mallipeddi	PEM	2003
Clive E. Malpas-Sands	CAI	1963
C.H. Malyon	Q	1952
Krishna Mandalia	Q	1999
Revd Robin Mann	F	1973
Mrs Rosemary K.Mann (née Bayes)		
	N/HH	1967/70
Duncan Mara		
Reshma Maraj	CAI	2003
Edo Marinus	SID	1999
Calvert Markham	CHU	1965
Dr Christos N. Markides	R	
Dr John Marks		
Lt Col (Retd) W.W. Marks	PET	1958
D.G. Marriott	PET	1948
Paul Marsh	JE	1962
Beresford Ivor de Lacy Marshall	EM	1959
His Hon. D. Marshall Evans QC	TH	1956
Elizabeth Marshall	W	1970
Noel Marshall		
Patrick Marshall	F	1965
Sir Roy Marshall	PEM	1942
Chris Martin	F	1976
Dennis Martin	PET	1952
Daniel Martin		
Darryl K.Q. Martin	ED	2004
Dr Graham Martin	TH	1957
Prudence Martin	G	1953
Dr Rainer E. Martin	CHU	1999
Roderick E. Martin	G	1983
David Marwood	CTH	1947
Veronique Marx	G	2001
Dr Balla Frederick Yumbu Pondejo Masele		
	G	1992
Julian P.V. Mash		
Richard Mash	JN	
Rosalind Mash	G	
Dr Vivian Mash	G	1959
Ann Mason (née Harroway)	G	1965
Stephanie Mason	EM	1981
Jawad Masood	HH	2004
Ms Caroline J. Mather	JN	2002
In memory of Mr Donald R. Mather		
	SID	1936
Hiroshi Matsuoka	CTH	2000
Mrs Syloo Ravi Matthai	N	1954
D.A. Matthews	DOW	1948

Name	Code	Year
P.C. Matthews	JN	1974
Dr H.J. Maxmin	F	1964
Dr Geoffrey J. May	F	1967
Simon Maybury	F	1975
David Maycock	CHR	1972
Dr Paul M. Mayhew	CL	2001
Sir John Mayhew-Sanders	JE	1950
Dr Sean McAlister	CL	1968
Ian M. McAlpine	CL	1962
Cedric McCarthy	F	1948
The Revd F.J. McCarthy	DOW	1949
Walter McCarthy		
Prof. A.J. McClean	CAI	1957
Scott McCleskey	SE	2001
Mr Justin John McConnachy LLM	CHU	1998
Alan McConnell-Duff	T	1965
L. Murray McCullough OBE	HH	2005
Roger B. McDaniel	JN	1954
Justin McDonnell		
Alan McFetrich	M	1961
Vicki McGlade (née Whitney)	G	1968
Neil McGregor-Wood	T	1948
Dr Cecil McIver	SID	1950
Eric McKenzie	F	1971
Jean McKenzie	N	1952
Captain Alfred Scott McLaren USN (Retd) PhD	PET	1981
Prof. Hugh J. McLean	K	1952
Ewan Douglas MacLeod	T	1957
Donald McMorland	CAI	1969
Vanessa McNaughton	EM	1988
Prof. K.M. McNeil	PEM	1962
S.J. McQuay	N	1985
Dr Janette McWilliam	CC	1997
Dr Cynthia L. Meachum	W	1985
Richard Craig Meade	W	1999
Henry Meadows	T	1959
E.M.T. Mealing	DAR	1970
Dr Melissa Medich	TH	1994
Joyance Meechai	W	2001
Antony Meier		
Tan Wu Meng	T	1996
Nandita Menon	LC	1985
Cecile Menterey-Monchau	F	2000
Dr Garry Edward Menzel	JN	1985
Canon R.E. Meredith	T	1952
Patricia E. Merriman	N	1944
Dr John E. Merwin	EM	1958
Prof. L. Mestel		
Andrew B. Methven	T	1988
Benedikt H. Meyer	SID	1992
Keith Michel	F	1967
Prof. Roger Middleton	W	1976
David Miles	F	1972
Martin W. Miles	M	1969
Mr Michael Milkowits	SID	2000
R.J. Milla	SE	1991
Alastair Miller	JN	1971
C. Ralph Miller	T	1936
Prof. David Miller	CL	1949
Elaine Miller	JN	1993
Dr J.M. Miller	SID	1966
Dr J.S. Miller	DOW	1947
James L. Miller	JN	1952
Prof. John Boris Miller	JN	1952
Dr Maynard M. Miller	JN	1957
Francis Joseph Mills IV	SE	2004
Nick Milner-Gulland	PET	1958
S. Jonathan Milo Brand	CHR	1974
Derick Mirfin	M	1950
Dr M.C. Mirow	CAI	1988
Kathryn Mitchell	HO	1999
Dr Thanos Mitrelias	W	1993
Michael J. Moeckel	JN	2002
Isabell Mossler	CTH	2004
Miss Mohanna		
Christopher Mole		
Anthony D. Monk	F	1972
Marilee Monnot	CHU	1995
Maria Victoria Monsalve	LC	1995
D.G. Montefiore	CL	1947
Francisco A.T.B.N. Monteiro	F	2005
Bohórquez-Montero	DAR	1997/2006
Kenneth B.C. Montgomerie	T	1956
Rahul Nath Moodgal	F	1994
Bernard John Moody	JN	1945
George C.J. Moore	Q	1966
Patrick Moore		
Stuart M.C. Moore	CHR	1977
Paul and Morwenna Moran	HH	1997
Dr David F. Morgan	CL	1962
Frank E. Morgan II	TH	1974
John D. Morgan	PET	1942
Peter Morgan MBE	TH	1956
David Morgan-Smith	T	1958
Dr Daniel Morgenstern	T	1993
Peter Morley	PEM	1950
Miss M.T. Morrell	N	1955
Mr Andrew W. Morris	PEM	2000
Christopher J.E. Morris	K	1944
Paul H. Morris	JN	1973
R.B. Morris	PEM	1975
Roger Morris	Q	1974
Amy Morrish	R	2003
Mr Kimball Morrison	CL	1988
Dr J.J. Morrissey		
Ian Mortimer	F	1948
Jenepher Wolff Moseley	G	1953
Andrew Moss	CHU	1962
David John Moss	JN	1965
Jairo H. Moyano	HH	1996
Mr James L. Moyes	EM	1971
Dr Judy S.E. Moyes	G	1972
Tiyanjana M. Mphepo	CLH	2003
Alison Mueller (née Sweeney)	CHU	1984
Graham Muir	SE	1975
J. Russell Muir	Q	1960
Prof. J.R. Mulryne	CTH	1955
Prof. John Mulvaney	CL	1951
Dr Mudiwa P. Munyikwa	SID	1983
Kieran Murphy	JN	1976
Paul Murphy	W	1999
R.S.F. Murphy		
Revd G.J. Murray	CTH	1954
Lindsay Elaine Murray (née Law)	DAR	1990
Prof. Robert G.E. Murray		
Mr M.D. Murrell		
Sally Musson (née Boxell)	DAR	1977
Yassar Mustafa	DOW	2005
Andy Mydellton MA	PEM	1997
Ms Isayvani Naicker PhD	CLH	2006
Hugh Naismith	F	1956
Hironori Nakamura	M/N	2001/03
Michael Napier	K	1945
Mr J. Naylor		
John M. Naylor	TH	1988
S.J. Naylor	T	1993
Andy Neale	CAI	1970
Mr David C. Neil-Smith	PEM	1975
John S. Neilson	CC	1977
Ana M.R. Neiva	G	1966
Richard Nelmes	JN	1962
David A. Nelson	PET	1954
Elaine P.C. Neo	CTH	1984
Heather S. Nesbit	PEM	2005
C.E. Nettlefold	T	1970
Karen E. Netzel (née Thacker)	EM	1994
John F. Newcombe	T	1946
Aryeh L. Newman	EM	1941
John Newman	EM	1964
L.A. Newman		
Mr R.H. Newman	TH	1978
John Newnham		
Dr Alison A. Newton (née Hinds)	N	1950
Dr Bruce A. Newton	PET	1948
Prof. David Peter Newton	PEM	1980
Heather R. Newton	PEM	2002
Margaret Ng Ngoi Yee		
Wan Fai Ng	F	1989
Abigail Nicholls	CAI	1991
A.E. Nicholson	TH	1975
Dr A.E. Nicholson	TH	1942
A.J. Nicholson	M	1947
N.M. Nicholson	N	1975
The Hon. Justice Robert Nicholson AO		
Constantinos K. Nicolaides	T	1990
Dr Chris R. Nicolay	TH	1996
Dr Dorothea Niedr e-Sorg	CAI	1988
Dr Peter Arnt Nielsen	F	1988
Bruce Nightingale OBE	K	1952
Dr Leena H. Nikkilä	G	1991
Gill Nixon	G	1972
Richard L. Nobbs	JN	1960
Virinda Nohria		
Mgr Prof. John C. Noordermeer OCS	ED	
Geoffrey R. Norman	CTH	1963
D.R. Norris	M	1962
R.T. Norris	JE	1968
Prof. Toby Norris	PEM	1954
Robin Norton	CTH	1976
Mercedes Nostas	K	1994
John E.B. Notley	JN	1973
Guy Nowell	SID	1975
Dr Conrad Nowikow	PEM	1974
John L. Nutt	JN	1969
Jean Nuttall (née Waterman)	N	1943
Stuart D. Oakley	SE	1969
Dr Werner Oberholzner	PEM	1980
H.C. Obersi	DOW	1951
Mugoma Joseph Okomba	DOW	1997
M.H.R.R. O'Connell	PET	1955
Rhona O'Connell	SE	
Dr Susie O'Connor	EM	2000
David Odling	F	1966
M.J. O'Donoghue		
P.A.H. O'Donovan	TH	1972
Shihoko Ogawa		
Masahiro Ohara		
Dr Sue O'Hare (née Allcock)	CL	1980
Revd Dr Michael P.K. Okyerefo	HO	2000
Richard Oldcorn	CHR	1956
Anne Oldroyd (née Holloway)	G	1951
Colin Oldroyd	DOW	1951
Mark Oliver	PET	1981
Carl Olsson	JN	1972
Ho Man On		
Keith Ong	M	2002
Richard F. Oppong	F	2003
Peter J. Orme	SID	1962
James S. O'Rourke IV PhD	CHR	1979
Miss M. Orr		
Charles E. Ortner	TH	1953
Mrs Ruth Osborn	G	1941
Neville Osmond	SID	1953
Stephen J. Osmond	PET	1974
Richard Ossei and Aminta Ossei (née Paiva)	Q/HH	2005
Judge Helen O'Sullivan	W	1998
Mr Andrew Overy	PET	1975
D.N.H. Owen		
Judith Owen (née Edge)	N	1969
Tom William Owen	DOW	1989
Awotunde Samuel Owolabi	CHU	1968
Dr Alan J. Oxley	PEM	1949
John Oyler	T	1953
Captain P.J. Pacey RN	JN	1969
Michael Pacold	T	1999
Malcolm Page	CHR	1955
Prof. Trevor Page	JE	1964
Stephen Paget-Brown	JE	1980
G.T. Pagone QC	TH	1982
Andrew L. Paine	JE	1960
Dr Valeria de Paiva	LC	1984
Ian Palfreyman	T	1966
Clifford Palmer	CHU	1994
Revd Graham Palmer	EM	1950
Dr Peter Panegyres	JE	1992
Dr Joesph Pang	Q	1969
E.C. Pank		
Andread Papademetris	R	1997
Mr Kon. Papakonstantinou	HH	1999
Dr Ares Papangelou	PET	1984
Dr Yannos Papantoniou	Q	1976
Sr Don Carlos L. Paredes y Albanil-Camara	M	1985
Anuradha Parekh	CHR	2002
A. Robert Pargeter	PEM	1934
Geoffrey Brooks Parish	SID	2002
David Park	CTH	1968
Sohee Park	F	1979
Adrian Parker	TH	1974
Colin Parker	T	1955
Dr David L. Parker	CL	1958
Hugh Parker		
Iain G. Mck. Parker	EM	1959
Mr J.V. Parker	CC	1973
Andrew Parkes	CHR	1958
R.D. Parkinson	CL	1964
Stephen Parkinson	EM	2001
Andrew Parnell	CHR	1972
John M. Parr	CC	1991
Richard J. Parrino	TH	1979
Simon Parry	CTH	2005
William Parry	DOW	1996
F.D. Parsons	JN	1976
J. Parsons	CTH	1936
Roger Parsons	JN	1960
Tim Parsons	SE	1975
Dr Rashmi Patel	CHR	2002
Shahpur Patell	PEM	1974
Amanda J. Patrick	HH	1991
Mr Mark Pattinson	T	1952
Stephen Pattison	SE	1973
Kyriacos E. Pavlou		
Prof. Milija N. Pavlović	JN	1974
Michael Payne	CC	1943
Roger W. Payne	DOW	1960
David Peacock	PEM	1949
J.D.C. Peacock		
Elizabeth Peake (née Rought)	N	1942
John M. Peake	CL	1942
Jonathan Pearce	F	1977
Dr A.R. Pears		
Michael Pearson	PET	1939
Patrick Pearson	T	1950

John R. Peberdy	JN 1949	Michael J.S. Preece	EM 1955

John R. Peberdy JN 1949
Sebastian Pechmann TH 2005
Mr David M. Peck R 1990
J. Houe Pedersen R 1994
Nirmala C. Peiris SE 1951
Nigel Pendrigh M 1980
John Penney Cmg CTH 1960
Oliver Pereira SE 1994
M. Jared Perkins CLH 1999
The Hon. Mrs Betty Perks (née Butler) G 1979
Revd Everard Perrens
Yvonne B. Perret
Prof. Edward B. Perrin CHU 1991
Dr Robert Perrin K 1948
Dr Robert K. Perrons F 2001
Mr C.N. Perry T 1985
Deborah Lily Perry (née Whitton) T 1984
Dr Melissa Anne Perry QC CAI 1986
Michael Perry CAI 1968
R.D. Perry CAI 1957
Dr Joseph E. Pesce PhD PET 1988
J.W.N. Petty CAI 1952
Amy L. Pflueger M 1995
Helen A. Pfuhl DAR 1996
Mr and Mrs R.C. Phelps
Grant G. Phillipp ED 1999
Peter S. Phillips F 1966
George and Alison Phillipson CHR/N 1971
Dr A.J.V. Philp SID 1988
Colin Kit Lun Phoon CHU 1985
Jeremy Pickles
Fionn Peter Alexander Pilbrow JN 1998
Philippe Pinguet TH 1977
Diego Pizano CL 1972
Ian Plaistowe Q 1961
Mr P. Geoffrey Plant Q 1988
Baroness Platt of Writtle CBE DL FR Eng G 1941
Prof. Jennifer Platt N 1958
Julian Platt CL 1960
Elizabeth Platts HO 1975
Sarah Platts CAI 2004
Max Plotnek JN 1987
Simon W. Plummer CC 1996
David Pockney Q 1940
Heidi Pocock N 2005
Derek Pomeroy SID 1954
Ian Pong JN 2005
Sonia Ponnusamy JN 1997
Dr O. Poole-Wilson T 2001
Dr Guy R. Pooley JN 1987
Winston C.F. Poon TH 1972
Adrian Pope DOW 1982
Nikolai Alexander Popescu T 2001
Charles and Amanda Porter CAI 1977/78
Stephen Porter SE 1973
Kenneth Portnoy CL 1965
Robert Posey JE 1965
Henry Hugh Potter PEM 1953
Dr Chris Potts CHU 1981
Richard C. Poulton PEM 1958
Dr B.D. Powell T 1944
Geoff Powell F 1958
Ian E. Powell EM 1977
Dr Mark E. Powell T 1985
Alan P. Power
Simon J.R. Powles JN 1977
Tamsin J. Powles CL 1975
Revd Dr M.J. Pragnell
Jeremy D. Preddy CHR 1978

Michael J.S. Preece EM 1955
Nick Prentice Q 1975
Mr Graham D.H. Preskett R
Rosemary Beal-Preston G 1967
K.M.R. Price SE 1957
Dr P.C. Price T 1949
Peter H.M. Price JN 1956
Paul J. Price EM 1951
Stephen C. Price Q 1976
Dr Edward Prince CHR 1949
Jason E. Prince F 1999
Ruth Prince PET 1997
Air Marshall Sir Charles Pringle JN 1937
John Pritchard R 1983
Keith Pritchard PEM 1970
Mark Pritchard R 2001
Revd R.H. Prosser T 1950
Graham Prothero JE 1980
Dr M.J. Provost T 1973
John W. Pryor F 1968
Daniel J. Pugh CL 2001
John Pugh CAI 1957
Robert D. Pugh JE 1971
J.S.W. Pulford JE 1952
Dr Malcolm Pullan T 1989
David Purchase SID 1961
Dr Noel Purdey F 1991
John Purkiss JN 1980
Dr Michael Purshouse SID 1970
Ian Purver PEM 1965
Dr A.M. Purves
I.W. Purvis Q 1941
The Hon. Mrs Betty Parks G 1978
Dr I.F. Pye PEM 1960
Andrew C. Quale Q 1966
J. Leslie Quie CHR 1952
Adam Quinton CC 1980
F.C.J. Radcliffe CAI 1958
Dr Yehia Raef CHU 1972
Prof. Evangelos Raftopoulos DOW 1974
Donald Ramsay
Gordon D. Ramsay CTH 1948
Margaret Mary Ramsay G 1978
Cheryl Denise Alexandra Ramsey G 1979
Munidasa P. Ranaweera CHU 1966
Jonathan T. Randle EM 1994
Thomas A. Randle
Srinivasa Ranganathan PET 1962
Mr Sahan V. Rannan-Eliya CHR
Damian Ranson CTH 1992
Dorrie L. Rapp PhD W 1973
Dr John C.A. Rathmell JE 1956
Michael Rattigan PEM 1970
Leela Madhava Rau
Peter Rawling PET 1968
Charles Rawlinson JE 1952
David Rayner PET 1977
C.R.M.S. Reading JN 1971
John Reddaway CC 1944
P.J.M. Redfern CAI 1969
John E. Redford CHR 1982
Michael Redmond JN 1955
E.N. Reed T 1988
Elizabeth Reed (née Langstaff) N 1934
David Rees CTH 1950
Susan V. Rees N 1957
R.M. Reese JN 1972
Norman Reeves TH 1946
David Reid JE 1991
Mr Donald S. Reid T 1951
Michaela Reid (née Kier) G 1953
Prof. Arnold E. Reif CL 1942

Colin Reisner T 1965
Marika V. Rella ED 1999
Mr Martin Rennison T 1949
Rachel Revell HO 2003
Antony H. Reynolds PEM 1983
Dr Beverley J. McKeon Reynolds
J. Reynolds SID 1948
Michael T. Reynolds T 1990
W.J. Rhodes Q 1948
Dr W.J. St E.-G. Rhys JN 1950
The Revd B.K. Rice N 1966
Prof. Alison Richard N 1966
David A. Richards JN 1978
David Alan Richards SE 1967
Elizabeth Jane Richards N 2005
Guy Richards CHR 1936
Prof. Keith S. Richards JE 1967
Dr Colin Richardson Q 1974
Maurice J. Richardson CC 1942
Philip David Richardson CHR 1999
Prof. Charles E.F. Rickett EM 1975
Janet Riddlestone (née Warham) N 1946
Michael H.E. (Revd) Ridgeon EM 1958
Andrew Ridgeway
Patrick Ridgwell
Dr Robin Ridsdill Smith Q 1952
Kenneth Rimmer TH 1953
Peter W. Riola D Litt
Frank C. Ripley JE 1964
Jane Ritchie N 1968
M.L. Rivaud-Pearce SE 1971
Dr Timothy Rix CL 1967
Dr Timothy Roach CL 1968
Ann Roberts (née Wilkinson) N 1956
Brian R. Roberts PEM 1950
Catherine Roberts CHU 1979
Christopher K. Roberts JE 1974
Dr Donald James Roberts JN 1948
Hugh T. Roberts
Ian W. Roberts CAI 1945
John S. Roberts CC 1950
Dr Mark S. Roberts DOW 1980
Nigel Roberts SE 1975
Peter Roberts PEM 1970
Dr Roy S. Roberts JN 1959
Dr Sue Roberts (née Watkins) N 1970
T.S. Roberts PEM 1960
Tony Roberts CL 1960
Dr W.J.C. Roberts CL 1957
John M. Robertson QC
Dr N.R.C. Roberton DOW 1957
Una A. Robertson (née Spearing) G 1958
St J.A. Robilliard EM 1972
A.J.M. Robinson
B.D. Robinson CHR 1953
Dr Craig Robinson DOW 1972
David N. Robinson F 1976
David P. Robinson PEM 1959
David R. Robinson JE 1956
E. Robinson CAI 1968
Peter F. Robinson 1971
Geoffrey W. Robinson CL 1966
N.F. Robinson PEM 1953
Virginia G. Robinson CHU 1978
Iain Jeffrey Rodger W 2001
Prof. Brian Rofe FREng JN 1954
Brian Rolfes EM 1993
Neville Rolt PEM 1967
Hayley Romain HO 1999
Prof. Jarlath Ronayne JN 1975
Gemma Ronte Q 1988
Hanno Ronte JE 1988

Philip Rosenbaum ED 2005
Dr Grahame Rosolen JN 1989
John Ross Martyn JE 1962
Dr Phillip Ross Smith T 1967
Jack R. Ross T 1951
Michael W. Ross
Norman Rosser JN 1945
Jeffrey Cade Roux CAI 1989
Prof. Arthur Rowe DOW 1952
Jos Rowe G 1957
J.M. Rowley K 1959
Edward Royle
Dr Michael Rudolf CL 1964
Mr R. Rule EM 1956
Dr Jenny Rumsey G 1965
Dr C.A.J. Runacres Q
M.A. Runacres JN
Michael J.H. Ruscoe CHR 1961
Philip Rushforth T 1991
Brian Scotney Russell OBE PET 1948
Graham E. Russell CTH 1968
Mrs Heather A. Russell (née Brown) N 1957
Prof. Ian Russell JN 1963
Dr James Russell CL 1958
Judith Russell N 1974
Mary Russell (née Knott) G 1977
Prof. Michael W. Russell
Fr. D.J. Ryan OP Q 2000
Melanie Ryan (née Brooker) EM 1992
Dr John F. Ryley EM 1945
Dr Leslie Rymer JE 1968
S.C. Lee JN 1991
Philip 'Satch' Sachtleben DAR 1978
Richard A. Sage T 1984
Timothy C.H. Sale Q 1959
Peter Salinson M 1961
Nick Sallnow-Smith CAI 1965
Graham Sampson CHU 1965
Martin H. Sandbach T 1965
P.E. Sanderson F 1958
Dr Robert E. Sandstrom DAR 2001
Ming San Lee R 1983
Dr Alister J. Sansum R 1995
A.J. Sargent PEM 1955
Dr Yuji Sato MD PhD 1997
H. Martin Saunders Q 1960
Reginald Saunders F 1946
Malcolm Savage TH 1961
Dr Khay Chee Saw CAI 1979
Steven Richard Scadding CL 1968
Christie Scates M 2001
Dr Frank L. Schäfer DAR 1998
Teng Chieh Schen
Dr Erik H. Schlie CL 1998
Prof. Roger M.L. Schmitt PEM 1970
Ernest Schofield
Carl John Schroeder SE 2004
Jonathan D. Schwartz Q 1986
Richard M. Schwartz CL 1972
Michael Schwarz CHU 1980
Prof. J.R. Schwyter EM 1989
Mr Peter G. Scopes JE 1949
Alex Scott CL 1983
Andres A. Torres Scott W 2001
James W. Scott CTH 1943
John Scott JN 1974
John E.S. Scott Q 1945
Nigel and Wendy Scott-Williams HH 1978
Dr R.E. Scraton JE 1952
Dr Geoffrey F.W. Searle PEM 1962
G.J. Seddon
Roger Russell Seggins EM 1964

J. Roberto Parra-Segura	DOW	2006
Sir Peter W. Seligman	CAI	1932
G. Clifford Seller	PEM	1945
Dr John T. Clark Sellick	JN	1950
Anna Sembos		
Mr A.K. Sen MA LLB FCA	CTH	1970
Vernon Oh Min Sen		
Prof. Kwadzo E. Senanu	DOW	1957
Carl Sequeira	CHU	2005
R. Raman Sethu	CAI	1984
Costas Z. Severis	JN	1968
Zenon C. Severis	JN	1999
Dr John R. Sewell	CHR	1967
Lindsay K. Shaddy		
Dr William S. Shand	JN	1955
Daniel Shane	JN	1996
Sutheshan Shanmugarajah	CC	2007
Duncan M.C. Sharp	F	2000
Ian P. Sharp	CAI	1953
Mr Marc J. Sharpe	G	1988
Miss Meera Shaunak	SE	2005
Miss Radha Shaunak	R	2005
Dora Joan Shawe (née Davies)	N	1944
Andrew M. Sheaf	M	1977
Sarah Alexandra Shellard	JN	1981
Adam Shelley	PEM	2001
Caroline Shelton	G	1960
Robert R. Shepherd	F	1953
G. Sheppard		
C. Sherwood	SID	1978
Hugh C. Shields	CAI	1983
Richard C. Shipley	SE	1959
Prof. Eric. M. Shooter	CAI	1942
David J. Shore	SE	1990
Faye L. Shorey	CTH	1998
Barry Shorthouse	F	1971
Alan Shrimpton	JN	1957
Dr M.E. Sidaway		
Mr Daljit Sidhu	EM	1980
Dr Holger Sievert	CHU	2005
Charles Simeons	Q	1940
Dr Ashok Singh	CHR	1989
Jasdeep Singh PhD	CHU	2002
Dr Ranjit Singh	CHR	1989
Dr Sonjoy Singh	SE	1984
Colin Singleotn	T	1961
Veturi Srikanth	TH	1998
Prof. Patrick Sissons	DAR	
Dr Thomas H.W. Siu	DAR	2004
Danny Sivers	K	2005
Dr Devinderjit Singh Sivia	JN	1981
Mr R.L. Skelton	M	1990
A. James Skinner	CL	1951
John R. Skinner	M	1994
Howard Skipp	PEM	1965
E.R. Slater	G	
Mrs P.H. Sledge	N	1953
Ven R.K. Sledge	PET	1949
Ian Smallbone	T	1988
John K. Smallcombe	PET	1943
A.G. Smith	JN	1955
Dr Alan E. Smith CBE	CHR	1964
Alastair J. Smith	JN	2002
Dr Brian Smith	T	1981
C.D.F. Smith	JN	1959
Revd C.H. Smith	EM	1950
David G. Smith	JE	1959
David H. Smith	JN	1949
Dr David L. Smith	SE	1982
Donna Smith	TH	1998
Duncan Smith	JN	1969
Elizabeth Smith MSP	CC	1992

Emily Sarah Smith	R	1996
Francis Skillen Smith	DOW	1957
Prof. George P. Smith II	W	1992
Ivor J. Smith	SID	1950
Dr Ian M. Smith	PET	1961
Ivo Smith	JE	1951
J. Harvey Smith	JN	1952
John M. (Jack) Smith	PEM	1947
Julian Smith	PET	1958
Leslie G. Smith	SID	1970
M.V. Smith		
Michael J. Smith	HO	1985
Dr N.J. Smith	JN	1965
Penelope Smith	K	1974
R. Graham Smith	T	1970
Prof. Raymond T. Smith	PEM	1943
Rodney Smith	JN	1963
Roger Edward Smith	CTH	1957
Stephen Smith		
Anthony Jack Smouha	M	1974
Helen Smyth	NH	2005
Jeffrey Smyth	Q	1960
Paul Smyth	JN	1970
Dr H.A. Snaith	M	1990
Dr Jeffrey K. Snell	T	1947
Prof. Anna Soci	CLH	1999
Dr Hilary Allester Soderland	PEM	2001
Dr Elizabeth Soilleux	JE	1991
Mr Ian C. Solomon	SID	1996
Nat Solomon	EM	1944
W.S. Soong	T	1998
Prof. A.H.A. Soons	JE	1974
Severin L. Sorensen	K	1986
Mr Basil D. South	EM	1957
Mr Peter H. South	EM	1954
Dr Stella G. Souvatzki	CLH	1993
Royston Spears	CTH	1991
Shanin Specter		1984
Philip Speer	SID	1970
Michael J. Spelman	JN	1959
Dr John Spencer	SID	1975
Lynden Spencer-Allen	DOW	2000
Naomi A. Spina	M	1990
Revd Dr Bryan D. Spinks	CHU	1980
Matthew J.T. Spriggs		
Ssegawa-Ssekintu Kiwanuka	JE	2005
Ljiljana Stancic (née Mihajilovic)	T	1999
John A. Stanley	F	1956
R.W. Stanley	CTH	1944
Michael Stannard	F	1960
Michael Stary	DOW	1950
Jane Stebbing	G	1978
John Stebbing	JN	1981
David Steed	JE	1952
Ron L. Steele	JN	1952
Helen Steers		
Benedict G. Stefaneli		
Dr B.E. Steinberg	K	1948
Ms Tracey L. Stephens	PEM	1999
Dr Marvin Stern	HH/PEM	2001
Alison Stevens (née Byrne)	N	1972
Christopher Stevenson		
D.J. Steventon	JN	1967
Prof. Alec T. Stewart	T	1952
David John Stewart	SE	1998
J.B.B. Stewart	M	1950
Dr John C. Stewart	CHR	1959
Dr Fred Stoddard	JN	1981
Mrs M. Stojanovic-Rathmell	N	1963
Nigel A. Stoke	PEM	1967
Valentin Stollyar	DOW	2006
Nathan Storfer-Isser	F	1994

James W. Storrar	DOW	1972
Anthony Strazzera	PEM	
M.J. Strickland	EM	1952
Prof. J. Stringer		
Dr Ruediger Stroh	CHU	1987
Dr George R. Struthers	JE	1968
Sidney M.A. Stubbs	ED	1984
Ann-Sofie Stude	Q	1990
Stephen Sugden	JN	1968
Jana Zuheir Sukkarieh	CHU	1994
Prof. Robert S. Summers		1991
Dr Walton Sumner II		
Sun-Fatt Ng	PET	1975
Mr John E. Sussams	CAI	1951
Dr Stephen K. Swallow	Q	1975
Dr Thomas Rex Sweatman	CHU	1969
Peter D. Sweeney	CTH	2004
Andrew E. Sweet	T	2005
Clive Swift	CAI	1959
David Swift	CAI	1953
Dr Mike Swift	DOW	1958
Dr Tim Swift	CHU	1978
Dr Kenneth Swinburne		1950
Bradford Swing	JE	1969
Dr Charles Swithinbank	PEM	1946
Dr Richard Sykes	CL	1964
Tomasz Szejner	W	2005
Dr James Talbot	PET	1992
Mr Stephen Talbot	CHR	2000
Mr Curtis S. Tamkin Jr	ED	2002
Mr Andrew K.S. Tan	JN	2005
Bok Huat Tan	DAR	1988
Dr Francis S.K. Tan	CL	1971
Fui Ching Tan	DAR	1997
Kai Sin Tan	CLH	2002
Dr Vincent Tang	Q	2000
Whai Shin Olivia Tang	N	1999
Dr Justice Tankebe	ED	2004
Sarah Alexandra Tasker	JN	1982
Mr Tat Man Ho	CTH	1982
James J. Tattersall	W	
R.B. Tattersall	PEM	1949
Barry T. Taylor	F	1999
Revd Bill Taylor	CC	1954
Bruce Taylor	DOW	1960
Ian C. Taylor	SID	1982
J. Graham Taylor	EM	1951
Julie J. Taylor	JE	1999
Kevin Taylor	CAI	1981
Mike Taylor	SID	1957
N.C. Taylor	M	2002
Simon Taylor FCMI	F	2000
Stephen Taylor	TH	1977
Susan Taylor	SID	1988
James F. Tearle	JN	1947
Dr Weng Hong Teh	CLH	2000
Prof. Meral Tekelioglu MD	CLH	1975
Osvaldo S. Tello Rodriquez	DAR	1994
Jiri Tencar	JE	2005
David Terry	K	1956
Mr P.A. Tett	CL	1960
Vijay K. Thakur	Q	1991
Dr Nadarajah Thedchanamoorthy		
	CHU	1962
Michael P. Thelen	DAR	1990
Nikos Theodoulou		
Phoebus Theologites	HH	1989
Eng San Thian	G	2002
Dr David G. Thomas	CL	1962
Graham V. Thomas	CHU	1961
Dr Alwyn R. Thompson	Kings	1965
C.J.B. Thompson		

David Thompson	CHU	2000
Ian C. Thompson	HH	1986
Jennifer Su Thompson	CHU	2000
Miss Lisa E. Thompson	EM	2000
David S. Thomson	SE	1990
Robert Thomson	JN	1952
Christopher Thorne	Q	1971
Valerie R. Thornhill	N	1954
Derek R. Thornton	CTH	1944
Jane Thorpe (née Hillier)	TH	1982
Mark C.M. Thorpe	Q	1960
M. Andrew Threadgold	T	1968
Ian Thubron		
Augustine Tibazarwa	F	1985
Dr Philip Tidswell	JN	1978
Mr G. Tierney		
Dr J.B.M. Tilman MA	T	1947
Keith Tilson	JN	1973
Dr Ralph E. Timms	CTH	1961
David Tindall	EM	1964
Mr Anthony J. Tinkel	CL	1957
Joseph F.D. Tinston	SID	2001
Miha Tisler		
John S. Titford	JN	1964
Prof. A. Ray Toakley	CLH	1982
Dr Peter F. Todd	EM	1961
Hiroaki Toh		1998
Mr A.J. Tomkins	EM	1958
Arthur Tompkins	CAI	1983
Dr Brian Tong	JN	1956
Yan Tordoff	CHU	1991
Ana Luisa Toribio Fierro	W	
Mladen Tosic	CAI	2000
Jonathan Towers	CL	1958
Edward Towne	M	1972
Geoffrey M. Townsend	DOW	1949
Jo Toy	CTH	1977
Kaeko Tozawa		
Dr Nicole Trask	G	2000
Miss Natalie C. Travers	HO	2001
Barbara Treacy	N	1943
Graham Tregonning	DOW	1969
J.E. Trice	CAI	1959
Dr Peter R.J. Trim	PEM	1995
Suely Abreu de Magalh Trindade	F	1997
Prof. Alan J. Troughton	JE	1946
Revd Raymond F. Trudgian	F	1957
Dr Donald E.S. Truman	CL	1956
Lawrence W.H. Tsang	JE	1990
Dr King-Jet Tseng	DAR	1990
Eleanna Tsertou	Q	2005
Ms Erini Tsianaka	CLH	2003
Solly Tucker	T	1957
Eldad Tukahirwa	DAR	1976
Farik Ismail Tunku	CTH	1986
N.M. Turcato-Covert		
Dr Sophie Turenne		
Dr C.J.G. Turner	SID	1957
James Turner Howe	JN	1944
John N. Turner	CHR	1954
Dr Martin R. Turner	F	1989
Dr P.D.M. Turner (née Watson)	G	1956
Robert G. Turner MD	K	1940
Mrs Shirley Turner	G	1950
Derek L. Turnidge	CTH	1956
Mr John Kithome Tuta	ED	1997
Ashish Tuteja	W	2000
Major George E. Twine	CTH	1930
John N. Tyacke	TH	1959
David Tyler	TH	1971
Jonathan Tyler		
Mary Tyndall		

Sidney Tyrrell (née Welsh) — N 1966
Katherine Underwood
Dr Peter J. Underwood — DOW 1976
Ana Margarida Urbano — CTH 1994
The Rt Revd Barry Valentine
Dr Valluri R.M. Rao — JE 1972
Revd Peter J. van de Kasteele — M 1958
Alison van Diggelen (née Gourlay) — W 1989
Dr Frank van Diggelen — W 1992
Laurence Van Someren — T 1958
Dr Samuel A. van Vactor — DAR 2004
Mr P.J. van Went — JN 1966
Luis Vargas — K 1958
Paul Vatistas — TH 1982
Prof. Jan Pieter Veerman LLM — Q 1973
Jean-Louis Velaise — PET 1981
Alan Vening — CC 1952
Prof. Rauf Versan — DOW 1977
Dr Eboo Versi — K 1978
Colin Vickerman OBE — CTH 1944
Maria Vidali — DAR 2004
Nicoline Videbaek MSc PhD — LC 1994
James E. Vigus — CL 1998
Martin Village — JE 1970
Dr M.J.P. Villalobos — DAR 1988
Dr Charles Villiers — CC 1957
Dr Amanda C.J. Vincent — DAR 1985
Ben Vincent — CAI 2006
Dr Prodromos Vlamis — EM 1999
Robin Voelcker
Prof. Peter L. Volpe — K 1956
Peter Voss — CAI 1964
John Wade — DOW 1950
Mr O.T. Wade
James W. Wadkin — Q 1965
Dr Anthony E. Wagstaff — Q 1946
Choon Wah Wong — JN 1996
Dr Michael L. Wain — JN 1969
Benjamin Waine — CAI 1996
Dr Jonathan P. Wainwright — CTH 1985
Ray Wainwright
Mrs Jennifer Wallace
Richard Walden — DOW 1968
Mr Hugh Richard Walduck — CTH 1959
E.B.D. Waldy — HH 1988
Dr Lionel Walford — CTH 1960
Uday Walia — PET 1994
Adrian Walker — EM 1971
Andrew Walker — T 1987
Christopher G. Walker — CAI 1952
Elizabeth A. Walker (née Saunders) — G 1960
Emma Walker — JE 1986
Graham R. Walker — M 1982
John G. Walker — CTH 1965
M. Jean Walker MA JP — NH 1970
Dr Raymond F. Walker — CAI 1963
Steve Walker — F 1973
Mrs T. Walker
Dr Cecil A.M. Walkley — DOW 1948
George Wall — CTH 1968
Oliver Wall — Q 1952
John Wallace — JN 1963
Wallace K.H. Yu — CHR 2005
Rob Walley — SE 1962
Martin W. Walsh PhD Cantab — CHR/CC 1974
Dr Karen D. Walton — W 1992
Dr R.B. Walton — CAI 1958
Ms L.K. Wan — CHR 1983
E. Peter Ward — T 1948
Ms Nuala C. Ward — DAR 2001
Peter M. Ward — CL 1942

Prof. Michael Waring — JE 1965
Prof. Michael Waring — DOW 1958
Dr M.H. Waring — M 1968
Mr Nigel M. Waring — DOW 1962
Dr Paul Waring — T 1976
The Revd Nigel Warner — JN 1969
Philip Warner — T 1944
Dick Warwick — SE 1953
Dr Ellis A. Wasson — TH 1972
Mr Derek H. Waters — TH 1942
Monica Waters — LC 1999
Ian Watkins — T 2006
Janet and Mark Watkins — N/Q 1971
Peter R. Watkins — EM 1950
Bob Watson — CHU 1974
Dr David Watson — PEM 1983
Eric Watson — T 1942
Geoffrey K. Watson — SE 1991
Michael Watson — TH 1972
Rachel Watson — EM 2005
Prof. Stephen R. Watson — EM 1961
Cedric Watts
Ronald Watts — TH 1962
Charles Watts-Jones — JN 1959
Lance V. Waumsley — SE 1966
Edward J. Wawrzynczak — JN 1980
Jane Way (née Whitehead) — G 1962
Peter Waymouth
Dr Ray Weatherby — TH 1969
Miss Kaarn J. Weaver — N 1968
Christopher Webb — SE 1969
Dr Eric Webb — CHR 1969
Michael Webb — TH 1992
Michael D. Webb
Nigel Webb
Brigadier F.R. Webster — CHR 1937
Mr Peter Webster — JN 1986
Timothy Webster — ED 1999
G.A.C. Weeden — JN 1951
Dr Terence Wei
Brian H. Weight — T 1969
Jeremy D. Weinstein — TH 1982
Richard H. Weiss — CL 1979
Prof. Lowell R. Weitkamp — TH 1960
Revd Barry Welch — DOW 2001
Dr Priscilla Jeanne Welford — N 1963
Dr Hilary Welland — N 1973
Alan Wells
Bernard Wells — CHR 1956
Mrs Niobe Wells (née Hopkins) — NH 1970
George W.S. Wen — K 1971
The Chevalier de Weryha-Wysoczanski — M 1998
Carolyn West — G 1973
Clay Matthew West — EM 1997
Colin West — JN 1973
Neil Westreich — CC 1970
Richard Whale — F 1998
Dr Ruth M. Whaley — G 1977
Michael Whatmough — Q 1954
James R. Whelan
Dr Nicola H.G. Whitaker
Mme Nicola Whitaker
Dr Bob Whitbread — CL 1957
Dr Colin Whitby-Strevens — TH 1965
Dr A.D. White — PET 1968
I.H. White
Ian Michael White — PEM
Nick J. White
Richard White — JN 1972
Prof. John S. Whitehead — SE 1972
David Whitfield — CHR 1973

Simon Whitworth — CTH 1970
Andrew S.D. Whybrow — T 1962
Robin A.F. Wight — M 1958
Richard Wightwick — CTH 1965
Prof. Aldin Wijffels — CAI 1987
Dr A. Ross Wilcock — CAI 1958
Juliette Wilcox — CAI 1985
G. Walter Wilde — Q 1948
Dr Kern Wildenthal — CTH 1968
Adrian J. Wilkes — DOW 1976
Dr Belinda J. Wilkes — JE 1978
Mr R.A. Wilkes BA — CTH 2003
Amb. Malcolm Wilkey — W 1990
Adrienne Wilkins — CHU 1975
Canon Dr Alan Wilkinson — CTH 1951
Roseanne Wilkinson — JN 1993
Roger S. Willbourn FRGS — SID 1972
Peter A. Willers — TH 1969
G.F. Willett — CTH 1946
Carol Anne Williams — DAR 1973
Dr David J. Williams — CHU 1979
Edward T. Williams MBE MA LLM — TH 1948
Prof. Fred Williams — JN 1958
James H. Williams Jr PhD — T 1968
Martin Williams — TH 1966
Dr Martin R. Williams
Dr Paul G.L. Williams — T 1964
Prof. Ray B. Williams — CHU 1964
Richard Alun Williams — JE 1998
Revd Dr Roger Williams — PEM 1991
Ruth A. Williams — N 1953
Trevor Williams — JN 1952
David K. Williamson — K 1998
Stephen W. Williamson QC — SID 1959
Tom Williamson — K 1998
Clive Willis — F 1957
Colin Willis — CAI 1954
Mike Willmott — SE 1968
Dr David Wilman — TH 1964
Mr A. Wilson
Revd Canon A.M.S. Wilson — JE 1952
Andrew J. Wilson — JN 1986
Arnold D.P. Wilson — SE 1951
Barry and Karen Wilson — F 1962
Daniel R. Wilson MD PhD — Q 1992
David G. (Wynn-) Wilson — JN 1950
Derek J. Wilson — JN 1977
E. Joan Wilson — G 1941
Gillian Wilson — JN 1985
Ian Wilson — CHU 1970
Kingsley D. Wilson — F 1996
L.S. Wilson — EM 1952
Peter T. Wilson — T 1958
Roderick Wilson — Q 1951
Sam Wilson — CL 1960
Dr Sandra J. Wilson — NH 1991
Steven John Wilson — TH 2005
Steve Wilson — CTH 1976
Mr T.J. Winchcomb — TH 1996
Tang Wing Sze Wincy — CHU 1992
Ward O. Winer — EM 1961
Dr Robin Wingate-Hill — W 1967
Michael A. Wingate-Saul — K 1958
Villiam Wing-Lam Lo — HH 2007
Diego Winkelried — JN 2005
Prof. Glyn Winskel — EM 1972
Dr Nitinant Wisaweisuan — JN 1996
John Withers — DOW 1957
Dr Robert S.M. Withycombe — SE 1965
Revd Tania Witter — G 1955
Michelle Witton — HH 1992

Dr Michael Wolff — JN 1945
Paul A. Wolter — TH 1974
Dr Richard A. Womersley — 1939
R.A. Womersley
Howie Wong — G 1990
Khai Cheng Wong — ED 1999
Kok Leong Wong (Croc) — F 1989
Mr Peter H.H. Wong — W 1989
Ting Hway Wong — JE 1992
Wai San Wong — NH 1998
Francesca Wood — EM 1982
John M.A. Wood — JN 1962
Dr M.D. Wood — CTH/CAI 1950
Mike Wood — T 1974
Dr Philip M. Wood — JN 1978
Vanessa Wood — NH 1980
Graham Woodard — DOW 1968
Philip Woodcock — TH 1958
Mr Denis Woodhams — T 1952
Mr John C. Woodhouse — JN 1970
Peter B. Woodhouse — JN 1960
Susi Woodhouse — N 1971
Dr David Woodings — EM 1962
Prof. Geoffrey Woodroffe — JN 1956
Mrs Rosemary Woodroffe (née Colquhoun) — G 1967
Enid Woolett
Dr J.A. Woolmore — CL 1992
W.H. Woolverton — K 1973
Gregory Wren
Ben H.B. Wrey — CL 1960
Dr Joanna Wright — N 1976
J. Wright
Mr James R.G. Wright — JN/CTH 1961
John D. Wyatt MA — JE 1951
Adrian 'Percy' Wykes — CTH 1984
Silvana Lourdes Perez Yalan — W 2001
Makiko Yamamoto — R 2005
Mrs Satoko Fukada Yamamoto
Prof. Lok C. Lew Yan Voon — R 1984
Yang Zhijie — HH 2005
Mr Rod Yarnell — EM 1956
David Yates — EM 1960
Prof. E.D. Yeboah — SE 1957
A.E.J. Yelland — CTH 1955
Fay Yelland — N 1954
Trevor E. Yelland — CHR 1956
Cheng Chuan Yeoh — JN 1978
Fiona Yeomans (née Main) — N 1975
Mr Byron Yeung — SE 1986
C.P. Yeung — DAR
Dr H.L. Yewlett — CTH 2005
Steve Yianni — K 1980
Alfred Yip — R 1987
G.C.M. Young
Irene B.K. Young — NH 1987
Peter Young — CAI 1950
Dr F. Ronald Young — JE 1943
William Y.P. Yu — HH 2004
Dr Yi Yuan — Q 1989
Dr Ying-Ying T. Yuan — NH 1966
Dr Ainslie Yuen — K 2000
C.N. Yuen — R 2002
Dr Irene Zadnik — CC 1989
Nathalie Zaidman — CAI 2002
Carsten Zatschler — JN 1993
Prof. G.J. Zellick — CAI 1967
Cesare A.P. Zetti — CTH 1986
Clara Yi Zhu — DAR 2000
Dr Mara L. Ziouvas — W 2002
Alexander P. Zorn — G 1998

Acknowledgements

The editors would like to thank the many people throughout the University and further afield who greeted our relentless requests for meetings, information and images with patience, constructive help and enthusiasm for this project. We would particularly like to thank the archivists at Churchill, Downing, Girton, Lucy Cavendish, Newnham and St John's (Caroline Herbert, Kate Thompson, Kate Perry, Karen Davies, Pat Ackerman and Jonathan Harrison), and Gillian Cooke, archivist at Cambridge Assessment. Many of the teaching departments searched for material and photographs, including English, Engineering, History, Mathematics and Philosophy. At the Department of Chemistry, Brian Crysell, John Holman and Nathan Pitt were extremely helpful, as was Dora Kemp at the McDonald Institute. Many Cambridge librarians assisted us, especially Anne Hughes at the Forbes Mellon Library, Boyd Spradbury at the Marshall Library and Sue Slack at Cambridge Central Library. The University Library was an invaluable source of wisdom and material, for which we thank, amongst others, Jacky Cox, Anne Taylor and Charles Aylmer. The staff of the University museums, Fiona Brown, Carly Farthing and Peter Greenhalgh at the Fitzwilliam, Lara Gisborne at Kettle's Yard, Julie Macarthur at the Zoology Museum, Ruth Horry at the Whipple, Sandra Jackson at the Sedgwick Museum, Grete Dalum-Tilds at the Museum of Classical Archaeology and Kelvin Fagan at the Cavendish Laboratory, dealt with the mounting pace of our needs with sympathy and efficiency.

Tom Watson at CUP, Paul Willcox at the Achilles Club and Stan Whitehead for the CURUFC went to great trouble to assist us with pictures. Several professional organisations and photographers were kind enough to allow us to use their material without charge, in particular the Musée d'Archéologie Nationale de Saint-Germain-en-

Laye, Boydell & Brewer, Bidwells, the Geoinformation Group, Adam Williamson and Peter Sanders. Also generous with their personal photographs, apart from those thanked elsewhere, were James Chell, Hugh Mellor, Lynden Spencer-Allen and Patrick Bateson. We would also like to thank Jocelyne Dudding, Tom Ebbutt, Simon Fairclough, Mark Goldie, Sally Hames, Paul Hammans, Claire Jarmy, Jane Kingsbury, Tony Lemons, Don Manning, Martin McBrien, Mark Mniszko, John Parker, Sophie Pickford, Jocelyn Poulton, Hannah Razzell, Charlotte Richer and Muhammad Suheyl Umar.

CUSU and the Union Society lent material and assisted us with research. Varsity Publications now has a remarkable electronic archive, and Michael Derringer, as Business Manager, provided invaluable assistance across a broad front, as well as supplying and taking his own photographs. We were helped towards images for drama and the Footlights by Tim Cribb, James Baggaley, Megan Prosser and Daniel Morgenstern. We are also grateful to Piers Brendon, Nicholas Bullock, Elisabeth Leedham-Green, Robert Macfarlane, Jeremy Mynott, John Naughton, Stephen Parkinson, Adrian Poole, Peter Richards and Brendan Simms for their general advice and wisdom.

The Cambridge University Development Office team, where Jenny Zinovieff was our point of contact, was supportive throughout, and we are particularly grateful to Rachel Kirkley who put us in touch with alumni and pursued specific needs with great energy and speed. Finally, we would like to express our appreciation to all the alumni who responded to our call for ephemera, photographs and reminiscences, in particular Will Adams, Julian Andrews, Rachel Beckett, Gwyn Bevan, Guy Brew, Kenneth Hastings, Charles Lysaght, Stephen MacDonnell, Elizabeth Mills, Gudrun Pollitt, Karl Sabbagh, Vicky Singh, Alexander Stillmark, Bill Treharne-Jones, Andrew Warner, Bridget Wheeler and Barbara Woroncow.

Picture Credits

Every effort has been made to contact the copyright holders of all works reproduced in this book.
However, if acknowledgements have been omitted, the publishers ask those concerned to contact Third Millennium Publishing.

Achilles Club 285L; **ADC** Theatre 298, 305, 307B; **Allied + Morris** 127, 130T; **Ancient** India and Iran Trust 117; Julian **Andrews** 13, 30, 41T, 44, 48, 52B, 56R, 70, 106, 116, 179B, 230, 259, 272, 273; Christopher **Angeloglou** 46L, 46R, 84TL, 96-7, 98L, 99B, 129L, 148R, 180, 190L, 192T, 300R, 309T; Peter **Ashley** 85BR, 293 BL; Antony **Barrington** Brown 75L, 232T; Courtesy of Sir Patrick **Bateson** 241R; **Biblioteca** Angelica, Rome MS 401, fol. 54r 34; Courtesy of Catherine **Bishop** 274; **Boydell** & Brewer 120R; Guy **Brew** 187L; **British** Library Newspapers/ Cambridge Evening News 184; Philip **Brown** 94L, 309R; **Cambridge** Assessment 326B; **Cambridge** Research Institute 155, 158T; By permission of **Cambridge** Science Park 248; **Cambridge** Union Society 191, 194L [Nicholas Hartman 194R]; Courtesy of the Syndics of **Cambridge** University Library 14–15, 93L, 125B, 135L, 145R, 146T, 149, 151B, 151T, 183C, 196, 198B, 200B, 201, 217L, 246, 265C, 297, 300L, 319R, 325 [Ackerman's *History of the University of Cambridge* 177; cam.a.815.4 244; cam.b.41.16.79 148L; David Loggan's *Cantabrigia illustrata* 1690 18–19, 33, 220T; *Gradus ad Cantabrigiam*, 1824 294T; James Gibb 220B; Matthew Parker sel.3.229 218; P.S. Lambourn (Views x.2 (26)) 221; University Archives Luard-187 35L; University Archives Luard-7 31]; Courtesy of the Syndics of **Cambridge** University Press 134, 202, 203, 204L, 205B; **Cambridge** Wittgenstein Archive 65, 135B, 137; **Cambridgeshire** Collection 37, 235, 265; Sir Hugh **Casson** Ltd 224; **Cavendish** Laboratory Museum 56L, 57; **CERN** 58; James **Chell** 239L, 240; Courtesy of the Master and Fellows of **Christ's** 128R; **Churchill** College Archives 84TR, 263T; Courtesy of the Master and Fellows of **Clare** and the Forbes Mellon Library 125T; **Clare** College Archives 32T; Courtesy of Tim **Clutton**-Brock 242; **Computer** Laboratory, Cambridge 74, 227; Peter **Cook** 72, 73B, 225, 226B; **Corbis** 103; Courtesy of the Master and Fellows of **Corpus** Christi 308B; Institute of **Criminology** 179T; **CUCC** 283T; **CUER** 71T; **CURUFC** archive 278; **CUSO** 318R; **CUWBC**

Archive/Newnham College Library 271B, 275T, 275L; **Department** of Chemistry, Cambridge 75R [John Holman 76R, 226T][Nathan **Pitt** 76L, 77, 250]; **Department** of Engineering, Cambridge 67, 71B; **Department** of Experimental Psychology, Cambridge 165R; Michael **Derringer** 14, 19, 23, 25R, 27R, 32B, 88, 111T, 118T, 121, 130T, 142B, 166, 188T, 189R, 205T, 284, 249, 258, 293, 297R, 306B, 307T, 314, 316T, 319, 322, 327L, 328; **Faculty** of Architecture 141, 142T; **Faculty** of English, Cambridge 133; **Fitzwilliam** Museum 20, 22, 24B, 35R, 197, 205, 206, 207, 208, 209, 211R, 316B, 317L; Ian **Fleming** 167; **Footlights** Dramatic Club 309L, 310–4; **fotogenix.co.uk** 27L; High-resolution aerial image of Cambridge kindly supplied by The **GeoInformation** Group. All rights reserved 332–3; **Getty** Images 45, 114, 321; **Ghim** Wei Ho 68L; Courtesy of the Mistress and Fellows of **Girton** 38B, 85R, 131; By permission of Paul **Gopal-Chowdhury** and the Master and Fellows of Gonville & Caius 59T; **Great** St Mary's Archive 255T; **Grete** Dalum Tilds/Museum of Classical Archaeology 210R, 211L; **Gurdon** Institute, Cambridge 239R; Dona **Haycraft** 234R; Courtesy of Peter **Hill** 150R; **Hulton** Picture Library 89; **Iqbal** Academy, Pakistan 261T; Tony **Jedrej** 50B, 66, 84B, 111B, 120L, 122, 126, 132, 175, 192–3, 312; **Judge** Business School 164; Dora **Kemp** 140R, 140B, 168; **Kettle's** Yard 212, 213, 214, 215, 253; By courtesy of the Provost and Fellows of **King's** 169; Hugo van **Lawick**, by permission of Jane Goodall 241L; Cambridge University **Library** Mass of St Gregory from a Book of Hours (Use of Rome), MS. Add. 4100, fos 115v–116 200; **London** Library 38T; Malcolm **Longair** 54, 60; E.J. Hill (By courtesy of the Mistress and Fellows of **Lucy** Cavendish) 83L; Jack **Luo** and Yong Qing Fu 80; Joanne **Maldonado-Saldivia**/Azim Surani 231; Loïc Hamon, **MAN**, Saint Germain-en-Laye 138; **Marks** Barfield 229; **Marlowe** Society 302, 303L; **Marshall** Library of Economics, Cambridge 170, 171L; **Mary** Evans Picture Library 198T; **Masons** News 36; Hugh **Mellor** 135T, 136; Mark **Mniszko** 82,236–7; Simon **Moore** 73T; **Museum** of Archaeology and Anthropology, Cambridge

165L; **Napp** Pharmaceuticals Ltd 251; **National** Portrait Gallery 232L; The **Nobel** Foundation 336; **PA** Photos 233; Nicholas **Patrick** 78; Courtesy of the Master and Fellows of **Pembroke** 232R; Sam **Perry** 279; **Peter** Sanders Photography 261B; Courtesy of the Master and Fellows of **Peterhouse** 123T; Sophie **Pickford** 264, 276, 286, 287T; **Plastic** Logic Ltd 250; Courtesy of the Master and Fellows of **Queens'** College 329; **Ramsey** and Muspratt Archives 172L; Ophelia **Redpath** 294B; Courtesy of Charlotte Roach 285R; Nicholas **Roberts** 182L, 183T; **Russell** Archives, McMaster University 137R; **School** of Clinical Medicine, Cambridge 236B; **Science** and Society Picture Library 26L; Hiroshi **Shimura** 4, 10, 12, 16, 17, 21L, 21R, 24T, 28, 39T, 47, 62, 83R, 85L, 86–7, 110R, 113, 144, 176, 219, 222–3, 243, 247, 252, 262B, 271T, 275B, 288–9, 290, 330; **Sir** Cam 42, 160, 254, 267L, 268, 296B; **SOAS** archives 29; Lynden **Spencer–Allen** 283B; Courtesy of the Master and Fellows of **St John's** 50T, 63, 146B; **Stanton** Williams Ltd 80–1; Jan **Stradtmann** 104T; David **Thomas** 299; Anna **Trench** 53B, 152R; By permission of the Master and Fellows of **Trinity** 61, 81, 128L, 134, 135R; **Trinity** College Library 145L; Courtesy of the Master and Fellows of **Trinity** Hall 292L; **University** Press and Publications Office, Cambridge 6, 234L, 260, 295, 327R; **Varsity** Publications 52T, 102R, 150L, 151R, 152L, 181, 188B, 189L, 189T, 190R, 280; Sir John **Walker** 238; Phil **Waterson** 154; Keith **Whelan** 95R; **Whipple** Museum of History of Science 217R, 324; Dan **White** 2, 23R; Ben **Wrey** 93

Text Permissions
By permission of George **Allen** and Unwin publishers 134L; By permission of **Faber** & Faber 18, 26, 127L; By permission of John **Murray** Publishers 112B; By permission of **Oxford** University Press 49; By permission of **Penguin** Publishing 115B; By permission of the **Random** House Group Ltd 100